CW00521755

How fascinating to examine the lives of Christian sisters from antiquity! Their steps call and inspire today's women to leave footprints along the same trail.

MARY A. KASSIAN
Author, *Girls Gone Wise*
Distinguished Professor of Women's Studies,
Southern Baptist Theological Seminary, Louisville, Kentucky

Her-Story provides a daily walk with Christian women from the first century to our present day. But as the reader takes this journey, we are ultimately taught and reminded not so much about women, but rather about our great God as He is clearly the focus for the lives of the women that Diana Lynn Severance has chosen. Throughout the book we are constantly taught and reminded that: God is always at work; it's a great joy and privilege to be involved in the ministry of reconciliation; living as a Christian is costly but God never leaves us; the centrality of the ministry of the word; the necessity of mission work to all nations and people's groups; and the importance of Christian character. This book is accessible to many because the readings each day are brief, interesting, and because there is such a variety of different Christian models of women. There are hundreds of women and so they have different gifting and are involved in many different types of ministries across the world and across different ages. By reading this book, hopefully many men and women today can be encouraged, refreshed, and challenged by the examples of their Christian sisters from the past since these women model what Christian discipleship looks like whatever age we live in, since our great God never changes.

JANE TOOHER
Ministry Department, Director of the Priscilla and Aquila Centre,
Moore Theological College, Sydney, Australia

Diana Severance has written a different kind of devotional — one that reminds us of the 'great cloud of witnesses' who have loved the Lord over the last two thousand years. But her specific focus is on the women who have followed Christ, a diverse collection spanning many generations, cultures, and lands. Readers will learn about a number of women both famous and obscure who labored for the advance of the gospel. This is an encouraging addition to anyone's daily Scripture reading and prayer time, a literary reminder to go and do likewise for the glory of God.

CAROLYN MCCULLEY
conference speaker and author of
The Measure of Success, Radical Womanhood,
and *Did I Kiss Marriage Goodbye?*
Washington, D.C.

What a gift to add to daily bible reading! Diana Lynn Severance has summarized a wealth of research on hundreds of edifying lives lived for Jesus without sentimentality and with deep effect. I was enriched in my mind, challenged in my heart as well as helped to see and love the Lord more. This is a book to treasure and share with all.

KATHY MANCHESTER
Pastor's wife, Mother and Educator, North Sydney, Australia

Diana Severance has written the most beautiful daily devotional book for women: *Her-Story*. She combines a collection of women throughout Christian history who have offered their lives, work, and personal sacrifice for Jesus Christ and His ministry. Beautifully-written, a reader (woman or man!) will daily read, worship, and learn about many Christians, both well-known and lesser known. I highly recommend Diana Severance's new book, published by Christian Focus.

DENISE GEORGE
Author, teacher, speaker
Birmingham, Alabama

Never have I read a daily devotional book that is a page-turner. This one is. Drawing on real life stories from New Testament times to now, the author sheds light on the convictions, commitments, struggles, joys, and yes sorrows of some 365 women who have trusted and served Christ. Read this for new insight into church history, fresh gratitude for God's glory in women's lives, and strong motivation to aspire to the levels of faith, love, sacrifice, and service on display in these fascinating vignettes. This gives not a sugary but rather a protein boost to pondering Scripture, to prayer, and to worship.

ROBERT W. YARBROUGH
Professor of New Testament
Covenant Theological Seminary
St. Louis, Missouri

Her-Story

366 DEVOTIONS *from* 21 CENTURIES *of the* CHRISTIAN CHURCH

DIANA LYNN SEVERANCE

CHRISTIAN
FOCUS

Unless otherwise stated, Scripture quotations taken from the *Holy Bible, English Standard Version*. Copyright © 2001 by Crossway, a publishing ministry of Good News Publishers. Used by permission of Good News Publishers. All rights reserved.

Copyright © Diana Lynn Severance 2016

Diana Lynn Severance has asserted her right under the Copyright, Designs and Patents Act, 1988, to be identified as Author of this work.

A CIP catalogue record for this book is available from the British Library.

paperback ISBN: 978-1-78191-750-3

First published in 2016

Reprinted in 2018 and 2020
by
Christian Focus Publications Ltd,
Geanies House, Fearn, Ross-shire
IV20 1TW, Scotland

www.christianfocus.com

Cover design by Sarah Bosman

Printed by Gutenberg, Malta

All rights reserved. No part of this publication may be reproduced, stored in a retrieval system, or transmitted, in any form, by any means, electronic, mechanical, photocopying, recording or otherwise, without the prior permission of the publisher or a licence permitting restricted copying In the U.K. such licences are issued by the Copyright Licensing Agency, 4 Battlebridge Lane, London, SE1 2HX, www.cla.co.uk.

Contents

Women in Late Antiquity

Women in the Early Middle Ages

Women in the Late Middle Ages

Women of the Reformation

Reform and Revival

A Benevolent Society

Victorian Christian Women

At the End of Two Millennia

*You shall love the Lord your God with all your heart
and with all your soul and with all your mind.*

~MATTHEW 22:37~

Preface

Women were an integral part of Jesus' life and ministry as described in all four Gospels, and they are integral to the life of the church wherever Christianity has spread. Women whose hearts were transformed by faith in Jesus now lived for God, and for others rather than themselves. In whatever position they found themselves, whether queens or slaves, they lived for their Savior and sought to bring others to Him. They did whatever was necessary in whatever place God had placed them: mentoring other Christians, supporting their husbands in Christian work, showing hospitality, instructing other women, teaching children, or helping those in need and distress. Many of the women accomplished what seemed to be impossible. They would have admitted as much, while recognizing that God gave them the strength to accomplish His will through them. Many of the women suffered persecution, torture, and even death for Christ. They were bright lights in a darkened world.

These glimpses of Christian women are arranged in a basic chronological order. Because of the sources available, women in more recent centuries predominate. Yet, we have a sisterly affection for those in early times. Though in material ways their world differed greatly from ours, we share many of the same trials, afflictions, and spiritual passions.

A verse of Scripture concludes each daily entry. The verse is a biblical commentary on the life of the lady or ladies of the day and can also become a personal prayer for our own Christian walk, as we seek to live lives that reflect a heart for God.

Diana Lynn Severance

JANUARY 1

'Another Year is Dawning'

∞ Frances Ridley Havergal, 1836-1879 ∞

Frances Ridley Havergal is one of the sweetest of hymn writers whose hymns continue to comfort, encourage, and enrich many. Frances' father was a clergyman known for his hymn writing and musical compositions, and Frances shared in this talent.

Frances gave an account of her hymn writing:

> Writing is praying with me; for I never seem to write even a verse by myself, and I feel like a little child writing. You know a child would look up at every sentence and say, 'And what shall I say next?' This is just what I do. I ask that at every line He would give me, not merely thoughts and power, but also every *word*, even the very rhymes. Very often I have a most distinct and happy consciousness of direct answers.[1]

In her personal life as well as in her writing, Frances had a deep humility. She wrote a friend:

> My experience is that it is nearly always just in proportion to my sense of personal insufficiency in writing anything that God sends his blessing and power with it. … I think he must give us that total dependence on him for every word, which can only come by feeling one's own helplessness and incapacity, before he can very much use us.[2]

Frances' faithful trust in the Lord is evident in her hymn for the New Year:

Another year is dawning:
Dear Master, let it be,
In working or in waiting,
Another year with thee.

Another year of leaning
Upon thy loving breast,
Of ever-deepening trustfulness,
Of quiet, happy rest.

Another year of mercies,
Of faithfulness and grace;
Another year of gladness
In the shining of thy face.

Another year of progress;
Another year of praise:
Another year of proving
Thy presence 'all the days'.

Another year of service,
Of witness for thy love;
Another year of training
For holier work above.

Another year is dawning
Dear Master, let it be,
On earth, or else in heaven,
Another year for thee.

So teach us to number our days that
we may get a heart of wisdom.
~ PSALM 90:12 ~

---

1. Mrs E. R. Pitman, *Lady Hymn Writers* (T. Nelson & Sons, 1892), p. 74.
2. Ibid, p. 75.

Women in the
New Testament

Woman of the Word

∞ Mary, 1st century ∞

One of the most popular subjects in Christian art is Gabriel's announcement to Mary that she would have a son. In most of the paintings, Mary is shown reading the Scriptures when Gabriel appears to her. As she is taking in the written Word of God, she also will conceive the Living Word of God. Often a dove is shown over Mary as well, symbolizing that her virgin conception would be by the Holy Spirit.

That Mary was a woman deeply rooted in the Scriptures is clear from the Gospel records. She was thoroughly acquainted with the prophecies of a coming Seed, a Messiah, who would bring blessing to all nations.[1] She knew that her bearing a child apart from the normal means of conception was impossible, but she believed God's Word spoken to her by Gabriel, knowing that God can perform the impossible.

Mary's song of praise when she met her cousin Elizabeth (Luke 1:46-55) reveals Mary's deep knowledge of the Scripture, for the song contains over thirty quotes or allusions to Scripture:

My soul magnifies the Lord,[2]
And my spirit rejoices in God my Savior,[3]
For he has looked on the humble estate of his
  servant,[4]
For behold, from now on all generations will
  call me blessed;[5]
For he who is mighty has done great things
  for me,[6]
and holy is his name.[7]
And his mercy is for those who fear him[8]
From generation to generation.
He has shown strength with his arm;[9]

He has scattered the proud in the thoughts
  of their hearts;[10]
He has brought down the mighty from
  their thrones
And exalted those of humble estate;[11]
He has filled the hungry with good
  things,[12]
and the rich he has sent away empty.[13]
He has helped his servant Israel,[14]
In remembrance of his mercy,[15]
as he spoke to our fathers,[16]
to Abraham and to his offspring forever.

The Gospel accounts of Jesus' birth show Mary was a woman of humility and faith in God's power, goodness, and the truth of His Word. Mary not only knew God's Word, but meditated on the events brought into her life and how God might be working in them (Luke 2:49-51).

Mary was at the foot of the cross when Jesus died. While on the cross, Jesus entrusted the care of his mother to the disciple John. After Jesus' ascension, she remained in Jerusalem, praying with the disciples in the Upper Room awaiting the promised Holy Spirit. In this last mention of Mary in the Scriptures, as in the first, she is shown obedient to God's Word.

*But when the fullness of time had come, God sent forth his
Son, born of woman, born under the law.*

~ GALATIANS 4:4 ~

1. Gen. 3:15; 12:1-3
2. II Sam. 2:1-10; Ps. 34:2.
3. Ps. 35:9; Hab. 3:18; Isa. 61:10.
4. Ps. 138:6.
5. Ps. 72:17.
6. Ps. 89:8; Zeph. 3:17; Ps. 71:19.
7. Ps. 99:3; 111:9; Isa. 57:15.
8. Deut. 5:10; Pss. 89:1-2; 103:17.

9. Pss. 89:10; 98:1; 118:16; Isa. 51:9.
10. Dan. 4:37.
11. Pss. 75:7; 107:40; 113:7-8; 147:6.
12. Pss. 34:10; 107:9.
13. Job 22:9.
14. Isa. 41:8-9; 44:21; 49:3.
15. Ps. 98:3; Mic. 7:20.
16. Gen. 17:9; Ps. 132:11.

First Two Women to Know Jesus as Lord

∞ Elizabeth and Anna, 1st century ∞

Among the first women who recognized Jesus as the Lord and Redeemer were two elderly women who had dedicating their lives to serving God. After Gabriel told Mary she would have a son, the promised Messiah, Mary left Nazareth to visit her relative Elizabeth in Judah. Gabriel had told Mary that Elizabeth and her husband Zachariah were to have a child, though Elizabeth had always been barren and was past child-bearing years. When Mary first saw her relative, Elizabeth, full of the Holy Spirit, exclaimed,

> Blessed are you among women, and blessed is the fruit of your womb! And why is this granted to me that the mother of my Lord should come to me? For behold, when the sound of your greeting came to my ears, the baby in my womb [John the Baptist] leaped for joy. And blessed is she who believed that there would be a fulfillment of what was spoken to her from the Lord. (Luke 1:42-45)

Elizabeth thus became the first woman recorded in Scripture to recognize that Mary's baby was the promised King and Lord prophesied of in the Hebrew Scriptures. Mary stayed with Elizabeth three months, and undoubtedly received much encouragement as she witnessed the birth of John the Baptist and the fulfillment of the angel's word to Zachariah.

After Jesus' birth in Bethlehem, Joseph and Mary followed Jewish law and took Jesus to the temple to be dedicated. There they were greeted by Simeon – who had been told by the Holy Spirit that he would not die until he had seen the Christ – and Anna. Anna was eighty-four and had been a widow for around sixty years. She had a devotion to God and spent her life in fasting and prayer and serving in the temple. Anna was in the temple when Simeon met Mary, Joseph, and the baby Jesus, and she heard his proclamation, 'Lord ... my eyes have seen your salvation that you have prepared in the presence of all peoples, a light for revelation to the Gentiles, and for glory to your people Israel' (Luke 2:29-32). Anna thanked God for beholding the promised Messiah and spread the news about him to those who were waiting for the fulfillment of God's promises for the redemption of Jerusalem.

You shall call his name Jesus.
He will be great and will be called the Son of the Most High. And the Lord
God will give to him the throne of his father David, and he will reign over
the house of Jacob forever, and of his kingdom there will be no end.

~ LUKE 1:31-33 ~

Spreading the Good News of Jesus

We don't know her name, only where she lived. We don't know a lot about her, but we do know her life was transformed by an encounter with Jesus by a well in Samaria. Though the Jews and Samaritans avoided each other with a certain hatred because of historic and religious differences, the Gospel writer tells us that Jesus needed to be in Samaria (John 4:4) undoubtedly to meet the woman at the well who would become his evangelist to the Samaritan people.

Jesus was thirsty and tired as he waited by Jacob's well for his disciples to go into the village to get some food. The land was where Jacob had pitched his tent; Jacob later gave the land to Joseph, whose bones were buried nearby when the Israelites returned from Egypt. When a woman from the village came to draw water from the well, she was surprised when Jesus asked her for a drink. After all, he was a Jew, and she was a Samaritan woman. The rabbis said a man should not even speak in public to his own wife! To her surprise, Jesus replied:

> If you knew the gift of God, and who it is that is saying to you, 'Give me a drink,' you would have asked him, and he would have given you the living water. … Everyone who drinks of this water will be thirsty again, but whoever drinks of the water that I will give him will never be thirsty again … The water that I will give him will become in him a spring of water welling up to eternal life (John 4:10, 13-14).

Now the woman was truly astonished. Was this man greater than Jacob who had made the well to begin with? Having an eternal water supply sounded wonderful! She asked Jesus for that water, so she wouldn't have to come daily to Jacob's well. Then, Jesus revealed he knew the woman's deepest needs. He asked her to call her husband. When she said she had none, he said that was true, since she had had five husbands and now was living with a man not her husband! Now the woman knew Jesus was a prophet, and she began asking the spiritual questions with which she had long struggled. The Jews and Samaritans have different worship practices—which is the right one? Jesus told her that salvation was of the Jews and the Father desired all to worship him in spirit and in truth. The woman knew that the Messiah, the Christ, was coming, and when he came, he would 'tell us all things.'[1] Jesus then revealed himself to the woman as he had not directly revealed himself to the Jewish people when he said, 'I who speak to you am he.'[2] Jesus clearly claimed his position as Messiah to the woman at the well in Samaria.

The woman became one of the first evangelists for Jesus. She ran back into the village, bringing many out to meet Jesus. Many Samaritans believed in Him because of the woman's testimony. Jesus stayed in the village two days, and many came to know that He indeed was the Savior of the world.

> 'If anyone thirsts, let him come to me and drink. Whoever believes in me, as the Scripture has said, "Out of his heart will flow rivers of living water".'
>
> ~ JOHN 7:37-38 ~

---

1. John 4:25.
2. John 4:26.

Tale of Two Sisters

∞ Mary and Martha, 1st century ∞

Though sisters, Mary and Martha were as different as two ladies could be. Martha was active and impulsive; Mary was meditative and reticent. Martha was busy with household chores, while Mary was sitting at Jesus' feet for instruction. Mary and Martha, along with their brother Lazarus, came from a family of some wealth. Martha had the gift of hospitality and welcomed Jesus and the twelve disciples into their home and provided for them. Yet, Martha's generous actions became corrupted by pride. She became self-absorbed in her service for Jesus so that she wasn't receiving her necessary spiritual food from Him. Her pride made her susceptible to the sins of anger, resentment, jealousy, distrust, and a critical spirit. She used herself as the perfect measure to judge others and began watching her sister Mary with a critical eye; she even impugned Jesus as not caring for her: 'Martha was distracted with much serving. And she went up to him [Jesus] and said, "Lord, do you not care that my sister has left me to serve alone? Tell her then to help me."' Jesus answered Martha with tenderness, 'Martha, Martha, you are anxious and troubled about many things, but one thing is necessary. Mary has chosen the good portion, which will not be taken away from her' (Luke 10:40-42). Martha was preoccupied with what she could do for Jesus, rather than what He could do for her.

When their brother Lazarus was ill, Mary and Martha sent word to Jesus, but he delayed in coming right away, arriving in Bethany after Lazarus died. Jesus was teaching Mary and Martha that His delays are not denials, and they witnessed the most compelling of Jesus' miracles when Jesus raised Lazarus from the tomb. Martha knew that Jesus was 'the Christ, the Son of God, who is coming into the world.'[3] After Jesus raised Lazarus, the Jewish leaders plotted to put Jesus and Lazarus to death. At another dinner in the home of Martha and Mary, Martha continued to serve Jesus, but no longer was distracted by her work. Mary anointed Jesus' feet with an expensive ointment. Her action expressed her thankfulness for Jesus raising Lazarus, as well as her anticipation of Jesus' coming death and burial. Mary, more than the other disciples and followers, understood Jesus' death was imminent.

In the Gospel accounts of Mary and Martha, we find two sisters in the ordinary events of life who meet Jesus and recognize Him as their Deliverer. They learned He is the resurrection and the life and deserves our true worship as well as our service.

'I am the resurrection and the life. Whoever believes in me, though he die, yet shall he live, and everyone who lives and believes in me shall never die.'

~ JOHN 11:25-26 ~

---

3. John 11:27.

First to See the Risen Lord

∞ Mary Magdalene, 1st century ∞

After Mary the mother of Jesus, Mary Magdalene is the woman most frequently mentioned in the Gospels. She is mentioned twelve times there and is often called 'Mary Magdalene,' after her hometown, a fishing village on the Sea of Galilee, and to distinguish her from the six other Marys among Jesus' followers. Mary at one time was possessed of seven demons, but Jesus healed her (Mark 16:9). She then became his faithful follower, joining the group of women who helped finance Jesus' ministry (Luke 8:1-3). She was in Jerusalem for the Last Passover and remained with Jesus' mother and other women at the crucifixion (Matt. 27:56, 28:1; Luke 23:55).

In the third century Hippolytus wrongly identified Mary Magdalene with Mary of Bethany, Lazarus's sister, and with the sinner at Jesus' feet in Luke 7:37-50. In 591, in a series of sermons, Pope Gregory I also combined these three different women as one and described her as a prostitute, leading many to equate her with the woman taken in adultery in John 8. Many writers and artists in the following centuries continued to identify these different women as one. In 1969, the Vatican officially recognized these were separate women.

Mary and some other women awoke early after the Sabbath following Jesus' crucifixion and went outside the city to Jesus' tomb, planning to complete the proper preparations of Jesus' body for burial. When they arrived, they saw the stone was rolled away from the tomb, and His body was not in the tomb. Mary was horrified and ran back into the city to tell the disciples that someone had stolen the body of Jesus. She then made her way back to the tomb, hoping to find out who had done this thing! As she approached the tomb again, two angels asked her why she was weeping. She replied 'They have taken away my Lord, and I do not know where they have laid him.'[4] Turning around, she saw Jesus, but through her tears and despair, she didn't recognize him. Thinking he was the gardener, she pleaded that if he had taken away Jesus' body to show her where and she would take care of it! When Jesus simply said her name, 'Mary,' she recognized her Lord and clung to him. Interestingly, the one she thought was the gardener had indeed taken away the body of Jesus – transforming it into his glorious resurrected body. Jesus commissioned Mary to go and tell the disciples that he was alive, so she ran back into the city with the glorious news. Mary became the first person to see the risen Jesus and the first to share this good news that he was alive with the disciples.

> *Blessed be the God and Father of our Lord Jesus Christ! According to his great mercy, he has caused us to be born again to a living hope through the resurrection of Jesus Christ from the dead, to an inheritance that is imperishable, undefiled, and unfading, kept in heaven for you …*
>
> ~ I Peter 1:3-4 ~

---

4. John 20:13.

First European Convert

∞ Lydia, 1st century ∞

On his second missionary journey, the apostle Paul revisited the cities in what is today Turkey, where people had come to Christ on his previous trip. At Lystra, Timothy joined Paul and Silas as the team planned to continue to take the gospel west into the Province of Asia. The Holy Spirit, however, constrained them and forbade their preaching the gospel in the region. They travelled 400 miles by foot before reaching Troas. There Paul had a vision at night of a Macedonian man saying, 'Come over to Macedonia and help us.'[5] Confidently knowing the direction the Lord was now leading them, Paul and his companions set sail for Samothrace and Neapolis. Stepping for the first time on the continent of Europe, they made their way to Philippi, the leading city of Macedonia.

It had been Paul's method to attend the synagogues of the towns through which he travelled and bring the gospel to the people there. Since there was no synagogue in Philippi, Paul and his companions went to the stream outside the city, where Jews often assembled for worship when a synagogue was not available. There they found a group of women meeting together, and Paul told them the message of Jesus. The Lord especially opened the heart of Lydia, a merchant from Thyatira who sold goods dyed with an expensive purple dye. She had become a worshipper of the Jewish God and recognized in Jesus the fulfillment of God's promises of old to His people. That day Lydia was baptized, becoming the first known European convert to Christianity.

Being a woman of some means, Lydia immediately urged Paul and his friends to stay at her house, telling them, 'If you have judged me to be faithful to the Lord, come to my house and stay' (Acts 16:15). Lydia's house then became the site of meetings of the first Christian church in Europe.

Some time later, after Paul healed a demon possessed girl who was earning money for her master by her wild utterances, merchants of the city had Paul and Silas arrested for disturbing the peace. They were beaten and thrown into prison. During the night, as the two were praying and singing hymns, an earthquake shook the city and the foundations of the prison, loosening the chains of the prisoners. When the jailer feared all the prisoners had escaped, Paul assured him all were there and took advantage of the opportunity to tell him the gospel: 'Believe in the Lord Jesus, and you will be saved …'[6]

When Paul and Silas were released from prison, they went back to Lydia's home. There they met with the Christians, were encouraged by their faith, and then departed for Thessalonica. Lydia was the first of many women throughout Christian history whose hospitality to others was her service to Christ.

The Lord opened her heart to pay attention to what was said by Paul.

~ ACTS 16: 14 ~

---

5. Acts 16:9.
6. Acts 16:31.

Aquila's Wife and Fellow Worker with Paul

∞ Priscilla, 1st century ∞

Aquila and Priscilla comprise a most fascinating couple in the New Testament. They are always mentioned together, for they were a team. Not only were they in the business of tent making together, but they loved God's Word and served the Lord together. Aquila was a Jew from Pontus. Priscilla (also called 'Prisca', the diminutive form of Priscilla) might have been a Gentile, possibly from the Roman family Prisca, and thus of a higher social status. They were living in Rome, but were forced to leave when Claudius expelled the Jews from Rome, possibly over disturbances in the capital city between the early Christians and Jews.

Aquila and Priscilla then went to Corinth. On his second missionary journey, Paul stayed with them while there. They shared the tent making business as well as the gospel ministry. It is not known when Aquila and Priscilla became Christians. Possibly they had been in Jerusalem at Pentecost and had taken the Christian faith back with them to Rome. It does seem, however, that they were Christians before they had met Paul. They were an encouragement to Paul during his eighteen-month stay in Corinth. When he went on to Ephesus, Aquila and Priscilla went with him.

After Paul left Ephesus, Apollos, an eloquent preacher of the Scriptures from Alexandria, arrived in town. Aquila and Priscilla went to hear him. Apollos taught accurately about Jesus, but his knowledge was incomplete, not knowing about Christian baptism and possibly not familiar with Pentecost and the ministry of the Holy Spirit. Aquila and Priscilla took Apollos aside and explained the way of God more accurately to him. Apollos went on to have a fruitful ministry in Corinth.

When Claudius died Aquila and Priscilla returned to their home in Rome. In his letter to the Romans, Paul sent greetings to the couple and noted that a church met in their house and that they had 'risked their necks for my life'. What this refers to is unknown. But whether in Corinth or Ephesus, Aquila and Priscilla had risked everything in rescuing Paul from some life-threatening difficulty.

Paul mentioned Aquila and Priscilla again in his last letter to Timothy. The couple had returned to Ephesus; possibly the persecution of Christians after Nero's burning of Rome caused them to leave Rome again. Priscilla and Aquila are an example of a married couple's oneness in the gospel. Knowing persecution and hardship, opening their homes to the church, and teaching the truth to others, they were willing to risk their necks for the gospel and became important building blocks of the earliest church.

Indeed, all who desire to live a godly life in
Christ Jesus will be persecuted …

~ 2 TIMOTHY 3:12 ~

Phoebe and Paul's Roman Friends

☜ 1st century ☞

Certainly the most influential of all of Paul's writings is his letter to the Romans. Samuel Taylor Coleridge thought this 'the most profound work in existence'. John Calvin wrote that, 'When anyone understands this epistle, he has opened to him … the understanding of the whole Scriptures.' The letter was important in the conversion of Augustine, Martin Luther, John Wesley, and countless others. In the concluding section of the book Paul sends greetings to twenty-eight named individuals in Rome. Even though Paul had never been to Rome, he knew quite a few of the Christians in the city. Of the twenty-eight people named, at least eight are women.

Paul began his greetings by commending Phoebe, 'our sister', who is 'a servant of the church in Cenchrea' (a port near Corinth). Phoebe was a businesswoman who probably brought Paul's letter to Rome. What a treasure she carried and preserved over the many Roman miles! Paul encourages the Roman Christians to 'help her in whatever she may need from you', because she has been a helper to him and many others.[7]

Paul greeted two husband and wife teams. Aquila and Prisca, whom Paul first met in Corinth, were back in Rome with a church meeting in their home. Paul recognized these friends and fellow workers 'risked their necks for my life', and all the churches were thankful for them. Paul also greeted Andronicus and Junia, fellow Jews who were believers before Paul's conversion and had been imprisoned with Paul at some point.

Paul mentioned Mary, Persis, Tryphaena and Tryphosa as workers in the Lord. Tryphaena and Tryphosa's names are from a common root meaning gentle or delicate, and they might have been sisters. Julia is also a woman to whom greetings were sent.

An intriguing greeting is Paul's to Rufus, 'chosen in the Lord; also his mother, who has been a mother to me as well'. Rufus was the son of Simon of Cyrene, who was forced by the Roman soldiers to help carry Jesus' cross (Mark 15:21). Rufus' mother would have been Simon's wife. Luke records that men from Cyprus and Cyrene were the first to bring the gospel to Antioch (Acts 11:20). Possibly Simon and Rufus were among these first missionaries. If so, possibly it was at Antioch that Rufus's mother had taken motherly care of Paul in his early Christian life.

Therefore, my beloved brothers, be steadfast, immoveable, always
abounding in the work of the Lord, knowing that in the Lord
your labour is not in vain.

~ 1 CORINTHIANS 15:58 ~

---

7. Romans 16:1-2.

Women in the
Early Church

Lady with Imperial Connections

∞ Domitilla, 1st century ∞

The catacombs of ancient Rome are fascinating repositories of ancient history. These underground burial chambers contain early Christian art and inscriptions which reflect the Christians' hope of resurrection and a new life in Christ. One of the most extensive and best preserved of the catacombs is that of Flavia Domitilla, who donated land for the catacombs along the Appian Way in Rome. Living at the end of the first century, Domitilla was the granddaughter of the Emperor Vespasian and wife of Titus Clemens, who shared the consulate with Vespasian's son Domitian. When Domitian became Emperor, he adopted Domitilla and Clemens' sons as successors to the throne. Domitilla was certainly among the powerful and well-connected in Rome.

We have tantalizing hints of Domitilla's Christian faith, not only in the donation of land for Christian burial, but also in the persecution she suffered for her faith. Christianity was not yet an accepted religion in the Roman Empire, and Christians periodically suffered persecution. A notable Christian persecuted under Emperor Domitian was the apostle John, who was exiled to the island of Patmos. Domitilla and Clemens' closeness to the imperial throne did not protect them from persecution. Clemens was executed, and Domitilla was banished to the island of Pandataria in the Tyrrhenian Sea. Their crime? 'Atheism' – or not believing in the gods of Rome. This was frequently a charge against Jews and Christians at this time.

The church of St Clement in Rome, constructed in the fourth century, is built on a large house from the first century, likely the house of Domitilla and Clemens. Very possibly this was the location of one of the early Christian house churches in Rome. In the first century, Christianity had spread throughout the Roman Empire and even reached those closest to the Emperor. They, along with Christians throughout the Empire, also endured suffering for the name of Christ.

'A servant is not greater than his master. If they persecuted me,
they will also persecute you.'

~ JOHN 15:20 ~

Bold Witness for Christ

∞ Blandina, d. 2 June 177 ∞

Throughout the history of the church, believers have kept others informed of church affairs by writing letters. One letter which has come down to us from the second century was written by Christians in Lyon, in what is now France, to Christians in Asia Minor, in what is now Turkey. Christians from Asia Minor had first brought the gospel to Lyon and continued to have an interest in their 'daughter church'. The letter we have dates from 177, and describes the bold witness of the martyr Blandina.

In 177, people in the towns of Lyon and nearby Vienne became very hostile to Christians. Mobs attacked and robbed the Christians, and they were stoned in the markets and public places. Under torture, servants of the Christians falsely accused them of cannibalism and incest, which led to the imprisonment and torture of more Christians. They were tortured in various ways before being sent to the arena to be publicly tormented before the people. Among these was the Christian slave girl Blandina.

The persecutors could not break Blandina and get her to renounce Christ, though her body was mangled and broken. She only gained strength from her persistent confession, 'I am a Christian, and there is nothing vile done by us.' After being tortured Blandina was put on a stake in the arena to be devoured by wild beasts. When the animals did not come near her, she was taken down and thrown again into prison. Other prisoners gained strength from her courage.

On the last day of the spectacle, Blandina was brought into the arena, scourged, and placed on a red-hot iron seat so her flesh burned. Finally, she was placed in a net and tossed about by a bull, and so she died. Even the pagans observed 'that never among them had a woman endured so many and such terrible tortures'.[1] Yet, in her weakness, Blandina was clothed with the strength of Christ. She would not deny Him and remained a bold witness for her Lord.

> 'My grace is sufficient for you, for my power is made perfect in weakness.'
> Therefore I will boast all the more gladly of my weaknesses, so that the
> power of Christ may rest upon me. For the sake of Christ, then, I am
> content with weaknesses, insults, hardships, persecutions, and calamities.
> For when I am weak, then I am strong.
>
> ~ 2 CORINTHIANS 12:9-10 ~

---

1. The letter describing the martyrdom of Blandina and the other martyrs from Lyon can be found in Eusebius, *Church History*, V, I-3. This can be read online at the Christian Classics Ethereal Library: http://www.ccel.org/ccel/schaff/npnf201.iii.x.ii.html.

'I am a Christian'

In 202, Roman Emperor Septimius Severus issued a decree forbidding anyone from converting to Judaism or Christianity. In the north African city of Carthage, a twenty-one-year-old named Perpetua was among those arrested for her recent conversion. Perpetua was from a respectable family, married, and had an infant son. Her father and the Roman officials pled with her to renounce her faith and offer sacrifices for the well-being of the Emperors, but Perpetua would not. She said, 'I am a Christian and cannot be called by any other name. Just as a pot cannot be anything other than a pot, so a Christian cannot be anything other than a Christian.'

When she was first imprisoned in the dungeon, Perpetua became quite despondent surrounded by absolute darkness. As she found renewed strength in Christ, however, she said the dungeon became like a palace. Perpetua gave her infant son into the care of relatives. She wrote down her thoughts and experiences, including several visions, while in prison, becoming the first Christian woman whose writings we have today. Her writings show she believed death, even death by martyrdom, is not an accident, but a call from God. God was sovereignly in control of human affairs. Through his death and resurrection Christ had won the victory over death and Satan, and Perpetua saw her death as sharing in that victory and ushering her into eternal life. Christ gave her the strength and power to endure.

On 7 March, 203, Perpetua, along with a slave girl named Felicitas, was sent into the arena in Carthage with a mad heifer released against them as the crowds cheered. Tossed about cruelly by the heifer for a time, she was put to death by having her throat cut. How could a twenty-one year old woman give up her life and her infant son? Perpetua's answer was, 'I am a Christian.' She was a witness to the truth, which was more important and powerful than torture and physical pain.

'They will lay their hands on you and persecute you, delivering you up to the synagogues and prisons, and you will be brought before kings and governors for my name's sake. This will be your opportunity to bear witness.'

~ LUKE 21:12-13 ~

Living and Dying for Jesus

∞ Agatha, d. 251 ∞

When Decius became Roman Emperor in 249 he hoped to restore something of the glory of Rome, including the traditional Roman religion. In 250, he issued an edict requiring everyone in the Empire to sacrifice to the Roman gods and burn incense to the Emperor in the presence of a magistrate; a certificate was issued to all who sacrificed.

It was during this time, in the town of Catana in Sicily, that Quintianus, the governor, set his lust and avarice on Agatha. Agatha was from a rich and noble family, was beautiful, and had dedicated herself to Jesus Christ. When she did not sacrifice to the gods, Quintianus had Agatha arrested. Agatha prayed, 'Jesus Christ, Lord of all things, you see my heart, you know my desire – possess alone all that I am. I am your sheep, you make me worthy to overcome the devil.'[2] Quintianus turned Agatha over to Aphrodisia, who ran a house of prostitution, thinking Agatha's virtue would soon be broken. Agatha, however, trusted in God for protection and continued to resist assaults against her. After a month, when Quintianus was informed of Agatha's constancy, he had her brought before him. Under questioning, Agatha courageously proclaimed she was a servant of Jesus Christ, who was her life and her salvation. Quintianus had her thrown into prison where she was stretched on the rack, tormented with iron hooks, and burned with torches. When she continued to resist and refused to sacrifice to the gods, Quintianus had her rolled naked over live coals and broken postherds. Agatha prayed, 'Lord, my Creator, you have protected me from the cradle; you have taken me from the love of the world, and given me patience to suffer; receive now my soul.' Agatha died soon after. Before her physical death, she had already died to the world and sought to live only for her Savior.

For to me to live is Christ, and to die is gain.

~ PHILIPPIANS 1:21 ~

---

2. Rev. Alban Butler, *The Lives of the Fathers, Martyrs, and Other Principal Saints*, Vol. 1. (D. & J. Sadler & Co., 1864).

Passing on a Godly Heritage

∞ Nonna, b. 305? d. 5 August 374 ∞

Nonna was born into a prosperous Christian family in Nazianzus, in Cappadocia (in modern Turkey). When she married Gregory, a wealthy land owner of the region, he was not a Christian. Nonna was deeply burdened that they did not share a oneness of spirit in the Lord and prayed diligently for her husband's salvation. Her prayers and her godly character softened Gregory's heart, and he did come to faith in Christ. Nonna and Gregory then enjoyed a spiritual union and oneness in the Lord and a beautiful marriage. Gregory was named Bishop of Nazianzus and faithfully served his flock. He used his wealth to build the church building in the community.

Nonna and Gregory had three children, all of whom served Christ's church and were noted for their godly lives. Even before her first son was born, Nonna promised him to the Lord, and she dedicated him to God immediately after his birth. This son, named Gregory after his father, became Archbishop of Constantinople, a noted Trinitarian theologian, and is counted among the Doctors of the church. Her second son, Caesarius, became a distinguished court physician in Constantinople. Nonna's daughter, Gorgonia, was also noted for her godly conduct and care for the poor; her two sons also became bishops in the church.

Gregory recognized his parents' beautiful marriage was a gift from the Lord:

> Had anyone from the ends of the earth and from every race of men attempted to bring about the best of marriages, he could not have found a better or more harmonious one than this. For the most excellent of men and of women were so united that their marriage was a union of virtue rather than of bodies: since, while they excelled all others, they could not excel each other, because in virtue they were quite equally matched. … She who was given by God to my father became not only, as is less wonderful, his assistant, but even his leader, drawing him on by her influence in deed and word to the highest excellence; judging it best in all other respects to be overruled by her husband according to the law of marriage, but not being ashamed, in regard to piety, even to offer herself as his teacher. … She … has acknowledged but one kind of beauty, that of the soul, and the preservation, or the restoration as far as possible, of the Divine image.[3]

Nonna was a woman of deeds as well as prayer. Both she and her husband came from families with wealth, and while Gregory devoted himself to his pastoral duties, Nonna administered their wealth, liberally helping the poor and those in need. She was a remarkable wife and mother – devoting herself to the church without neglecting her responsibilities to her husband and children.

> *Likewise wives, be subject to your own husbands, so that even if some do*
> *not obey the word, they may be won without a word by the conduct of*
> *their wives, when they see your respectful and pure conduct.*
>
> ~ I Peter 3:1-2 ~

---

3. Gregory Nazianzus, 'Select Orations, Sermons, Letters; Dogmatic Treatises', trans. in *Nicene and Post-Nicene Fathers*, 2nd Series, ed. P. Schaff and H. Wace (Repr. Grand Rapids, MI: Wm. B. Eerdmans, 1955), VII, pp. 256-257.

First Christian Queen

∽ Helena, c. 250 – c. 330 ∾

Helena was almost eighty when she took her journey to the Holy Land in 326-328, but she began a path of pilgrimage many have followed over the centuries. Helena's origins and birthplace are uncertain, though there is some evidence she was the daughter of an innkeeper from Bithynia in Asia Minor. She became the wife of the Roman military leader Constantius, and on 27 February, about 272, their son Constantine was born.

On the rising political path to become Emperor, Constantius divorced Helena some time before 289; her lower social position was a hindrance to his political advancement. Their son Constantine, however, always maintained a respect and love for his mother. It is likely that when Constantine converted to Christianity, he encouraged his mother in the Christian faith as well. After Constantine became Emperor in 306, he brought Helena to the imperial court and gave her the title Augusta. He had coins struck with her likeness on them and the inscription 'most noble lady Helena'.

Not only did Constantine allow freedom of religion within the Empire, he also actively sponsored the building of churches. He encouraged Helena to travel to the Holy Land and seek out Biblical sites which churches could commemorate. Helena attended the dedication of the Church of the Nativity in Bethlehem and visited the place many revered as the tomb of Jesus, where the Church of the Holy Sepulcher was being built. On the Mount of Olives she dedicated the Church of the Ascension. Constantine apparently gave Helena limitless access to the imperial treasury for her travels, and she freely distributed funds to the poor along the way as well as providing lavish offerings to the churches she visited. Like many Christian queens after her, Helena used her position and wealth to help the needy and encourage the Christian faith of her people.

In 330, two years after returning from her Holy Land pilgrimage, Helena died surrounded by Constantine and his three sons.

> *But far be it from me to boast except in the cross of our Lord Jesus Christ,*
> *by which the world has been crucified to me, and I to the world.*
>
> ~ GALATIANS 6:14 ~

Faithful to Death

∞ Agnes, 291-304 ∞

One of the revered martyrs of the early church is a thirteen-year-old girl named Agnes. Agnes was raised in a Christian family and early gave herself to Christ. A lovely girl from a family of means, Agnes had many suitors, including the son of the Prefect Sempronius, but she rejected them all, wishing to remain a virgin and serve Christ only. One of the suitors, angered by Agnes' rejection, turned her name in to the authorities as a Christian.

In 303, Emperor Diocletian had issued an edict requiring all to follow Roman religious practices and sacrifice to the Roman gods. As a Christian, Agnes would not deny her Savior. Since it was against Roman law to execute a virgin, tradition says the judge sent Agnes to a brothel, where he thought her virginity would be quickly taken from her. Though stripped naked and humiliated, all who attempted to do harm to Agnes were in some way prevented, and her chastity was preserved. Legend says some attempting to rape her were struck blind or dead.

After a formal trial, Agnes was sentenced to death. She was executed on 21 January 304. When the wood would not burn at her execution, she was beheaded. Agnes was buried beside the Via Nomentana in Rome, and a large catacomb grew up around her tomb. The story of Agnes's faithfulness to Christ in the face of death inspired many. Even pagans were shocked at the brutal execution of the teenager, and their disapproval might have curbed the Diocletian persecutions somewhat. Ambrose, Prudentius and others wrote poems and works extolling Agnes's chastity and faithful witness (for the original meaning of the word *martyr* is indeed 'witness').

Later in the fourth century Constantina, daughter of Emperor Constantine I, had a basilica built over Agnes' tomb; it was remodeled in the seventh century and remains in Rome today. Early in Christian art, Agnes was represented with a lamb, the Latin word for lamb being *agnus*.

'Blessed are the pure in heart, for they shall see God.'
~MATTHEW 5:8~

Three Sisters Standing Bold for the Scriptures

∽ Agape, Chionia, and Irene, d. 5 April 304 ∽

In 303, the Roman Emperor Diocletian issued an edict which ordered the destruction of all Christian Scriptures and churches throughout the Empire and forbade Christians to assemble for worship. Three sisters living in Thessalonica – Agape, Chionia, and Irene (whose names mean love, purity, and peace) – hid the Scriptures they had in their house and fled to the mountains, where they remained in hiding for almost a year before they were discovered and turned over to the authorities. The court records of their examination before Dulcetius, the governor, remain and give testimony to the women's faith. When Dulcetius asked Agape why she would not eat meat sacrificed to the gods, Agape replied, 'I believe in the living God, and will not by an evil action lose all the merit of my past life.'[4] Chionia said, 'I believe in the living God, and for that reason did not obey your orders.' Irene said she did not obey Caesar's orders 'for fear of offending God'. Agape told the governor, 'It is not proper to obey Satan; my soul is not to be overcome by these discourses.' When asked who had drawn them to embrace such foolishness, the sisters replied, 'Almighty God and his only Son our Lord Jesus Christ.'

Dulcetius said they were bound to obey Caesar's edicts, then he read the sentence for Agape and Chionia: 'I condemn Agape and Chionia to be burned alive, for having out of malice and obstinacy acted in contradiction to the divine edicts of our lords the emperors and Caesars, and who at present profess the rash and false religion of Christians, which all pious persons abhor.' Irene was sent back to prison.

After Agape and Chionia were consumed by fire, Irene was again brought before Dulcetius. He told her, 'Your madness is plain, since you have kept to this day so many books, parchments, codicils, and papers of the scriptures of the impious Christians.' He urged her to take warning from the deaths of her sisters, promising her freedom if she would worship the gods and obey the Emperor. Irene refused, saying, 'those who renounce Jesus Christ, the Son of God, are threatened with eternal fire.' She told the governor, 'Almighty God ... has commanded us to love him even unto death; on which account we dare not betray him, but rather choose to be burnt alive, or suffer anything whatsoever ...'[5]

Dulcetius promised Irene a slow death. He ordered that she 'be exposed naked in a brothel'. But, God protected her, and no indecency was done to her. Dulcetius finally ordered Irene to be burnt alive. On 5 April, 304, two days after her sisters' deaths, Irene went to her death singing psalms and celebrating the glory of God.

> *Therefore, since we are surrounded by so great a cloud of witnesses, let us also lay aside every weight, and sin which clings so closely, and let us run with endurance the race that is set before us, looking to Jesus, the founder and perfecter of our faith ...*
>
> ~ HEBREWS 12:1-2 ~

---

4. As recorded in Rev. Alban Butler, *The Lives of the Saints*, Vol. IV, 1866.

5. Alban Butler, *The Lives of the Fathers, Martyrs, and other Principal Saints Compiled from Original Monuments and Other Authentic Records*, volume 4 (London: John Murphy, 1821), pp. 26-30.

Women in
Late Antiquity

Using the Classics to Proclaim Christ

∞ Faltonia Proba, c. 306 – c. 353 ∞

Proba belonged to an influential Roman family, and many of her relatives had important positions in the government. Her grandfather had been a consul in 310; her father was Roman consul in 322; her brother was consul in 341. Proba married Clodius Celsinus Adelphus, who was prefect of Rome in 351. The couple had two sons who became imperial officers. After her marriage, Proba converted to Christianity. Through her influence, her husband and sons became Christians as well.

When Julian became Emperor in 361 he sought to restore the traditional Roman religious practices which the Christian Emperors since Constantine had abandoned. Julian was the last pagan ruler of the Roman Emperor; and during his brief reign, he passed numerous measures to restore paganism. Among them was the School Edict of 362. In this Julian required that all public teachers be approved by the Emperor and that Christians not be allowed to teach classical Greek and Latin texts, such as Homer and Virgil, which were foundational to ancient education. Christian teachers who taught from the classics often used them to teach grammar and style, but also used them to show the foolishness of the pagan gods. With disdain, Julian said if Christians 'want to learn literature, they have Luke and Mark. Let them go back to their churches and expound on them.'[1]

It was probably partially in response to Julian's edict that Proba wrote her Christian poem known as *A Cento from Virgil to the Praise of Christ*. In her poem, Proba presented the story of the early chapters of Genesis and the life, death, burial, and ascension of Jesus—all with lines taken from works by the Latin poet Virgil. She created the poem for her son, but hoped it would be used by his children as well. Indeed, Proba's *Cento* was widely used in schools in later centuries and well into the middle ages. Readers could learn Christian truth while also learning the Latin style of Virgil.

Rather than ask the Muses for inspiration, Proba began her poem with a prayer for God to aid her in her work. Jesus was central to Proba's poem, with the Old Testament events anticipating His coming. Words Virgil had used to foretell the glory of Rome, Proba shaped to tell of God speaking to Jesus at his baptism and establishing the coming Kingdom of God:

> Listen, my Son,
> I bear you witness; in whatever place
> The rising and setting sun surveys the sea,
> Either side, from East to West – happy
> At your offerings made complete, you shall
> Behold all regions turned and ruled
> Beneath your feet. Govern your subjects with
> Authority.[2]

Proba's work is the earliest poem known written by a Christian woman. Her poem is also very possibly the first printed work composed by a woman, for it was printed in 1472, very soon after the development of the printing press.

See to it that no one takes you captive by philosophy and empty deceit, according to the human tradition, according to the elemental spirits of the world, and not according to Christ. For in him the whole fullness of deity dwells bodily.

~ COLOSSIANS 2:8-9 ~

---

1. Peter Brown, *The World of Late Antiquity* (New York: W. W. Norton, 1971), p. 93.

2. Elizabeth A. Clark and Diane F. Hatch, 'Jesus as Hero in the Vergilian *Cento* of Faltonia Betitia Proba', *Vergellius*, No. 7, 1981, 35.

Faithful to Mother's Prayers

∞ Monica, c. 333-387 ∞

Monica was deeply concerned about her son Augustine. Though she had instructed him in the Christian faith as a child, as he entered his teenage years he grew increasingly rebellious. He was becoming promiscuous and began to embrace Manichaeism, a dualistic philosophical religion from Persia.

Monica's husband, Patricius, died when Augustine was about sixteen. Patricius had become a Christian not long before his death. Monica's exemplary Christian behavior and her prayers were used to turn Patricius's heart to Christ. Monica was so concerned about Augustine's following the false teaching of Manichaeism that she talked with the bishop and begged him to speak with Augustine about the errors of that philosophy. The bishop refused, saying Augustine was not ready to listen. However, he assured the concerned mother that 'it cannot be that the son of these tears shall perish'.

Augustine decided to leave Carthage and go to Rome to advance his career. Monica pled with him not to go; she feared that the corruption and decadence of the imperial city would only further entice Augustine from the truth in Christ. Augustine then slipped away to Rome without telling Monica, and she intensified her prayers. She later followed Augustine to Italy, settling with him in Milan.

Ambrose was bishop of Milan, and Monica grew spiritually under his preaching. In time Augustine did come to faith in Christ, after reading sections of Paul's epistle to the Romans. Augustine was baptized by Ambrose in 387. Monica was overjoyed and felt she was no longer needed on earth.

When Augustine and Monica decided to return to North Africa, they stopped at the Italian port of Ostia along the way. There they conversed about eternity, sharing a vision of the Eternal, and knowing that 'eye hath not seen, nor ear heard, neither have entered into the heart of man the things which God hath prepared for them that love Him' (1 Cor. 2:9 KJV). Monica became ill of a fever and died before the ship sailed. Her persistent prayers were answered, and her son Augustine became perhaps the leading Christian theologian of all time.

> *Her children rise up and call her blessed; her*
> *husband also, and he praises her ...*
>
> ~ PROVERBS 31:28 ~

Early 'Bible' Society' in Rome'

Marcella (325-410) had an insatiable desire to learn the Scriptures and live a life devoted to Christ. Her husband died just a few months after their marriage, and Marcella refused all other suitors. She lived with her mother in the family's palatial home on the Aventine hill in Rome, but lived in the utmost simplicity. She began a ladies' Bible study in her home, which became a place of prayer and psalm-singing for many.

When the Christian scholar Jerome was in Rome, Marcella constantly asked him questions about the Bible and theology – what were the meanings of the Hebrew words *Allelulia, Amen, Selah*? What were the ephod and teraphim? What are the Hebrew names for God? What was the sin against the Holy Spirit? Even when Jerome left Rome, Marcella sent letters to him with her questions; over fifteen of Jerome's replies to her letters remain. Jerome was astonished at Marcella's knowledge of Scripture and her desire to learn more.

Lay people and church leaders alike came to Marcella to better understand Scripture. She had scribes working in her home copying Scriptures; her home became a kind of 'Bible Society' where people could come and obtain copies of the Scriptures. One woman whom Marcella particularly helped was Paula, an aristocratic woman descended from the founder of Rome and related to the leading Roman families. Paula had been married when she was seventeen and had four daughters and a son. When her husband died, she was overwhelmed with grief. Marcella comforted her and shared with her the hope of the gospel in Jesus. Paula became a vibrant Christian and a supporter of Jerome in his translation work and ministry.

In August 410, when Marcella was eighty-five, Alaric the Goth sacked Rome. When the Goths came to Marcella's home demanding gold, she told them she had none, pointing out to them her simple dress. Thinking she was hiding her wealth, they severely whipped her. Marcella died a few days later. Her life had awakened many to the Scriptures.

For whatever was written in former days was written for our instruction, that through endurance and through the encouragement of the Scriptures we might have hope.

~ ROMANS 15:4 ~

Lover of Scripture

∞ Paula, 347-404 ∞

Paula was a self-indulgent noble Roman whose ancestors included the leading families in Rome. When she was seventeen she married into another wealthy, established family. She had four daughters and a son before her husband died. Paula was in her early thirties and was overwhelmed with grief at her husband's death. At her time of grief, her Christian neighbor Marcella urged her to find her comfort in Jesus. Through Marcella's witness, Paula converted to Christianity. Though she had tremendous wealth (she owned the towns of Nicopolis and Actium!), she began living simply and giving her wealth to charity. No longer did she wear rich silks and the finest jewels or have eunuchs carry her in a litter through the streets of Rome.

Jerome was then in Rome, and Paula became his student and patron. She knew Greek and studied Hebrew so she could sing the psalms in the Hebrew original. She had a passion for studying the Scriptures and was a great help to Jerome in his work of translating the Scriptures into the common or vulgar Latin (hence the *Vulgate* translation), financing his rare manuscripts and books. Jerome dedicated several of his translations and commentaries to Paula and her daughter Eustochium. Some people took offense at having women's names on studies of Scripture, but Jerome wrote,

> These people do not know that while Barak trembled, Deborah saved Israel; that Esther delivered from supreme peril the children of God. I passed over in silence Anna and Elizabeth and all other holy women of the Gospel, but humble starts compared with the luminary, Mary. Is it not to women that our Lord appeared after His resurrection? Yes, and the men could then blush for not having sought what women had found.[3]

When two of her daughters died, Paula, again deeply grieving, decided to leave Rome and follow Jerome to the Holy Land. She took her daughter Eustochium with her, leaving her youngest daughter and son to be cared for in Rome. When Paula and Eustochium reached the Holy Land, they traveled to many biblical sites, places associated with Jesus and places associated with biblical women – Caesarea, where Phillip's daughters prophesied; Joppa, where Peter raised Dorcas; Bethany, the home of Mary and Martha; the well of Samaria.

In Bethlehem Paula founded three convents. She made the copying of manuscripts a major work in the convents, thus beginning a tradition of manuscript copying in the monasteries which continued through the Middle Ages. Paula also founded a hospice to shelter pilgrims, orphans, the sick, the poor and the elderly.

When Paula died in 404, six bishops carried her body to its grave in Bethlehem. People came from throughout the region to her funeral, including the poor who came displaying clothes she had given them. Jerome noted Paula was an example of how to eradicate feminine self-indulgence and remake a patrician lady into a vessel of grace.

All Scripture is breathed out by God and profitable for teaching, for reproof, for correction, and for training in righteousness that the man of God may be complete, equipped for every good work.

~ 2 TIMOTHY 3:16-17 ~

---

3. *Preface* to *Commentary on Sophonius*, as quoted in H. J. Mozans, *Woman in Science* (New York and London: D. Appleton & Co., 1913), p. 34.

First Hospital in Europe

∞ Fabiola, ? – 399 ∞

Fabiola belonged to one of Rome's most ancient patrician families. She early married a man who was so cruel and vicious no one could live with him, so she obtained a divorce under Roman law. She then remarried. After her second husband died, she became convicted that she should not have remarried, since the laws of the church stipulated she was not to remarry while her first husband was still alive. In great repentance, Fabiola made a public confession of her sin before the church. She then sold all her property and began to use her wealth to care for the poor, also giving large sums of money to churches and monasteries.

Fabiola erected a hospital in Rome, the first hospital in Europe, and often cared for the patients herself. She didn't shirk from treating the most loathsome sores or diseases. Jerome in his eulogy of Fabiola commended her compassion and noted:

> The poor wretch whom we despise, whom we cannot so much as look at, and the very sight of whom turns our stomachs, is human like ourselves, is made of the same clay as we are, is formed out of the same elements. All that he suffers we too may suffer. Let us then regard his wounds as though they were our own, and then all our insensibility to another's suffering will give way before our pity for ourselves.[4]

Fabiola also worked with Pammachius, a Roman senator, to establish a hospice for travellers at the Roman port of Ostia, where those in distress could find a place of refuge.

Fabiola was not part of the group of women who supported Jerome while he was in Rome, but she went to join Jerome in Bethlehem for a time, staying with Paula and Eustochium. There she earnestly studied the Scriptures, asking Jerome numerous questions. She wondered why in the book of Numbers the forty-two stopping places of the Israelites in the wilderness were listed. Jerome said he did not know, but would study the matter. After her death, he wrote a treatise on the subject and dedicated it to Fabiola's memory.

Fabiola returned to Rome, where she died in 399. Thousands of people came to honor her, appreciating all she had done for them. Jerome wrote that 'Her triumph was more glorious far' than those of conquering emperors. 'They had conquered physical force, she had mastered spiritual iniquities.'

'And I tell you, make friends for yourselves by means of unrighteous wealth,
so that when it fails they may receive you into the eternal dwellings.'

~ LUKE 16:9 ~

---

4. Jerome, Letter 77, 'To Oceanus', *From Nicene and Post-Nicene Fathers*, Second Series, Vol. 6, ed. Philip Schaff and Henry Wace, trans. W. H. Fremantle, G. Lewis and W. G. Martley (Buffalo, NY: Christian Literature Publishing Co., 1893), revised and edited for *New Advent* by Kevin Knight, http://www.newadvent.org/fathers/3001077.htm.

Travels to the Holy Land 381-384

∞ Egeria, 4th century ∞

In the nineteenth century explorers in the Holy Land began documenting the remains of ancient Capernaum, the town near the Sea of Galilee where Jesus taught and performed so many of his miracles. In 1866, the ruins of the synagogue were identified. From the descriptive writings of Egeria, scholars knew the house of Peter was nearby.

Little is known about Egeria, but in 381 she began a journey from Spain to the Holy Land. The journey took her three years, and we have some of the letters she wrote describing her travels. Wanting to deepen her understanding of Scriptures, Egeria traveled with her Bible in hand to where biblical events occurred. Local guides and religious people helped her find biblical sites. When she found a particular site, she read the pertinent Scriptures about that place. Egeria went to Mount Sinai, climbing to the top to see where the glory of the Lord shone to Moses. She visited Mount Nebo, where Moses died, and Haran, where Abraham had lived.

Egeria was in Jerusalem for Holy Week and described in detail the practices and ceremonies of the six churches in Jerusalem associated with the life of Jesus. She found there was a greater emphasis on the preaching of the Scripture in Jerusalem than at home in Spain. The liturgy associated with Holy Week particularly focused on the Gospel records, increasing the people's understanding of the Scriptures.

At Capernaum, Egeria visited the synagogue and the nearby church, which she said had once been Peter's house. In 1968, archaeologists working in Capernaum excavated underneath the remains of the Byzantine church near the synagogue and found the remains of a first century house. The house showed clear evidence that one of the rooms had been used for community gatherings of the early Christians. Egeria's description of her travels in the fourth century helped point the way to the uncovering of Peter's house, where Jesus had taught and where he had performed some of his miracles.

But grow in the grace and knowledge of our Lord and Savior Jesus Christ.
To him be the glory both now and to the day of eternity.

~ 2 PETER 3:18 ~

What Women These Christians Have!

∽ Anthusa, 4th century ∾

Antioch in Syria was the fourth largest city in the Roman Empire, the place where 'Christian' was first used to describe the followers of Jesus, and the place where Paul began his first missionary journey. In the fourth century, Antioch was also where Anthusa lived with her husband Secundus. Secundus was a leader in the Imperial Army in Syria. With his important position and Anthusa's ample dowry, the couple enjoyed a comfortable life. Together they had a daughter and a son, named John. But, shortly after John's birth, when Anthusa was twenty, Secundus died. Anthusa was left to raise her children alone. She refused to remarry, looking to God for her direction and guidance, and devoting her attention to the upbringing of her children. Apparently her daughter died early, and John became the focus of Anthusa's care. When he was yet a child, Anthusa instilled a love of the Scriptures in her son, and the boy became intimately acquainted with the Bible. Anthusa also sent her son to the leading classical teacher of the day, Libanus.

Even though Libanus was a pagan, he was greatly impressed by Anthusa's selflessness and her dedication in educating and caring for her son, exclaiming at one point, 'Ah! What wonderful women there are among the Christians.' John was a brilliant student, and Libanus wanted him to succeed him at the school. John, however, was drawn to a life of service within the church and became one of the most excellent preachers of antiquity. His sermons were clear expositions of Scripture, coupled with practical applications of biblical truth. Even today, over sixteen-hundred years after they were first preached, his sermons on various books of the Bible are spiritually invigorating and profitable to read. Because of his eloquence, he was given the name of 'Chrysostom', which means 'golden tongued'. John Chrysostom became Archbishop of Constantinople and had an important ministry in the imperial court. Anthusa's devotion to serve God as a single mother in the training of her son bore much fruit in Chrysostom's own day, and through the centuries.

Her children rise up and call her blessed ...
~ PROVERBS 31:28 ~

From Riches to Rags

∞ Olympias, 368-408 ∞

Olympias was born into a wealthy family in Constantinople (today's Istanbul) in 368. Both of her parents died when Olympias was a young girl, and she was raised by her Uncle Procopius, who was a devout Christian. As a beautiful lady and the wealthiest heiress in Constantinople, Olympias had many suitors for marriage. At sixteen she married Nebridius, a noble man of good character. When Nebredius died twenty months after the marriage, Olympias took this as a sign she was not to be married, though again she had many suitors. Emperor Theodosius wanted her to marry a relative of his; when she refused, he confiscated her property. Olympias somewhat sarcastically thanked the Emperor for relieving her of a heavy responsibility and encouraged him to use the wealth to support the church and the poor. Theodosius relented and returned the property to Olympias.

Olympias lived simply and used her vast wealth to care for the sick and poor and help churches throughout Greece, Asia Minor and Syria. She built a hospital and orphanage and purchased hundreds of slaves, only to give them their freedom. She supported and became a close friend and co-worker with John Chrysostom, the eloquent preacher and bishop of Constantinople. She was an encourager to him when he was exiled from Constantinople for speaking against the extravagance of Empress Eudoxia. Olympias herself was harassed for her support of Chrysostom. Her assets were seized, and she went into exile. When Olympias puzzled over the suffering she now faced, Chrysostom wrote her to reflect on the examples of Job, Abraham, Joseph, and John the Baptist:

> May the endurance of these spiritual athletes become a teacher of patient endurance for you. Seeing that the entire life of these noble and lofty men is woven through with these kinds of sufferings, don't be disturbed or alarmed – neither by your own particular trials, nor those trials common to all. For the Church has been nourished from the very beginning in this fashion, and in this way has grown.[5]

Olympias died in exile and poverty on 25 July, 408.

> *As for the rich in this present age, charge them not to be haughty,*
> *nor to set their hopes on the uncertainty of riches, but on God, who*
> *richly provides us with everything to enjoy. They are to do good, to*
> *be rich in good works, be generous and ready to share, thus storing*
> *up treasure for themselves as a good foundation for the future, so*
> *that they may take hold of that which is truly life.*
>
> ~ 1 TIMOTHY 6:17-19 ~

---

5. Christopher Hall, 'Letters from a Lonely Exile', *Christian History*, 1994, Issue 44.

Generational Faithfulness

⚭ Macrina the Younger, 4th century ⚭

Macrina married into a wealthy family in Pontus, near the Black Sea. However, her family's wealth did not protect it from the persecution of Christians led by Diocletian in the fourth century. Macrina and her husband hid in the forests of Pontus for some time while the persecutions raged, yet they survived the onslaught and emerged from the trials to establish a notable Christian family. Several of Macrina's grandchildren became leaders in the church. Her granddaughter and namesake, Macrina the Younger, was beautiful and intelligent. As a child she memorized the Psalms and many other portions of Scripture.

The oldest of ten children, the younger Macrina helped her mother administer the family estate after her father's death. Betrothed at age 12, her fiancé died before their marriage and Macrina decided to remain unmarried, devoting herself to Christian work. Macrina's brother Peter became Bishop of Sebaste; brother Basil became Bishop of Caesarea; and brother Gregory became a famous theologian.

Macrina the Younger established the first monastery for women in the East as well as a hospital which ministered to both the physical and spiritual needs of the people. Macrina's brother Gregory wrote *The Life of Macrina*, which described her many Christian works and the spiritual encouragement she gave to her family throughout her life. In *The Life*, Gregory recorded Macrina's dying prayer:

Thou, O Lord, hast freed us from the fear of death. Thou has made the end of this life the beginning to us of true life. Thou for a season dost rest our bodies in sleep and wake them again. Thou givest our earth, which Thou hast fashioned with Thy hands, the earth to keep in safety. One day Thou will take again what Thou hast given, transfiguring with immortality and gracing our mortal remains. Thou hast saved us from the curse and from sin, having become both for our sake. ... O Thou who hast power on earth to forgive sins, forgive me, that I may be refreshed and may be found before Thee when I put off my body, without defilement on my soul. But may my soul be received unto Thy Hands spotless and undefiled, as an offering before Thee.[6]

'Death is swallowed up in victory'.
'O death, where is your victory?
O death, where is your sting?' ...
But thanks be to God, who gives us the victory
through our Lord Jesus Christ.

~ 1 CORINTHIANS 15:54-55, 57 ~

---

6. As quoted in Edith Deen's *Great Women of the Christian Faith* (A Barbour Book, 1959), pp. 13-14. Also available online at http://www.tertullian.org/fathers/gregory_macrina_1_life.htm.

Women in the
Early Middle Ages

Christian Queen among Barbarians

⚬ Clothilde, 474-545 ⚬

The history of how the barbarian tribes moving across Europe in the first centuries of the Christian era converted to Christianity often centers around the queens. Frequently, a Christian queen influenced her husband to become a Christian, and he then led many of his people out of paganism into the Christian faith. In fact, there are letters from various Popes who corresponded with Christian queens and encouraged them to bring their kingly husbands into the Christian fold, citing 1 Corinthians 7:14: '... the unbelieving husband is made holy because of his wife'.

Clothilda was one such queen at the turn of the fifth and sixth centuries. A Burgundian princess, Clothilda, was married to Clovis, the King of the Franks, as part of a political alliance. While Clovis was seeking to expand the Frankish kingdom, Clothilda sought the expansion of Christ's kingdom and maintained her Christian faith at the Frankish court. Clothilda encouraged Clovis to turn away from his idols to the Creator of all:

> The gods you venerate are nothing, as they are unable to provide the needs of others. They are idols made of wood, stone, or metal. ... They are magicians, their power does not have a divine origin. The God who must be worshiped is he whose Word brought out of nothing the heavens, the earth, the sea, and all they contain ... It is by his will that the fields produce their harvests, the trees, their fruits, the grapevines, their grapes. It is by his hand that the human race was created. Thanks to his liberality, all creation has been set to serve man, is submitted to him and showers him with its blessings.[1]

Clovis continued to trust his gods and ignored the Christian God.

When Clothilda bore Clovis a son, the infant was baptized, then died shortly after. Clovis angrily claimed that if the child had been dedicated to his gods, he would not have died. Clothilda replied, 'I thank God, Creator of all things, who has deigned to honor my unworthiness by opening his kingdom to this child to whom I gave birth.' Clovis continued his refusal to believe in the Christian God. One day, however, he was losing a fierce battle with the Alemanni. In desperation, he raised his eyes to heaven and cried to Christ for help. The Alemanni fled, and Clovis won the battle. Clovis told Clothilda that Christ had won the battle for him, and he wanted to follow Christ. He proclaimed his faith to the Frankish people and urged them to forsake their idols and worship the Creator of heaven and earth. Many replied, 'O pious king, we reject our mortal gods, and we are ready to follow the immortal God.' Clovis, his sisters, and three thousand of the Frankish people, were baptized on Christmas Day, 496.

> *If any woman has a husband who is an unbeliever, and he*
> *consents to live with her, she should not divorce him. For the*
> *unbelieving husband is made holy because of his wife, and the*
> *unbelieving wife is made holy because of her husband.*
>
> ~1 CORINTHIANS 7:13-14~

---

1. Richard Fletcher, *The Barbarian Conversion from Paganism to Christianity* (New York: Henry Holt & Co., 1997), pp. 104, 123.

From Turmoil to Peace'

⋘ Radegund, c. 518-587 ⋙

Born the daughter of Berthachar, a king of Thuringia, Radegund was thrown into the tumultuous conflicts among the Germanic tribes and the Merovingian Franks. Radegund's uncle killed her father in battle and took Radegund to his house when she was eleven. When the Merovingian Clothar defeated the Thuringians in 531, he took Radegund and her brother captive. Among the Merovingians, Radegund was introduced to Christianity and learned to read Latin, the language of the educated of her day. Once she was of age, Clothar took Radegund as his wife, though he had several concubines as well. When Clothar murdered Radegund's brother, probably because he had some rights to the Thuringian kingship, Radegund fled the court. She begged the bishop of Soissons to consecrate her as a deaconess and provide protection for her from Clothar. With some hesitation, the bishop consented.

Radegund later established a monastery at Poitiers where she lived as a simple nun. For her monastery she adopted the rule of Caesarius of Arles. When the Abbess of Arles sent the rule to Radegund, she also sent a covering letter of encouragement and permeated with Scripture quotations, including the following:

> 'Our lord God, who raises the broken and loosed the fettered and illuminates the blind' [Ps. 146:7-8], let him direct you on the right road, let him teach you to do his will, let him grant that you walk in his precepts and keep his mandates and meditate on his law, as the psalmist says: 'And on his law he will meditate day and night' [Ps. 1:2] and: 'the lucid precept of the LORD illuminating eyes, the irreprehensible law of the LORD converting souls' [Ps. 19:7-8]. As attentively as secular men hear when royal precepts are read, so attentively listen when divine readings are read. Let the whole mind, the whole thought, the whole meditation be on the precepts of the LORD; solicitously fear that: 'Cursed are those who fall away from your commands' [Ps. 119:21]; and who would not keep one or the least of the Lord's mandates will be called least in the kingdom of heaven. Fulfill this: 'May meditation of the heart always be in your sight [Ps. 19:14]. Hide your words in my heart that I may never sin against you' [Ps. 119:11]. And since the LORD deigned to choose you, ladies dearest to me in Christ, as his heirs, give thanks to him and bless him always. Abstain from all vice, from all sin; since 'who commits sin is the servant of sin' [John 8:34]. Love and fear the Lord for 'the eyes of the LORD are always on those who fear him and his ears [open] to their prayers' [Ps. 34:18, 33:16]. Let your heart be pure, your heart peaceable; be mild and humble, patient , obedient. ... [T]here is no greater, better, more precious nor more splendid doctrine than the reading of the gospel. ... Hear the apostle: 'who wish to live piously in Christ, suffer persecution'[2 Tim. 3:12]. As God rejoices in the beginnings of your conversion, so the devil grieves about it, who has thousands and thousands of arts of harming and seeks God's food for himself; so pray incessantly that God resist him. ... Call on God continually: 'God, incline to my help; LORD, hasten to help me. God, do not withdraw from me; my God, look to my help. Be my helper, do not abandon me. Help me and I shall be safe' [Pss. 70:2, 71:12, 119:117]. ....[2]

Radegund lived peacefully in the monastery for thirty years, dying in 587.

> *The fear of the LORD is clean, enduring forever; the rules of*
> *the LORD are true, and righteous altogether.*
>
> ~ PSALM 19:9 ~

---

2. 'A letter from Caesaria, abbess of Arles', http://epistolae.ccnmtl.columbia.edu/letter/915.html.

First Christian Queen in England

∞ Bertha, 539 – c. 612 ∞

Bertha's marriage to King Ethelbert was a political one. Ethelbert had so increased the size of his Anglo-Saxon Kingdom that he could make an alliance with the Franks, the most powerful state in Europe. The alliance was sealed by Bertha, daughter of the Frankish King, coming to England and marrying Ethelbert. Ethelbert was not a Christian, and part of the marriage agreement included the stipulation that Bertha would be able to continue to live and worship as a Christian in the Anglo-Saxon court. Bertha's private chaplain, Liuhard, went with her to Canterbury, capital of the Anglo-Saxon kingdom.

In Canterbury, Bertha found an abandoned church left over from Roman times. She renovated the church for her use, dedicating it to Saint Martin of Tours; Bertha had grown up near Tours, so this was a reminder of home. St. Martin's in Canterbury is the oldest church in the English-speaking world. Letters of Pope Gregory suggest that Augustine's Christian mission to England in 595 was sent at Bertha's request. Upon his arrival in England, Augustine used the Church of St. Martin's as his mission headquarters.

Queen Bertha's great-grandmother, Queen Clothilda, had been influential in bringing her husband Clovis, King of the Franks, into the Christian fold. Bertha undoubtedly saw her Christian duty similarly to seek Ethelbert's conversion. Pope Gregory wrote Bertha a letter encouraging her in this, and even complaining that she was so slow in bringing her husband to Christ:

> They who desire, after earthly dominion, to obtain the glory of a heavenly kingdom ought to labour earnestly to bring in gain to their Creator. ... For, as through Helena of illustrious memory, the mother of the most pious Emperor Constantine, He kindled the hearts of the Romans into Christian faith, so we trust that He works in the nation of the Angli through the zeal of your Glory. And indeed you ought before now, as being truly a Christian, to have inclined the heart of our glorious son, your husband, by the good influence of your prudence, to follow, for the good of his kingdom and of his own soul, the faith which you possess, to the end that for him, and for the conversion of the whole nation through him, fit retribution might accrue to you in the joys of heaven. ... Since, by the will of God, now is a suitable time, so proceed, with the co-operation of divine grace, as to be able to make reparation with increase for what has been neglected. Wherefore strengthen by continual hortation the mind of your glorious husband in love of the Christian faith; let your solicitude infuse into him increase of love for God. ... Now we pray Almighty God that He would both kindle the heart of your Glory with the fire of his grace to perform what we have spoken of, and grant you the fruit of an eternal reward for work well-pleasing to Him.[3]

Through Bertha's encouragement, Ethelbert did convert to Christianity and encouraged Augustine in his mission to again establish the Christian faith in England.

> *After this I looked, and behold, a great multitude that no one could number,*
> *from every nation, from all tribes and peoples and languages, standing*
> *before the throne and before the Lamb, clothed in white robes, with palm*
> *branches in their hands, and crying out with a loud voice, 'Salvation belongs*
> *to our God who sits on the throne, and to the Lamb!'*

~ REVELATION 7:9-10 ~

---

3. 'To Bertha, Queen of the Angli', Book XI, Letter 29, *Nicene and Post-Nicene Fathers, Second Series*, Vol. 13, ed. Philip Schaff and Henry Wace (Buffalo, N.Y.: Christian Literature Publishing Co., 1898), p. 57.

From Slavery to the Throne

∽ Bathildis, c. 631-680 ∽

In 641, an eleven-year-old Anglo-Saxon girl named Bathildis was among those captured by invading armies from Denmark. Bathildis was sold as a slave to Erchinoald, the Mayor of the Palace for King Clovis II of France. Bathildis diligently and humbly carried out her duties, earning the respect of her fellow servants as well as Erchinoald, her master. When Erchinoald's wife died, he wanted to marry Bathildis, which she did not want. She ran away and hid herself, taking on a disheveled appearance to hide her natural grace and beauty. When Erchinoald married another woman, Bahildis returned to her station as a servant and continued to humbly carry out her duties. When the young king Clovis noticed Bathildis, he wanted to marry her. She did not refuse, and Clovis and Bathildis were married in 649. The Anglo-Saxon slave girl became Queen of France.

As Queen, Bathildis kept her servant's heart and her humility. Daily she had a time of prayer, and she encouraged Clovis to provide donations for the poor. Clovis assigned Abbot Genesius to Bathildis' side to aide her in charitable giving. Bathildis bore three sons: Clotaire III, Childeric II, and Thierry III. All three would hold positions of kingship within the Frankish Kingdom. The oldest, Clotaire, became King at the age of five, when his father died around 658. Bathildis became regent during Clotaire's minority. As regent, Bathildis continued to encourage Christianity among the people, as well as feeding the hungry and clothing the poor, selling her jewels when necessary to raise the needed funds. Bathildis brought about many important reforms. She fought corruption in the church by discouraging simony, the practice of purchasing church offices. She prohibited the practice of killing unwanted children, and no longer could Christians be sold as slaves in Frankish lands.

Bathildis also provided land and support for the building of many abbeys, including the abbeys of Chelles, Saint-Denis, and Corbie. When Clotaire ascended to the throne as King of France, Bathildis retired to the abbey of Chelles. She gave up her royal rank and spent the rest of her life in serving the poor. Bathildis died in 680, before she was fifty. Her life was a model of humility, mercy, gentleness, and Christian love.

Humble yourselves before the Lord, and he will exalt you.

~ JAMES 4:10 ~

Abbess of Whitby

∞ Hilda, 614-680 ∞

The Venerable Bede in his *Ecclesiastical History of the English Nation* tells of Hilda, the seventh-century Abbess of Whitby, who had an important role in training leaders in the Anglo-Saxon Church. Hilda's father had been poisoned when she was a toddler, and she was raised at court by Queen Ethelberga, who saw that Hilda was educated in the Christian faith. A member of the royal family, Hilda was baptized along with King Edwin, her uncle, during Easter of 627.

When Hilda was thirty-three, Aidan, Irish founder of the monastery at Lindisfarne, asked Hilda to start a small monastery in Northumbria. Following a pattern found in the East, Anglo-Saxon monasteries were double monasteries, with monks and nuns in separate communities but under one administration. Women were often abbesses and seen as exercising a maternal role in their oversight of the monasteries. Hilda later established the double monastery at Whitby, one of the most famous monasteries in England. Bede writes that 'Those under her direction were required to make a thorough study of the Scriptures and occupy themselves in good works, to such good effect that many were found fitted for Holy Orders and the service of God's altar. Five men from this monastery later became bishops.'[4]

One of the people Hilda mentored was Caedmon, an uneducated herdsman on the monastic lands. Hilda recognized Caedmon's gift for poetry and brought him into the Abbey to teach him the Scriptures. In a day when only those educated in Latin could read the Bible, Caedmon wrote poems in English about Genesis, Exodus, and Christ's life and teachings, making the Bible understandable for the common people.

Hilda was an excellent administrator and woman of wisdom. Kings and princes often sought her advice. Because of Whitby's prestige, in 664 King Oswiu called a Synod to settle the conflicts between practices in the Celtic and Roman churches, to meet at Whitby. There it was decided that the English church would follow the Church of Rome in calculating the date of Easter and observing the monastic tonsure. Though Hilda had followed the Celtic practices, she abided by the Synod's decision.

Bede wrote that all who knew Hilda called her mother, 'on account of her piety and grace … She never failed to return thanks to her Maker or publicly or privately to instruct the flock committed to her charge.'

> *Make me to know your ways, O Lord; teach me your paths. Lead*
> *me in your truth and teach me, for you are the God of my salvation;*
> *for you I wait all the day long.*
>
> ~ Psalm 25:4-5 ~

---

4. Venerable Bede, 'Of the Life and Death of the Abbess Hilda', *Ecclesiastical History of the English Nation* (Book 2, mxxii), available at http://www.liturgies.net/saints/hildaofwhitby/bede.htm.

Wifely Prayers and a King's Conversion

ⓢ Ethelberga, d. 647 ⓢ

The Anglo-Saxon princess Ethelberga came from a line of queens who had been important in bringing their husbands to the Christian faith. Ethelberga's great-great-grandmother was Clothilda, a Burgundian princess who married the pagan Clovis, King of the Franks. Through Clothilda's prayers, example and gospel witness, Clovis converted to Christianity and encouraged his people to do likewise. Ethelberga's mother, the Frankish princess Bertha, was married to the Anglo-Saxon King Ethelbert with the expectation that she would be the means of bringing him to Christ. When Ethelberga, now an Anglo-Saxon princess, married the Northumbrian King Edwin, she similarly was expected to bring Christianity to his kingdom. Part of the marriage arrangement was that Ethelberga would be able to freely practice her Christian faith, and she brought her chaplain Paulinus with her to Northumbria.

Pope Boniface wrote Ethelberga to encourage her in her Christian faith and advised her on how to win her husband to the faith:

> ... You likewise carefully refrain from the worship of idols and the deceits of temples and auguries, and having changed your devotion, are so wholly taken up with the love of your Redeemer, as never to cease lending your assistance for the propagation of the Christian faith.

Boniface encouraged Ethelberga not to defer winning her husband for the gospel,

> to the end that you may thereby enjoy the rights of marriage in the bond of a holy and unblemished union. For it is written, 'They two shall be in one flesh.' How can it be said that there is unity between you, if he continues a stranger to the brightness of your faith by the interposition of dark and detestable error?
>
> Wherefore, applying yourself continually to prayer, do not cease to beg of the Divine Mercy the benefit of his illumination to the end, that those who the union of carnal affection has made in a manner but one body, may, after death, continue in perpetual union, by the bond of faith. Persist, therefore, illustrious daughter, and to the utmost of your power endeavour to soften the hardness of his heart by insinuating the Divine precepts; making him sensible how noble the mystery in which you have received by believing .... Inflame the coldness of his heart by the knowledge of the Holy Ghost, that by the abolition of the cold and pernicious worship of paganism, the heat of Divine faith may enlighten his understanding through your frequent exhortations; that the testimony of the holy Scripture may appear the more conspicuous, fulfilled by you, 'The unbelieving husband shall be saved by the believing wife.'

The Pope encouraged Ethelberga with his prayers and asked her to let him know when her husband was converted. He also sent her a gift of a silver mirror and a gilt comb.[5]

Edwin did convert to Christianity, and on Easter 627 he was baptized at York, along with his young son and others in the royal family. In 633, the King of Mercia invaded Northumbria, and Edwin was killed at the Battle of Hatfield. Ethelberga and her children managed to escape, and found refuge with her brother in Canterbury. Ethelberga's daughter Enflaeda broke with family tradition and married a Christian king – Oswald, King of Bernicia and Deira, near Northumbria. She used her position, however, to advance the Christian faith. After her husband's death, she succeeded Hilda as abbess of the monastery at Whitby.

> 'Let your light shine before others, so that they may see your good works and give glory to your Father who is in heaven.'
> ~ MATTHEW 5:16 ~

---

5. Letter in Bede's, *Ecclesiastical History of the English Nation*, Book 2, Chapter 11.

First Female English Author

∾ Walburga, c. 710-777 ∾

In eighth-century England a wealthy Christian family in Wessex became important in bringing the gospel to the German tribes on the continent. Richard and Winna, the sister of Boniface, 'Apostle to the Germans', had three children: Willibald, Winnibald, and Walburga. About 721, Richard set off with his two sons on a pilgrimage to the Holy Land. He left eleven-year-old Walburga in the care of the abbess of Wimborne Abbey. Richard died from a fever in Italy, but his two sons continued and spent several years in the Holy Land and Constantinople. Walburga remained a member of the community of nuns at Wimborne Abbey for twenty-six years and received an education which well prepared her for her future missionary work in Germany.

In bringing Christianity to Germany, Walburga's uncle Boniface not only preached the gospel but established a series of monasteries which became centres of learning and the foundation for the German church. Boniface appealed to Tetta, abbess of Wimborne, to choose women to aid him in his missionary work, and Tetta chose Walburga and Leoba. When they set sail from England, the weather was fair, but soon the ship was caught in a fierce storm. Walburga knelt on the deck and prayed, and soon the sea became calm. The sailors were still talking about this answer to prayer when they reached the continent, and Walburga received a special welcome.

After his pilgrimage to the Holy Land, Walburga's brother Willibald founded a double monastery (for men and women) at Heidenheim am Hahnenkamm, and Walburga became a nun there. When Willibald died in 751, Walburga became abbess of the double monastery. Walburga wrote an account of Wilibald's life and of his travels in Palestine. Because of this, many consider Walburga the first female author of England and Germany.

If I take the wings of the morning and dwell in the uttermost parts of the sea, even there your hand shall lead me, and your right hand shall hold me.

~ PSALM 139:9-10 ~

FEBRUARY 3

Dedicated to God

∞ Leoba, c. 710-782 ∞

Dynne and Aebbe were an elderly couple in Wessex who never had children. When Aebbe amazingly became pregnant, she dedicated the child in her womb to God. Little Leoba was taught the Scripture from her infancy and later was brought to be educated in a monastery. Her biographer, Rudolf of Fulda, wrote that Leoba:

> had no interests other than the monastery and the pursuit of sacred knowledge. She took no pleasure in aimless jests and wasted no time on girlish romances, but, fired by the love of Christ, fixed her mind always on reading or hearing the Word of God. Whatever she heard or read she committed to memory, and put all that she learned into practice. ... She prayed continually, knowing that in the Epistles the faithful are counseled to pray without ceasing. When she was not praying she worked with her hands at whatever was commanded her, for she had learned that he who will not work should not eat. However, she spent more time in reading and listening to Sacred Scripture than she gave to manual labour.[6]

Leoba was well read in the Church Fathers as well as in the Scriptures.

Boniface, the English missionary who brought the gospel to the Anglo-Saxons in Germany, was related to Leoba's mother. When he learned of Leoba's virtue and learning, he asked her to come to Germany and help in establishing Christianity there. Leoba arrived in Germany in 748, and Boniface installed her as abbess of the convent in Bischofsheim. There she trained many nuns who went on to become abbesses throughout Germany. She was known both for her humility and service to the nuns and for her wisdom and learning. Rudolf wrote that:

> When she lay down to rest, whether at night or in the afternoon, she used to have the Sacred Scriptures read out at her bedside, a duty which the younger nuns carried out in turn without grumbling. It seems difficult to believe, but even when she seemed to be asleep they could not skip over any word or syllable whilst they were reading without her immediately correcting them. Those on whom this duty fell used afterwards to confess that often when they saw her becoming drowsy they made a mistake on purpose to see if she noticed it, but they were never able to escape undetected.[7]

Leoba's reputation for learning and godly living spread far and wide, and she often was summoned to the Frankish court, where she was highly respected by King Pepin and his successor, Charlemagne. Because of her wisdom and knowledge of Scripture, the princes and nobles of both the church and state discussed spiritual matters with her. Charlemagne's queen Hiltigard would have liked for Leoba to remain at court to help her in her own spiritual growth, but 'Leoba detested the life at court like poison'. She always returned to the quiet of the convent where she could devote her time to prayer and study.

Take the helmet of salvation, and the sword of the Spirit, which is the word of God, praying at all times in the Spirit, with all prayer and supplication.

~ EPHESIANS 6:17-18 ~

---

6. C. H. Talbot, *The Anglo-Saxon Missionaries in Germany, Being the Lives of SS. Willibrord, Boniface, Leoba, and Lebuin together with the Hodoepericon of St. Willibald and a selection from the correspondence of St. Boniface* (London and New York: Sheed and Ward, 1954), as found at the Medieval Sourcebook, http://www.fordham.edu/halsall/basis/leoba.html.

7. Ibid.

Wise Words from a Loving Mother

⊙ Dhuoda, mid-9th century ⊙

Dhuoda married Bernard of Septimania in the imperial palace of Aachen on 29 June 824. The couple had two sons, William and Bernard, when Dhuoda's husband became involved in the conflicts as Charlemagne's descendants competed for control of his crumbling empire. Four grandsons – Charles, Louis, Pepin, and Lothair – were at war, and the Frankish nobility had divided loyalties. When Dhuoda's husband pledged allegiance to Charles the Bald in 841, fourteen-year-old William was sent to Charles's court as a pledge of good faith, while infant Bernard went with his father to Aquitaine. Dhuoda was left alone to oversee the family lands in Uzés.

Dhuoda seems to have been in failing health, and her mother's heart yearned to give advice or share words of wisdom with adolescent William. Unable to speak to him in person, Dhuoda wrote a *Manual* for William to have even when she was gone. She began her work with a chapter on the sublimity of God, since He is foundational to all of life. She wrote on the nature of the Trinity, faith, hope, and charity, and the nature of prayer. She included a chapter on vices and virtues, examining the trials of life, such as false riches, persecutions, temptations, sickness and danger, and how to virtuously face each. Whatever trials came, God could be glorified. Throughout the *Manual*, Dhuoda included biblical illustrations and Scripture references, as well as many quotes from classical authors.

Dhuoda included an extensive section on prayer, encouraging William to pray for the clergy, kings, and his feudal rulers. She showed how reading the Psalms could be the basis for personal prayer and included a sample prayer William could say at any time:

> Mercy-giving and Merciful, Just and Pious, Clement and True, have pity on Your creation, whom You created and redeemed with your blood, have pity on me, and grant that I may understand, believe, love, fear, praise and thank You and be perfect in every good work through proper faith and goodwill, O Lord, my God. Amen.[8]

Dhuoda encouraged William to always be 'strong and brave in Christ'.

Dhuoda's *Manual* shows the passion of a mother's heart and the wisdom of a mother longing for her children to follow in the ways of truth. How long Dhuoda lived after sending William the *Manual* in 843 is unknown. Did she ever know the fate of her husband and William? Bernard was accused of treason for supporting Pepin over Charles and executed in 844. William later was beheaded for treason in 849. Dhuoda's younger son, Bernard, survived the tumult. His son, William the Pious, founded the abbey of Cluny and worked for reform of the Church.

> *So flee youthful passions and pursue righteousness, faith, love, and peace*
> *along with those who call on the Lord from a pure heart.*
>
> ~ 2 TIMOTHY 2:22 ~

---

8. Excerpt found in Amy Oden, *In Her Words* (Nashville: Abingdon Press, 1994), p. 96.

First Christian Playwright

∽ Hrotsvit, c. 935-1000 ∾

Hrotsvit had lived at the abbey of Gandersheim since childhood and received an excellent education. At the abbey, noblewomen were schooled in the liberal arts and read classical literature, as well as Scripture and the lives of the saints. Hrotsvit was a canoness, which meant she never did renounce the secular world. Though she lived in the abbey, she was not cloistered. She could keep her property, retain her servants, and remain a member of her family. Emperor Otto had encouraged the building up of the abbey libraries, so Hrotsvit had access to the best scholarly works.

Hrotsvit wrote literary works in many different forms – eight legends, six plays in classical form, two epics, and a short poem, all written in Latin. Adapting the style of the Latin author Terrence, Hrotsvit was the first Christian author to write plays. Her plays are as delightful today as they were a millennium ago when first written and continue to be published in German, French, English, Hungarian, Italian, and Dutch. Her sources and subjects covered a wide range of time periods, from early Christian through tenth-century Spain. A key theme of Hrotsvit's work was the conflict between paganism and Christianity. In several of her works, Christian martyrs are shown to have truly triumphed in their defeat of Satan and their victory in Christ. Hrotsvit's plays included the earliest literary account of a man making a pact with the devil, the forerunner of the *Faust* story. Hrotsvit obviously delighted in portraying scenes in which pagan Roman authority could not stand against the power of Christ, especially when shown through the courage and wisdom of young virgins. These were writings that were appreciated and enjoyed in the abbey, as well as at Emperor Otto's court. Hrotsvit explained her reason for writing:

> I do not deny that by the gift of the Creator's grace I am able to grasp certain concepts of the arts because I am a creature capable of learning, but I also know that through my own powers, I know nothing. I also know that God gave me a sharp mind ... and that thus, the Giver of my talent all the more justly be praised through me, the more limited the female intellect is believed to be. This alone was my intention in writing, my only thought; this alone was the reason why my work was wrought.[9]

In the preface to her plays, Hrotsvit wrote that she preached 'Christ's glory and strength as it works through His saints to the extent He grants me the ability to do so'.

> *Do not be unequally yoked with unbelievers. For what partnership has righteousness with lawlessness? Or what fellowship has light with darkness? What accord has Christ with Belial? Or what portion does a believer share with an unbeliever? What agreement has the temple of God with idols? For we are the temple of the living God ...*
>
> ~ 2 CORINTHIANS 6:14-16 ~

---

9. As quoted in Brenda Johnson, 'Hrotsvit of Gandersheim Tenth Century Poet and Playwright' (Mount Saint Agnes Theological Center for Women, 2001). Some of Hrotasvit's plays and writings can be found at www. fordham.edu/halsall/basis/roswitha-toc.html.

Pearl of Scotland

∽ Margaret of Scotland, c. 1045-1093 ∾

Margaret, whose name means 'pearl', was born about 1045 in Hungary, the daughter of the exiled English Prince Edward Atheling of the Royal House of Wessex and Agatha, the niece of the Holy Roman Emperor Henry III. Margaret was raised at the court of the King of Hungary. When Edward the Confessor became King in England her family was able to return to England. After the English defeat at the Battle of Hastings and the death of her husband, Agatha was returning to Hungary with her children, but a storm drove the ship up the Firth of Forth to Dunfermline. Malcolm II, King of Scotland, warmly received the family. Malcolm was the son of Duncan I, who was killed by Macbeth. Malcolm had lived in exile until he defeated and killed Macbeth in 1057, and succeeded to the throne. Malcolm's wife had died, and when he met Margaret, then about twenty-three, he offered to marry her.

Malcolm had a rough nature. He could not read or write, and he relished savage attacks on the English. Margaret, however, was able to refine Malcolm's ways. As the *Anglo-Saxon Chronicle* recorded, 'She was to increase God's praise in the land and to direct the king from the erring path and to bend him to a better way, and his people with him; and to suppress the evil customs which the people did formerly used. ...'[10] Turgot, Bishop of St. Andrews, wrote that Malcolm:

> could not but perceive from her conduct that Christ dwelt within her; nay, more, he readily obeyed her wishes and prudent counsels in all things. Whatever she refused, he refused also; whatever pleased her, he also loved for the love of her. Hence it was that, although he could not read, he would turn over and examine books which she used either for her devotions or her study; and whenever he heard her say that she was fonder of one of them than the others, this one he too used to look at with special affection, kissing it and often taking it in his hands. Sometimes he sent for a worker in precious metals, whom he commanded to ornament the volume with gold and gems, and when the work was finished, the King himself used to carry the volume to the Queen as a kind of proof of his devotion.[11]

One such book, now in the Bodleian Library, was a volume of the Four Gospels on vellum, illuminated with gold capital letters, and bound with precious stones.

Margaret, as she lived her life as a servant of God, gave new life to Christianity in Scotland. She rose early and spent time in reading the Psalms and prayer before beginning each day. She created a comfortable home for her family, established charities and spiritual refuges for the poor and suffering. In her encouragement of trade for the nation, she also introduced the wearing of plaid, which has come to characterize the dress of Scotland.

I hear of your love and of the faith that you have toward the Lord Jesus and for all the saints, and I pray that the sharing of your faith may become effective for the full knowledge of every good thing that is in us for the sake of Christ.

~ PHILEMON 5-6 ~

---

10. *The Anglo-Saxon Chronicle: Newly Translated by* F. E. C. Gomme (London: George Bell and Sons, 1909), p. 179

11. Turgot, Bishop of St Andrews, *The Life of Margaret of Scotland*, trans. William Forbes-Leith, S. J. (Edinburgh: David Douglas, 1896), 2.13.

Laying up Treasures in Heaven

∾ Elizabeth of Hungary, 1207-1231 ∾

When she was only four, the Hungarian Princess Elizabeth was betrothed to Ludwig, son of the Landgrave of Thuringia. Elizabeth went to live with Ludwig's family and grew up in the Wartburg Castle, made famous later as the place where Martin Luther translated the Bible into German. Growing up together, Ludwig and Elizabeth often called each other 'Brother' and 'Sister'. When she was seven, Elizabeth's mother was murdered in a political assassination; Elizabeth, even as a child, prayed for the murderers.

Elizabeth was fourteen when she married Ludwig, who was twenty-one. Ludwig's motto was 'Piety, Chastity, and Justice', and he shared Elizabeth's compassionate heart and desire to help those in need. When Thuringia suffered a famine in 1226, Elizabeth fed the people from her own resources, even selling some of her jewels and her silver cradle to provide food for the suffering. Ludwig appreciated Elizabeth's care for the people, and when some of the courtiers criticized Elizabeth's munificence, Ludwig replied, 'Let her do good and give to God whatever she will, so long as she leaves me Wartburg and Nurnberg. Alms will never ruin us.'[12]

Elizabeth bore four children. At the birth of each child she carried the baby to the Chapel, where she thanked God for the delivery of the child and recited Psalm 127:3-4: 'Behold, children are a heritage from the LORD, the fruit of the womb a reward. Like arrows in the hand of a warrior are the children of one's youth.'

Ludwig died of a fever in 1227, on his way to the Sixth Crusade; Elizabeth became a widow when she was only twenty. When Ludwig's body was returned to Thuringia, she prayed:

> I give Thee thanks, O Lord, that Thou has been pleased to grant Thy handmaid the great desire I had to behold the remains of my beloved, and in Thy compassion to comfort my afflicted soul. I do not repine that he was offered up by himself and by me for the relief of Thy Holy Land, although with all my heart I love him. Thou knowest, O God, that I would set his presence – most delightful to me – before all the joys and enchantments of this world, had Thy graciousness yielded him to me. But now I lay at Thy disposal him and me, as Thou wilt. Nay. Though I could call him back at the cost of the smallest hair of my head, I would not call him back against Thy will.[13]

With her dowry money Elizabeth established a hospital; she also she built a leprosarium and established an orphanage, the first in eastern Europe. Disliking idleness, Elizabeth occupied much of her time in spinning, where she could also spend time in prayer. Elizabeth died when she was twenty-four. Her brief life was lived in Christian service for others. At her funeral, many of the poor, the blind, lepers, and the lame came to show their thankfulness for young Elizabeth of Hungary.

> *'Do not lay up for yourselves treasures on earth, where moth and rust destroy and where thieves break in and steal, but lay up for yourselves treasures in heaven, where neither moth nor rust destroys and where thieves do not break in and steal.'*
>
> ~ MATTHEW 6:19-20 ~

---

12. As quoted in Edith Deen, *Great Women of the Christian Faith* (Uhrichsville, OH: Barbour Books, 1959), p. 46.
13. Ibid, p. 48.

Women in the
Late Middle Ages

Good Queen Anne

∽ Anne of Bohemia, c. 1367-1394 ∽

As the oldest daughter of Emperor Charles IV and sister to Wenceslaus, King of Bohemia and Emperor of Germany, Anne of Bohemia easily became a pawn in the marital bargaining of the diplomats in fourteenth-century Europe. King Richard II of England, who came to the throne in 1377 at the age of ten, early set his heart on marrying Anne. When he was thirteen he sent negotiators to arrange the alliance. Richard set such a high value on Anne that rather than Anne bringing a dowry, Richard sent a large sum to Bohemia on condition that Anne would become his bride. The agreement was made and Anne, with a Bohemian entourage, sailed for England.

The Peasants Revolt was raging through much of England when Anne arrived, wreaking destruction in London itself. When the revolt was put down, Anne, not yet married to Richard, pled with him to be merciful to the common people who had joined in the uprising, revealing her gentle nature as soon as she arrived in England. Anne and Richard were married in the Chapel Royal of Westminster Palace on 14 January 1382. Richard loved Anne greatly and was ever faithful to her. The people loved her as well. She was a lady concerned about the poor and daily fed thousands of them from her own funds.

When Anne was growing up in Bohemia, she knew several preachers who spoke out strongly for the need to reform the church. From such reformers, Anne learned to reverence the Bible. She had copies of the Gospels in Bohemian, English, and Latin and read them daily, along with commentaries. John Wycliffe, the English Oxford scholar and reformer, praised Anne for her reading of the Scriptures, comparing her with Mary who sat at Jesus' feet.

In May 1382, at the instigation of the Pope, William Courtenay, Archbishop of Canterbury, convened a synod in the Blackfriars area of London to condemn the teachings of John Wycliffe. Wycliffe looked to the Scriptures as the norm for the Christian faith and refuted many of the doctrines of the Roman church, such as papal hierarchy, purgatory, and transubstantiation (that the bread and wine of communion became the body and blood of Christ). When Wycliffe's teachings were condemned as heresy by the synod, the Archbishop began arresting and imprisoning his supporters. Anne quietly pled with Richard not to arrest Wycliffe, quoting Scripture that 'The one who receives a prophet because he is a prophet will receive a prophet's reward, and the one who receives a righteous person because he is a righteous person will receive a righteous person's reward' (Matt. 10:41-42). Wycliffe was allowed to remain unmolested in his parish of Lutterworth, where he spent his last years overseeing the translation of the Scriptures into English and writing Christian works.

King Richard was greatly distressed when Anne fell ill from the plague and died on 7 June, 1394. At her funeral, Arundel, Archbishop of York, remarked on Anne's study of the Scriptures, commenting, 'A lady of such extraordinary piety it was never my happiness to know.'[1] When many of her household returned to Bohemia after her death, it was with the writings of John Wycliffe. Bohemian students who had attended Oxford also became familiar with Wycliffe's teachings. The biblical teachings of John Wycliffe were taken up by Czech reformer John Hus, a forerunner of the Reformation of the sixteenth century. Anne's love and support for the truth of the Scriptures became a light to both England and Bohemia.

> *'Let your light shine before others, so that they may see your good works and give glory to your Father who is in heaven.'*
> ∽ MATTHEW 5:16

---

1. James Anderson, *Ladies of the Reformation* (London: Blackie and Son, 1855), p. 52.

Treasuring the Scriptures

∞ Lollard women, 14th – 15th centuries ∞

In the mid-fourteenth century, a movement arose in England which questioned the supreme authority of the Roman Church and many of the Church's doctrines. John Wycliffe, an Oxford scholar, wrote and spoke out against the wealth, greed, and corruption of the Church as well as against the teachings on transubstantiation,[2] praying to the saints, and confessing to a priest. Wycliffe replaced the authority of the Church with the authority of the Scriptures. He and his followers made the first complete translation of the Bible into English and sent out preachers to carry the Bible to the people. Followers of Wycliffe's teachings became known as Lollards, the meaning of which is still debated and unclear.

Lollardy was a family, not a monastic, affair, and the evidence indicates women often attended Lollard meetings with their husbands. In Bristol, for example, Christina and William More, members of the governing class of the city, shared interests in the Lollard cause. They even supported a Lollard chaplain in their home for a time. When Christina became a widow in 1412, she continued to manage her husband's estate and show patronage. In 1414, she was among eight 'heretics' brought before the Bishop; she was probably spared execution because of her social position.

There is evidence some women learned to read specifically so that they could read the Scriptures and Lollard literature. Several Lollard women were active in book distribution. In the day before printing, when all books were manuscripts, copies of the Scriptures themselves were scarce, and women learned long Scripture passages which they could recite in meetings. There are records too of daughters continuing the missionary work of their Lollard fathers and learning Scripture passages to recite. Some married couples are known to have worked among the people spreading the truth of the Scriptures or holding meetings where the Scriptures could be taught. The clerical authorities were horrified the Scriptures were being opened to the 'inferior' understanding of women.

> *I delight to do your will, O my God;*
> *your law is within my heart.*
>
> ~ PSALM 40:8 ~

---

2. Transubstantiation is the teaching that during the Mass the substance of the bread and wine becomes the literal body and blood of Jesus.

Beloved of God

∞ Joan Broughton, c. 1414-1494 ∞

Since so many of his teachings were also those of the later reformers, John Wycliffe (c. 1330-1384) has been called the 'Morning Star of the Reformation'. A philosopher and preacher at Oxford, Wycliffe opposed the papal hierarchy and the luxurious living of the clergy as well as the doctrines of purgatory and transubstantiation (that the bread and wine of communion is transformed into the body and blood of Jesus) as being not found in Scripture. He encouraged the reading of Scripture by the ordinary people, not just elite scholars. He and his followers were the first to translate the Bible into English. After his death the Church authorities condemned Wycliffe and his teachings, dug up his bones and burned them, throwing the ashes into the River Swift. The Constitutions of Oxford in 1408 forbade the Bible in English.

Yet, many continued to cherish manuscripts of the forbidden English Bible and follow Wycliffe's teachings of a Christianity rooted in the Scriptures. Joan Broughton was a disciple of his teachings who was tried for heresy in 1494, the ninth year of the reign of King Henry VII. The Church threatened to burn Joan alive unless she repented of her support of Wycliffe's doctrines. Joan obstinately replied that she was so beloved by God and his angels that the fires that threatened would not hurt her. John Foxe noted that, 'she set nothing by their menacing words, but defied them, for she said she was blessed of God, and of his holy angels; that she feared not the fire.'[3] Joan was executed at Smithfield on 28 April, 1494, becoming the first female martyr in England. As the fire came around her, she cried for God to take her soul into His holy hands. Joan's daughter, Lady Jane Yonge, wife of a merchant and mayor of London, was also executed the same year.

> *These all died in faith, not having received the things*
> *promised, but having seen them and greeted them from afar,*
> *and having acknowledged that they were strangers and exiles*
> *on the earth. For people who speak thus make it clear that*
> *they are seeking a homeland ... they desire a better country,*
> *that is, a heavenly one. Therefore God is not ashamed to be*
> *called their God, for he has prepared for them a city.*
>
> ~ HEBREWS 11:13-14, 16 ~

---

3. Thomas Timpson, *British Female Biography: Being Select Memoirs of Pious Ladies in Various Ranks of Public and Private Life* (London: Aylott and Jones, 1846), p. 103.

Mother Faithful in Teaching her Children

∞ widow Smith, martyred 4 April 1519 ∞

After the death of John Wycliffe, who made the Scriptures available in English and trained lay preachers in Christian truth, the English clergy in 1408 passed what became known as the 'Constitutions of Oxford'. These laws said the English Bible was illegal and anyone found with copies of the Bible in English were to be charged with heresy. Many hungered for the Scriptures, however, and pockets of Wycliffe's followers could be found in England up until the Reformation, when the Bible began to circulate freely in the land.

In Coventry, a small group of Christians had learned portions of the Bible and taught their children the Scriptures in English. The Franciscans were annoyed that common laymen, and even a woman, should be involved in religious instruction. In 1519, the bishop had four shoemakers, a hosier, a glover, and widow Smith, with all their children, arrested. The children were taken to Grey Friars' monastery while their parents were taken to the abbey of Mackstoke. The children were examined separately about what they had been taught. When they confessed they had been taught the Lord's Prayer, the Apostle's Creed, and the Ten Commandments in English, the examiner angrily demanded they were to have nothing to do with such teaching.

The five men were condemned to be burned alive, but the judge had compassion on widow Smith and spared her for the sake of her young children. The examiner was escorting Mrs Smith to her home at night, when he heard rubbing in her clothing. He reached his hand up her sleeve and found a piece of parchment. Drawing to a lighted window, he saw the parchment contained the Lord's Prayer, Apostle's Creed, and the Ten Commandments in English. Angrily, he drew the widow after him and took her before the bishop, who immediately gave the sentence of death.

On 4 April, 1519, widow Smith was burnt alive, along with the five men from Coventry, for teaching her children the Lord's Prayer in English.

> And these words that I command you today shall be on your
> heart. You shall teach them diligently to your children, and shall
> talk of them when you sit in your house, and when you walk by
> the way, and when you lie down, and when you rise.
>
> ~ DEUTERONOMY 6:6-7 ~

Women of the
Reformation

Caring for a Beggar

∞ Ursula Cotta, d. 1511? ∞

Ursula Cotta had been watching the small group of choir boys go from house to house, singing in hopes that some would offer them food for their song. The boys had only received harsh words and were told to move on, and many of the boys had scattered. She recognized one who yet stood near her door. She had seen him in the choir at St. George's and noted the melodiousness of his voice and the fervency of his devotion. Ursula invited the youngster into her home.

Ursula was the daughter of a Burgomaster of Hefield; her husband Conrad was a man of substance and a leading man in the town of Eisenach. She learned that the young teenager, whose name was Martin Luther, was from Mansfeld, where his father was a leaseholder of copper mines and a representative on the local council. His father was ambitious for his son, hoping he'd become a lawyer, and so had sent him to school in Eisenach. Though Martin had relatives in Eisenach, they were so poor they could not care for him, and he often didn't have enough to eat. Singing at the houses was one way of trying to get food. Ursula's heart was filled with compassion for the boy, who burst into tears at her unexpected kindness to him.

Ursula not only gave Martin a good meal, but invited him to stay with her and her husband. Martin stayed with the Cottas almost four years while attending school at Eisenach, encouraged and strengthened by Ursula's motherly affection for him. Noticing Martin's musical talents as well as his tendency to depression, Ursula gave Martin a flute, which he soon learned to play beautifully. Years later, Martin wrote, 'Music is the gift of God, not of man. It puts the devil to flight, and makes the soul joyful; it draws away wrath, impurity of thought, pride and other evil passions. Next to theology, I assign to music the highest place and the highest honor.'[1]

In 1501, Martin left the Cotta home for the University of Erfurt. He was tremendously grateful for Ursula Cotta's kindness to him. Years later, when he was known throughout Europe as a leader of the Reformation, Martin Luther recalled Ursula with deep emotion, noting: 'There is nothing on earth more charming than the heart of a woman in which piety resides.' A nineteenth-century writer praised Ursula, saying, 'The love, the piety, and the compassion of this excellent lady saved a spirit which ultimately gave the pure and unadulterated WORD to millions for an everlasting blessing and inheritance! Glorious woman! What a priceless work hast thou accomplished for the world!'[2]

She opens her hand to the poor
and reaches out her hands to the needy.

~ PROVERBS 31:20 ~

---

1. G. P. Disosway, 'Ursula, Wife of Conrad Cotta', *Ladies' Repository*, vol. 23, issue 3 (March 1863), p. 159.
2. Ibid, p. 159.

Martin Luther's Rib

∞ Katherine Luther, 1499-1552 ∞

The movement to reform the church, begun by Martin Luther in 1517, brought about a renewed emphasis on Scriptures, a revival of congregational singing, and clergy marrying and establishing families. The church had forbidden clerical marriage for centuries, but Luther noted there was no biblical reason for such an injunction. He encouraged his clerical friends to marry. However, because of the threats on his life, Luther didn't see marriage in his future. Katherine von Bora changed that.

When she was five, after her mother's death and her father's remarriage, Katie was sent to a nunnery for her education. Later she was moved to the Marienthron convent; she was consecrated as a nun at sixteen. Some of Martin Luther's writings were brought to the convent by a merchant as he delivered goods. When Katherine and some of the other nuns began questioning the teachings of the convent as unscriptural, they wrote to Luther for help in leaving the cloister. Luther sent Leonhard Köppe, a merchant who delivered herring to the convent, to secretly pick up the eleven women on 4 April, 1423, the evening before Easter. When the women were brought out, Luther wrote Köppe, 'You have liberated these poor souls from the prison of human tyranny at just the right time – Easter, when Christ liberated the prison that held His own.'[3] Some of the former nuns returned to their families; the rest were placed in families in Wittenberg.

After two years, all had married except Katherine. One young man who wanted to marry Katherine was opposed by his family. When Luther and his friends tried to match Katherine with a Pastor Glatz, Katie refused, saying he was arrogant and opportunistic and she had no respect for him. Then, she said she would not marry anyone unless she married Martin Luther! To Katie, Martin was her liberator and someone she could trust. Luther finally consented to marry Katie, saying it would 'please his father, rile the pope, cause the angels to laugh and the devils to weep'.[4]

Martin and Katie were married 13 June, 1525. Their wedding invitation stated, 'marriage was an act of confession and obedience to God's act of creation'. The twenty years of Luther's marriage became a model of Christian and pastoral marriage. Katie, who bore Luther six children, elevated the position of motherhood. She managed a large household, and cared for and comforted Luther in his many trials. Luther had many terms of endearment for Katie; a frequent one was his 'rib'. He also called her his *Galatians*, for she relieved his burdens and brought him much freedom. Luther wrote a friend, 'My wife is compliant, accommodating, and affable beyond anything I dared to hope. I would not exchange my poverty for the riches of Croesus.'[5]

And the rib that the LORD God had taken from the man he made into a
woman and brought her to the man. Then the man said, 'This at last is
bone of my bones and flesh of my flesh; she shall be called Woman, because
she was taken out of Man.'

~ GENESIS 2:22-23 ~

---

3. As quoted in Rudolf and Marilynn Markwald, *Katherina von Bora* (St. Louis, MO: Concordia Publishing House, 2002), p. 50.

4. Ibid, p. 70.

5. As quoted in Philip Schaff, *History of the Christian Church*, vol. VII (1859), p. 460. The expression 'as rich as Croesus' comes from the fabulous wealth of the ancient Greek King Croesus.

Boldly Defending the Scriptures

∞ Argula von Grumbach, 1492 – c. 1554 ∞

Argula von Grumbach was from a noble Bavarian family. When she was ten, her father gave her a beautiful German Bible printed by the famed printer, Koberger. Franciscan preachers warned her not to read it, claiming she would only get confused trying to understand it. Argula, however, read and learned much from the Scriptures. When she became a lady-in-waiting at the court of Queen Kunigunde, sister of the Emperor, she met John von Staupitz, the mentor of Martin Luther, and learned that Christ's merits alone, not anything in ourselves, provide salvation.

When works by Martin Luther began to be available, Argula read everything Luther wrote and even began corresponding with him on theological issues. She was firmly persuaded that the Scriptures should be the source of all Christian truth, and Luther pointed the way to the Scriptures. The Bavarian court in Munich was not receptive to Luther's teachings or Protestant ideas, and Protestant teachings were forbidden at the University of Ingelstadt.

Arsacius Seehofer, an eighteen-year-old student at the University, had visited Wittenberg and brought back many of Luther's writings with him. Seehofer was arrested and charged with heresy. He could have been executed, but the courts offered him confinement to a monastery if he recanted, which he did. On 22 September, 1523, Argula wrote an extensive letter to the University faculty protesting these actions against Seehofer. Her letter was published as a booklet and became a bestseller, going through fourteen editions in two months! With over eighty Scripture references in her lengthy letter, Argula argued staunchly against this attack on Scripture itself:

> How in God's name can you and your university expect to prevail when you deploy such foolish violence against the word of God; when you force someone to hold the holy Gospel in their hands for the very purpose of denying it as you did in the case of Arsacius Seehofer? When you confront him with an oath and declaration such as this, and use imprisonment and even the threat of the stake to force him to deny Christ and his word?[6]

Argula said the University was like the false prophets in Ezekiel 13: 'Woe to the fools, to those who prophesy according to their own conceits. They see useless things, and teach lies. They say, "The Lord says," when I have neither spoken nor sent them.'[7] The laws which conflicted with the Bible were foolishness, the wisdom of man, as Paul described in 1 Corinthians. Argula exclaimed:

> Ah, but what a joy it is when the Spirit of God teaches us and gives us understanding – God be praised – so that I came to see the true, genuine light shining out. … What I have written to you is no woman's chit-chat. But the word of God; and (I write) as a member of the Christian Church, against which the gates of Hell cannot prevail. … God give us his grace, that we all may be saved, and may (God) rule us according to his will. Now may his grace carry the day, Amen.[8]

The publication of Argula's powerful letter made her the first Protestant woman writer.

We must obey God rather than men.
~ ACTS 5:29 ~

---

6. Peter Matheson, ed. *Argula von Grumbach: A Woman's Voice in the Reformation* (Edinburgh: T & T Clark, 1995), p. 76.

7. Ibid, p. 78.

8. Ibid, pp. 86, 90.

'Church Mother'

∞ Katherine Zell, 1497/98 – 1562 ∞

An effect of the Protestant Reformation which initially stirred much controversy was the marriage of priests. The Roman Church required that priests be celibate and unmarried. However, when the Reformers turned to the Scriptures as the Christian's standard and rule, they discovered that the Church's demands for priestly celibacy had no biblical basis. Among the early Reformers to marry was Matthew Zell, the first Protestant preacher in Strasbourg. On 3 December, 1523, Matthew married Katherine Schütz, a native of Strasbourg who had come to faith in Christ through Zell's preaching.

Katherine was devoted to her husband and only wanted to be 'a little piece of the rib of the sainted Master Zell'. She wrote that she and Matthew were 'of one mind and of one soul. … What bound us together was not silver and gold. Both of us possessed a higher thing, Christ was the mark before our eyes.'[9]

Strasbourg and the Zell home soon became a refuge for persecuted Protestants. In 1524, when the Hapsburg forces moved against Kenzingen to arrest the Protestant pastor, 150 men protected the pastor and fled with him to Strasbourg. Many found refuge with Katherine and Matthew, and Katherine joyfully fed fifty to sixty for several weeks. Visitors and refugees were constantly at the Zell home, and Katherine delighted in serving them.

When the Hapsburgs took over Kenzingen, Katherine wrote a letter of encouragement to the women remaining in the town. She cited examples of courageous women in Scripture and encouraged them to look to the Word of God as sufficient for salvation, finding comfort from the beatitudes that there is a special blessing to those persecuted for righteousness. At the same time, Katherine published a defence of Matthew Zell's marriage to her. She defended him not as her husband, but as a brother in Christ. Katherine emphasized from the authority of the Scripture the rightness of his marriage. She said she wrote out of love for her neighbor, to refute the lies which might cause some to not listen to Zell's preaching of the gospel.

Katherine wrote several other works, including meditations on the Lord's Prayer and the Psalms for a man with leprosy, whom she cared for outside the town. Katherine once called herself a 'church mother'. It seems a fitting description. She devoted her life to her husband and others, showing abundant hospitality to strangers, charity to those in need, and biblical counsel to those in the church.

> 'Blessed are you when others revile you and persecute you and
> utter all kinds of evil against you falsely on my account. Rejoice
> and be glad, for your reward is great in heaven, for so they
> persecuted the prophets who were before you.'
>
> ~ MATTHEW 5:11-12 ~

---

9. James I. Good, *Women of the Reformed Church* (Sunday School Board of the Reformed Church in the United States, 1901), pp. 46-47.

First Woman Protestant Hymn Writer

∽ Elisabeth Cruciger, c. 1500-1535 ∽

Elisabeth von Meseritz, the daughter of a Polish nobleman, was a nun at Belbuck Abbey near Treptow. While John Bugenhagen was the biblical lecturer at Belbuck, he read some of the writings of Martin Luther and became a supporter of the Reformation. Elisabeth and her family soon embraced Bugenhagen's evangelical teachings. When Bugenhagen left Belbuck and moved to Wittenberg, those in the cloister holding Protestant sympathies were suppressed.

In the early 1520s, Elisabeth fled the Abbey and went to Wittenberg for refuge.

In 1524, Elisabeth married Casper Cruciger, a favourite pupil of Martin Luther's. Shortly after their marriage Casper became preacher at St Stephen's Church, Magdeburg. In 1528, he was called back to Wittenberg and became one of the professors of theology at the university. In Wittenberg, Elisabeth became close to Katie Luther and the other Reformers' wives. She had two children. Her son, Casper the Younger, was a theologian who later succeeded Philip Melanchthon at the University; daughter Elizabeth marred Luther's son Johannes.

Before her marriage to Casper Elisabeth wrote a hymn which was shown to Martin Luther, who enthusiastically approved of it. The hymn was published in the first Lutheran hymnal in 1524, and has remained a popular hymn to this day. 'Lord Christ the Only Son of God' is rich with Scriptural and theological content:

> The only Son from heaven,
> Foretold by ancient seers,
> By God the Father given,
> In human form appears.
> No sphere His light confining,
> No star so brightly shining
> As He, our Morning Star.
>
> O time of God appointed,
> O bright and holy morn!
> He comes, the King anointed,
> The Christ, the virgin-born,
> Grim death to vanquish for us,
> To open heav'n before us
> And bring us life again.

> O Lord, our hearts awaken
> To know and love You more,
> In faith to stand unshaken,
> In Spirit to adore,
> That we, through this world moving,
> Each glimpse of heaven proving,
> May reap its fullness there.
>
> O Father, here before You
> With God the Holy Ghost
> And Jesus, we adore You,
> O pride of angel host:
> Before You mortals lowly
> Cry, 'Holy, holy, holy,
> O blessed Trinity!'

Elisabeth wrote the first Protestant hymn written by a woman, but many women hymn writers would follow.

> *Shout for joy to God, all the earth: sing the glory of his*
> *name; give to him glorious praise!*
>
> ~ PSALM 66:1 ~

Fourteen-page Marriage Proposal!

∞ Anna Bullinger, c. 1504-1564 ∞

Anna Adlischweiler's father died in battle when she was eight. Her mother dedicated little Anna to God and placed her in the cloister at Oedenbach at Zurich. Anna's mother was sick and boarded at the cloister. During this time the Reformation came to Zurich, and the gospel was preached freely in the churches. In 1522, Ulrich Zwingli came to the cloister and preached a sermon to the nuns on 'The Clearness and Certainty of the Word of God'. Zwingli began to care for the spiritual needs of the women, and soon the town council gave orders that the nuns could leave the cloister if they chose and take their property with them. Many did leave, but Anna remained to care for her mother.

One day the chaplain brought Heinrich Bullinger, a young parish minister, into the convent. When Heinrich met Anna, his heart was moved. Later Heinrich wrote Anna a marriage proposal of fourteen-and-a-half pages! Heinrich described his health and economic status. He then gave his thoughts on marriage as a means of holiness, an opportunity 'to exercise all virtue, faith, love, compassion, hope, patience, moderation, discipline, and all godliness in Christ'. Bullinger wrote:

> You alone are the only one I have fixed upon. God alone knows whether you are meant for me and my choice rests on your manner of speaking and conduct. I have come to imagine you as a woman of breeding in whom the fear of God dwells and with whom I would like to live in love and in suffering and in everything God wills.[10]

Heinrich commended himself as not a drunkard, gambler, or a priest of Rome:

> The sum of it all is, that the greatest, surest treasure that you will find in me, is fear of God, piety, fidelity, and love, which with joy I will show you, and labor, earnestness and industry, which will not be wanting in temporal things. Concerning high nobility and many thousand gulden, I can say nothing to you. But I know that what is necessary to us, will not be wanting. For Paul says, 'We brought nothing into the world and we will take nothing out.' Therefore, if we have clothing and food it is enough.[11]

Within ten days Heinrich received Anna's answer – it was 'Yes'.

Heinrich and Anna were married in 1529. Their marriage became a model of Christian marriage to the growing Reformed movement in Europe.

He who finds a wife finds a good thing and
obtains favor from the Lord.

~ PROVERBS 18:22 ~

---

10. Patrick Miller, 'Bullinger – Family Man', *Annex* (2004), p. 7.

11. As quoted in James I. Good, *Famous Women of the Reformed Church* (Birmingham, AL: Solid Ground Christian Books, 2007, reprint of 1901 edition), p. 34.

Refuge for the Persecuted

∞ Anna Bullinger, c. 1504-1564 ∞

Heinrich Bullinger was pastor of the church at Bremgarten in the Swiss Canton of Zurich when he married Anna Adlischweiler in 1529. The couple was extremely happy, and two daughters were born to them in the next years. In 1531, their peace was shattered by the defeat of the Protestant forces at the Battle of Kappel and the brutal death of Ulrich Zwingli, pastor of the church at Zurich. Knowing they especially sought out pastors for torture, Bullinger fled to Zurich just before the Catholic soldiers entered Bremgarten. The soldiers plundered Bullinger's house and quartered soldiers with Anna and her two little daughters, a year-and-a-half and six-months old. Anna knew she could not stay there and was determined to be with her husband. The soldiers at the gate of the town would not let Anna leave, but Anna forcefully took the key from the soldier, opened the gate and fled. Heinrich was overjoyed when Anna and the girls reached Zurich.

Heinrich was chosen as successor to Zwingli at the church in Zurich and pastored the church for almost forty years. During many of those years, Zurich was a refuge for persecuted Protestants from Italy, France, England, and throughout Europe. Many of the refugees stayed with the Bullingers, and Anna oversaw a large household which included many besides her eleven children. Their home was almost like a hotel: the Bullingers lovingly cared for Zwingli's widow and children, who stayed with them, along with Heinrich's parents! In addition, young men whom Heinrich trained in the ministry often stayed with the Bullingers. Theologians from other cantons such as John Calvin, William Farel, and Martin Bucer also enjoyed the hospitality of the Bullinger home.

Anna managed the limited funds to care for her family and minister to others in need. In Zurich Anna became known as 'mother'. Throughout Europe she became known as 'Zurich-mother'. With other ministers' wives, she cared for the poor, sick and needy.

When Heinrich was stricken with the plague in 1564, all thought he would die, but Anna nursed him back to health again. She herself, however, weakened, sickened and died on 25 September. Her life remains an inspiration of love and hospitality to others.

> *Love one another with brotherly affection ... serve*
> *the Lord. Rejoice in hope, be patient in tribulation,*
> *be constant in prayer. Contribute to the needs of*
> *the saints and seek to show hospitality.*
>
> ~ ROMANS 12:10-13 ~

Sister of the King

∞ Marguerite of Navarre, 1492-1549 ∞

Marguerite, born in 1492, was two years older than her brother Francis, who became King Francis I of France in 1515. There was a great love and bond between the brother and sister, and each protected the other in various ways throughout their lives. Francis once remarked, 'My sister Marguerite is the only woman I ever knew who had every virtue and every grace without any admixture of vice.'

King Francis's reign was marked by a series of wars, known as the Italian Wars, involving France, the Holy Roman Emperor, England, and the Papal States and Italian states. During one of those conflicts, at the Battle of Pavia, on 24 February, 1525, Francis's forces were severely defeated and he was taken captive to Madrid, where he spent the next year as a prisoner. Marguerite prayed for his release and wrote him a letter of encouragement:

> The further they remove you from us, the greater becomes my firm hope of your deliverance and speedy return, for the hour when men's minds are most troubled is the hour when God achieves His masterstroke ... and if He now gives you, on the one hand, a share in the pains which He has borne for you, and, on the other hand, the grace to bear them patiently, I entreat you, Monseigneur, to believe unfalteringly that it is only to test your love for Him and to give you leisure to think about how much He loves you. ... He has permitted this trial, after having united you to Him by tribulations to deliver you for His own glory – so that, through you, His name may be known and sanctified, not in your kingdom alone, but all Christendom.[12]

Francis asked that Marguerite be allowed to come to him, and she made her way to Spain as quickly as possible. When she arrived in Madrid, her brother was deathly ill, depressed and constantly repeating Isaiah 38:1-2: 'In those days Hezekiah became sick and was at the point of death. ... Then Hezekiah turned his face to the wall and prayed to the LORD.' Marguerite assembled all the household in the king's room, and they all knelt in prayer for the king, then received communion. The king recovered to reign in France twenty-two more years.

Then they cried to the Lord in their trouble, and he delivered them from their distress. He sent out his word and healed them, and delivered them from their destruction.

~ PSALM 107:19-20 ~

---

12. As quoted in Edith Deen, *Great Women of the Christian Faith* (Uhrichsville, OH: Barbour Books, 1959), p. 19.

Protector of the Faith

∞ Marguerite of Navarre, 1492-1549 ∞

Marguerite, Queen of Navarre, was an important protector of the early movement for Reformation of the Church in France. King Francis I held Marguerite, who was his sister, in high esteem and there was a great affection between two. Marguerite learned of biblical truth from Jacques Lefèvre d'Éstaples, who preached a return to the Christianity of Christ and the Apostles. Lefèvre's commentary on the epistles of Paul clearly delineated the doctrine of justification by faith five years before Martin Luther began the Reformation in Germany. Lefèvre became Marguerite's spiritual advisor and encouraged her in her biblical studies.

Marguerite's marriage to Henry of Navarre was an arranged political marriage, and Henry did not share Marguerite's Reformed faith. Marguerite regularly had preaching services and communion in her chambers. One day, Henry came into the service and reprimanded Marguerite about her religious meetings, striking her on the face. Marguerite told the King of France, her brother, about her treatment, and Francis readied an army to bring against the King of Navarre. Henry begged Marguerite's forgiveness and promised to study the Reformation teachings. Soon, Henry joined Marguerite in Bible studies and protected those suffering persecution for their faith.

Though Marguerite herself never broke with the Roman Church, hoping for a reform of the Church while preserving its unity, she brought preachers to Navarre who were of the Reformation persuasion – rejecting indulgences, prayers to the saints, and the sacrifice of the Mass, while looking to the Scriptures for truth and salvation in Christ alone. Marguerite corresponded with John Calvin and other Reformers, who encouraged her in her stand for the gospel. She often used her influence with King Francis to obtain release of ministers imprisoned for their Protestant faith, though towards the end of his reign Francis became more implacable against those favoring the Reformation.

In 1531, Marguerite published *The Mirror of the Sinful Soul*, religious poems based on David's words, 'Create in me a clean heart, O LORD'. The poems rehearse the sinfulness of the soul, while praising God's power and goodness and looking forward to a world regenerated by Jesus Christ. In 1544, an eleven-year-old Princess Elizabeth in England translated Marguerite's work and bound it with a decorative embroidered cover as a present for Queen Catherine Parr.

Have mercy on me, O God,
According to your steadfast love; according to your
abundant mercy blot out my transgressions. Wash me
thoroughly from my iniquity, and cleanse me from my sin!

~PSALM 51:1-2~

Artist's Friend

∞ Vittoria Colonna, 1490-1547 ∞

People the world over are familiar with Michelangelo's magnificent paintings and sculptures – of David, Moses, the Pieta, and the Sistine Chapel. However, few have heard of the spiritual encouragement the artist received from his friendship with the Italian poet Vittoria Colonna.

Vittoria was from the distinguished Colonna family of Naples. When she was four years old she was betrothed to Fernando d'Avalos of Pescara; the two were married when Vittoria was nineteen, on 27 December, 1509. They enjoyed two beautiful years on the island of Ischia until Fernando was called to command troops in the Italian Wars. For the next thirteen years Fernando was rarely home, becoming chief commander of the Hapsburg armies in Italy. During these years, Vittoria and Fernando exchanged impassioned letters and poems. When Fernando died of his war injuries in 1525, Vittoria wrote a series of sonnets extolling Fernando's greatness and his bravery in battle. In time, her sonnets became more religious. Vittoria was among a group in Italy who wanted to reform the Roman Church while maintaining the Church's unity. She believed salvation was an inner experience and that justification was by faith in Christ. Resisting the Church's emphasis on external rituals, Vittoria also opposed the corruption in the Church. Her sonnets *Triumph of the Cross of Christ* reveal the Christ-centerdness of Vittoria's Christian faith.

When Michelangelo met Vittoria he was drawn to her purity and piety in the middle of Rome's corruption. Vittoria in turn recognized the spiritual ministry of Michelangelo's art. She wrote him, 'Painting, better than any other means, enables us to see the humility of the saints, the constancy of the martyrs, the purity of the virgins, the beauty of the angels, the love and charity with which the seraphim burns. It raises and transports mind and soul beyond the stars, and leaves us to contemplate the eternal sovereignty of God.'[13] Michelangelo claimed that Vittoria's life and example made him a better Christian. In her last illness, he visited her daily. At her request, Michelangelo repeated in her last hours the prayer she had written:

> Grant, I beseech Thee, Lord, that I may always adore Thee with that abasement of soul which befits my humbleness, and with that exaltation of mind which Thy Majesty demands, and let me ever live in the fear which Thy justice inspires and in the hope which Thy mercy allows, and submit to Thee as Almighty, yield myself to Thee as Allwise, and turn to Thee as to supreme Perfection and Goodness. I beseech Thee, most tender Father, that Thy most living fire may purify me, that Thy most clear light may illumine me, and that Thy most pure love may so avail me that, without hindrance of mortal things, I may return to Thee in Happiness and Security.[14]

Vittoria died 25 February, 1547.

> *For God has not destined us for wrath, but to obtain salvation through*
> *our Lord Jesus Christ, who died for us so that whether we are awake*
> *or asleep we might live with him. Therefore encourage one another*
> *and build one another up, just as you are doing.*
>
> ~ I THESSALONIANS 5:9-11 ~

---

13. Quoted in Edith Deen, *Great Women of the Christian Faith* (Uhrichsville, OH: Barbour Books, 1959), pp. 77-78.

14. Quoted in Maud F. Jerrold, *Vittoria Colonna: With Some Account of Her Friends and Her Times* (London: J. M. Dent & Company, 1906), p. 295.

Princess Protects the Persecuted

∽ Renée of France, 1510-1575 ∽

Renée, born 25 October, 1510, was the second daughter of King Louis XII of France and Anne of Brittany. Her mother died when she was four, but Renée's aunt (and the King's sister), Marguerite of Navarre, showed much love to the young princess. Marguerite was sympathetic to the teachings of the Reformation, and through her Renée also came to know many of the early French Reformers. Renée's governess, Mme De Soubise, was an Englishwoman who taught Renée the English Scriptures from the Bible translated by John Wycliffe.

When she was eighteen Renée was married to Ercole of Este, Duke of Ferrara, a member of one of the most powerful families in Italy. Ferrara in the sixteenth century was a center of Renaissance culture. The Dukes of Ferrar were patrons of the arts, and their court was a place of refinement and intellectual pursuits. Ferrar also was a place of religious conflict. The Dukes possessed their land as a fief under the papacy, hence they had a strong alliance with the Roman Pope. Yet Protestant sympathies could be found. At her court, Renée, who became sympathetic to Protestant writings and preaching while still in France, protected many Protestants fleeing persecution.

When exiled from France, John Calvin, under the assumed name of Charles d'Esperville, came and stayed at the Court of Ferrar for a month. Renée's husband, however, was not sympathetic to the Reformation and had Calvin arrested for heresy. Renée secretly had Calvin recaptured and taken to a place of safety. Calvin maintained a correspondence with Renée until his death almost thirty years later. He even wrote her from his deathbed, encouraging her to stand firm in her faith against the Catholic Inquisition around her. His successor, Theodore Beza, continued to write Renée and encourage her to use her position to protect those following the Scriptures.

As the Inquisition came to Ferrar, the Duke took the children from Renée and had her placed in solitary confinement. Under this pressure Renée dissimulated her Protestant faith and made confession to a Jesuit priest, re-establishing her position among the Catholics. When, after her husband's death, she spoke out in favor of the Reformers, her son, then the Duke, required her to become Catholic or leave Italy. Renée chose to return to France. The people of Ferrar mourned her leaving, for she had always been very charitable and kind to them.

The Protestants, known in France as Huguenots, were being persecuted more violently there than in Italy. Renée stayed away from the royal court at Paris and lived in her ancestral castle Montargis, sixty miles east of the capital. The castle became known as Hôtel Dieu, the 'Hotel of the Lord', for the many Protestants Renée sheltered and fed there. At times there were 300 eating at her table. She built a chapel and hired two Protestant ministers. When King Charles IX later required that the fugitives under her care leave the castle, Renée hired wagons and provisions to help the Protestants flee the country. Born to royalty, Renée sought to use her position and wealth to help the cause of the King of Kings.

This is the true grace of God. Stand firm in it.

~ I Peter 5:12 ~

Peace in persecution

∞ Olympia Morata, 1526-1555 ∞

Olympia Morata was about sixteen when Renée, the Duchess of Ferrara, invited her to come to the court as a companion and tutor for her daughter, Anna, who was seven. Olympia's father, Fulvio, was a professor at the University of Ferrara – one of the oldest in Italy. Fulvio recognized Olympia's intelligence and gift of language and had given his daughter the best classical education while also teaching her from the writings of the Reformers Martin Luther and John Calvin.

When the Inquisition was brought to Ferrara Olympia, along with other Protestants, was banished from the Ferrara court. Olympia looked upon her banishment as the means of weaning her heart from the world and increasing her longings for heaven.

In 1550, Olympia married Andrew Grunthler, a German doctor who had studied at Ferrara and who shared Olympia's faith and love in Jesus Christ. They settled in Schweinfurt in Bavaria, Andrew's native town, and enjoyed three years of peace before war came. The town endured a siege of fourteen months, bringing food scarcities and outbreaks of a fever which killed half of the population. Olympia wrote, 'We have found one consolation only, in the Word of God, which has sustained us, and because of which I have never looked back to the flesh-pots of Egypt. I would rather await death here than enjoy all the pleasures of the world elsewhere.'[15] When the town fell, Olympia escaped with her husband and younger brother. Along the road they suffered many hardships; Olympia said she felt like the queen of beggars. When they did reach Heidelberg, Olympia's health was broken, and she suffered from frequent fever and pain. Yet, she kept up a correspondence with friends and family in Italy and beyond. Her letters show her persistent faith and peace in the midst of much suffering, as well as her warm concern for others. To her former student, Anne, now the Duchess of Guise, she wrote:

> I sincerely hope that you will devote yourself to sacred studies, which alone are able to join us to God and to console us in this vale of tears. ... Riches, honors, and the favors of kings are nothing. Only that faith which we have in Christ can save us from eternal death. It is not enough to know the history of Christ. The devil knows that. It must be the sort of faith which is active in love.[16]

She wrote her sister Vittoria:

> There is trouble everywhere. Germany is raped. England suffers persecution. O my dear sister, may I be able to pray with David in the 90th Psalm, 'Teach us to number our days that we may get us a heart of wisdom.' Remembering that the span of our life is but toil and trouble and we soon fly away, may I give myself to the contemplation of things eternal.[17]

A letter to a dear friend concluded, 'The godly here must bear the cross. May God give faith and constancy that we may overcome the world.'[18]

Olympia died in 1555, not quite twenty-nine. A teacher and friend collected and published some of her poems, writings, and letters, dedicating them to Queen Elizabeth I of England.

'In the world you will have tribulation. But take heart, I have overcome the world.'

~ JOHN 16:33 ~

---

15. 'Olympia Morata', *The Bulwark or Reformation Journal*, Vol. 10 (1881), p. 194.
16. Quoted in Roland Bainton, *Women of the Reformation in Germany and Italy* (Minneapolis: Fortress Press, 1971), p. 262.
17. Ibid.
18. Ibid, p. 266.

Loving Christ More

⊙ Isabela Bresegna, 1510-1567 ⊙

The daughter of a Spanish noble, Isabella Bresegna was born to wealth and influence. Educated in Naples, in 1517, she married Garcia Manriquez, a Spanish captain. The couple had four children; two sons and two daughters. Garcia was frequently absent on military duties, and Isabella capably administered their estate. In 1536, Isabella heard Bernardino Ochino preach in Naples and heard for the first time the biblical truth of justification by faith. She joined the followers of Juan de Valdés and embraced the teachings of the Reformation.

In 1547, Garcia was appointed governor of Piacenza. Isabella helped him in governing and frequently hosted preachers supportive of Martin Luther's teachings. When Piacenza was taken over by the French, Isabella and her family moved to Milan. The Inquisition had begun in Rome in 1542, and persecution against those with Reformation ideas was intensifying throughout Italy. In 1557, Isabella fled across the Alps, leaving behind her family. Her husband, brother, and sons urged her to return, but she said she would only live where there was freedom of conscience.

Isabella first went to Tübingen, then to Zurich, where Ochino was pastor of an Italian congregation. Later she settled in Chiavenna and attended an evangelical church pastored by Agostino Mainardi. Many expatriates who shared Isabella's Protestant faith visited her in exile, and she was joined by one of her sons. Several reformers dedicated writings to her. Caelius Secundus Curio compiled the works of another Italian evangelical woman, Olympia Morata, and wrote a dedication to Isabella.[19] In it Curio praised Isabella as 'one of the most highborn of women' who 'kept the integrity of her religion amid the dangers and losses which her confession of the gospel of God brought in its wake'. As wife of the governor of Piacenza, she gave 'famous examples of temperance, chastity, modesty, charity, patience. Therefore all the citizens of Piacenza bewailed your departure as that of a pious parent.' In Milan Curio noted some attacked Isabella to turn her away from her faith, but 'whatever was thrown at you as a hindrance merely drove you in the direction you were headed. And whatever was meant to extinguish the light that God had kindled in you merely fanned the flames.' Though Isabella loved her children and husband, Curio praised her for loving Christ more and serving Christ with a clear conscience.

> *'If anyone comes to me and does not hate his own father and mother*
> *and wife and children and brothers and sisters, yes, and even his*
> *own life, he cannot be my disciple. Whoever does not bear his own*
> *cross and come after me cannot be my disciple.'*
>
> ~ LUKE 14:26-27 ~

---

19. See Olympia Morata, *The Complete Writings of an Italian Heretic*, edited and translated by Holt N. Parker. (Chicago and London: University of Chicago Press, 2007), p. 67.

Persuaded by the Word of God

∞ Paula and Claudine Levet, 1530s ∞

In the early days of the Reformation in Geneva, Antoine Froment opened a school to teach young people. Using the classroom as a platform to expound the Scriptures, many adults began attending the classes to hear the Word of God. Paula Levet was one who became very zealous for the Scriptures after hearing Froment preach. She urged her sister-in-law, Claudine, to come and listen, but Claudine had a horror that she might be bewitched by Froment and led into error. Finally, Paula persuaded Claudine to come and listen out of love for her. However, Claudine dressed to protect herself, placing rosemary leaves in her hair, and hanging crosses and rosaries around her neck. She wasn't going to let the enchanter bewitch her!

Claudine sat in the hall ready to mock and deride everything Froment said. As Froment read from the Bible and then simply expounded the words, Claudine crossed herself several times and whispered prayers to ward off Froment's influence. Yet, as he spoke, Claudine began to hear the gospel, and it found its way into her heart. Afterwards, she spoke with Froment and asked him if all he said was in that book. Froment said it was and loaned her his New Testament. Claudine put it underneath her cloak, still covered with her many amulets.

Back at her home, Claudine began reading the Scriptures, remaining in her room three days without eating, but praying and consuming the Word of God. She began to see that forgiveness for sins was in Christ, apart from the superstitions which had guided her life before. Claudine called for Froment to visit her, and she told him how God had opened her heart to His truth. Froment was greatly strengthened by seeing her newborn faith in God's Holy Word.

Claudine's newfound faith and perspective in life brought a change which all could see. Previously she had spent much time and funds on the finest fashions and dress. She now sold much of her finery and gave her money to the poor. Many of her friends couldn't understand this change, but she invited them to her home, gave each of them a New Testament, and began to see the gospel change their lives as it had hers. So the gospel spread in Geneva.

Claudine's husband, Aimee Levet, came to faith in Christ as well through his wife's witness and her changed life. The church authorities hated the influence the couple now had for the reformation of Geneva, and some zealots broke into Aimee's apothecary shop, threw away all the drugs and had Aimee placed in prison. Such opposition only strengthened the Levets' faith in the gospel and the Word of God.

> *For I am not ashamed of the gospel, for it is the power of God for salvation to everyone who believes, to the Jew first and also to the Greek. For in it the righteousness of God is revealed from faith to faith, as it is written, 'The righteous shall live by faith.'*
>
> ~ ROMANS 1:16-17 ~

Blessing after Dark Night

∽ Anna Reinhardt Zwingli, 1487-1538? ∽

Anna Reinhard was a beautiful woman with a noble character to match. Yet when Hans von Knonau, who came from a distinguished family in Zurich, wanted to marry her, his father strongly objected, having chosen another bride for his son more in keeping with the family's social station. Hans ignored his father and married Anna in 1504; his father disinherited him. Hans became a soldier and fought with the Swiss army in Italy in the wars against France.

He returned from the campaigns in broken health and died in 1517. Anna was a widow with three children to support; two daughters and a son.

Anna's house was not far from Ulrich Zwingli's church in Zurich, and she became a regular attendant there, growing spiritually from Zwingli's expositional sermons. Zwingli noticed the precociousness of Anna's son Gerold and began teaching him Greek and Latin. Soon Zwingli began to notice the Christian graces of Gerold's mother. Zwingli married Anna in 1522, becoming one of the first priests of the Reformation to marry. Zwingli became a father to Anna's children, and Anna and Zwingli had four children together. In 1523, Zwingli wrote for Gerold, 'Directions for the Education of a Young Nobleman', the first Reformed work on education.

Anna was a model minister's wife, caring for the poor and needy as well as supporting her husband in his work. The Zwingli home was always open to the many Protestant refugees who had fled to Zurich. When Zwingli and other ministers in Zurich began translating the Bible, Zwingli read Anna the proof sheets every evening. She treasured her copy of the Bible when the translation was printed and encouraged each family to have a copy.

In October 1531, the army of the Catholic cantons moved against Zurich. Zwingli was called upon to go along with the Zurich forces as a chaplain. Anna was fearful as she said her farewell, but said, 'We shall see each other again if the Lord will. His will be done. And what will you bring back when you come?' Zwingli replied, 'Blessing after dark night.'[20] These were Zwingli's last words to her. Zurich was defeated at the Battle of Kappel on 11 October. Zwingli was killed early in the battle, his body later quartered and burned. Anna's son Gerold also died on the battlefield, along with a brother and brother-in-law, while a son-in-law was wounded and died later. Anna's sorrow seemed overwhelming, yet she turned to her Savior for comfort and sustenance.

Heinrich Bullinger succeeded Zwingli as pastor in Zurich. He brought Anna and her children into his home and cared for her as a son would a beloved mother. In around 1538, Anna died peacefully. Leaving the dark night of earth, she found the blessing of the new day in heaven.

> *Weeping may tarry for the night,*
> *but joy comes with the morning.*
>
> ~ PSALM 30:5 ~

---

20. James Isaac Good, *Women of the Reformed Church* (Sunday School Board of the Reformed Church in the United States, 1901), p. 14.

Excellent Companion

∞ Idelette Calvin, d. 1549 ∞

In 1533, Idelette Stordeur, her husband Jean, and several other Anabaptists, fleeing religious persecution in Liege, Belgium, sought refuge in Geneva, Switzerland. Each Swiss canton chose which religion to follow. The council in Geneva chose a Reformed faith, but would not accept the Anabaptists. When Jean was banned from the town in 1537, the Stordeurs took refuge in Strasbourg. The next year John Calvin himself was forced to leave Geneva and similarly found refuge in Strasbourg.

In Strasbourg Calvin not only preached two sermons on Sundays but lectured every day, while also working on the second edition of his *Institutes* and a *Commentary on Romans*. After hearing Calvin preach, the Stordeurs left the Anabaptist congregation and joined with Calvin. Calvin visited with them in their home and nurtured them in the Scriptures.

Calvin was twenty-nine when he came to Strasbourg, and many of his friends were urging him to marry. Calvin was open to his friends' suggestion, but he had some qualifications of his own: '... he wished a wife who would be gentle, pure, modest, economical, patient, and to whom the care of her husband would be the chief matter'. Calvin's friends recommended several possibilities, but each had drawbacks. One was too wealthy and didn't know French (Calvin's native language); another was ten years older than he; another he simply didn't like. Pastor Bucer then suggested Idelette to Calvin. Her husband had died of the plague in the spring of 1540. Idelette was a godly widow with two young children, a woman of character, and intelligent. Idelette and John Calvin were married in Strasbourg, 1 August, 1540.

When Calvin accepted the call to return to Geneva, the Geneva Council sent a two-horse carriage to bring Idelette, the children, and their possessions to Geneva. The council also furnished them with a new house. Idelette planted a vegetable and herb garden in the back as well as some flowers. Calvin always enjoyed showing Idelette's garden to visitors. Idelette brought a calm and stability to Calvin's life. She cared for him, encouraged him, and fervently prayed for his safety.

Idelette bore several children to Calvin, but they all died in infancy. Her own health weakened, and in 1549 she too died. Calvin was grief-stricken and later wrote a friend, 'My grief is very heavy. My best life's companion has been taken from me. Whenever I faced serious difficulties, she was ever ready to share with me, not only banishment and poverty, but even death itself.'[21]

> *House and wealth are inherited from fathers,*
> *But a prudent wife is from the* LORD.
>
> ~ PROVERBS 19:14 ~

---

21. Quotes cited in William J. Petersen, 'Idelette: John Calvin's Search for the Right Wife', *Christian History* (Vol. V, No. 4), p. 15.

Anne of a Thousand Days

∽ Anne Boleyn, 1507-1536 ∽

Anne Boleyn became King Henry VIII's second wife and Queen of England when she was twenty-six. Executed for treason when she was twenty-nine, she was queen for only a thousand days. Nevertheless, she had an important influence on the development of Christianity in England.

Anne's father was a diplomat in the court of England's King Henry VII, and Anne was educated at the French court from the age of six. Anne first began to study the Scriptures in France, reading Lefèvre's French translation of the Bible and French commentaries on Scripture. Anne's personal books which remain give evidence of her evangelical faith: a Lefèvre Bible, inscribed with Romans 5:12-18 and John 1:17; an English New Testament translated by William Tyndale (which was banned in England at the time), a book of Huguenot poetry by Clément Marot, and a commentary on Ecclesiastes.

When Anne returned to the English court as a young woman she caught the eye of Henry VIII, who had decided his marriage with Catherine of Aragon was a sin since she had been married to his brother before his death. Henry petitioned the Pope for an annulment while at the same time pursuing Anne. Henry pursued Anne for six years, but Anne refused to become his mistress. She did undoubtedly encourage Henry to break with the papacy when the Pope would not grant an annulment for Henry's first marriage. Only when Henry's divorce from Catherine seemed certain to receive the approval of Parliament did Anne yield to Henry and the two were secretly married, followed by a more public ceremony.

Anne considered herself providentially placed to encourage the Reformation in England, and there was wide-spread opinion that she helped bring about the reform of the Church of England. When Henry dissolved the monasteries, Anne worked for the resulting funds to be used for the poor. She also encouraged the ladies of the court to sew clothes for the poor, thinking there should be no idleness among them. She encouraged Henry to appoint several evangelical bishops and deans and tried to convince him that William Tyndale was a friend. Anne's personal chaplains included the Reformers Hugh Latimer and Matthew Parker. The sincerity of Anne's humility and desire to be true in her faith was evident by her exhortation to her chaplains to freely tell her what they 'saw in her amiss'.

Anne gave birth to a daughter, the future Queen Elizabeth I, but then suffered at least two miscarriages, the last one a son. Henry became persuaded that Anne had bewitched him and began flirting with Jane Seymour. Anne was falsely accused of adultery with five men, including her brother. She was beheaded at the Tower of London 19 May, 1536, seventeen days after her arrest. Her last words were 'To Jesus Christ I commend my soul; Lord Jesus receive my soul.'

> But my foes are vigorous, they are mighty, and many are those
> who hate me wrongfully. Those who render me evil for good
> accuse me because I follow after good. Do not forsake me, O
> Lord! ... Make haste to help me, O Lord, my salvation!
>
> ~ Psalm 38:19-22 ~

Only Woman Named on Geneva's Reformation Monument

∽ Marie Dentière, c. 1495-1561 ∾

During the four-hundredth anniversary of John Calvin's birth, in 1909, an impressive Reformation Wall was built on the grounds of the University of Geneva, with larger than life statues depicting many of the leaders of the Reformation throughout Europe. In 2002, the name of Marie Dentière was inscribed on the wall, making Marie the only woman recognized on the massive monument.

Marie was born in Tournai, in Flanders, in the last decade of the fifteenth century. From a noble family, she entered an Augustinian nunnery as a young woman. When she studied some of Martin Luther's writings, Marie accepted the Scriptural teaching of salvation by faith and left the convent. To avoid punishment and persecution she fled to Strasbourg where she met and, in 1528, married Simon Robert, a priest who had also accepted the teachings of the Reformation. Simon became pastor to the French reformed church in Valais, and Marie helped in his pastoral work, often accompanying him on his evangelistic trips. She learned Hebrew and Latin, and helped Simon with a Bible translation. Marie and Simon had five children before Simon's death in 1533. Marie later married Antoine Froment, a friend of Simon's, who was working in Geneva with reformer William Farel.

Marie was active in public evangelism, reaching out to women with the truth of the gospel. In 1535, with Farel, Marie visited the Poor Claire's convent in Geneva and spoke to the nuns about the freedom she had found in Christ, including the beauty of marriage and a family. When William Farel and John Calvin were expelled from Geneva in 1538, Marguerite of Navarre, sister to King Francis I of France, apparently contacted Marie to find out details of the expulsion. Marie wrote an epistle to Marguerite which was intended as a message for Francis as well as for a wider audience. Marie noted that though women are not to preach in public, they are not forbidden to write and admonish one another in love. The Samaritan woman and Mary Magdalene certainly were important in sharing their faith with others. Marie encouraged Marguerite that salvation is by faith in Christ alone and all spiritual authority is in Him. She wrote that the Church had usurped the authority of Christ and established a new idolatry with pilgrimages, indulgences, veneration of saints, the sacrifice of the Mass, and forbidding to marry. Marie wrote that women, equally with men, were able to read and interpret Scripture. In her joy in studying Scripture, Marie also wrote Marguerite that her daughter had written a Hebrew grammar to help girls in their study of Scripture.

Shortly before her death, in 1561, Marie wrote a preface to John Calvin's sermon on women's apparel, in which she exhorted women to avoid materialism and covetousness in dress:

> You will find that those who are the most concerned about adorning their bodies, are little concerned that their spirits be adorned with true, solid virtues, As for us, we should not seek the ornament of garments, but of good behavior. As for women, who are in that regard more covetous than men, may they understand that too much daring has always been associated with immodesty; likewise, on the contrary, simplicity in clothes has always been a mark of chastity and continence.[22]

For all that is in the world – the desires of the flesh and the desires of the eyes and the pride in possessions – is not from the Father but is from the world. And the world is passing away along with its desires, but whoever does the will of God abides forever.
~ 1 John 2:16-17 ~

---

22. Marie Dentiere, Mary B. McKinley, trans., *Epistle to Marguerite de Navarre and Preface to a Sermon by John Calvin* (Chicago: University of Chicago Press, 2004), p. 93.

Bible Study in the Palace

The drama surrounding the life and six wives of King Henry VIII of England has been frequently portrayed in movies, novels and plays. Often ignored, however, are the spiritual undercurrents of the life at Court. On 12 July, 1543, King Henry married Catherine Parr, his sixth and last wife. She was a devout Christian who patiently tried to influence the King in reforming the Church of England. She was an important mothering influence for Henry's children, particularly Edward and Elizabeth, and directed their education.

Catherine's chaplain was Miles Coverdale, an early Bible translator and editor of the 'Great Bible' which King Henry had ordered to be placed in every church in England. At a time when the Bible was only just becoming available in English, and reading the Bible was still heavily restricted, the English Bible was readily available for anyone to read in the Queen's apartments. Catherine gathered around her ladies-in-waiting who were interested in theology and Bible study.

Catherine encouraged the translation into English of the *Paraphrases* of Desiderius Erasmus, a commentary on Scripture gleaned from many of the early church fathers. The queen, who was fluent in Latin, French, and Italian, did part of the translation herself. King Edward, who succeeded his father Henry as king, proclaimed that a copy of the *Paraphrases*, along with the Bible, be placed in every English church.

Catherine was the first English queen to publish a book, *Prayers and Meditations*, under her own name. Her *Lamentations of a Sinner*, written after Henry's death, lamented the life lived apart from Christ. Though Catherine lived at the height of English society, she wrote of the true Christian's experience whatever his social standing:

> I will call upon Christ, The Light of the world. The Fountain of Life, the Relief of all careful consciences, the Peacemaker between God and man, and the only health and comfort of all repentant sinners. ... I have certainly no curious learning to defend the matter ..., but a simple and earnest love to the truth inspired of God, who promiseth to pour his Spirit upon all flesh; which I have, by the grace of God ... felt in myself to be true ...[23]

For the grace of God has appeared, bringing salvation for all people,
training us to renounce ungodliness and worldly passions, and to
live self-controlled, upright, and godly lives in the present age.

~ TITUS 2:11-12 ~

---

23. Paul Zahl, *Five Women of the English Reformation* (Grand Rapids: William B. Eerdmans Publishing Co., 2001), p. 50.

Faithful unto Death

∞ Helen Stark, d. 1544 ∞

The Scottish Parliament early took action to prevent the spread of the teachings of the Reformation. In 1525, the Parliament forbade the importation of Lutheran books, hoping to suppress such 'heresies'. When the prohibitions were ineffective, the religious authorities resorted to executing those adhering to such doctrines as justification by faith or the authority of the Scriptures. In 1528, Patrick Hamilton was burned at the stake at Saint Andrews, becoming the first martyr to the Reformation in Scotland. Hamilton's courageous stand for the truth only helped spread the Reformation in Scotland.

On 15 December, 1543, Parliament took further action, exhorting all prelates within the realm to take action against all persons heretical to the established church according to the laws of the Church, which included punishment by death. On 25 January, Cardinal Beaton went to Perth, where there were many of the Reformed faith. Six people were soon accused and arrested: Robert Lamb, a merchant; William Anderson, a maltman; James Finlayson; James Hunter, a flesher; James Ranoldson, a skinner; and Ranoldson's wife, Helen Stark. A semblance of a trial was held the following day. All were charged with holding meetings for the exposition of the Scriptures, against the Act of Parliament which forbade disputations on the meaning of the Holy Scriptures. Other charges against the individuals included treating the image of St Francis disrespectfully and eating a goose during a fast day. Helen was accused of refusing to pray to the Virgin Mary during childbirth, saying she would pray to God alone in the name of Christ. All six of the accused were found guilty of violating the Act of Parliament and condemned to death, the men by hanging and Helen by drowning.

Many in the town of Perth interceded for the lives of the condemned, but without success. As the six were taken to the place of execution, they comforted each other with the assurance that they would soon eat together in the kingdom of heaven. Helen asked that she might be able to die with her husband, but her request was denied. As she went to the place of execution with him, she exhorted him to remain constant in the cause of Christ. Kissing him, she said,

> Husband, be glad: we have lived many joyful days, but this day, on which we must die, ought to be the most joyful of all to us both, because now we shall have joy for ever. Therefore I will not bid you good night, for we shall suddenly meet with joy in the kingdom of heaven.[24]

After the execution of the men, Helen was taken to a pool of water. She had several children, including a nursing infant, which she prayed the townspeople to care for. She was then tied in a sack and drowned in the water. As one writer reflected,

> After a momentary struggle her redeemed spirit, emancipated from all its sorrows, was rejoicing before the throne of God; and may we not affirm that, next to the Saviour, among the first to welcome her into that happier state of being were her own husband and his fellow-sufferers, who had reached it, perhaps, hardly an hour before?[25]

> *'Then they will deliver you up to tribulation and put you to*
> *death, and you will be hated by all nations for my name's sake.*
> *… But the one who endures to the end will be saved.'*
>
> ~ MATTHEW 24:9, 13 ~

---

24. James Anderson, *Ladies of the Reformation* (London: Blackie and Son, 1855), p. 532.

25. Ibid, p. 533.

Firm in Her Faith

∞ Anne Askew, 1521? – 1546 ∞

Twenty-five-year-old Anne Askew had a passion for the Scriptures and sharing them with others, which often brought ridicule upon her. Her husband, who did not share her evangelical faith, tired of her devotions and forced her to leave the house. Anne went to London, where she became part of Queen Catherine's Bible study in the palace. She was also active in distributing Bibles, tracts, and religious books.

It was a time of unsettled change in England. King Henry VIII had removed England from the authority of the Roman Church and placed himself at the head of the Church of England. Yet, the Church still largely followed Roman Catholic doctrine and the Roman Mass. In 1545, Anne Askew was arrested and examined about her attitude to the Mass. Anne quoted Scripture to support her faith that Christ died once and for all as a sacrifice for sin and the Mass was not a re-sacrifice of the body and blood of Jesus. Anne was released, but arrested again the following year and interrogated under torture. She boldly maintained her faith under great torture. When urged to believe that the priest during the Mass did transform the bread and wine into the body and blood of Christ, Anne replied, 'I have read that God made man; but that man can make God, I never read, nor I suppose, ever shall read.'

Anne was taken to the Tower of London where she was commanded to tell the names of other ladies at court who shared her beliefs, but she would not name any. She was put on the rack and her body stretched to try and break her will, but she never cried out even as her bones were dislocated. When she was taken to be executed by burning at Smithfield on 16 July, 1546, her body was so broken she could not walk, but had to be carried. Anne thanked the Lord that He had given her strength to persevere. Before her death she prayed for her persecutors, that their blind hearts would be opened to the mercy and goodness of the Lord.

But we have this treasure in jars of clay, to show that the
surpassing power belongs to God and not to us.

~ 2 CORINTHIANS 4:7 ~

Converted in a Palace Bible Study

∽ Catherine Willoughby, 1519-1580 ∽

Catherine was born 22 March, 1519, into the nobility of Tudor England. Her father was William, Lord Willoughby de Eresby; her mother was Maria de Salinas, who had come to England from Spain with Catherine of Aragon as her lady-in-waiting. When Catherine's father died, she inherited his vast estate. At fourteen she became the wife of Charles Brandon, Duke of Suffolk, and in 1543 she became lady-in-waiting to Queen Catherine Parr, Henry VIII's sixth wife.

Queen Catherine established for her household a regular regime of prayer, Bible reading, and studies in theology. It was in these palace Bible studies that Catherine Willoughby began to understand the centrality of Scripture to the Christian faith. She recognized the abuses and corruptions in the Roman Catholic Church and embraced the biblical truth of justification by faith alone. By 1546, Catherine had an English New Testament translated by William Tyndale; she was instrumental in distributing New Testaments throughout the court and sponsored the publication of other evangelical tracts and books, including Queen Catherine's *Lamentations of a Sinner*.

At court Catherine met Hugh Latimer, who occasionally preached for Henry VIII, and invited him to her home at Grimsthorpe to preach to her household and the community. Between 1550 and 1553 Latimer preached thirty-seven sermons at Grimsthorpe on topics Catherine specifically requested: the centrality of Scripture, God's sovereignty, the importance of Christ's sacrificial death, the priesthood of all believers, justification by faith alone, and prayer. Latimer did not hesitate to also address sinful proclivities in Catherine – her sharp tongue, quick temper, and excessively luxurious dress. Catherine recognized and repented of her sinfulness, comforted by Christ's sacrificial death when considering her many sins.

In 1551, Catherine's sons Charles and Brandon both died of the sweating sickness. Catherine was deeply grieved, but could write, 'I give God thanks for … all his benefits … and truly take this last (and to first sight most sharp and bitter) punishment not for the least of his benefits.' Her sons' deaths taught her to know more of God's power, love, and mercy. She had come to know that 'in sickness, adversities, persecutions, or what else in the world can happen to us that they be sent of God for our profit and that nothing can happen amiss to his elect children.'[26]

Seven years after her husband died Catherine married Richard Bertie, who shared her Reformation beliefs. When Mary Tudor became Queen, Bishop Stephen Gardiner interrogated Bertie, urging him and Catherine to return to the Roman Catholic Church. Catherine and her husband fled to Europe to escape looming persecution, returning to England when Elizabeth became Queen.

If we confess our sins, he is faithful and just to forgive us our sins
and to cleanse us from all unrighteousness.

~ 1 JOHN 1:9 ~

---

26. Melissa Franklin Harkrider, *Women, Reform, and Community in Early Modern England: Catherine Willoughby, Duchess of Suffolk, and Lincolnshire's Godly Aristocracy, 1519-1580* (Woodbridge, Suffolk: The Boydell Press, 2008), p. 57.

Bold Testimony for Christ

∞ Elizabeth Dirks, d. 1549 ∞

When she was a child, Elizabeth Dirks was placed in the convent of Tienge, near Leer in Germany. There she received a good education. When she heard about a heretic being burned for repudiating the sacraments, Elizabeth obtained a Latin Bible and diligently read it to try to find the truth. She became certain that the monastic or convent life was not found in Scripture. Disguised as a milkmaid, she escaped the convent and found refuge in a home of Anabaptists in Leer. Anabaptists received their name because they believed in believer's baptism and re-baptized people when they came to faith in Christ, even if they had been baptized as an infant.

Elizabeth was arrested for heresy on 15 January, 1549. During her interrogations she confidently answered with Scripture. When asked if the priests had power to forgive sin, Elizabeth replied, 'No, my lords; how should I believe this? I say that Christ is the only priest through whom sins are forgiven'.[27]

When asked if she was saved by baptism, she replied, 'No, my lords, all the water in the sea cannot save me. All my salvation is in Christ, who has commanded me to love the Lord my God, and my neighbor as myself.' She repeatedly was pressed to name who had baptized her and who her friends were, but she answered, 'No, my lord, do not press me on this point. Ask me about my faith and I will answer gladly.'[28] When she would not voluntarily confess the names of her associates, screws were applied to her thumb and fingers until blood spurted from the fingernails. The torturers then crushed her leg bones with screws until she fainted. Since she would not confess, she was condemned to die. She was tied in a bag and drowned in the river. Her moving testimony of her faith in Christ, however, continued to be told long after her death, even to this day.

'And when they bring you before the synagogues and the rulers
and the authorities, do not be anxious about how you should
defend yourself or what you should say, for the Holy Spirit will
teach you in that very hour what you ought to say.'

~ LUKE 12:11-12 ~

---

27. Hebrews 7:21.

28. Denis R. Janz, ed. *Reformation Reader* (Minneapolis, MN: Fortress Press), pp. 228-230.

Suffering for the Incorruptible Word of God

∞ Lysken Dirks, d. 19 February, 1552 ∞

During the sixteenth century a large number of Anabaptists in the Netherlands were slain for their faith in the Word of God and their testimony for Jesus Christ. Among those was Lysken Dirks, a young lady of eighteen who married a fellow-Anabaptist, Jeronimus Segerson, about 1550. The Anabaptist minister married the couple, but since they were not married by a Catholic priest, many considered their marriage unlawful.

In 1551, both Lysken and her husband were imprisoned. Kept in separate cells, they never saw each other again after their arrest. They wrote each other, however, and their remaining letters are beautiful witnesses to their faith. In one of his letters, Jeronimus encouraged Lysken:

> My most beloved wife, Lysken, submit yourself to present circumstances; be patient in tribulation, and instant in prayer, and look at all times to the precious promises everywhere given us, if we continue steadfast to the end ... Fear not the world, for the hairs of your head are all numbered. Men have no power, except it be given them from above. ... O, my heartily beloved wife, abide faithful to the Lord, even unto death; for the crown is not at the beginning, nor in the middle, but at the end.[29]

The priests urged both Jeronimus and Lysken to recant their beliefs. After one session with the priests, Jeronimus wrote Lysken warning her about those who would destroy her peace in Christ:

> Christ himself hath warned us that in the last days many false prophets and false Christs shall arise, insomuch that, if it were possible, they should deceive the very elect ... Christ hath warned us also against the doctrine of the Pharisees, and of those that come in sheep's clothing, but inwardly are ravening wolves ... I therefore beseech you, my dear wife, from the bottom of my heart, ... that you give no heed to them, and have nothing to do with them.[30]

When the priests sought to get Lysken to recant her beliefs, she always answered them with Scripture. The priests told her she should not be meddling with the Scriptures but should mind her sewing. In a letter to her husband, Lysken wrote:

> The Lord is faithful, saith Paul, who will not suffer us to be tempted above that we are able. Blessed be God, the father of our Lord Jesus Christ, who hath counted us worthy to suffer for His name, ... yea, we know, as Paul saith, 'If we suffer, we shall also reign with him; if we be dead with him, we shall also live with him ... herewith I commend you to the Lord, and to the word of his grace and glory, whereby he will glorify us, if we remain therein to the end. The grace of the Lord be with us.'[31]

Jeronimus was burned at the stake on 2 September, 1551. Lysken was pregnant and was delivered of her child before her execution. Leaving her trial, she told the crowd, 'know that I do not suffer for robbing, or murder, or any kind of wickedness, but solely for the incorruptible Word of God.'[32] On 19 February, 1552, Lysken was placed in a sack and drowned in the river Schledt.

For what credit is it if, when you sin and are beaten for it, you endure? But if when you do good and suffer for it you endure, this is a gracious thing in the sight of God.

~ I PETER 2:20 ~

---

29. James Anderson, *Ladies of the Reformation* (London: Blackie and Son, 1855), p. 606.

30. Ibid, pp. 608-609.

31. Ibid, pp. 612-613.

32. Ibid, p. 616.

Standing for Christ in Difficult Days

∞ Lady Jane Grey, 1537-1554 ∞

Jane Grey was born in 1537, the same year Henry VIII's son Edward and heir to the throne was born. As a great-granddaughter of Henry VII, Jane was fourth in line to the throne of England after Henry VIII's own three children. Jane was given the best possible education, learning French, German, Latin, and Greek, as well as embroidery, music and fine arts. When she was nine years old her parents sent her to court where she lived with Catherine Parr, Henry VIII's last wife. From Catherine, Jane received the love and nurture she did not receive from her ambitious parents. Catherine regularly held Bible studies among the ladies of the court, and here Jane came to faith in Christ.

When Jane was sent back home after the deaths of Henry VIII and then Catherine, her parents told her she was worthless and treated her cruelly. Jane found escape in her studies and even corresponded with leading Reformation figures Heinrich Bullinger and Martin Bucer. Henry VIII's successor, young Edward VI, strongly supported the Reformation in England. Realizing his health was failing and he probably would not live long, Edward sought to change Henry VIII's will to assure the throne would remain Protestant and not revert to Catholicism. Bypassing Mary and Elizabeth, he made Jane Grey his heir. John Dudley, the king's advisor, seeking to assure his own power, then married his son Guildford to Jane. Jane was against the marriage, but her mother forced her to marry him. When Edward died in June 1553, Jane was then proclaimed Queen. She had not been told that she was to be the heir and fainted when she was told. Jane resisted, but then did accept the royal throne. Edward's older sister Mary, however, would not relinquish her right to the throne and came to London with an army. When the people supported Mary as Queen, even Jane's former supporters retreated from her; she relinquished her claim to be queen after nine days, but Jane and Guildford were accused of treason and imprisoned in the Tower of London.

The evening before her execution, Jane distributed her personal affects. She gave her sister Katherine her Greek New Testament. In it she wrote of the importance of the Scripture in teaching us how to live and die. She concluded:

> Now as touching my death, rejoice, as I do, my dearest sister, that I shall be delivered of this corruption, and put on incorruption; for I am assured that I shall, for losing a mortal life, win one that is immortal, everlasting, and joyful; the which I pray God grant in his most blessed hour, and send you his all-saving grace to live in his fear, and to die in true Christian faith, from which, in God's name, I exhort you never swerve, neither for hope of life nor fear of death; ... if you will cleave to him he will stretch forth your days to an uncircumscribed comfort, and to his own glory, to the which glory God bring me now, and you hereafter, when it shall please him to call you. Farewell, once again, my beloved sister, and put your only trust in God, who only must help.[33]

Before Jane was beheaded on 12 February, 1554, she recited Psalm 51. The Lord was glorified in the life and death of this gentle sixteen-year-old.

The sacrifices of God are a broken spirit; a broken and
contrite heart, O God, you will not despise.

~ PSALM 51:17 ~

---

33. W. H. Davenport Adams, *Stories of the Lives of Noble Women* (London: T. Nelson & Sons, 1891), pp. 164-165.

Marian Martyrs

∞ Catherine Hutt, Joan Horne, and Elizabeth Thackvill, d. 16 May, 1556 ∞

The English Protestants gave Queen Mary I the nickname 'Bloody Mary' for the almost three hundred Protestants executed for their faith under her reign. At least forty-five of those executed were women. Among these were three women from the county of Essex. Catherine Hutt, Joan Horne, Elizabeth Thackvill, and Margaret Ellis quit attending the local parish church because they no longer could believe in the sacrament of the Mass, that the communion bread and wine was transformed into the literal body and blood of Christ. This brought them under suspicion of heresy, so that the Essex county justices of the peace sent them to the Bishop of London for trial in 1556.

Under examination, the women said they could not believe in the Mass; Christ's natural body was in heaven, not in the bread used in the sacrament. Catherine Hutt said she did not approve of the service in Latin, and she did not believe the Roman Church administered the sacraments according to God's Word, making an idol out of the Mass. Each was required to give their opinion of the Mass and return to the Roman Catholic faith. Catherine said the sacrament of the papists was not truly God, but made with man's hands. Joan Horne said she did not believe the sacrament to be Christ himself but simply bread. Saying she detested the abominations of the Papacy, she was condemned to death. Elizabeth Thackvill and Margaret Ellis answered similarly. All were condemned on 13 April.

Margaret Ellis died in prison. The other three women were taken to Smithfield on 16 May. There they were fastened to one stake. The fagots were lit, and their bodies consumed by the flames. They committed their spirits to God, joyfully suffering death for the truth of God's Word and looking forward to their life eternal with their Savior, whose body they knew to be in heaven.

'Truly, truly, I say to you, if anyone keeps my word,
he will never see death.'

~ JOHN 8:51 ~

Blind faith

∞ Joan Waste, 1534-1556 ∞

Joan Waste was born blind in 1534, though her twin brother Roger had his sight. Her father was a barber and also a rope maker. When a teenager, Joan was able to help her father in making ropes and also learned to knit various articles of clothing. Under King Edward's reign church services began to be in English, and the Scriptures were read during the services. Joan daily went to the church and learned much Christian truth from the sermons and Scripture reading. She bought an English Bible for herself and paid people to read it to her, enabling her to memorize many passages of Scripture.

When Queen Mary came to the throne the Latin Mass was restored and English Bibles were again forbidden. Joan, however, clung to the Scriptures and the teaching of the many godly men she had previously heard preach in the church. For refusing to attend Mass or confess to a priest, Joan was arrested and placed in the prison in Derby. The bishop's officials came and spoke with her many times, trying to persuade her of the errors of her ways, and she was finally brought before the bishop himself. She was especially accused of not recognizing the body and blood of Christ in the bread and wine of communion. Joan answered her accusers by saying she believed what the Scriptures taught and was ready to forfeit her life for her faith. Joan was condemned as a heretic, and 1 August, 1556, was appointed for her execution. Joan, then twenty-two, walked to the execution spot holding the hand of her twin brother. After kneeling and praying fervently for Christ to have mercy upon her, she called upon the multitude to pray for her. She was hanged and the fire lit below her. When the fire burned the rope, she fell into the fire, and, as John Foxe wrote, 'the glorious light of the everlasting Sun of righteousness beamed upon her departed spirit.'[34] One historian noted, 'And thus did this injured faithful woman quit the mortal stage of earth to inherit a life of immortality, the sure and certain reward of all those who suffer for the sake of the glorious gospel of the blessed God.'[35]

Precious in the sight of the LORD *is the death of his saints.*

~ PSALM 116:15 ~

---

34. John Foxe, *Acts and Monuments*, chapter 26.
35. Thomas Timpson, *British Female Biography* (London: Aylott and Jones, 1846), p. 120.

Welcome the Cross of Christ!

∞ Joyce Lewis, d. 10 September, 1557 ∞

Among the early martyrs under Queen Mary was Laurence Saunders of Northamptonshire. Saunders had obtained a licence to preach under King Edward, ministering at Lichfield Cathedral and then in London. When Queen Mary came to the throne, he warned England of its lukewarmness to the gospel of Christ and impending difficulties under the new queen. Saunders was arrested, convicted of heresy, and taken to Coventry, where he was burned at the stake on 8 February, 1555. He kissed the stake as he was being chained to it and said, 'Welcome the cross of Christ, welcome everlasting life.'[36]

In the crowd watching the execution was Joyce Lewis. She was disturbed by Saunders' execution and impressed by his steadfast faith in the face of such suffering. She began to question a religion which would inflict such cruelty, which she could not believe was from God. Wanting to know the truth, she went to visit John Glover, whose younger brother was martyred a few months after Saunders. Glover pointed out to her some of the errors in the Roman Church and encouraged her to study the Scriptures, finding truth in the Word of God. Reading the Scriptures, Joyce became a convert to the gospel of Jesus Christ, and her faith began to be molded by the Word of God.

One day in church, Joyce turned her back on the altar and expressed disapproval of the ceremonies. This was reported to the Bishop of Lichfield, and a summons was issued for Joyce to appear. When the officer came to the door, Joyce's husband held a knife to his chest, grabbed the warrant and destroyed it. The officer left, only to return later with a larger arresting body for both Mr and Mrs Lewis. When the Lewises were brought before the bishop, Mr Lewis apologized and was dismissed. Joyce, however, refused to apologize or express support for the Mass. Because she was a person of some importance, the bishop gave her a month to reconsider her stance, only requiring her husband to put forth a bond of £100.

As the month drew to a close, friends urged Joyce's husband to have her move elsewhere to avoid being arrested again. But he did not want to forfeit his £100. The bishop examined Joyce several times, but she could not agree to the Roman Church's ritual, which she could not find in God's Word. She said if she could find it in Scripture, she would follow it. The bishop told her she must be a heretic if she only believed what was found in Scripture. Joyce was kept in prison a year. On 10 September, 1557, she was taken out to her place of execution. She went with all cheerfulness. As she had seen Saunders do two years before, she kissed the stake, saying, 'Welcome the cross of Christ!' She spoke to the people saying:

> Good people, I would not have you think, that I expect to be saved because I offer myself here to death for the Lord's cause, but I believe to be saved by the death and passion of Jesus Christ; and this my death shall be a testimony of my faith to you all here present.[37]

As the fire arose about her, she said, 'My soul doth magnify the Lord, and my spirit doth rejoice in God my Savior.'[38] Those watching were amazed at her peace and her very quick passing.

> *Do not think that I have come to bring peace to the earth. I have not come to bring peace, but a sword. ... And a person's enemies will be those of his own household.'*
> ~ MATTHEW 10:34, 36 ~

---

36. John Foxe, *Acts and Monuments*, Book 11.
37. Thomas Timpson, *British Female Biography* (London: Aylott and Jones, 1846), p. 128.
38. See Luke 1:46-47.

Suffering Persecution

∞ Phillipine von Graboren, c. 1534-1558 ∞

King Henri II of France was determined to stamp out the Huguenots (French Protestants) from his country, seeing them as heretics and a threat to the stability of his kingdom. In 1547, he created a special court to judge heresy cases. In 1551, he issued the Edict of Chateaubriant, which called on civil and ecclesiastical courts to punish all heretics, placed restrictions on the meetings of Protestants, and offered rewards to informants – who could gain one third of the Protestant's property! Printing and distribution of Protestant books, even discussing religious topics at work or in the field, were all forbidden. Yet the movement to reform the church grew. In 1557, King Henri stiffened the persecution of the Huguenots and issued the Edict of Complégne, which made death the penalty for all heresy convictions.

On the night of 4 September, 1557, a mob broke into a meeting of 400 French Protestants on St Jacques Street in Paris. The angry mob thought the French defeat at the Battle of Saint-Quentin the previous month was in part caused by the French Protestants. Though some Huguenots managed to escape the mob, over one hundred and thirty were arrested. Among them was Phillipine von Graboren, a twenty-three-year-old widow whose husband, an elder in the Huguenot Church, had recently died.

Phillipine remained in prison a whole year. Priests regularly visited her, trying to persuade her to convert to the Roman Catholic faith and encouraging her to attend Mass, confess to a priest, and pray to Mary and the saints. Phillipine, firm in her faith in the Scriptures, said she could not find such practices in them: 'I will believe only what is found in the Old and New Testaments.'[39] Because of her continued resistance, Phillipine was put in solitary confinement, and her trial was expedited. On 27 September, 1558, she was sentenced to death, along with two elders of the Huguenot Church who had been arrested with her. All three were tortured.

The day of their execution, the three prisoners put on their best clothing, saying they were not going to a funeral but to a wedding as they met Jesus Christ the bridegroom. At the place of execution, Phillipine's tongue was cut out (a frequent punishment for heretics), her face and feet were burned with torches, then she was strangled and her body burned. Phillipine's brief life on earth ended in a steadfast testimony of faith in her Savior and His Word. Eternity was before her.

'Whoever loves his life loses it,
and whoever hates his life in this world will keep it for eternal life.
If anyone serves me, he must follow me;
and where I am, there will my servant be also.'
~ JOHN 12:25-26 ~

---

39. James I. Good, *Famous Women of the Reformed Church* (The Sunday School Board of the Reformed Church of the United States, 1901), p. 97.

Steadfast in the Faith

∽ Jeanne d'Albret, 1528-1572 ∾

On Christmas Day, 1560, Jeanne d'Albret publicly professed her conversion to the teachings of the Reformation, turning away from the tradition of the Roman Church. As the daughter of Marguerite of Navarre, Jeanne had been frequently exposed to preachers of the Reformation as a child. After she became Queen of the small kingdom of Navarre in her own right, Jeanne proclaimed Calvinism the official religion of the territory and offered protection to the Huguenots, as French Protestants were called.

Married to Antoine de Bourbon in 1549, Jeanne and Antoine invited ministers from Geneva to come to their province and preach. The ministers found there a freedom to preach the Word not allowed elsewhere in France. This inevitably brought persecution and criticism. Antoine wavered and went back and forth between Protestant and Catholic leanings, depending on the political winds, but Jeanne remained firm in her faith as she worked to spread the truth of the gospel among her people. She established a college of theology, and the chaplains in her court translated the Bible into the Béarnaise dialect, spoken by the Basques of Lower Navarre. This was the first time the Basques had a Bible in their own language. Jeanne did not consider the teachings of the Reformation a new religion, but a restoration of the ancient, biblical Christian teachings.

Jeanne herself regularly read and studied the Scriptures. In 1560, John Calvin wrote her from Geneva:

> Unless we betake ourselves daily to the Holy Scriptures the truth that we once knew oozes away little by little till it is all gone, except that God shall come to our aid. In His infinite wisdom He has seen fit to prevent you from descending to such a pass.[40]

Both her husband and Catherine d'Medici, the Queen Mother, sought to persuade Jeanne to return to her Catholic faith, but Jeanne remained firm in wanting to follow the Scriptures rather than tradition. At one point she fled the French court because of Catherine's plot against her life. A Huguenot army protected her as she returned to Navarre. The Papacy also sent an ambassador to get Jeanne to return to the Roman Church and summoned her to appear in Rome.

Jeanne's son Henry married Margaret of Valois, princess of France, and later became King Henry IV. Though Henry returned to the Catholic faith in order to retain his crown and preserve peace, he did issue the Edict of Nantes in 1598, which protected the Protestant Huguenots.

Therefore, as you received Christ Jesus the Lord, so walk in him,
rooted and built up in him and established in the faith, just as you
were taught, abounding in thanksgiving.

~ COLOSSIANS 2:6-7 ~

---

40. Edith Deen, *Great Women of the Christian Faith* (Uhrichsville, OH: Barbour Books, 1959), p. 87.

Standing Firm in the Scriptures

ⲟ Alice Driver, c. 1528-1558 ⲟ

Alice Driver, a native of the area of Woodbridge, Suffolk, was a country girl who had often driven her father's plough before marrying Edward Driver of Grundisburgh. She had been able to obtain an English Bible and read it diligently, which was a criminal act under the reign of Queen Mary. Alexander Gooch, a weaver in Woodbridge, also had believed in the Scriptures. Refusing to admit the Pope was head of the Church, he no longer attended Mass and had to go into hiding. Justice Noone pursued Alexander and Alice, who hid from the authorities in a haystack. When the authorities plunged a pitchfork into the hay, they found the pair, who were taken to Bury St Edmunds.

When Alice, who was then about thirty, was first taken before chief judge Sir Clement Higham, Alice told him Queen Mary was like Jezebel in her persecution of Christians. For that Sir Higham had Alice's ears cut off. Alice was happy to be counted worthy to suffer for the name of Christ. Carried to the jail in Ipswich, Alice was brought before Dr Spenser, who asked Alice why she was brought there. Alice replied, 'Wherefore? I think I need not tell you; for ye know it better than I.' When Dr Spenser said he did not know, then Alice said there certainly was much wrong done then, 'thus to imprison me, and know no cause why; for I know no evil that I have done, I thank God; and I hope there is no man that can accuse me of any notorious fact that I have done.'

Dr Spenser then asked Alice what she thought of the sacrament, whether it was indeed the flesh and blood of Christ. Alice replied she had not read any such thing in Scripture about a sacrament. She could not see that when Jesus gave the bread to His disciples at the Last Supper it was His body. For if He gave them His body, how could He be crucified the next day? Did He have two bodies? According to St Paul in 1 Corinthians 11, the taking of the bread is to be done in remembrance of Christ, but it is not the eating of His body. Alice always answered her judges with Scripture, so that they were silenced and just looked at each other. At their silence, Alice said:

> Have you no more to say? God be honoured! You are not able to resist the Spirit of God in me, a poor woman ... in the defence of God's truth, and in the cause of my Master Christ, by his grace I will set my foot against the foot of any of you all, in the maintenance and defence of the same, and if I had a thousand lives, they should go for payment thereof.[41]

Alice was taken away to prison again 'as joyful as the bird of day, praising and glorifying the name of God'.

On 4 November, 1558 Alice Driver and Alexander Gouch were taken to the stake, praying and singing psalms as they went. They were among the last of the nearly 300 Marian martyrs, for Queen Mary died two weeks after their execution.

Stand therefore, having fastened on the belt of truth, and having put on the breastplate of righteousness ...

~ Ephesians 6:14 ~

---

41. 'Alice Driver and Alexander Gouch', John Foxe, *Acts and Monuments of the Christian Church*, p. 385, www.exclassics.com/foxe/foxe388.htm.

Last of the Marian Martyrs

∞ Elizabeth Prest, martyred 17 November 1558 ∞

Elizabeth Prest was from Cornwall, of the laboring class. She had come to accept the Reformation truths, but her husband and children remained part of the Roman Church. Her husband forced her to continue attending Mass, which afflicted her conscience since she considered it contrary to God's Word. She prayed for God's help, and finally left her husband and family.

She traveled around supporting herself by labor and spinning. After some time she returned to her family, but was soon accused of heresy and arrested. She was brought before the bishop and repeatedly examined and urged to repent of her rebellion. The bishop particularly examined her on the Mass and the priest's power to transform the bread and wine into the body and blood of Jesus. Elizabeth appealed to the Apostle's Creed, which said that Christ sits at the right hand of his Father, until he comes again:

> If it be so, he is not here on earth in a piece of bread. If he be not here, and if he do not dwell in temples made with hands, but in heaven, what, shall we seek him? If he did offer his body once for all, why make you a new offering? If with once offering he made all perfect, why do you with a false offering make all imperfect? If he be worshipped in spirit and in truth, why do you worship a piece of bread? If he be eaten and drank in faith and truth, if his flesh be not profitable to be among us, why do you say you make his flesh and blood, and say it is profitable for body and soul? Alas, I am a poor woman, but rather than I will do as you, I would live no longer.[42]

Elizabeth was imprisoned, but priests continued to visit her in prison, encouraging her to repent and save her life. She replied:

> No, that I will not; God forbid that I should lose the life eternal for this carnal life. I will never turn from my heavenly husband to my earthly husband; from the fellowship of angels to mortal children and if my husband and children be faithful, then I am theirs. God is my father! God is my mother! God is my friend most faithful![43]

Elizabeth Prest was burned at the stake outside the walls of Exeter on 17 November, 1558. Queen Mary died the same day. Elizabeth thus became the last of the Marian martyrs, for with Queen Mary's death, all those imprisoned for their faith were released from prison.

> 'Whoever loves father or mother more than me is
> not worthy of me, and whoever loves son or daughter
> more than me is not worthy of me.'
> ~ MATTHEW 10:37 ~

---

42. Thomas Timpson, *British Female Biography* (London: Aylott and Jones, 1846), p. 128.
43. Ibid, p. 131.

Heiresses of the Reformation: the Puritan Era

A Praying Queen

∞ Elizabeth I, Elizabeth Tudor, 1533-1603 ∞

Elizabeth was twenty-five when she ascended the throne of England on November 17, 1558. Her youth had been a tumultuous one fraught with dangers. She was only four when her father, King Henry VIII, had her mother, Anne Boleyn, beheaded. Elizabeth was then declared illegitimate. With each changing political wind Elizabeth's position changed. However, Henry VIII's sixth wife, Catherine Parr, was a patient, caring Christian woman who became like a mother to Elizabeth, providing spiritual nurture and love. Elizabeth reciprocated her kindness. On New Year's Eve, 1544, the eleven-year-old Princess Elizabeth presented Queen Catherine with a translation she had done of Marguerite of Navarre's *The Mirror of the Soul*, bound beautifully with her own embroidery work. In her dedication to the Queen, Elizabeth wrote that Marguerite, 'doth perceive how of herself and of her own strength she can do nothing that good is or prevailed for her salvation, unless it be through the grace of God.'[1] The following year, Elizabeth's gift to Queen Catherine was her own translation into English of the first chapter of John Calvin's *Institutes*.

When Elizabeth's half-sister became Queen Mary I, Elizabeth again found herself in political disfavor. Fearing a Protestant uprising around Elizabeth, Mary imprisoned Elizabeth in the Tower of London and then put her under house arrest for a year before allowing her back in court. One can understand Elizabeth's deep sense of gratitude to God when she did become queen, having survived the vagaries of the Tudor court. On the day of her coronation, she made a heartfelt prayer:

> O Lord, almighty and everlasting God, I give Thee most hearty thanks that Thou hast been so merciful unto me as to spare me to behold this joyful day. And I acknowledge that Thou hast dealt as wonderfully and as mercifully with me as Thou didst with Thy true and faithful servant Daniel, Thy prophet, whom Thou deliveredst out of the den from the cruelty of the greedy and raging lions. Even so was I overwhelmed and only by Thee delivered. To Thee (therefore) only be thanks, honor, and praise forever, amen.[2]

Elizabeth frequently wrote out her prayers. One from early in her reign reflects her conviction that God had placed her on the throne of England for His purposes:

> God, my Father and Protector, greatly do I feel myself a debtor to thy mercy for having called me early by the preaching of the Gospel of Jesus Christ to the true worship and sincerity of Thy religion, to the end ... I might be made Thy instrument for replanting and establishing in this part of the world, where it hath pleased Thee that I reign in the name of Thy kingdom, Thy worship, and most holy religion. I pray Thee, my God and good Father ... may it please Thee to remove all impediment and resistance of unbelief from my people ... giving me efficacious men as, apt and sufficient instruments, so that I may be able to do as I desire, uprooting every wicked seed of impiety, to spread, plant, and root Thy holy Gospel in every heart, increasing throughout this Thy earthly kingdom, that heavenly one of Jesus Christ, to whom be evermore honor and glory, amen.[3]

> *By me kings reign, and rulers decree what is just; by me*
> *princes rule, and nobles, all who govern justly.*
> ~ PROVERBS 8:15-16 ~

---

1. Elizabeth I, *Collected Works* (Chicago & London: The University of Chicago Press, 2000), p. 7.
2. Elizabeth I, *Collected Works* (eds. Leah S. Marcus, Janet Mueller, Mary Beth Rose), Chicago & London: The University of Chicago Press, 2000, 54-55. Throughout her life Elizabeth wrote private prayers (in English, French, Italian, Spanish, Greek, and Latin!), some of which were collected and published during her lifetime.
3. Ibid, pp. 153-154.

Following the Law of God

∞ Elizabeth I, 1533-1603 ∞

In ancient Israel the king was required to make a copy of the law of God to have with him all the days of his rule: 'and he shall read in it all the days of his life, that he may learn to fear the LORD his God by keeping all the words of this law and these statutes, and doing them ...' (Deuteronomy 17:18-19). Queen Elizabeth I in many ways followed this Scriptural admonition for rulers.[4] As a child she learned Scripture and theology, as well as Latin, Greek, and French. As an adolescent she translated religious works into other languages, including the works of Margaret of Navarre, Catherine Parr, and John Calvin. As she translated Psalm 13 into English from the Vulgate, she undoubtedly found comfort in the Lord's steadfast love during her sometimes dangerous political surroundings.

Throughout her life Elizabeth frequently turned to the Scriptures. When imprisoned in the Tower of London under Queen Mary, her written prayers reflect Matthew 6:25: 'do not be anxious about your life, what you will eat or what you will drink, nor about your body, what you will put on. Is not life more than food, and the body more than clothing?' When she later learned that Mary had died and she would become queen, she quoted Psalm 118:23: 'This is the LORD's doing; it is marvelous in our eyes.' As a reigning monarch she looked to King Solomon as an example and prayed with him: 'Give your servant therefore an understanding mind to govern your people, that I may discern between good and evil, for who is able to govern this your great people?' (1 Kings 3:9). When the Spanish Armada came to defeat, Elizabeth compared the deliverance of England with the deliverance of Israel and the destruction of Pharaoh's forces in the Red Sea. Elizabeth was thankful for her many personal blessings and the blessings to her kingdom, while also recognizing that 'Everyone to whom much was given, of him much will be required, and from him to whom they entrusted much, they will demand the more' (Luke 12:48).

In 1563, Elizabeth published a collection of sayings on royal rule, taken from Scriptural, classical, patristic, medieval and humanistic sources. She began with an extensive quote from Romans 13 on the duty of obedience to rulers.

Elizabeth's writings and speeches reflect an extensive knowledge of Scripture, which undoubtedly provided strength and wisdom for her forty-four-year reign.

> *The king's heart is a stream of water in the hand of the LORD;*
> *he turns it wherever he will.*
>
> ~ PROVERBS 21:1 ~

---

4. Examples of Elizabeth's knowledge and use of Scripture is taken from Brad Walton's 'Elizabeth', in *Handbook of Women Biblical Interpreters*, ed. Marion Ann Taylor (Grand Rapids, Michigan: Baker Academic, 2012).

Imparting Wisdom to her Sons

∞ Ann Bacon, 1528-1610 ∞

When Sir Anthony Cooke, an early supporter of the Reformation in England, became the tutor to the young Edward VI, his daughter Ann assisted as governess. Sir Anthony had personally educated his five daughters along with his four sons, and the daughters came to be recognized as the most learned women in England.[5] Ann herself was fluent in Latin, Greek, Hebrew, Spanish, Italian, and French. She translated into English and had printed some sermons of the Italian reformer Barnardine Ochine as well as Bishop Jewell's *Apologie of the Church of England* from the Latin.

Ann married Sir Nicholas Bacon, and the couple had two sons – Anthony and Francis. Both of them played leading roles in Elizabethan society, while Francis' influence continues into our own day as a pioneer of the scientific method and an expositor of the natural law, foundational to the American system of law. Both Anthony and Francis were educated at home, with their parents providing them Christian nurture as well as intellectual foundations.

Some of Ann's letters to her sons have survived, and they show that even into their adulthood, she was most concerned about their spiritual welfare and Christian character. In 1590, when Francis was almost thirty, she wrote him:

> This one chiefest counsel your Christian and natural mother doth give you even before the Lord, that above all worldly respects you carry yourself ever at your first coming as one doth unfeignedly profess the true religion of Christ, and hath the love of the truth now by long continuance fast settled in your heart, and that with judgment, wisdom, and discretion, and are not afraid or ashamed to testify the same by hearing and delighting in those religious exercises of the sincerer sort. ... If you will be wavering (which God forbid, God forbid), you shall have examples and ill encouragers too many in these days. ... Beware, therefore, and be constant in godly profession without fainting, and that from your heart: ... Be not speedy of speech nor talk suddenly, but where discretion requireth, and that soberly then. For the property of our world is to sound out at first coming, and after to contain. Courtesy is necessary, but too common familiarity in talking and words is very unprofitable. ... And you have little enough, if not too little, regarded your kind and no simple mother's wholesome advice from time to time. And as I do impute all most humbly to the grace of God whatsoever he hath bestowed upon me, so dare I affirm that it had been good for you every way if you had followed it ere this. But God is the same, who is able to heal both mind and body, whom in Christ I beseech to be your merciful father and to take care of you, guiding you with his holy and most comfortable spirit, now and ever.

Ann added in a postscript:

> I trust you with your servants, use prayer twice in a day, having been where reformation is. Omit it not for any. It will be your best credit to serve the Lord duly and reverently, and you will be observed at the first now. Your brother is too negligent herein, but do you well and zealously; it will be looked for of the best learned sort, and that is best.[6]

My son, keep your father's commandment, and
forsake not your mother's teaching.

~ PROVERBS 6:20 ~

---

5. Ann's older sister Mildred became the wife of William Cecil, Lord Burleigh, privy councilor to Queen Elizabeth. See March 18 on Mildred Cooke Burleigh.

6. James Spedding, *The Letters and the Life of Francis Bacon* (London: Longmans, Green, and Co., 1890), pp. 112-113.

Husband's Tribute

∞ Mildred Cooke Burleigh, 1526-1589 ∞

Mildred Cooke was the eldest daughter of Sir Anthony Cooke, an English scholar, mentor of Edward VI, and supporter of the Reformation in England. Sir Anthony educated Mildred and her four sisters at home, providing them an education equal to his four sons. Mildred was fluent in Greek, Latin, and French, and regularly read works by the early church fathers, especially John Chrysostom and Basil the Great, in the original Greek. In 1545, Mildred married William Cecil, Lord Burleigh, who became Queen Elizabeth's Privy Councilor and Lord High Treasurer of England. The two were most happily married forty-three years. Mildred died 4 April, 1589. Five days after her death, Lord Burleigh wrote a 'Meditation' on her life.

He realized he could not recover her mortal existence, for her body rested dead in the earth, and her soul was taken to heaven awaiting the resurrection, at which time 'her body shall be raised up, and joined with her soul, in an everlasting, unspeakable joy, such as no tongue can express, nor heart can conceive'. Burleigh wrote,

> I ought to thank Almighty God for his favour in permitting her to have lived so many years together with me, and to have given her grace to have had the true knowledge of her salvation by the death of his son Jesus, opened to her by the knowledge of the Gospel, whereof she was a professor from her youth.
>
> I ought to comfort myself with the remembrance of her many virtues and godly actions, wherein she continued all her life, and especially that she did of late years sundry charitable deeds, whereof she determined to have no outward knowledge whilst she lived.[7]

Burleigh then 'with mine own handwriting' did list the many secret charities Mildred had supported, many of which he himself had not been aware until after her death. The charitable acts he described included funding scholarships for St. John's College and Westminster College, Cambridge; funding loans to the poor in certain industries in London; funding preachers of St John's College; and regular support of food for the poor of Cheshunt. Four times a year she sent funds for food to all the prisons in London, as well as clothing for the poor in London and Cheshunt. She also 'provided a great number of books, whereof she gave some to the University of Cambridge – namely, the great Bible in Hebrew, and four other tongues; and to the College of St John's very many books in Greek of divinity and physic, and of other sciences'.[8] She provided wool and flax to the women in Cheshunt parish and oversaw their making into yarn and cloth. Shortly before her death she bought a large quantity of wheat to be distributed among the poor.

Burleigh wrote out this tribute 'for my comfort in the memory thereof, with assurance that God had accepted these and she was enjoying their fruits in heaven'. He signed the Meditation 'Written at Collings' Lodge, by me in sorrow, W.B.'[9]

'Do not lay up for yourselves treasures on earth, where moth and rust destroy and where thieves break in and steal, but lay up for yourselves treasures in heaven, where neither moth nor rust destroys and where thieves do not break in and steal.'

~ Matthew 6:19-20 ~

---

7. Julia Kavanagh, *Women of Christianity: Exemplary for Acts of Piety and Charity* (London: Smith, Elder, and co., 1852), p. 149.

8. Ibid, p. 151.

9. Ibid, p. 152.

Daily Meditating on the Word

∞ Grace Mildmay, 1552-1620 ∞

When Grace Sherington was growing up, her mother daily read her Bible and encouraged Grace in her daily Bible reading. Throughout her life Grace followed her mother's advice. In the morning she read one chapter each in Moses, the Prophets, the Gospels, and the Epistles, in addition to the Psalms for the day. She also regularly read three other books given her by her mother – John Foxes's *Book of Martyrs*, Wolfgang Musculus's *Common Places of Christian Religion*, and Thomas à Kempis's *Imitatio Christi*. Grace daily submitted herself to God and His Word, and with humility she looked to God for leadership and strength.

Grace's marriage was arranged by her parents. When she was fifteen Grace was married to Anthony Mildmay, then eighteen or nineteen. Anthony was often away from home, serving in Parliament and going on diplomatic missions for the Queen. Grace could have lived a life at the royal court, but she chose to remain on the family estate of Apethorpe in Northamptonshire. She thought the temptations at court would draw her away from a truly Christian life.

As lady of the manor at Apethorpe, Grace spent much time caring for the poor and sick. Her medical records survive, and her notes are a remarkable collection on the causes of diseases, their remedies, and specific medicines for their treatment. Recipes for different ointments and balms indicate she produced these medicines in large quantities. One recipe called for over 150 different seeds, roots, spices and gums, eighteen pounds of sugar and nuts, and over eight gallons of oil, wine, and vinegar! Grace never charged for her care or her medicines, and she became renowned for both her medicinal skill and charity. Spiritual counsel often accompanied her physical treatment, and she looked to Christ as the true Healer.

After her husband died in 1617 Grace wrote an autobiography for her daughter and granddaughters, one of the first known autobiographies written by an English woman. She had kept a journal throughout her life and was able to reflect on her spiritual growth since childhood. She called her spiritual meditations the 'consolation of my soul, the joy of my heart, and the stability of my mind'.[10] Her life had a peace and strength which was a testimony to her personal relationship with Christ. Grace's daily reading and meditation on Scripture were foundational to her life, and she encouraged her grandchildren to follow in their path. She wrote her granddaughter:

> Whoever in the beginning of his life sets the word of God always before his eyes and makes the same his delight and counsellor, and examines all that he sees, all that he hears, all that he thinks, and all that he loves, wishes or desires by the said word of God, he shall be sure to be preserved in safety.[11]

I will meditate on your precepts
and fix my eyes on your ways.
I will delight in your statutes;
I will not forget your word.

~ PSALM 119:15-16 ~

---

10. Retha M. Warnicke, 'Lady Mildmay's Journal: A Study in Autobiography, and Meditation in Reformation England', *Sixteenth Century Journal*, vol. 20, No.1 (Spring 1989), p. 57.

11. Quoted in Norman Leslie Jones, *English Reformation* (Oxford: Blackwell Publishers, 2002), p. 25.

Mother's Last Letter to her Son

☞ Maeyken Wens, executed 6 October 1573 ☜

In April 1573, the authorities in Antwerp arrested Maeyken Wens, along with several other women, for worshiping together contrary to the established Roman Catholic Church. The women were Anabaptists, a branch of the Protestant Reformation. Anabaptists did not baptize infants, but believed baptism should only follow personal conversion. They also did not believe the church and government should be joined. Maeyken was the wife of Mattheus Wens, a mason by trade and one of the Anabaptist ministers in Antwerp, and had nine children. The oldest, Adriaen, was about fifteen while the youngest, Hans, was about three.

After her arrest priests and secular authorities subjected Maeyken to torture and sought to cause her to reject her Anabaptist beliefs. When she steadfastly held to her faith a sentence of death was pronounced on 5 October.

The following day Maeyken and the other women were brought to the place of execution. A screw was placed on her tongue to keep her from speaking to the people from the stake. Adriaen brought little Hans to see the last of their mother, but when his mother was brought forth, Adriaen fainted. When he came to, little Hans was standing over him and his mother had been burnt to ashes. Adriaen went to his mother's stake, found the tongue screw among the ashes, and kept it as a remembrance.

But Adriaen had a better remembrance in the letters his mother had written to him from prison. Here he continued to have his mother's counsel for life:

> My dear child Adriaen my son. I leave you this for a testament, because you are the oldest, to exhort you that you should begin to fear our dear Lord, for you are getting old enough to perceive what is good or evil. … My son, from your youth follow that which is good and depart from evil: do good while you have time, and look at your father, how lovingly he went before me with kindness and courteousness, always instructing me with the Word of the Lord. … Hence, my dear son; beware of that which is evil, that you will not have to lament afterwards, 'Had I done this or that; for then, when it is as far as it now is with me, it will be too late.' Hear the instruction of your mother: hate everything that is loved by the world and your sensuality, and love God's commandment, and let the same instruct you, for it teaches, 'If any man will come after me, let him deny himself,' that is, forsake his own wisdom, and pray, 'Lord, thy will be done.' If you do this, the anointing of the Holy Ghost will teach you all that you are to believe. 1 John 2:27. Believe not what men say, but obey that which the New Testament commands you, and ask God to teach you His will. Trust not in your understanding, but in the Lord, and let your counsel abide in Him, and ask Him to direct you into His ways. My child, learn how you are to love God the Lord, how you are to honor your father, and all other commandments which the Lord requires of you. Whatsoever is not contained therein, believe not; but whatever is contained therein, obey. Join yourself to those that fear the Lord, and depart from evil, and through love do all that is good. … This I, Maeyken Wens, your mother, have written, while I was in prison for the Word of the Lord; the good Father grant you His grace, my son, Adriaen. Wherefore, let them that suffer according to the will of God commit the keeping of their souls to Him in well doing, as unto a faithful Creator. 1 Peter 4:19.[12]

But our citizenship is in heaven, and from it we await a Savior, the Lord Jesus Christ, who will transform our lowly body to be like his glorious body, by the power that enables him even to subject all things to himself.

~ Philippians 3:20-21 ~

---

12. T. J. Van Bright (trans. Joseph F. Sohn), *Martyrs Mirror*, 981-982. www.homecomers.org/mirror/martyrs143.htm.

Mother of Kings and Queens

⭕ Charlotte de Bourbon, 1546-1582 ⭕

During the life of Charlotte de Bourbon, Protestant and Catholic forces in France fought each other not only religiously, but also politically and militarily. In her own family, Charlotte's father, Louis, Duke of Montpensier, was a staunch Catholic while her mother, Jacqueline de Longwy, was sympathetic to Protestant beliefs. Charlotte's mother secretly taught her and her sisters the Scriptures and the Reformed faith. Intent that his children remain Roman Catholic, the Duke sent his daughters to convents. Charlotte, who was only thirteen, begged to stay with her mother, but there was no changing her father's mind. Charlotte was sent to the royal convent of Jouarre to be raised as a nun.

While in the convent Charlotte retained her mother's biblical faith and teachings. A dissident priest at the abbey was sympathetic to the Reformed faith and also taught from the Scriptures. When twenty-six, at the time of the St Bartholomew's Day massacre in 1572, Charlotte managed to flee the convent. She found refuge with Frederick, the Protestant Electorate of the Palatinate. Frederick treated her kindly and allowed her to practice her Protestant faith freely. Charlotte's father was furious and demanded she return to the Roman Catholic faith, even calling on the King of France to force her to submit. Charlotte remained firm in her faith and under Frederick's protection.

William of Orange, a strong Protestant and leader of the Dutch revolt against the Spanish Hapsburgs, heard of Charlotte's faith and considered marrying her. Since she was part of the French nobility, marriage to Charlotte would also add to William's position in Europe. Charlotte's father at first was opposed to the match, but then came around, as did the King of France, and provided a nice dowry for his daughter.

Charlotte and William, married 24 June, 1575, were unusually well suited to each other. Both had a love for the Protestant faith and liberty; both showed a benevolence and sympathy for those in need. Charlotte loved William, and he treated her with kindness and tenderness. William's brother wrote a friend that the prince looked well in spite of the many political troubles he faced:

> Of a surety it is a most precious consolation and a wondrous relief that God should have given him a wife so distinguished by her virtue, her piety, her vast intelligence – in a word, so perfectly all that he could wish; in return he loves her tenderly.[13]

In 1580, King Philip of Spain outlawed William and placed a price of 25,000 crowns on his head to anyone who could bring him to him dead or alive. William was accused of being a rebel, bringing the Reformed religion to the Netherlands, a heretic, and profanely marrying a nun. On 10 July, 1581, an assassin did shoot William in the head. Though seriously injured, William survived, in part through the loving, constant care of Charlotte. Though William recovered, Charlotte's health was broken by the ordeal and she died 5 May, 1582.

William and Charlotte had six daughters. One of them, Louise Juliana, is the ancestress of the current British royal family.

> 'Whoever loves father or mother more than me is not worthy of me, ...
> whoever does not take his cross and follow me is not worthy of me.'
>
> ~ MATTHEW 10:37-38 ~

---

13. James Anderson, *Ladies of the Reformation* (London: Blackie and Son, 1855), p. 652.

Afflicted on Every Side

∞ Louise de Coligny, 1555-1620 ∞

The second half of the sixteenth century in France was marked by wars of religion between Protestant and Catholic forces. The battles were both political and military, and often were quite brutal. Gaspard de Coligny, a French nobleman, became the leader of the Huguenot or Protestant cause, along with his wife Charlotte de Laval. The motto of Charlotte was 'as for me and my house, I will serve the Lord', and the Colignys reared their three children in the fear and admonition of the Lord. Daughter Louise was a beautiful girl and had many suitors for her hand in marriage. Her father recommended she accept one of his young officers, Charles De Teligny. Others might be richer and have more titles, but Teligny was a man of Christian conviction and character.

Louise and Charles were married in 1571. The following year, in August 1572, the French king's sister Margaret married the Protestant Henry III of Navarre. Political tensions between the Catholics and Huguenots in Paris were taut. On 22 August an assassin shot Gaspard de Coligny in the street. Coligny was injured, but survived. Two days later, however, Coligny was attacked at his lodgings and brutally murdered. Thousands of other Huguenots in the city and throughout France were killed in what became known as the St Bartholomew's Day massacre (the massacres began the eve of the feast of Bartholomew the Apostle). Also killed in the uprising was Charles De Teligny. With both her father and husband brutally murdered, Louise managed to escape to Geneva. All of her father's property had been confiscated, and Louise was now an impoverished orphan (her mother had died several years previously) and widow. The French offered to return her property if she renounced her Huguenot faith, but Louise refused. She finally found a refuge in Heidelberg, where Elector Frederick III of the Palatinate offered her protection. There Louise remained in quiet and safety for eleven years.

After the death of his wife Charlotte de Bourbon, William Prince of Orange proposed to Louise. Though poor, she was of noble ancestry. She also was strong in her Protestant faith and was a lady of good character. Louise accepted, travelled to Antwerp, and was married on 12 April, 1583. It was a happy marriage, made even more so by the birth of a son, Prince Frederick Henry, the following year.

There had been an assassination attempt on Prince William in 1582, and Charlotte always feared her husband would be assassinated. The King of Spain had placed a large reward out for his life. On 10 July, 1584 Louise's fears were realized; William died within moments of being shot in the palace. At thirty-two Louise was again a widow. Yet she trusted God throughout her afflictions. She raised her son in Christian truth and also cared for the daughters of William by his previous marriage. Her son Frederick became Prince of Orange and an ancestor of the British royal family today.

> We are afflicted in every way, but not crushed; perplexed, but not driven
> to despair; persecuted, but not forsaken; struck down, but not destroyed;
> always carrying in the body the death of Jesus, so that the life of Jesus may
> also be manifested in our bodies.
>
> ~ 2 CORINTHIANS 4:8-10 ~

Living and Dying Well

∞ Charlotte Duplessis Mornay, 1550-1606 ∞

Charlotte Duplessis, a widow with a young daughter, was in Paris during the St. Bartholomew's Massacre of 1572 and barely escaped with her life. The assassination of leading Huguenots (French Protestants) began the night of 23-24 August and continued for weeks as the Huguenots were hunted down by the Roman Catholic forces. Charlotte had sent her daughter to her Catholic grandmother, and she managed to escape to a Catholic friend's house shortly before the soldiers arrived at her own home. Charlotte found a hiding place, and when soldiers arrived at the friend's house, they never found her. At another refuge she hid in the hollow space under the roof of an outhouse, listening to the cries of men, women, and children being murdered in the street.

After escaping Paris, Charlotte met Philippe de Mornay, a leading French Protestant who had also escaped the St Bartholomew's Massacre. The two were married 3 January, 1576. Philippe went on to become an advisor of King Henry of Navarre, who became King Henry IV of France. Philippe drafted the Edict of Nantes, which for a time provided religious tolerance for Protestants. He also served as a diplomat for the French King to England and Flanders. Charlotte went with Philippe in all his travels, providing important hospitality to dignitaries they met. She encouraged Philippe also in his writing of apologetic works for the Protestant cause.

Charlotte and Philippe had eight children, with three living past infancy. When her son Philip was in Holland, Charlotte wrote him:

> My son, God is my witness that even before your birth, He inspired me with a hope that you would serve Him; and this to you ought to be some pledge of His grace and an admonition to perform your duty. Your father and I have also taken care to instruct you in every branch of useful learning, to the end that you may not only live, but also shine in His church. You are young, my son, and divers imaginations present themselves to youth, but always remember the saying of the Psalmist, 'How shall a young man direct his way? Certainly by conducting himself according to thy word, O Lord.' Nor will there be wanting persons who will desire to turn you aside therefrom to the left hand or the right. But also say with the Psalmist, 'I will associate only with those that keep thy laws. Thy laws, O God, shall be the men of my counsel.'[14]

Philip died in battle fighting the Dutch. Charlotte never completely recovered from the shock and died a few months later on 15 May, 1606.

When she realized she was dying Charlotte told her husband, 'I am going to God, persuaded that nothing can separate me from His love. I know that my Redeemer liveth. He has triumphed.' Her pastor reminded her of Christ's words: 'Father, into thy hand I commend my spirit.' Charlotte added the words from Psalm 31, 'For thou hast redeemed me, O eternal God of truth.' Her last word was, 'Jesus'. Her husband said of her, 'She assisted me to live well, and by her pious death, she has taught me how to die well.'[15]

Into your hand I commit my spirit;
you have redeemed me, O LORD, faithful God.

~ PSALM 31:5 ~

---

14. Quoted in James I. Good, *Famous Women of the Reformed Church* (The Sunday School Board of the Reformed Church in the United States, 1901), p. 92. Charlotte quotes from Psalm 119:9, 63.

15. Ibid, pp. 93-94.

Away, Vain World

∞ Elizabeth Melville, c. 1578 – c. 1640 ∞

Elizabeth Melville's ancestors were among the earliest supporters of the Reformation in Scotland; many were also important members of the courts of Mary, Queen of Scots, and her son James VI. Elizabeth actively supported the resistance to the royal authority of James VI and Charles I over the church in Scotland, maintaining an extensive correspondence with many leaders of the Presbyterian opposition, including Samuel Rutherford. Elizabeth also used her considerable poetic talents to write verse supporting Reformation truths, sending personalized poems to those imprisoned for their faith. When John Welsh was imprisoned in the Castle of Blackness for holding a Christian assembly in Aberdeen in 1605, Elizabeth wrote an acrostic poem of encouragement (the first letters of the lines spell out M. Jhona Welsh):

My dear brother, with courage bear the cross,
Joy shall be joined with all thy sorrow here,
High is thy hope, disdain this earthly dross,
Once shall you see the wishéd day appear.

Now it is dark, the sky cannot be clear,
After the clouds it shall be calm anon;
Wait on his will whose blood hath brought thee dear –
Extol his name, though outward joys be gone.

Look to the Lord, thou are not left alone,
Since he is thine, what pleasure canst thou take?
He is at hand, and hears thy every groan:
End out thy fight, and suffer for his sake.

A sight most bright thy soul shall shortly see,
When store of glory thy rich reward shall be.

In 1603, with the publication of her poem *Ane Godlie Dreame*, Elizabeth became the first Scottish woman to have a work printed. Her poem in some ways anticipates Bunyan's *Pilgrim's Progress*, in that Elizabeth has a dream in which she is guided through the difficulties of this world to the celestial mansion. The poem concludes with the encouragement:

Rejoice in God, let not your courage fail,
Ye chosen saints that are afflicted here:
Though Satan rage, he never shall prevail –
Fight to the end and stoutly persevere.

Your God is true, your blood is to him dear,
Fear not the way since Christ is your convoy:
When clouds are past, the weather will grow clear;
Ye sow in tears, but ye shall reap in joy.[16]

Elizabeth added a short poem to *Ane Godly Dream*, which said in part:

Away, vain world, bewitcher of my heart!
My sorrow shows my sins make me to smart:
Yet will I not despair, but to my God repair –
He has mercy aye, therefore will I pray;
He has mercy aye, and loves me,
Though by his troubling hand he proves me ....

What shall I do? Are all my pleasures past?
Shall worldly lusts now take their leave at last?
Yes, Christ these earthly toys shall turn in heavenly joys;
Let the world be gone, I will love Christ alone,
Let the world be gone, I care not:
Christ is my love alone, I fear not.[17]

And the world is passing away along with its desires, but whoever does the will of God abides forever.

~ 1 JOHN 2:17 ~

---

16. Ibid, p. 61.
17. Ibid, p. 62.

MARCH 25

Should Women be Educated?

∞ Anna Maria van Schurman, 1607-1678 ∞

The Reformation's focus on the Scriptures encouraged literacy and education of both men and women. Anna Maria Schurman was an example of an educated Christian woman. Raised in a Dutch Reformed family, she was drawn to Christ at an early age. In her autobiography she recalls a time when she was about four years old:

> While collecting herbs with the maid whose chore this was, I sat down on the bank of a certain stream. When she suggested it, I recited from memory the response to the first question of the Heidelberg Catechism. At the words 'that I am not my own but belong to thy most faithful servant Jesus Christ', my heart was filled with such a great and sweet joy and an intimate feeling of the love of Christ that all the subsequent years have not been able to remove the living memory of that moment ... I thirsted constantly from childhood on with an honest and sincere desire for the true practice of devotion.[18]

Anna was educated at home with her two brothers and became something of a child prodigy. Besides her native Dutch she spoke French, English, and Spanish fluently. She was translating Latin by 10 and also learned Greek, Hebrew, Chaldaic, Syriac, Turkish, and Persian. She was a skilled painter and her poetry was praised by leading poets of her day. She was the first woman to attend a Dutch University, though while attending the University of Utrecht she listened to the lectures behind a curtain so as not to distract the male students! Yet, with her many talents Anna Maria remained humble.

In her most famous work, *Whether a Christian Woman Should be Educated?*, Anna Maria developed numerous arguments for the education of women. Since women have reason, they are capable of understanding the arts and sciences. Unlike beasts, a woman's face is raised to heaven, so she is suitable for knowledge and contemplation. Women are homemakers, and education and study is most suitable to a woman at home by herself. Education is suitable for pursuing virtue and prudence and leads to true greatness of soul.[19] Women were not just to learn spinning and weaving but theology, nature, Scripture history, languages and biographies.

Towards the end of her life, however, Anna Maria wondered if she had spent too much time on trying to learn everything, when she should have spent more time on the 'one thing necessary' of which Jesus spoke (Luke 10:42).

The fear of the LORD is the beginning of wisdom,
and the knowledge of the Holy One is insight.

~ PROVERBS 9:10 ~

18. From *Eukleria* 2.1 in Van Schurman, Anna Maria, *Whether a Christian Woman Should be Educated and other writings from her intellectual circle*, ed. and trans. Joyce L. Irwin (Chicago and London: The University of Chicago Press, 1998), pp. 79-80.

19. Anna Maria Van Schurman, *Whether a Christian Woman Should be Educated and other writings from her intellectual circle*, ed. and trans. Joyce L. Irwin (Chicago and London: The University of Chicago Press, 1998), pp. 25-37.

Native American Convert to Christianity

☞ Pocahontas, c. 1595-1617 ☜

In 1607, 133 men aboard the *Susan Constant*, the *Godspeed*, and the *Discovery* sailed from England to America. They had a three-fold mandate from the sponsoring London Company: find gold and precious metals; discover a water route to the Pacific; and bring the Christian gospel to the natives. The first years were ones of hardship and difficulties for the settlers at the place they named Jamestown. Often when starvation seemed imminent, only the food supplied by the natives sustained the colonists. Pocahontas, young teenage daughter of chief Powhatan, often visited the English settlement and brought help and food to the colonists.

In 1609, war broke out between the English and the natives, and during the conflict, the English captured Pocahontas, holding her hostage for a year while negotiating the release of English captives and stolen weapons and tools. Pocahontas became fluent in English and felt at home among the colonists. She was very receptive to Christian instruction from Alexander Whitaker, the colony's minister. John Rolfe, one of the Jamestown settlers strongly interested in advancing the honor of God and propagating the gospel in the new colony, developed an attachment for Pocahontas, but wasn't certain if marriage was God's will. He wrestled with himself, wondering if marrying a heathen woman would be like the Israelites of old marrying the Canaanites – something the Lord had definitely forbidden. He wrote a letter to Sir Thomas Dale, an officer of the colony back in England, laying bare his thoughts. He noted Pocahontas's 'great appearance of love to me, her desire to be taught and instructed in the knowledge of God, her Capableness of understanding, her aptness and willingness to receive any good impression'. Rolfe trusted God's gracious providence and prayed to be a help in converting the unregenerate to regeneration, 'which I beseech God to grant for his dear son Christ Jesus' sake'.[20]

Pocahontas did convert to Christianity and was baptized, taking the biblical name of Rebecca. On 5 April, 1614, she and John Rolfe were married, restoring a time of peace between the natives and the English. For two years the Rolfes lived on Rolfe's Varina Farm. One son was born to them, named Thomas. In 1616, the Rolfes travelled to England, where Rebecca became the sensation of London society and was received at court by the Queen (but not by King James; the king was displeased with Rolfe for marrying a princess without his permission!).

Before the planned return to America, Rebecca took ill and died. Her funeral was held at St George's church at Gravesend. The church today contains two stained-glass windows commemorating the young American woman. One is of the Old Testament matriarch Rebecca, with a smaller picture depicting Pocahontas's baptism. The other window is of Ruth, the Moabitess, who left her native people to follow the God of Israel.

> *For where you go I will go, and where you lodge I will lodge. Your*
> *people shall be my people, and your God my God.*
>
> ~ RUTH 1:16 ~

---

20. Letter from John Rolfe to Thomas Dale, *Virginia Magazine of History*, vol. XXII (1914), pp. 150-157.

Mother's Advice

∞ Dorothy Leigh, died c. 1615 ∞

The Puritans recognized that women had an important role in shaping the spiritual education of their children; the sixteenth-century Geneva Bible, the first English study Bible, has a marginal note at Deuteronomy 21:18 which states, 'it is the mothers dutie also to instruct her children'. Reflecting this are the numerous advice books mothers wrote for their children in the seventeenth century. The first of these was *The Mother's Blessing*, written by Dorothy Leigh and first published posthumously in 1616. It was easily the bestselling book by a woman in the seventeenth century, going through seven editions in its first year and twenty-three editions between 1616 and 1674.

Little is known about Dorothy. She was married to Ralph Leigh, a soldier who was killed in Ireland in 1597 fighting under the Earl of Essex. In his will Ralph urged Dorothy to see that their three sons be 'well instructed and brought up in knowledge'. Dorothy had a sense that her own life might not last long, so she wrote out her advice for her sons as a way of carrying on her husband's wish. The book was published after her death; her sons were probably in their early twenties at that time. The lengthy title of the work, typical for the day, clearly tells its purpose: *The Mothers Blessing Or The godly counsaile of a Gentle-woman not long since deceased, left behind for her Children: containing many good exhortations, and godly admonitions, profitable for all Parents to leave as a Legacy to their Children, but especially for those, who by reason of their young yeeres stand most in need of Instruction.*

Dorothy covered a variety of topics, all within a Scriptural framework: how to reform morals, manners and religion; the importance and method of prayer; the proper and improper use of wealth; need to restrict business dealings and marriage to the godly; and the faults of worldly ministers. She encouraged the daily reading of the Scriptures as important to the nourishment of their souls:

> Labour for the spiritual food of the soul, which must be gathered every day out of the word, as the children of Israel gathered Manna in the wilderness. ... For as the children of Israel must needs starve, except they gath'red every day in the wilderness and fed of it, so must your souls, except you gather the spiritual Manna out of the word every day, and feed of it continually: for as they by this Manna comforted their hearts, and strengthened their bodies, and preserved their lives; so by this heavenly Word of God, you shall comfort your souls, make them strong in Faith, and grow in true godliness, and finally preserve them with great joy, to everlasting life, through Faith in Christ; whereas, if you desire any food for your souls, that is not in the written Word of God, your souls dies with it even in your hearts and mouths; even as they, that desired other food, died with it in their mouths [Num. 11.3] were it never so dainty: so shall you, and there is no recovery for you.[21]

Dorothy used many analogies to develop her teachings. In a chapter on how to 'rule our corruptions', she wrote of the importance of the Holy Spirit in the Christian life, noting:

> without [the Holy Spirit] we are like a house which is built fair on the outside: but there are no windows to show any light at all into it, and then the house is good for nothing, because there remains nothing but darkness in it: even so dark is the earth of *Adam*, which we are made of ...[22]

One of Dorothy's sons, William, became a minister and was rector at Groton, Suffolk, under the patronage of Puritan John Winthrop.

Hear, my son, your father's instruction, and forsake not your mother's teaching, for they are a graceful garland for your head and pendants for your neck.

~ PROVERBS 1:8-9 ~

---

21. As found in Sylvia Brown, ed., *Women's Writings in Stuart England* (Thrupp, Stroud: Sutton Publishing, 1999).
22. *The Mother's Blessing*, ch. 30.

Seventeenth Century Love Letters

∽ Margaret Winthrop, c. 1591-1647 ∾

John Winthrop was the organizer and first governor of the Massachusetts Bay Colony. A staunch Puritan with a heart for God, he sought to glorify God in every area of his life, including marriage. However, his first wife died after eleven years of marriage, leaving behind four children. Winthrop remarried, but his second wife died a year later. Both marriages had strengthened Winthrop's spiritual life and caused him to appreciate more the love Christ had for him. On 24 April, 1618, John married Margaret Tyndall. This marriage lasted thirty years, and we have evidence of the Winthrops' deep Christian love and affection from surviving letters to each other. John often had to be in London on business, and the Winthrops communicated through letters. In addition to accounts of mundane affairs at home or in business, the letters are filled with encouragements in the things of the Lord. Each recognized that their marriage and love was God's gift, and they sought to live for His honor and glory.

In 1620, John wrote Margaret, 'O, ye sweet wife, let us rather hearken to the advice of our loving Lord who calls upon us first to seek the kingdom of God, and tells us that one thing is needful. Without it, the gain of the whole world is nothing.'[23] In 1628, Margaret wrote John, 'You do daily manifest your love to me and care for my spiritual good, as well as temporal. ... I desire God I may choose the better part which cannot be taken from me, which will stand me in stead when all other things fail for me.' After a series of difficulties and the long absence of John, Margaret wrote, 'it pleases the Lord to exercise us with one affliction after another in love; lest we should forget ourselves and love this world too much, and not set our affections on heaven where all true happiness is for ever'.

As they anticipated moving to New England, John wrote Margaret in 1629, 'My comfort is that you are willing to be my companion in what place or condition soever, in weal or in woe. Be it what it may, if God is with us, we need not fear. His favour, & the kingdom of heaven will be alike & happiness enough to us & ours in all places.' When the ship was ready to sail in 1630, Margaret was pregnant and stayed behind for a year, yet she encouraged John in his work: 'Husband cheer up your heart in the expectation of God's goodness to us, & let nothing dismay or discourage you. If the Lord be with us, who can be against us? My grief is the fear of staying behind you, but I must leave all to the good providence of God.'

There was a most joyous reunion with John when Margaret arrived in New England in August, 1631. Margaret and John lived in Boston for fifteen years. Margaret died 13 June, 1647 when an epidemic swept through the colony. The next day John wrote in his diary that she had 'left this world for a better, being about fifty-six years of age; a woman of singular virtue, prudence, modesty, and specially beloved and honoured of all the country.'

However, let each one of you love his wife as himself,
and let the wife see that she respects her husband.

~ EPHESIANS 5:33 ~

---

23. Quotes from letters taken from Joseph Hopkins Twichell, ed., *Some Old Puritan love Letters: John and Margaret Winthrop, 1618-1638* (New York: Dodd, Mead & Co., 1894).

Mother's Legacy

∽ Elizabeth Jocelin, 1596-1622 ∽

Elizabeth Brooke's mother died when Elizabeth was a young child. Elizabeth was then raised by her grandfather, William Chaderton, who was at the time Bishop of Lincoln. Grandfather Chaderton, who had previously been Professor of Divinity at Cambridge and President of Queen's College, had an academic bent and saw that Elizabeth received the best education with a strong Christian foundation. In 1616, when she was twenty-one, Elizabeth married Tourell Jocelin of Cambridgeshire. Six years later, when she was pregnant, Elizabeth had a premonition that she might not survive childbirth. In that eventuality, she wrote a 'Mother's legacies to her unborn child' and left it with a letter to her husband. Elizabeth's daughter was born 12 October, 1622; nine days later Elizabeth died, probably of puerperal fever.

Elizabeth's concerns for her unborn child were primarily spiritual: 'I never aimed at so poor an inheritance for thee as the whole world: ... the true reason I have so often kneeled to God for thee, is that thou might be an inheritor of the Kingdom of Heaven.' Elizabeth's foundational instruction was from Ecclesiastes 12:1, 'Remember also your Creator in the days of thy youth.' A child should establish a relationship with God 'before the world, the fleshe and the divell take hould on thee'. Elizabeth then outlined a pattern of how time should be spent each day, with time for prayer, meditation, study, lawful recreation and conversation. Elizabeth warned against the sins of covetousness, idleness, pride, envy, wantonness, lust, and drunkenness, recognizing that service to God requires a constant self-examination. Elizabeth then counseled on the importance of obedience to parents and the duties of charity which should be performed in the world.

Not knowing whether her child would be a boy or girl, Elizabeth wrote advice for both. If a son, she wrote, 'I humbly beseech Almighty God ... that thou may serve him as his Minister.' If the child were a daughter, she wrote her husband:

> I desire her bringing up may be learning the Bible ... good housekeeping, writing, and good workes: other learning a woman needs not: though I admire it in those whom God hath blessed with discretion, yet I desired not much on my owne, having seen that sometimes women have greater portions of learning than wisdom. ... But where learning and wisdom meet in a virtuous disposed woman she is the fittest closet for all goodness. ... Yet I leave it to thy will. ... If thou desire a learned daughter, I pray God give her a wise and religious heart, that she may use it to his glory, thy comfort, and her own salvation.[24]

Elizabeth Jocelin's *The Mother's Legacy to Her Unborn Child* was published in 1624, with Rev. Thomas Goad providing an *Approbation* and life of Elizabeth. It went through numerous editions into the nineteenth century. In 1904, it was even cited in a report by the US Bureau of Education among early English writers on education.[25]

Hear, my son, your father's instruction, and forsake not your mother's teaching, for they are a graceful garland for your head and pendants for your neck.

~ PROVERBS 1:8-9 ~

---

24. Betty Travitsky, 'New Mother of the English Renaissance', in Cathy N. Davidson and E. M. Bronerm, eds., *The Last Tradition: Mothers and Daughters in Literature* (New York: Frederick Ungar Publishing Co., 1980), pp. 39-40.

25. House of Representatives, *Annual Reports of the Department of the Interior for the fiscal year ended June 30, 1904 – Report of the Commissioner of Education*, Volume 1 (Washington: Government Printing Office, 1905), p. 666.

Puritan Marriage

∞ Lucy Hutchinson, 1620-1681 ∞

On her wedding day Lucy Apsley was taken ill of smallpox, and the wedding was delayed as her life hung in the balance. Lucy did survive smallpox, but her visage was marred and deformed from the disease. Colonel John Hutchinson looked beyond the wreck of Lucy's beauty to her honor and virtue, and the two were married on 3 July, 1638. Lucy later wrote of their courtship:

> Never was there a passion more ardent and less idolatrous: he loved her better than his life, with inexpressible tenderness and kindness; had a most high, obliging esteem of her, yet still considered honour, religion, and duty above her; nor ever suffered the intrusion of such dotage as should blind him from marking her imperfections.[26]

Colonel Hutchinson was a trusted officer of Oliver Cromwell and one of the commissioners of the trial of Charles I. At the Restoration he was imprisoned and Lucy worked tirelessly to secure his release and to be with him during his confinement. Though she was not allowed to stay with him, she took lodgings near him and visited him daily. During his imprisonment Colonel Hutchinson spent much of his time reading his Bible, making many notes along the way. Lucy later compiled these into a commonplace book, with Scriptures organized under different headings.

In spite of Lucy's care Colonel Hutchinson fell ill from the damp, miserable conditions of his cell and died 11 September, 1664. The Hutchinsons had eight children, and Lucy wrote *The Life of Colonel Hutchinson* for them to learn to emulate their father's virtues and character. In her introduction she wrote that their father's

> example was more instructive than the best rules of the moralists; for his practice was of a more divine extraction, drawn from the Word of God, and wrought up by the assistance of His Spirit. He had a noble method of government, whether in civil, military, or domestic administration, which forced love and reverence even from unwilling subjects, and greatly endeared him to the souls of those who rejoiced to be governed by him. He had a native majesty that struck awe into the hearts of men, and a sweet greatness that commanded love.[27]

Lucy lovingly described their marriage relationship:

> His affection for his wife was such, that whoever would form rules of kindness, honour, and religion, to be practiced in that state, need no more but exactly draw out his example. Man never had a greater passion or a more honourable esteem for woman ... but he managed the reigns of government with such prudence and affection, that she who would not delight in such honourable and advantageous subjection must have wanted a reasonable soul. He governed by persuasion, which he never employed but in things profitable to herself. He loved her soul better than her countenance; yet even for her person he had a constant affection. ... When she ceased to be young and lovely, he showed her the most tenderness. He loved her at such a kind and generous rate ... yet even this, which was the highest love any man could have, was bounded by a superior feeling; he regarded her, not as his idol, but as his fellow-creature in the Lord, and proved that such a feeling exceeds all the irregularities in the world.[28]

Let marriage be held in honor among all,
and let the marriage bed be undefiled ...

~ HEBREWS 13:4 ~

---

26. Sarah Josepha Hale, *Lessons from Women's Lives* (London: William P. Nimmo, 1877), p. 46.
27. Ibid, p. 51.
28. Ibid, pp. 51-52.

Looking to Heaven

☜ Mary Love, d. 1660 ☞

When Mary Stone's father, a wealthy London merchant, died Mary became the ward of John Warner, the Sheriff of London. Warner invited Christopher Love, a Welsh non-conformist preacher, to be his chaplain. Over the next six years, a bond of Christian affection developed between Mary and Christopher. Christopher taught and catechized the children and servants of the household and was instrumental in the conversion of several family members. He also served as an army chaplain with the Parliamentary forces from 1642-1645. After completing his army service Christopher Love and Mary Stone were married 9 April, 1645, at St Giles of the Field Church in London. An ordained Presbyterian minister, Christopher became a lecturer at St Ann's Aldersgate and then pastor at St Lawrence Jewry. The Loves had four children, though two died as infants. Mary was pregnant with their fifth child in 1651, when Christopher was arrested for treason and condemned to death. Like many Presbyterians, Christopher had become disillusioned with Parliament and had corresponded with Charles II's forces about overthrowing Cromwell and restoring the monarchy. Though the six other ministers involved in the plot were released after a brief imprisonment, Christopher remained in the Tower of London under sentence of death. Mary and others petitioned Parliament for leniency, but a reprieve of only a few weeks was granted.

The letters Christopher and Mary wrote to each other during his imprisonment reveal a passionate, Christian love with roots in and eyes on eternity. In her last letter, written the day before Christopher was executed, Mary wrote:

> God hath put heaven into thee before He hath taken thee to heaven. Thou now beholdest God, Christ and glory as in a glass; but tomorrow, heaven's gates will be opened and thou shalt be in the full enjoyment of all those glories which eye hath not seen, nor ear heard, neither can the heart of man understand. God hath now swallowed up thy heart in the thoughts of heaven, but ere long thou shalt be swallowed up in the enjoyment of heaven. And no marvel there should be such quietness and calmness in thy spirit while thou art sailing in this tempestuous sea, because thou perceivest by the eye of faith a haven of rest where thou shalt be richly laden with all the glories of heaven. O lift up thy heart with joy when thou layest thou dear head on the block in the thought of this: that thou are laying thou head to rest in thy Father's bosom which, when thou dost awake, shall be crowned not with an earthly fading crown but with a heavenly eternal crown of glory. ...
>
> O let not one troubled thought for thy wife and babes arise within thee. Thy God will be our God and our portion. He will be a husband to thy widow and a father to thy children: the grace of thy God will be sufficient for us.
>
> Now my dear, I desire willingly and cheerfully to resign my right in thee to thy Father and my Father, who hath the greatest interest in thee. And confident I am, though men have separated us for a time yet our God will ere long bring us together again where we shall eternally enjoy one another, never to part more. ...[29]

What no eye has seen, nor ear heard,
nor the heart of man imagined ...
God has prepared for those who love him ...

~ I CORINTHIANS 2:9 ~

---

29. Don Kistler, *A Spectacle unto God: The Life and Death of Christopher Love (1618-1651)*, (Soli Deo Gloria Publications, 1998), pp. 84-85.

Abounding in the Work of the Lord

∞ Mary Tracy Vere, 1581-1671 ∞

Born 18 May, 1581, Mary Tracy was the youngest of fifteen children. Her mother died three days after she was born, and her father died when she was eight. As an orphan, Mary found comfort and care in her heavenly Father, adopting for her motto, 'God will provide'. As her life unfolded she always looked to her God for sustenance.

When she was nineteen Mary married William Hobby, son of Henry VIII's Privy Counsellor. The couple had two sons before Henry died. Mary then married Sir Horatio Vere, a devout Christian gentleman and military leader aiding Holland in its war with Spain. Mary and Horatio were supremely happy in their marriage and had five daughters. Mary lived several years in Holland with Horatio during the Spanish war. Here she worshiped with the English Puritan church pastored by William Ames.

Mary's two sons died young. When her oldest son, a promising student at Emmanuel College, Cambridge, died at the age of twenty-two, a friend wrote Mary a letter filled with Christian solace:

> God hath taken away your well-beloved and only son, I confess this is such a cross as must needs affect the heart of a loving mother. But remember that he hath given you his own and only Son, to be your wisdom, righteousness, holiness, and redemption. He hath adopted you to be his daughter and heir, and fellow-heir with Jesus Christ. He hath given you his word, his Holy Spirit, and hope and assurance of eternal life. Besides these unspeakable mercies, the Lord hath blessed you with a gracious and worthy husband, with many hopeful children .... God is the father of your child; he gave him his life, and breath, and being; you were appointed to be his nursing mother, and that for a few days; which now being ended, he hath taken him into his own kingdom; and therefore you should not be so much grieved that you part with him now, as thankful that you enjoyed him so long, and that he now enjoyeth everlasting life in the heavens, whither yourself also shall come within a while.[30]

Mary used her position and wealth to help others materially and to secure appointments of faithful ministers to important positions. Her influence helped secure James Ussher's position as Archbishop of Armagh and Primate of Ireland. William Gurnall, the esteemed Puritan who delivered the sermon at Mary's funeral, stated that 'she had silver for the penniless, food for the sick, salves for the wounded'. Her well-ordered house reflected her Christian heart. Twice daily the family, including the servants, met together for worship – reading the Word, praying and singing psalms. Mary's life was a quiet life, but one lived in the light of God, throughout her ninety years.

Therefore, my beloved brothers, be steadfast, unmovable,
always abounding in the work of the Lord, knowing that
in the Lord your labor is not in vain.

~ 1 CORINTHIANS 15:58 ~

---

30. W. H. Davenport Adams, *Stories of the Lives of Noble Women* (London: T. Nelson & Sons, 1891), pp. 51-52.

Making a Home in the Wilderness

∞ Ann Mountfort Eliot, 1604-1687 ∞

When Archbishop William Laud began restricting the biblical preaching and lectures of Puritans in England, many found a refuge in America. Among these was John Eliot, who immigrated to Massachusetts in 1631. Eliot left behind his fiancée, Ann Mountfort; the two had been introduced by Rev. Thomas Hooker, who also would find his way to America and become a founder of Connecticut. Eliot settled in Roxbury, near Boston. The following year Ann followed him to America. The two were married shortly after her arrival; their marriage in October 1632 was the first recorded in the town of Roxbury.

John and Ann's love was rooted in the Savior, and their fifty-five years of marriage became a model for all. One daughter and five sons were born to the Eliots, and their home became a miniature church. Daily prayers and Scripture reading were held in the family. After the Bible reading, each child was encouraged to note what it learned from the Scripture that day. Ann was skilled in providing clothing and food for her family, and she also became skilled in medicine and surgery. Often she and John found themselves together at the bedside of an ill patient, he laboring for the health of the soul while she provided for the health of the body.

John Eliot not only pastored the church at Roxbury but also brought the gospel to the native Algonquians. He learned the Algonquian language and translated the Scriptures into their language, making the Algonquian Bible the first Bible printed in America. Eliot's missionary work became a pattern for William Carey in India. Ann cared for the children and home while John was on his missionary travels and provided an atmosphere that allowed John to work on his translation. Cotton Mather wrote of John Eliot's love for Ann: 'The wife of his bosom he loved, prized and cherished with a kindness that strikingly represented the compassion which he thereby taught others to expect from the Lord Jesus Christ.'[31]

As the couple aged together, neighbors called them Zacharias and Elizabeth. When Ann died in 1687 John wept uncontrollably, saying over her grave, 'Here lies my dear, faithful, pious, prudent, prayerful wife. I shall go to her; but she shall not return to me.'[32] John did follow Ann three years later.

I remember the devotion of your youth, your love as a bride,
how you followed me in the wilderness,
in a land not sown.

~ JEREMIAH 2:2 ~

---

31. Rev. Thomas Timpson, *Memoirs of British Female Missionaries* (London: William Smith, 1841), p. 4.

32. Lydia Howard Sigourney, *Examples of Life and Death* (New York: Charles Scribner, 1852), pp. 178-179.

APRIL 3

Jesus, My Redeemer Lives!

∞ Louisa Henrietta of Brandenburg, 1627-1667 ∞

Louisa Henrietta was born in the early years of the Thirty Years War, that conflict which raged across Central Europe between 1618 and 1648, and her life would be lived in the thick of that political and religious conflict. Born in The Hague, Louisa's grandfather was William I, Prince of Orange, who had led the revolt bringing independence from Spain to the Dutch Republic. On her mother's side she was descended from Admiral Coligny, a leader of the French Protestants. With her noble heritage, Louisa's marriage became a matter of diplomatic negotiations. When an engagement with Charles II of England came to nothing, Louisa was married to Frederick William, Elector of Brandenburg. Frederick's early years had been spent in Holland, and he had known Louisa as a girl and knew of her devotion to the Bible and the Reformed faith. The two were married in The Hague on 7 December, 1646.

Louisa and Frederick lived at Cleves in western Germany for a couple of years, where a son was born and soon died, to their parents' great sorrow. In 1848, with the end of the Thirty Years War, the couple journeyed to Frederick's capital of Berlin, a journey taking six months. Adding to their personal sorrow, they were surrounded by the devastation of war on every side. People were poor and starving; fields were desolate. In her deep sadness Louisa drew closer to her Savior, and during this time wrote a hymn weaving together themes from Psalm 46, Job 19:25, 27, and 1 Corinthians 15, which has become a favorite German hymn, 'Jesus, my Redeemer, lives':

Jesus, my Redeemer, lives,
Christ, my trust, is dead no more!
In the strength this knowledge gives,
Shall not all my fears be o'er;
Calm, though earth's long night be fraught
Still with many an anxious thought? ...

Close to Him my soul is bound,
In the bonds of hope enclasped;
Faith's strong hand this hold hath found,
And the Rock hath firmly grasped.
Death shall ne'er my soul remove
From her refuge in Thy love. ...

Ye who suffer, sigh and moan,
Fresh and glorious there shall reign;
Earthly here the seed is sown,
Heavenly it shall rise again;
Natural here the death we die,
Spiritual our life on high. ...

Only see ye that your heart
Rise betimes from earthly lust;
Would ye there with Him have part,
Here obey your Lord and trust.
Fix your hearts above the skies,
Whither ye yourselves would rise.[33]

For I know that my Redeemer lives, and at the last he will stand upon the earth.
And after my skin has been thus destroyed, yet in my flesh I shall see God, whom I
shall see for myself, and my eyes shall behold, and not another.

~ JOB 19:25-27 ~

---

33. James I. Good, *Famous Women of the Reformed Church* (Birmingham, AL: Solid Ground Christian Books, 2007, reprint of 1901 edition by The Sunday School Board of the Reformed Church in the United States), pp. 224-226.

Persecuted for Christ

∽ Margaret Wemyss, Lady Colvill, 17th century ∾

The 1680s in Scotland has been called 'The Killing Time'; it was a time when the government forces of Kings Charles II and James VII sought to impose their will on church government and practices. Church ministers had to either accept the royal authority and bishops over the church or leave their parishes. About one third of the ministers refused to conform, believing Jesus Christ was the head of the church, not the king or any bishop. These ministers, intent on teaching the Scriptures, met in private homes or in fields and woods with the people faithful to the Scottish Covenant of 1638. These meetings were outlawed, and those participating were often persecuted with fines, imprisonments, and even death.

Margaret Wemyss, widow of Robert, Lord Colvill, was faithful in attendance at the preaching of the gospel at these field conventicles, as well as providing hospitality for the ministers in her home. In 1674, soldiers broke up a meeting in the Lomonds of Fife and later falsely claimed the people had violently resisted the authorities. The king issued an order to punish the ringleaders. Lady Colvill was among those listed to appear before the privy council and was fined. Yet Lady Colvill continued to attend preaching meetings and entertain ministers in her home. When the persecutions intensified she and other Covenanters hid themselves in the mountains, greatly injuring her health.

When the privy council resolved to take her son away from her, since they considered her a fanatic for diligently teaching him the Word of God and instructing him in the truth of Christ, she sent him away to safety before he could be taken by the authorities. This irritated the government more, and they fined her heavily. When she didn't pay she was imprisoned in the tollbooth of Edinburgh. There she was in a dark, damp room which required a candle to see even in the daytime. After some weeks she petitioned for a better room, and her room was changed. After three months in prison, her health was so broken she was in danger of death. She was temporarily released, but required to return to prison in a few weeks.

In spite of her imprisonment and enduring hardship, Lady Colvill never wavered in her faithfulness to Christ and His Word. She was honored to be able to suffer for Christ.

Beloved, do not be surprised at the fiery trial when it comes upon
you to test you, as though something strange were happening to you.
But rejoice insofar as you share Christ's sufferings, that you may
also rejoice and be glad when his glory is revealed.

~ 1 PETER 4:12-13 ~

Looking to the Lord in All of Life

⚭ Anne Bradstreet, house burned 10 July, 1666 ⚭

Anne Bradstreet was eighteen when she came to America with her husband Simon and her parents, Thomas and Dorothy Dudley, in 1630, on board the *Arbella* as part of the Puritan migration led by John Winthrop. Throughout her life Anne wrote poetry, writing biblical reflections to life's ordinary events – the birth of a child, marriage, or the care of children. On 10 July, 1666, when her house burned, Anne again put her thoughts in poetry:

In silent night when rest I took,
For sorrow ne'er I did not look,
I waken'd was with thundering noise
And Pietous shrieks of dreadful voice.
That fearfull sound of 'fire' and 'fire' … .
And to my God my heart did cry
To strengthen me in my Distresse
And not to leave me succourlesse.

Then coming out beheld a space,
The flame consume my dwelling place.
And when I could no longer look,
I blest his Name that gave and took,
That layd my goods now in the dust;
Yea, so it was, and so 'twas just.
It was his own; it was not mine;
Far be it that I should repine … .

Anne described how when looking at the ruins of her house she recalled where she had sat, where the trunk or table had been – all now ashes. There shall be no more guests under the roof or sitting at the table, or a bridegroom's voice heard within the walls:

In silence ever shalt thou lye;
Adieu, Adieu, All's vanity.

Then she began to rebuke herself, for certainly her wealth was not on earth and moldering dust. She needed to raise her thoughts 'above the skye':

Thou hast an house on high erect,
Fram'd by that mighty Architect,
With glory richly furnished,
Stands permanent tho' this bee fled.
It's purchased, and paid for too
By him who hath enough to doe.

A Price so vast as is unknown,
Yet, by his Gift, is made thine own.
Ther's wealth enough, I need no more;
Farewell my Pelf, farewell my Store.
The world no longer let me Love,
My hope and Treasure lyes Above.[34]

Anne had learned to seek the Lord and His ways, whatever came her way – the burning of her house led her to reflect more on the heavenly home and treasure stored above.

> *Do not lay up for yourselves treasures on earth, where moth and rust destroy and where thieves break in and steal, but lay up for yourselves treasures in heaven, where neither moth nor rust destroys and where thieves do not break in and steal. For where your treasure is, there your heart will be also.*
>
> ~ MATTHEW 6:19-21 ~

---

34. *The Poems of Mrs Anne Bradstreet* (The Duodecimos, 1897), pp. 343-345.

Puritan Wife, Mother and Poet

⌀ Anne Bradstreet, 1612-1672 ⌀

Anne Bradstreet was among the leaders of society in early colonial Massachusetts. Both her father and husband served as governors of the colony at different times. Her husband Simon was gone frequently on government business, and on one occasion, Anne wrote a poem 'To My Dear and Loving Husband':

If ever two were one, then surely we.
If ever man were loved by wife, then thee;
If ever wife was happy in a man,
Compare with me, ye women, if you can.
I prize thy love more than whole mines of gold

Or all the riches that the East doth hold.
My love is such that rivers cannot quench,
Nor ought but love from thee, give recompense.
Thy love is such I can no way repay,
The heavens reward thee manifold, I pray.

Simon and Anne had eight children, all of whom survived to adulthood – a very rare occurrence in a day when most families lost several children to disease. Though Anne's children did become seriously ill they recovered, as Anne wrote in 'Upon my Daughter Hannah and Her Recovering from a Dangerous Fever':

Bles't be Thy Name who did'st restore to
Health my Daughter dear
When Death did seem ev'n to approach
And life was ended near.

Grant she remember what thou'st done
And celebrate thy praise
And let her conversation say
She loves Thee all her days.

Having eight children, Anne was wise enough to recognize that each child was different and required different parenting:

Diverse children have their different natures; some are like flesh [or meat] which nothing but salt will keep from putrefaction; some again like tender fruit that are best preserved with sugar; those parents are wise that can fit their nurture according to their Nature.[35]

In the epitaph Anne wrote for her mother, Dorothy Dudley, she pictured the Puritan ideal of woman:

A worthy matron of unspotted life,
A loving mother and obedient wife,
A friendly neighbour, pitiful to poor,
Whom oft she fed, and clothed with her store;

To servants wisely awful, but yet kind,
And as they did, so reward did find.
A true instructor of her family,
The which she ordered with dexterity.[36]

Though Anne gained some fame for her poems, and was America's first published poet, when she wrote her autobiography for her children she didn't even mention her poetry. Her life before God was primarily as a wife and mother. Shortly before her death she wrote in her journal:

Upon the Rock Christ Jesus will I build by faith, and if I perish, I perish. But I know all the powers of Hell shall never prevail against it. I know whom I have trusted, and whom I believe, and that he is able to keep what I have committed to his charge.[37]

But I am not ashamed, for I know whom I have believed, and I am convinced
that he is able to guard until that Day what has been entrusted to me.
~ 2 TIMOTHY 1:12 ~

---

35. Helen Campbell, *Anne Bradstreet and her Time* (Boston: D. Lathrop Company, 1891), p. 355.
36. John Harvard Ellis, ed. *The Works of Anne Bradstreet in Prose and Verse* (Charlestown: Abram E. Cutter, 1867), pp. 394, 28, liii.
37. Ibid, p. 293.

Sovereignty and Goodness of God

∞ Mary Rowlandson, 1637-1711 ∞

When King Philip, leader of the Wampanoag Confederacy, attacked isolated homesteads in Massachusetts throughout the summer of 1675, Rev. Joseph Rowlandson went to Boston and urged the government to provide protection for Lancaster and other frontier communities. While he was away, on the morning of 10 February, 1676, warriors attacked Lancaster. The Rowlandson house was one of the five or six garrison houses into which the fifty families of the town crowded. When fire was set to the house Mary Rowlandson and her sister took their four children to leave the house, but when they opened the door, the bullets were coming fiercely. Mary saw her brother-in-law fall dead, her nephew killed, and her sister shot. Mary herself was shot through the side; the little six-year-old Sarah she carried in her arms was hit by the same bullet. That morning thirteen were killed and twenty-four became captives and servants of the Indians. In the trek north Mary and Sarah were separated from her other two children, Joseph and Mary. After a week, little Sarah died from her wounds.

After a raid on another settlement one of the Indians brought Mary a Bible rescued from one of the burning houses and asked if she would like it. Mary recognized this as a 'a wonderful mercy of God to me in those afflictions, in sending me a Bible'. After eleven weeks of travelling with the Indians Mary was ransomed for £30. She was reunited with her husband in Boston, and her children were released soon after. They relocated to Wethersfield, Connecticut, where Rev. Rowlandson became pastor.

Mary wrote an account of her captivity, *The Sovereignty and Goodness of God, together with the Faithfulness of His Promises Displayed*, which was published in 1682. The narrative describes in vivid detail the horrors of Mary's captivity, but throughout is a trust and recognition in God's sovereign working. The first day after the raid and her capture, she wrote,

> God was with me, in a wonderful manner, carrying me along, and bearing up my spirit that it did not quite fail. ... The Lord renewed my strength still, and carried me along, that I might see more of his power; yea, so much that I could never have thought of, had I not experienced it.[38]

Fifty-nine Scriptural quotations are scattered throughout. Many of them were promises from the Psalms Mary trusted in during her captivity, and expressed her piteous state: 'My wounds stink and are corrupt ... . I am troubled; I am bowed down greatly; I go mourning all the day long' (Ps. 38:5-6, kjv). Others were promises that she would survive the ordeal: 'I shall not die, but I shall live, and recount the deeds of the Lord' (Ps. 118:17). Mary concluded her narrative:

> When God calls a Person to any thing, and through never so many difficulties, yet he is fully able to carry them through and make them see, and say they have been gainers thereby. And I hope I can say in some measure, As *David* did, It *is good for me that I have been afflicted*. ... I have learned to look beyond present and smaller troubles, and to be quieted under them, *as Moses* said, *Exodus* 13.13. *Stand still and see the Salvation of the Lord.*[39]

> *Wait for the Lord;*
> *be strong, and let your heart take courage; wait for the Lord!*
> ~ Psalm 27:14 ~

---

38. Mary Rowlandson (Neal Salisbury ed.), *The Sovereignty and Goodness of God* (Boston: Bedford Books, 1997), pp. 72-73.
39. Ibid, p. 112.

Penn's Farewell Letter to His Wife

⟠ Gulielma Springett Penn, 1644-1694 ⟠

In 1681, the Quaker William Penn received a large grant of land in America with a right of sovereign, sole proprietorship, except the power to declare war. Penn saw this land, which the king named Pennsylvania, as a refuge for Quakers, who were under persecution in England. Penn spent the next year drawing up the Frame of Government and drafting a charter of liberties for the colony. On this first voyage to America he would have to leave his wife Gulielma and children behind in England. Before setting sail, not knowing whether he would ever see them again, Penn wrote a farewell letter on 4 August, 1682 to 'My dear Wife and Children'.[40] Penn reminded Gulielma,

> remember thou was the love of my youth, and much the joy of my life, the most beloved, as well as most worthy, of all my earthly comforts. And the reason of that love was more thy inward than thy outward excellences (which yet were many). ... I can say it was a match of providence's making, and God's image in us both was the first thing and the most amiable and engaging ornament in our eyes. Now I am to leave thee, and that without knowing whether I shall ever see thee more in this world. Take my counsel into thy bosom and let it dwell with thee in my stead while thou lives.

Penn's first counsel was, 'Let the fear of the Lord, and a Zeal and love to His glory, dwell richly in thy heart.' He encouraged Gulielma to be diligent in worship meetings and also that once a day the family should meet and 'wait upon the Lord, who has given us much time for ourselves'. By keeping a regular schedule, household affairs should be easier:

> Consider what income you have and what your daily requirements are, and live within that: I need not bid thee be humble, for thou are so; nor meek and patient, for it is much of thy natural disposition. But I pray thee, be often in retirement with the Lord and guard against encroaching friendships ... that which might seem engaging in the beginning, may prove a yoke and a burden too hard and heavy in the end.

Penn had specific counsel for the care of the children:

> Above all things, endeavour to breed them up in the love of virtue and that holy plain way of it which we have lived in, that the world, in no part of it, get into my family. I had rather they were homely than finely bred, as to outward behaviour. ... Next, breed them up in a love one of another. Tell them, it is the charge I left behind me, and that it is the way to have the love and blessing of God upon them ... tell them it was my counsel, they should be tender and affectionate one to another.

No expense should be spared on their learning. Someone should teach them at home rather than them going to school, where 'too many evil impressions' can be received. Penn also wrote out lengthy words of counsel for the children, especially to be obedient to their mother, 'for she has been exceeded by none in her time for her plainness, integrity, industry, humanity, virtue, and good understanding, qualities not usual among women of her worldly condition and quality'.

So William Penn wrote farewell to his 'dearly beloved wife and children', signing off with 'Yours, as God pleases, in that which no waters can quench, no time forget nor distance wear away, but remains forever.' Penn was in America two years, returning to England in 1684 and reuniting with Gulielma and the children. Gulielma, who was always frail in health, died in 1694. Penn returned to his colony in 1702.

> *Beloved, let us love one another, for love is from God,*
> *and whoever loves has been born of God and knows God.*
> ⟠ 1 JOHN 4:7 ⟠

---

40. Maria Webb, *The Penns and Penningtons of the Seventeenth Century* (London: F. Bowyer Kitto, 1867), pp. 340-343.

Heart for God

∽ Madame Jeanne Guyon, 1648-1717 ∽

A French aristocrat who moved in the highest court circles, Jeanne Guyon maintained a heart for God under much opposition and the temptations of the world. Educated in a French convent, Jeanne came upon a Bible there when she was about ten years old. She began reading the convent Bible and memorized large portions of Scripture. When she was fifteen Jeanne's father arranged her marriage to M. Jacques Guyon, a man of great wealth.

Jeanne's mother-in-law ruled their home like a tyrant and constantly criticized Jeanne to her husband. Jeanne realized that God could use this adversity for good in her own soul, as he had used Joseph's slavery in Egypt, and God used her acerbic mother-in-law to develop Jeanne's humble spirit. She turned to God in prayer and read devotional books which turned her mind to Christ. The deaths of two of her children caused her to trust God's hand in her life even more.

Jeanne's husband died when she was twenty-eight, leaving her with three children – one just months old. Her husband also left her with a wealthy estate, and Jeanne started to use her fortune to help others, providing food and nursing, and establishing hospitals. She began traveling in Europe speaking to people about the importance of seeking Christ by faith, not by outward ceremonies. She wrote forty books about the importance of the Christ-transformed life, an inward holiness, and a total surrender to God. She wrote:

> There are but two principles of moral life in the universe, one which makes ourselves, or the most limited private good, the center; the other, which makes God, who may be called the universal good, the center. When self dies in the soul, God lives; when self is annihilated, God is enthroned.[41]

As Madame Guyon's writings increased in popularity, the church authorities became alarmed and accused her of heresy. She was imprisoned for seven years, including two years in solitary confinement in the Bastille. She was broken in health when released, though her spirit remained resilient. In her last will she wrote:

> It is to Thee, O Lord God, that I owe all things; and it is to thee, that I now surrender up all that I am. Do with me, O my God, whatsoever Thou pleases. To Thee, in an act of irrevocable donation, I give up both my body and my soul, to be disposed of according to thy will. Thou seest my nakedness and misery without Thee. Thou knowest that there is nothing in heaven, or in earth, that I desire but Thee alone. Within Thy hands, O God, I leave my soul, not relying for my salvation on any good that is in me, but solely on Thy mercies, and the merits and sufferings of my Lord Jesus Christ.[42]

Rejoice always, pray without ceasing, give thanks in all circumstances;
for this is the will of God in Christ Jesus for you.

~ I THESSALONIANS 5:16-18 ~

---

41. Quoted in Edith Deen, *Great Women of the Christian Faith* (Uhrichsville, OH: Barbour Books, 1959), p. 136.
42. Ibid, p. 140.

He Does All Things Well

Marion Fairlie Veitch, 1638-1722

Marion Fairlie endured many hardships during the religious and political turmoil in Scotland during the seventeenth century. Her diary reveals the Scriptures which sustained her throughout these troubles. From a godly family, Marion was thankful for the blessing of early being brought to faith:

> It pleased God, of his great goodness, early to incline my heart to seek him, and bless him that I was born in a land where the gospel was at that time purely and powerfully preached as also, that I was born of godly parents, and well educated. But above all things, I bless him that he made me see, that nothing but the righteousness of Christ could save me from the wrath of God.[43]

On 23 November, 1664, Marion married William Veitch, a nonconforming minister. Some of Marion's friends discouraged the marriage, saying the times were such that she would be reduced to severe straits by persecution and hardship. Marion, however, decided to trust God for all her temporal provisions as well as her spiritual blessings. Towards the end of her life she could testify that God not only 'provided well for me and mine, but made me in the places where my lot was cast useful to others, and made that word good, "as having nothing, and yet possessing all things" (2 Cor. 6:10).'

When married just two years, persecution fell upon Marion and her husband. As a participant in the Covenanters' resistance to the king's forces at Pentland Hills, William was declared guilty of treason and worthy of death. He found safety for some years in England, where Marion and her two sons were able to follow four years later. They had lost their land in Scotland, and Marion prayed that the Lord would sustain them, giving them food to eat, and clothes to put on, and He did indeed. On 19 January, 1679, however, a party of dragoons came to the house at night, broke in the windows, came into the house and captured William, eventually taking him to Edinburgh on charges of high treason. During the break-in Marion remained calm, persuaded that the men could not do anything that God did not permit. The Scripture from Mark 7:37, 'He has done all all things well,' came to mind. Remembering Psalm 56:11 – to trust in the Lord and fear not what man can do – brought her perfect peace.

In the months ahead, whenever she began to fear, Marion returned to the Scriptures for comfort. Job 23:14 (KJV) encouraged her that 'he performeth the thing that is appointed for me'. Whenever doubt assailed her, she again found comfort in God's Word, recalling Psalm 43:5.

The King released William after several months in prison. He then spent some years in exile in Holland, before the Glorious Revolution of 1688, after which he returned to Scotland and became minister of Dumfries. Marion's prayers of William returning to Scotland and preaching freely there had been answered. Marion died the day before William in 1722. Their fifty-eight years of marriage had seen many difficulties and afflictions, but always God's promises provided strength in times of trial.

> *Why are you cast down, O my soul, and why are you in turmoil within me?*
> *Hope in God; for I shall again praise him, my salvation and my God.*
>
> ~ Psalm 43:5 ~

---

43. *Memoirs of Mrs William Veitch* (Edinburgh: General Assembly of the Free Church of Scotland, 1846), p. 1.

United in Soul and Spirit

∞ Margaret Baxter, 1631-1681 ∞

Margaret first met the Rev. Richard Baxter when she was eighteen or nineteen and Richard was pastor of the church in Kidderminster. Margaret had been staying in Oxford with her sister but in 1652 moved to Kidderminster to be with her mother. After her social life in Oxford, Margaret found Kidderminster not to her liking. Spending all her thoughts on fancy apparel and reading romances, Kidderminster seemed boring. But under Rev. Baxter's preaching Margaret realized that she was not converted. She began to read serious books and cast aside her romances. Then Margaret became very ill with consumption and lay dying. Baxter called for the people to set aside 30 December, 1659 as a day to fast and pray for Margaret's recovery. God heard their prayers, and Margaret amazingly recovered. She recognized that God had delivered her and that he had a special claim on her life.

Margaret and her mother came to so depend on Baxter's preaching for their spiritual food that when Baxter moved to a church in London they followed him there. Margaret's mother died in 1661, and Margaret became very melancholy. Baxter counseled her with the Scriptures. When the 1662 Act of Uniformity forced two thousand Puritan ministers from their pulpits in the Church of England for refusing to conform to the *Book of Common Prayer*, Baxter was among them. Without a congregation to oversee, perhaps Baxter felt free to marry as he had not previously. Margaret and Richard Baxter were married 24 September, 1662.

Margaret's melancholy left her as she found perfect contentment with her husband and managing the affairs of his household. Margaret's well-ordered home provided Richard with the calm needed for his extensive writing. Every morning as they rose and every evening as they went to bed they sang a psalm of praise together. Richard valued Margaret's kind temper and unselfishness. She cared not only for the physical needs of the poor, but instructed them in Christian truth and distributed religious books among them. She established a school for the poor in London, one of the first free public schools in the city. Richard also valued Margaret's discerning and quick insight to problems. When Richard was imprisoned for holding an illegal religious meeting, Margaret persuaded the jailer to let her stay with him in jail, and her happiness brought light to the prison.

When Margaret died in 1681 Baxter was consumed with grief. Within a month of her death he wrote a memorial of her life in which he noted, 'we lived in inviolated love and mutual complacency, sensible of the benefits of mutual help. These near nineteen years I know not that ever we had any breach in point of love, or point of interest. ...'[44] Historian Frederick Powicke found 'the simple truth was that they loved each other – with a love of that high spiritual character which unites soul to soul, and transfigures life, and is immortal.'[45]

> *Wives, submit to your own husbands, as to the Lord. For the husband is the head of the wife even as Christ is the head of the church, his body, and is himself its Savior.*
>
> ~ EPHESIANS 5:22-23 ~

---

44. Richard Baxter, *Memoirs of Mrs Margaret Baxter* (London: Richard Edwards, 1826), p. 52.
45. Frederick Powicke, 'A Puritan Idyll, or the Rev. Richard Baxter's Love Story' (*Bulletin of the John Rylands Library*, vol. 4, 1918), p. 444.

Remembering those in Prison

∞ Helen Johnston, Lady Graden, d. 1707 ∞

Helen Johnston's father, Sir Archibald Johnston, was a man of prayer who regularly led his family in prayer and devotions to Christ. Active in support of the Scottish National Covenant of 1638, he was a strong opponent of the attempts by the Stuart kings to bring control of the Church under the Crown. A member of the House of Lords under Cromwell, he was a prominent leader in the struggle for religious and civil liberty. After the monarchy was restored to Charles II, Johnston privately admonished the new king about his moral conduct. The king took great offence, and charges of treason were made against Johnston. Though he fled to the continent he was found, arrested, and brought back to Scotland, where he was executed in 1663.

Four years before her father's death in 1659, Helen was married to George Hume, who also was a Covenanter, a supporter of the Scottish National Covenant. The Stuart monarchs placed stiff penalties on those who failed to attend the parish church, attended 'conventicles' or unauthorized religious meetings, or housed and protected unconforming ministers. In 1678, George Hume was imprisoned for supporting nonconformity; he died the following year. In 1684, Helen was fined over £26,000 for her support of unauthorized preachers and meetings, much more than any others were fined for similar 'offences', probably because of the hatred the king still harbored against her father.

In 1683, Helen's cousin and brother-in-law, Robert Baillie, a godly man with strong Christian faith, had been arrested for participation in the Rye House Plot, an attempt to assassinate King Charles II and his brother James. Examined by Charles himself, Baillie denied any knowledge or participation in the plot, and there was no evidence of his participation. Nevertheless, he was fined £6,000 and imprisoned. During his imprisonment Baillie's health worsened, and he was dying. Helen petitioned the courts to allow her to go to the prison and care for him. The courts only allowed this if she remained imprisoned with him, so for two months Helen remained imprisoned, caring for her ailing cousin. She read the Scriptures to him and comforted him with the promises and hopes of the gospel. Baillie endured his sufferings with patience and even joy, as he anticipated the glories of his eternal home.

In the final hours before his execution for treason on 24 December, 1684, Baillie was filled with joy and the peace of Christ. Helen thought his face seemed to shine, and in his prayers he sounded like one already in heaven. She saw in him God's strength made perfect in weakness. As she had been with Baillie in prison on 24 December, 1684, Helen provided Christian companionship, accompanying him to his execution in Edinburgh.

> 'I was naked, and you clothed me, I was sick and you visited
> me, I was in prison and you came to me.' ... And the King
> will answer them, 'Truly, I say to you, as you did it to one of
> the least of these my brothers, you did it to me.'
>
> ~ MATTHEW 25:36,40 ~

Wigtown Martyrs

∞ Margaret Wilson and Margaret MacLauchlan, d. 1685 ∞

When Charles II restored the Stuart monarchy to the throne of Scotland in 1660 he quickly moved to replace the presbyteries and synods of the Church of Scotland with an episcopal church government. All were required to take an oath of allegiance recognizing Charles as head of the Church of Scotland. Any who refused were culpable of death. The numerous executions of those refusing to swear the required loyalty oath to the king has been called 'the Killing Time' in Scotland's history, lasting from 1660 to 1688.

Among those executed were eighteen-year-old Margaret Wilson and sixty-three-year-old Margaret MacLauchlan, both of Wigtown. Margaret's parents had a prosperous farm and took the oath recognizing the king's headship of the church, but their teenage children would not conform. They contended that Jesus Christ, not the king, was head of the Church. Since parents were considered responsible for their children, they were heavily fined and given strict orders not to allow the children in the house. Margaret, her sixteen-year-old brother Thomas, and her thirteen-year-old sister Agnes went to live secretly in the mountains, meeting as they could in open air conventicles with other Christians.

In February 1685, Margaret and Agnes went secretly to Wigtown to visit some friends, were discovered, arrested and placed in prison. When they were brought before the magistrates they were sentenced to be tied to posts in the Solway where they would be drowned when the tide came in. The girls' father was able to pay £100 and have Agnes freed, because of her age. But no effort of his could change the verdict against Margaret.

On 11 May, 1685, Margaret was tied to the post in the Solway. Sixty-three-year-old Margaret MacLauchlan, who also refused to recognize the king's headship of the Church, was tied nearby. As the waters approached, Margaret Wilson sang from Psalm 25:

> Let not the errors of my youth,
> Nor sins remembered be:
> In mercy for thy goodness' sake,
> O Lord, remember me.
> The Lord is good and gracious,
> He upright is also:
> He therefore sinners will instruct
> In ways that they should go.

Before the waters engulfed her, she recited the words of Romans 8 (KJV), concluding with, 'For I am persuaded, that neither death, nor life, nor angels, nor principalities, nor powers, nor things present, nor things to come, nor height, nor depth, nor any other creature, shall be able to separate us from the love of God, which is in Christ Jesus our Lord.'

Who shall separate us from the love of Christ? Shall tribulation, or distress, or persecution, or famine, or nakedness, or danger, or sword? As it is written, 'For your sake we are being killed all the day long: we are regarded as sheep to be slaughtered.'

~ ROMANS 8:35-36 ~

Importunate *Wife*

∞ Elizabeth Bunyan, ? – 1692 ∞

Elizabeth married John Bunyan in 1659, when she was seventeen or eighteen and he was thirty-one. Bunyan's first wife had died the previous year, leaving him with four young children, the oldest being Mary – a little girl of five who was born blind. Elizabeth loved and cared for the children as for her own. Barely a year after their marriage, John was in the Bedford jail, arrested for preaching without a licence. At the time of Bunyan's arrest, Elizabeth herself was pregnant. The trauma of the arrest caused Elizabeth to go into labor; the child was born premature and died within days.

Elizabeth shared Bunyan's commitment to Christ and was a great encouragement during his imprisonment. Bunyan had been arrested briefly before in 1658, but had been released. With the accession of Charles II in 1660, the requirements to worship according to the Church of England were strictly enforced. Bunyan had been able to preach freely under the Commonwealth, and he would not desist preaching.

Once Elizabeth recovered from the trauma of her husband's imprisonment and the loss of her child she began to look for ways to help her husband and obtain his release. Bunyan later wrote that Elizabeth's persistence was like the importunate widow in Jesus' parable (Luke 18:1-8). Though a country girl, she traveled to London and presented a request for his release at the House of Lords. The Lords would not act, telling Elizabeth she needed to present her case to the local judiciary. In August 1661, Elizabeth presented her case before Judge Matthew Hale and three other judges in Bedford. Hale told her he would look into the matter, but didn't think there was anything he could do. Elizabeth was determined to have the case considered; the next day she took the bold move of throwing her petition into the window of the judges' coach as it passed by! On the third day of the assizes, Elizabeth again came before the judges and begged for her husband's release. She pled, 'My Lord, I have four small children that cannot help themselves of which one of them is blind, and have nothing to live upon but the charity of good people.' Judge Hale was sympathetic, especially when he heard that Elizabeth had just lost a child. The other judges, however, were adamant, one even saying that Bunyan's preaching was the doctrine of the devil. Elizabeth replied, 'My lord, when the righteous judge shall appear, it will be known that his doctrine is not the doctrine of the devil.'

When Elizabeth left the assizes in tears she said it was 'not too much because they were so hard-hearted against me and my husband, but to think what a sad account such poor creatures will have to give at the coming of the Lord, when they shall there answer for all things whatsoever they have done, whether it be good or bad.'[46] Bunyan remained in prison ten more years. Elizabeth was allowed to visit him and bring the children. Little blind Mary even learned to find the way to the prison alone, often bringing soup to her father. Bunyan wrote numerous Christian books while in prison, and Elizabeth helped to find publishers for them. His most famous work – *The Pilgrim's Progress*.

... they ought always to pray and not lose heart.

~ LUKE 18:1 ~

46. As quoted in Edith Deen, *Great Women of the Christian Faith* (Uhrichsville, OH: Barbour Books, 1959).

Loyal Wife and Queen

∞ Queen Mary II, 1662-1694 ∞

On November 4, 1677, Mary, eldest daughter of King James II of England, was married to her cousin Prince William of Orange when she was sixteen. It was a political marriage cementing an alliance between England and the Netherlands. Some reports indicate Mary cried throughout the wedding as she was so distressed at marrying William, who was eleven years her senior, rather austere and, to be blunt, not particularly handsome. However, Mary came to love her husband and became noted for her loyalty and submission to him. She saw her marriage to William as important in supporting the Protestant faith in both her native England and the wider Europe.

The first twelve years of her marriage was lived in the Netherlands, where the Dutch people loved Princess Mary for her piety and virtue. Mary had two miscarriages early in her marriage which made her infertile, a source of sadness the remainder of her life.

After the death of her uncle, King Charles II, Mary's father came to the throne in 1685, as King James II of England and Ireland, and VII of Scotland. King Charles had converted to Roman Catholicism on his deathbed, and James brought more Catholic sympathizers into government. James wrote his daughter Mary a lengthy letter encouraging her to convert to Roman Catholicism. Though very respectful to her father, Mary replied at length, answering point by point James' arguments. She ably refuted the absolute authority and infallibility of the Roman Church and wrote of the importance of the Scriptures. Her faith was firm, and she was confident, as the Savior said, the gates of hell would not prevail against his true church.

With James wanting to establish not only Roman Catholicism but also an absolute monarchy within the kingdom, Parliament encouraged Prince William to invade England and depose James, claiming the throne for himself. The Glorious Revolution of 1688 did bring about the change in government; King William and Queen Mary were crowned in 1689.

The English came to love Mary as had the Dutch. Desiring the glory of God and the welfare of her people, Mary used her position to strengthen the Reformation in England. She secured appointments of bishops in the Church of England faithful to the Scriptures. Mary endowed the College of William and Mary in Virginia, hoping it would graduate students who would preach the gospel to the American natives. She also strongly supported Thomas Bray and the SPCK (Society for Promoting Christian Knowledge). On a lighter note, Queen Mary is known for encouraging the style of blue and white porcelain in England and the keeping of goldfish as pets.

Mary contracted smallpox and died in 1694, at the age of thirty-two. At her death, Mary was greatly mourned by the English people, and the poet John Milton wrote:

> When faith and love, which parted from her never,
> Had ripen'd her just soul to dwell with God,
> Meekly she did resign this earthly load
> Of death call'd life, which us from life doth sever.[47]

'I will build my church,
and the gates of hell shall not prevail against it.'

~ MATTHEW 16:18 ~

---

47. James A. Huie, *Records of Female Piety: Comprising sketches of the lives and extracts from the writings of women eminent for religious excellence* (Edinburgh: Oliver & Boyd, 1841), p. 101.

Encouraging the Body of Christ

∞ Anne Dutton, 1692-1765 ∞

When Anne Williams was growing up in Northampton, England her parents instructed her in 'the Doctrines and Worship of the Gospel'. As she grew she wrestled with the fear and guilt of her sinful nature and enjoyed the joy and peace from the grace and forgiveness she found in Christ. Pastor John Skepp especially edified Anne. She carefully wrote down notes from the sermons and her thoughts as she grew in the knowledge of Christ. She came to see writing as a gift God had given her to encourage others in their faith.

Anne married Thomas Cattell in 1715, and the couple moved to London. Four years later, Cattell died suddenly of a stroke. The next year Anne married Benjamin Dutton of Bedfordshire. In 1732, Benjamin became pastor of the Baptist church in Great Gransden, Huntingdonshire, and the church expanded greatly. Anne began writing letters of counsel and encouragement to numerous correspondents, as well as theological tracts, poems and hymns. All of her writings dealt with the journey which was the Christian life and reflected the biblically-rooted spirituality of the Puritans.

Benjamin Dutton went to America to raise funds for a new church building in Gransden and to find a publisher for Anne's *Letters on Spiritual Subjects*. After successfully raising the needed funds, Benjamin sailed for home; but his vessel was shipwrecked on the homeward voyage, and he drowned. Anne surrendered herself to 'Mercy's Ocean', and knew God would use each crisis to conform her more to Christ.

Anne corresponded with leaders of the evangelical revival such as Howell Harris, John Wesley, and George Whitefield as well as ordinary Christians in need of spiritual encouragement and comfort. She comforted them in their faith and strengthened them in their struggle with sin. She wrote that meditation on God's Word, prayer, and watchfulness were important spiritual practices for every Christian. By watchfulness, she meant to watch the first stirrings of sin and 'kill 'em in the *Bud*'. Temptations were not to be dallied with. The Christian must not have a place for sin in the heart, enlarging the room in the soul for God:

> When we would be *something* in ourselves, *separate* from God, we become *nothing* that's *Good*, nothing but *Evil*. When we are willing to be *nothing* in ourselves and *all* in God, we possess *Being*, enjoy the great I AM, and in Him possess our *own Souls*. And the *lower* we sink to nothing in *ourselves*, the *lighter* we rise to Being in God, and the *more* our Holiness and Happiness increases.[48]

Many of Anne's letters and essays were published, and today she is recognized as probably the most influential woman of her day. She used the gift of writing and her knowledge of God's Word to build up and encourage the Body of Christ.

Therefore encourage one another and build one
another up, just as you are doing.

~ 1 THESSALONIANS 5:11 ~

---

48. Anne Dutton, *Some Thoughts about Sin and Holiness*, in *Meditations and Observations upon the Eleventh and Twelfth Verses of the Sixth Chapter of Solomon's Song* (1743), pp. 61-62, as quoted by Michael Sciretti's 'Anne Dutton as Spiritual Director', The Center for Christian Ethics at Baylor University, 2009.

Bringing the Warmth of Christ to a Frozen Land

∽ Ann Egede, 1691 – c. 1734 ∽

At the end of the first millennium A.D., Erik the Red established a Danish settlement on Greenland (his naming the frigid area Greenland was a marketing ploy to attract later settlers). The settlement lasted for several centuries, then it wasted away. In the early eighteenth century, the Christianization of Greenland became a burden and concern for Rev. Hans Egede, pastor of the church at Vogen, Norway. He wanted to assemble a team to again bring the gospel to the Inuit on Greenland. Most people, including Hans' wife Ann, thought it was a foolish idea to try to travel in such dangerous waters to an inhospitable land. Yet, Hans deeply felt a call to bring the gospel to the Inuit. Ann, sensing her husband's burden, prayed for God's leading and came to accept Hans' mission. She then cheerfully gave him her unfailing encouragement and support in the work to which God had called him.

For ten years Hans prayed and appealed to enlist support from the government, merchants, and Christian leaders for the Greenland mission. Finally, when all was approved and the day came to say farewell to his congregation, there were many tears. Ann remained calm and cheerful as she prepared to leave behind her family and friends while bringing her four young children into the frozen land. May 1721, the Egedes left Bergen on the ship *Hope*, though many said their mission was hopeless. After enduring seas with heavy storms and dense fog, *Hope*, with two other smaller ships, arrived in Greenland 3 July.

Not only was the environment uninviting, but the language was difficult. At first the Egedes tried to communicate by drawing pictures. Famine was imminent, and Ann was able to provide medical care to some of those in need. After ten months all the Danes and Norwegians who had accompanied the Egedes, hoping to establish trade decided to return to Denmark. Should the Egedes return too? Hans resolved to return to protect Ann and the children from further hardship, but Ann said, 'No.' They should remain in Greenland and not neglect the charge they had prayed for for so long. A month after the merchants left a supply ship from the King of Denmark came to sustain their little settlement.

The Egedes endured many difficulties in Greenland. The winters were unbearably cold. The Inuit were critical and mocking to the truth of the gospel. Yet, Hans and Ann persevered in their calling. Hans began a Greenland grammar and translated portions of the Gospels. He traveled among the many settlements, leaving Ann often alone to care for the children. Yet she never complained. She loved her husband, loved God, and maintained a cheerful spirit under trying circumstances. Slowly the gospel began to penetrate the darkness.

In 1733, a smallpox epidemic killed two or three thousand of the natives over a period of eight months. Hans and Ann and their now older children helped provide medicine and prepare the people spiritually for death. One man, once a staunch critic, told Hans, 'You have done for us what our own people would not do. When we hungered, you have fed us. You have buried our dead. You have told us of a better life.'[49] After caring for many, Ann herself succumbed to illness. On her deathbed, as in life, she encouraged her children and husband to trust and find their comfort in God.

A glad heart makes a cheerful face,
but by sorrow of heart the spirit is crushed.

~ PROVERBS 15:13 ~

---

49. Lydia Howard Sigourney, *Great and Good Women* (Edinburgh, n.d.), p. 91.

Eighteenth Century Manual for Christian Women

∞ Cotton Mather's Ornaments for the Daughters of Zion, 1692 ∞

In 1692, Cotton Mather, the prolific Puritan writer and American pastor, published *Ornaments for the Daughters of Zion*. The book's extensive subtitle expressed the work's aim and purpose: 'The character and happiness of a virtuous woman: in a discourse which directs the female sex how to express the fear of God in every age and state of their life and obtain both temporal and external blessedness.' Mather's book provides a distinctively Puritan reflection on Christian womanhood.

Mather began with a discussion of the character of a virtuous woman, founded in a conviction that there is a God. From the creation she can see the wisdom, power, and goodness of God, and this produces a reverence for God. She recognizes God's providence in preserving all things and working through the discord of the world to accomplish His purposes. She seeks to please God in all things and considers being a servant of God the highest of callings. She 'perfumes' every room of her house with prayer, and she cherishes the Scriptures, sermons, and the attendance at worship.

The longest portion of Mather's work dealt with counsel and advice. Some of the advice could fit either sex: pray constantly that the fear of God be implanted in your soul. Let every action of the day be done in the fear of God, and end the day in communion with God:

> Throughout all the day, interweave a conscience of Duty into all your Motions, all your affairs. Let every meal, every sleep, every visit, and all your domestick business, though it be but the rocking of a cradle, be done with an eye to this, *This is the thing wherein I may perform a Service to God, and expect a Blessing from God: This is what my God would have me to be about.*[50]

Mather also had advice on the importance of proper speech:

> Proverbs 10:20, 'The Tongue of the Just, is as choice Silver.' So your speech ought likewise to be rare, like silver, which is not so common as copper or iron is. Be careful that you don't speak too soon, because you cannot fetch back and eat up, what is uttered; but study to answer. And be careful that you don't speak too much. …[51]

Mather spent some time discussing clothing as well. A woman's fashion shouldn't prejudice her health and should be consistent with modesty. She should not overexpose parts of her body. An old woman shouldn't dress as a young woman. If a woman spent more time on her clothes than she did in praying or working out her own salvation, then the clothes had become a snare to her soul.

The most important thing for a virtuous woman was her faith in Christ. Such a woman maintained the fear of God in every stage and condition of her life. The single woman, the wife, the mother, and the widow each in her own way and station should manifest the fear of the Lord.

Serve the Lord with fear, and rejoice with trembling.

~ PSALM 2:11~

---

50. Cotton Mather, *Ornaments for the Daughters of Zion* (Cambridge: S.G. & B.G., 1692).
51. Ibid.

Reform and Revival

Train up a Child

∽ Susanna Wesley, 1669-1742 ∾

One of the outstanding examples of a Christian mother is Susanna Wesley. Born 20 January, 1669, the youngest of twenty-five children, Susanna was the daughter of Dr Samuel Annesly, a prominent London minister. At the age of twenty she married Samuel Wesley, a Church of England minister. Their marriage went through many difficulties. Susanna bore nineteen children, only nine of whom reached adulthood. One daughter was deformed for life. Samuel considered himself a scholar and poet and accumulated a large debt seeking preferment in the Church. He could be very imperious with Susanna as she worked to keep the home and family together.

In her difficulties, however, Susanna recognized the omnipotent goodness of the Lord working for her spiritual and eternal good. Even with her many household responsibilities and the care of her children and a difficult husband, Susanna always spent an hour a day in private devotions. Six days a week, six hours a day, she devoted to the education of her children, sometimes even writing their textbooks herself. Every school day began and ended with the singing of a psalm and a Scripture reading. Weekly, she had a private, spiritual conversation with each one of her children. Her greatest desire was to be an 'instrument of doing good' to her children.

Growing up under Susanna's methodical instruction and discipline, two of Susanna's sons, John and Charles, became the founders of Methodism. John, along with George Whitefield, was a leader of the Great Awakening which renewed the Christian faith in Britain. Charles wrote numerous hymns, many of which continue to be sung today.

Susanna died July 23, 1742 at the age of 73, surrounded by her children. Charles wrote her epitaph, which began:

> In sure and stedfast hope to rise
> And claim her mansion in the skies,
> A Christian here her flesh laid down,
> The cross exchanging for a crown.

Train up a child in the way he should go;
even when he is old he will not depart from it.

~ PROVERBS 22:6 ~

What Shall I Give to the Lord?

∽ Selina Hastings, Countess of Huntington, 1707-1791 ∾

Lady Selina Shirley was born into privilege on 24 August, 1707, during the reign of Queen Anne. When she was nine Selina was deeply affected by attending the funeral of a playmate, and she began to pray and read her Bible regularly. She prayed that when she married she might marry someone of a serious nature, not consumed with frivolity. On 3 June, 1728, Selina married Theophilus Hastings, 9th Earl of Huntington, thus becoming the Countess of Huntington.

In 1738, when she was thirty-one, Selina suffered a serious illness. During this time she became close to her sister-in-law, Lady Margaret Hastings, who was the wife of Rev. Benjamin Ingham, a Methodist minister. Selina was converted through the ministry of Rev. Ingham and dedicated the rest of her life to God. She became a regular supporter of John and Charles Wesley and George Whitefield, leaders of the Great Awakening in England. The Church of England at the time needed a renewed spiritual life, and Selina worked to encourage revival among all classes of society. She began by reaching out to the aristocracy of which she was a part – holding meetings and inviting Whitefield or other evangelical speakers to present the gospel with power and clarity. She also began Bible studies for women in her community and instructed her servants in the truth of Christ.

Two of Selina's seven children died in a smallpox epidemic in 1743, at the ages of eleven and thirteen. Selina prayed that God would increase her faith and 'animate my heart with zeal for His glory, enlarge my sphere, and make me more faithful in the sphere in which I serve'.[1] In 1746, her husband died, leaving her a wealthy widow, though only thirty-nine. Selina determined to use both her time and money for the Lord's service.

Faced with spiritual deadness in the established church, Selina used a special privilege she had as a Peer of the Realm to establish a chapel in connection with any of her houses. Since she had numerous houses she began to use this privilege and established chapels throughout England as well as providing ministers who would preach the Scriptures. Preachers in the chapels did not have to be ordained in the Church of England, and Selina supported evangelical preachers of many denominations – Methodists, Moravians, Dissenters, and Anglicans. Selina carefully oversaw the chapels, corresponding and meeting with the ministers to encourage them in the gospel work. She wrote one minister, 'The salvation of souls and exalting the praises of our Blessed Lord and Savior has alone [been] the ground of my heart.'[2] She established Treveca College to train evangelical ministers.

Selina gave over £100,000 to Christian work, but she gave of herself as well. When Charles Wesley's wife contracted smallpox, Selina nursed her to health again. She spent time with George Frederick Handel in his last illness and encouraged him in the Lord. She supported Whitefield's Bethesda orphanage in Georgia, and was greatly interested in the missionary work among the native Americans. As she wrote in her last will, 'The grand view and desire of my life has been the good of all mankind.'[3]

Everyone to whom much was given, of him much will be required, and from him to whom they entrusted much, they will demand the more.

~ LUKE 12:48 ~

---

1. Quoted in Edith Deen, *Great Women of the Christian Church* (Uhrichsville, OH: Barbour Books, 1959), p. 152.
2. John R. Tyson, 'Lady Huntington's Reformation', in *Church History* (Vol. 64, No. 4, Dec. 1995), p. 584.
3. *Women of the Christian Church*, p. 156.

APRIL 21

Uncommon Union

∞ Sarah Edwards, 1710-1758 ∞

Jonathan Edwards first met Sarah Pierpont, a beautiful girl with a distinguished Puritan ancestry, when he was twenty, right after his graduation from Yale. Though Sarah was only thirteen, Jonathan was attracted to her joyfulness, sweetness, and occupation with spiritual thoughts. In fact, he wrote a little encomium to her in the front of his Greek grammar:

> They say there is a young lady in [New Haven] who is beloved of that Great Being, who made and rules the world, and that there are certain seasons in which this Great Being, in some way or another invisible, comes to her and fills her mind with exceeding sweet delight, and that she hardly cares for anything except to meditate on him. ...
>
> Therefore, if you present all the world before her, with the richest of its treasures, she disregards it and cares not for it, and is unmindful of any pain or affliction. She has a strange sweetness in her mind, and singular purity in her affections; is most just and conscientious in all her conduct; and you could not persuade her to do anything wrong or sinful if you would give her all the world. ... She is of a wonderful sweetness, calmness and universal benevolence of mind. ...
>
> She will sometimes go about from place to place, singing sweetly and seems to be always full of joy and pleasure; and no one knows for what. She loves to be alone, walking in the fields and groves, and seems to have someone invisible always conversing with her.[4]

Obviously Jonathan was smitten with Sarah! He courted her for four years, and the two were married on 28 July, 1727.

Jonathan was pastor of the Congregational Church in Northampton, Massachusetts and often spent up to thirteen hours a day in his study. He trusted Sarah to manage the household, which came to include three sons and eight daughters, as well as frequent guests and students coming to study with Jonathan. Sarah was industrious and managed affairs efficiently. Jonathan valued Sarah's conversation and religious affections. Sarah often visited him in his study, and daily at four p.m. the two would go for a walk or ride horseback together, when Jonathan could more fully share his studies from the day with her. Nightly, after all had gone to bed, they would pray together. When George Whitefield visited the Edwards, he wrote, 'A sweeter couple I have not yet seen. ... She talked feelingly and solidly of the Things of God and seemed to be such a Help meet for her Husband.' Whitefield began to pray he could have such a wife!

In 1758, when Jonathan accepted the position of President of the new college at Princeton, Sarah stayed behind in Massachusetts preparing for the family's move. Before her arrival, Jonathan fell ill and died on 2 March, 1758, from complications of a smallpox vaccination. Jonathan's last words were, 'Give my kindest love to my dear wife, and tell her that the uncommon union which has so long subsisted between us has been of such a nature as I trust is spiritual and therefore will continue forever.' When the news came to Sarah, she revealed the spiritual depth Jonathan had so valued in her, 'The Lord has done it: He has made me adore his goodness that we had him so long. But my God lives and he has my heart.'[5] Sarah contracted dysentery and died seven months later.

An excellent wife is the crown of her husband,
but she who brings shame is like rottenness in his bones.

~ PROVERBS 12:4 ~

---

4 Elisabeth Dodds, *Marriage to a Difficult Man: The Uncommon Union of Jonathan and Sarah Edwards* (Laurel, MI: Audobon Press, 2001), p. 74.

5. George Marsden, *Jonathan Edwards* (New Haven and London: Yale University Press, 2003), pp. 494-495.

Family Consecrated to Christ

∞ Sarah Edwards, 1710-1758 ∞

Pastor Jonathan Edwards and his wife Sarah had eleven children. That all of them survived to adulthood is a testimony in part to Sarah's wise management of her household. All who visited the Edwards home were impressed with the liveliness of the children as well as their courteousness. Sarah had a way of governing her children without loud or angry words. As Samuel Hopkins, a young minister who lived with the family for a time, wrote:

> She seldom punished them; and in speaking to them, used gentle and pleasant words. If any correction was necessary, she did not administer it in a passion, and when she had occasion to reprove and rebuke, she would do it in few words, without warmth and noise. ... In her directions in matters of importance, she would address herself to the reason of her children, that they might not only know her ... will, but at the same time be convinced of the reasonableness of it. She had need to speak but once; she was cheerfully obeyed: murmuring and answering again were not known among them.
>
> In their manners they were uncommonly respectful to their parents. ... The kind and gentle treatment they received from their mother, while she strictly and punctiliously maintained her parental authority, seemed naturally to ... promote a filial respect and affection, and to lead them to a mild tender treatment of each other. Quarrelling and contention, which too frequently take place among children, were in her family unknown.[6]

Hopkins noted that, 'Her system of discipline was begun at a very early age and it was her rule to resist the first, as well as every subsequent exhibition of temper or disobedience in the child ... wisely reflecting that until a child will obey his parents he can never be brought to obey God.'

Twice daily, in morning and evening, the family, led by Jonathan, read the Scriptures and prayed together. From a very early age the children were given chores appropriate to their abilities, and the entire family worked well together. Sarah and Jonathan were at one in the rearing of the children, and the love they had for each other encouraged the children's love and respect. Jonathan wrote, 'Every family ought to be ... a little church, consecrated to Christ and wholly influenced and governed by His rules. And family education and order are some of the chief means of grace.'[7]

In 1900, a study was made of the more than 1,400 Edwards family descendants. They included thirteen college presidents, sixty-five professors, 100 lawyers and a dean of a law school, thirty judges, sixty physicians and a dean of a medical school, and eighty holders of public office. The latter included three U.S. Senators, mayors of large cities, governors of three states, and a Vice President of the United States. Members of the family wrote 135 books and edited eighteen journals and periodicals. Many were pastors and hundreds became overseas missionaries. Others were leaders in industry and business.

Her children rise up and call her blessed; her husband also, and he praises her: 'Many women have done excellently, but you surpass them all.'

~ PROVERBS 31: 28-29 ~

---

6. Quoted in Elisabeth D. Dodds, *Marriage to a Difficult Man: The Uncommon Union of Jonathan & Sarah Edwards* (Laurel, MS: Audobon Press, 2003), pp. 35-36.

7. Ibid, p. 45.

Singing Psalms in Prison

∞ Marie Durand, c. 1711-1776 ∞

When King Henry IV of France issued the Edict of Nantes in 1598 he hoped to end the wars of religion and over thirty years of civil turmoil. With the Edict the Huguenots, as the French Protestants were known, were given civil and religious liberties. Almost a century later, in 1685, King Louis XIV revoked the Edict of Nantes, again making Protestantism an illegal religion in France. Protestant churches were destroyed, and the Huguenots had to worship in secret. Protestant preachers were executed and others who maintained their faith were imprisoned or sent to the galleys.

Marie Durand was born into a Huguenot family thirty years after the revocation of the Edict of Nantes. In 1719, when Marie was about eight, a neighbor's house was raided during a Protestant worship service and all those in attendance were taken away, including Marie's mother, who was never heard from again. For the next three weeks soldiers occupied the Durand house, where little Marie lived with her father. After the soldiers left Marie's father brought the Bible from its hiding place and continued to educate his little daughter in the Scriptures.

Since he was a preacher, the authorities were especially on the lookout for Marie's brother Pierre. When they couldn't find him, they arrested and imprisoned his father. In 1730, Marie also was arrested and imprisoned in the Tower of Constance in Aigues Mortes, France; she was nineteen. In 1732, her brother Pierre was discovered and hanged.

Though Marie was among the youngest of the imprisoned women she became their spiritual leader. Her faith lightened the darkness of the prison. She was able to obtain a psalter and read it daily to the prisoners. She prayed with the women and led them in the singing of hymns, praising God in their dungeon. Marie also wrote numerous letters to church and government officials appealing for better treatment of the prisoners and restoration of their freedom. At any time Marie could have gained her freedom by renouncing her faith. Marie, however, scratched the word 'Resist' on the prison's stone walls (which can be seen today).

On 26 December, 1767 Prince de Beauveau, the new commandant of the province, visited the notorious Tower of Constance. Moved with compassion for the suffering women, he released the forty prisoners immediately. King Louis XV protested the move, but de Beauveau did not rescind the release. After being a prisoner for thirty-eight years Marie was able to return home. She died ten years later, in 1776.

'Let your light shine before others, so that they may see your good
works and give glory to your Father who is in heaven.'

~ MATTHEW 5:16 ~

Made useful in the World

∞ Sarah Osborn, 1714-1796 ∞

In 1722, when she was eight years old, Sarah Haggar came to New England with her mother, joining her father who had come to America earlier. The Haggars settled in Newport, Rhode Island, which remained Sarah's home throughout her life. When she was eighteen Sarah married Samuel Wheaton, a sailor. The couple had one son, but Samuel died at sea shortly after. Sarah began teaching school in order to support herself and her baby. Nine years later, in 1742, Sarah married Henry Osborn, a widower with three children. Unfortunately, both Henry's health and business soon declined, and her son died when eleven. Sarah kept a school and began boarding students in order to care for her family, all the while thanking God for 'the veins of mercy which I could see running through all my afflictions'.[8]

In 1737, Sarah had come to repentance, saw herself lost without Christ, and by grace accepted him 'upon his own terms'. In the Great Awakening of the 1740s Sarah's faith was reinvigorated by the preaching of George Whitefield and Gilbert Tennent. She organized a Religious Female Society to encourage the women of the First Church of Newport in their spiritual growth. Weekly they met in Sarah's home, where they read the Bible and other religious literature, prayed and conversed about spiritual things. Others began coming to Sarah for her counsel and prayer, so that soon there were meetings at her home every evening. She began scheduling the groups in categories so as to avoid conflicts: Monday was for teenage girls; Tuesday a large number of boys came; Wednesday was the regular Female Society Meeting; Thursday and Saturday afternoons she catechized children; and Friday a number of heads of family met for 'prayers and religious conversation'. On Saturday evening a number of young men met, and a group of slaves met in another room. A group of free blacks, an 'Ethiopian Society' met in her kitchen on Tuesday evenings. Sarah did not find these gatherings in her home burdensome, but refreshing. Some criticized her for taking too much authority for herself, but she said she would readily relinquish any of the meetings if a minister would like to take them over. No one came forward, and Sarah's work continued. Ever since the revival meetings of the 1740s Sarah had a 'longing to be made useful in the world'.

Sarah and her Female Religious Society were influential in encouraging Samuel Hopkins, a student of Jonathan Edwards, and having him installed as pastor in Newport. Hopkins helped Sarah in the publication of devotional works during her lifetime and published her memoirs after her death. At the conclusion of her spiritual autobiography Sarah wrote, 'If a word in these lines ever prove useful to one soul, after my decease, it will be ten thousand times more than I deserve from the hands of a bountiful God: To him alone be all the glory.'[9]

> For God has not destined us for wrath, but to obtain salvation through
> our Lord Jesus Christ, who died for us so that whether we are awake
> or asleep we might live with him. Therefore encourage one another
> and build one another up, just as you are doing.
>
> ~ 1 THESSALONIANS 5:9-11 ~

---

8. Samuel Hopkins, *Memoirs of the Life of Mrs Sarah Osborn, who died at Newport, Rhode Island, on the second day of August 1796, in the eighty third year of her age* (Worcester, MA: Leonard Worcester, 1799), p. 19.

9. Ibid, p. 56.

From Peasant to Countess

∞ Anna Nitschmann, 1715-1760 ∞

In the early fifteenth century John Huss sought to reform the Church in Bohemia and Moravia, lands which are now the Czech Republic. A forerunner of Martin Luther and the Reformation, Huss believed in justification through faith alone, wanted church services in the language of the people, and rejected Roman Catholic doctrines of indulgence and purgatory. Huss was declared a heretic at the Council of Constance in 1415 and burned at the stake. His followers organized as the 'Bohemian Brethren', and a large majority of the people in Bohemia and Moravia became members of this early Protestant group. Opposition arose from the Hapsburg Emperors, war ensued, and the Jesuits took control of the educational system. Brethren either fled across northern Europe or began to operate underground. In 1722, a small group of the illegal Brethren found refuge in Herrnhut, the lands of Count Nicholas Ludwig von Zinzendorf, in eastern Germany.

Among the early refugees to Herrnhut were David Nitschmann and his children Johann and Anna. David and Johann had been imprisoned for their faith in Moravia before they found their way to Herrnhut in 1725. Anna was ten when she came to Herrnhut. Count Zinzendorf had organized the community, separating the sexes and assigning each to a particular group – Little Boys, Little Girls, Older Boys, Older Girls, Single Brothers, Single Sisters, Married Brothers, Married Sisters, Widowers, or Widows. Each group had its own leaders and worship services. When friction and disharmony arose after a couple of years the leaders prayed for harmony, and after a communion service on 13 August, 1727, a spiritual awakening spread among the people. At that time twelve-year-old Anna Nitschmann dedicated her life to the Lord's service and began organizing the ministry for Single Sisters. Two years later Anna was chosen by lot, as was the custom among the Brethren, to be chief eldress of all the women at Herrnhut. At fourteen she became leader of the Moravian women!

The Moravians sent out the first Protestant missionaries, and Anna became part of the 'Pilgrim congregation' to carry the message of Christ anywhere. She traveled to many foreign lands, including America, where she helped found Bethlehem and Nazareth, Pennsylvania. Anna was offered marriage twice, but refused. However, a year after Count Zinzendorf's wife died, he asked Anna to marry him, and she agreed. They were married in 1757, a nobleman and a commoner united together in Christ.

Only let each person lead the life that the Lord has assigned to him,
and to which God has called him.

~ I CORINTHIANS 7:17 ~

England's First Woman Hymnwriter

∞ Anne Steele, 1717-1778 ∞

Anne Steele lived a very quiet life. Born in Broughton, Hampshire in 1717, she lived in the village her entire life. Suffering from frequent illness, she had a very imaginative, soaring soul in a very weak body. Her mother died when she was three, but Anne remained very close to her father. Mr Steele, a Baptist minister in Broughton, early recognized Anne's gift for writing poetry. When, in 1757, Anne sent some of her poems to London to be published, Mr Steele wrote in his diary:

> I entreat a gracious God, who enabled and stirred her up to such a work, to direct her in it, and to bless it for the good and comfort of many. I pray God to make it useful, and to keep her humble.

Later, when some of Anne's poems were printed, Mr Steele again confided to his diary:

> I earnestly desire the blessing of God upon that work, that it may be made very useful. I can admire the gifts that others are blessed with, and praise God for his distinguishing favours to our family. I have now been reading our daughter's printed books, which I have earnestly desired might be accompanied with the divine Spirit in the perusing.[10]

Anne was reluctant to have her name published, so her poems were published under the name 'Theodosia', meaning 'God's gift' in Greek. She donated all the profits from her publications to charity. Three themes could be found throughout Anne's poems: the creation revealing the glory of God, faith and comfort in suffering, and the promised hope of eternal glory in Christ. Her hymns were very popular in the nineteenth century and could be found in many hymnals. When an Episcopal church in Boston published its own hymnal in 1808, fifty-nine of the 152 hymns were by Anne Steele. She has been recognized as the first woman writer whose hymns were widely used in hymn-books and the greatest Baptist hymn-writer.

Anne's poems reflect her own spiritual struggles and physical sufferings mixed with faith in her Savior's grace and mercy, as seen in the following:

When sins and fears prevailing rise,
And fainting hope almost expires,
Jesus, to thee I lift mine eyes,
To thee I breathe my soul's desires.

Art thou not mine, my living Lord?
And can my hope, my comfort, die,
Fixed on thine everlasting word –
The word that built the earth and sky?

If my immortal Saviour lives,
Then my immortal life is sure;
His word a firm foundation gives –
Here let me build and rest secure.

Here let my faith unshaken dwell,
Immovable the promise stands;
Nor all the powers of earth or hell
Can e'er dissolve the sacred bands.

Here, O my soul, thy trust repose:
If Jesus is for ever mine,
Not death itself, that last of foes,
Shall break a union so divine.

Behold, God is my salvation; I will trust, and will not be afraid;
for the LORD GOD is my strength and my song, and he has become my salvation.

~ ISAIAH 12:2 ~

---

10. Emma Raymond Pitman, *Lady Hymn Writers* (T. Nelson and sons, 1892), p. 70.

From a Slave to Freedom in Christ

∽ Rebekka Protten, 1718-1780 ∽

Rebekka was born about 1718 on the Caribbean island of Antigua to a white father and an African, slave mother. When she was about seven she was kidnapped and sold to Lucas van Beverhout, a Dutch planter on the island of St Thomas. Beverhout placed Rebecca as a servant in his house. The Beverhouts taught Rebekka about Christianity; they also taught her to read, and she read the Bible with eagerness. Rebekka wanted to be a Christian, but neither the Dutch Reformed nor the Lutheran Church on St Thomas would allow people of color in their congregations. When a Roman Catholic priest visited the island, Rebekka implored him to baptize her. It was then she was given the name 'Rebekka'. When Rebekka was about fifteen, Adam Beverhout, Lucas's son, gave Rebekka her freedom, though she continued to work for the family.

Moravian missionaries came to work among the slaves of St Thomas in 1732; Friedrich Martin joined the mission four years later. Rebekka responded to the gospel preaching and the spiritual equality the Moravians so clearly believed in. She became an evangelist herself, walking among the sugar fields and preaching the gospel to the slaves there. She was largely instrumental in the foundation of the first black Protestant church in the Americas on St Thomas in 1737.

In 1738, Rebekka married Matthäus Freundlich, one of the German Moravian missionaries. Friedrich Martin conducted the ceremony. The Dutch authorities did not like the social equality preached by the Moravians, fearing it would stir up a slave rebellion. There was also great dislike for interracial marriage, though there was no law against it. One pastor brought charges that Martin was not properly licensed to conduct the marriage, contending Rebekka and Matthäus were not legally married at all. Friedrich Martin, Matthäus, and Rebekka were jailed.

In January 1739, Count Ludwig von Zinzendorf, leader of the Moravian movement in Europe, arrived on St Thomas with additional missionaries. He used his influence with the governor of the island to have Rebekka and the two other missionaries freed. Zinzendorf encouraged Rebekka and her husband to become missionaries to the Gold Coast of Africa. The couple returned to Germany with Zinzendorf for further training. In Germany Rebekka also was a Bible teacher among the Moravian women. However, before the Freundlichs left for Africa, Matthäus died. Zinzendorf then encouraged Rebekka's marriage to Christian Protten, an African. The two were married in 1746 and went to Christiansborg on the Gold Coast. There they established a school for African children. Though born a slave, Rebekka had been set free. She used her freedom to bring others to the true freedom which can only be found in Jesus Christ.

For freedom Christ has set us free; stand firm therefore,
and do not submit again to a yoke of slavery.

~ GALATIANS 5:1 ~

Youth is Like a Flower

⊙ Jerusha Edwards, 1730-1748 ⊙

New England pastor Jonathan Edwards wrote a friend in Scotland that his second daughter, Jerusha, was 'generally esteemed the flower of the family'. Born 26 April, 1730, Jerusha could claim a rich Puritan heritage; both of her grandfathers were ministers, as was her father. When Jerusha was ten English evangelist George Whitefield stayed for a time with the Edwards in Northampton, Massachusetts. Whitefield's preaching brought revival to the Northampton community, and Edwards asked Whitefield if he would also particularly speak to his children about faith in Christ. Jerusha's conversion came through the influence of these conversations with Whitefield.

Young men were frequently in the Edwards home, coming to learn from Jonathan and train for the ministry under him. Samuel Hopkins was one future pastor who also tutored the Edwards' children while learning from their father. In 1743, Hopkins presented Jerusha with her own Bible. He must have noticed the thirteen-year-old's spiritual sensitivities to present such a gift to her. Some years later, in May 1747, David Brainerd, another young minister, came to the Edwards' home. Brainerd was a missionary who had a fruitful ministry among the Delaware Indians in New Jersey but was suffering from consumption. Jerusha cared for Brainerd during his stay at the Edwards, and accompanied him to Boston and back on a trip for his health. Jerusha and Brainerd developed a close attachment, sharing the same spiritual interests and hearts eager to serve Christ. One Sunday in October, as Brainerd weakened, he told Jerusha, 'Dear Jerusha, are you willing to part with me? I am quite willing to part with you: I am willing to part with all my friends. … I have committed … all my friends to God, and can leave them with God. Though, if I thought I should not see you and be happy with you in another world, I could not bear to part with you. But we shall spend an happy eternity together.'[11] Five days later, David Brainerd died.

Jerusha followed him in death four months later. After suffering five days with an acute fever, she breathed her last on 14 February, 1748; in two months she would have turned eighteen.

Her father preached her funeral sermon from Job 14:2: youth is 'like a flower that is cut down'. The flower cut down as a 'fit emblem of a young person in the bloom of life, with amiable, pleasant, and promising qualifications, not only with a blooming body but mind also; with desirable natural and moral endowments.' Jerusha was 'very indifferent about all things whatever of a worldly nature' and set her heart on another world. Both her words and deeds showed she was 'ever more ready to deny herself, earnestly inquiring in every affair which way she could most glorify God'. Edwards took comfort that she had set her love in Christ. He buried her next to the grave of David Brainerd.

Remember also your Creator in the days of your youth ….

~ ECCLESIASTES 12:1 ~

---

11. George Marsden, *Jonathan Edwards* (Yale University Press, 2003), p. 326.

Providence's Special Gift

⊂∞ Mary Catlett Newton, 1729-1790 ∞⊃

When John Newton and Mary Catlett were infants, their mothers were best friends and talked about their children growing up to marry each other. John's mother died when he was seven. His father remarried, and the Newtons and Catletts moved apart. John's father was a sea captain, and from the time John was eleven, his father was taking him to sea. When he was seventeen, John's father arranged for him to go to Jamaica and help manage a plantation there. Before he left, the Catletts invited John for a visit. He hadn't seen them since his mother's death and decided to visit them. When seventeen-year-old John laid eyes on fourteen-year-old Mary, he lost his heart. In fact, he overstayed his visit and missed his ship for Jamaica!

John's affection for Mary never lessened to any degree. When he became rebellious, a scoffer at all things Christian and swore worse than all the sailors, the one element of purity in his life was his affection for Mary. John found work on a ship involved in the African slave trade and lived for a time on the African coast, demoralized and often despairing of life itself. He knew he was unworthy of Mary, but thinking of her gave him hope. On 21 March, 1748, during a fierce storm at sea, when all despaired of life, John sought the Lord in prayer and was 'delivered out of deep waters'. When he reached England he sent a marriage proposal to Mary. Her reply was cautious, but that it was not a refusal made John's spirit soar. John later wrote Mary, 'Then, my dearest Mary, on that very day, I began to live indeed, and to act, in all my concerns, with a spirit and firmness to which I before was a stranger.'[12] John began to grow as a Christian, spending time in prayer and Bible study on his next voyage.

John Newton and Mary Catlett were married 1 February, 1750. John continued for a time in the slave trade, but he was called upon occasionally to preach or give his testimony of Christ transforming his life. In 1764, he became pastor of the church in Olney and began the rise to one of the leading evangelical preachers in England. Today he is most often remembered as the author of the hymn 'Amazing Grace' and a leading abolitionist.

John always considered Mary a special gift from providence. He considered their marriage 'as a talent to be improved to higher ends, to the promoting his will and service upon earth, and to the assisting each other to prepare for an eternal state'.[13] Newton wrote Mary that every prayer of his included gratitude to the Lord for their marriage:

> Your affection, and its consequences, are continually upon my mind, and I feel you in almost every thought. ... I trust the Lord had a further design than our accommodation in the present life, in bringing us together, even that we might be joint witnesses and partakers of his grace, and fellow-heirs of his salvation. Our earthly connection must cease but an eternal union in happiness, is an important prospect indeed![14]

John and Mary were married almost forty years. When Mary died in 1790, John said he was thankful she was spared to him so long. He considered her as a loan from God, who had a right to take her again whenever He pleased.

Have you not read that he who created man from the beginning created them male and female, and said, 'Therefore a man shall leave his father and his mother and hold fast to his wife, and the two shall become one flesh'?
~ MATTHEW 19:4-5 ~

---

12. John Newton, *Letters to a Wife* (Philadelphia: William Young, 1797), letter of September 2, 1750.

13. Ibid, February 6, 1754.

14. Ibid, May 5, 1768.

Promoting Christian Education for Children

∞ Sarah Trimmer, 1741-1810 ∞

Though largely forgotten today, Sarah Trimmer was tremendously important in developing Christian literature and educational material for children as well as adults. She was the author of at least forty books, many continuing in print decades after her death. Sarah was raised in a godly family. Her father, Joshua Kirby, was an artist and tutor in perspective to the Prince of Wales, later King George III.

In 1762, Sarah married James Trimmer. The Trimmers had twelve children, eleven of whom survived infancy, and Sarah was responsible for their education. It was while educating her own children that Sarah began writing textbooks and stories for children. Her first book, printed in 1780, was *An Easy Introduction to the Knowledge of Nature, and Reading the Holy Scriptures, Adapted to the Capacities of Children* (eighteenth-century books had very expansive titles!). In it Sarah surveyed the natural world as a means 'to open the mind by gradual steps to the knowledge of the SUPREME BEING, preparatory to their reading the holy scriptures'.[15] In the book, a mother and her son take a series of nature walks and gain a growing awe at the nature the Creator has made.

Being an artist's daughter, Sarah always had an appreciation for pictures in teaching young children. She developed a series of prints of Scripture history which were sold in book form or separate prints for a child's room. The prints included descriptions providing instruction on the illustrations. The series included sets of prints on ancient history, Roman history, English history, the New Testament, and the Old Testament.

Sarah's most popular work, first published in 1786, was *Fabulous Histories* or *The Story of the Robins*. This story of a robin family and a human family learning to live together continued in print until the beginning of the twentieth century. In the story, both the children and baby robins are encouraged to seek virtue and shun vice.

Sarah was also active in the beginning of the Sunday School movement for poor children, founding the first Sunday School in Old Brentford in 1786. She also established charity schools for the poor, which met during the week. She took great joy in the opportunity to educate the children in Christian truth and wrote a course teaching the children the principles of the Christian faith from Scriptures. Her work among the poor was so successful that Queen Charlotte asked for a meeting with Sarah to learn how to establish poor schools at Windsor. This led to Sarah writing *The Economy of Charity*, laying out her educational program. Many of Sarah's books were published by the Society for the Promotion of Christian Knowledge and were used throughout the British Empire to provide children with a Christian education, foundational to all of life.

> *We will not hide them from their children, but tell to the*
> *coming generation the glorious deeds of the LORD, and his*
> *might, and the wonders that he has done.*
>
> ~ PSALM 78:4 ~

---

15. Sarah Trimmer, *An Easy Introduction to the Knowledge of Nature and Reading the Holy Scriptures. Adapted to the Capacities of Children* (London: Longman and O. Rees, 1799), pp. v-vi.

Alone' yet Not Alone'

∞ Regina Leininger, c. 1745 – ? ∞

Sebastian Leininger, his wife Regina, and their four younger children left their home in Wurttemberg, Germany, boarding the ship *Patience* on 18 June, 1748, and arriving in Philadelphia on 16 September, 1748. They purchased land in Berks County, Pennsylvania, in the valley of the Susquehanna River, where they established their farm. Devout Lutherans, Sebastian daily read the Bible with his family and led them in prayers and singing the beloved German hymns.

When the family awoke on 16 October, 1755, they in no way foresaw how their lives were to be torn by tragedy. After morning prayers, the mother with baby Christian left for the mill to grind flour; ten-year-old Regina and twelve-year-old Barbara cleaned up the cabin, while Sebastian and oldest son Johannes Conrad prepared to work in the fields. Hearing the growl of their dog, the Leiningers opened the door to discover Delaware Indians on the warpath approaching the cabin. The dog was tomahawked and killed, as were Sebastian and Johannes; Regina and Barbara were taken away captive. When mother returned from the mill with baby Christian, she found her house and cattle burned, father and son killed, and her two daughters missing.

Regina and Barbara were separated and taken away by different Indian parties, but a little two-year-old captive was placed on Regina's back for her to carry through the woods. The bushes tore their clothing to tatters, and the captives walked until their feet were torn and painful. When they reached the village Regina was given as a slave to a cruel woman who had her gather all the wood for winter. She was given no clothes and was always hungry, forcing her to catch anything to eat, including rats and mice. In this wretched life, Regina remembered the prayers and passages from Scripture and the hymns she had learned at home:

> These divine truths began to uncoil in her soul, as a seed germinates in the ground and puts down roots and pushes upward when the earth is warmed by the sun. The Word of God she had learned by heart now transformed itself into sap, yea, spirit and life, and gave peace and rest and comfort to her heart in the midst of affliction. The wretched mode of life was an excellent bridle to curb the sinful flesh and its leaping passions, and thus the Word of our highly exalted Redeemer, that had been implanted in her when she was young, was all the more able to become spirit and life in the inner man.[16]

Regina and the younger child with her often prayed together under the trees, and Regina felt assured she would be restored to her people.

Barbara managed to escape her captors and made her way to Philadelphia in 1759. Regina was captive for nine years until the French and Indian War ended in 1763, and Britain controlled all the territory of western Pennsylvania. The hundreds of captives were brought together and their families encouraged to come and meet them. Regina was now nineteen, and her mother did not at all recognize her among the captives. However, when Mother Regina began singing the old German hymn 'Alone Yet not Alone', Regina ran to her, and mother and daughter were reunited:

Alone, yet not alone am I,	He comes the weary hours to cheer,
Though in this wilderness so drear;	I am with him, and he with me;
I feel my Saviour always nigh, –	Even here alone I cannot be.

'I will not leave you as orphans; I will come to you. Yet a little while and the world will see me no more, but you will see me. Because I live, you also will live.'
~ JOHN 14:18-19 ~

---

16. From the *Journals of Rev. Henry Melchior Muhlenberg*, February 1765, as quoted in Irene Reed, ed., *Berks County Women in History Profiles*, vol. 1, pp. 171-172. Mother and Daughter Leininger came and visited Rev. Mulhlenberg on 27 February, 1765, and he wrote a detailed account of Regina's story in his journal.

Redeemed and Living for God's Glory

∞ Willielma Campbell, 1741-1786 ∞

By education, background, and temperament, Willielma Campbell was well suited to the fashionable life which was to be hers when she married John viscount of Glenorchy in 1761. In the first years of their marriage they toured throughout Europe and spent two years in Italy. She loved the balls and amusements of the nobility and vivaciously entered into every gaiety. The Glenorchy estate of Great Sugnal was not far from Hawkstone, seat of Sir Richard Hill and his family. Willielma admired the Hills for their piety and became friends with Caroline Hill. She wanted to be religious as the Hills were, but did not want to give up her worldly amusements.

In the summer of 1765, Willielma contracted a violent fever which appeared to be fatal. She described her thoughts as she faced death:

> During the course of the fever, the first question of the Assembly's catechism was brought to my mind, 'What is the chief end of man?' as if some one had asked it. When I considered the answer to it – 'To glorify God and to enjoy him, for ever,' – I was struck with shame and confusion. I found I had never sought to glorify God in my life, nor had any idea of what was meant by enjoying him forever.[17]

Caroline Hill congratulated Willielma on the discovery of her sinful nature and directed her to Jesus as Savior. Willielma began searching the Scriptures, committed her soul to God and prayed to be taught the true way of salvation. She opened her Bible to Romans 3 and she saw our sinful nature and the way of redemption through Jesus' sacrifice:

> The eyes of my understanding were opened, and I saw wisdom and beauty in the way of salvation by a crucified Redeemer. I saw that God could be just, and justify the ungodly. The Lord Jesus now appeared to me as the city of refuge, and I was glad to flee to him as my only hope.[18]

Willielma grew in her Christian faith. Much as the Countess of Huntingdon, she became a patroness of evangelical work in Scotland, establishing numerous ecumenical chapels where Presbyterian, Methodist, and Anglican ministers all preached. She also donated large amounts of funds to the Scottish SPCK (Society for the Promoting of Christian Knowledge) and funded the education of ministers. One birthday she prayed:

> I now beseech thee, O Lord, to accept of my soul, body, reputation, property, and influence, and every thing that is called mine, and do with them whatever seemeth good in thy sight. I desire neither ease, health, nor prosperity, any further than may be useful to thy glory. Let thy blessed will be done in me, and by me, from this day forth. O let me begin this day to live wholly to thee! Let thy grace be sufficient for me, and enable me to overcome the world. And to thee be ascribed the honour and glory, now and for evermore.[19]

For ... all have sinned and fall short of the glory of God,
and are justified by his grace as a gift,
through the redemption that is in Christ Jesus ...

~ ROMANS 3:23-24 ~

---

17. *Records of Female Piety*, p. 188.
18. Ibid, p. 189.
19. Ibid, p. 198.

First African-American Female Poet

⫷ Phillis Wheatley, 1753-1784 ⫸

She was about seven or eight when she arrived in Boston from Africa on the ship *Phillis*, 11 July, 1761. Small and frail, the ship's captain didn't think she would live long and was willing to sell her for a pittance. Her front teeth were missing (hence the surmise she was seven or eight), and her meager clothing was a piece of dirty carpet. John Wheatley, a prominent Boston tailor, bought the little girl as a servant to help his wife Susanna. Mrs Wheatley named her 'Phillis', after the ship which brought her to America. Because of her frail condition Phillis Wheatley was only required to do light housework. The Wheatley teenagers, Nathaniel and Mary, began teaching her to read and write. The family soon discovered she was quite precocious. Soon she was reading the Bible, as well as Greek and Latin classics in the original languages. The Wheatleys attended the Old South Meeting House, and in 1771, Phillis became a member of the congregation.

Phillis also had a talent for poetry, writing in couplets of iambic pentameter. In 1770, she wrote an elegy upon the death of evangelist George Whitefield which was frequently reprinted in England and America. When Nathaniel Wheatley went to London on business in 1773 Phillis accompanied him, partly for her health and also to seek a publisher for her poems. In London she met with many leading figures, including the Lord Mayor of London and Selina Hastings, the Countess of Huntingdon, who had been a supporter of Whitefield's work in America. The Countess encouraged Phillis's work, and when her poems were published they were dedicated to the Countess of Huntingdon.

Phillis and Nathaniel returned to America, where Phillis eagerly awaited the arrival of her published book, *Poems on various Subjects, Religious and Moral*. Interestingly, the books arrived 29 November, 1773, on the *Dartmouth*, along with 114 chests of East India Company tea which would end up in Boston Harbor, courtesy of the Boston Tea Party, on 16 December. Among the published poems was 'On Being Brought from Africa to America':

> 'Twas mercy brought me from my pagan land,
> Taught my benighted soul to understand
> That there's a God – that there's a Saviour too;
> Once I redemption neither sought nor knew.
> Some view our sable race with scornful eye –
> 'Their colour is a diabolic dye.'
> Remember, Christians, Negroes black as Cain
> May be refined, and join the angelic train.[20]

After the publication of her poems the Wheatleys gave Phillis her freedom, though she continued to live with the Wheatleys until the death of Mr and Mrs Wheatley. She then married John Peters, a free black who was unsuccessful at numerous occupations. They had three children; two died early. When her husband was placed in a debtors' prison, Phillis tried to support herself as a cleaning woman. Her health failed, however, and she died at the age of thirty-one. Her infant son died three and half hours later. Phillis had joined 'the angelic train'.

There is neither Jew nor Greek, there is neither slave nor free, there is no
male and female, for you are all one in Christ Jesus. And if you are Christ's,
then you are Abraham's offspring, heirs according to promise.

GALATIANS 3:28 29

---

20. *Memoir and Poems of Phillis Wheatley, a Native African and a Slave* (Boston: George W. Light, 1834), p. 42.

Prayers for 'Deliverance'

∞ Anna Schinz Lavater, 1742-1815 ∞

Rev. Casper Lavater was a leading pastor in Zurich during the second half of the eighteenth century. As a young pastor, he wrote a friend describing the kind of person he sought as an ideal wife:

> She must have a good heart, for of the most importance is her moral character. She must, therefore, be mild, quiet and modest. She need not be beautiful, if she is only pleasant, healthful, neat and gentle. She must understand well domestic management, although it is not necessary for her to be learned – a pedant I detest. She must be teachable, compliant and determined to assist and not to hinder me in my official duties. She must aid me in my labors in visiting the sick.[21]

Casper found such a wife in Anna Schinz, whom he married at Zurich on 3 June, 1766. From a child Anna had a sensitive conscience to the things of God. Her brother built her a little house in the garden where she regularly spent time in Bible reading and prayer. She delighted in bringing food and happiness to a disabled neighbor.

In addition to being an assistant pastor in Zurich, Rev. Lavater's position included being pastor of the Orphan House and prisoners. Anna ably helped her husband in caring for the orphans. During a two-year period of famine Anna always had soup on the fire for the poor who frequently came to the parsonage for alms and sustenance. The companionship and oneness of soul between Anna and her husband in the Lord's service was exemplary.

Rev. Lavater often had consumptive symptoms and was in ill health, but Anna nursed and cared for him to regain his strength. One time when Rev. Lavater was visiting friends in Richterswil on Lake Zurich, he wrote Anna that he was enjoying perfect health. The next day, however, Anna had an overwhelming anxiety for her husband. She shared her anxiety with her father-in-law, who told her there was nothing to be concerned about; her husband had just written he was in perfect health. Nevertheless, Anna's anxiety persisted when she returned home. She fell on her knees weeping and in prayer for her husband. It was exactly at that time that Rev. Lavater was crossing Lake Zurich in a boat when suddenly the calm waters were convulsed by hurricane-force winds, the mast of the boat was shattered, and the boatmen all feared they were going down. As Lavater knelt on the boat in prayer, he thought death was imminent. He thought of his wife and children and prayed for God to deliver the boat from the fearful storm. He was praying in the boat the same time Anna was praying in Zurich. The Lord answered their prayers, and Anna was able to welcome her husband home to Zurich with great joy.

> *'And whatever you ask in prayer, you will receive, if you have faith.'*
>
> ~ MATTHEW 21:22 ~

---

21. James Isaac Good, *Women of the Reformed Church* (Sunday School Board of the Reformed Church in the United States, 1901), p. 255.

Conversion Story

∞ Rose Binney Salter, c. 1744-1822 ∞

Jonathan Edwards, a leading theologian and preacher during the Great Awakening, owned as many as six African slaves. Among them was Rose.

Rose had several children but they, one by one, were taken ill and died. She was deeply afflicted by the loss and Pastor Stephen West, who had succeeded Edwards at the church in Stockbridge, visited her. She soon asked Pastor West if she could be baptized. After conversing with her, Pastor West concluded her motives were not to join the church in faith, but to try to earn God's favor and heal what she thought was His anger against her. Rose admitted that was true. Pastor West told her that baptism was not just a ceremony to get right with God, but was a ceremony to show the heart was given to God, who freely gave His mercy and favor.

Some time later Rose thanked Pastor West and expressed her conviction of her own sinfulness. Yet she was agitated without the peace of Christ which comes from His forgiveness. One day, however, when Pastor West visited Rose, he immediately saw a peaceful countenance and a pleasant smile and knew there had been an alteration in her heart and mind. Rose described the dejection and sense of sinfulness which oppressed her, to the point that she was afraid to go to sleep, thinking she would wake up in hell. She tried to pray, but couldn't say a word. She went out to milk her cow, and when she leaned down, the sun shone in the pail as she had never seen it before. The trees had a beauty she had never noticed, and it seemed as if God was everywhere.

Rose made a public profession of her faith in Christ and joined the Stockbridge church in 1771. All could see the change in Rose's countenance, and Rose herself rejoiced to see the growth in the church which came from the outpouring of the Holy Spirit on the town.

Soon after, Rose became ill. Pastor West told her she might get better, or perhaps it was her time to die. What did she think about dying? Rose replied,

> If I do get well, I hope I shall be *content*; but I had set my mind tudder way. I tink if I cou'd do any good in de world, I be quite willing get well. But such poor creature as I can't do any good 'tall, in de world. But God know what best: if it be God's will I get well again, I hope I be *content*.

Pastor West concluded his account:

> In this calm and happy frame of mind I left her. This was the last conversation I ever had with her; for on the night following she expired and, as I trust, through the merits of that divine Redeemer, whose power and grace had been so remarkably displayed upon her, was received into the arms of everlasting mercy.[22]

It is my eager expectation and hope that I will not be at all ashamed,
but that with full courage now as always Christ will be honored in my body,
whether by life or by death.

~ PHILIPPIANS 1:20 ~

---

22. Stephen West, 'Conversion of an African Woman' (*The Theological Magazine, or Synopsis of Modern Religious Sentiment*, January-February 1797), pp. 191-195.

German Woman from Ireland Sparks Churches in America

⧜ Barbara Heck, 1734-1804 ⧜

When Barbara's son Samuel came into the room on 17 August, 1804 he found his mother's body in her chair, with her German Bible on her lap. At the age of seventy Barbara had gone to be with the Lord to whom she had committed her life over fifty years before.

Barbara Ruckle's parents were 'Irish Palatines', German Protestants who had fled persecution in Germany and found refuge in Ireland under Queen Anne; there Barbara was born in 1734. The Germans in Ireland were industrious farmers, but as they began to prosper, resentment against them grew. They were heavily taxed and rents were raised on their farms.

John Wesley visited Ireland some twenty times and, able to preach in German, had a rich ministry among the Germans there. Barbara became a convert to Methodism, as did Paul Heck. The two were married in 1760, shortly before sailing to New York on the ship *Perry*. New York at the time had a population of 14,000 Dutch, English, German, Spanish, and Afro-Americans. Barbara was astonished at the spiritual laxness of the place and saw the same spirit seeping into many of the relatives who had emigrated with her. She encouraged her cousin Philip Embury, who had been a Methodist lay leader in England, to preach to the people; she would gather the congregation. The first meeting had four people – Barbara, her husband, a laborer, and a black female servant. When the commander of the British forces at Albany, Captain Thomas Webb, came to town, he met with the small group of Methodists and began to preach as well. When the congregation outgrew the home they were meeting in, Barbara designed what became one of the earliest Methodist meeting houses in the New World. At the dedication, Embury preached from Hosea 10:12:

> Sow for yourselves righteousness;
> reap steadfast love;
> break up your fallow ground,
> for it is time to seek the Lord.

By 1768 that meeting house was outgrown and yet another was built.

When the American War for Independence broke out, the Hecks moved to be among loyalists in northern New York and founded a Methodist society in Salem. Barbara and her husband later moved to Augusta, Canada, where they began the earliest Methodist society in Canada. One hundred years after her death, a memorial monument was placed on Barbara's grave which read, 'Barbara Heck put her brave soul against the rugged possibilities of the future and under God brought into existence American and Canadian Methodism, and between these her memory will always form a most hallowed link.'

> *'Blessed are the dead who die in the Lord from now on.'*
> *'Blessed indeed', says the Spirit, 'that they may rest from their*
> *labors, for their deeds follow them!'*
>
> ~ Revelation 14:13 ~

A Benevolent Society

Faithful to the Scriptures

∽ Vehettge Magdalena Tikhule, d. 3 January 1800 ∾

One of the first modern groups to send missionaries to other nations was Count Zinzendorf's community of Moravian Brethren in Germany called Herrnhut. When Zinzendorf heard of the degradation of the Khoi people in South Africa, he asked George Schmidt to go and bring the gospel to them. Schmidt was twenty-seven when he left for South Africa in 1737. Before finding a refuge with Zinzendorf at Herrnhut, he had spent six years of brutal imprisonment for his Christian faith in Moravia.

The Dutch who had settled South Africa despised the Khoi, whom they derisively called Hottentots, and ridiculed Schmidt's missionary efforts among them. Schmidt built a native-style house in what was called the Valley of Baboons, living and farming among the Khoi. He established a school, and soon there were four men, two women, and four children in regular attendance. At a time when many of the Dutch were illiterate, the Khoi were learning to read and write! Every evening Schmidt visited among the Khoi people, teaching them about the Savior and helping them in their work. The Dutch ridiculed and resented Schmidt, and at one time raised an armed group to do away with him and the Khoi people.

In 1742, five years after coming to the Valley of Baboons, Schmidt baptized five Khoi who understood the gospel and had put their faith in Jesus Christ. Among them was Vehettge, who took the baptismal name of Magdalena. Magdalena had been one of the most faithful attendees at school. Her husband was a hunter among the Khoi and had helped Schmidt establish his home among them. The Dutch continued to resist Schmidt's teaching among the Khoi, and in 1744 Schmidt was forced to leave the country.

In the ensuing years Magdalena gathered the people under the pear tree Schmidt had planted near his home and read them the New Testament. The people then prayed together. In 1792, almost fifty years after Schmidt had to leave South Africa, three Moravian missionaries were allowed into the country. They went to the Valley of the Baboons, wondering if there was anyone there who would remember Schmidt or the gospel he had brought to the Khoi. They were amazed when they met an old lady who remembered Schmidt, saying he had given her the name of Magdalena. She brought out the New Testament Schmidt had given her and introduced the missionaries to her daughter and granddaughter. She had taught both to read from that New Testament, and they now read the gospel to the people.

Today the Valley of Baboons is called the Valley of Grace.

> *Oh how I love your law! It is my meditation all the day.*
> *Your commandment makes me wiser than my enemies, for*
> *it is ever with me. I have more understanding than all my*
> *teachers, for your testimonies are my meditation.*
>
> ~ PSALM 119:97-99 ~

Modern Female Education

∽ Hannah More, 1745-1833 ∾

Though born to a schoolmaster near Bristol, England, Hannah More came to enjoy life in the highest levels of British Society, all the while maintaining her Christian faith and morals. Educated by her father and older sisters, Hannah learned to read by the age of four, early learned Latin, and later learned French, Italian, and Spanish. A clever writer and conversationalist, Hannah met several learned men when they visited Bristol and began to move in the social circle of writer Samuel Johnson, painter Sir Joshua Reynolds, actor David Garrick, and statesman Edmund Burke. When in her twenties, she published pastoral plays and poetry which were praised by critics and brought a nice income from their copious sales.

Hannah was engaged to be married to an older man, but he kept postponing the wedding and finally broke off the engagement after three years. The two remained friends, and he bestowed an annuity on Hannah which allowed her to retire to a country home, Cowslip Green, near Bristol, where she could spend much of her time writing. Hannah became friendly with the evangelical Clapham Sect, a group of Anglican social reformers which included William Wilberforce and Zachary Macaulay. She corresponded regularly with Pastor John Newton, and her writings took on a more Christian focus. Hannah wrote a series of moral tracts, publishing three a month between 1795-1797, which were especially aimed at the poor and taught virtues of trust in God, industry, soberness, humility, contentment, and reverence for the British Constitution. The Revolution was in full force in France, and Hannah's works exposed the foolishness of the ideas underlying the Revolution. The British government purchased thousands of copies for distribution.

Hannah and her sisters began a number of Sunday Schools for the poor in their neighborhood, raising money for them and directing them. The schools taught the basics of reading and writing as well as the basics of the Christian faith.

In 1799, Hannah published *Strictures on the Modern System of Female Education*, which went through twenty editions in just a few years. Hannah emphasized the importance of Christian instruction in women's education. She wrote that women owed their elevation in society to Christianity, whose principles exalted the soul as well as the mind. Only Christianity taught the moral laws which were foundational to true and desirable knowledge. Hannah inveighed against a preoccupation with external beauty, noting a true education should prepare a woman for when beauty will inevitably fade. The last three chapters of her work were especially devoted to the importance of Christianity. She showed how an understanding of human nature's corruption, Christ's redemption, and the necessity of a changed heart by divine influence were what produced a truly Christian character.

Hannah's moral and religious writings and the establishment of Sunday Schools greatly contributed to the development of Christian knowledge and literacy in England and America. She also exemplified a Christian caring for her neighbor by contributing vast amounts of money to the poor.

> *Whatever is true, whatever is honourable, whatever is just, whatever is*
> *pure, whatever is lovely, whatever is commendable, if there is any excellence,*
> *if there is anything worthy of praise, think about these things.*

~ PHILIPPIANS 4:8 ~

Providing Education for the Poor

∞ Hannah More's Sunday Schools, from 1801 ∞

When 170 young people showed up for the opening of Hannah More's first Sunday school in Cheddar in 1789, Hannah knew there was nothing she could do for them, but the grace of God could do much. Several of the older youth already had criminal records. Three were the children of a person recently hanged for his crimes. Many were thieves – all were 'ignorant, profane, and vicious beyond belief!'[1] When the clergyman came into the room and saw these dissolute youth kneeling in prayer, he was moved to tears.

Divine grace did work in Hannah's schools, which she operated with the help of her sister. In 1801, Hannah wrote to William Wilberforce, who financially supported her schools, describing some of her methods. The Sunday school, which was an all day affair, was for both basic instruction in reading as well as spiritual development of the poor and uneducated of the region. The day began with prayer and reading from a spiritual tract. Then there was instruction in the Bible. Hannah always began the Bible instruction for new students in the parables, beginning with the three parables in Luke 15. First the literal sense of the parables was explained, then the young people were taught to make practical applications. Once they had some experience in Bible study, a long time was spent on the first three chapters of Genesis, establishing the doctrine of the fall of man. Students read the same passage frequently, so that important texts became fixed in their minds. Hannah wrote Wilberforce she encouraged the young people:

> by little bribes of a penny a chapter to get by heart certain fundamental parts of Scripture – such as the ninth of Isaiah, fifty-third of Isaiah, and fifty-first Psalm – the beatitudes, and, indeed, the whole sermon on the mount – together with the most striking parts of our Saviour's discourses in the Gospel of St. John. It is my grand endeavour to make everything as entertaining as I can, to try to engage their affections; to excite in them the love of God; and particularly to awaken their gratitude to their Redeemer.[2]

When the students became tired, Hannah had them stand up and sing a hymn to refresh themselves.

The Sunday schools were all day affairs, beginning in the morning and ending at five o'clock with a prayer and hymn. Students who came four Sundays without intermission received a penny on the fourth Sunday. Little books and Bibles were given as rewards for those who had learned their lessons. Once a year they were also given an article of clothing – a hat, a pair of shoes, or a shirt. By God's grace, many of the young people in Cheddar became Christians and lived productive lives because of the instruction they received in Hannah's Sunday schools.

The fear of the LORD is instruction in wisdom,
and humility comes before honor.

~ PROVERBS 15:33 ~

---

1. Hannah More in a letter to William Wilberforce, October 14, 1789. Thomas Timpson, *British Female Biography* (London: Aylott and Jones, 1846), p. 171.

2. Ibid, p. 173.

Washington's Mother and Wife

∞ Mary Ball, 1708-1789 and Martha Washington, 1731-1802 ∞

George Washington, often called the 'Father of his Country', played several important roles in the founding of the United States – commander of the Continental Army achieving victory in the War for Independence, President of the Constitutional Convention framing the government for the new country, and first President of the United States of America. All recognized Washington as a gentleman of impeccable Christian character, a character shaped in childhood especially by his mother.

George's father died when he was eleven. On his deathbed, Augustine Washington gave George three books on prayer. As a single mother, Mary Ball Washington educated her five children at home and continued the family practice of regularly reading sermons together as a family – a practice George continued even when President. Among the books Mary Ball used in educating George were *The Sufficiency of a Standing Revelation*, *The Wisdom of God Manifested in the Works of Creation*, and Sir Matthew Hale's *Contemplations, Moral and Divine*. In later life Mary Ball lived near her daughter's family in Fredericksburg, Virginia. She frequently walked to a nearby outcropping of rocks to pray, so that these became known as the Prayer Rocks. When George knew he had been chosen President, he and his wife Martha went to visit his mother and tell her the news. She was ill and weak at the time and didn't think she would live long. When George saw she was ill, his first thought was to decline the Presidency and care for his mother. She, however, told him to fulfill the duty heaven had foreordained for him and go with a Mother's blessing.

Washington had married the widow Martha Custis in 1759. Martha too was a lady of Christian character. Throughout her life, every day after breakfast she spent an hour reading the Scriptures and in thanksgiving and prayer. Visitors often noticed her face especially sweet and peaceful when she came from her devotions. In the evenings, the Washingtons read together a chapter and psalm from the family Bible and knelt in an evening prayer. Martha's maid often sang a hymn in this evening gathering. On Sunday evenings Washington read a sermon to the family. During the War for Independence Martha always went to the encampments during the winter (when there was little fighting) to be near George, establishing a home away from home for him in the army. As the first First Lady of the United States, Martha was a model of kindness and Christian virtue.

> *Women should adorn themselves in respectable apparel,*
> *with modesty and self-control, not with braided hair and*
> *gold or pearls or costly attire, but with what is proper for*
> *women who profess godliness – with good works.*
>
> ~ I TIMOTHY 2:9-10 ~

She Gave All She Had

∞ Sally Thomas, 1769-1813 ∞

The early nineteenth century saw a growing interest in bringing the gospel to the far reaches of the globe. In 1792, the Baptist Missionary Society was formed in England, and the following year William Carey and his family set sail for India. Carey's interest in missions had been aroused by reading accounts of the work of David Brainerd and John Eliot among the Native Americans. In turn, Christians in America were stirred to an interest in foreign missions by Carey's work in India. In the summer of 1806, Samuel Mills and four other Williams College students held a prayer meeting for world missions which led to the establishment of the American Board of Commissioners for Foreign Missions (ABCFM) four years later. In 1812, the ABCFM sent out its first missionaries from the United States to India.

Christians throughout New England became supporters of the foreign mission work and were eager for news from the foreign lands. In Cornish, New Hampshire, the family of Daniel Chase regularly prayed for the missionaries. The pastor of the Cornish Congregational Church, Rev. Joseph Rowell, had great sympathy with the ABCFM; two of his sons later became foreign missionaries. The Chase family was friends with Samuel Mills' cousins and sister and was able to keep up with the news of the missionary work through them.

Sally Thomas, a servant working for the Chase family, was a devout Christian who was thoroughly interested in the gospel work among foreign lands. Sally had come to work for the Chase family in her early twenties and worked for them twenty years until her death in 1813. Sally earned fifty cents a week, out of which she could buy her clothes and personal items. When Sally died in 1813 she had saved $345.83; in her will, she left this to the ABCFM. Hers was the first legacy received by the missionary society which became the largest mission society in America in the nineteenth century. That Sally gave so much when she had so little inspired many others to support Christian missions.

> *Jesus looked up and saw the rich putting their gifts into the offering box, and he saw a poor widow put in two small copper coins. And he said, 'Truly, I tell you, this poor widow has put in more than all of them. For they all contributed out of their abundance, but she out of her poverty put in all she had to live on.'*
>
> ~ LUKE 21:1-4 ~

Transformed into Glory

∽ Mary Chambers Coultart, 1787-1817 ∽

Mary Ann Chambers came to faith in Christ when she was twenty-three. When she later united with an Independent Church near Stourbridge, Massachusetts, she wrote a prayer in her diary:

> O! that his Spirit may lead and guide me, and enable me to glorify him in my daily walk! May I never bring any disgrace upon the Christian name or profession! Hold thou me up, and I shall stand: if thou leave me, I must perish. Guide me, dearest Lord, by thy counsel, and at last receive me to glory. Preserve the church thou hast formed here from hypocrisy; may they all be numbered as thine in the day when thou makest up thy jewels. Make us very useful to each other, and enable us to show forth to an ungodly world whose we are, and whom we serve.[3]

Mary's brother Hiram was preparing for work as a missionary and Mary, who longed to be of some service in missionary work herself, encouraged Hiram in his calling, writing him:

> O! to be employed for and by God in converting the heathen! What an honour! Should you cross the seas to be the instrument of saving one soul, even the hazard of your life, you will be more than repaid for your trouble. Can you hear the poor destitute heathen cry, 'Come, tell us of salvation through Jesus Christ,' and yet be deaf to hear it? Cannot you follow the steps of your Redeemer? He left the abodes of glory for you; for you he suffered more than you possibly can. ... My dear brother, count not then your life dear to you, so that you may win souls to Christ. I do, indeed, love the missionary cause; it is nearer my heart than anything else: my soul seems in the work.[4]

When Mary was introduced to Rev. James Coultart, who was preparing to go to Jamaica in Christian work, Rev. Coultart found in her a perfect companion to his work. They were married 6 February, 1817, and departed for Jamaica the following month. Before leaving England Mary again wrote her brother Hiram:

> Had I ten lives, and those ten laboured indefatigably for twenty years, and were made useful only to one soul, eternity would be too short to praise God for it. Who can know the value of a soul, but a Saviour, who in his human nature sweat drops of blood, caused by the heavy load of guilt he sustained.[5]

The congregation in Jamaica was large, and Mary rejoiced to hear her husband preach the Word of life to a congregation of over a thousand black and brown Jamaicans thirsty for the Word. However, within five months after arriving in Jamaica, Mary fell ill with a fever from which she did not recover. In her last letter to her brother, Mary wrote that she anticipated with real delight the time when she would see Jesus as he is, would no more grieve the Holy Spirit, and would be transformed into his glorious image:

> I do long to live without sin; I think
>   I can say –
> Haste, my Beloved, fetch my soul
>
> Up to thy bless'd abode;
> Fly, for my spirit longs to see
> My Saviour and my God.[6]

Mary breathed her last on 8 October, 1817.

> *And we all, with unveiled face, beholding the glory of the Lord, are being transformed into the same image from one degree of glory to another. For this comes from the Lord who is the Spirit.*
>
> ~ 2 CORINTHIANS 3:18 ~

---

3. Rev. Thomas Timpson, *Memoirs of British Female Missionaries* (London: William Smith, 1841), pp. 8-9.
4. Ibid, p. 10.
5. Ibid, p. 13.
6. Ibid, p. 17.

Beginning of Sunday Schools in the United States

⊗ Isabella and Joanna Graham, 1742-1814 and 1770-1860 ⊗

When Isabella Graham's husband, a British army surgeon, died in America in 1772, Isabella had three daughters under the age of five and was pregnant with a son. Isabella returned to her native Scotland and supported herself by teaching and administering a large boarding school in Edinburgh. John Witherspoon, Isabella's former pastor from Paisley, Scotland who had emigrated to America to become President of the College of New Jersey (later named Princeton University), encouraged Isabella to return to America. In 1789, Isabella moved to New York City, where she established a school for young women. In ensuing years Isabella founded and supported several benevolent societies in New York – the Society for the Relief of Poor Widows with Small Children, the Orphan Asylum Society, the Magdalene Society for the mentally ill, and the Society for the Promotion of Industry among the Poor.

Isabella's second daughter, Joanna, had immigrated to America with her mother and worked with her on many of her benevolent projects. Joanna married Divie Bethune, a Scottish immigrant with an import-export business in New York City. He liberally supported the Christian benevolent works of Isabella and Joanna. On a business trip to England in 1802 the Bethunes learned more about the Sabbath or Sunday schools, first established by Robert Raikes in England in the 1780s. The schools were mainly for the poorer children who were not given an education or spiritual instruction in their homes. Many of the children were factory workers whose only day not working was Sunday.

In 1803, Joanna and Isabella began a Sunday school in New York and encouraged other women to begin similar schools. In 1804, a group of women from various denominations formed a society for the education of poor girls in Philadelphia. The curriculum included reading, writing, sewing, Scripture memorization, hymns, and the catechism.

The clergy were at first opposed to the Sabbath schools. Many were appalled at the idea of lay people, especially women, teaching the Bible. Some thought it was breaking the Sabbath to study or teach on Sunday. Others thought Sabbath schools usurped the rights of parents and churches. Yet, the Sunday school movement grew. When Joanna felt an organization was needed to encourage Sunday schools her husband told her, 'My dear wife, there is no use in waiting for the men; do you gather a few ladies of different denominations and begin the work yourselves.'[7] On 24 January, 1816, Joanna organized in New York a Female Sunday School Union. In six years, there were 600 teachers in the city with about seven thousand students, and thirty graduates were training for the ministry. The next year Joanna was instrumental in establishing the American Sunday School Union.

Isabella Graham and Joanna Bethune were examples of the tremendous influence women can have from their own personal initiative.

Blessed is the one who considers the poor!
In the day of trouble the LORD delivers him.

~ PSALM 41:1 ~

---

7. Nancy Hardesty, *Great Women of Faith* (Nashville: Abingdon, 1980), p. 73.

First Female Missionary Society

∞ Mary Webb, 1779-1861 ∞

Mary Webb was an unlikely candidate to begin a movement which helped spread the gospel around the globe. When she was five Mary had a severe illness which threatened her life. Though she did recover, her legs were paralyzed and she was confined to a wheelchair the remainder of her life. Mary's father died when she was thirteen, leaving the family in poor financial condition. Thomas Baldwin, a neighbor and pastor of Boston's Second Baptist Church, befriended the family, showing special compassion to Mary. Mary came to faith in Christ and was baptized in 1798. Two years later she read a sermon given at the annual meeting of the Massachusetts Missionary Society in Boston by Dr Nathanel Emmons. Emmons' sermon on 2 Chronicles 15:7 (KJV), 'Be ye strong therefore, and let not your hands be weak: for your work shall be rewarded,' called for the spread of the gospel and building up the kingdom of Christ in the world. The sermon spawned in Mary a passion for missions. Convinced that her physical disability was no excuse for inaction, she suggested to Pastor Baldwin a plan for organizing women to support missions.

With Baldwin's approval, on 9 October, 1800, when she was twenty-one, Mary Webb and thirteen other women from the Baptist and Congregational churches organized the Boston Female Society for Missionary Purposes. This was the first women's missionary organization in the United States and the progenitor of numerous other societies throughout the land. With a membership fee of two dollars per year, the women planned to use their funds to purchase Bibles, Testaments, and other religious books for missionaries to use. Mary remained the Secretary-Treasurer of the society for over fifty years, writing thousands of letters of counsel, encouragement, and business to further the cause of missions.

Though confined to a wheelchair, Mary was able to motivate others and organize them for effective work. She later helped organize the Female Cent Society, in which each member contributed one cent a week to missions. In 1811, she helped organize the Corban Society to raise money to educate poor but worthy young ministers. In 1812, she organized the Fragment Society to collect clothing and bedding for needy children. In 1818, she helped establish a refuge for women caught in alcoholism and immorality. When Second Baptist Church began a Sunday school in 1816, Mary became its superintendent. Mary in her wheelchair was a familiar sight in Boston as she ministered to many of the poor and suffering. Though her legs were indeed weak, following the admonition of 2 Chronicles, her hands were strong and worked for the Lord.

But you, take courage!
Do not let your hands be weak, for your work shall be rewarded.

~ 2 CHRONICLES 15:7 ~

Showing the Love of Christ to Prisoners

∽ Sarah Martin, 1791-1843 ∽

Sarah Martin's parents died when she was young, and she was cared for by a loving grandmother. At fourteen, she spent a year learning dressmaking and then earned her living traveling around to families in the village of Caister and also Yarmouth, three miles away. In her work Sarah sometimes passed the prison in Yarmouth, and her heart went out to those confined there. Often she thought how she would like to go and read the Scriptures with the prisoners, knowing only God's Word could alleviate their unhappy condition. In August 1819, a woman was convicted and imprisoned for neglecting and beating her nursing infant. The story of this woman's unhappy sin spurred Sarah to go to the prison and visit her.

Sarah was a quiet, gentle person, and at first could not gain entrance to the prison. With persistence, however, she was able to visit the poor woman, who was very surprised by this stranger's visit. When Sarah told her she had come to share with her God's mercy in Christ, the woman burst into tears. The woman's welcoming of Sarah convinced her that this was a needed ministry among the prisoners. She began going to the prison regularly, reading the Scriptures to the prisoners. She then began teaching them reading and writing. Feeling the blessing of God was on her work, Sarah gave up a day in her dressmaking labors to work among the prisoners.

On her grandmother's death, Sarah had an annual income which helped her establish her residence in Yarmouth and spend more time in the prisons, distributing Bibles, testaments and books of Christian nourishment. As her dressmaking business began to decline with Sarah's growing prison work, Sarah was faced with how she was to sustain herself. Convinced her work with the prisoners was the right thing for her, she trusted God to provide for her, saying,

> I had learned from the Scriptures of truth that I should be supported; God was my master, and would not forsake his servant. He was my father, and could not forget his child. I knew also that it sometimes seemed good in his sight to try the faith and patience of his servants, by bestowing upon them very limited means of support, as in the case of Naomi and Ruth; of the widow of Zarephath and Elijah; and my mind, in the contemplation of such trials, seemed exalted by more than human energy; for I had counted the cost; and my mind was made up. If, whilst imparting truth to others, I became exposed to temporal want, the privation so momentary to an individual, would not admit of comparison with following the Lord, in thus administering to others.[8]

Sarah encouraged the prisoners to organize regular Sunday services, reading the Scriptures to each other. After about three years, she began to develop work programs for the prisoners. She began with the women preparing baby clothes which could be sold, as well as shirts, coats, and other articles. Men began making straw hats and tailoring clothing. Sarah then established a fund for setting up employment for the prisoners after they were discharged.

Men old in age and in crime could be seen to soften under Sarah's gentle influence. Through her, many began learning the Scriptures and had lives transformed through Christ and His Word.

For this reason I remind you to fan into flame the gift of God, which is in you …
for God gave us a spirit not of fear but of power and love and self-control.

~ 2 TIMOTHY 1:6-7 ~

---

8. Sarah Josepha Hale, *Woman's Record: or Sketches of all Distinguished Women, from 'the beginning' until* A.D. *1850* (Sampson Low, Son, and Co., 1853), p. 412.

MAY 16

Light to Her 'People'

∞ Catherine Brown, c. 1800-1823 ∞

In 1816, missionary Cyrus Kingsbury appeared before the Council of the Cherokees and offered to establish a school among them. The Cherokees were agreeable to the proposal, and in the spring of 1817 a school was established at Chick-a-mau-gah, near present day Chattanooga, Tennessee. The missionaries named the mission Brainerd in memory of David Brainerd, the eighteenth-century missionary to the native Americans. When seventeen-year-old Catherine Brown (her English name) heard of the school, she begged her parents to let her attend. Though the school was 100 miles from Catherine's Creek Path community, her parents did allow her to go. Catherine had learned to converse some in English and read monosyllable words, which only whetted her appetite for learning.

When Catherine came to the school she had almost no religious understanding. She thought whites and Cherokees were different races, and that the white people's religion was of no concern for the Cherokees. It was some time before she came to understand that Jesus died for the Cherokees as well as the white people. Catherine was diligent in her studies, and within a few months she was able to read the Bible intelligibly and soon was reading the Scriptures with eagerness and understanding. Catherine desired to know and do the will of God. In December 1817, she trusted the Lord Jesus for her pardon from sin. She began praying with the missionaries and assisting in teaching the younger children in school. She especially prayed for the salvation of her people and her family. On 25 January, 1818, Catherine was baptized; Mr Kingsbury preached the sermon from Galatians 3:28.

Catherine was the first convert to Christ at the mission, and her growth in Christian faith was a great encouragement to the missionaries. Her story and letters were often written and printed in the *Missionary Herald*. In 1820, Catherine accepted a teaching position at a new mission school in the settlement of Creek Path. Her brothers and parents became Christians largely through her influence and prayers. Her brother David attended Andover Seminary and became the first native Cherokee pastor.

When Catherine's brother Jonathan became ill with tuberculosis, Catherine left teaching to care for him. His death brought great sorrow, but Catherine wrote her brother David:

> I hope you will lean on the Saviour, who is able to give the consolation which you need, and recollect we are in the hands of an infinite, wise and good Being, who will order everything for his own glory, and the best good of his children. Since we are the children of a glorious and holy God, may we be submissive to all the dispensations of his Providence, not only in prosperity, but also in adversity, and say, The will of the Lord be done. ... O! may we follow his example, as far as he followed Christ, and live devoted to God; be in constant readiness for our own departure, that we may at last meet our brother around the throne of that blessed Redeemer, who hath brought us from death unto life eternal.[9]

Catherine contracted tuberculosis when caring for Jonathan and joined him before the throne of the Redeemer the following year.

There is neither Jew nor Greek,
there is neither slave nor free, there is no male and female,
for you are all one in Christ Jesus.

~ GALATIANS 3:28 ~

---

9. 'Extract of a Letter from Catherine Brown, to her Brother David' (*The Religious Intelligencer*, Vol. 6, April 1822), pp. 741-742.

Caring for the Poor and Sick

⤷ Eleanor Brennan, 1792-1859 ⤶

Eleanor Brennan's father, a sailor, died at sea before Eleanor was born, and her mother was frail and sickly. Eleanor, or Nelly, as she was called, was always a serious girl. As did many widows in that day, Mrs Brennan bought a mangle, or ringer washing machine, to take in washing for a living. Nelly soon helped her mother in the business. When Mrs Brennan became quite ill, Nellie moved her mother's bed into the washing room so she could both care for her mother and work at earning an income. When Nelly was sixteen her mother died, leaving her an orphan. Nellie was so poor she had to obtain a loan to have the funds to bury her dear mother. Rev. Thomas Howard, Rector at St. George's Church in Douglas, Isle of Man, brought the comfort of the Scripture to Nelly. She came to know Jesus as Savior and consecrated herself to his service. She faithfully attended the daily, early morning worship service at St. George's before diligently working in the laundry business.

When a dreadful cholera epidemic swept through the Isle of Man in 1832, Nellie brought physical and spiritual comfort to many. Others fled the island or were afraid to go into the rooms of the ill and dying, but Nelly was fearless in bringing aid and support to the sufferers. She had yielded her life to her heavenly Father, and she trusted him to do all things well with her. As Nelly cared for the bodies of the suffering, she also cared for their souls, praying with them and bringing them words of life from the Scripture. Rev. Howards noted that:

> There were very few houses I was sent for to visit in which I did not see Nelly sitting by the bed of the sick and the dying, endeavouring to direct them to that blessed Saviour from whom alone they could obtain comfort and salvation. Nothing could be more disinterested, benevolent, or humane than her attention to the sick at that time. ... But her charity was truly Christian charity; it proceeded from pure love to her fellow-creatures. She well knew at the time that she was exposing her own life to the imminent danger; but she rose above every selfish consideration.[10]

Doctors found Nelly very helpful in faithfully carrying out their instructions for the afflicted.

When someone marveled at the work she did, Nelly simply said, 'I use the means for preserving health, and pray to the Lord to keep me in safety; and blessed be his holy name, he has enabled me to go in and out among them poor things thirty-nine years in safety.'[11] However, Nelly did suffer financially during the epidemic. When some of her customers learned she was visiting cholera patients, they no longer gave her their business, for fear of bringing home the contagion in their laundry.

After the epidemic there were many orphans in Douglas who Nelly helped or managed to find care for. All she sought to bring to the Savior. Many others who had survived the epidemic began meeting in Nelly's home for prayer, thanksgiving and praise to the Savior whom she served so faithfully.

'Blessed are the poor in spirit,
for theirs is the kingdom of heaven.'

~ MATTHEW 5:3 ~

---

10. Joseph Johnson, *Noble Women of Our Time* (London: Thomas Nelson and Sons, 1882), p. 253.

11. Ibid, p. 258.

Caring for Those in Prison

⊙ Elizabeth Fry, 1780-1845 ⊙

Elizabeth Fry had heard that conditions inside London's Newgate prison were grim, but she was totally unprepared for the horrible condition she found when she visited the prison in 1813. Three hundred women and their children were in four rooms built to hold half that number. The women were in rags, and babies born in the prison were unclothed and filthy. There was no order, and bullies ran the place. Eating, sleeping, and all living were in the same crowded rooms. Women in prison for petty crimes were in the same room with women convicted of murder. Elizabeth immediately set to work to reform the prison with her own funds and donations. She gathered clothes and supplies for the women and started classes in sewing and knitting to encourage them to be productive. By selling their work, they could buy soap and more food. Elizabeth organized classes so that the more educated prisoners could teach the less educated.

Daily Elizabeth came and read the Bible to the women. She often began with Isaiah 53:6-7 (KJV), 'All we like sheep have gone astray; we have turned everyone to his own way; and the LORD hath laid on him the iniquity of us all ...' Readings from Psalm 24 and 27, in which God sustains the Psalmist's faith, and Psalm 69, a prayer in affliction, were also routinely read. Elizabeth read to the women from Jesus' Sermon on the Mount and the parable of the Vineyard in Matthew 20. All these Scriptures were to cause the women to understand that holiness, justice, and strength were all from God.

Elizabeth clothed her prison work in prayer in and out of the prison:

> O Lord, may I be directed what to do and what to leave undone and then may I humbly trust that a blessing will be with me in my various engagements. ... Enable me, Lord, to feel tenderly and charitably toward all my beloved mortals. Help me to have no soreness or improper feelings towards any. Let me think no evil, bear all things, hope all things, endure all things. Let me walk in all humility and Godly fear before all men, and in Thy sight. Amen.[12]

When John Randolph visited London from America, he thought all the magnificent London sites sank into insignificance compared to seeing Elizabeth Fry at Newgate:

> I have witnessed there, sir, the miraculous effects of true Christianity upon the most depraved of human beings – bad women, sir who are worse, if possible, than the Devil himself. And yet the wretched outcasts have been tamed and subdued by the Christian eloquence of Mrs Fry. Nothing but religion can effect this miracle, sir.[13]

Elizabeth's work went beyond Newgate. She worked with Parliament for a Prison Reform Act, ministered to those about to be deported to Australia, and established a training school for nurses in London. Always she recognized that only by the truths of Scripture was a real reformation of lives possible; only the Scripture could change a human heart.

> *Remember those who are in prison,*
> *as though in prison with them, and those who are mistreated,*
> *since you also are in the body.*
>
> ~ HEBREWS 13:3 ~

---

12. Quoted in Edith Deen, *Great Women of the Christian Faith* (Uhrichsville, OH: Barbour Books, 1959), p. 166.
13. Ibid, p. 166.

America's First Woman Hymn Writer

∞ Phoebe Hinsdale Brown, 1783-1861 ∞

Phoebe never had much of the world's goods or favor. Born Phoebe Hinsdale on 1 May, 1783 in Canaan, New York, she was orphaned at the age of two. Phoebe was at first cared for by a loving grandmother, but was then placed in the care of an older sister and her husband, who was a jailer with a harshness often bestowed on little Phoebe. Phoebe was never allowed to attend school and could not read or write. When she was eighteen she left her sister and found a way to attend school for three months, learning with the much younger students. Though that was the extent of her schooling, she managed to educate herself, especially by reading and studying her Bible.

When she was twenty-two, in 1805, Phoebe married Timothy Brown, a house painter. Timothy worked hard, but the Browns were poor. When they later moved to Ellington, Massachusetts, they at first lived in a small, unfinished house on the edge of the village. Four children had been added to the family, and a sick sister came to live with them as well. At the evening's twilight, Phoebe enjoyed walking in woods near her home which belonged to a large estate. There was seldom anyone there after dark, and there Phoebe felt alone with God and could spend uninterrupted time in prayer, without bothering anyone. The lady of the mansion noticed Phoebe coming every evening and sent a servant to reproach her for coming on the grounds. Phoebe was crushed, and went home in tears. That evening, she wrote, 'My Apology for my Twilight Rambles, addressed to a Lady':

> Yes, when the toilsome day is gone,
> And night with banners gray
> Steal silently the glade along,
> In twilight's soft array –
>
> I love to steal awhile away
> From little ones and care,
> And spend the hours of setting day
> In gratitude and prayer. …
>
> Thus when life's toilsome day is o'er,
> May its departing ray
> Be calm as this impressive hour
> And lead to endless day.

Some years later, the evangelist Dr Asahel Nettleton was preparing a volume of *Village Hymns*, and Phoebe Brown's pastor recommended several of Phoebe's poems for Nettleton. Four of Phoebe's hymns were included in this early hymn collection. 'Go, messenger of love' was a hymn encouraging missions and the spread of the gospel throughout the world. Phoebe prayed that her little son, seven years old when she wrote the hymn, might serve the Lord as a missionary. Her prayer was answered when Samuel Brown became a missionary to China and then the first American missionary to the Japanese. Samuel Brown said that to his mother, 'I owe all I am, and if I have done any good in the world, to her, under God, it was due.'[14]

They ought always to pray and not lose heart.

~ LUKE 18:1 ~

---

14. Hezekiah Butterworth, 'A Country Sunday School' (*Sunday School Times*, June 13, 1889), p. 373.

Wife, Mother, and Hymnwriter

☞ Anna Schlatter, 1773-1826 ☜

Anna Bernet was one of twelve children born into a prominent manufacturing family in St Gall, Switzerland. Her father died when she was seven, and her mother died suddenly the following year. Her Heavenly Father cared for the orphaned girl and drew her to Himself. When she was thirteen, Anna read a sermon which convicted her of her sins, leading her to repentance.

When Hector Schlatter later proposed marriage, Anna was very hesitant and spent much time in prayer about whether or not to accept. Though a respectable citizen, Hector followed a rationalist form of Christianity, placing more faith in his own reason than the Bible. Encouraged by her pastor to accept Hector's proposal, and hoping to lead him to a saving knowledge of Jesus, Anna married Hector on 18 February, 1794. Four days later, on 22 February, Anna said she gave herself entirely, 'with all that I am and have, living and dying' to God:

> And the peace of God higher than all knowledge filled my soul. I was a new creature. Everything appeared to me in a different light. Prayer was my delight, the reading of the Bible my highest pleasure, and the Gospel to me a treasure, whose key I never before had had.[15]

Anna prayed earnestly for the conversion of her husband. When Hector's father died, he began to soften and began to read the Bible. He began to see that his own morality could not save him, and he became a follower of Jesus.

With ten children (not counting the three who died very young), Anna's life was a busy one. In addition to caring for the children she assisted her husband in the shop, made all the clothing, stockings, and bedding for the household, as well as taking care of all the cooking and household chores. During those years she wrote hymns and songs which continue to be found in German hymnals. One, translated into English, was a hymn 'On Awaking':

Now, in thy name, Lord Jesus Christ,
I from my couch arise;
To thee, who omnipresent art,
I lift my hands and eyes.

How much of toil and work and care
Awaiteth me to-day!
Teach me to order everything,
I ask of thee always.

According to thy mind and will,
Though small the work may be,
And, 'mid the crowd, O may mine eye
Be fixed alone on thee. ...

And should the load of cares oppress,
I will in thee abide;
And do thou bid the storm within
My anxious heat subside.

Teach me in all to see thyself,
And only wait on thee;
If at thy word I tread the waves,
And sink, uphold thou me.

Ah, never let me sink, O Lord!
Thou knowest I am thine!
And if my spirit fail today,
Say to me, 'Thou art mine.'[16]

As her children grew, Anna became more active in Bible distribution and established the first Women's Missionary Society in Europe.

Fear not, for I have redeemed you; I have called you by name, you are mine.

~ ISAIAH 43:1 ~

---

15. James I. Good, *Famous Women of the Reformed Church* (Birmingham, AL: Solid Ground Christian Books, 2007, printing of 1901 edition).

16. Emma Raymond Pitman, *Lady Hymn Writers* (London, Edinburgh, and New York: T. Nelson and Sons, 1892), pp. 135-136.

Faithful to the Recurring Duties of Life

∞ Amelia Sieveking, 1794-1859 ∞

When a cholera epidemic swept through Hamburg in 1831, Amelia Sieveking volunteered her help at the infirmary of St Ericus, soon taking over the supervision of the female cholera patients. Amelia was the daughter and grand-daughter of Hamburg senators, and at the time, it was unprecedented for a lady of her station to take on such work. Amelia's mother died when she was five, and her father when she was fifteen, but she was left with an independent inheritance which made her life comfortable. Yet Amelia looked for an occupation that would satisfy her mind and heart:

> I used to dream that I should one day do something great in the eyes of the world, but now that I know it is not in my power to do anything extraordinary, I will try to fulfill with double faithfulness the little, common, daily-recurring duties of life.[17]

When she was nineteen Amelia had begun a school without fees. Besides regular academic instruction, the students knit stockings and made shirts for those fighting in the conflict with France. After the death of her brother Gustave, in 1817, Amelia had a time of soul searching. She read Thomas à Kempis's *The Imitation of Christ*, Francke's *Directions for Reading the Bible* and then immersed herself in the Bible itself. She had a childlike faith and recognized she was an adopted child of God through Jesus Christ.

During the cholera epidemic she called for Christian ladies to come and assist in the infirmary, but no one came. Once the epidemic was over, Amelia organized the Female Association for the care of the Poor and Sick. Through this society Christian ladies were organized to visit the homes of poor invalids and their families, providing material help and spiritual guidance. From twelve original ladies, the organization expanded to fifty-three within ten years and eighty-five by the time of Amelia's death in 1859. Affiliates arose in other German cities. Amelia had shown women of means how to live a life of Christian service to others.

Amelia's work among the poor, sick, and prisoners became renowned, so much so that when the Crown Princess of Denmark visited Hamburg, she sought out Amelia for her advice on caring for discharged prisoners. After the Princess became Queen, Amelia sent her a copy of her book *Conversations on the Holy Scripture*. In her accompanying letter she wrote:

> One mission I believe to be common to all women, whether their station be high or low, though according to the differences of their station it may be very differently carried out. It is the mission of love based on faith, humble and willing to render any service, and which by its gentle magic softens the opposing rudeness of a world agitated by wild passions, ay, and draws down heaven to this poor earth, building a paradise in its own heart, though it may not enjoy one in the outer world.[18]

Let all that you do be done in love.

~ I CORINTHIANS 16:14 ~

---

17. L. A. Holdrich, 'Amelia Sieveking' (*Ladies Repository*, Vol. 25, Issue 3, March 1866), p. 133.
18. Ibid, p. 136.

Cheerful Giver

∞ Emily H. Tubman, 1794-1885 ∞

William Tubman, nineteenth President of the Republic of Liberia, is often recognized as the 'father of modern Liberia' since his presidency brought important economic growth and political stability to the country. Tubman's grandparents were freedmen who settled in Liberia in 1844, largely through the philanthropy of Emily Tubman.

Emily lived a long, rich life. Born in 1794 during the presidency of George Washington, she lived under twenty presidents, dying in 1885 at the age of ninety-one. Her father came to Kentucky shortly after the state entered the Union.

When she was twenty-four Emily traveled with some cousins to Augusta, Georgia, where she met Richard C. Tubman. Tubman, an Englishman, had a southern plantation and made a large fortune through the exportation of cotton, indigo, and tobacco. Emily and Richard were married in 1818, and Emily became a lovely part of Augusta society. When the Marquis de Lafayette, French statesman and friend of Washington, toured the United States, Emily arranged the banquet and celebrations in Augusta in his honor.

But high society was not Emily's passion. A devout Christian and student of the Bible, she used her wealth to support Alexander Campbell's restoration movement, known as the Disciples of Christ. Numerous church buildings throughout Georgia were built with her aid. When her husband died in 1836, his will declared his desire that all the slaves be freed. Since Georgia had strict laws against freed slaves living within the state, Emily found the best way to provide their freedom was to colonize the freed slaves in Liberia. When Emily gave the slaves a choice, whether or not they wanted to go to Liberia, about a third decided to go to Liberia; seventy-five remained in Georgia. Emily arranged for the travel and supported the former slaves in Liberia for a time. They named their farming community in Liberia, Tubman Hill. Recognizing her remaining slaves in America needed more than simply freedom, Emily provided them with land and provisions until they were able to care for themselves.

Emily believed she was only the steward, not the owner, of her wealth, and she freely gave. A minister visiting her home when she was seventy-seven wrote of her spiritual conversation and life:

> It is beautiful to look on such a life, rising so sweetly and grandly above the ordinary plane of selfishness on which the world, and too largely the Church, moves; and it is blessed beyond expression to look on the freshness, heartiness, and gladness, unwithered by age, with which a life is invested and crowned that has thus devoted itself.[19]

Remember the words of the Lord Jesus, how he himself said, 'It is more blessed to give than to receive.'

~ Acts 20:35 ~

---

19. Edith Deen, *Great Women of the Christian Faith* (Uhrichsville, OH: Barbour Books, 1959), p. 184.

Protestant Mission in Canada

⌘ Henriette Odin Feller, 1800-1868 ⌘

By the nineteenth century Geneva had departed from the vibrant Christianity it had known under John Calvin and become a bastion of rationalism. When Robert Haldane, a Scottish evangelist, stopped at Geneva on his way home from India in 1816, his preaching led to a religious revival returning many to the Scriptures. Among those was Henriette Odin.

In 1822, Henriette married Louis Feller, a forty-one-year-old widower with three children, the oldest of whom was fourteen. Louis was director of the Lausanne police. When an 1824, law was passed persecuting the dissidents who chose to follow the Scriptures rather than the rationalistic established church, Louis was responsible for punishing the dissidents. Henriette could not bear to see the dissidents hunted down and, with her husband's tacit approval, protected them whenever she could.

Henriette suffered greatly during this time when her baby daughter died, then her husband, sister, and mother within a few years. Henriette herself contracted typhoid fever. While taking a rest cure in the Jura she read her Bible constantly and became convinced of the need to leave the established church. The next year, in 1828, restrictions against the dissidents were lifted, and Bible studies and prayer meetings flourished as the revival spread. Henriette found solace in evangelism. The Societé des Missions Evangéliques de Lausanne was formed, and the London Bible Society advised it to send missionaries to the Indians of Lower Canada. In August 1835, Henriette left for Canada along with Louis Roussy, a former student at a missionary institute.

The first year was especially difficult as the Roman Catholic clergy denounced them, doors were closed against them, they were forced to close the schools they established, and they were ill-treated. In 1836, they moved the mission base to Grande-Ligne, ten miles south of Saint-Jean in Quebec Province. It was a more rural area without the controlling priests. Henriette and Louis established a school and medical clinic and gained the confidence of the community. Within a year there were sixteen converts and others sympathetic to the Protestant mission. Henriette was known as 'Mother' to the students, who flourished under her affection and Christian devotion.

Henriette spent thirty-two years as a Protestant missionary in Canada. Her last years were marked by weakness from pneumonia and paralysis, yet she continued to guide the mission from her room. At the time of her death in 1868, the mission at Grande-Ligne had 400 members, nine churches, seven pastors, and many evangelists and colporteurs. God's providence had led a Scottish evangelist to bring revival to French-speaking Geneva, which then touched Henriette to bring the truth of the Scriptures to French-speaking Canada.

'You will be hated by all for my name's sake.
But not a hair of your head will perish.
By your endurance you will gain your lives.'

~ LUKE 21:17-19 ~

Hungry for the Word

⋘ Mary Jones, 1784-1864 ⋙

December 1784, Mary Jones was born to Jacob and Mary Jones, poor weavers in Wales. Mary's father died shortly after her fourth birthday, and Mary and her mother faced hardship in the coming years. Mary soon learned to weave and help her mother with the household chores. Together they attended the local Methodist church, where Mary came to personal faith in Christ when she was eight. When she was ten a school was begun about two miles from Mary's home, and as often as her work at home would allow, Mary walked to school, eager to learn to read so she could read the Bible. When a Sunday school was established at the church Mary regularly attended, faithfully memorizing the catechism and entire chapters of the Bible.

The only Bible in her Welsh community besides the one in the church belonged to a farm family two miles from Mary's home. The farmer's wife gave Mary permission to come and read it whenever she liked, as long as she removed her clogs before coming into the parlor. For six years, at least once a week, Mary walked to the farmhouse to read and memorize portions of Scripture.

During those six years Mary also saved every penny she could with the hopes of buying a Bible for herself. This was no small accomplishment, considering Mary's poverty and the difficult economic times. However, Mary's desire to have a Bible of her own was very strong. In 1800, when she had finally accumulated more than the seventeen shillings needed to purchase a Bible, Mary walked to Bala, twenty-five miles away, to purchase a Bible from Thomas Charles. She walked barefoot most of the way in order to save her shoes (and then had to make the return twenty-five-mile trip home!).

Mary's desire for the Scriptures and the sacrifices she made to obtain her personal copy of the Bible made a strong impression on Thomas Charles. He told Mary's story to a meeting of the Religious Tract Society in London, and the committee began to consider founding a society to publish and distribute Bibles. Out of this meeting and discussion, the British and Foreign Bible Society was founded in 1804. For over two hundred years the Bible Society has published and distributed Bibles all over the world, believing everyone benefits from knowing and understanding the Scriptures.

Mary married in 1813 and had at least six children, though most died young. She and her husband were both weavers and always lived a simple life. Mary's passion for the Scriptures never waned. When she died a widow in 1864, the Bible she had bought from Thomas Charles was on the table by her side. Today Mary's Bible is in the Library of the British and Foreign Bible Society.

Your word is a lamp to my feet and a light to my path.

~ PSALM 119:105 ~

Victorian Christian Women

Women's Record

∞ Sarah Josepha Hale, 1788-1879 ∞

After Sarah Hale's husband died in 1822, she wore black in mourning the rest of her days. Sarah was left with five small children to raise and care for. At first she tried to support her family through dressmaking, then she turned to writing. She became the editor of *Ladies' Magazine* in 1828, and in 1837 became editor of the widely popular *Godey's Lady's Book*. Sarah authored over thirty books of her own, but her most well-known work is undoubtedly the little nursery rhyme, 'Mary had a Little Lamb'.

In 1854, Sarah published the multi-volume *Women's Record: Sketches of all distinguished women from the creation to A.D. 1854*. In it she featured at least 2,500 women, only about 200 of whom were from heathen nations. In her introduction she noted that, 'Wherever the Bible is *read*, female talents are cultivated and esteemed. ... God's Word is woman's shield, His power her protection, and His gifts her sanction for their full development, cultivation and exercise.'[1] Sarah further claimed that:

> The Bible is the only guarantee of women's rights, and the only expositor of her duties. Under its teachings men learn to honour her. Wherever its doctrines are observed, her influence gains power. ... If the Gospel is the supreme good revealed to the world, and if the Gospel harmonizes best with the feminine nature, and is best exemplified in its purity by the feminine life, giving to the mother's instinctive love a scope, a hope, a support, which no religion of human device ever conferred or conceived, then surely God has, in applying this Gospel so directly to her nature, offices, and conditions, a great work for the sex to do. 'Christ was born of a woman'; woman must train her children for Christ. Is this an inferior office?[2]

Sarah wrote that there were three ways in which male and female were different in creation. Their mode of creation was different; the materials from which each was formed were different; and the functions for which each were designed were dissimilar. She thought that women were especially designed to wield a moral influence and inspire men in 'whatsoever things are lovely, pure, and of good report'. Because of woman's moral influence, her education was of utmost importance:

> If the mind which stamps the first and most indelible impression on the child is in a state of mental darkness, how can the true light be communicated? A mother will teach the best she knows to her son; but if she does not understand the true, she will, of necessity, imbue his mind with the false ... [3]

Sarah used her influence in numerous ways. She was a leader in the establishment of Thanksgiving as a national American holiday, worked toward the building of the Bunker Hill Monument, and founded the Seaman's Aid Society to help families of Boston sailors who died at sea.

In 1879, a year after retiring as editor of *Godey's*, Sarah died at the age of ninety. The same year Thomas Edison recorded the first speech ever recorded on his new invention of the phonograph. The words were the opening lines of 'Mary had a Little Lamb'.

Woman is the glory of man. For man was not made from woman, but woman from man. Neither was man created for woman, but woman for man.

~ 1 CORINTHIANS 11:7-9 ~

---

1. Sarah Josepha Hale, *Women's Record: Sketches of all distinguished women from the creation to A.D. 1854* (New York: Harper & Brothers, Pubs., 1853), p. ix.
2. Ibid, p. viii.
3. Ibid, p. xlvii.

Just as I am

⚮ Charlotte Elliott, 1789-1871 ⚭

Charlotte Elliot had been an invalid for years before her death on 22 September, 1871. Though confined to bed and often racked with pain, she had an impact on the lives of thousands of people both before and after her death.

Charlotte was born into a Christian family in Clapham, England in 1789. As a young lady she gained some popularity as a portrait painter and writer of verse, but her health began to fail when she was in her thirties. Bedridden and in pain, she often became despondent, overcome by feelings of uselessness. When Dr Caesar Malan, an evangelist from Geneva, visited the Elliotts in Brighton, England in 1822, he counseled Charlotte about her need for a Savior. He told her, 'You must come just as you are, a sinner, to the Lamb of God that taketh away the sin of the world.' Every year thereafter, Charlotte celebrated this day as the day of her conversion.

Fourteen years later Charlotte's brother, Rev. Henry Venn Elliott, was raising funds to establish St Mary's Hall in Brighton, to be a girls' school for daughters of poor clergy. As everyone bustled about preparing for bazaars and fund-raising projects, Charlotte felt helpless, though she desired to help. It was then that Dr Malan's words came back to her, and the verses of the hymn 'Just as I Am' came to mind:

> Just as I am, without one plea
> But that Thy blood was shed for me,
> And that Thou bidd'st me come to Thee,
> O Lamb of God, I come! I come!
>
> Just as I am, and waiting not
> To rid my soul of one dark blot,
> To Thee whose blood can cleanse each spot,
> O lamb of God, I come! I come! ...
>
> Just as I am, Thou wilt receive,
> Wilt welcome, pardon, cleanse, relieve,
> Because Thy promise I believe,
> O Lamb of God, I come! I come!

The hymn was published the same year in *The Invalid's Hymn Book*, which included 115 of Charlotte's hymns. The funds received were used for St Mary's Hall. The hymn was also printed and widely distributed in leaflet form. One day Charlotte's doctor brought her a tract with the hymn, thinking the words would comfort her in her suffering, not realizing she was the author!

This one hymn brought many to Christ; Charlotte's brother once said, 'In the course of a long ministry, I hope to have been permitted to see some fruit of my labours; but I feel more has been done by a single hymn of my sister's.'[4] Charlotte died at the age of eighty-two in 1871, having been an invalid for fifty years. At her death, among her papers were found a thousand letters from people who had been particularly blessed by 'Just as I am'.

> 'Whoever does not take his cross and follow me is not
> worthy of me. Whoever finds his life will lose it, and
> whoever loses his life for my sake will find it.'
>
> ~ MATTHEW 10:38-39 ~

---

4. Kenneth W. Osbeck, *101 Hymn Stories* (Grand Rapids, MI: Kregel Publications, 1982), p. 147.

Long Walk for Freedom

Captain Lopouloff was a respected officer in the Russian army who had fought valiantly in several of the Russian military engagements of the late eighteenth century. For reasons which are no longer known, he was sentenced to perpetual exile in Siberia under Czar Paul I. With his wife and Prascovia, his three-year-old daughter, Captain Lopouloff was confined to Ischim, Siberia and given an allowance of ten kopeks a day. He repeatedly petitioned the governor of Siberia, even sending the petition by an officer who could represent his case, but no response ever came.

As Prascovia grew she learned to help her mother more about the house and gained work in the village to supplement the family's resources. When she was about fifteen she began to realize how wretched her father was about his exile, and she daily prayed he might be comforted and might return to his home. One day during her prayers, like a bolt of lightning, she thought she might go to Petersburg and obtain her father's pardon from the Czar. When she broached the idea to her father, he scoffed at her and ridiculed the very thought. Nevertheless, she daily began praying that he would relent and allow her to make the trip on his behalf.

After three years, during which her mother was seriously ill and needed Prascovia's frequent care, Prascovia broached the subject again. This time her father did not laugh at her, but asked her to not leave them. Her father did allow Prascovia to apply for a passport, not thinking this would be granted to her. When, six months later, her passport did arrive, he locked it up and would not let her go. Prascovia trusted that the God who brought her the passport would change her father's heart. Finally, on 8 September, with her parents' reluctant blessings, Prascovia left Ischim and began the long walk to Petersburg.

The first night she was terribly tired and lonely, but she thought of God's care for Hagar in the wilderness and courageously trudged on. When she asked people the way to Petersburg, they laughed at her, the distance was so great. Prascovia suffered through winter storms, hunger, sickness, angry dogs, and even a plunge into the Volga River. Yet, along the way she did find people who befriended her – nursing her to health, providing warmer coverings and letters of introduction to people at the next stop in the road, and even giving her funds for the journey. After eighteen months, Proscovia reached Petersburg.

Trusting God all the way for guidance and direction, Proscovia was introduced to Empress Mary, mother of Czar Alexander, who took an interest in Proscovia's story and introduced her to the Czar. Czar Alexander graciously received Proscovia, agreed to revise her father's trial, and gave the girl 5000 rubles. Prascovia's health was ruined by her ordeal and she died a few years later, but she died joyous at having gained her father's freedom by trusting God and His providence.

And after you have suffered a little while, the God of all grace, who
has called you to his eternal glory in Christ, will himself restore,
confirm, strengthen, and establish you. To him be the dominion
forever and ever. Amen.

~ I PETER 5:10-11 ~

Prayerful for Souls to Know the Savior

∽ Harriet Winslow, 1796-1833 ∽

When the revival known as the Second Great Awakening swept through the towns and villages of New England, thirteen-year-old Harriet Lathrop found herself under conviction of her sin and placed her trust in Jesus for the salvation of her soul. On 9 April, 1809 she made a public profession of her faith and joined the church in Norwich, Connecticut. She began to spend much time in prayer and Bible study and sought to serve God in whatever ways she could. She began evangelizing among her friends and established a female prayer circle. She helped found the Society for the Relief of Poor Women and Children, began teaching in a school for poor children, and organized the first Sabbath school in Norwich. In 1814, when she was eighteen, Harriet wrote,

> When I reflect on the multitudes of my fellow-creatures who are perishing for lack of vision, and that I am living at ease, without aiding in the promulgation of the Gospel, I am almost ready to wish myself a man, that I might spend my life with the poor heathen. But I check the thought, and would not alter one plan of Infinite Wisdom. I could, however, cheerfully endure pain and hardship for them and for my dear Redeemer. Has he not given his life for multitudes now perishing as well as for my soul? And oh, how basely ungrateful and selfish in me, to sit down quietly in the care of self, without making any exertion for their salvation. But what can I do – a weak, ignorant female? One thing only do I see. My prayers may be accepted. Yes, I will plead with my heavenly Father, that he may be a Father to the poor benighted heathen.[5]

For several years Harriet felt drawn to missionary work and prayed for God's clear direction. When she met Rev. Miron Winslow, a graduate of Andover Theological Seminary and a member of the American Board of Commissioners for Foreign Missions, she met a kindred soul who also was burdened for the heathen in foreign lands. Harriet and Miron were married 11 January, 1819. In June they sailed for Ceylon, modern Sri Lanka, where they helped found the Missionary Seminary and the Female Central School – the first boarding school in Asia.

Harriet wrote the arithmetic and geography lessons for the school and oversaw the sewing and household arts. Daily she prayed individually for the children, and all who graduated were Christians. She wrote in one journal entry:

> Would that I had a heart to continue instant in prayer! Lord, take away my sloth, my unbelief, my hardness of heart, my distrust of thee; and grant me humility, activity, tenderness of heart, and strong faith. Can I not say, Lord, thou knowest that I desire above every thing to be like my Redeemer; to have his Spirit, to be filled with his fulness, that I may glorify thee among this people.[6]

Harriet Winslow died in childbirth on 14 January, 1833, joining in heaven the five children who had preceded her, and leaving behind her dear husband and three daughters. Three of her younger sisters became missionaries in Ceylon, and two are buried beside her in Oodooville, awaiting the glorious resurrection.

> Far be it from me that I should sin against the LORD by ceasing to
> pray for you, and I will instruct you in the good and the right way.
> Only fear the LORD and serve him faithfully with all your heart. For
> consider what great things he has done for you.
>
> ~ 1 SAMUEL 12:23-24 ~

---

5. H. W. Pierson, ed. *American Missionary Memorial* (New York: Harper & Brothers, 1853), pp. 190-191.
6. Ibid, pp. 197-198.

Mother of the Serampore Mission
⟶ Hannah Marshman, 1767-1847 ⟵

William Carey, often called the Father of Modern Missions, was sent out from England to India by the Baptist Missionary Society in 1793. Six years later he was joined by William Ward, a printer, and Joshua Marshman, a schoolteacher. The three settled in the Danish colony of Serampore, near Calcutta, and have often been called the 'Serampore Trio'. Together they translated and printed the Bible in Bengali, Sanskrit and other major languages and dialects, as well as established Serampore College, the first degree-granting institution in Asia. Important to the success of the mission was Joshua Marshman's wife, Hannah. Hannah was the first woman to leave England for missionary work. Being the first, she had no manual to guide her, but she importantly established a pattern for later women missionaries to follow.

Carey called Hannah 'a prodigy of prudence', and her stability and courage were a great strength to the fledgling missionaries. Shortly after arriving, Hannah and her husband noticed that Carey's four boys were undisciplined and were not being educated. Carey's wife suffered mentally and was not able to care for them. Hannah and Joshua provided important nurture for the boys, as well as an education.

When she went to the market, Hannah wondered where the women were. She began to realize that women were all kept at home and did not go out in public. If the women were to be reached with the gospel, they must be visited at home, so Hannah began visiting the homes to bring the gospel to the women, thus beginning the pattern of Zenana[7] missions. Hannah also established a school for girls, the first in India, training older students to teach the younger girls. The boarding school she established became an important source of financial support for the missionaries. In 1819, Hannah worked in Calcutta for the establishment of the Society for the Education of Native Females, to encourage the education of Indian women.

Hannah had twelve children, though six died in infancy. Her oldest son, John Clark Marshman, became an important educator and publisher in India; his *Guide to the Civil Law* was the civil code of India for years. He paid tribute to his mother:

A woman of feeling, piety, and good sense, of strong mind …, fitted in every respect to be an associate in the great undertaking to which the life of her husband was devoted – and withal so amiable a disposition that nothing was ever known to have ruffled her temper.[8]

Hannah served forty-seven years in India and was the last of the early missionaries, surviving her husband Joshua's death in 1837 by ten years. When she lay dying, she told her daughter she had no fears: 'Has He not said that He will save to the uttermost those that come unto him and will not cast away any?' She said, 'Should you speak of me after my death speak to the people and tell them, He sent from above, he took me, he drew me out of many waters," then she asked to be read the end of *The Pilgrim's Progress*, describing the pilgrims passing over the river to the Eternal City. She said, 'I wish myself among them,' and soon she was.

He holds his priesthood permanently, because he continues forever.
Consequently, he is able to save to the uttermost those who draw near to God
through him, since he always lives to make intercession for them.
~ HEBREWS 7:24-25 ~

---

7. 'Zenana' is a Persian word meaning 'of the women'. It was used to refer to the part of the house reserved for the women, especially in a Hindu or Muslim family. In order to evangelize women Christian missionaries established zenana missions, with trained female missionaries providing health care and teaching the women in their homes.
8. Quoted in Edith Deen, *Great Women of the Christian Faith* (Uhrichsville, OH: Barbour Books, 1959).

MAY 30

Mother's Challenge to her Children

∞ Mary Forbes Winslow, 1774-1854 ∞

Born in Bermuda to Dr and Mrs George Forbes, Mary was an only child. When she was seventeen she married Lt Thomas Winslow. Shortly after her marriage, Mary was brought to trust in Christ for her salvation and began a spiritual journey which can be traced in her letters and diaries, many of which have been collected by her son Octavius.

Mary and Thomas had thirteen children; three died before their first birthday. Though Thomas had a comfortable income and property after he retired from the army, he lost much of it in poor investments. Thomas' spirits were crushed by this reversal, but Mary sought the Lord's direction, knowing He was a loving Father to them, and suggested they move the family to America, where the opportunities seemed brighter. Mary courageously offered to go ahead and prepare a home there, with Thomas to follow. Having letters of introduction to leading Christians in New York who could help her, Mary, her ten children, and the servants left Gravesend for New York in June 1815. Throughout the voyage the Winslow group had morning and evening worship, and the captain often joined them in prayer. Soon after her arrival in New York Mary's infant daughter died. Before she was even buried, Mary received news that her husband had died across the Atlantic. Now a widow in a strange land with nine children to care for, Mary went through a time of intense despair.

Years later, in a letter to her children, Mary traced the hand of providence in her life, describing this dark time and encouraging her children to look completely to their God:

> In the days of my deep sorrow you know that God gave me a promise. In the dark hours of the night, when sleep had forsaken my eyes, and my heart was overwhelmed with anxious care, then did He bow the heavens, and in condescending mercy, spoke peace and consolation to my tried soul. He then, in that most blessed and eventful hour, promised to be a Father to my fatherless children, and to be my God. And O how He has fulfilled that promise! Who has supplied all your wants? Who has poured abundance into your lap? Has not God done it? Why were you not left destitute, and dependent in a strange land? Who has the gold and silver at His command? Not you. Who has all hearts at His disposal? Not you. Who has preserved you, while crossing a mighty ocean, from a watery grave? Has not God been the Guide of your youth? Has He not watched over you by day and by night, by sea and by land? Has He not supplied all your wants? Dare not say, oh *dare* not say, 'My talents, my industry, my exertions have gotten me these things.'

Mary then challenged her children to live their lives for His glory:

> Give God the glory and acknowledge it was Him, and Him alone. But what have been the returns? What have you done with what God has given you? He has poured richly into your lap, but what returns have you made for all His goodness to you? Have you made any? Have you laid out what He has given you to the glory of His blessed name? Have you remembered and acknowledged Him in all your ways? Have you gone to Him as your reconciled Father in Christ Jesus? Do you know Him? Do you love Him – Oh, do you *love Him who has been so good to you, watching over you by day and by night!* Do you love Him?[9]

All of Mary's children did come to faith in Christ, and three of her sons became ministers of the gospel. A mother's fervent prayers were answered.

> Not to us, O LORD, not to us, but to your name give glory, for the
> sake of your steadfast love and your faithfulness!
>
> ~ PSALM 115:1 ~

---

9. Mary Winslow (Octavius Winslow, ed.), *Christian experience; or, Words of loving counsel and sympathy* (London: William Hunt and company, 1868), pp. 252-254.

Living with Eternity in View

∞ Anna Jane Linnard, 1800-1833 ∞

Anna Jane Linnard, born in Philadelphia in 1800, had little use for religion or church as a child and was always happy to miss services. She found the company of good people so disagreeable; she could not imagine how she could ever bear being with the saints and angels in heaven. Yet, at the age of nineteen, Anna was brought to Christian faith through the tragic death of an older sister. She resolved henceforth to live her life for God and began regularly studying the Scriptures, often with Matthew Henry's or Thomas Scott's commentaries, and serving others in numerous ways. She taught Sunday school and was active in numerous benevolent societies. She served as Secretary of the Auxiliary Female Bible Association of Philadelphia and of the Female Domestic Missionary Association. She regularly distributed Bibles and tracts to those she met and visited the poor in the city, bringing them physical help and conversing with them about the need of their souls for salvation in Christ.

Anna dressed with simplicity and plainness for two reasons. First, it saved money and allowed her to spend more on the poor. Secondly, it would discourage the poor from being extravagant in their dress, spending for finery what could best be used for food and necessities. In 1823, she wrote a friend on the subject:

> So much for dress. Alas! What care, what expense, what time is spent by more than half the world in clothing and adorning these poor frail bodies, while the everlasting interests of the soul are either entirely neglected, or, at best, occupy but little thought or attention. If we could but have realizing views of eternity, and could, with the eye of faith, see things invisible to sense, as present, how little would it concern us, of what the robe which covered our bodies was composed. We should then, indeed, 'take no thought wherewithal we should be clothed', save with that 'meek and quiet spirit which is, in the sight of God, of great price'. But oh, how trifling and groveling are the pursuits, even of christians! A christian! One, whose privilege it is to soar above this world, through regions of immortality, whose professed home is heaven – God's glory his aim! How ought a christian to live! I once met with an idea that struck me as forcible: speaking of the pursuits of christians, the writer asked, what would be thought of the man who was travelling to a far country, to receive the inheritance of a great kingdom, where honour, glory, and power, awaited him, who should be seen to stop at every step to gather chips and pebbles?… let us seek to live above this vain, dying world, and bear the cross, always keeping in mind that solemn saying of our Lord, 'Who soever doth not deny himself, and bear his cross, cannot be my disciple.'[10]

Anna's diaries and letters are filled with similar meditations and exhortations on the Christian life. During the twelve years she lived after her conversion, Anna tirelessly dedicated herself to know God and to serve Him. The American Sunday-school Union published anonymously her book *Helen Maurice: or, the Benefit of Early Religious Instruction*, which sold over 9,500 copies by the early 1830s and appeared posthumously in a second edition in 1837. Anna went to be with her Savior on 16 June 1833; she was thirty-three.

And why are you anxious about clothing? Consider the lilies of the field, how they grow: they neither toil nor spin, yet I tell you, even Solomon in all his glory was not arrayed like one of these. But if God so clothes the grass of the field, which today is alive and tomorrow is thrown into the oven, will he not much more clothe you, O you of little faith?

~ MATTHEW 6:28-30 ~

---

10. *Christian Biography*, vol. 6 (London: Religious Tract Society), pp. 34-35.

Living for Christ

ᢒᢒ Anne Randolph Meade Page, 1781-1838 ᢒᢒ

Anne Randolph Meade was born into a wealthy Virginia family. Her mother gave Anne and her siblings a solid upbringing in the things of Christ. In 1799, Anne married Matthew Page, a member of the Virginia legislature. Matthew had a large estate of 2,000 acres on which he built a plantation home he named 'Annfield' after his wife.

Anne resisted the frivolities and frequent parties of her husband's friends and acquaintances. She felt alienated when friends would get together and never speak of Christ or of his salvation, and she determined to speak boldly of Christian truths to all she met – strangers, children, overseers, masters, slaves, and friends. However, sometimes she feared she was too aggressive and prayed to God, 'Teach me to pray more for my friends when I feel anxious concerning them, and talk less.'[11] One Sunday she returned home after church, not going to the elaborate Sunday dinner to which she had been invited, and went to her room to give her thoughts to spiritual things. Anne later wrote:

> While thus engaged in my chamber, an old blind negro woman was led in, who was a dear child of God. We began a conversation in which she used expressions respecting entire confidence in Christ, which made an indelible impression upon my mind. ... I think I owe her, under God, much of my religious joy in after years. Dark old creature, I often visited her in her cottage, and witnessed the evidences of her triumphant faith. She was a living example of Christ formed in the soul. The hope of glory.[12]

Anne believed slavery was wrong, but her husband would not let her free any of the 200 slaves on their plantation. Anne, however, was most devoted to their education and care. Daily she had Scripture reading and prayer with all the slaves and members of the household. She was an early supporter of colonization, sending the slaves back to their African homeland, and she prepared her slaves for skills and education which would help them live a life of freedom in Africa.

After her husband's death, Anne worked tirelessly for African colonization. She freed all of her slaves, sending them to Liberia in three waves, and giving each provisions for a year to get established in their new country. At her death many wrote testimonials of Anne's Christian character and life. One published in the *Christian Statesman* read:

> From the time when this most excellent woman regarded herself as the disciple of Christ, her life was a beautiful and impressive example of the purest and most sublime virtues of Christianity. Her humility was profound – her zeal intense – her love to the Savior and his cause surpassing all other affections – her charity as large as the wants and miseries of our nature. Her religious sentiments seemed blended with all her thoughts and feelings, and inwrought into the very frame and constitution of her being. For her to live was Christ; all other objects were subordinated to the advancement of his cause. Compared with his favour she counted all things but loss. Her service was not a service of fear, but of confidence – of gratitude – of love.[13]

'If you abide in my word, you are truly my disciples,
and you will know the truth, and the truth will set you free.'
~ JOHN 8:31-32 ~

---

11. Charles Wesley Andrews, *Memoir of Mrs Anne R. Page* (Philadelphia: Herman Hooker, 1844), p. 69.
12. Ibid, p. 17.
13. Ibid, p. 96-97.

Life of Usefulness

∞ Ann Hasseltine Judson, 1789-1826 ∞

Ann Hasseltine first met Adoniram Judson in 1810, when he boarded briefly at her father's home in Bradford, Masschusetts during a church association meeting. Adoniram was a passionate young man consumed with a desire to bring the gospel to the heathen in distant lands. Ann herself had a strong desire to live a life of usefulness. In 1806, when she was seventeen, she was awakened to a sense of her own sinfulness and looked to Jesus for redemption. Reading Hannah More's *Strictures in the Modern System of Female Education*, Ann was convicted that her life should not be lived for herself but in useful service for others. She began diligently studying the Scriptures and works by writers such as Jonathan Edwards and Philip Doddridge. When Adoniram Judson wrote a letter to Ann proposing marriage, for two months she struggled how to reply. She would not only be marrying Adoniram, but she would be marrying into a totally different life in a foreign land away from family and friends. Though many counseled Ann against accepting Adoniram's proposal, Ann decided this was what God would have her do. She wrote, 'O, if [God] will condescend to make me useful in promoting his Kingdom, I care not where I perform his work nor how hard it be. *"Behold the handmaid of the Lord; be it unto me according to thy word."*'[14]

Adoniram and Ann were married 5 February, 1812, and sailed for India two weeks later. When they visited William Carey's mission in India, Ann saw the school for girls Hannah Marshman had established. She knew that schools and education would be her work by Adoniram's side.

Not being allowed to establish themselves in India, the Judsons established a mission in Burma. Ann became fluent in Burmese and Siamese and helped Adoniram in his Bible translation. She established a Sabbath Society for women and gathered with them to read the Bible. She translated tracts and a catechism into Burmese and was the first to translate any portion of the Bible into Siamese. When war broke out between England and Burma, Adoniram was imprisoned as a spy. Ann, with a small baby, regularly visited him, bringing food to him and other prisoners. Adoniram was to be executed and was moved to different prisons, while Ann faithfully followed and tried to secure his release. When the war ended and Adoniram was released, Ann's health was broken; she died two months later. Her life of service to others and bringing the gospel to the lost inspired many to follow her path in missionary work.

> *Do nothing from selfish ambition or conceit, but in humility count others more significant than yourselves. Let each of you look not only to his own interests, but also to the interests of others.*
>
> ~ PHILIPPIANS 2:3-4 ~

---

14. James D. Knowles, *Memoir of Ann H. Judson, Missionary to Burma* (Boston: Gould, Kendall, and Lincoln, 1846), p. 48.

JUNE 3

Forsaking All for Christ

∞ Harriet Newell, 1793-1812 ∞

One of the most influential books of the nineteenth century was the *Memoirs of Mrs Harriet Newell*, composed by Harriet's husband Samuel. The Newells were, along with Adoniram and Ann Judson, among the earliest missionaries sent to foreign lands from the United States. Based on her letters and journals, Harriet's *Memoirs* reveal a young woman who had given herself completely to bring the gospel of Christ to those who had never heard.

While attending Bradford Academy in Massachusetts, Harriet came under conviction she was a sinner and was drawn to Jesus as Savior. About that day of 29 June, 1809, she wrote, 'I then made the solemn resolution, as I trust, in the strength of Jesus, that I would make a sincere dedication of my all to my Creator, both for time and eternity.'

Harriet's friend Ann came to faith in Christ about the same time. Harriet was deeply moved when Ann agreed to marry Adoniram Judson and join him in mission work in India. Harriet's heart ached for those who were spiritually perishing without the knowledge and light of the gospel. She prayed, 'Great God, direct me! O make me *in some way* beneficial to immortal souls.'[15]

A few years later, in February 1812, Harriet married Samuel Newell, one of the founders of the American Board of Commissioners of Foreign Missions, and the newlyweds set off for India with Adoniram and Ann Judson. Britain and America were at war at the time. Though the young missionaries did land in India and met with British missionary William Carey and his team, the East India Company would not allow them to remain in the country. The Newells were able to find a ship and head for Mauritius. By this time Harriet was pregnant, and while at sea she gave birth to a little daughter, who died within five days. Harriet died shortly after landing; she was barely nineteen years old.

Harriet was the first American missionary to die in a foreign field, and her story of dedication and sacrifice moved many hearts. Many could trace their call to the mission field from Harriet Newell's example.

> 'Whoever does not take his cross and follow me is not
> worthy of me. Whoever finds his life will lose it, and
> whoever loses his life for my sake will find it.'
>
> ~ MATTHEW 10:38-39 ~

---

15. John D. Knowles, *Memoir of Ann H. Judson, missionary to Burma* (Boston: Gould, Kendall, and Lincoln, 1846), p. 43.

JUNE 4

Princess Mourned

∽ Princess Amelia, House of Hanover, 1783-1810 ∽

King George III of Britain enjoyed a happy, harmonious marriage with his queen consort Charlotte of Mecklenburg-Strelitz. The couple had fifteen children, the youngest of whom, Amelia, was born at Windsor Castle in 1783. Though the king was affectionate with all of his children, Amelia became his favorite. Possibly the deaths of her four-year-old brother Octavius and her two-year-old brother Alfred months before she was born made Amelia even more precious to her father.

In 1798, when she was fifteen, Amelia began to show symptoms of tuberculosis. Though she often suffered greatly, she never complained and patiently looked to her Savior. Her condition later was compounded by the measles in 1808 and erysipelas in October 1810. As it became apparent Amelia was dying, the king daily visited her bedside, always directing his conversations with Amelia to spiritual things and the hope of eternal life through Jesus Christ. An attendant on Amelia described the king's visits:

> His majesty speaks to his daughter of the only hope of a sinner being in the blood and righteousness of Jesus Christ. He examines her as to the integrity and strength of that hope in her own soul. The princess listens with calmness and delight to the conversation of her venerable parent, and replies to his questions in a very affectionate and serious manner.
>
> If you were present at one of these interviews, you would acknowledge with joy that the gospel is preached in a palace, and that under highly affecting circumstances. Nothing can be more striking than the sight of the king, aged and nearly blind [from cataracts] bending over the couch on which the princess lies, and speaking to her about salvation through Christ, as a matter far more interesting to them both than the highest privileges and most exalted pomps of royalty.[16]

Knowing that her death was very near, Amelia called a jeweller to her to make a mourning ring containing a lock of her hair with the inscription, 'Remember me, when I am gone'. When her father visited her, she put the ring on his finger without saying a word. The king was so moved and shocked and became so mentally disturbed by Amelia's death, that the Prince of Wales acted as regent for the last ten years of the King's life.

The nation greatly mourned Princess Amelia's death. The Rev. Dr Collyer wrote of the nation's grief:

... Around Amelia's royal hearse,
No feigning, heartless mourner weeps;
No hireling hand shall write the verse
Upon the tomb where greatness sleeps!

A nation feels the monarch's grief, –
A princess dead, the country mourns;
Nor can Britannia find relief,
Till to her Sovereign health returns.

Behold, we bow beneath the rod –
The nation weeps, but not despairs;
Succour must come from thee, O God!
Our sins forgive, accept our prayers![17]

But we do not want you to be uninformed, brothers, about those who are asleep,
that you may not grieve as others do who have no hope.
For since we believe that Jesus died and rose again, even so, through Jesus,
God will bring with him those who have fallen asleep.

~ 1 THESSALONIANS 4:13-14 ~

---

16. Thomas Timpson, *British Female Biography* (London: Aylott and Jones, 1846), p. 83.
17. Ibid, p. 85.

Heart and Hands for Missions

∽ Sarah Doremus, 1802-1877 ∽

Sarah Doremus had a heart for serving others in the name of Christ and worked tirelessly to help others both at home and abroad. In 1821, Sarah married Thomas Doremus, a wealthy New York businessman. Both were members of the Dutch Reformed Church and lived lives devoted to Christ. They had eight daughters and one son and adopted several other children as well. Sarah cared for her children and things of her house while actively seeking to bring the Word of Christ to others. A simple list of her numerous philanthropic and Christian involvements is amazing. In addition to regularly teaching Sunday school, Sarah organized or presided over numerous Christian organizations.

In 1828, she aided the Greek Christians who were suffering under Turkish persecution. In 1834, after hearing a missionary's call from Chinese women – 'Are there no females who can come and teach us?' – she organized the Society for the Promoting Female Education in the East. In 1840, she began working with the women's ward of the New York City prisons and eventually organized the Women's Prison Association, to help discharged women prisoners. She worked with the prison association for thirty-two years, often serving as President, and helped many discharged women prisoners return to an honorable life. In 1841, she began thirty-six years of service as manager of the City and Tract Society, which evangelized among the poor. She also was active in the City Bible Society of New York, which distributed Bibles to the poor. She helped establish in New York the Nursery and Child's Hospital in 1854 and the Woman's Hospital of New York State in 1855. During the Civil War she helped in distributing supplies to the hospitals in New York.

In 1860, Sarah became the first President of the Woman's Union Missionary Society of America for Heathen Lands, especially to send out single women missionaries. With New York being the port for many missionaries departing for or returning from foreign lands, Sarah often was at the port welcoming home missionaries or seeing them off on their mission. Her home became a temporary haven for many missionaries on their journey, and her numerous activities with missions led her to be known as the 'Mother of Missions'. Once when her husband gave her an expensive shawl, she asked if she could have the money instead. She used the money to buy materials for fancy work embroidery, which she loved, and made articles which then sold for $500, which she donated to missions in Hawaii. Helen Montgomery wrote of Sarah:

> Perfectly consecrated to Christ's service, she yielded her life into His control, and the fullness of His power flowed through her life unhindered. A heart at leisure from itself to soothe and sympathize was hers. Her powers were not frittered, but directed.[18]

Having a reputation for good works: … she has brought up children, has
shown hospitality, has washed the feet of the saints, has cared for the afflicted,
and has devoted herself to every good work.

~ I TIMOTHY 5:10 ~

---

18. Quoted from Helen Montgomery, *Western Women in Eastern Lands* in Edith Deen, *Great Women of the Christian Faith* (Uhrichsville, OH: Barbour Books, 1959), p. 372.

Name of Jesus

When Rev. Eber Tucker, a Baptist home missionary, brought the gospel to Petersburgh, New York in the second decade of the 1800s, Lydia and her sister were among the first to have their hearts opened to the truth in Christ. They evangelized their friends and neighbors and helped found the Baptist Church at Petersburgh in 1820. Lydia became a successful Sabbath school teacher.

When she married John C. Baxter, Lydia moved to New York City. A son was born to the couple in 1837. A few years later Lydia became ill and was bed-ridden for the rest of her life. In spite of her great pain, she always had a cheerful disposition. Preachers, evangelists, song-leaders, and other Christians would visit simply from the encouragement she gave them! When people asked how she was so cheerful under such suffering, Lydia replied, 'I have some very special armour.' She would then explain:

> I have the name of Jesus, and I use that name as my special protection. When the tempter tries to make me blue or despondent, I mention the name of Jesus, and ask him to give me the soothing balm of his presence, and I soon drop off to sleep. The name 'Jesus' means Savior and it comes from the same Hebrew root from which the names Joshua and Joash come. When I remember that, and all that the name of Jesus signifies about the nature or personality of God, I can conquer any foe.[19]

Lydia was an eager student of Scriptures and could unfold the importance of Jesus' name from numerous passages. Jesus promised his followers, 'that whatever you ask the Father in my name, he may give it to you' (John 15:16). The apostles preached that 'there is no other name under heaven given among men by which we must be saved' (Acts 4:12). The apostle Paul looked forward to the time when 'at the name of Jesus every knee should bow' (Phil. 2:10).

From her experience of the strength through suffering provided by her 'special armour', the name of Jesus, Lydia wrote the enduring hymn:

Take the name of Jesus with you,
Child of sorrow and woe;
It will joy and comfort give you;
Take it then where'er you go.

Refrain: Precious name, O how sweet!
Hope of earth and joy of heaven.

Take the name of Jesus ever,
As a shield from ev'ry snare;
If temptations round you gather,
Breathe that holy name in prayer.

At the name of Jesus bowing,
Falling prostrate at His feet,
King of Kings in heav'n we'll crown Him
When our journey is complete.

And whatever you do, in word or deed,
do everything in the name of the Lord Jesus,
giving thanks to God and the Father through him.

~ COLOSSIANS 3:17 ~

---

19. Edgar McFadden, 'Take the Name of Jesus with You' (*The Examiner*, July 1986, Vol. 1, No. 4), http://www.theexaminer.org/volume1/number4/nameof.htm.

JUNE 7

Wool and Bible Bees

∽ early 19th century ∽

Women were important contributors to the nineteenth-century missionary and Bible societies. In her *The Book and Its Story*, published in 1853, for the Jubilee of the British and Foreign Bible Society, 'L.N.R.' (Ellen Ranyard) provides stories about various contributors to the Bible Society. Among them is the story of the old woman and the wool:

> A poor widow living on the side of the Black Mountains, in Caemarthenshire, attended a public meeting. She had only one shilling in her possession, part of which she intended to lay out to buy wool for making an apron, and the other part for candles, that she might see to spin it in the evenings, after finishing her day's work with the farmers. Having heard the speakers describe the sad condition of the poor heathen without Bibles, she felt for them so much, that she determined to give six-pence out of her shilling to the collection, thinking that she would do without the apron for some time longer, and spin her wool by daylight, when the summer evenings came. As the speaker proceeded, the old woman felt more and more, till at last she determined to give the shilling altogether 'because,' she said, 'I can do better without an apron, than the heathen can without the word of God.' She cheerfully gave her shilling, went home, and slept comfortably that night. At daybreak the following morning, a neighbouring farmer called at her door, and said, 'Peggy, we have had a dreadful night; several of my sheep have been carried away by the flood. There are two lying quite dead in the hedge of your garden. You may take them if you like, and you will get some wool upon them.' She thankfully accepted the gift; and thus she had enough wool to make three or four aprons, and tallow to make candles to spin it. As no one knew what she had done the day before but herself and her God, she looked upon that occurrence as a very kind providence towards her.

In a following account, L.N.R. told this story about the Bible-bees:

> In the year 1809, at the formation of a Bible Association, at Barton, in Lincolnshire, before Mr and Mrs W. went to the meeting, Mrs W. said to Mr W, 'We must give a guinea to the Bible Society.' 'Nay,' said her husband, 'that is too much; the rich do not give more than a guinea, and we are not rich; it will even look like ostentation in us to give so much.' 'Still,' said Mrs W., 'if you will not give it, I *will*.' 'And where are you to get it?' said he. 'I have it by me,' said she; 'do you not remember that you gave me a guinea, with which to buy a hive of bees; now, I will give that guinea to the Bible Society.' 'Then,' said Mr W., 'you will go without your bees.' So they went to the Bible-meeting, and the guinea was given.
>
> They had no sooner reached home, than the wife said to her husband, 'Oh! See! A swarm of bees has settled on our beech tree: if no one claims them in four-and-twenty-hours, the swarm will be mine.' No one did claim them, and they were hived. A day or two afterwards, Mr W. said to his wife, 'It appears to me very remarkable that Providence should send to us, just now the swarm of bees. Suppose we dedicate these bees to the Bible Society?' To this Mrs W. gladly gave her consent. The first year, the hive produced two swarms, and they gave two guineas to the Bible Society; the second year the three hives produced ten swarms, and they gave ten guineas to the Bible Society. [20]

When the bee owners moved, the bees were left under the care of others and continued to provide contributions to the Bible Society in ensuing years.

> *The point is this: whoever sows sparingly will also reap sparingly, and whoever*
> *sows bountifully will also reap bountifully. Each one must give as he has decided*
> *in is heart, not reluctantly or under compulsion, for God loves a cheerful giver.*
>
> ~ 2 Corinthians 9:6-7 ~

---

20. L.N.R., *The Book and Its Story* (London: Samuel Bagster and Sons, 1853), pp. 263-265.

Duty of Every Christian

֍ Laura Haviland, 1808-1898 ֍

The year 1845 was a dark period in Laura Haviland's life. Within six weeks her husband, her mother, her sister, her father, and her baby all died of erysipelas, and she herself was extremely ill with the deadly skin disease. Though Laura did recover, she was then a widow at the age of thirty-six with seven children to care for. With courage and trust in God Laura continued serving others as she and her husband had done.

Born in Canada in 1808, when Laura was seven her family moved to New York. When she was seventeen Laura married Charles Haviland. They followed Laura's parents to southeastern Michigan in 1829, settling in the area of Raisin. Laura was instrumental in establishing the first anti-slavery society in Michigan in the 1830s, and the Havilands' home became the first station in Michigan on the 'Underground Railroad', a network of secret safe houses for slaves fleeing to Canada for their freedom. Laura personally escorted several of the slaves to Canada herself. Protecting the slaves became a criminal act after the passage of the Fugitive Slave Law in 1854, and at one time irate slave owners put a $3,000 bounty on Laura, dead or alive.

Though Laura had no formal schooling, she had been a voracious reader since a child and was self-educated. She taught her own children as well as orphans of the county. In 1836, she and her husband founded the Raisin Institute, a school for area children open to all regardless of race, sex, or creed, a very radical concept in that day.

When the Civil War came Laura ministered to wounded soldiers and former slaves. After the war, when many former slaves fled north, Laura worked among the refugees in Kansas, helping provide education for them. Laura even went to Washington, D.C. to gain financial support from Congress for the enterprise. In recognition of her humanitarian and educational work among the freed slaves, the poor, and the needy, Haviland, Kansas and Haviland, Ohio were both named in her honor.

Laura's autobiography, *A Woman's Life Work*, recounts a life filled with great tragedy, unbelievable adventure, and examples of principled courage. In it Laura summarized her thinking of a Christian's responsibility:

> Is it not the duty of every Christian to bring his or her religion into every line of life work, and act as conscientiously in politics as in church work? Sanctified common sense is loudly called for in the highway of holiness. In whatever condition or station in life we find ourselves, are we not our brother's keeper in a more extensive view than we are prone to conceive?[21]

Eleven years after her death, in 1898, a statue of Laura Haviland was erected in front of City Hall at Adrian, Michigan. A drinking fountain is at the statue's feet with Jesus' words from Matthew 25:35: 'I was thirsty and ye gave me to drink.'

'You shall love your neighbor as yourself.'
Love does no wrong to a neighbor:
therefore, love is the fulfilling of the law.

~ ROMANS 13:9-10 ~

---

21. Laura Smith Haviland, *A Woman's Life Work: Labor and Experiences of Laura S. Haviland* (Cincinatti: Walden & Stowe, 1882), p. 454.

JUNE 9

Delighting to Submit to God's Will

∞ Elizabeth Barrett Browning, 1809-1861 ∞

Elizabeth Barrett, the oldest of twelve children, was educated at home. Sharing her brother's tutor, she learned to read the Greek and Latin classics as well as Dante in their original languages. She also learned Hebrew and read the Bible in its original Hebrew and Greek. The Barretts were dissenting Congregationalists, and the family regularly attended services at the Dissenting Chapel. Throughout her life, Elizabeth regularly read seven chapters of the Bible daily.

Elizabeth began writing poetry as a child and, with her father's encouragement, published an epic poem when still a teenager. By the time she was twenty Elizabeth began struggling with lifelong pulmonary problems which left her weak and frail. She learned, however, that suffering and pain were tools God often used for spiritual growth. In suffering she learned to find delight in submitting to God's will:

> I praise Thee while my days go on;
> I love Thee while my days go on;
> Through dark and dearth, through fire and frost,
> With emptied arms and treasure lost,
> I thank Thee while my days go on:[22]

Elizabeth's illness caused her to become a virtual recluse, confined to her bedroom; but there she wrote poetry for various periodicals. In 1838, *The Seraphim and Other Poems*, the first volume of her mature poetry, was published. References to God and her Christian faith were frequent in these poems. One editor asked Elizabeth to mention God and Jesus Christ a little less since this did not accord with his secular publication. Elizabeth, however, would not restrict her Christian expressions:

> The Christian religion is true or it is not, and if it is true it offers the highest and purest objects of contemplation. And the poetical faculty, which expresses the highest moods of the mind, passes naturally to the highest objects. Who can separate these things? Did Dante? Did Chaucer? Did the poets of our best British days? Did anyone shrink from speaking out Divine names when the occasion came?[23]

After reading a collection of Elizabeth's poems in 1844, poet Robert Browning wrote her to tell her how much he admired her poetry. A friend arranged a meeting between the two, and a courtship followed. Elizabeth, an invalid and six years older than Robert, at first could not believe he loved her; but in 1846 the two were married and went to live in Italy, where Elizabeth's health improved some. Elizabeth's most famous works, *Sonnets from the Portuguese* and her verse-novel *Aurora Leigh*, were written after her marriage. Her fame was so great that she was seriously considered for poet laureate after the death of Wordsworth; however, Tennyson was chosen instead.

For I consider that the sufferings of this present time
are not worth comparing with the glory that is to be revealed in us.

~ ROMANS 8:18 ~

---

22. Elizabeth Barrett Browning, 'De Profundis', XXI-XXIII.
23. Martha Foote Crowe, *Modern Poets and Christian Teaching: Elizabeth Barrett Browning* (New York: Eaton and Maine, 1907), p. 25.

Serving the Lord with Gladness

⋙ Gertrude Reichardt, c. 1788 – c. 1864 ⋘

When Theodor Fliedner became pastor in Kaiserswerth, Germany in 1821, it was a time of economic crisis, and the town was so poor it could not support the church and its normal ministries. Fliedner traveled in Germany, the Netherlands, and England to collect donations for his community. From the Mennonites in the Netherlands he learned about the early church office of deaconess, and from Elizabeth Fry in England he found an example of Christian work among the poor and imprisoned. Fliedner came back to Kaiserswerth not only with funds but also ideas for working among the impoverished and sick in his own town. In 1833, he opened a House of Refuge for released female prisoners and for women who had fallen into prostitution. In 1836, Fliedner opened a deaconess training centre which became a model of female service around the world.

The first to apply for deaconess training was Gertrude Reichardt, a forty-eight-year-old daughter of a doctor who had often helped her father in his work. Fliedner, recognizing Gertrude had organizational skills as well as experience in helping the sick and destitute, appointed her superintendent of the deaconess training centre. In installing Gertrude into her office, Fliedner preached on Psalm 100:2: 'Serve the LORD with gladness.'

At Kaiserswerth, deaconesses were trained in nursing skills and in teaching Christian truths. Florence Nightingale studied nursing at Kaiserswerth, graduating in 1851. Within Fliedner's and Gertrude's life times the Kaiserswerth complex came to include a Mother House, which provided dwellings for the deaconesses and a hospital, an Infant School, a Female Orphanage, the House of Refuge, a home for Protestant Insane Women, a workers' retreat called Salem, and a House of Rest for aging deaconesses. Interestingly, the German name for the House of Rest was *Feier-Abend Hause*, which means 'the House of the evening which precedes a great festival'. The name itself looked forward to the great heavenly festival and homecoming which awaited those aged women.

When Theodor Fliedner died in 1863, Kaiserswerth had become a model for the re-establishment of deaconesses around the world. Gertrude, now in her seventies, was then one of the aged deaconesses in the House of Rest. She testified that:

> Still the Lord is faithful and near to all who call upon Him. I am old and weak; but the consolations of the Lord are always near and always strong. He will not forsake me even in the valley of the shadow of death, as He did not forsake Pastor Fliedner, who with joy has entered into his rest.[24]

Serve the LORD with gladness!
Come into his presence with singing!

~ PSALM 100:2 ~

---

24. Jan de Liefde, *Six months among the charities of Europe*, vol. 1 (London: Alexander Strahan, 1865), p. 109.

Pioneer Missionary Wife

∞ Lucy Thurston, 1795-1876 ∞

Lucy Goodale's father arranged her meeting with Asa Thurston on 23 September, 1819. Lucy was a well-educated, pious Christian; Asa was a recent graduate from Andover Seminary.

The two were married a few weeks after meeting, and on 23 October, 1819 set sail for Hawaii to bring Christianity to the islands! The voyage took five months, and during the voyage Lucy's admiration, respect, and love for her new husband grew and intensified.

The Thurstons were part of the first missionaries sent out to Hawaii, which was still in the thrall of idol worship. Drunkenness and debauchery were rampant among the people, flamed by the sailors from the numerous trading vessels stopping at the islands. Lucy and Asa mostly served on the island of Kona. They had six children, and while reaching the native Hawaiians with the gospel of Christ they also protected their children from the paganism around them. The missionaries' Christian home became an example of Christian marriage and family life which the Hawaiians could emulate.

Lucy and fellow missionary Elizabeth Bishop held Friday Female Meetings teaching the native women the Scriptures as well as domestic skills, such as sewing. By 1830, 2,600 women were in attendance.

Lucy endured many physical difficulties while in Hawaii – tuberculosis, partial paralysis, and breast cancer. Because of her recent paralysis, the doctor who operated on her for breast cancer advised against her having an anaesthetic. She uncomplainingly endured the surgery, stating, 'God's left hand is underneath my head. His right hand sustains and embraces me. I am willing to suffer.'

Shortly before her death, in 1876, Lucy wrote a soon-to-be married granddaughter:

> It is very beautiful to have two lives mingle and flow into one, producing a union of hearts. May you … become the light of your husband's house, the center of home, that sacred spot of love and harmony, of comfort, quiet, and ease, that wealth alone cannot give, nor poverty take away.[25]

Lucy was such a light in her home and was an example to many in Hawaii and beyond of a Christian wife and mother. Her children and grandchildren continue to be influential in Hawaiian life.

> *Let your adorning be the hidden person of the heart with the imperishable*
> *beauty of a gentle and quiet spirit, which in God's sight is very precious.*
> *For this is how the holy women who hoped in God used to adorn*
> *themselves, by submitting to their own husbands.*
>
> ~ 1 PETER 3:4-5 ~

---

25. Betty Fullard-Leo, 'Lucy Thurston: Missionary Wife', *Coffee Times* (Spring/Summer 1999).

Missionary to the Jew and the Greek

༄ Mary Briscoe Baldwin, 1811-1877 ༄

Born in a Virginia mansion in the Shenandoah Valley on 20 May, 1811, Mary Briscoe Baldwin early devoted her life to Christ. Mary was connected with some of the leaders of Virginia. President James Madison was her mother's uncle. Bishop Meade of the Protestant Episcopal Church, also a relative, influenced Mary and helped her in her spiritual life. When she was ten Mary's parents died, and the twelve children were separated to different homes. This was a sad trial for Mary, but she continued steadfast in her Christian commitment. When she was about twenty, while visiting some relatives in Stanton, Pennsylvania, Mary 'grew weary of fashionable life'. She wanted to be engaged in some useful Christian endeavor, and her thoughts turned to being a missionary, but she thought that position too heavenly for her to attain. Meanwhile, Mary taught at a ladies' boarding school at Stanton.

Mrs Hill, a missionary with her husband in Athens, needed assistance in the school she had established there, and she told of her need to the Protestant Episcopal Society. Mary considered Mrs Hill's request, and, after much thought, she 'rose up with a firm and steady purpose of heart and said, "I will go."'[26] Her salary was only $250, but Mary was able to supplement this with her own funds. She became one of the earliest single lady missionaries from the United States. When she arrived in Greece, Mary was stirred to be in the land where Paul had preached about the 'unknown God' on Mars Hill and proclaimed salvation by Jesus Christ.

Mary took over the entire sewing department of Mrs Hill's school. The girls loved Mary, and the parents appreciated the girls were learning skills enabling them to support themselves. Always most important to Mary was the teaching of the Bible, by which the girls could be good daughters and become good wives and mothers. Many also became teachers. Mary later established a boarding school for higher-class girls in Athens, donating much of her own fortune to see the success of the school. When Crete revolted against Turkey in 1866, many Cretans took refuge in Athens. Mary worked with the refugees, establishing schools, Sunday schools, and providing the women and girls with sewing and knitting materials. When the Cretans returned home, Mary began to think thirty-three years in Greece was sufficient. She then went to Joppa, where her nephew was consul. For eight years she worked in the Protestant schools which had been established there, raising funds for a boys school as well. She rejoiced to be in the Holy Land where so much of the Biblical history occurred. Mary always thought 'the position of a missionary of the Gospel of Christ the very highest privilege which could be bestowed upon me while on earth'.[27]

Mary died on 21 June, 1877, after forty-two years of missionary service. She is buried near the Jordan Valley. The inscription on her tomb reads, 'There is no difference between the Jew and the Greek: for the same Lord over all is rich unto all that call upon him.'

For in one Spirit we were all baptized into one body
– Jews or Greeks, slaves or free –
and all were made to drink of one Spirit.

~ I CORINTHIANS 12:13 ~

---

26. Annie Ryder Gracey, *Eminent Missionary Women* (New York: Eaton and Mains, 1898), p. 72.
27. Ibid, p. 77.

Solitary Light in a 'Dark Place'

∽ early 19th century ∾

Robert Moffatt spent twenty-three years as a missionary in South Africa with the London Missionary Society. During that time he translated the Bible into Setswana, and the British and Foreign Bible Society aided in its publication. Thousands of copies of the Psalms and New Testament in Setswana were sent into Southern Africa, and as literacy spread, thousands were able to read the Word of God in their own language. There is a power in the Word alone, and it showed its power among the people. Jesus and the apostles speak clearly in the Word. As Moffatt looked over the vast interior of Africa, with the Bible now in many villages, he rejoiced that:

> When taught to read they have in their hands the means not only of recovering them from their natural darkness, but of keeping the lamp of life burning even amidst comparatively desert gloom. In one of my early journeys with some of my companions, we came to a heathen village on the banks of the Orange River, between Namaqua-land and the Griqua country. We had travelled far, and were hungry, thirsty, and fatigued. From the fear of being exposed to lions, we preferred remaining at the village to proceeding during the night. The people at the village rather roughly directed us to halt at a distance. We asked for water, but they would not supply it. I offered the three or four buttons which still remained on my jacket for a little milk; this also was refused. We had the prospect of another hungry night at a distance from water, though within sight of the river. We found it difficult to reconcile ourselves to our lot, for in addition to repeated rebuffs, the manner of the villagers excited suspicion. When twilight drew on, a woman approached from the height beyond which the village lay. She bore on her head a bundle of wood, and had a vessel of milk in her hand. The latter, without opening her lips, she handed to us, laid down the wood, and returned to the village. A second time she approached with a cooking vessel on her head, and a leg of mutton in one hand, and water in the other. She sat down without saying a word, prepared the fire, and put on the meat. We asked her again and again who she was. She remained silent till affectionately entreated to give us a reason for such unlooked for kindness to strangers. The solitary tear stole down her sable cheek, when she replied, 'I love Him whose servant you are, and surely it is my duty to give you a cup of cold water in his name. My heart is full, therefore I cannot speak the joy I feel to see you in this out-of-the-world place.' On learning a little of her history, and that she was a solitary light burning in a dark place, I asked her how she kept up the life of God in her soul in the entire absence of the communion of saints. She drew from her bosom a copy of the Dutch New Testament, which she had received from Mr Helm when in his school some years previous, before she had been compelled by her connexions to retire to her present seclusion. 'This' she said, 'is the fountain whence I drink; this is the oil which makes my lamp burn.'[28]

Moffat noticed the Bible had been printed by the British and Foreign Bible Society. He and his companions had a joyous time of prayer and fellowship with this solitary light in Africa, nourished by God's Word. Moffat rejoiced, 'Glory to God in the highest, and on earth peace, good will to men!'

And we also thank God constantly for this, that when you received the word of God, which you heard from us, you accepted it not as the word of men but as what it really is, the word of God, which is at work in you believers.

~ 1 THESSALONIANS 2:13 ~

---

28. Robert Moffat, *Missionary Labours and Scenes in Southern Africa* (London: John Snow, 1842), pp. 618-620.

First Protestant Missionary to Mexico

∽ Melinda Rankin, 1811-1888 ∾

Only a few years before Melinda Rankin was born in New Hampshire in 1811, the United States bought the vast Louisiana Purchase from France, encouraging the westward movement of the country which would characterize the nineteenth century. Melinda became part of the missionary arm of that westward movement.

In 1840, Melinda moved to Kentucky and established schools in the Mississippi Valley, then, in 1842, moved to Mississippi and Alabama, where she established schools and worked among the poor. The Bible was always an important part of the education in the schools Melinda began. After the Mexican-American War concluded in 1848, Melinda talked with many of the returning soldiers, who told her there was a hunger for the Bible in Mexico. During the War the American Bible Society had distributed over 7,000 Bibles to American troops and Mexican civilians. Melinda was eager to take the gospel and the light of the Scriptures into Mexico, but it did not allow missionary activity. Nevertheless, Melinda left Mississippi for Texas.

Melinda taught at the Huntsville Female Academy and published a book, *Texas, 1850*, descriptive of the land and institutions of Texas. In her preface she specifically stated that she was furnishing this description to:

> enlist Christian sympathy and co-operation in aid of evangelizing a country which is destined, evidently, to exert an important influence over other contiguous countries. Texas occupies a very important position in regard to the unevangelical portions of our own continent.[29]

Melinda urged Christians in the eastern part of the United States to:

> do a great deal more, in strengthening the hands and encouraging the hearts of Christians, who are occupying the destitute fields in Texas. The growing importance of Texas is a matter of serious consideration. … Whether the blessings of the gospel will accompany all the changes which will evidently take place, is a question of infinite importance.[30]

Melinda went and settled at Brownsville, Texas, on the border with Mexico. There she established a school and found ways to have Bibles brought into Mexico, though that was against Mexican law at the time. Melinda was encouraged when one day a mother of one of her students came and brought her the statue of a saint. The woman said she had prayed to it all her life, but it had never done any good, and she would like to exchange it for a Bible!

In 1857, when religious liberty was allowed in Mexico, Melinda moved to Monterrey, Mexico and began the first Protestant mission in the country. She worked establishing schools, distributing Bibles, and encouraging the growth of native teachers. In 1872, after twenty years, Melinda retired and returned to the United States because of ill health. She had hoped to live out her life in Mexico and die there, saying, 'it had been the long cherished desire of my heart that I might make my last resting place with the Mexican people, and with them rise in the morning of resurrection, as a testimony that I had desired their salvation.'[31]

In the way of your testimonies I delight …

~ PSALM 119:14 ~

---

29. Melind Rankin, *Texas, 1850* (Boston: Damrell & Moore, 1850) pp 3-4

30. Ibid, p. 5.

31. Annie Ryder Gracey, *Eminent Missionary Women* (New York: Eaton & Mains, 1898), p. 65.

Model Missionary Wife

∞ Jessie McClymont Inglis, 1811-1885 ∞

Jessie McClymont, born in Corriefechloch, Scotland in 1811 received an excellent education and upbringing to become a missionary's wife. After completing her schooling at fourteen, Jessie helped her mother in the domestic affairs and in bringing up the younger children of the large family. Ministers and missionaries were often guests at the McClymont home, and Jessie developed skills in hospitality. When she was about eighteen Jessie made a profession of faith in Christ and joined the church. She regularly read and studied her Bible.

On 11 April, 1844, Jessie married John Inglis, who was being sent out to New Zealand by the Reformed Presbyterian Mission. The couple left for New Zealand three months after their marriage. After eight years in New Zealand they relocated to the New Hebrides, joining John and Charlotte Geddes in their work on Aneityum, the southernmost of the New Hebrides islands. As they settled into what would be twenty-five years on the island, Jessie devoted herself to being first a wife and then a missionary. She took her household duties seriously in keeping a comfortable home with well-prepared food, knowing this would be important in maintaining their health in the debilitating climate.

Jessie and John shared the same perspectives on all the issues of life, creating a most harmonious marriage. In part this was due to their reading together in the evenings. Reading each other biographies (especially missionary biographies), theology works, and simply what news periodicals might come to hand brought unity to their thinking. Jessie learned the Aneityunese language and was able to help John in his translation work and other writing. John did not write anything which Jessie did not proofread and critique. Working with John Geddes, the translation of the New Testament was completed in 1873; the Old Testament was completed in 1879. In addition, an abridged version of *The Pilgrim's Progress*, a hymnal, grammar and other books were printed.

Jessie noticed that arrowroot grew on the island, though the natives knew nothing about its use. She learned how to prepare it, taught the natives, and they began preparing and shipping the arrowroot to New Zealand. Sale of the arrowroot helped pay for the printing of the Aneityunese Bible.

In addition to her own domestic affairs, Jessie taught a girls' class reading and the memorization of the Scriptures as well as a sewing class for women. Once a lady in Scotland sent out some cloth for a dress to be given to the student who led in the memorization of the first six chapters of Acts. Rather then one student, there were six girls who memorized the chapters without a mistake, requiring fabric for six dresses! Many of Jessie's students went on to become excellent teachers themselves. Jessie was able show the natives the value of girls and halted the infanticide of girls which had prevailed on the island. After eight years on the island, 1,800 people had turned away from heathenism to Christ. Jessie had assisted in the making of all of the clothes they then wore.

Do not grow weary in doing good.

~ 2 THESSALONIANS 3:13 ~

Saving Women from the Cannibals

∝ Mary Ann Lyth, 1811-1890 ∝

In 1836, Mary Ann Hardy married the Rev. Richard B. Lyth and sailed for the South Sea Islands where the Lyths became missionary pioneers. Rev. Lyth was the first medical missionary on the islands. Mary Ann uncomplainingly shared the hardships, perils, and strong faith of her husband while living among cannibalistic natives.

The first three years of the Lyths mission were spent in Tonga, where Mrs Lyth learned the Tonga language. The Tonga were very receptive to the gospel. Thousands converted to Christianity and then eagerly wanted to send the gospel to the Fijians. The Lyths were then sent to Somosomo, Fiji, where they learned the Fijian language. Rev. Lyth established a hospital there; Mary Ann nursed the sick and trained the natives in nursing. The Fijians were frequently at war with each other, and often the cannibal death-drum could be heard. Bodies were sometimes dragged in front of the mission house as a sacrifice before they were cooked to be eaten. When Commodore Wilkes of the United States Exploring Expedition visited Somosomo, he remarked upon the patience and courage of Mary Ann and the other missionary wives:

> nothing but a deep sense of duty and a strong determination to perform it could induce civilized persons to subject themselves to the sight of such horrid scenes as they are called upon almost daily to witness. I know no situation so trying for ladies to live in, particularly when pleasing and well informed, as we found at Somosomo.[32]

After five years at Somosomo the Lyths moved to Lakemba, where many of the natives had become Christians and a school was established to train local pastors and teachers. Mary Ann taught the wives, teaching them a Bible lesson they could repeat back in their own villages, as well as sewing and knitting. After eight years in Lakemba the Lyths went to Viwa, where Mary Ann assisted in Bible translation.

> On one occasion, when her husband was away, fourteen native women captured as prisoners of war were about to be killed, offered as sacrifice, and eaten. Mary Ann and another missionary wife, Mrs Calvert, determined to rescue the women. As they approached the camp, they could already hear piercing shrieks and knew the butchery had begun. Nevertheless, they rushed through the cannibalistic crowds to the house of King Tanoa. Though it was forbidden for women to enter, they came in with a whale's tooth in each hand as offerings and pled for the lives of the captured women. King Tanoa was amazed at their approach and said, 'Those who are dead *are dead*, but those who are alive *shall live*.' Five of the women were rescued. Only when she looked back on the event later did Mary Ann realize the great danger she had been in.

The work on Fiji did bear fruit, and a Christian church was firmly established on the island.

For one will scarcely die for a righteous person –
though perhaps for a good person one would dare even to die –
but God shows his love for us in that
while we were still sinners, Christ died for us.

~ ROMANS 5:7-8 ~

---

32. Annie Ryder Gracey, *Eminent Missionary Women* (N.Y.: Eaton & Mains, 1898), p. 42.

Abiding in Love

∞ Mary Custis Lee, 1808-1873 ∞

Growing up, Mary Custis was surrounded by stories of George Washington, who had adopted her father, George Washington Parke Custis, who was Washington's stepson. The Custis home at Arlington was filled with Washington memorabilia, and visitors always wanted Mary's father to tell about growing up at Mount Vernon. Mary was a vivacious girl who loved learning. With a special gift for languages, she could easily read French, Latin, and Greek. In the summer of 1830, Mary experienced two very important events. Robert E. Lee, her third cousin whom she had known since childhood, proposed marriage. Robert was a West Point graduate and a man of excellent character; Mary accepted his offer.

Also that summer, Mary's Uncle Fitzhugh, master of Ravensworth plantation, died. Aunt Maria was devastated by his death, sank into despair, and became a shell of her former self. Mary began praying that God would comfort her aunt. There was such desolation at Ravensworth, Mary prayed that God would change not only her aunt's but her own heart. She wrote in her journal:

> I first prayed to my God to change my heart & make me His true & faithful servant until my life's end. I was led on by His blessed spirit from day to day more & more to desire His favour, to see my base ingratitude & unworthiness to Him who so loved us as to give His only son to die for us, to see my utter helplessness, to cast all my hopes upon my Savior, to feel a willingness to give up all I had formerly delighted in for His sake & afterwards through His grace not to desire them, to feel my heart melted with love to God.[33]

The prayers Mary recorded in her journal that summer reveal a heart renewed by Christ and seeking to serve Him in every way:

> O my Father, let me thank Thee for Thy mercies to me, that Thou hast drawn me to Thee by the cords of love – What shall I render to the Lord for all His goodness? I would say my vows in His courts this day. I would dedicate my life to Him. I would live with a single eye to His service – yet – O my Saviour, thou who has borne our human nature knowest how weak we are, how utterly unable to do anything of ourselves. Thou wilt pity me & support me … enable me to feel that what Thou has promised Thou wilt surely perform, for Lord in whom shall we trust, if not in Thee? Keep me from spiritual pride, selfishness, indolence. Make my heart soft to receive Thy holy word & never suffer it to turn again to the world. Oh I dread that snare, but if Thou uphold me I shall be safe. Make me humble, my Saviour. Make me to abhor and hate myself on account of sin and above all make me love Thee more & more …[34]

Mary's devotion to Christ continued throughout her life. Mary and Robert were married on 31 June, 1831, and regular Bible reading and family worship were part of their daily lives as they raised three sons and four daughters. Robert became a leading soldier in the United States and then in the Confederate States during the Civil War. Mary suffered from arthritis and was confined to a wheelchair in later life, but her joy in the Lord remained throughout her days.

God is love, and whoever abides in love abides in God,
and God abides in him.

~ 1 JOHN 4:16 ~

---

33. John Perry, *Lady of Arlington: The Life of Mrs Robert E. Lee Sisters* (Oregon: Multnomah Publishers, 2001), p. 76.
34. Ibid, p. 72.

Wife of the Bishop of Jerusalem
∞ Maria Zeller Gobat, 1813-1879 ∞

Samuel Gobat was a Swiss Lutheran missionary in Abyssinia (modern Ethiopia) when he met Maria Zeller at her father's home in Zofingen, Switzerland. Maria's father was a noted educator, pietist, and director of the schools in Zofingen. Samuel thought Maria eminently qualified to be the wife of a missionary, and accordingly the two were married on 23 May, 1834, when Maria was twenty-one.

The trip to Maria's new home in Abyssinia was a tortuous one – thirty-six days in a small boat in the Red Sea, followed by riding camels through the desert. Samuel became ill before the Gobats reached their destination of Adowa. Maria bestowed great love and nursing care on Samuel, but he became bedridden for two years; during this time their first child was born. As Samuel appeared to be dying, it was decided to return to Europe. Once again they traveled through the hot desert and in the small boat to reach Cairo. Samuel bought a goat to provide milk for the baby along the way, but the goat died. The baby died too and was buried in Cairo.

Samuel did regain his health in Switzerland, and Maria and Samuel went on to have nine more children. For two years Samuel was assigned to Malta, where he superintended the translation of the Bible into Arabic. He was appointed Vice Principal of the Malta Protestant College; but before he assumed his position, he was nominated by Frederick William IV to be Bishop of Jerusalem, which was a joint bishopric for Anglicans, Lutherans and Calvinists under the Anglican Church of England and the United Evangelical Church in Prussia. Samuel was Bishop in Jerusalem for thirty-three years, and Maria and Samuel thought of Jerusalem as their home.

Maria was ever Samuel's helper, especially in the numerous schools and orphanages he established in the Holy Land. Her hospitality to many travelers to the Holy Land was one way she let the light of Christ shine in her life. A prayer she had written, found among her papers, reveals the longing of her heart:

> O Lord, long-suffering and gracious, how many years hast thou added to my life, and yet I still am an unfruitful fig-tree; although thou, O Heavenly Gardener, hast not failed to dig, to prune, and to do all that ought to have made me fruit-bearing to thine honour and glory. Oh! Spare me yet, and continue Thy working in me til I have wholly yielded to Thy constraining love. O Lord Jesus, Lamb of God, make me feel assured that Thou hast taken my sins on Thee, so that I am now free from condemnation. Oh, give me grace to be taught by Thy Holy Spirit, to be led by him, and not to resist his admonitions, his warnings. This is one of the causes, I am afraid, of my not enjoying more the gracious promises of Thy Holy Word, and possessing that peace which passeth all understanding. Let me wrestle and pray, and not faint till I have *fully* found, and with Thee, and in Thee, everlasting life. Let me be a mother in Israel, a priestess in Thy house, and in my family. O Lord, let me be a true Mary, sitting at Thy feet, especially now, when I cannot be a Martha, being unable to go out and serve Thee, visiting the members of our congregation. Let me be a Mary, being Thy servant, and keeping Thy words.[35]

After suffering a stroke during a visit to Europe, Samuel died in Jerusalem. Maria died less than twelve weeks later, joining him before the throne of the Lamb.

'Martha, Martha, you are anxious and troubled about many things, but one thing is necessary. Mary has chosen the good portion, which will not be taken away from her.'

~ LUKE 10:41-42 ~

---

35. Emma Raymond Pitman, *Heroines of the Mission Field* (London, Paris & New York: Cassell, Petter, Galpin & Co., 1880), pp. 79-80.

Jesus Christ for Every Man

∞ Catherine Marsh, 1818-1912 ∞

In 1853, three thousand navvies (laborers) began work on moving the Crystal Palace from Hyde Park to Sydenham. Two hundred of them were lodged in Beckenham, where Catherine Marsh lived in the rectory. Miss Marsh, for such she was always called, was the youngest daughter of an elderly clergyman. She and her father lived with her sister and brother-in-law, Rev. F. Chalmers, who was the rector of Beckenham. Miss Marsh was a most caring nurse to her ailing father, often spending long evening hours reading the Scriptures to him.

When the navvies descended on Beckenham, many of the neighbors feared the rough influence the workmen would have on the town, but Miss Marsh, with great evangelistic spirit, was most concerned about their souls. One Sunday evening she went to visit a cottage belonging to a family, knowing some of the navvies were lodged there. A gruff man answered the door, and Miss Marsh found herself inside a room filled with hardy laborers. One young man brought a chair, and she began to pleasantly converse with the men. She asked them if they had been to church that morning. When they said they hadn't even thought about it, Miss Marsh reviewed the sermon for them. As the dignified lady sat among the rough workers, she spoke with warmth and feeling about the Savior and the things of God. One young man said he had always thought of God as an angry God, but she spoke of him as a friend. When she offered to pray with the men, the younger man was ready, but he said one of the other men never opened his mouth except to swear. Miss Marsh offered to pray with him too. As she knelt with all the men in the room and offered her prayers to God, two or three of the men were sobbing. Miss Marsh had not only spoken to them about the Savior, but her manner showed a care and concern for them which they had not known. Miss Marsh began Cottage Bible readings in the barn of the rectory, and many of the navvies began walking in Christian faith.

Miss Marsh wrote extensively and published over fifty works, including the very popular *English Hearts and English Hands*, recounting stories of the Lord's work among the navvies. The work influenced many other women at the end of the nineteenth century to reach out to others in Bible work, including Ellen Ranyard, the foundress of the Bible Women and Nurses' Mission in London, and Agnes Weston, who worked extensively among the sailors.

During the cholera epidemic of 1866, Miss Marsh spent many weeks counseling and consoling those in the London Hospital. She established one of the earliest convalescent homes in England at Brighton. Promising many dying parents she would care for their children, she established an orphanage in Beckenham. To young and old, Miss Marsh always had a comforting Scripture and word of encouragement from the pages of God's Word. She knew Jesus Christ was for every man.

She was full of good works and acts of charity.

~ Acts 9:36 ~

More Love to Thee

∞ Elizabeth Prentiss, 1818-1878 ∞

Elizabeth Prentiss was both a daughter and wife of prominent Presbyterian ministers. She was active in caring for the sick in body and soul in her husband's church, as well as with the numerous responsibilities of her own family. Beginning with her father's death when she was nine years old, Elizabeth learned the lessons which could be learned through suffering. Often in ill health, when she was twenty-two she commented that 'I never knew what it was to feel well.' Throughout her life she suffered from insomnia, leading to restless nights and weary days. Yet, she learned that suffering could often be a way of God preparing his children for further service, and joy came to characterize her life.

In 1852, her four-year-old son Eddy died; within three months Elizabeth bore a little girl who died shortly after birth. Later, found among her manuscripts was a scrap of paper entitled 'My Nursery, 1852':

> I thought that prattling boys and girls
> Would fill this empty room;
> That my rich heart would gather flowers
> From childhood's opening bloom.
> One child and two green graves are mine,
> That is God's gift to me:
> A bleeding, fainting, broken heart –
> That is *my* gift to Thee.[36]

In the years that followed Elizabeth did indeed give her heart to God by authoring children's books that taught moral truths of Christianity. For several years she wrote a children's book a year, often using examples and allegories to teach simple moral principles. Many of the works were translated and published into French and German as well. All of her books were born in prayer; Elizabeth never sat down to write anything without first praying, 'that I might not be suffered to write anything that would do harm, and that, on the contrary I might be taught to say what would do good.'

Elizabeth's most famous work, *Stepping Heavenward*, first published in serial form in *The Chicago Advance*, was published as a book in 1869. It went through numerous printings in England, Germany, Australia, Switzerland, and France, as well as the United States. The story of the heroine Katy's loves, mistakes, despairs, successes and gradual, steady progress in Christian devotion and service continues to encourage women today. In the preface to *Stepping Heavenward* Elizabeth explained the purpose of her writings:

> The aim of [my] writings, whether designed for young or old, is to incite patience, fidelity, hope and all goodness by showing how trust in God and loving obedience to his blessed will brighten the darkest paths and make a heaven upon earth.

Elizabeth did not seek worldly fame or position. She repeatedly prayed that God would 'crowd the self out of me by taking up all the room himself'. It is fitting that she is perhaps best known today as the author of the hymn, 'More Love to Thee'.

'I love you, O LORD, my strength.'

~ PSALM 18:1 ~

---

36. George Lewis Prentiss, *More Love to Thee: The Life and Letters of Elizabeth Prentiss* (New York: A. D. F. Randolph & Co., 1882), p. 138.

JUNE 21

Chinese Girls' School in Singapore

∽ Sophia Cooke, 1814-1895 ∼

St Margaret's Primary School, the oldest girls' school in Singapore and East Asia, was founded in 1842 by Maria Dyer, a missionary with the London Missionary Society. Here orphan girls had the opportunity to receive an education and learn the truth of God in Christ Jesus. The school held on after Maria had to leave Singapore and began to flourish with the arrival of Sophia Cooke in 1853. Sophia had been a governess in England for twenty years and was thirty-nine when she arrived in Singapore.

When Sophia came to what was then known as the Chinese Girls' School, there were twenty girls at the boarding school. Sophia quickly learned the Malay language and enthusiastically developed the educational standards of the school. The girls were taught Scripture and from an early age learned the importance of serving others. Sophia often took the students with her on her hospital visits, bringing handmade gifts or flowers. Sophia saw the school as a place to train girls to become Christian wives and mothers. In the 1860s, two day schools were begun for women and children. One school was run by older students from the Chinese Girls' School; the other was run by a former pupil.

Sophia had the gift of bringing others together in Christian service. In 1857, she and a few other ladies formed the Ladies' Bible and Tract Society to encourage each other in Christian work. The Society published a quarterly magazine, *The Christian in Singapore*. Sophia began a monthly meeting for graduates of the Chinese Girls' School, which later was reorganized and became the Young Women's Christian Association (YWCA) in Singapore.

With many sailors visiting Singapore's port, Sophia saw the opportunity to reach out to them with both physical aid and the gospel. In 1882, she and Mr Hocguard, a Brethren Missionary, organized a Sailors' Rest. Many sailors came to Christ through the Wednesday Bible classes conducted there. Sophia used Bible study notes from Dwight L. Moody and introduced many of the sailors to the hymns of Ira Sankey.

When Sophia returned to England for a visit in 1880 the Society for Promoting Female Education in the East, Sophia's mission agency, thought she would retire, but Sophia had more work to do in Singapore, where she returned and worked until her death in 1895. Sophia had plenteously sown the seed of the gospel and saw much fruit during her forty-two years in Singapore.

Older women likewise are to be reverent in behavior, not slanderers or slaves to much wine. They are to teach what is good, and so train the young women to love their husbands and children ...

~ Titus 2:3-4 ~

Bible Women for London

∞ Ellen Ranyard, 1809-1879 ∞

Raised in a Christian home, Ellen White early developed a concern for the poor. As a teenager she visited poor families to bring them the gospel and whatever aid she could. When she was sixteen, she and her friend Elizabeth Saunders visited the sick in a poor neighborhood and both caught a fever, from which Elizabeth died. Ellen continued her visitation to the poor, especially working with the Bible Society and supplying the poor with Bibles.

In 1839, Ellen married Benjamin Ranyard, and the couple had one son, Arthur Cowper Ranyard, who became a noted astronomer. In 1852, Ellen wrote *The Book and its Story, a Narrative for the Young*. This popular book not only told the story in the Bible, but also told the story of the Bible in our English translations. In 1857, Ellen formally organized her work among the poor and established the Bible and Domestic Female Mission. The Mission had a two-fold purpose: 'to supply the poorest of the population with copies of the Holy Scriptures, and also to improve their temporal condition by teaching them to help themselves rather than look to others.'[37]

Ellen's innovations in organizing the work among the London poor became a pattern for later organizations. One idea which missionaries around the world would use was that of the 'Bible woman'. The Bible woman was from the poor herself, living in the district, and a Christian of the highest character, but without a family to care for. She was given a three-months training. Her first work was to see who did not have the Scriptures and provide inexpensive copies for them to purchase – in small weekly installments if necessary. Each Bible woman was under a Superintendent from the middle class who received the weekly reports and directed the Bible woman, who also could take subscriptions for clothing and bedding, as well as provide instructions in needlework, cooking, and cleanliness. Ellen believed the reform of mothers was most important if the conditions of the poor were to be improved. By 1867, there were 234 Bible women working in London, the first group of paid social workers in the city.

In 1868, Ellen began a program of Bible nurses, who were trained in London hospitals before being assigned to one of London's districts. The Bible nurses held mothers' meetings, referred patients to doctors, and encouraged medical self-help among the poor. Ellen regularly published periodicals which recounted the work being done on the streets of London by the Bible women and Bible nurses. In all her work, Ellen was most concerned in providing the Word of God to the people, 'Let us sow them wherever we are able the imperishable seed of the word, broadcasting it in humble faith and prayer.'[38]

You have been born again, not of perishable seed but of imperishable,
through the living and abiding word of God.

~ I PETER 1:23 ~

---

37. L N R [pen name used by Ellen Ranyard], *The missing link, or Bible-women in the homes of the London poor* (New York: Robert Carter & Brothers, 1860), p. 297.

38. Quoted in E. Platt, *The Story of the Ranyard Mission, 1857-1937* (London: Hodder and Stoughton, 1937), p. 1.

Modiste for the First Lady

∽ Elizabeth Keckley, 1818-1907 ∾

When Elizabeth Keckley moved to Washington, D.C. in 1860, planning to work as a dressmaker, she never expected to become acquainted with – much less close friends with – the President of the United States or his wife. Elizabeth was born a slave in 1818 in Virginia. Only late in life would she learn her father was the master of the plantation, Armistead Burwell. Her mother was one of fifty slaves on the plantation. Elizabeth learned sewing from her mother and became quite skilled in dressmaking. As a teenager, she was loaned out to Burwell's son, a Presbyterian pastor. His wife did not like Elizabeth and enlisted a neighbor to beat her to subdue her 'stubborn pride'. Elizabeth was flogged weekly for three weeks, until the neighbor broke down in tears saying it was a sin to beat her any more. During these years, a white man forced himself on Elizabeth, and she had a son by him.

Elizabeth then was loaned to Robert Burwell's sister, Ann Garland, and moved with the family to St Louis in 1847. Elizabeth helped the Garlands through some desperate financial times and virtually supported the family through her sewing. She married James Keckley, but he was prone to dissipation, and the couple separated after a few years. She enrolled her son in Wilberforce University, affiliated with the African Methodist Episcopal Church and the first college owned and operated by African Americans. She was able to buy her freedom and moved to Washington, D.C. to work as a seamstress.

Elizabeth quickly gained work in the nation's capital and was commissioned to make dresses for Mrs Robert E. Lee, Mrs Jefferson Davis, and Mary Todd Lincoln. Mrs Lincoln was very fond of clothes, and soon Elizabeth was coming regularly to the White House to help dress and care for Mrs Lincoln's appearance, becoming a close friend. Elizabeth published an autobiography in 1868 in which she described some of the scenes she had observed while with the Lincolns. One day, President Lincoln came into the room with a look of dejection, having just come from the War Department and found all the news dark. Lincoln lay down on the sofa and picked up a little Bible to read. After a quarter of an hour, Elizabeth looked at the President and noticed has face was more cheerful:

> The dejected look was gone, and the countenance was lighted up with new resolution and hope. The change was so marked that I could not but wonder at it, and wonder led to the desire to know what book of the Bible afforded so much comfort to the reader. Making the search for a missing article an excuse, I walked gently around the sofa, and looking into the open book, I discovered that Mr Lincoln was reading that divine comforter, Job. He read with Christian eagerness, and the courage and hope that he derived from the inspired pages make him a new man. I almost imagined that I could hear the Lord speaking to him from out of the whirlwind of battle: 'Gird up thy loins now like a man: I will demand of thee, and declare thou unto me.' What a sublime picture was this! A ruler of a mighty nation going to the pages of the Bible with simple Christian earnestness for comfort and courage, and finding both in the darkest hours of a nation's calamity. Ponder it, O ye scoffers at God's Holy Word, and then hang your heads for very shame![39]

> *I know you can do all things,*
> *and that no purpose of yours can be thwarted.*
>
> ~ JOB 42:2 ~

---

39. Elizabeth Keckley, *Thirty years a slave, and four years in the White House* (New York: Carleton & Co. Publishers, 1868).

Queen Finds Assurance of Salvation

∞ Queen Victoria, 1819-1901 ∞

After a service in St Paul's Cathedral in London, Queen Victoria asked her chaplain, 'Can one be absolutely sure in this life of eternal safety?' The chaplain answered, 'No, there is no way that anyone can be absolutely sure.' The conversation was later published in the *Court News*. When minister John Townsend read the conversation, he prayed for wisdom and then wrote the Queen the following letter:

> To Her Gracious Majesty, our beloved Queen Victoria, from one of your most humble subjects: With trembling hands, but heart-filled love, and because I know that we can be absolutely sure now for our eternal life in the home that Jesus went to prepare, may I ask your Most Gracious Majesty to read the following passages of Scripture: John 3:16; Romans 10:9-10. I sign myself, your servant for Jesus' sake, John Townsend.

Townsend had others pray with him for the Queen after sending his letter.

About two weeks later, Townsend received this letter from the Queen:

> To John Townsend: I have carefully and prayerfully read the portions of Scripture referred to. I now believe in the finished work of Christ for me, and trust by God's grace, to meet you one day in that place He has prepared for us in heaven. Victoria Guelph.[40]

The Queen's assurance of salvation and eternal felicity came from the Scriptures. She began keeping with her a little booklet by George Cutting, 'Safety, Certainty and Enjoyment', which she would share with others to help them find the same assurance in Christ. Cutting's classic tract noted there were three classes of people: Those who are saved and know it; those who are not sure of salvation, but are anxious to be sure, and those who are not only unsaved, but totally indifferent about it. Cutting clearly presented the biblical understanding of salvation through trust in Jesus Christ and eternal assurance because of God's promises.

When Queen Victoria was later visiting one of her Royal Estates, an elderly woman approached her and timidly asked, 'Your Majesty, will I see you in Heaven one day?' Victoria smiled and answered, 'By the all-availing blood of Jesus, you most assuredly shall, my dear! I have His word on it!'

The Queen was deeply grieved by the death of her beloved husband, Prince Albert. Victoria ever after wore black. She gave orders, however, that she was not to be buried in black; she was to be buried in white and in her wedding veil, looking forward to the Marriage Supper of the Lamb. Above the door of the Royal Mausoleum at Frogmore where Albert and then Victoria were buried, Victoria had inscribed, 'Farewell best friend, here at last I shall rest with thee, with thee in Christ I shall rise again.'

Because, if you confess with your mouth that Jesus is Lord and
believe in your heart that God raised him from the dead, you will
be saved. For with the heart one believes and is justified and with
the mouth one confesses and is saved.

~ ROMANS:10:9-10 ~

---

40. Letters sited in Robert E. Coleman, *The Heart of the Gospel* (Baker Books, 2011), pp. 197-198.

Beloved Partner

❧ Mary Moffat, 1795-1871 ❧

It was at the Moravian School at Fairfield that Mary Smith's attraction to missions was planted. When she met Robert Moffatt, who was working as a gardener while his application to the London Missionary Society was being processed, the two young people felt a calling to serve together in missionary work and became engaged. Robert's parents were not enthusiastic about his missionary plans. Mary encouraged them: 'Surely you would be willing to be deprived of an earthly comfort, to have more of the consolation of the spirit of God.' When her own family at first disapproved of her joining Robert in missionary work, she wrote her brother, 'Surely it ought to afford consolation that I am now united to one who counts not his life dear to himself.'[41]

Robert sailed for South Africa in 1816 and joined missionaries at Afrikaner's Kraal. Mary, after finally obtaining her parents' approval, went out to South Africa three years later. Robert met Mary in Cape Town, and the two were married on December 27, 1819. Mary wrote, 'Oh, my cup of happiness seems almost full; here I have found in him all my heart could desire.'[42]

The 'honeymoon' was a seven-week, 700-mile trip north by oxcart. Mary trusted, 'the Lord will not disappoint my hopes but will grant me the honour of doing something for Him in Africa'. Soon they moved farther north to the Kuruman Valley. Living conditions were primitive, but Mary learned to make her home in a mud hut and, with irrigation, made their Kuruman home an oasis in the desert. She established a school for the children as well as working to teach the women to read and to sew, encouraging modesty in their dress. Robert worked diligently in learning the language and translating the Bible into Tswana.

Mary was truly a partner with Robert in their work and always an encourager to him in times of discouragement. There were no converts for many years, and the Moffats began to think they were simply preparing the soil for the next missionaries who would harvest the fruit. In faith, however, Mary wrote friends in England to send out a communion set. The communion set arrived three years later, just days before the first converts were to be baptized in February 1829. The timing seemed a special 'mark of the Divine approbation'.

Robert and Mary had ten children, two of whom died in infancy. Oldest daughter Mary married the famous missionary and explorer David Livingston; son John continued his parents' work at Kuruman, and other children continued in various aspects of Christian work. After over fifty years in Africa, Robert and Mary returned to England in 1870. Within five months Mary, suffering from bronchitis, breathed her last and entered eternity. The Lord had abundantly answered her desire, 'the honour of doing something for Him in Africa'.[43]

'If anyone serves me, he must follow me;
and where I am, there will my servant be also.
If anyone serves me, the father will honour him.'

~ JOHN 12:26 ~

---

41. John S. Moffat, *The Lives of Robert & Mary Moffat* (London: T. Fisher Unwin, 1885), p. 53.

42. Ibid, p. 68.

43. 'Mary Moffat', *Gospel Fellowship Association*, https://www.gfamissions.org/missionary-biographies/moffat-mary.html.

Doing All Things Heartily as to the Lord

 Catherine Tait, 1819-1878

Catherine Tait's husband Archibald had been Dean of Carlisle since 1849, diligently pastoring the people while also restoring the cathedral. Catherine was busy with her growing family of seven children as well as caring for the poor in the community. Together they prayed daily as a family, especially that all the children might be found in Christ. Early each morning Catherine had a time of private devotion, reading the Scriptures and communing with her Savior in prayer. Daily she attended the parish church services, which led to her knowing most of the psalms by heart.

Catherine had a buoyant, cheerful nature, but she and her husband were engulfed in tragedy in 1856. Within five weeks, five daughters died of scarlet fever. In her deep grief Catherine yet rejoiced, confident her children were with Jesus. She accepted everything as from the Lord, and He gave her strength and solace at such a loss.

Catherine endlessly gave of herself to others. She visited the poor in their homes and helped them with their needs. When her husband became Dean of London she continued her interest in the poor, reading to old people in the workhouse and working in hospitals. She organized a Ladies Diocesan Society to coordinate women's charitable work and gathered the women in her home for weekly religious services. Concerned for orphans after the cholera plague, she worked with Mrs Gladstone to provide a home for children. The children visited her home on Sundays, and she read *The Pilgrim's Progress* to them.

When her husband became Archbishop of Canterbury, Catherine organized a system for the ladies or children of the upper classes to befriend a particular child in the orphanage, providing both funds and friendship for them. She had a large garden next to the Archbishop's residence and frequently sent vegetables from it to those in need. The archbishop described his wife's life:

> According to the grace given to her, she did her work as to the Lord, without any ostentation; − giving of her abundance with cheerfulness; ruling her house with diligence; charitable and cheerful; abhorring that which is evil; cleaving to that which is good; kindly affectioned in sisterly love; preferring others to herself; not slothful in business; fervent in spirit; serving the Lord; rejoicing in hope, patient in all trials; continuing instant in prayer; distributing to the necessities of those in need; given to hospitality; blessing by her gracious words and demeanour; rejoicing with them that rejoiced, and weeping with them that wept; not minding high things; accessible and kind to those of low estate; never recompensing evil for evil; providing things honest in the sight of all men.[44]

Catherine's three daughters followed their mother in Christian devotion and caring for others. Her son Craufurd was a man of outstanding character who became a pastor and for a time his father's chaplain. More sorrow came when Craufurd became ill and died in 1878, at the age of twenty-nine. Catherine died a few months later, gathered to paradise with her six children who had gone before.

The joy of the LORD is your strength.

~ NEHEMIAH 8:10 ~

---

44. Joseph Johnson, *Noble Women of Our Time* (London: Thomas Nelson and Sons, 1992), pp. 301-302.

JUNE 27

Bringing the Gospel to the Nations

∞ Sarah Boardman Judson, 1803-1845 ∞

Sarah Hall was nine when Adoniram and Ann Judson left Boston for India, becoming the first foreign missionaries sent out from the United States. There was a great deal of interest in this missionary undertaking, and Sarah was caught up in the prospect. When three years later Adoniram and Ann's little boy Roger died at eight months, Sarah, full of compassion, wrote a poem on the infant's death. On 4 June, 1820, Sarah made a public profession of her faith in Jesus as her Savior. When Ann Judson later visited New England in 1823, Sarah wrote a poem in her honor, which Sarah read during one of the meetings at which Ann spoke. During Ann's stay in the States, Sarah and she corresponded frequently.

When Sarah heard of the death of missionary James Coleman, shortly after his arrival in India in 1822, she wrote a poem, published in the *Christian Watchman*, on his passing. George Boardman, a student at Andover Seminary, sought out the young lady who had so movingly written of Coleman. George was even more impressed by Sarah in person and soon proposed that she marry him and accompany him to India as a replacement for Coleman. George Boardman and Sarah Hall were married 3 July, 1825, and soon sailed from Boston for Burma.

The British/Burmese War was raging when the Boardmans landed in Calcutta and they waited two years there, occupying themselves with language study, before they could go to Burma. They arrived in Burma in 1827; Ann Judson had died a few months previously. The Boardmans were assigned a mountainous region there and pioneered a mission among the Karen people. Many came to faith in Christ through George's evangelism, and Sarah began several schools in the community. Both translated Scripture; Sarah prepared a hymnbook, including some hymns she had written herself. When George died of tuberculosis in 1831 Sarah remained in Burma with their little son George and continued the mission work. Three years later, on 10 April, 1834 the two widowed missionaries, Adoniram and Sarah, were married. Sarah continued her translation work; her translation of *The Pilgrim's Progress* into Burmese continues in use today.

When Sarah's health was failing in 1844 Adoniram realized he must take her back to the United States. She died 1 September, 1845, during a stop on Mauritius. Knowing she was dying, she wrote her last poem for Adoniram:

We part on this green islet, love –
Thou for the eastern main,
I for the setting sun, love –
Oh, when to meet again! …

But higher shall our raptures glow,
On yon celestial plain,
When the loved and parted here below
Meet ne'er to part again.

Then gird thine armour on, love,
Nor faint thou by the way –
Till the Boodh[45] shall fall, and Burmah's
   sons
Shall own Messiah's sway.

Thus it is written, that the Christ should suffer and on the third
day rise from the dead, and that repentance and forgiveness of sins
should be proclaimed in his name to all nations …

~ LUKE 24:46-47 ~

---

45. The Buddha.

First Single Woman sent from America as a Missionary

∞ Betsey Stockton, 1798-1865 ∞

Betsey came into the Stockton family as a child slave with her mother. When the Stockton's daughter Elizabeth married Ashbel Green, Betsey went with her to her new home. The Greens treated Betsey as one of the family, even educating her at home with their own son. Ashbel, who, in 1812, became president of the College of New Jersey, later Princeton University, had a large library where Betsey enjoyed spending her time reading.

When a religious revival swept through Princeton in 1816 Betsey was converted to faith in Christ. Ashbel noted Betsey's previous thoughtlessness and wildness left her as she 'met with a saving change of heart'. In 1818, Ashbel gave Betsey her freedom; she continued to live with the family, but as a paid domestic servant. As Betsey grew in the Christian faith she had a desire to be a missionary to Africa. However, in 1821, Charles Stewart, a recent Princeton graduate, visited Ashbel and discussed with him the idea of joining the new mission in the Sandwich Islands, or Hawaii. The idea of Betsey accompanying them was also discussed, and Ashbel wrote letters of recommendation for them both. Betsey's Sabbath school teacher also wrote a recommendation for Betsey, describing her as:

> pious, intelligent, industrious, skillful in the management of domestic affairs, apt to teach, and endued with a large portion of the active, persevering, self-sacrificing, spirit of a missionary. ... [She] has a larger acquaintance with sacred history and the mosaic Institutions, than almost any ordinary person, old or young, I have ever known (by *ordinary person* you will understand me to mean such as are not clergymen or candidates for the ministry).[46]

In 1821, Betsey Stockton was part of the second group of missionaries sent to Hawaii by the American Board of Commissioners of Foreign Missions. She was the first single woman and first black woman sent out by the ABCFM.

In her journal, written especially for Ashbel Green, Betsey described the five month voyage to Hawaii (they sailed about nine and a half miles an hour!). Descriptions of her sense of loneliness, her joy in Sabbath worship, and her delight in the beauties of the natural world – the whales, sharks, sea birds, and phosphorous oceans – are all interwoven with reflections on God's Word. Sailing around Cape Horn, Betsey wrote:

> We were called to witness one of the most sublime scenes that ever the eyes of mortals beheld – no language could paint it – it was the setting of the sun. The scene kept changing from beautiful to more beautiful, until I could think of nothing but the bright worlds above, to which the saints are hastening. As soon as it was over, and the sun had disappeared, we were assembled on the quarter deck for prayers. Here my soul found free access to the throne of grace, and rose with delight in the contemplation of that God who is the author of all our joys, and of all our good.

Betsey and the missionary group arrived in Hawaii on 24 April, 1823. Betsey established a school with four English and six Hawaiian students. When the Stewarts had to return home two years later because of Mrs Stewart's declining health, Betsey returned with them.

Back in the United States Betsey taught for a decade in Princeton's black public school and served as a Sabbath school teacher for twenty-five years, inspiring others to serve Christ either at home or on the mission field.

And the gospel must first be proclaimed to all nations.

~ MARK 13:10 ~

---

46. Betsey Stockton's Journal, in David W. Wills and Albert J. Raboteau, eds., *African-American Religion: A Historical Interpretation with Representative Documents*, http://www3.amherst.edu/~aardoc/Betsey_Stockton_Journal.html, accessed September 5, 2014.

JUNE 29

Conversion of Sandwich Islands' Queen

⤳ Elizabeth Kaahumanu, 1773-1832 ⤳

Kaahumanu was born on the island of Maui about 1773, but grew up on Hawaii, where her father was in the king's army. When she was thirteen her father gave her in marriage to King Kamehameha, twenty years her senior. According to the customs of the islands, Kamehameha could have as many wives as he wanted. He eventually married seventeen times, but he always considered Kaahumanu his favorite wife. Kaahumanu was an encourager to the king in his goal of uniting all of the Sandwich Islands under his one rule.

The ancient Hawaiian code of laws, *kapu*, restricted women in many ways. Women and men could not eat together. Women were forbidden to eat certain foods, such as coconuts or bananas. The penalty for breaking *kapu* could be very severe, and often included death. When Europeans began stopping at the islands at the end of the eighteenth century, Kaahumanu noticed they did not observe *kapu* but nothing ever happened to them. Maybe the Hawaiian gods were not as powerful as was once thought.

When King Kamehameha died in 1819, his son Liholiho became king, but Kaahumanu was his guardian and regent. Kaahumanu took advantage of the opportunity to abolish *kapu* with its restrictive taboos. She challenged the new king to eat with her. When he did, the gods did not strike him. Kaahumanu then began removing the idols and destroying the sacred sites.

The next year, 1820, Christian missionaries came to Hawaii from America. To them it seemed providential that the old pagan religion of the islands was being destroyed in preparation for the people receiving the gospel. The missionaries began putting the native language into a written form, wrote grammars for the schools they established, and began translating the Scriptures into the native tongue. Kaahumanu quickly learned to read and gradually came to believe the truth of the gospel. She was baptized on 5 December, 1825, taking the Christian name of Elizabeth. She worked to encourage her people in the Christian faith and established new laws based on the Ten Commandments to replace the old taboos. She built churches and schools and spread Christianity among the people. The people saw a change in Kaahumanu and called her the 'new Kaahumanu'. She asked, 'What shall I render unto the Lord for all his benefits towards me?' Transformed by the gospel, she answered, 'I will make his Word the man of my counsel, and will endeavor to induce all under my influence to honor and obey it."[47]

Kaahumanu died in the early morning of June 5, 1832. Shortly before her death, missionary Hiram Bingham gave her the newly printed first edition of the New Testament in Hawaiian.

> *Oh how I love your law! It is my meditation all the day.*
> ~ PSALM 119:97 ~

---

47. Hiram Bingham, *A Residence of Twenty-One Years in the Sandwich Islands: or the Civil, Religious, and Political History of those Islands* (Canandaigua, N.Y.: H. D. Goodwin, 1855), p. 435.

Book of Heaven for the Nez Percé

⟶ Eliza Spalding, 1807-1851 ⟵

After the United States purchased the Louisiana Territory from France in 1803, President Thomas Jefferson sent Meriwether Lewis and William Clark on an exploratory expedition to the northwest to map the land, study the flora and fauna of the region, and establish peaceful trade with the Native Americans. Beginning their journey in St Louis in May 1804, the expedition returned to St Louis in September 1806. Among the natives with whom good relations were established were the Nez Percé. In conversations the explorers told the Nez Percé about the wider world, including something about the Bible, which they called 'The Book of Heaven'. The Nez Percé waited many years for the white men to bring them this Book of Heaven, but no one brought it to them. A tribal council decided to send a delegation to bring this book to the tribe. The four men sent were Black Eagle, Man of the Morning, Rabbit Skin Leggins, and No Horns on the Head.

The men traveled over a thousand miles, across rivers and mountains and through strange and hostile tribal lands. In October 1832, they reached St Louis and were able to find General Clark. After a few days the men presented their request. Would General Clark give them the Book of Heaven and tell them about his God? General Clark was eager to satisfy the men, but there was not a Bible in any language they could understand. Black Eagle and Man of the Morning died during that winter. Before departing in the spring, No Horns on the Head rose at the farewell dinner and gave a speech in which he said:

> I came to you over the trail of many moons, from the setting sun. I came with one eye partly open for my people who sit in darkness. I go back with both eyes closed. How can I go back blind to my blind people? ... When I tell my poor blind people after one more snow, in the big council, that I did not bring the Book, no word will be spoken by our old men or by our young braves. One by one they will rise up and go out in silence. My people will die in darkness and they will go on a long path to other hunting grounds. No White Man will go with them, and no White Man's Book of Heaven will make the way plain. I have no more words.[48]

Reports of the appeal of the Nez Percé spread. In 1836, the American Board of Commissioners of Foreign Missions sent out five missionaries to the Oregon territory – Dr Marcus Whitman and his wife Narcissa, the Rev. Henry Spalding and his wife Eliza, and William Gray. The 3,000 mile journey from New York took six months; Narcissa and Eliza became the first white women to cross the Rocky Mountains, the continental divide. Thirty years after the Lewis and Clark expedition, the Whitmans settled among the Cayuse Indians, and on 29 November, 1836 the Spaldings settled among the Nez Percé, in modern Idaho.

Eliza and Henry Spalding quickly learned the Nez Percé language and began teaching the gospel to the people, who were eager to hear Christian truth. Eliza developed a written language for the Nez Percé and began translating portions of Scripture and hymns into their language. At times there were over two hundred in the school she established. She could only manage this by teaching a small group of students who then were responsible for teaching others. With her husband Henry she translated the entire book of Matthew as well as many stories from the Bible. At last, the Nez Percé were receiving portions of the Book of Heaven.

'Ask, and it will be given to you; seek, and you will find; knock, and it will be opened to you. For everyone who asks receives, and the one who seeks finds, and to the one who knocks it will be opened.'

~ MATTHEW 7:7-8 ~

---

48. 'The Saint Louis Delegation of 1831' (Baker City, OR: Bureau of Land Management, National Historic Oregon Trail Interpretive Center).

Pioneer Missionary in Turkey

⬿ Elizabeth Baker Dwight, 1806-1837 ⬾

Elizabeth Baker's parents were Unitarians, and she had no one in her family who could answer her spiritual questions as a young girl. Yet she longed to know the truth and was drawn to the gospel preaching of Dr Justin Edwards in Andover, Massachusetts. Converted at the age of seventeen, she joined the Congregational Church and grew in grace, striving to use her time and talents for Christ.

In 1830, Elizabeth married Harrison O. Dwight, a graduate of Andover Seminary and a missionary with the American Board for Commissioners of Foreign Missions. On 21 January, 1830, just a few weeks after their marriage, Elizabeth and Harrison sailed from Boston for Malta, where they spent two years and where their first son was born. The couple would later be blessed with three additional sons. On 5 June, 1832, they were transferred to Constantinople, becoming part of the early mission team in the capital of the Ottoman Empire.

Soon after her arrival in Constantinople Elizabeth contracted chronic diarrhoea, leaving her weak and unable to do the teaching among the native children she had hoped to do. In a letter to a fellow missionary wife who similarly suffered, Elizabeth wrote:

> It certainly requires as much grace to *suffer*, as it does to *labour*, and perhaps suffering is more necessary for us, and better for the cause of Christ. I cannot do even the one half that is needful for the instruction of our own dear children; and then, to think how much might be done for perishing souls about us, and to be able to accomplish nothing, is truly humbling. How different this from the picture of a missionary life as we viewed it in America![49]

Elizabeth had begun a school in Constantinople but had to disband it because of her ill health. Along with two other missionary wives in the city she organized a maternal association, where mothers could meet and discuss the proper Christian nurture of their children and how to lead them to conversion. Elizabeth recognized that the example of the life of the Christian wife and mother was an important witness to the surrounding heathen:

> The heathen want not only ministers of the word, but *pious, well-educated families*, in all the various departments of life, to be the living, bright examples of Christianity. ... Then would the dwelling of domestic love, the altar of morning and evening sacrifice, the school-room of virtuous and religious knowledge, the Sabbath school, the sanctuary of public worship, preach more powerfully than volumes of abstract teaching.[50]

Perhaps her lack of Christian nurture in her own family growing up made Elizabeth value the importance of Christian families more.

When the bubonic plague swept through Constantinople in 1837, Elizabeth's third son died, and she contracted the disease as well. Her devoted husband cared for her during her last days. When she died on 8 July she was only thirty-one. One writer noted she 'had hardly become habituated to the missionary cross, when she was called to wear its crown'.[51]

We rejoice in our sufferings, knowing that suffering produces endurance,
and endurance produces character, and character produces hope,
and hope does not put us to shame, because God's love has been poured into
our hearts through the Holy Spirit who has been given to us.
~ ROMANS 5:3-5 ~

---

49. Rev. H. G. O. Dwight, *Memoir of Mrs Elizabeth B. Dwight* (New York: M. W. Dodd, 1849), p. 154.

50. Ibid, p. 170.

51. Sarah Josepha Hale, *Women's Record; or Sketches of all Distinguished Women, from 'the beginning' till* A.D. *1859* (New York: Harper and Brothers, 1853), p. 292.

Seeking Constant Reference to Eternity

∽ Sarah Lanman Huntington Smith, 1802-1836 ∽

Sarah Lanman Huntington, born in Norwich, Connecticut in 1802, had a heritage of Christian service. Ancestor John Robinson had been the pilgrims' pastor in Leyden; her grandfather was a member of the American Board of Commissioners of Foreign Missions, the first foreign-sending missionary organization in the United States. Sarah began teaching Sunday school when she was fourteen, but not until four years later did she know her forgiveness for sin in Christ. After trusting Christ alone for her salvation, she wrote, 'All is changed. I am in a new world of thought and feeling. I begin to live anew. Even our beautiful Norwich has new charms, and, in sympathy with my joyousness, wears a new, a lovelier aspect.'[52]

Two years later Sarah began visiting some of the Mohegan Indians near Norwich and started a Sabbath school among them. She encouraged a missionary to come and establish a church there and even appealed to the Connecticut and federal governments to aid in the schools there. Sarah had an interest in missions among the natives farther west, but Eli Smith directed her attention to the East. Smith, along with H. G. O. Dwight, had just completed a pioneer exploration of the Middle East for establishing Christian missions there. In 1833, Eli and Sarah were married. A month after her wedding Sarah left home for Beirut, where she arrived 28 January, 1834.

Sarah was eager to serve the cause of Christ with her husband. She wrote:

> To make and receive visits, exchange friendly salutations, attend to one's wardrobe, cultivate a garden, read good and entertaining books, and even attend religious meetings for one's own enjoyment; all this does not satisfy me. I want to be where every arrangement will have unreserved and constant reference to eternity. On missionary ground I expect to find new and unlooked-for trials and hindrances; still it is my choice to be there. And so far from looking upon it as a difficult task to sacrifice my home and country, I feel as if I should 'flee as a bird to her mountain'.[53]

In Beirut, Sarah began a school for Egyptian, Arab and Turkish children and established the first school for girls in the Ottoman Empire. Sarah's work among the Mohegans had prepared her for this new endeavor. Sarah learned Arabic, French, and Italian to communicate with the various cultures in the Middle East as well as help Eli with his translation work. Failing health, however, caused Sarah to return to the United States, with Eli accompanying her. Their vessel was wrecked north of Cyprus. Ill with consumption, Sarah suffered constant seasickness from the tempestuous winds. She died in Smyrna shortly after their arrival, on 30 September, 1836. The American flags on ships in the harbor were lowered in her honor. As she faced death, Sarah wrote:

> Who would not wish to die like those
> Whom God's own Spirit deigns to bless?
> To sink into that soft repose,
> Then wake to perfect happiness.[54]

For from him and through him and to him are all things. To him be glory forever. Amen.

~ ROMANS 11:36 ~

---

52. Daniel C. Eddy, *Daughters of the Cross or Woman's Mission* (Boston: Wentworth & Co., 1856), p. 122.
53. Sarah Josepha Hale, *Woman's Record, or Sketches of all distinguished women from 'the beginning' till A.D. 1850* (New York: Harper & Brothers, 1853), p. 512.
54. *Daughters of the Cross*, p. 135.

JULY 3

Maternal Associations

∞ 19th century ∞

Ann Louisa and Edward Payson, pastor of the Congregational Church Portland, Maine, had eight children together. Concerned with the children's spiritual development, as well as the spiritual welfare of other children in the church and community, Ann Louisa had the idea of forming a woman's organization devoted to the spiritual development of their children. In 1815, she sent out a circular inviting mothers to unite in prayer for their children and meet to discuss methods of training them in truth of the Lord. Thus the Portland Maternal Association was born. The following year, a similar maternal organization was formed in the Old South Church in Boston. The idea spread to other New England villages, and home missionaries began establishing maternal organizations among the Cherokees and native Americans.

The early missionaries in Hawaii established regular mother's meetings to help mothers provide for their children both physically and spiritually. By 1833, 1,500 Christian mothers in Hawaii had bonded together to pray for their children. Missionaries formed similar organizations in India, Ceylon, Turkey, South Russia, and South Africa. At monthly meetings helpful topics were discussed such as 'Lent Treasures', 'Influence of a Mother's Example and Prayer', 'Two Opposite Ways of Correcting a Fault'. In 1833, a *Mother's Magazine* began to be published which included helpful articles on child rearing and spiritual development.

At a Maternal Association meeting in Boston's Park Street Church in 1839, advice was given on child-rearing during the first six years:

> At this early period the habit of submission to lawful authority can be formed. A cheerful subjection, from principle, to parental authority, is the first step in religious education, which, if neglected, all subsequent effort will be of little avail.[55]

Susan Huntington, wife of the pastor of the Old South Church in Boston, was a strong supporter of the Boston Maternal Association. In 1815, she offered this advice on child rearing:

> It appears to me that three simple rules ... would make children's tempers much more amiable than we generally see them. First. Never to give them anything improper for them, because they strongly and passionately desire it: and even to withhold proper things, until they manifest a right spirit. Second. Always to gratify every reasonable desire, when a child is pleasant in its request; that your children may see that you love to make them happy. Third. Never to become impatient and fretful yourself, but proportion your displeasure exactly to the offence.[56]

The standard preamble for the constitutions adopted by these associations often began:

> Deeply impressed with the great importance of bringing up our children in the nurture and admonition of the Lord, we the subscribers, agree to associate for the purpose of devising and adopting such measures as may be best calculated to assist us in the right performance of this duty.[57]

The rod and reproof give wisdom,
but a child left to himself brings shame to his mother.

~ PROVERBS 29:15 ~

---

55. Louise O. Tead, 'The International Union Maternal Association', *American Motherhood* (Vol. 22, April 1906), p. 344.

56. Benjamin B. Wisner, ed., *Memoirs of the Late Mrs Susan Mansfield Huntington* (Boston: Crocker and Brewster, 1826), pp. 127-129.

57. *Constitution of the Maternal Association of Sherburn*, July 1833. Old Sturbridge Village Research Library. Edited by Old Sturbridge Village, http://resources.osv.org/explore_learn/document_viewer.php?DocID=1017.

This I Do for My Savior

☞ Sarah D. Comstock, 1812-1843 ☜

Since her conversion at the age of eighteen Sarah Davis always had compassion for the lost. Longing for their redemption, she eagerly gave them the good news of salvation in Jesus. This compassion for the lost naturally led to an interest in the salvation of the heathen in foreign lands. In 1832, Sarah applied as a missionary to the American Baptist Missionary Society. At the same time, Grover S. Comstock, a minster's son and lawyer, applied for missionary work in Burma (today's Myanmar). The two attended a Burmese language school a missionary had set up in Hamilton, New York and then were married on 24 June, 1834. The Comstocks sailed for Burma 2 July, 1834. Sarah knew she would probably never see her family and friends again, but she was eager to serve her Savior in this way and wrote:

> What though trials, suffering, and danger be my earthly lot? Shall I fear to follow where my Savior leads? Shall I shrink from persecution and reproach, or tremble before the stake, if the cause of him who withheld not his life for me requires this at my hands? Gratitude forbids it. Yes, and it seems even a privilege to be cast into the furnace for the sake of walking with Jesus. Though of myself I can do nothing, my strength being perfect weakness, yet I can do all things, and bear all sufferings, if my Lord be there. Though unworthy the high honor, yet I feel it will be my privilege to wear out life in winning souls to God.[58]

After a voyage of five months the Comstocks arrived in Burma. They spent some time in further language study and then set up their mission station in Arracan. In addition to his itinerant work among the villages, Grover established an English school for boys while Sarah established a school in the native language. She also translated and had printed a 'Scripture Catechism' and 'Mother's Book' in Burmese.

Sarah was especially skilled in engaging the women in conversation and telling them the truth of the gospel. Four children were born to Sarah and Grover, increasing Sarah's domestic responsibilities.

After six years only one person had come to faith in Christ, but Grover and Sarah were not discouraged. Though the visible results of their work were few, Sarah wrote:

> We trust the seed we are now sowing, sometimes in hope, and sometimes with a faint heart, will spring up and yield a glorious harvest. It would be pleasant, it would cheer our hearts, to see converts multiplied, but it should be our chief concern to do *our* part faithfully, and then be willing to leave the event in God's hands.[59]

Sarah and Grover faced a most difficult decision when they realized the moral dangers their children would face growing up in Arracan. In 1843, when a fellow missionary was returning to the States, they reluctantly sent their two oldest children with him. Sarah kissed the little ones farewell, lifted her eyes to heaven in a prayer, and gave them to Grover to walk to the ship saying, 'This I do for my Savior.' Remaining in Arracan to bring the gospel to the lost was a sacrifice for Sarah as her children left for America.

Soon after, Sarah contracted dysentery and, after a week's illness, died 28 April, 1843. The two thousand people who came to mourn Sarah's death were indicative of the love of Christ so many had seen in her. Sarah's two youngest children died within a few months, and Grover became ill and died on 25 April, 1844. The two oldest children were safe in America with family members.

Thanks be to God for his inexpressible gift!

~ 2 CORINTHIANS 9:15 ~

---

58. Mrs A. M. Edmond, *Memoir of Mrs Sarah D. Comstock, Missionary in Arracan* (Philadelphia: American Baptist Publication Society, 1854), p. 35.

59. Ibid, p. 179.

JULY 5

Women's Mission Societies: Support and Prayer for Missions

⚭ 19th century ⚭

Very early in the growth of missions in the nineteenth century, women at home formed societies to support the missionary enterprise in whatever way they could. Women contributed the money they had earned from the sale of eggs or butter to Female Cent or Mite Societies organized to support missionaries, Dorcas Societies (named after the Christian woman Peter healed in Acts 9), or produced needlework they could sell to raise funds for missions.

The earliest known legacy a woman left for missions was made by Sally Thomas, a housemaid. She earned 50¢ a week, and over a lifetime saved $345.88 which she bequeathed to the American Board of Commissioners of Foreign Missions (ABCFM). In 1827, a small group of women in Brookline, Massachusetts, began praying for the Christianization of Japan. Japan was a closed society and wouldn't open to foreigners for another twenty-five years. Nevertheless, the women continued to pray for Japan and regularly set aside funds for a Japanese mission. Over the years they contributed $600 to the ABCFM for a mission in Japan. The ABCFM invested the money, and the women continued to pray. Forty years after the women had begun to pray, the funds had grown to $4,104.26. In 1869, the ABCFM sent its first missionaries to Japan – Daniel and Mary Greene. In 1871, freedom of religion was introduced to Japan, allowing preaching of the gospel and the establishment of churches.

The Greenes established a church in Kobe, Japan which continues as an international church today. Daniel was a member of the committee which translated the New Testament into Japanese; he also edited a Chinese New Testament for use by Japanese readers. In 1881, he was stationed at Kyoto, where he was a theological instructor in the Doshisha English School. The persistent prayers and faithful contributions of the women in Brookline, Massachusetts, bore fruit for the Lord's work around the globe.

He who supplies seed to the sower and bread for food will supply and
multiply your seed for sowing and increase the harvest of your righteousness.
You will be enriched in every way to be generous in every way, which
through us will produce thanksgiving to God.

~ 2 Corinthians 9:10-11 ~

First American Woman Missionary in China

◌ Henrietta Hall Shuck, 1817-1844 ◌

Henrietta Hall, born in 1817, was raised in a loving Christian home. When she was about thirteen Harriet began to seriously consider spiritual things, prompted by a question a teacher wrote on the board, 'Where shall I be a hundred years' hence?' The teacher encouraged the students to give their answers individually at a later time. Henrietta made a confession of faith in Christ and was baptized shortly afterwards.

When she was sixteen Henrietta decided to become a missionary. Soon afterwards she met Lewis Shuck, a young theological student. Lewis too had his heart set on being a missionary in a foreign land. When Lewis was accepted as a missionary by the American Baptist Board of Foreign Missions, he proposed to Harriet to marry him and accompany him to China. It was difficult for Harriet to separate from her dear family, anticipating she would likely never see them again, but her love for Christ and His work were stronger. She wrote, 'The sincere prayer of my heart is, "Oh, that I were qualified to become a missionary of the Cross".'[60]

Harriet and Lewis were married 8 September, 1835, and sailed for China on 22 September. Harriet would be the first American woman missionary to China. After six months they reached Singapore and began learning the Malay and Chinese languages. A month after the birth of her first child, the couple set out for Macao, a small peninsula south of Canton where the Chinese permitted foreigners. In 1842, after Hong Kong was ceded to the British, Henrietta and Lewis moved to the thriving settlement. Lewis preached and established several chapels, while Harriet established a boarding school for boys and girls – all the while taking care of her growing family of four children. Harriet's letters home are filled with the love of Christ. In her last letter home she wrote,

> I rejoice to be able to say that recently, more than ever, I have enjoyed the smiles of the Saviour; I have felt so much happiness, so much joy, in committing all my cares into the hands of him who, I know, cares for me. How delightful to know that God is our Friend, and that all things shall work together for our good.[61]

Harriet was quite ill after the birth of her fourth child, but was recovering her strength and continued her work missionary work. However, on the night of 26 November, 1844, at the age of twenty-seven, she suddenly took ill and died. In a letter to her father, Lewis wrote of Harriet's last hours:

> Her mind was engaged in prayer to the last, and as there was scarcely a pain or a struggle, but purely sinking and prostrations, she literally fell asleep in Jesus, yea, almost like Enoch, translated, for having walked with God. He took her in kindness, to himself, without the usual suffering and distress. ... She seems to have passed away like a glorious meteor, and her light still shineth.[62]

Humble yourselves, therefore, under the mighty hand of God
so that at the proper time he may exalt you,
casting all your anxieties on him, because he cares for you.

~ 1 Peter 5:6-7 ~

---

60. Marjorie Dawes, 'Henrietta Hall Shuck', in A. S. Clement, ed., *Great Baptist Women* (London: The Carey Kingsgate Press, 1955), p. 109.

61. Ibid, p. 114.

62. Ibid, pp. 114-115.

Educating for Christ

∞ Mary Lyon, 1797-1848 ∞

The oldest college for women in the United States, Mount Holyoke Female Seminary in Massachusetts, was founded by Mary Lyon in 1837. Mary had a passion for learning as well as for Christian service. From one of her teachers, Rev. Joseph Emerson, she had come to realize that the Christian faith was all-encompassing and included history, science, and every area of knowledge. From reading Jonathan Edwards' *History of Redemption*, Mary came to understand the broad scope of God's redemptive plans, moving towards the coming Kingdom of God.

Mt Holyoke opened for students 8 November, 1837. While providing the best possible education for the young ladies, Mary realized the school must be affordable. She planned for the students to do much of the maintenance of the school – the washing, cleaning, and cooking.

Mary established a curriculum on Christian principles, demonstrating that history and science supported the truth of the Bible. Daily there was morning and evening Bible reading, and three times a week Mary addressed the ladies on important biblical themes. Concerned about the salvation of each of her students, Mary regularly met with the ladies individually to set before them the claims of Christ or encourage them in their Christian walk. In all her work, Mary leaned upon God in prayer and depended 'hourly for light and strength and for success on our Heavenly Father through Jesus Christ our Redeemer'.[63]

Mary encouraged one graduating class:

> Never be hasty to decide that you can not do, because you have not physical or mental strength. Never say you have no faith or hope. Always think of God's strength when you feel your weakness, and remember that you can come nearer to him than to any being in the universe. ... And, wherever you are, remember that God will be with you, if you seek to do good to immortal souls.[64]

Many of the graduates of Mount Holyoke became missionaries to Persia, India, Ceylon, Hawaii, and Africa. They carried with them the Christian lessons they learned from Mary Lyon and modeled Christian virtues and marriage and family life for societies around the globe.

> *... to reach all the riches of full assurance of understanding*
> *and the knowledge of God's mystery, which is Christ,*
> *in whom are hidden all the treasures of wisdom and knowledge.*
>
> ~ Colossians 2:2-3 ~

---

63. Sarah Stow, *History of Mount Holyoke Seminary, South Hadley, Mass. During its First Half Century, 1817-1887* (Springfield: Springfield Printing Company, 1807), p. 107.

64. Fidelia Fisk, *Recollections of Mary Lyon, with selections from her instructions to the pupils of Mt. Holyoke Female Seminary* (Boston: American Tract Society, 1866), p. 86.

Mother of a Thousand Daughters

∞ Eliza Agnew, 1807-1883 ∞

When Eliza Agnew was eight years old, she was in geography class and first learned about Harriet Newell, a former pupil in the New York City school who went out as one of America's first missionaries to the East. Eliza resolved then that when she was grown she should go to the East and help others as Harriet Newell had wanted to do. Eight years later, on 28 December, 1823, Eliza gave her life to Christ at a revival meeting at the Orange Street Presbyterian Church. She began teaching in the church's Sabbath school and was active in the distribution of Scripture and tracts.

In 1816, the American Board of Commissioners of Foreign Missions (ABCFM) sent out their second mission, this time to Ceylon (modern Sri Lanka). In 1824, some of the missionary wives opened a school for girls. They were much scorned by the natives, who thought girls were incapable of learning to read and it was useless to send them to school. Nevertheless, this first school for girls in Asia opened in Uduvil with twenty-nine girls and grew to over one hundred pupils. The missionary wives asked for funds for a better building and to send someone to oversee the school.

Eliza Agnew's parents had recently died, and she knew the school in Ceylon was where she belonged. She applied and received the appointment from the ABCFM. In 1839, she sailed from Boston on the *Black Warrior*. She knew she would never see her country again as she set off on the five-month voyage to Ceylon. When she arrived in Ceylon and assumed the position as principal of the school, she was an enigma to the natives as a single woman. One child asked her, 'Where is Mr Agnew?' Yet, Eliza knew this was where the Lord wanted her to be, and she remained in Ceylon, without a furlough, over forty years.

Eliza cared for the spiritual and physical needs of her students in addition to providing intellectual instruction for them. She began each morning with prayer, and the students could hear her in the next room to theirs praying for the school and each one of them by name. Whenever a problem would arise, Eliza's response often was, 'I'll tell it to the Master,' and she would bring the problem to the Lord in prayer. Over one thousand girls came under her care, and she taught the children and grandchildren of her early students. All of the 600 girls who had completed the entire course at the school became Christians. Many became teachers themselves and became wives of Christian pastors and leaders, who in turn brought up their children in the fear and admonition of the Lord. The people of Ceylon affectionately called Eliza 'Mother of a Thousand Daughters'.

> *'If anyone would come after me, let him deny himself*
> *and take up his cross daily and follow me.*
> *For whoever would save his life will lose it,*
> *but whoever loses his life for my sake will save it.'*
>
> ~ LUKE 9:23-24 ~

Only One Life

∞ Mary Elizabeth Hawes Van Lennep, 1821-1844 ∞

Growing up in the home of a minister in Hartford, Connecticut, Mary Elizabeth Hawes was familiar with the Bible from an early age. When her younger brother died, ten-year-old Elizabeth quoted Scripture to comfort her mourning parents in their sorrow. About this time Elizabeth also became a Christian; her father watched as she began to grow in grace and increase in godliness. When she was accepted into the church, Elizabeth felt an obligation to serve in some way. She labored to earn money, which she gave for missions. She also founded a society to sew and knit clothing for those serving as missionaries.

In the summer of 1841, Elizabeth suffered an illness from which it was feared she would not recover. This became a time of reflection for her. Faced with her own mortality, she realized she must lay up her treasures in heaven, not spend her life in the vanity of earthly pleasures and joys. At the same time, a revival swept through the church and the town, and many, both young and old, were coming to faith in Christ. Elizabeth saw the worth of every soul and the bliss of heaven which could be theirs.

Henry van Lennep was a young man who studied for a time with Elizabeth's father. Henry was born in Smyrna, Turkey and returned to the United States for his education. On September 4, 1843, Elizabeth and Henry were married. The next month they sailed on the *Stamboul* for Turkey. Though leaving behind her home, family, and friends with the likelihood she would not see them again, Elizabeth and Henry were delighted Rev. Hawes made the trip with them. He had joined a team from the ABCFM reporting on missions throughout Syria and Turkey. It was a joy having her father's sermons and presence with them on the two month voyage.

The *Stamboul* arrived at Smyrna in December. After his visit to the various mission stations, Rev. Hawes returned to America in the spring. Elizabeth lovingly clung to her father as they said their farewells, sensing they would not meet again. She wrote her father a parting letter, saying that they would never be separated, for they were united by the Father in heaven:

> O my dear father! It is good to be in his hands; to know no will but his; to work just where he appoints, and just how he appoints. We thank God that he has brought you here. You will never know the good you have done, in this world. It has been a sweet comfort to Henry and me; and every word of yours is treasured in our memory. I thank you for every counsel you have ever given me; for every prayer you have prayed for me; for all the sermons I have heard you preach; for all our pleasant talks together.
>
> Dear father, you will not be sorry that we are working on missionary-ground, when you get to heaven … tell all my young friends that there is a great and blessed work to be done in this world, and that they have but one life to do it in.[65]

In August Elizabeth contracted a severe case of dysentery; she died a month later, on September 27, 1844. Her last words were 'O, how happy!' She then recited the lines from the hymn, 'Jesus, lover of my soul, Let me to thy bosom fly.'

> *So we do not lose heart. Though our outer self is wasting away, our inner self is being renewed day by day. For this light momentary affliction is preparing for us an eternal weight of glory beyond all comparison …*
>
> ~ 2 CORINTHIANS 4:16-17 ~

---

65. Edward A. Lawrence, *The Life of Rev. Joel Hawes* (Boston, 1881), pp. 183-184.

Singing a New song

∽ Cecil Frances Alexander, 1824-1895 ∽

Cecil Frances Humphreys showed a gift for poetry from childhood. Her father encouraged her writing, and over her lifetime Cecil Frances wrote over four hundred poems. Alfred Tennyson said he would have been proud to have written her narrative poem on 'The Burial of Moses'.

In 1848, Cecil Frances published *Hymns for Little Children*, containing three hymns still very popular today. She wrote her hymns as a tool for teaching children spiritual truths of the Apostle's Creed, the Ten Commandments, and the Lord's Prayer. The phrase 'Maker of Heaven and Earth' in the Creed was explicated in the favorite children's hymn:

All things bright and beautiful,
All creatures great and small,
All things wise and wonderful,
The Lord God made them all.

Each little flower that opens,
Each little bird that sings,
He made their glowing colours,
He made their tiny wings. ...

He gave us eyes to see them,
And lips that we might tell,
How great is God Almighty,
Who has made all things well.

The phrase 'was conceived by the Holy Ghost, born of the Virgin Mary' was elaborated in the Christmas hymn,

Once in royal David's City,
Stood a lowly cattle shed,
Where a mother laid her Baby,

In a manger for His bed.
Mary was that mother mild,
Jesus Chirst her little Child. ...

The phrase 'suffered under Pontius Pilate, was crucified, dead, and buried' was expounded in the hymn,

There is a green hill far away,
Without the city wall,
Where the dear Lord was crucified,
Who died to save us all. ...

O dearly, dearly has He loved,
And we must love him too,
And trust in His redeeming Blood,
And try His works to do.

Though many were written for children, Cecil Frances's hymns became favorites of adults and still can be found in many hymnals.

In 1850, Cecil Frances married the Rt. Rev. W. Alexander, Bishop of Derry and Raphoe, who became Archbishop of Armagh and Primate of Ireland. All of the profits from her writing were given to charity, especially the Derry and Raphoe Diocesan Institution for the Deaf and Dumb. Her gentle presence could often be found ministering to the poor and sick of the city. She exemplified the words of another of her hymns:

Jesus calls us; o'er the tumult
Of our life's wild, restless sea,
Day by day his clear voice soundeth,
Saying 'Christian, follow me.' ...

Jesus calls us! By thy mercies,
Saviour, may we hear thy call,
Give our hearts to thine obedience,
Serve and love thee best of all.

He put a new song in my mouth, a song of praise to our God.
Many will see and fear, and put their trust in the LORD.

~ PSALM 40:3 ~

Writing to Right the Treatment of Slaves

∽ Harriet Beecher Stowe, 1811-1896 ∽

Harriet Beecher was the seventh of thirteen children and the second daughter of one of the most influential families in nineteenth-century New England. Her father, Lyman Beecher, was a founder of the American Bible Society, a nationally prominent Presbyterian minister, an abolitionist, and leader of the Second Great Awakening. When Harriet was four, her mother died, and Harriet became very close to her older sister Catherine. When Catherine established the Hartford Female Academy, Harriet wrote books for the Academy and later taught in the school.

In 1832, Lyman moved his family from Connecticut to Cincinnati, Ohio, where he became head of Lane Theological Seminary. In Ohio Harriet came to know some of the slaves who ran away from their southern masters to find freedom in the North. The plight of the slaves moved her deeply. At Lane, Harriet met Calvin Stowe, a clergyman, abolitionist and professor at the Seminary. The two were married in 1836. In 1850, they moved to Maine where Calvin became a professor at Bowdoin College.

When the Fugitive Slave Act was passed in 1850, requiring northerners to return escaped slaves to their masters, Harriet's sister-in-law wrote her, 'Now Hattie, if I could use a pen as you can, I would write something that would make this whole nation feel what an accursed thing slavery is.'[66] Harriet vowed, 'I will write something. … I will if I live.'

In February 1851, while taking communion in church, Harriet imagined a godly, Christ-like slave being beaten to death while praying for his persecutors. This was to become the climax of her novel *Uncle Tom's Cabin*, when Tom is brutally beaten by the diabolic Simon Legree. *Uncle Tom's Cabin* humanized and personalized the evils of slavery and aroused the entire nation over the issue. For Harriet, the issue was always a spiritual one. After the novel was published, she wrote:

> This story is to show how Jesus Christ, who liveth and was dead, and now is alive and forever-more, has still a mother's love for the poor and lowly, and that no man can sink so low but that Jesus Christ will stoop and take his hand. Who so low, who so poor, who so despised as the American slave? The law almost denies his existence as a person, and regards him for the most part as less than a man – a mere thing, the property of another. … He can do nothing, possess nothing, acquire nothing, but what must belong to his master. Yet, even to this slave Jesus Christ stoops, from where he sits at the right hand of the Father, and says, 'Fear not, thou whom man despiseth, for I am thy brother. Fear not, for I have redeemed thee, I have called thee by thy name, thou art mine.'[67]

Harriet took the principles of the gospel and applied them to the slavery issue.

Fear not, for I am with you; be not dismayed, for I am your God;
I will strengthen you, I will help you,
I will uphold you with my righteous right hand.

~ Isaiah 41:10 ~

---

66. Charles Edward Stowe, *Life of Harriet Beecher Stowe* (Boston & New York: Houghton, Mifflin, & Co., 1891), p. 145.
67. Ibid, p. 154.

African-American Christian Poets

∞ 19th century ∞

The Christian Recorder was a weekly newspaper published in Philadelphia by the African Methodist Episcopal Church from 1854 to 1902. Many black women writers published poems and articles in the *Recorder*. Julia C. Collins' *The Curse of Caste*, the first novel written by a black woman, was serialized in the paper. In the following poem, written in the middle of the Civil War, Belle Goode prays for spiritual cleansing and guidance:

The Anxious Young Pious Mother

If I loved thee, oh! my Saviour,
The vain heart of mine would be
Free from every carnal pleasure,
And content to follow thee.

If I loved thee, oh! my Saviour,
I would strive to please thee here,
Then my soul would find acceptance,
In a higher, brighter sphere.

If I loved thee, oh! my Saviour,
Earth would be a pleasant place,
But alas! 'tis sad and dreary,
With no smile from thy dear face.

If I loved thee, oh! my Saviour,
I would delight in all that's good,
Ever willing to obey thee,
Then I'd love thee as I should.

Thou hast said, exalted Master,
They who love thy law will keep,
Help me Lord, incarnate Saviour,
To learn of thee, low at thy feet.

Wilt thou let thy Holy Spirit,
Change this sinful heart of mine,
Then my weary burdened soul,
Will be renewed by divine grace.

Then, dear Saviour, wilt thou guide me?
O'er the rugged path of life,
Make me humble, make me prayerful,
Cleanse my heart from every vice.

At the assassination of Abraham Lincoln, Angeline Demby recognized this as no accident, but all part of God's plan, though they would mourn the President's loss:

We mourn, to learn that we are struck
With such appalling wo[e];
We bow beneath the mighty stroke;
'Twas God who willed it so.

A Martyr to sweet Freedom's laws,
A patriot true and brave,
With noble brow and form erect,
Is stricken to the grave.

The grave shall not environ him;
His spirit is with God;
It took its flight at early morn,
When Jesus spoke the word.

'Come unto me, beloved Son,
You filled your place of trust;
I call you hence, come unto me;
I'll raise you from the dust.'

The nation mourns a patriot slain!
Lord, heal the broken heart.
We cannot bear this stunning pain,
Unless thou heal the smart.

Thy balm apply to bleeding hearts;
Our comfort Thou shalt be.
It was thy will that we should part
With him who made us free. ...

God opposes the proud,
but gives grace to the humble.

~ JAMES 4:6 ~

Conversion and Call to Service

⟨⟨ Florence Nightingale, 1820-1910 ⟩⟩

Florence Nightingale, the daughter of wealthy English landowners, was named after the city of her birth, Florence, Italy. Her father took personal responsibility for the education of Florence and her sister, teaching them Greek, Latin, French, German, Italian, history, philosophy and mathematics. When she was about sixteen Florence read *The Cornerstone* by American Congregational minister Jacob Abbott, who wrote numerous books for children. Central to *The Cornerstone's* theme was that Jesus Himself was the foundation and cornerstone of salvation. Florence was moved by Abbott's descriptive reflections on Jesus' crucifixion. He showed that all the characters at the crucifixion, including the Pharisees, Peter, and Judas, had followers and imitators in Florence's own day. Florence was converted and began studying the Scriptures. She made a detailed chronology of Jesus' last days and made it available to friends and family who requested it.

Florence also read Abbott's *The Way to Do Good, or the Christian Character Mature*. The first chapter in this narrative of the boy Alonzo showed that the Christian has no hope in his own works, but only in the undeserved mercy of Christ. Because of Christ's mercy, the Christian seeks to do good to others. Abbott wrote:

> Upon the cornerstone of faith in Jesus Christ, as the atoning sacrifice for sin, there is reared the superstructure of holy life and action; and a holy life is one which, from the impulse of love to God, is occupied with doing good to man.[68]

In his story Abbott included principles of personal piety, examples of working among the poor and ministering among the sick, which deeply affected Florence.

A year after her conversion, on 7 February, 1837, Florence felt a distinct call to serve God. Later, as she cared for the sick in her own family or on her family's estate, she felt that her calling was to nursing. Her parents were not pleased. They were Unitarians and did not share Florence's Christian faith. They also believed nursing was for working class women, not for women of Florence's station. In time, however, they came to accept Florence's call to serve God through nursing. Florence once told her father:

> Nay, it strikes me that all truth lies between these two: man saying to God, as Samuel did, Lord, here am I, and God saying to man as Christ did, in the storm, Lo it is I, be not afraid. And neither is complete without the other. God says to man in suffering, in misery, in degradation, in anxiety, in imbecility, in loss of the bitterest kind, in sin, most of all in sin, Lo, it is I, be not afraid. This is the eternal passion of God. And man must say to him, Lord here am I to work at all these things. ... The Bible puts into four words of one syllable what whole sermons cannot say so well. The whole of religion is in God's Lo, it is I, and man's Here am I, Lord.[69]

As each has received a gift, use it to serve one another,
as good stewards of God's varied grace ...

~ I PETER 4:10 ~

---

68. Jacob Abbott, *The way to do good: or, the Christian character mature* (Boston: William Peirce 1836), p. 3.

69. Lynn McDonald, 'Florence Nightingale: Faith and Work', keynote address for the 7th Annual Conference, Canadian Association for Parish Nursing Ministry, Toronto, 27 May 2005, http://www.uoguelph.ca/~cwfn/spirituality/faith.htm.

JULY 14

Lady with a Lamp

∞ Florence Nightingale, 1820-1910 ∞

Early in her Christian life Florence Nightingale felt a call to serve God in nursing. Florence's family did not at first approve of Florence leaving her life of comfort to serve those in need and often destitute. At last, however, Florence's father accepted his daughter's call and settled an annual stipend of £500 (roughly $50,000 in present dollars) upon her so she could freely pursue her career.

Florence became superintendent of the Institute for the Care of Sick Gentlewomen in Upper Harley Street, London in 1853. That same year the Crimean War began, with Russia invading Turkey. France and Britain then sent soldiers to aid Turkey. Many of the British soldiers soon succumbed to cholera and malaria. Florence volunteered to go to Crimea as a war nurse. At first the government resisted the offer, but it finally agreed. Florence organized thirty-eight nurses and went to Crimea. There she found the conditions at the soldiers' hospital horrific. The first winter she was there 4,077 soldiers died, many deaths caused by poor living conditions. Florence immediately worked to improve sanitation, and the death rates declined. Florence kept careful statistics of the diseases and health conditions, providing evidence to government for improving army hospitals. The London *Times*, noting her management and endurance, reported: 'When all the medical officers have retired for the night and silence and darkness have settled down upon those miles of prostrate sick, she may be observed alone, with a little lamp in her hand, making her solitary rounds.'[70] One soldier commented that before Florence came there was a lot of cussing and swearing, but with her presence, the hospital became 'as holy as a church'.

When she returned to England, Florence began a campaign to improve nursing in military hospitals, publishing *Notes on Nursing* to gain support for her reforms. In 1860, she founded the Nightingale School and Home for Nurses at St. Thomas's Hospital. Nursing was a calling Florence received from God, and she saw her work as a service to God. That Christ identified himself with the poor and weak of society was always an example to her:

> I don't think any words have had a fuller possession of my mind through life than Christ's putting himself in the place of the sick, the infirm, the prisoner – and the extension which the Roman Catholic Church (especially) gave to these words, as it were *God* putting Himself in the place of the leper, the cripple and so forth, telling us that we see Him in them. Because it is so true.

In her Bible Florence commented on 1 John 4:10-11:

> We love him, because he first loved us. What we ordinarily want is a belief of God's love to us. We do not realize to ourselves all that Christ's death shows us of God's love; we do not believe that our own single individual soul is and ever has been the direct object of the infinite love of the most high God. It is hard, both because of our own *littleness*, and because of our own *hardness*. But, if this belief once takes possession of our hearts, then are we redeemed indeed.[71]

> *In this is love, not that we have loved God but that he loved us*
> *and sent his Son to be the propitiation for our sins.*
> *Beloved, if God so loved us, we ought also to love one another.*
>
> ~ 1 JOHN 4:10-11 ~

---

70. Edith Deen, *Great Women of the Christian Faith* (Uhrichsville, OH: Barbour Books, 1959), p. 217.

71. Quotes from Florence Nightingale are taken from Lynn McDonald, 'Florence Nightingale: Faith and Work', keynote address for the 7th Annual Conference Canadian Association for Parish Nursing Ministry, Toronto, May 27, 2005, http://www.uoguelph.ca/~cwfn/spirituality/faith.htm.

Jesus Loves Me

∞ Anna Warner, 1827-1915 ∞

In 1944, John F. Kennedy's Patrol Torpedo boat collided with a Japanese destroyer; Kennedy and his crew managed to swim to an island three and a half miles away. After a few days, natives discovered them and led a rescue boat to the island, and the men were saved. One of the rescued men then put his arms around the two natives, and the three together sang, 'Jesus loves Me, this I know, / For the Bible tells me so …' The natives had learned the song from missionaries, and this was a common bond between them and the Americans.

The simple children's song, one of the first hymns missionaries often teach new converts, has had a global influence. Amy Carmichael, who later became a missionary to India, was converted at a children's mission in Yorkshire, England after hearing this hymn. 'Jesus Loves Me' was a favorite with Francis Schaeffer, who recognized intellectuals need the simple message of Jesus as much as children. After the founding of the People's Republic of China in 1949, Christians were severely persecuted and the outside world had little reliable information about the church in China. The Communist Chinese, however, did allow a rather cryptic message to reach some Americans; it said 'The This I Know People' are safe. The Chinese Christians knew the words of the simple children's song would have meaning to other Christians.

'Jesus Loves Me' was written by Anna Warner and first appeared in *Say and Seal*, a children's novel written by Anna's sister, Susan. Susan's and Anna's father was a prominent New York lawyer and businessman; their mother died a year after Anna was born. When, in 1837, their father suffered great economic losses in a financial depression, the family had to sell their New York home. They moved to what was to have been a summer residence on Constitution Island, in the Hudson River near West Point. This became the sisters' home for close to eighty years.

To help with the family finances Susan and Anna both began writing, mostly children's books. After Harriet Beecher Stowe, Susan was the most popular American female author of the nineteenth century. Her novels taught religious and moral values, providing fictional examples of how to live a moral, Christian life in a world filled with darkness. Anna wrote devotional commentaries on Psalm 23 and men and women of the Bible, but her most remembered work is her simple poem, 'Jesus Loves Me'. Located opposite West Point Military Academy, the sisters also taught Bible studies to the cadets for many years. They are the only non-military people buried in the West Point cemetery. Constitution Island was donated to West Point after Anna's death.

> *For God so loved the world, that he gave his only Son,*
> *that whoever believes in him should not perish*
> *but have eternal life.*
>
> ~ JOHN 3:16 ~

Bible for the Creeks

◌ Ann Worcester Robertson, 1826-1905 ◌

Samuel Austin Worcester and his wife Ann Orr were Congregational missionaries to the Cherokee Indians in Tennessee when Ann Eliza was born 7 November, 1826. They later moved to the Cherokee capital in New Echota, Georgia. Samuel was imprisoned for a time for resisting Georgia's claim to jurisdiction over Cherokee territory. When he was released he moved his family to Indian territory (present day Oklahoma), where he established a mission station at Park Hill.

From her father Ann had the conviction that the Indians needed to have the Bible in their native languages. In Georgia, Samuel had begun translating the Bible into Cherokee and writing a Cherokee grammar. When her father's translation work and grammar, along with the printing press, were lost when the boat carrying most of their possessions sank in the Arkansas River, Ann knew what the loss of his translation work meant to her father. The press eventually was recovered, however, and the Worcesters established the first printing press in Oklahoma.

When she was fifteen Ann was sent to an Academy in Vermont for her education. There she became proficient in Greek as well as Latin. Little did she know how these studies would be important to her later work. In 1846, Ann returned to help her parents teaching in Park Hill. On 16 April, 1850, she married William Robertson, a Presbyterian minister and teacher, and moved to the Tullahassee Mission, near present day Muskogee, Oklahoma. The couple had four children while at the Tullahassee Mission. There Ann learned the Muskogee language, spoken by the Creek and Seminole Indians, and helped in all aspects of the mission. With her husband she oversaw the boarding school, with over a hundred students. She also taught in the school – one year she taught Latin, Arithmetic, and 'Watts on the Mind' – while overseeing the numerous household chores of that period.[72]

Ann was often ill, but used those periods of forced inactivity to study the Creek language. William said that was her amusement! With her husband she translated a number of school books, hymnals, and Christian tracts into Muskogee, but her real delight was translating the Bible from the Greek. To her, the Creek language was not the invention of man but the 'Creator's gift to man'. The first edition of the New Testament in Muskogee was printed in 1887. In 1892, Ann was awarded an honorary Ph.D. by the University of Wooster for her linguistic studies, the first woman in the United States to receive an honorary Ph.D.

Ann continued her biblical translation work, translating the psalms and historical books and revising the New Testament translation. She had almost completed her fifth revision of the New Testament when she died in 1905. Her labors provided the words of life to the Creeks and Seminoles.

Lord, to whom shall we go? You have the words of eternal life, and we have believed, and have come to know, that you are the Holy One of God.

~ JOHN 6:68-69 ~

---

72. The famed hymn writer Isaac Watts also wrote books on theology and logic. His textbook *Logic, or the Right use of Reason in the Enquiry After Truth with a variety of Rules to Guard Against Error in the Affairs of Religion and Human Life, as well as in the Sciences,* went through numerous editions and became a standard textbook, still in use today.

Planting the Gospel along the Nile

∽ Mary Louisa Whately, 1824-1889 ∽

Mary Louisa Whately first went to Egypt for her health in the winter of 1860, when she was thirty-six. The sites and culture of the place were a fascination to her, and soon she was drawn to helping the women and children among the poor. Mary had been teaching and helping the poor in various ways since she was a teenager. Her father, who became Archbishop of Dublin in 1831, had opened a school for the poor children in Dublin, and Mary had taught there along with her siblings. During the years of the terrible Irish famine, 1846-1851, Mary and her family worked tirelessly in bringing relief to the poor. It was during this time that Mary had an increased desire to actively work for God in some way. At the end of the Crimean War, quite a number of destitute Italians found their way to Dublin. Mary and her sister visited them in their homes and in the hospitals, teaching them the truth of the gospel. Mary became skilled in explaining biblical truth to those of different religions and customs. All of this prepared Mary for the great work she would begin in Egypt.

In 1860, Mary moved to Cairo and bought a house in the lower-class area of Cairo. Here she established a girls' school, the first school in Egypt for Muslim girls. The following year she opened a school for Muslim boys. Christian teaching was an integral part of the schools' instruction. Mary hired her Arabic teacher, Mansoor Shakoor, and his brother Joseph to help in the teaching. The Shakoor brothers were Christian missionaries from Syria.

With the Shakoors at the schools, Mary took time periodically to visit the towns and villages along the Nile, traveling the river in a *dahabyeh*, a little boat, with an English flag on it. In the villages, Mary and her companion read or told Bible stories to the women and children. Soon, when the people in the village saw the little boat coming, they would run down to the landing places crying, 'Here are the people of the Book!' and 'Have you books for us?' 'Come to our house and read to us!' Portions of Scripture were given to the men and boys who could read. Later, in some of the villages, Mary heard people say, 'Bring out the aged, that they may hear the Word of God before they die!'

Mary Whately spent almost thirty years in Egypt, giving of herself and her substance for the education of the poor and the spread of the gospel. One traveler visiting Mary's schools wrote that in his experience Mary Whately's Mission was the most outstanding in the East:

> It has reached *the very heart of Islam*, and has been the first to plant the Gospel of our Divine Master in the very midst of the Mohammedan families in Egypt. Such a thing was never heard of before, nor has been done by any one since the rise and progress of the Mohammedan religion. God has manifestly watered the seed, and blessed it also, which she scattered in faith in Egypt, and even before she was called away to the higher service, the fruits of her labours of love began to appear.[73]

And let us not grow weary of doing good, for in due season we will reap,
if we do not give up. So then, as we have opportunity,
let us do good to everyone, and
especially to those who are of the household of faith.

~ GALATIANS 6:9-10 ~

---

73. E. R. Pitman, *Missionary Heroines in Eastern Lands* (London: S. W. Partridge & Co., 1884), p. 160.

From Every Nation, Tribe, and Language

∞ Catherine Winkworth, 1827-1878 ∞

Scripture assures us that the Kingdom of Heaven includes people from every nation, tribe, and language. Today, praising God together across the language barriers is helped by good translators. Catherine Winkworth was one such translator.

Born in London on 13 September, 1827, Catherine was the fourth daughter of a successful silk merchant. Both her parents were pious Christians, and hymn singing became a traditional evening recreation for the family. Catherine's mother died when she was fourteen. At that time, Catherine and her sister Selina were sent to Dresden for a year to study German and German culture. Catherine continued her German studies when she returned to England, where her family had moved to Manchester. Her tutor required her to translate German poetry into English, giving Catherine valuable training for her later hymn translations.

Christian Karl Josias, Baron von Bunsen, the German ambassador to England, became a friend of the Winkworth family. He gave Catherine a copy of a collection of hymns and prayers he had published in 1833. Catherine translated many of these into English, publishing them, in 1855, as *Lyra Germanica: Hymns for the Sundays and Chief Festivals of the Christian Year*. The work sold out in two months and went on to enjoy twenty-three editions. Catherine published a second volume of hymn translations, *Lyra Germanica: The Christian Life*, in 1858. A decade later she published a history and compilation of German devotional verse from the ninth through the eighteenth century, *The Christian Singers of Germany*. This work included biographical sketches of many of the hymn writers, as well as additional translations of their works. Catherine later produced a work on chorales which included the tunes for the German hymns.

Through Catherine's translations many German hymns have become part of English hymnody. A favorite is the hymn by German Reformed theologian Joachim Neander, based on Psalm 103, 'Praise to the Lord, the Almighty':

> Praise to the Lord, the Almighty, the King of creation!
> O my soul, praise him, for he is thy health and salvation!
> All ye who hear, now to his temple draw near,
> Join me in glad adoration.

> Praise to the Lord, who o'er all things so wondrously reigneth,
> Shelters thee under his wings, yea, so gently sustaineth!
> Hast thou not seen how thy desires e'er have been
> Granted in what he ordaineth? ...

> Praise to the Lord! O let all that is in me adore him!
> All that hath life and breath, come now with praises before him!
> Let the amen sound from his people again,
> Gladly for e'er we adore him.

And they sang a new song, saying,
'Worthy are you to take the scroll and to open its seals,
for you were slain, and by your blood you ransomed people for God
from every tribe and language and people and nation,
and you have made them a kingdom and priests to our God,
and they shall reign on the earth.'

~ REVELATION 5:9-10 ~

JULY 19

Life of Living for Others

∞ Susan Law McBeth, 1830-1893 ∞

Born in Dourne, Scotland in 1830, Susan Law McBeth immigrated to America with her parents in 1832. The family settled in Wellesville, Ohio. Three more daughters and a son were added to the family. Daily they read the Scriptures together, and they regularly worshiped at the Presbyterian church. The McBeths were staunch abolitionists, and the cellar of their home was a stop on the Underground Railroad at a crossing of the Ohio River from Virginia. When Sue was seventeen, her father died. Sue went to work in a millinery to help support herself while also attending Steubenville Female Seminary. Sue was an excellent scholar and teacher. She taught for several years at the Wellsville Institute and then at the Fairfield Female Seminary in Iowa, a branch of the University of Iowa.

When the Presbyterian Board of Foreign Missions invited Sue to work among the Choctaws in Indian Territory, she hesitatingly accepted and set off by herself on the long journey. Sue taught young girls at the Goodwater Mission in Indian Territory. When the outbreak of the Civil War forced the abandonment of the Mission Sue returned to Fairfield University as a temporary assistant director. She became one of the first women to join the U.S. Christian Commission, providing medical relief for Civil War soldiers. Sue ministered at the Jefferson Barracks near St Louis, where 18,000 combat victims were treated during the war. Providing spiritual sustenance as well as medical services, Sue wrote numerous tracts for the soldiers which were later published as *Seed Scattered Broadcast: Incidents at a Camp Hospital*. After the war Sue headed a home for seamstresses in St Louis. She was engaged to Eben Law, a doctor from Mississippi who had been a prisoner of war in Illinois. A month before the wedding date, Eben died suddenly of typhoid fever. When Sue heard the news she had a stroke and was paralyzed for a time. Ever after she walked with a limp. When in 1873 the Presbyterian Board of Foreign Missions again called her, this time to the Nez Percé in Idaho, Sue accepted the challenge.

In her teaching among the Nez Percé, Sue specialized in training young braves for the ministry; the first Nez Percé ordained were those Sue had taught. The braves called her 'Pika', meaning 'mother', and treated her with great affection. In 1880, they built and gave her a three-room frame house. Sue worked on a dictionary of Nez Percé words as well as a grammar for the Nez Percé vernacular. In 1879, Sue's younger sister Kate joined her, opening a school for young women to teach them homemaking skills, reading and the Bible. When Sue died of Bright's Disease in 1893, Kate sent Sue's Nez Percé dictionary and grammar to the Smithsonian Institute.

Do not neglect to do good and to share what you have,
for such sacrifices are pleasing to God.

~ HEBREWS 13:16 ~

Giving the Son to the Heathen

∞ Eleanor Macomber, 1801-1840 ∞

Growing up at Lake Pleasant, New York, Eleanor Macomber early had a desire to devote herself to serving Christ and bringing others to a knowledge of Him. In 1830, when she was twenty-nine, the Baptist Missionary Board sent her as a teacher among the Ojibwas at Sault de Ste Marie, Michigan. She worked there for four years, but poor health caused her to return to New York. With her health recovered, in 1836 the Mission Board sent Eleanor to Burma to work among the Karen people.

It was unusual for a single woman to go out as a missionary in the early nineteenth century. It was even more unusual for her to be the lone missionary at her station, but Eleanor was stationed at Dong-Yahn, about thirty-five miles from Maulmain, where other missionaries were stationed. Drunkenness was rampant among the people there, as were sensuality and vice. Eleanor began by holding Sabbath worship weekly, in which she told of the cross and the salvation in Christ. Daily she opened her home to morning and evening prayers. Within a year there were ten converts, four men and six women, and others were becoming interested in the gospel. Eleanor also established a school, which opened with a dozen pupils. A church was established with the new converts, and a missionary from Maulmain came to hold Sabbath worship. Eleanor trained the natives to do the work of evangelism, and the message of the gospel spread. Gradually, the drunkenness and sensuality disappeared, replaced by Christian virtues.

Eleanor didn't just stay at Dong-Yahn, but she went out into the surrounding areas, climbing hills and mountains and crossing ravines and rivers to bring the message of salvation to isolated groups. Her love for the people and zeal for the gospel gained her respect among the people. Eleanor recognized that in her mission as a single woman:

> Never were the power and mercy of God more manifestly displayed, and never did his saving grace shine through a more feeble instrumentality. But God can work according to his will; and, blessed be his name, the heathen shall be given to his Son.[74]

After four years among the Karen, Eleanor died of jungle fever on 16 April, 1840. She was deeply mourned by the Karen people.

Do you not know that the unrighteous will not inherit the kingdom of God?
Do not be deceived: neither the sexually immoral, nor idolaters, nor adulterers,
nor men who practice homosexuality, nor thieves, nor the greedy, nor drunkards,
nor revilers, nor swindlers will inherit the kingdom of God.
And such were some of you.
But you were washed, you were sanctified,
you were justified in the name of the Lord Jesus Christ and by the Spirit of our God.

~ I CORINTHIANS 6:9-11 ~

---

74. Daniel C. Eddy, *Daughters of the Cross or Women's Mission* (Boston: Wentworth & Co., 1856), p. 149.

Laying all on the Altar

☙ Phoebe Palmer, 1807-1874 ❧

Phoebe Worrall was born in New York City to Henry and Dorothea Worrall, both active in the Methodist Episcopal Church. Phoebe herself joined the church as a young girl and remained a strong member throughout her life. When she was nineteen she married Dr Walter Palmer, also of Methodist upbringing. The first three of their children died in infancy, one in horrible circumstances.

On 29 July, 1836, Phoebe had rocked little eleven-month-old Eliza to sleep and then put her gently in her crib. Shortly after, Phoebe heard screaming from the nursery. Running in, she found that a careless servant tried to fill an oil lamp while it was burning. When the flames exploded upward, the servant threw the lamp from her, and it landed in the crib – covering little Eliza with burning oil. Phoebe took the child in her arms, but she died soon after. Phoebe, filled with anger and grief, cried out to God in her anguish. Perhaps she had loved her children too much, placing them as idols in her affections in place of God. She then resolved to surrender everything to God, writing in her diary:

> Never before have I felt such a deadness to the world, and my affections so fixed on things above. God takes our treasures to heaven, that our hearts may be there also. And now I have resolved that the time I would have devoted to her [Eliza] shall be spent in work for Jesus.

A year later, July 27, 1837, Phoebe wrote,

> Last evening, between the hours of eight and nine, my heart was emptied of self, and cleansed of all idols, from all the filthiness of the flesh and spirit, and I realized that I dwelt in God, and felt that he had become the portion of my soul, my ALL IN ALL.[75]

Phoebe developed what became known as 'altar theology'. If the Christian consecrated oneself entirely to God, then God would sanctify and perfect her. Phoebe and her sister began holding a weekly Tuesday Meeting for the Promotion of Holiness, where people met for Bible reading, prayer and testimonies. Originally attended by women, the meeting grew to include hundreds – men and pastors among them.

Phoebe wrote numerous books, including *The Way of Holiness*, which were very popular. She also spoke extensively at camp meetings and revival campaigns, while also organizing groups to support the poor and indigent. Her teaching on Holiness or Christian Perfection, as distinct from gradual sanctification, was adopted by many Methodists, the Salvation Army, and the Keswick movement.

> *I appeal to you therefore, brothers, by the mercies of God,*
> *to present your bodies as a living sacrifice,*
> *holy and acceptable to God,*
> *which is your spiritual worship.*
>
> ~ Romans 12:1 ~

---

75. As quoted in Charles Edward White, 'Holiness Fire-Starter: Transformed by her child's fiery death, Phoebe Palmer lit the flames of revival on two continents', *Christian History and Biography* (Issue 82, Spring 2004), p. 19.

JULY 22

Society for Promoting Female Education in the East
∞ 1837-1899 ∞

In 1834, Rev. David Abeel, a missionary with the Dutch Reformed Church, published a pamphlet, 'An Appeal to Christian ladies on behalf of female Education in China', calling on Christian women in the West to aid their suffering sisters in the East whose lives were degraded and without the hope found in the gospel of Jesus Christ. Women were not considered capable of learning, so received no education. They were the virtual slaves of their husbands, who had absolute authority over them. In India they were not allowed to eat with their husbands, and the law expressly allowed their husbands to beat them. There was also a regular trafficking in females; infanticide was common, and many found refuge in suicide. Abeel appealed to Christian women to come and help the plight of the East, bringing instruction and the gospel to elevate the women to be the instructors of their children and the companions of their husbands.

Heeding Abeel's appeal, in 1837 the Society for Promoting Female Education in the East (SPFEE) was organized in Britain. Its stated purpose was:

1. To collect and to diffuse information on the subject.

2. To prepare and send out pious and intelligent women, as trainers and superintendents of native female teachers.

3. To assist those who may be anxious to form female schools in accordance with the rules of this Society, by grants of money, books, and superintendents.

In addressing Christian women, SPFEE further described the needs which it hoped to address:

... to rescue the weak from oppression, and to comfort the miserable in their sorrow to give to the infant population of India and China the blessing of maternal wisdom and piety; to teach the men of those nations, that those who are now their degraded slaves, may be their companions, counsellors, and friends; ... to make them acquainted with the Bible, which now they cannot read; to place them under the instruction of the missionary, from which they are at present excluded to bring them to the knowledge of Christ; and to prove that his grace can do more in a few years to bless them, than the centuries of heathenism could do to degrade them.

Sending out and supporting female missionaries to the East was a way of showing thanksgiving to God for His providence and grace in bringing the message of the gospel to women in the East under such suffering:

Wives, who are happy in the affectionate esteem of your husbands; mothers, who enjoy your children's reverence and gratitude; children, who have been blessed by a mother's example and a mother's care; sisters, who have found in brothers your warmest friends ... impart your blessings to those who are miserable because they are without them. If your minds are intelligent and cultivated, or your lives are useful and happy, and if you can look for a blessed immortality beyond the grave, do not, for the love of Christ, whose sufferings have been the source of all your blessings and of all your hopes, do not refuse to make Him known, that the degraded millions of the east may, like you, 'be blessed in Him', and, like you, may 'call Him blessed'.[76]

Husbands, live with your wives in an understanding way, showing honor to the woman as the weaker vessel, since they are heirs with you of the grace of life, so that your prayers may not be hindered.

~ I PETER 3:7 ~

---

76. All quotes from 'An Appeal to the Christian Ladies on Behalf of Female Education in China, India, and the East', *Baptist Magazine and Literary Review* (Volume 26, 1834), p. 478.

Apostle to the Zenanas

∞ Hannah Catherine LaCroix Mullens, 1826-1861 ∞

Especially among the Brahmin class, the lives of women in India were very restricted. Women were kept in the *zenana* or women's quarters in the inner part of the house. The outer part of the house was for the men and guests. The women lived separated lives, not being allowed to be seen in public or even to eat with men in a social setting. Secluded and apart from the world, missionaries early realized the need to reach the women within the *zenana* and bring them the light of the gospel of Christ.

Hannah LaCroix Mullens was able to develop a fruitful ministry among the women of Bengal. Born in Calcutta on 1 July, 1826, Hannah was the daughter of Rev. A. LaCroix, who served in India with the London Missionary Society for many years. Hannah early became fluent in Bengali, and by the age of twelve she was teaching a class of young children in her parents' garden. When she was about thirteen, particularly moved by a native Christian's prayer for the children of missionaries, Hannah resolved to devote her life to the Savior. On 19 June, 1845, when she was nineteen, Hannah married Rev. Dr Mullens of the London Missionary Society. The two had a warm companionship, reading and studying together as they sought to reach the natives with the truth of Christ.

Hannah established a Girls' Boarding School at which the girls were taught reading, writing, biblical truths, and needlework. She wrote a little book in Bengali for native Christian women which became quite popular. The story was about two families, one Christian and one unchristian, in a Bengali village. Details of village life were very true to the times, and through her story Hannah was able to show the transforming power of the gospel in the lives of believers. The book went through many printings and in a few years was translated into twelve Indian languages.

One day a Brahmin – an upper-class Hindu – was visiting Hannah's father. Hannah was in the room sewing and embroidering a pair of slippers. The Brahmin admired the needlework and wished his wife could be taught such work. This was Hannah's entrée into the *zenana* of the Brahmin's home. Besides teaching needlework, she brought the women the gospel of Christ. Soon her visits to Brahmin *zenanas* consumed most of her time, and Hannah had to turn over much of the work of the Girls' Boarding School to another. At one time, Hannah provided spiritual care for eighty native women and seventy girls in the *zenanas* and girls' school.

Suddenly ill in 1861, Hannah died at the age of thirty-five on 20 November, 1861. There were 150 Christian converts from Hinduism at her funeral, and the sermon was delivered by an Indian Christian pastor.

Whatever you do, do all to the glory of God.

~1 CORINTHIANS 10:31~

Foreign Lady with the Big Love Heart

∞ Lottie Moon, 1840-1912 ∞

Charlotte Moon, who everyone called Lottie, was born into an old and wealthy Virginia family on 12 December, 1840. She was raised in the plantation home of Viewmont, not far away from Thomas Jefferson's Monticello and James Madison's Montpelier. There was no church near their home in Lottie's early years, but her mother always had services in the parlor on Sundays for her children, neighbors, and servants. Viewmont's library was filled with good books which Lottie enjoyed reading. Reading *The Lives of the Three Mrs Judsons*, describing the Judsons' work in Burma, planted an early desire to become a missionary.

Lottie attended Hollins College, where she graduated with the highest grades in her class and was proficient in Latin, Greek, French, Spanish and Hebrew. While in college, when she was eighteen Lottie believed in Jesus as her Savior and Lord and was baptized in the First Baptist Church in Charlottesville, Virginia. She continued at Hollins to receive a Master's Degree in 1861, among the first Southern women to receive such a degree. Lottie completed her schooling just at the time the Civil War was beginning. During the war she helped her mother on the plantation and in nearby hospitals cared for many of those wounded in the fighting. When the War ended Lottie taught in schools in Virginia, Kentucky, and Georgia.

Lottie's younger sister Edmonia accompanied missionaries T. P. and Martha Crawford to China in 1872. That an unmarried woman could work in missions was becoming a possibility. The following year Lottie joined Edmonia and the Crawfords in Tengchow, China. Edmonia became ill and had to return home in 1875, accompanied by Lottie, but Lottie soon returned, opened a school, and did evangelistic work among the villages. She wore Chinese dress and adopted Chinese customs while among the people. At first the people called her 'The Old Devil Woman', but in time they gave her names such as 'The Heavenly Book Visitor' and 'The Foreign Lady with the Big Love Heart'. On one occasion, two men walked many miles to find the lady who knew the 'Words of Life'.

In September 1887, Lottie, always operating with minimal funds, wrote a letter to the Southern Baptists pleading with them,

> Why should we not ... instead of the paltry offerings we make, do something that will prove that we are really in earnest in claiming to be followers of him who, though he was rich, for our sake became poor? ... Is not the festive season when families and friends exchange gifts in memory of the Gift laid on the altar of the world for the redemption of the human race, the most appropriate time to consecrate a portion from abounding riches and scant poverty to send forth the good tidings of great joy into all the earth?[77]

Lottie was hoping enough could be raised to send another missionary; in the first year $3,000 were given, enough for three missionaries! This special Christmas offering continues today in Lottie Moon's name.

Lottie endured the hardships of the early twentieth century with the Chinese people – the Russo-Japanese War, the Boxer Rebellion, and famine. In 1912, Lottie gave all she had for food to the Chinese. Becoming malnourished and starved herself, she died in December 1912.

'Look, I tell you, lift up your eyes, and see that the fields are white for the harvest.
Already the one who reaps is receiving wages and gathering fruit for eternal life ...'

~JOHN 4:35-36~

---

77. Lottie Moon letter, September 15, 1887 (*Foreign Mission Journal*, December 1887), p. 10.

JULY 25

Counted Worthy

∽ Fidelia Fiske, 1816-1864 ∾

In 1843, missionary Justin Perkins visited Mount Holyoke Seminary and told of the need for a woman to come to Persia and educate girls there. Several qualified ladies applied, but Fidelia Fiske's humble request, 'If counted worthy, I should be willing to go,' helped secure her acceptance. Fidelia had long had an interest in missions, in part from conversations with an uncle who was a missionary in the Holy Land. Fidelia was one of the first pupils at Mount Holyoke Seminary and began teaching there after her graduation, leading many of her pupils to Christ.

On 1 March, 1843, Fidelia departed Boston for Persia, with Mr and Mrs Perkins. By June they had reached Urmia, where Fidelia was the first single-woman missionary. When the missionaries had first come to the region in 1835, there was only one woman who could read among the people. Fidelia was replacing the missionary Mrs Grant, who had first opened a school but had since succumbed to illness and died. Women had a very poor position in the society. They were told that it was a disgrace for them to learn to read. Many were forced into early marriages in which their husbands freely beat them. The lack of cleanliness, proclivity to lying and quarrelsomeness among the women led Fidelia to write:

> I felt pity for the women before going among them, but anguish when, from actual contact with them, I realized how low they were. I did not want to leave them, but I did ask, 'Can the image of Christ ever be reflected from such hearts?'[78]

Fidelia established a boarding school for girls, teaching them cleanliness and morals as well as reading and basic education. The Bible was the important tool for learning to read, and the students memorized large portions of the Scripture. Many of the students were converted to Christ under Fidelia's teaching. Fidelia not only cared for the spiritual nurture of her students, but she regularly visited their mothers, prayed with them, and encouraged them with the Scriptures. She was in frequent prayer for the people, and the students at Mount Holyoke supported her in prayer as well. One year the Mount Holyoke students made fifty garments for the girls in Persia. Fidelia remained in Persia for fifteen years until she had to return to the United States in 1858 because of poor health. Before she left, however, three of her early students and their husbands went into Kurdistan as missionaries – fruit of her labors.

Fidelia always hoped to return to Persia, but her health worsened. She died on 26 July, 1864. Her last words, mirroring a passion of her life were, 'Will you pray?'

At her funeral, Rev. Dr Kirk said,

> I wish to speak carefully, but I am sure I can say I never saw one who came nearer to Jesus in self-sacrifice. If ever there should be an extension of the eleventh chapter of Hebrews, I think that the name of Fidelia Fiske would stand there.[79]

Now faith is the assurance of things hoped for,
the conviction of things not seen.

~ HEBREWS 11:1 ~

---

78. Mrs J. T. Gracey, *Eminent Missionary Women* (New York: Earton & Mains, 1898), p. 26.
79. Ibid, p. 23.

JULY 26

First Protestant Girls' School in Shanghai

∞ Eliza Jane Bridgman, 1805-1871 ∞

From her childhood days growing up in Connecticut, Eliza Gillett had wanted to be a missionary. Reading Claudius Buchanan's *Christian Researches in Asia* opened up the world of India to Eliza, and she eagerly read any missionary publications which came her way. In 1821, when she was sixteen, Eliza came to personal faith in Christ during the religious revival at Trinity Church, New Haven and was confirmed. The following year Eliza moved with her mother to New York City, where she became a member of St George's Episcopal Church. Eliza taught a Bible class at the church and became principal of a boarding school for girls. The same year, Eliza participated in the farewell party for the second group of missionaries who went to the Hawaiian Islands. Dr Milnor, rector at St. George's, was a member of the Board of Missions of the Protestant Episcopal Church and encouraged Eliza's interest in missions.

At the time, however, American mission boards were very reluctant to send out unmarried women as missionaries. However, when the Episcopal Church organized its China Mission and recruited its staff of missionaries, Eliza was among three single women teachers included. Eliza and her missionary companions sailed from New York for China on the *Horatio* on 14 December, 1844.

When the group arrived in Hong Kong, Eliza and a married couple were lodged with Elijah Coleman Bridgman, the first American missionary to China. Bridgman had been serving in China with the American Board of Commissioners of Foreign Missions since 1830, and was working on a Bible translation. Unmarried, he had been praying that God would send him a wife. Believing Eliza was the answer to that prayer, he proposed; and the two were married on 28 June, 1845.

Eliza learned Cantonese and, in 1850, opened the first Protestant day school for girls in Shanghai. The girls were taught reading, writing, singing, domestic skills, and Christian truth. Many of the girls became Christians and later wives of Christian pastors in China. After her husband's death in 1861 Eliza opened Bridgman Academy in Peking, which later became the Women's College of Yenching University. She contributed large amounts of her own funds to support the school and the Peking mission station.

At her death in 1871, Eliza was highly respected by the Chinese. Her truthfulness, justice, and abounding charity to the poor touched many hearts.

What does the LORD your God require of you, but to fear the LORD your God, to walk in all his ways, to love him, to serve the LORD your God with all your heart and with all your soul, and to keep the commandments and statutes of the LORD, which I am commanding you today for your good?

~ DEUTERONOMY 10:12-13 ~

Whitman Massacres

∽ Narcissa Whitman, 1808-1847 ∽

When Narcissa heard Rev. Samuel Parker speak about his missionary work among the western Indians, she was drawn to become a part of the mission work. Narcissa had made a profession of faith in Christ when she was eleven during a religious revival in the Prattsburg Presbyterian Church, and she had a desire to serve the church in some way. Rev. Parker introduced Narcissa to Marcus Whitman, a medical doctor who had applied to become a medical missionary. Marcus soon proposed marriage, and Narcissa accepted. The couple were married on 18 February, 1836; the day after the wedding they began their long journey from New York to the Pacific Northwest.

Narcissa's diary described the journey and scenery in vivid detail. Traveling only fifteen or twenty miles a day, she at times felt the trip was like the Israelites' journey through the wilderness to the Promised Land. On 4 July the party crossed the Continental Divide, and on 1 September, over six months after leaving home, they reached Fort Walla Walla, a Hudson Bay Trading post in the Columbia River. Narcissa was overjoyed to be near the place where they could teach the natives about the Savior. On the first Sabbath she wrote her family:

> This has been a day of mutual thanksgiving with us all. This first Sabbath in September, a Sabbath of rest, first completing a long journey, first in the vicinity of our future labors. All of us here before God. It is not enough to us alone to be thankful. Will not beloved friends at home unite with us in gratitude and praise to God for His great mercy? It is in answer to your prayers that we are here, and are permitted to see this day under such circumstances.[80]

In addition to the normal housework of the day (making soap, washing, ironing, cookng, etc.), Narcissa learned the Nez Percé language, taught classes in church, and helped her husband in Indian camp meetings. A little daughter was born to the Whitmans whom they named Alice Clarissa. However, when she was two, the little toddler went to the river to get some water and drowned. In her sorrow Narcissa prayed, 'Lord it is right; it is right. She is not mine but Thine; she has only been lent to me for a little season, and now, dearest Savior, Thou hast the best right to her; Thy will be done, not mine.'

Narcissa mothered and cared for several Indian children as well as seven orphans whose parents had died on the Oregon Trail. One of the settlers who stayed with the Whitmans in 1844-1845 wrote that Narcissa 'was always gentle and kind to the Indians, as she was to every one else. She took an interest in every one at the mission, especially the children. Every one loved her, because to see her was to love her.'

In 1847 a measles epidemic swept through the region. Not having developed an immunity to the disease, many of the Indians, especially the children, died. Dr Whitman who treated them was blamed for these deaths, and on 29 November, 1847, a Cayuse came into the Whitmans' home and killed Narcissa, Marcus and several of the children. Narcissa's last words were, 'Tell my sister that I died at my post.'

For if we live, we live to the Lord, and if we die, we die to the Lord.
So then, whether we live or whether we die, we are the Lord's.

~ ROMANS 14:8 ~

---

80. All direct quotes are from Edith Deen, *Great Women of the Christian faith* (Uhrichsville, OH: Barbour Books, 1959), pp. 208-213.

First Lady of Texas

∽ Margaret Lea Houston, 1819-1867 ∽

Seventeen-year-old Margaret Lea was among the crowd cheering the arrival of General Sam Houston to New Orleans. On 21 April, 1836, Houston's Texian army of volunteers had defeated the armies of Generalissimo Santa Anna of Mexico in an amazing battle lasting eighteen minutes, thereby securing Texas' independence from Mexico. Houston's ankle was shattered in the battle, and he came to New Orleans for treatment. Seeing the Texas hero, Margaret Lea thought to herself that one day she would meet the hero of the Battle of San Jacinto.

Two years later Margaret Lea and Sam Houston met at a garden party in Mobile, Alabama. At forty-six Sam was then President of the Republic of Texas, a man of worldly success with a rough past. He had resigned as Governor of Tennessee after his wife left him shortly after the wedding. He then took an Indian wife and lived among the Cherokee, who called him 'Big Drunk' because of his drinking. He went to Texas in 1832 and was swept up in the Texas Revolution, signing the Texas Declaration of Independence on his forty-third birthday – 2 March, 1836. At twenty Margaret was a quiet, intellectual young lady who read constantly. She was a graduate of Judson College, named after Ann Hasseltine Judson, the first female missionary from the United States. Margaret's father, Temple Lea, had been a lay Baptist pastor, and Margaret had been baptized at the Siloam Baptist Church in Marion, Alabama when she was nineteen. Her Christian faith was at the center of her life, whereas Sam rarely thought of God and had drifted from his Presbyterian upbringing. No two could be more opposite, yet their attraction was strong. Margaret became Mrs Sam Houston in 1840 and moved to Texas, where Sam was President, and would later be Governor and Senator, when Texas became part of the United States.

From the beginning of their marriage, in her quiet way Margaret set about reforming Sam. He agreed to quit drinking, and he kept his promise out of love for her. Margaret also frequently shared passages of Scripture with Sam and freely discussed her Christian faith with him in a winsome manner. When he was in the Senate, Sam gave Margaret D'Aubigne's *History of the Reformation*, which captivated her. She urged him to get a copy for himself so they each could be reading it and share notes. She saw so many similarities between him and Luther and had 'great hopes that the same spirit which brought the great reformer out of darkness into marvellous light, will dawn upon your soul and fill your heart with Heavenly peace.'[81]

Margaret's Christian life drew Sam to Christ, and he began regularly reading the New Testament and works of Christian apologetics. His rough, worldly scepticism fell away in the light of the gospel of Christ. Sam Houston testified of his faith in Christ by his baptism in Independence, Texas on 19 November, 1854. Margaret's faithful witness and prayers had been answered.

> But if we walk in the light, as he is in the light,
> we have fellowship with one another,
> and the blood of Jesus his Son cleanses us from all sin.
>
> ~ 1 JOHN 1:7 ~

---

81. Madge Thornall Roberts, *The Personal Correspondence of Sam Houston, 1848-1852* (University of North Texas Press, 1996), p. 21.

'I Gave My Life for Thee'

∽ Frances Ridley Havergal, 1836-1879 ∽

Frances Ridley Havergal was born into a Christian home, the youngest of William and Jane Havergal's five children. William was a composer and hymnwriter as well as a clergyman, and Frances partook of her father's musical and poetic talents. Trusting Christ as Savior when she was thirteen, she lived a Christian life of earnestness and sweet devotion. She was a precocious child, and her father gave her the best education, sending her to schools in England and Germany.

On 10 January, 1858, Frances was studying in Dusseldorf, Germany when she first saw the painting 'Ecce Homo' by Domenico Feti. 'Ecce Homo' is Latin for 'Behold the Man', the words Pontius Pilate had said when he presented Jesus to the crowd (John 19:5). Feti's painting was of a beaten Jesus with a crown of thorns around his head. Underneath the painting, Feti wrote in Latin, 'This have I suffered for you; now what will you do for me?' Frances, quite moved by Feti's painting and his question underneath, took out a pencil and a scrap of paper and wrote stanzas for a hymn:

> I gave My life for thee,
> My precious blood I shed,
> That thou might'st ransomed be
> And quickened from the dead;
> I gave, I gave My life for thee –
> What hast thou giv'n for Me?
>
> My Father's house of light,
> My glory-circled throne
> I left, for earthly night,
> For wand'rings sad and lone;
> I left, I left it all for thee –
> Hast thou left aught for Me?

> I suffered much for thee,
> More than thy tongue can tell,
> Of bitt'rest agony,
> To rescue thee from hell;
> I've borne, I've borne it all for thee –
> What hast thou borne for Me?
>
> And I have brought to thee,
> Down from My home above,
> Salvation full and free,
> My pardon and My love;
> I bring, I bring rich gifts to thee –
> What hast thou brought to Me?

When Frances read through what she had written later, she didn't think it was worth much and threw the paper into the fire, but it fell out of the fire and was found by her father, who wrote music for the hymn.

This was the first of many hymns which Frances wrote as she sought to live her life for the Christ who had given His life for her.

> '... even as the Son of Man came not to be served but to serve,
> and to give his life as a ransom for many.'
>
> ~ MATTHEW 20:28 ~

Example of Persevering Faithfulness

∞ Josephine Lemmert Coffing, 1833-1913 ∞

In 1905, over five hundred people gathered in Hadjin, Turkey to bid farewell to missionary Josephine Coffing, who was returning to the United States after forty-eight years in Turkey. The emotional farewell from many of Mrs Coffing's students and friends was a great contrast to her first reception in Hadjin over forty years earlier.

Josephine and her husband, Rev. Jack Coffing, first came to Turkey in 1857, settling in Aintab (Gaziantep). Their role was to develop Sunday schools in the region. When they arrived in Aintab there were about forty in attendance at Sunday school. Under their guidance attendance grew to 1,400. Even the Muslim donkey boys began singing the children's gospel songs in the street. Once the Sunday schools were well established in Aintab, the Coffings relocated to Hadjin in the Taurus Mountains.

The mountain area was controlled by robber bands, and the Turkish government had little authority in the region. Kazan Oghloo, the robber chieftain, told the Coffings they had to leave Hadjin. He feared that if the Christians gained influence in the town, the robber business would decline. When the Coffings, who were living in a tent, continued to build their house, the robbers came and physically pulled them out of the tent and threw all their possessions into a ravine. Forced out of Hadjin, the Coffings went to Marash. The following year, when Rev. Coffing was traveling through the robber-infested area, he and his servant were shot and killed.

Josephine felt she must continue in Turkey to complete the work she and her husband had begun together. For fourteen years she oversaw the young women's seminary at Marash as well as the Sunday schools in the region, with over six hundred pupils. She tirelessly traveled in the surrounding villages bringing the gospel of Christ to the children.

When a church was established in Hadjin, in 1872, it was an amazing and joyous time for Josephine. She wrote a friend:

> Can you doubt that these were among the happiest days of my life? Cannot I say that 'It is good to wait on the Lord.' More than one of those who were formed into the church trace their first impressions to the truth to the hymns sung during that day when the mob pulled our tent down over our heads. 'Cast thy bread upon the waters; for thou shalt find it after many days.' [Eccles. 11:1, KJV][82]

In 1880, Josephine was able to return to Hadjin, where she and her husband had been ejected twenty years before. She established Sunday schools there and in the surrounding villages. Her forty-eight years of faithful service in Turkey mirrored the faithfulness of her Lord.

Let us hold fast the confession of our hope without wavering,
for he who promised is faithful. And let us consider how to
stir up one another to love and good works …

~ HEBREWS 10:23-24 ~

---

82. Gordon and Diana Severance, *Against the Gates of Hell* (Wipf and Stock, 2012), p. 93.

Songs from Trial and Tribulation

∽ Lina Sandell Berg, 1832-1903 ∽

Sweden, during the nineteenth century, was moved by waves of Pietism and revival which encouraged a personal faith in Jesus Christ, not simply an adherence to the ceremonies of an established church. It was during this time that Carolina Sandell was born on 3 October, 1832, at Fröderyd. Her father was a parish pastor and as a child, Lina, as she was called, loved most to spend time in her father's study. As an adult Lina became her father's secretary and assisted him in his pastoral duties.

In 1858, Lina accompanied her father to visit a friend in Jönköping. The evening they boarded the boat, Lina read Psalm 77 as part of her devotions and thought the verse 'Your way was through the sea, your path through the great waters; yet your footprints were unseen' was especially beautiful. The next morning, as Lina and her father were on deck, a large wave came up, swept her father overboard and Lina saw him drown before her eyes. Lina was stricken with horror, but gradually the words from Psalm 77 came to mind again. With this great sorrow, Lina immersed herself in the Scriptures, finding there the love of God her Father. From her broken heart flowed songs rich with spiritual power. Within the year, fourteen of her hymns were published. One which became a favorite in Sweden and throughout the world was, 'Children of the heavenly Father.' After the loss of her earthly father, Lina's relationship with her heavenly Father became even more important to her:

Children of the heav'nly Father
safely in his bosom gather;
nestling bird nor star in heaven
such a refuge e'er was given. ...

Neither life nor death shall ever
from the Lord his children sever;
unto them his grace he showeth,
and their sorrows all he knoweth. ...

More secure is no one ever
Than the loved ones of the Saviour:
Not yon star on high abiding
Nor the bird in home-nest hiding.

Lina went on to write over six hundred hymns. Many of the tunes were written by Oscar Ahnfelt, a singer in the Swedish revival movement. Famous singer Jenny Lind sang many of Lina's hymns. 'Day by Day' continues to be a favorite today:

Day by day and with each passing moment,
Strength I find to meet my trials here;
Trusting in my father's wise bestowment,
I've no cause for worry or for fear.
He whose heart is kind beyond all measure
Gives unto each day what he deems best –
Lovingly, its part of pain and pleasure,
Mingling toil with peace and rest.

Help me then in every tribulation
So to trust your promises, O Lord,
That I lose not faith's sweet consolation
Offered me within your holy Word.
Help me, Lord, when toil and trouble meeting,
E'er to take, as from a father's hand,
One by one, the days, the moments fleeting,
Till I reach the promised land.

And because you are sons,
God has sent the Spirit of his Son into our hearts,
crying, 'Abba! Father!'

~ GALATIANS 4:6 ~

Christ Alone

∞ Christina Rossetti, 1830-1894 ∞

Christina Rossetti is recognized as one of the leading English poets of the nineteenth century. Her devotional poems, all grounded in her Christian faith, blended an appreciation for the beauty of the natural world with an acknowledgment of the sin and suffering also inflicting our lives. Christina's mother, Frances Polidori, was born to an English woman and a political exile from Italy. Frances in turn married the Italian poet and political exile Gabriele Rossetti. Gabriele became professor of Italian at Kings College, Oxford. Frances, who had been a governess before her marriage, educated their four children at home. She regularly read to her children from the Bible, *The Pilgrim's Progress*, and the works of St Augustine. In the evenings the family discussed literature and painting. Though their lives often bordered on poverty, the Rossetti children had a rich heritage. All four of the children became writers, and brother Dante Gabriel became a painter. Dante, along with brother William, became a founder of the art movement known as the Pre-Raphaelite Brotherhood.

Even before she could write Christina created stories which her mother wrote down for her. When she was twelve her grandfather published some of her early poems. In her lifetime Christina wrote over nine hundred English poems and sixty poems in Italian. She had several suitors at different times, but rejected them all because they did not share her evangelical Christian faith. For many years, before illness afflicted her, Christina volunteered at the Magdalene Asylum in Highgate, helping former prostitutes. In 1871, Christina was stricken with Graves disease, which disfigured her face and threatened her life. She survived and lived twenty-three more years, which she continued to spend in devotional writing. One of her most beautiful poems is 'None Other Lamb', based upon the scene in Revelation 5:

> None other Lamb, none other name,
> None other hope in heaven or earth or sea,
> None other hiding-place from guilt and shame,
> None beside Thee.
>
> My faith burns low, my hope burns low;
> Only my heart's desire cries out in me
> By the deep thunder of its want and woe,
> Cries out to Thee.
>
> Lord, Thou art Life, though I be dead;
> Love's fire Thou art, however cold I be:
> Nor heav'n have I, nor place to lay my head,
> Nor home, but Thee.

In Jesus, the Lamb of God, Christina found her life, her love, her home.

Worthy is the Lamb who was slain, to receive
power and wealth and wisdom and might and honor and glory and blessing!

~ REVELATION 5:12 ~

Widow Helping Widows

⬤ Eizabeth Bowen Thompson, d. 1869 ⬤

From her childhood Elizabeth Bowen had an interest in the Bible and in Christian work. When a young woman, she was invited by Sir Culling Eardley to work with the Syro-Egyptian Mission. Here she met Dr James Bowen Thompson, who had opened and directed the British Syrian Hospital at Damascus from 1843 to 1848. The two were married and settled in Antioch, Syria.

In Syria, Elizabeth gained firsthand knowledge of the lack of education and training among the Syrian women. She opened a school for the women in her home to teach them literacy as well as the truth of Christ. Elizabeth conducted the school for eighteen months. When her husband volunteered his medical services to the British in the Crimean War, Elizabeth accompanied him, leaving the operation of her school in the hands of native teachers. Almost immediately after the Thompsons arrived in Balaklava, Dr Thompson was stricken with the fever and died shortly after. Elizabeth buried her husband 'under a spreading tree, commanding a fine view of the Bosporus and Constantinople',[83] and went home to England.

Her husband's death seemed part of her preparation for her ministry to widows and orphans. She understood something of the loss the widows suffered. In 1860, the Druse in Syria attempted to kill every Marionite Christian male between the age of seven and seventy, leaving the women and children to die. Eleven thousand Christians had been massacred, leaving behind twenty thousand widows and orphans. Elizabeth felt she must return to Syria to offer help and solace to these widows.

Elizabeth established the Society for the Betterment of Syrian Women and remained in Syria for eight years.[84] Financing her work with her own funds as well as donations of friends and family members, Elizabeth administered an amazing work of relief. She established eight schools in Beirut and several in outlying villages, as well as teacher training schools. Those who were not refugees saw the value of the education provided in Elizabeth's schools and wanted to be able to attend as well. The fees she charged these wealthier people helped sustain the work for the poor. Prayer and Bible reading was an important part of the education of the women and girls. After visiting the schools Canon Tristram wrote, 'Nowhere has the experiment of female education in the East been tried with more success, and nowhere has it been conducted on more uncompromising and thoroughly Christian principles'.[85]

Exhausted by her work, Elizabeth returned to England, where she died on 14 November, 1869. In one of her last prayers she said, 'And now, Lord, let none of those who know me, and none of those who love me, ever think of me as going through the grave and gate of *death*, but through the gate of *glory!'*

> *Religion that is pure and undefiled before God, the Father, is*
> *this: to visit orphans and widows in their affliction, and to keep*
> *oneself unstained from the world.*
>
> ~ JAMES 1:27 ~

---

83. E. R. Pitman, *Missionary Heroines in Eastern Lands* (London: S. W. Partridge & Co., 1884).

84. The Society for the Betterment of Syrian Women became today's Middle East Christian Outreach .

85. *Missionary heroines in Eastern Lands*, pp. 68-69.

AUGUST 3

Advocate

∞ Charitie Bancroft, 1841-1923 ∞

Born in 1841, Charitie was the fourth child of Charlotte Lees and Rev. George Smith, who was minister of the Colebrooke church in the Aghalurcher Parish of the Church of Ireland. Charitie early showed a gift for poetry and in 1860, in the aftermath of the Irish Revival, published 'O for the robes of whiteness' in a leaflet form. In 1867, Charitie moved with her family when her father became rector of St. Columba's at Tattyreagh. She continued to write devotional poems, which she published in 1867, entitled *Within the Veil*.

Charitie's 'The Advocate', written when she was twenty-two, continues to draw Christians to their Savior today. The poem is rich with biblical allusions and references:

> Before the throne of God above (*Hebrews 4:15-16*)
> I have a strong and perfect plea.
> A great High Priest whose name is Love (*Hebrews 4:14*)
> Who ever lives and pleads for me. (*Hebrews 7:25*)
> My name is graven on His hands, (*Isaiah 49:6*)
> My name is written on His heart.
> I know that while in Heaven he stands
> ⟩ No tongue can bid me thence depart. (*Romans 8:34*)
>
> When Satan tempts me to despair (*Luke 22:31-32*)
> And tells me of the guilt within,
> Upward I look and see Him there (*Acts 7:55-56*)
> Who made an end of all my sin. (*Colossians 2:13-14*)
> Because the sinless Saviour died
> My sinful soul is counted free.
> For God the just is satisfied (*1 John 2:1-2*)
> To look on Him and pardon me. (*Romans 3:24-26*)
>
> Behold Him there the risen Lamb, (*Revelation 5:6*)
> My perfect spotless righteousness, (*1 Corinthians 1:30; 1 Peter 1:18-19*)
> The great unchangeable I AM (*Hebrews 13:8; John 8:58*)
> The King of glory and of grace, (*Psalm 24:8*)
> One with Himself I cannot die.
> My soul is purchased by His blood (*Hebrews 9:11-12; Revelation 5:9*)
> My life is hid with Christ on high, (*Colossians 3:3*)
> With Christ my Saviour and my God! (*Titus 2:13*)

Certainly Charitie was a young woman rich in biblical understanding. Not much else is known about her. In 1869, she married Arthur Bancroft in Edinburgh, Scotland. After his death she then married a Mr de Cheney, who also died – leaving her a widow a second time. Charitie accompanied her brother, Dr Thomas Smith, to California. She died in Oakland, California on 20 June, 1923, at the age of eighty-two. She then met the King of Glory face to face, Him who had been her advocate throughout her life.

> *But if anyone does sin, we have an advocate with the Father,*
> *Jesus Christ the righteous. He is the propitiation for our sins,*
> *and not for ours only but also for the sins of the whole world.*

~ 1 JOHN 2:1-2 ~

Abounding in Every Good Work

∞ Miss de Broen, 1870s ∞

Paris was in turmoil in 1871, as the French forces surrendered to the Germans at the city gates and Napoleon's II's Second Empire collapsed. Many were fearful of the reinstitution of the monarchy. Revolutionists, mostly socialists and communists, easily won the municipal elections and in the spring established a commune system in the city. As the revolutionists continued to oppose French authority, national troops came in May to put down the rebellion. 20,000 insurrectionists were killed, 38,000 were arrested, and thousands more were deported.

Miss de Broen,[86] a worker at London's Mildmay Mission established by Rev. Pennfather, was in Paris during the German siege and the subsequent uprisings, and had a growing conviction that she needed to devote herself to mission work in France. She visited Père la Chaise the day after 500 communists had been shot and thrown into a ditch as a common grave. The grief and despair of the women and children were intense, and many cried out in rage and revenge. One woman cried, 'I have lost everything.' Miss de Broen quietly replied, 'Not the love of God.' She walked among the women telling them that Jesus was the only comforter.

Miss de Broen had no funds to begin a mission, but she knew that if God had placed the matter in her heart, He would supply. She soon met two Englishmen who had come to Paris with funds Quakers had raised to help the victims of the war in France. They turned all the money over to Miss de Broen, and she was able to begin work. She rented rooms in Belleville and invited the women to come. She would pay them five pence for three hours of sewing. At the first meeting, only three women came, but eight were at the second, and more at each following meeting. Miss de Broen taught them the Scriptures as they sewed. In a few months the sullenness and moroseness of these poor, illiterate, forsaken women began to be replaced with the peace and love of Christ.

Starvation and hunger were rampant after the siege and fighting, and Miss de Broen's mission to the poor expanded rapidly. Souls were converted, lives were transformed, and families were restored. A night school was established, where often a father learned his letters along with his son. A medical mission was established with a physician. In the waiting room evangelists and Bible women read and explained the Scriptures. A gospel service was held every morning in the waiting room, and many people heard the Word of God in this way. Miss de Broen's report for 1888 showed 30,000 treated at the medical mission, 2,214 attending the sewing classes, 29,729 at gospel meetings, 4,575 at Sunday schools, 8,727 at week-day schools, with total expenditures of £2,728! God did indeed provide for the work he had placed in Miss de Broen's heart.

> God is able to make all grace abound to you,
> so that having all sufficiency in all things at all times,
> you may abound in every good work. As it is written,
> 'He has distributed freely, he has given to the poor; his
> righteousness endures forever.'
>
> ~ 2 CORINTHIANS 9:8-9 ~

---

86. Unfortunately, I have not been able to find the first name of this lady. She is simply called 'Miss de Broen' in several different accounts of her mission.

I Need Thee Every Hour

∞ Annie Sherwood Hawks, 1835-1918 ∞

Born in Hoosick, New York in 1835, Annie Sherwood's gift of writing poetry was evident from an early age; by the time she was fourteen, her poems were being published in local newspapers. In 1859, Annie married Charles Hawks, and the couple had three children. They lived in Brooklyn, New York and attended Hanson Place Baptist Church, pastored by Dr Robert Lowry. Dr Lowry was also a gifted musician. He encouraged Annie in her poetry and said he would write music for the poems she wrote.

Annie recorded the story behind her most famous hymn, 'I Need Thee Every Hour':

One day as a young wife and mother of thirty-seven years of age, I was busy with my regular household tasks during a bright June morning, in 1872. Suddenly, I became filled with the sense of nearness to the Master, and I began to wonder how anyone could ever live without Him, either in joy or pain. Then, the words were ushered into my mind and these thoughts took full possession of me – 'I need Thee every hour …'

When Annie showed the words to Dr Lowry, he was very much impressed and composed music for them, adding the refrain:

Refrain: *I need Thee, O I need Thee,*
Ev'ry hour I need Thee!
O bless me now, my Saviour –,
I come to Thee!

I need Thee ev'ry hour,
Most gracious Lord;
No tender voice like Thine
Can peace afford.

I need Thee ev'ry hour,
Stay Thou near by;
Temptations lose their pow'r
When Thou art nigh.

I need Thee ev'ry hour,
In joy or pain;
Come quickly and abide,
Or life is vain.

I need Thee ev'ry hour,
Most Holy One;
O make me Thine indeed,
Thou blessèd Son!

The hymn was published in 1872. Ira Sankey used it in the Moody-Sankey campaigns in both the United States and Great Britain. Annie later described how the hymn brought comfort to her when her husband died in 1888:

I did not understand at first why this hymn had touched the great throbbing heart of humanity. It was not until long years after, when the shadow fell over my way, the shadow of a great loss, that I understood something of the comforting power in the words, which I had been permitted to give out to others in my hours of serenity and peace.[87]

'Abide in me, and I in you. As the branch cannot bear fruit by itself, unless it abides in the vine, neither can you, unless you abide in me. I am the vine; you are the branches. Whoever abides in me and I in him, he it is that bears much fruit, for apart from me you can do nothing.'

~ JOHN 15:4-5 ~

---

87. Kenneth W. Osbeck, *101 More Hymn Stories: The Inspiring True Stories Behind 101 Favorite Hymns* (Kregel Publications, 1985), pp. 132-133.

Sunbeam

∞ Elizabeth Clephane, 1830-1869 ∞

Elizabeth Clephane had the nickname of 'Sunbeam' in the community of Melrose, Scotland where she lived. Though often ill and weak herself, Elizabeth brought joy to the many sick and dying she visited and comforted. She also freely distributed the funds she had among those needier than she. Elizabeth loved poetry and enjoyed writing verse as well. Most of her poems were published posthumously. One of her poems, 'Beneath the Cross of Jesus', was written a year before her death at the age of thirty-nine, in 1869. The rich Biblical symbolism in the hymn reflects Elizabeth's deep love of Scripture:

> Beneath the cross of Jesus I fain would take my stand, (*Isaiah 32:2*)
> The shadow of a mighty rock within a weary land; (*Psalm 63:1*)
> A home within the wilderness, a rest upon the way (*Jeremiah 9:2; Isa. 28:12*)
> From the burning of the noon day heat and the burden of the day. (*Isa. 4:6; Matt. 11:30*)
>
> O safe and happy shelter! O refuge tried and sweet! (*Isa. 4:6*)
> O trysting place where Heaven's love and Heaven's justice meet! (*Psalm 85:10*)
> As to the exiled patriarch that wondrous dream was given, (*Genesis 28:10ff.*)
> So seems my Saviour's cross to me – a ladder up to heaven! (*John 3:51*)
>
> There lies beneath its shadow, but on the further side, (*Psalm 36:7*)
> The darkness of an open grave, that gapes both deep and wide;
> And there between us, stands the cross, two arms outstretched to save, (*Exodus 6:6*)
> Like a watchman set to guard the way from that eternal grave.
>
> Upon that cross of Jesus mine eye at times can see
> The very dying form of One who suffered there for me;
> And from my smitten heart with tears two wonders I confess –
> The wonders of redeeming love, and my own worthlessness.

Elizabeth's concluding stanzas spoke of the release of death and the glory above, but went on to say she didn't now ask for that, but asked:

> ... for thy strength to do the work my God hath set for me
> No faithful servant he who seeks for rest before,
> Who faints ere yet the day is done and the evening work is o'er.
>
> I ask a living faith within me to abide;
> I ask thee for a holy heart, and a spirit purified;
> Two willing hands to serve, a patient mind to bear,
> And hallowed, earnest lips to speak for Jesus everywhere.

When 'Beneath the Cross of Jesus' was published in *The Family Treasury* in 1872, editor William Arnot prefaced the hymn with these words:

> These lines express the experiences, the hopes, and the longings of a young Christian lately released. Written on the very edge of this life, with the better land fully in the view of faith, they seem to us footsteps printed on the sands of Time, where these sands touch the ocean of eternity. These footprints of one whom the Good Shepherd led through the wilderness into rest may, with God's blessing, contribute comfort and direct succeeding pilgrims.[88]

Walk as children of light
(for the fruit of light is found in all that is good and right and true).

~ EPHESIANS 5:8-9 ~

---

88. Rev. William Arnot, ed., *The Family Treasury* (London: Thomas Nelson and Sons, 1872), pp. 398-399.

Teacher Par Excellence

∽ Emeline Dryer, 1835-1925 ∾

When she suffered a severe case of typhoid fever, in 1870, Emeline Dryer, an educator *par excellence*, had a distinguished position as head of the women's faculty at Illinois State Normal University (now Illinois State University). Neither Emma, as she was known, nor her doctors had little hope she would recover, but recover she did. Emma realized the Lord had spared her for a purpose, and she felt called to commit her life to Christian work rather than secular teaching:

> [I]n a recent typhoid fever, I had prepared to die, and recovering from that sickness, saw the needs of this dying world, as never before, and especially the fallen, wretched condition of the masses around me. And I understood that the heathen in foreign lands were in a far worse condition than the masses in our cities, and in our own country. And in my earnest, prayerful meditations, God gave me new light from the Scriptures, and taught me.[89]

Emma left behind her good salary and secure position and moved to Chicago to live by faith in God's provision and direction.

In Chicago Emma met Dwight L. Moody and his wife, also named Emma, and the three became instant friends. Moody admired Emma's willingness to leave all earthly achievement behind for the sake of working to help others in need. When the 1871 fire destroyed much of Chicago, including all that Emma herself owned, she devoted herself to helping those in need. Moody invited all the youth to his church and enlisted Emma as teacher of the young people. He also urged her to become head of the Chicago Women's Aid Society and superintendent of the Women's Auxiliary of the YMCA, forerunner of the YWCA.

In England, Moody had been impressed with the deaconesses program that William Pennefather had established, providing an important women's ministry within the church. Before he left for England again in 1873, Moody encouraged Emma to open a school to train women for evangelistic work and home or foreign missions. Moody helped find funding for the school, while Emma set the school in operation. She organized Bible conferences for nationally-acclaimed teachers to come to Chicago and train women for evangelism and work on the mission field. In 1883, with Moody's permission, Emma organized the 'May Institute', weekly meetings for prayer and discussions about the Bible and church work. Many discussed the need for a school to train lay workers – men and women – for the church. With roots in Emma's Bible training for women and the prayer meetings, in 1886 Dwight L. Moody established the Chicago Evangelization Society, which later became Moody Bible Institute.

As for you, always be sober-minded, endure suffering, do the
work of an evangelist, fulfill your ministry.

~ 2 TIMOTHY 4:5 ~

---

89. Quoted from Dyer's memoirs in Barbara Dobschuetz, 'Emma Dryer and the Moody Church', *Fides et Historia* (Vol. 33, no. 2, Summer-Fall, 2001), p. 44.

Missionary Daughter and Wife

∞ Mary Moffatt Livingston, 1821-1862

The oldest daughter of pioneer missionaries Robert and Mary Moffatt, also named Mary, was born in Griquatown, South Africa in 1821. She grew up in Kuruman, where her parents had established a mission among the Botswana people. From her mother Mary learned the skills of making a home in Africa, and as a young woman she taught in the school at Kuruman.

David Livingstone had been inspired to be a missionary and had come to Africa after hearing Mary's father speak in Scotland about the great opportunities of expanding Christianity's influence northward in Africa. When Livingstone later visited the Moffatts at Kuruman, he was attracted to their daughter Mary. In January, 1845, the two were married in the mission church at Kuruman.

The newlyweds' first home was at Mabotsa, where Mary again taught school as she had at Kuruman. David was not satisfied with the work at Mabotsa and wanted to move more to the interior. During the first three years of marriage the family moved three times, finally settling at Kolobeng. Each year another child was born. David was restless and always moving on, exploring what lay behind the next horizon. Mary tried to stay with him in his explorations, crossing the Kalahari Desert twice and twice giving birth along the journey! The family had returned to Kolobeng when their fourth child, Elizabeth, was born. The baby was weak and soon died. Mary then had a stroke, and her face and left side were paralyzed. She recovered, but was much weakened.

David was intent on exploring the water system of the Zambezi, convinced that this would be the pathway for expanded Christian missions and trade. Mary herself wanted to be with Livingstone, but she was unable to physically endure the journey. Livingstone sent his wife and four children to Britain as he continued his explorations of the Zambezi.

In Britain, Mary faced poverty and loneliness, separated from her husband for four years. During those years Livingstone explored Central Africa, mapping the interior of the Continent for future mission and commercial enterprises. At the end of 1856, he returned to England, and at last he and Mary were reunited. David was celebrated everywhere, and Mary was now by his side. At one dinner in his honor, he announced he was returning to Africa for another exploration and Mary would be with him. He noted that 'She had always been the main spoke in his wheel', and he was glad she would be able to accompany him on this trip.

Mary, however, was pregnant and became ill at sea returning to Africa. She gave birth to her sixth child in her parents' home in Kuruman. Her ill health required her to return to Scotland, where she became quite depressed. She longed to be with her husband and children. When Mary did return to Africa and rejoined David, she soon fell ill again. David remained by her side; after some days Mary fell into a coma. David wept like a child when she died. He wrote in his journal, 'I loved her when I married her, and the longer I lived with her I loved her the more. … Oh, my Mary, my Mary! How often we have longed for a quiet home, since you and I were cast adrift at Kolobeng; surely the removal by a kind Father who knoweth our frame means that He rewarded you by taking you to a better home, the eternal one in the heavens.'[90]

In this you rejoice, though now for a little while, if necessary, you have been grieved by various trials, so that the tested genuineness of your faith – more precious than gold that perishes though it is tested by fire – may be found to result in praise and glory and honor at the revelation of Jesus Christ.

~ I Peter 1:6-7 ~

---

90. Quoted in Edith Deen, *Great Women of the Christian Faith*, (Uhrichsville, OH: Barbour Books, 1959), p. 197.

Leader of Her People

∞ Ranavalona II, 1829-1883 ∞

Envoys of the London Missionary Society first arrived in Madagascar in 1818. King Radama I, wanting to benefit from closer contact with European nations, encouraged the missionaries to build schools on the island. A school was established in the palace, where many of the children of the military and ruling class first heard the gospel of Jesus Christ,

Ramoma, born in 1829 into the ruling Merina family of Madagascar, early accepted the Christian teachings and persevered in her faith even when it was banned. In 1835, a new ruler, concerned the missionaries and European influence were weakening the ancestral religion and the monarchy, prohibited Christianity in the kingdom. Soon all the missionaries were forced to leave the country. Christians were persecuted by being sold into slavery, tortured, or even executed. Ramoma quietly maintained her Christian faith.

In 1868, Ramoma succeeded her cousin as queen and took the name Queen Ranavalona II. The night before her coronation the new queen had a private prayer meeting with her Prime Minister and leading pastors, all who had suffered much under the persecutions. In prayer Ramoma placed in God's hands the heavy burden of ruling the island. During her coronation Ramoma removed all the royal idols but had a Bible placed on a table to show this as the foundation of her rule.

After her coronation the Queen sent a letter to the missionaries of the London Missionary Society and promised them she would do whatever she could to help them, encouraging their return to Madagascar. She issued a Code of 101 articles which provided freedom of religion while also repealing some of the traditional practices, such as polygamy. She required all children, including girls, be educated through the age of fourteen. In 1869, Ranavalona burned the royal idols, replacing their authority with the Bible.

On the four walls of the Queen's bedroom were written in gold letters texts from Scripture in Malagassy, 'Glory to God in the highest, and on earth peace among those with whom he is pleased. ... God is with us.' She genuinely looked to God to help her in ruling Madagascar.

> *Blessed be the name of God forever and ever, to*
> *whom belong wisdom and might.*
> *He changes times and seasons; he removes kings*
> *and sets up kings ...*
> *~ DANIEL 2:20-21 ~*

Mrs Dwight L. Moody

∽ Emma Revell, 1842-1903 ∾

The Civil War was in its second year when Emma Revell and Dwight L. Moody were married, 28 August, 1862. The two had met three years before when Moody was recruiting teachers for his Sunday school at Chicago Avenue and Wells Street. Moody's Sunday school was the largest of its day, with an average attendance of 650 and sixty volunteer teachers. The Sunday school had such a reputation that President-elect Lincoln visited the school shortly after his election in 1860.

Born in London, Emma came to Chicago with her parents when she was seven. By the time she was fifteen she was teaching Sunday school, and at seventeen she was a teacher in the Chicago public schools. As Dwight L. Moody's preaching and work as an itinerant evangelist expanded, Emma was a constant encourager and support to Moody's Christian work and numerous educational endeavors – Moody Church and Moody Bible Institute (both named in his honor after his death), Moody Press in Chicago, and the Northfield and Mount Hermon Schools in Massachusetts. His evangelistic meetings attracted large crowds in both England and the United States.

When the Chicago fire broke out in 1871, Emma was at home alone with their two small children. She sent the children to stay with friends for safety, but she was full of concern that they were indeed safe. Moody's church and home were both destroyed by the fire, and Emma's hair began turning white that very night. The Moodys then moved to Northfield, Massachusetts, where another son was later born.

Oldest son Paul Dwight Moody, who became a minister and later President of Middlebury College in Vermont, wrote of his mother:

> Our home seemed so ideal, and the secret of it was my mother. My father's admiration for her was as boundless as his love for her. Till the day of his death he never ceased to wonder at two things – the use God had made of him despite what he considered his handicaps, and the miracle of having won the love of a woman he considered so completely his superior. He was impulsive, outspoken, dominant, informal, and with little education when they met. She was intensely conventional and conservative, far better educated, fond of reading, and self-effacing to the last degree. Yet they presented a common front.[91]

Paul noted that his mother continued her helpful support during Moody's many travels:

> When away from Northfield she was equally busy making a home-away-from-home for my father; shielding him from interruptions, bores, and cranks always in abundance; writing his letters; handling all his money; paying his bills; and doing all in her power to set him free for the work he was doing, in which she took the greatest pride and interest. Only the closest and oldest of his associates knew the extent to which he leaned upon her. She did not intend that they should.[92]

An excellent wife who can find?
She is far more precious than jewels."

~ PROVERBS 31:10 ~

---

91. Emma Moody Powell, *Heavenly Destiny: The Life and Story of Mrs D. L. Moody* (Chicago, IL: Moody Press, 1943), p. 258.

92. Ibid, p. 255.

To Whom Much was Given

∞ Nettie McCormick, 1835-1923 ∞

Nancy Fowler's father was killed in an accident months after her birth, and her mother died when she was eight. Nettie, as she was called, was then raised by her grandmother, Maria Fowler, in Clayton, New York, on the St Lawrence River. From an early age Nettie had a serious disposition, dedicating herself to the service of God and not wanting to waste her life in idleness and frivolity. She joined the Presbyterian Church as a girl, thanked the Lord for her Sunday school class, sang in the church choir, and played the church melodeon.

When she was twenty-two Nettie visited relatives in Chicago where she met Cyrus McCormick, the inventor of a mechanical reaper and founder of the company which became International Harvester. Cyrus was forty-six and a bachelor, but when he met Nettie he knew she was the lady he wanted to spend his life with. Nettie was hesitant; Cyrus was a successful businessman with a strong will. Cyrus persuaded her that he could be strong-willed with gentlemen in business dealings, but with her he claimed, 'I do not think there is a man in the world who would strive more to please you than I should do – no one whose disposition and manner would be more under your control and influence than would mine as your husband.'[93]

Nettie and Cyrus were married 26 January, 1858, and enjoyed twenty-six years together. The couple had seven children, two of whom died as infants and two of whom suffered from schizophrenia, bringing much sorrow to Nettie. When Cyrus died in 1884 he left Nettie a large estate, which she regarded as a sacred trust under God to use for purposes serving Him. She continued to support the numerous causes she and Cyrus had supported, such as Dwight L. Moody, Moody Bible Institute, and Presbyterian Seminary of the Northwest (which was renamed McCormick Seminary). Nettie provided large support to the Student Volunteer Movement under John Mott, Southern Mountain Schools, Alborz College in Teheran, hospitals in Siam and Persia, theological schools in Korea, and many other Christian projects.

When she became deaf later in life she didn't complain, but said it gave her time to think and kept her from hearing 'mean things'. A woman of prayer, Nettie had a trust in God's guidance and providence, once writing a sick relative, 'We plan – and God steps in with another plan for us – and He is all wise and the most loving friend we have, always helping us.'[94]

'Everyone to whom much was given, of him much will be required,
and from him to whom they entrusted much, they will demand the more.'
~ LUKE 12:48 ~

---

93. Stella Virginia Roderick, *Nettie Fowler McCormick* (Rindge, New Hampshire: Richard R. Smith Publisher, 1956), p. 48.

94. Ibid, p. 143.

AUGUST 12

Telling the Message of Jesus

❰ Phoebe Rowe, 1856-1897 ❱

Phoebe Rowe's sweet, clear voice brought peace and joy to many in India as she shared the gospel of her Savior in song, word, and deed. One of her sweetest hymns was 'I Leave it all with Jesus', which began:

I leave it all with Jesus,
For he knows
How beside me
Through my foes;
Jesus knows,
Yes, he knows.

I leave it all with Jesus,
For he knows
Every trial,
Self-denial,
All these blows;
Jesus knows,
Yes, he knows.

Phoebe was born 21 June, 1856, in Agra, India. Her father was a Scotsman. Her mother was Indian and died when Phoebe was two. Phoebe's father educated her himself. When she was thirteen a visiting Baptist minister explained the gospel to Phoebe, and she gave her life to Jesus. From the moment of her conversion, Phoebe took every opportunity to share the good news of Christ with others. When she was sixteen her father died.

Isabella Thoburn had established a girls' school in Lucknow, India in 1870 and needed another teacher; Phoebe was recommended. She came to the Lucknow school in 1872, and continued as a teacher there for ten years. Her fluency in Hindustani, her gentleness, and her love of Christ endeared her to all. Through her ministry, in 1874, every boarder at the school became a Christian. In her spare time Phoebe went out among the poor people to share the gospel, talking with them along the byways and markets, visiting them in their homes, or simply talking under the trees. Often she began gathering people by singing in her sweet voice.

In 1882, Phoebe became a full missionary with the Methodist's Women's Foreign Missionary Society. She was able to devote all of her time to evangelism in the zenanas (women's quarters) and muhullas (laboring class neighborhoods) of northern India. She also regularly conducted classes to train native women as 'Bible women', who could take the Bible and read it to the village people. In her Bible Phoebe had written, 'God being my helper, I will comfort the feeble-minded, support the weak, and be patient toward all.'[95] The Christ-likeness of Phoebe's spirit came from her daily, morning and evening, spending time with her heavenly Father.

When Phoebe died, in 1897, Isabella Thoburn wrote, 'She was a worthy ambassador of our King and His messages were ever on her lips. To all alike, rich and poor, young and old, the high and low, she told the old, sweet story of Jesus. And many who heard believed and will stand with her among the white-robed throng before the throne praising God for evermore.'[96]

In your hearts honor Christ the Lord as holy,
always being prepared to make a defence
to anyone who asks you for a reason for the hope that is in you,
yet do it with gentleness and respect.

~ I PETER 3:15 ~

---

95. Isabella Thoburn, *Phoebe Rowe* (Cincinatti: Curts and Jennings, 1899), p. 33.

96. Isabella Thoburn, 'Memoir of Phoebe Rowe', *Report, Woman's Foreign Missionary Society, North India Conference*, p. 112.

AUGUST 13

Child of the King

∽ Harriet E. Buell, 1834-1910 ∽

Harriet Buell looked forward to the annual camp meetings near her small cottage in Thousand Island Park, New York. The opening service on Sunday morning in 1876 was particularly inspirational. Preaching from Romans 8:17, the evangelist developed the theme that Christians are heirs of God and joint heirs with Christ. His excitement over this truth grew until he concluded by shouting, 'Christian friends, we are the children of a King! Our Heavenly Father's a King! Poor ones, take heart, you'll have a palace someday built for you by Jesus Himself!'

As Harriet walked to her camp tent after the meeting, exalting in the realization she was a child of the King, she composed the following hymn:

> My Father is rich in houses and lands;
> He holdeth the wealth of the world in His hands!
> Of rubies and diamonds, of silver and gold,
> His coffers are full – He has riches untold!
>
> I'm a child of the King! A child of the King!
> With Jesus my Saviour, I'm a child of the King!
>
> My Father's own Son, the Saviour of men,
> Once wandered o'er earth as the poorest of them;
> But now He is reigning forever on high,
> And will give me a home in heav'n by and by.
>
> A tent or a cottage – why should I care?
> They're building a palace for me over there!
> Though exiled from home, yet still may I sing:
> All glory to God, I'm a child of the King.

Harriet sent the poem to the *Northern Christian Advocate*, which printed it in 1 February, 1877. Methodist minister John Sumner later wrote the music for the hymn.

In 1883, Peter Bilhorn was traveling up the Missouri River to Bismarck to do some evangelistic work among the cowboys out West. One Sunday on the way, the boat stopped at Blunt and unloaded some freight. Bilhorn took out his organ and sang a few songs on the wharf, including 'I'm a Child of the King'. Two years later, Bilhorn sang the song in Dwight L. Moody's church in Chicago, when a man at the back rose up and said, 'Two years ago I heard that song at Blunt, Dakota; I was then an unsaved man, but that song set me to thinking, and I decided to accept Christ, and I am now studying for the ministry.'[97]

> *The Spirit himself bears witness with our spirit that we are*
> *children of God, and if children, then heirs – heirs of God*
> *and fellow heirs with Christ, provided we suffer with him in*
> *order that we may also be glorified with him.*
>
> ~ ROMANS 8:16 ~

---

97. Ira Sankey, *My Life and the Story of the Gospel Hymns* (Harper & Brothers, 1906), pp. 258-259

Advice to a Young Convert

CO Sarah Jackson Davis Tappan, 1852 CO

Among the benevolent societies established in New York in the first part of the nineteenth century was the American Female Guardian Society and Home for the Friendless. The Society was organized and operated entirely by women to help four distinct classes of the needy: friendless and deserving young women; destitute children between the ages of three and fourteen; motherless and orphan infants; and dependent mothers with children who should not be separated. The Society published a monthly magazine as well as Christian books of help to the young women in their care. One of the Society's most popular publications was *Letters to a Young Christian*, first published in book form in 1852. This was the reflective work of Sarah Jackson Davis, widow of a former mayor of Boston and second wife of Lewis Tappan, the wealthy businessman and Christian abolitionist.

Sarah's *Letters* written to a new Christian named Eugenia were practical encouragements on living the Christian life. She began by noting:

> In the first place, you want to be a *Bible Christian*. Now do not look among the members of the church to find out what that is; go straight to the Bible. There you read 'whosoever he be of you that forsaketh not all that he hath, he cannot be my disciple [Luke 14:33, KJV]. ... Thou shalt love the Lord thy God with all thy heart, and with all thy soul and with all thy mind, This is the first and great commandment.' [Matt. 22:37-38, KJV][98]

Sarah also reminded Eugenia that the Christian was to live a life dead to sin and alive to God (Rom. 6:11). She encouraged her to read Romans 12, 1 Corinthians 13, and the Sermon on the Mount to see the full portrait of a Bible Christian. The standard of piety in the current church was so much lower than what the Scripture demanded that the young convert should look to the Scriptures, not to the church, for the standard of Christian living.

In her *Letters* Sarah laid out for Eugenia practical guidelines for living a life totally consecrated to God, covering everything from trusting the promises; crucifying fleshly desires; looking to the Bible as the only standard; living in sweet communion with the Father through prayer; choosing associates, especially a spouse, wisely; faithfully discharging duties to family, relations, church, and community; taking care of the physical nature, and doing all to the glory of God. The standard is high, but God has given His Spirit to enable us to fulfill His will. He is able to do exceedingly abundant above all that we ask or think, according to the power that works in us. The way to true holiness is narrow, but:

> Does not your heart burn with desire to be all that it is your privilege to be? All that God would have you to be? Does it not look infinitely desirable to be holy? ... The provisions of the Gospel are sufficient to meet every want of the soul.[99]

Now to him who is able to do far more abundantly than all that we ask or think,
according to the power at work within us,
to him be glory in the church and in Christ Jesus
throughout all generations, forever and ever. Amen.

~ EPHESIANS 3:20-21 ~

---

98. Sarah Jackson Davis, *Letters to a Young Christian* (New York: American Female Guardian Society, 1852), p. 13.
99. Ibid, p. 113.

AUGUST 15

Calm in the Midst of Storms

∽ Maria Dyer Taylor, 1837-1870 ∽

Maria and Hudson Taylor had only been in Yangzhou a few months, in 1868, when a mob, opposing foreigners in their midst, stormed the house. The mob set the house on fire and a tall, strong man, naked to the waist attacked. He snatched the wedding ring from Maria's finger, then another attacker tried to throw one of the missionaries off the roof. Maria and Emily Blatchley dragged him back into the room, but an attacker picked up a brick and was about to dash in the man's head. Maria stood up to him, raised her hand to stop the blow and said, 'Would you strike a defenceless woman?' The man, amazed that she spoke his own language, dropped the brick. Maria – who was six months pregnant – and other missionaries fled, jumping out the window to the ground fifteen feet below. Maria feared she would have a miscarriage and was faint from loss of blood, but later said, 'God was our stay, and He forsook us not. That confidence He gave me – that he would surely work good for China out of our distress.'[100]

The mandarin sent the missionaries to Zhenjiang. When another missionary visited them, he found:

> Mrs Hudson Taylor was sitting down in the middle of the room amidst all this confusion as composedly as possible, going on with the composition of the Ningbo Dictionary. She had a wonderful power of concentration. … She struck me as remarkable for her Christian faith and courage. She had a delicate, sweet face – a fragile body, but a sweet expressive face of indomitable perseverance and courage.[101]

Maria Dyer was the perfect wife for Hudson Taylor. The youngest child of missionary parents, she was born in Penang, Malaya in 1837. At nine, both of her parents had died, and Maria and her older sister Burella went to live with an uncle and aunt in England. After their education in England, Buella and Maria both sailed for China in 1852 to teach at a girls' school in Ningbo. On the voyage to China Maria placed her trust in Christ alone as her Savior. She also began the study of the Ningbo dialect, in which she became quite fluent.

Maria met Hudson Taylor the day after he arrived in Ningbo in 1854. The two were married on 23 January, 1858. Maria became Hudson's companion and partner in ministering to the Chinese. In 1865, Maria fully supported Hudson in the founding of the China Inland Mission (CIM) and served as Hudson's secretary in the mission work.

During their twelve and a half years of marriage the love between Maria and Hudson remained passionate. Even in business notes and letters, Hudson often wrote, 'My heart yearns for you.' Before Maria's death of cholera in 1870 the Taylors had nine children. The four who reached adulthood all became CIM missionaries.

> *'In the world you will have tribulation.*
> *But take heart; I have overcome the world.'*
>
> ~ JOHN 16:33 ~

---

100. A. J. Broomhall, *Hudson Taylor and China's Open Century*, Vol. 5: *Refiner's Fire* (Sevenoaks, UK: Hodder & Stoughton and OMF, 1985), p. 100.

101. Ibid, p. 106.

Rescue the Perishing

∞ Fanny Crosby, 1820-1915 ∞

Fanny Crosby had a heart for the poor and humble people. Blind since infancy, Fanny never pitied herself but sought to bring the light of the gospel to others less fortunate. Though she was able to live in nicer surroundings, she usually lived in tenement buildings near New York's Bowery district. At least once a week she invited neighbors to an evening of hymn singing and Bible reading. She regularly visited the Howard Mission and Home for Little Wanderers on Little Bowery Street. Sometimes she simply sat in the audience and talked to the men informally. At other times she was the speaker. She always began her talks with, 'God bless your dear hearts; I'm so happy to be with you.' Always she talked with excitement in a personal, intimate way about the love of the Savior. She ended her talks with the Mizpah blessing, 'May the Lord watch between me and thee, when we are absent, one from another.'[102]

One hot summer evening in 1869, Fanny addressed a large group of men at the mission. The thought kept coming to her mind that 'some mother's boy must be rescued that night or he might be eternally lost'. She made a plea that 'if there was a boy present who had wandered from his mother's home and teaching, he should come to me at the end of the service'. After the service, a young man of eighteen came to see Fanny and asked, 'Did you mean me, Miss Crosby? I promised my mother to meet her in heaven, but as I am now living, that will be impossible.' Fanny prayed with him, and he arose with new light and life, having been reconciled to God and assured that he would see his mother in heaven.[103]

A few days before, composer William Doane had sent Fanny a tune for her to compose a new hymn to be titled, 'Rescue the perishing', based on Luke 14:23. With the thoughts of the young man at the mission, Fanny wrote:

> Rescue the perishing,
>   Care for the dying,
> Snatch them in pity from sin and the grave;
>   Weep o'er the erring one,
>   Lift up the fallen,
> Tell them of Jesus the mighty to save.
>
> Down in the human heart,
>   Crushed by the tempter,
> Feelings lie buried that grace can restore;
>   Touched by a loving heart,
>   Wakened by kindness,
> Chords that are broken will vibrate once more.
>
> Rescue the perishing,
>   Duty demands it;
> Strength for thy labour the Lord will provide;
>   Back to the narrow way,
>   Patiently win them;
> Tell the poor wand'rer a Saviour has died.

'Go out into the highways and hedges,
and compel people to come in, that my house may be filled.'

~ LUKE 14:23 ~

---

102. Genesis 31:49.

103. Kenneth W. Osbeck, *Amazing Grace* (Grand Rapids, Michigan: Kregel Publications, 1990), p. 297.

Guide Through Life

∞ Fanny Crosby, 1820-1915 ∞

One day, Fanny Crosby, the blind hymn writer, desperately needed five dollars but had no idea where the money was going to come from. As she always did, Fanny prayed about her problem. Shortly after, a stranger came to the door and put something in Fanny's hand. When she showed her companion, she learned it was the five dollars she had prayed for. Fanny knew there was no way to explain this except that God had put into the heart of that man to bring the money. Fanny thought God's leading so wonderful that she wrote a poem, which Robert Lowry put to music. The hymn was first published in 1875 and continues to encourage many to trust the Lord for guidance and direction through life:

> All the way my Saviour leads me; what have I to ask beside?
> Can I doubt His tender mercy, who through life has been my Guide?
> Heavenly peace, divinest comfort, here by faith in Him to dwell!
> For I know whate'er befall me, Jesus doeth all things well.
>
> All the way my Savior leads me, cheers each winding path I tread,
> Gives me grace for ev'ry trial, feeds me with the living bread.
> Though my weary steps may falter, and my soul athirst may be,
> Gushing from the Rock before me, lo! a spring of joy I see.
>
> All the way my Saviour leads me; Oh the fullness of His love!
> Perfect rest to me is promised in my Father's house above.
> When my Spirit, clothed immortal, wings its flight to realms of day,
> This my song through endless ages: Jesus led me all the way.

Fanny had learned that she could depend upon God for her every need. As a baby she had an eye infection which a doctor treated with hot poultices, which scarred her eyes, making her blind for life. She had learned that her blindness was not simply an accident, but something God could use in her life for His glory. She once said that her blindness was the best thing that had happened to her. Certainly her life would not have been as useful if she had not been blind.

Fanny entered the New York Institute for the Blind at the age of twelve, and then went on to teach at the Institute for twenty-three years. She became something of a celebrity there, writing poems for every conceivable occasion, and meeting many dignitaries who came to the school such as Henry Clay, Winfield Scott, John Tyler, and John Q. Adams. Ex-President Martin van Buren took her out to dinner on several occasions. Fanny had dinner with President and Mrs Polk at the White House and was impressed with the Christian faith of Mrs Polk. Fanny knew Grover Cleveland, later President, when he was a secretary at the Institute as a young man. In all these encounters and events of her life Fanny looked to Jesus as her comfort and guide.

> *For this God is our God forever and ever;*
> *he will be our guide even to the end.*
>
> ~ PSALM 48:14 (NIV) ~

Gospel in Patchwork

∞ Harriet Powers, 1837-1910 ∞

Harriet was born into slavery near Athens, Georgia in 1837. Her owners, the Lesters, had eight slaves on their plantation. Harriet's mother was the cook for the Lesters, and early Harriet learned to do work around the house. By the time she was twelve she was also working on the farm, hoeing, weeding, and picking crops. She learned to pick the seed from the cotton before carding it for her mother to spin.

When Harriet was eighteen she married Amsted Powers, a slave on a farm ten miles away. Though marriages were not legal among slaves, both masters approved the marriage and Amsted was able to visit Harriet twice a week. Most likely the two met at church, which was a seven mile walk from Harriet's home. At church the white people sat on one side and the slaves on the opposite side. Harriet learned much of the Bible from the sermons, but she also read the Bible regularly herself. She had learned to read from the Lester children.

Harriet had two children before the Civil War, and three after. The Powers lived on the Lester land after the War, but by 1880 they were able to buy four acres of land, where they raised hogs, cotton, and potatoes. The following year Harriet was able to buy a sewing machine. With this she not only sewed clothes, but created story quilts which were machine appliquéd and then hand quilted. Some of her designs illustrated Bible stories, as Harriet sought to 'preach de Gospel in patchwork'.[104]

In 1886, Harriet exhibited one of her quilts at the county fair in Athens, Georgia. The quilt was divided into eleven rectangles and began with the beginning of sin, the story of Adam, Eve, and the serpent. Harriet placed a peacock in the Garden of Eden to symbolize the 'proudness' which led to their sin. One scene showed Cain slaying Abel, with Abel's blood spilling to the ground. Her last Old Testament scene was Jacob dreaming of the ladder to heaven, with an angel descending. Harriet then had five scenes from the life of Jesus. Underneath the scene of Abel's murder, Harriet showed Jesus' crucifixion between two thieves, with Jesus' blood flowing from his side, to blot out the sin of the world.

In 1891, when the Powers came into financial difficulties, Harriet reluctantly sold this quilt to Jennie Smith, an art teacher in Athens, for $5. Jennie had the quilt exhibited in 1895 at the Cotton States Exhibition in Atlanta. Some ladies who saw the quilt commissioned Harriet to create another Bible quilt for Charles Hull, a pastor dedicated to teaching African Americans and President of Union Theological Seminary.. Though Harriet did many other quilts, including one of the Last Supper, only these two Bible story quilts remain. One is in the Boston Museum of Fine Arts; the other in the Smithsonian National Museum of American History.

But now, O Lord, you are our Father;
we are the clay, and you are our potter;
we are all the work of your hand.

~ Isaiah 64:8 ~

---

104. Kristen Frederickson & Sarah Webb, *Singular Women: Writing the Artist* (Berkeley & Los Angeles: University of California Press, 2003), p. 87.

God's Image Carved in Ebony

∽ Amanda Berry Smith, 1837-1915 ∽

Amanda's grandmother was a praying woman. Born a slave, she prayed that her family might enjoy freedom. Amanda's mother and father belonged to different masters in Long Green, Maryland. Amanda's father worked in the fields on the plantation, then late at night made brooms and husk mats to sell, earning money to buy his freedom and that of his wife and five children. Often he had only a few hours sleep, but his hard work did enable him to bring his family to freedom. Amanda's father always read the Bible to the family on Sunday mornings, and Amanda's mother taught Amanda to read by the age of eight.

When she was about thirteen Amanda went to work for a widow with five children, near York, Pennsylvania. At a Methodist revival meeting on 17 March, 1856, she gave herself to the Lord, resolving to live for Him. Though still a servant girl, her life was lived for Christ:

> One day I was busy with my work and thinking and communing with Jesus, for I found out that it was not necessary to be a nun or be isolated away off in some deep retirement to have communion with Jesus; but, though your hands are employed in doing your daily business, it is no bar to the soul's communion with Jesus. Many times over my wash-tub and ironing table, and while making my bed and sweeping my house and washing my dishes I have had some of the richest blessings. Oh, how glad I am to know this, and how many mothers' hearts have cheered when I told them that the blessing of sanctification did not mean isolation from all the natural and legitimate duties of life, as some seem to think. Not at all. It means God in you, supplying all your needs according to His riches in glory by Christ Jesus; our need of grace and patience and long suffering and forbearance, for we have to learn how not only to bear, but also to forbear with infirmities of ourselves and others as well. [105]

During the Civil War Amanda's husband joined the Northern Army and never returned. She then married James Smith, an unstable minister who left the ministry. After James' death in 1869 Amanda began helping organize Holiness camp meetings, praying with the sick, and working as an evangelist. She had a beautiful singing voice and began to be called on to sing or speak at evangelistic meetings. Sometimes she would feel very awkward when called to sing before a crowd of people; after all, she was only a washerwoman. But she calmed her fears by remembering that she was royalty and related to the King of Kings.

In 1876, some friends invited Amanda to go to England for the meetings at the Keswick Convention. Just the thought of crossing the vast ocean frightened her at first, but she realized she could trust God for the passage. She ended up spending over two years in Britain, participating in evangelistic meetings throughout the land. The way then opened up for Amanda to go to India and finally Africa. Everywhere Amanda went she carried with her the light of Christ and the challenge to live for Him. A minister who knew her well described her as 'God's image carved in ebony'.[106]

My God will supply every need of yours
according to his riches in glory in Christ Jesus.

~ PHILIPPIANS 4:19 ~

105. Amanda Berry Smith, *The Story of the Lord's Dealings with Mrs Amanda Smith, the Colored Evangelist* (Chicago: Meyer & Brothers, Publishers, 1893), p. 103.

106. Edith Deen, *Great Women of the Christian Faith* (Uhrichsville, OH: Barbour Books, 1959), p. 239.

Praying Teenager becomes a Woman of Prayer

⊙ Amelia Taylor Broomhall, 1835-1918 ⊙

Amelia Taylor was born into a Christian family which dutifully trained the children in the Christian faith. Her father was a chemist and a Methodist lay preacher. Her brother Hudson was two years older, while her sister Louisa was five years younger. As toddlers, Hudson had helped Amelia learn to walk, and brother and sister remained close throughout their lives.

When he was fifteen Hudson went to work in a bank. An older bank clerk ridiculed his professed Christianity, and Hudson began to drift from God, becoming a sceptic. The whole church business grew bothersome to him. Amelia tried to reason Hudson out of his scepticism, but without success. Not being able to persuade him, Amelia decided to pray for him three times a day.

One day shortly after, Hudson read a tract which convicted him and brought him to submit to Christ in faith. Amelia was the first person Hudson told of his conversion.

When Hudson later went to China as a missionary he hoped Amelia would soon join him. Amelia, however, received a marriage proposal from Benjamin Broomhall, a friend of Hudson's, and the two were married in 1859. Though Amelia and Benjamin both had a strong interest in missions, they did not feel called to the mission field. They did work together to provide important home support to the China Inland Mission (CIM), which Hudson established in 1872. Benjamin became General Secretary to CIM, serving in that capacity from 1878 to 1895.

Amelia was the consummate wife and helper to Benjamin's work, providing a well-run household, even with ten children. Their home became a welcoming, hospitable place for mission candidates and visiting missionaries. When Hudson and his wife needed to devote themselves to the famine relief in China, Amelia took care of their six children, adding them to her ten! While Benjamin was coordinating missions activities and speaking throughout Britain in support of the missionary work in China, Amelia was behind the scenes, lifting up the mission in prayer, as she had prayed for her brother Hudson when a young teenager.

I urge that supplications, prayers, intercessions, and thanksgivings be made
for all people, for kings and all who are in high positions,
that we may lead a peaceful and quiet life, godly and dignified in every way.
This is good, and it is pleasing in the sight of God our Savior,
who desires all people to be saved and to come to the knowledge of the truth.

~ 1 TIMOTHY 2:1-3 ~

A.L.O.E.

⤲ Charlotte Maria Tucker, 1821-1893 ⤳

Charlotte Maria Tucker was born into a life of wealth and ease. Her father, Henry St George Tucker, was a director of the East India Company and his friends included many notable in society, including the Duke of Wellington. Charlotte's father did not approve of girls' schools, so Charlotte was educated at home by governesses. In a family with ten children Charlotte early became a teacher herself as she taught her younger siblings. Charlotte and her siblings produced a family magazine and wrote and performed plays together. Though Charlotte was encouraged to participate in society's teas and dinner parties, she preferred caring for her younger siblings or various nieces and nephews whose parents were in India.

In 1848, Charlotte began visiting Marylebone workhouse, central London, doing social work among the poor. After her father died in 1851 Charlotte began publishing children's books under the *nom de plume* A.L.O.E. – A Lady of England. Many of her works were allegories or stories illustrating biblical principles. *The Claremont Tales* illustrated the beatitudes. *Angus Tarlton* illustrated the fruits of the Spirit. From 1854-1893 Charlotte published 142 books, mostly for children. She used the profits from her writing to support social work among the poor.

Charlotte had for some time thought about doing missionary work in India and decided to embark in 1875, at the age of fifty-four. She had sufficient funds to be self-supporting and went as an independent missionary. India would be her home for the rest of her life. Charlotte studied Hindustani and quickly learned the grammar, but never was able to converse with ease. Locating herself at Batala, north-east of Lahore, Charlotte helped support the Baring High School for native Christian boys and founded a school for Indian boys not yet Christians. She wrote booklets – mostly allegories – for translation into native Indian dialects and use in the zenanas which she regularly visited.

Charlotte died in India in 1893, having lived a life for her Savior in service and help to others.

> *Whatever you do, work heartily, as for the Lord and not for men,*
> *knowing that from the Lord you will receive the inheritance as your reward.*
> *You are serving the Lord Christ.*

~ COLOSSIANS 3:23-24 ~

AUGUST 22

Caring for the Least of These

∞ Agnes Elizabeth Jones, 1832-1868 ∞

When Agnes Elizabeth Jones was born on 10 November, 1832, she was a feeble baby and not expected to live. However, Agnes gained strength and grew to be a blessing and help to many. Her father was in the military, and when Agnes was a young girl, his career took him to Mauritius, where he was stationed for six years. There Agnes saw many Christian refugees who had been expelled from Madagascar, and at the age of seven she wanted to do mission work to help the people.

During a family tour of Germany, France, and Switzerland in 1853 Agnes spent a week at the Deaconess's Institute of Kaiserswerth, a training program for nurses. Agnes increasingly felt caring for the poor and sick was her particular area of service for her Savior. She wrote in her journal:

> To hold ourselves ever in readiness to serve Him; to think nothing too small, and so we shall be ready for greater works and further submission, if he sees fit to call us to any great work. ... Enable me to grow in the knowledge of what may help others, but, above all, in the knowledge of thee, my Saviour, from whom comes the will to work for thee.[107]

After leaving Kaiserswerth Agnes sought to make herself useful until God opened up the work he would have her do: 'I want a life-work to employ the faculties which God has given me; they are not many or great mentally, but they are his gift, and I desire to devote them to his service.'[108] Agnes found further training as a Nightingale probationer at St Thomas' Hospital in London. While there she established a Bible study for the nurses. Bringing spiritual solace to her patients brought Agnes great joy.

After serving as superintendent of two London hospitals, in 1865 Agnes became superintendent of the Liverpool Workhouse and oversaw the first staff of twelve Nightingale nurses from St Thomas' Hospital. Agnes depended on the Lord's strength for the task. She noted a hymn which expressed her trust:

> I know not the way I am going.
> But well do I know my Guide;
> With a child-like trust I give my hand
> To the mighty Friend by my side.
>
> The only thing I can say to him,
> As he takes it, is 'Hold it fast;
> Suffer me not to lose my way,
> And bring me home at last.'

At Liverpool Agnes supervised seventy wards with 1,400 people. She provided spiritual as well as physical care for the people, establishing regular Bible readings for the patients and a Bible class for the nurses. The work, however, weakened Agnes, and she contracted typhus. She went to her Savior on 19 February, 1868.

Florence Nightingale recognized Agnes did all for the Savior and wanted her life to be spent usefully:

> The light with which the loving Agnes was enlightened directed her to duty, not to selfish ease, personal comforts, or pleasures. And in doing that duty her heavenly Father remembered her with blessings that filled her with divine love, and converted a workhouse into 'the very gate of heaven'.[109]

And the King will answer them,
'Truly, I say to you, as you did it to the least of these my brothers, you did it to me.'
~ MATTHEW 25:40 ~

---

107. Joseph Johnson, *Noble Women of Our Time* (London: Thomas Nelson & Sons, 1882), pp. 27-28.
108. Ibid, p. 31.
109. Ibid, p. 47.

Building a Nation's Homes

∞ Lucy Webb Hayes, 1831-1889 ∞

Lucy Webb Hayes knew that the home was foundational to the health of a nation and civilization. In her own home Lucy not only exemplified Christian virtues, but she worked to encourage others to build strong families.

In 1850, Lucy graduated with first honors from Wesleyan's Women's College; her commencement essay, 'The Influence of Christianity on National Prosperity', reflected Lucy's Christian faith and her concerns for the welfare of the nation. In 1852, Lucy married lawyer Rutherford Hayes. The couple made their home in Fremont, Ohio, where they were active members of the Methodist Church. Both were anti-slavery, and when the Civil war broke out Rutherford joined the Union forces. Lucy worked in camp hospitals throughout the war and spent two winters at camp with her husband, nursing him back to health. After the war Rutherford served as governor of Ohio. Lucy used her influence to help establish a state home for Soldiers' Orphans. Three of the Hayes' children died as toddlers, but four sons and a daughter lived to maturity.

In 1877, Rutherford was inaugurated the nineteenth President of the United States, and in her role as First Lady Lucy continued to radiate her Christian faith. In the White House, Lucy and Rutherford continued their practice of reading a Bible chapter and saying prayers together after breakfast. Together they decided there would be no alcoholic beverages served in the White House, a practice which gained Lucy the nickname of 'Lemonade Lucy' and the administration as 'the cold water regime'. On Sunday evenings Lucy regularly held hymn sings at the White House, with hymn books distributed and Vice President Wheeler often choosing and directing the hymns.

In 1880, Lucy was reluctantly persuaded to be President of the Women's Home Missionary Society, newly organized at the Trinity Methodist Episcopal Church in Cincinnati. One purpose of the society was to repair the wrongs of slavery, and provide domestic and family training for black girls and women. Several model homes were established with a Christian matron to instruct the women and girls in home industries, chastity, purity of thought, and Christian principles. Though reluctant at first to take the mantle of President, Lucy came to use her influence to promote strong families. In 1886, at the Fifth Annual meeting of the Society, Lucy reminded the members:

> The corner-stone to practical religion is the Golden Rule . ... Within our [America's] borders are Africans, Asiatics, and Europeans. The apostles were told that repentance and remission of sins should be preached among all nations in Christ's name, and they were also told that the beginning should be at Jerusalem. Is not the meaning and spirit of this divine injunction clear and plain? This command is obeyed by all whose work is done where it will accomplish most to win souls from the paths of sin to the paths of righteousness. ... If, by reason of our neglect of home-work, the stream of unchristian tendencies from abroad, and the flood of indifference and vice of our own country, shall overwhelm the institutions of our fathers, the missions of every Christian church, both home and foreign, will suffer alike by the common calamity. If our eyes are to be gladdened by the sight of heathen lands rapidly becoming Christian, we must direct our efforts and strain every nerve to protect from heathenism our own land. ... With America and American homes what they should be, we need not greatly fear the evils that threaten us from other lands. We can easily shun or safely meet them, if our duty is faithfully done in behalf of the weak, the ignorant, and the needy of our own country. [110]

By wisdom a house is built,
and by understanding it is established.

~ PROVERBS 24:3 ~

---

110. Mrs John Davis, *Lucy Webb Hayes, A Memorial Sketch* (Cincinnati: Cranston Stowe, 1890), pp. 87-90.

Auntie Wright

∞ Laura Maria Sheldon Wright, 1809-1886 ∞

Growing up along the Connecticut River in Vermont in the early nineteenth century, Laura Sheldon often played with the local Native American children. Even as a child Laura had a serious nature and always wanted to be useful. When she was ten she began holding prayer meetings with her playmates. After finishing school Laura began organizing 'infant schools' for young children in Newbury, Vermont and lived with the family of Rev. Clark Perry. Rev. Perry's friend and classmate at Dartmouth, Asher Wright, was a missionary to the Seneca, part of the Iroquois Confederation, in New York. When Asher's first wife died after only a brief marriage, Rev. Perry suggested to him that Laura would be a good wife for him in his missionary work. Though they had never met, Asher wrote Laura proposing she consider being his wife! In her carefully considered response, Laura wrote in part,

> As regards the missionary enterprise I must say I have always taken a lively interest in all its concerns. I have thought of devoting myself to that object ever since I was a child, but as no opportunity has yet offered and no special providence has yet pointed plainly the path of duty, I have often almost concluded that God had nothing for me to do in heathen lands and that my sphere of usefulness was evidently elsewhere. I humbly hope I have long sincerely loved the cause of Christ, and that I have devoted my all to his service. I trust that I love the souls of the heathen, and am willing to leave the friends of my youth and encounter the toils and hardships of missionary life, if by so doing I can be useful to them.
>
> In the present case there is apparently an opportunity for an intelligent, pious female possessing a heart devoted to the work to accomplish much good; but whether I am that female remains to be decided. I believe, however, that if I commit my cause to God and sincerely desire divine direction, he will order it all in infinite wisdom. ...[111]

Laura and Asher corresponded for a year. Then Asher came to Newbury, where the two were married January 21, 1833. The next day the Wrights were off to western New York, a journey of fifteen days and nights. Along the way, Laura began learning the native language, greatly impressing the first Indians they met at the Mission House.

Laura and Asher worked together among the Seneca Nation for over forty years. Asher was an excellent linguist and developed an alphabet for the Seneca language. Laura helped him in the work teaching the children and writing a series of schoolbooks as well as a bilingual journal that was published between 1841 and 1850. When starvation and epidemics orphaned numerous Seneca children, Laura took them into her home as her own. The number of orphans became so numerous that she persuaded Philip E. Thomas, a merchant of Baltimore, to provide funds for an orphanage, which at first was called the Thomas Asylum for Orphan and Destitute Indian Children, later called the Thomas Indian School. Recognizing the problem alcohol caused among many of the Indians, Laura also founded the Iroquois Temperance League. Laura manifested the love of Christ in her respect and all her treatment of the Iroquois, who affectionately called her Auntie Wright.

> *Who will not fear, O Lord, and glorify your name?*
> *For you alone are holy.*
> *All nations will come and worship you,*
> *for your righteous acts have been revealed.*
> ~REVELATION 15:4~

---

111. Mrs Harriet S. Caswell, *Our Life Among the Iroquois* (Boston & Chicago: Congregational Sunday-School and Publishing Society), p. 18.

AUGUST 25

Mother of the Salvation Army

∞ Catherine Booth, 1829-1890 ∞

Catherine Mumford, the only daughter of five children, was a precocious little girl. She could read by the age of three and read voraciously. By the time she was twelve she had read through the Bible eight times. She also enjoyed reading theology and church history. When she was sixteen she was converted and joined the Wesleyan Church.

One Sunday, she heard an itinerate evangelist, William Booth, preach and was impressed. When a friend told Booth, a correspondence ensued between William and Catherine. Catherine had definite ideas about what she wanted in a husband. He must be a true Christian and a man of common sense; she could never respect a fool or someone mentally her inferior. He must totally abstain from liquor. Husband and wife must have a oneness in viewpoints and tastes, without any idea of lordship of one over the other. In May 1852, Catherine and William were engaged. Shortly before their marriage, Catherine wrote William a note of encouragement:

> Don't let controversy hurt your soul. Live near to God by prayer. Oh, I do feel the importance of spiritual things, and am in a measure living by faith in the Son of God! Just fall down at His feet and open your very soul before him, and throw yourself right into His arms.[112]

A few months after their wedding, Catherine wrote William:

> I believe that if God spares you and you are faithful to His trust, your usefulness will be untold, and beyond our present capacity to estimate. God seems to be preparing you in your own soul for greater things yet.[113]

The couple set some rules for their marriage: They were not to have any secrets affecting the relationship between each other or their family. They were not to have two separate budgets but share their resources. And they were not to argue in front of the children.

When William began working among the impoverished in the East End of London, Catherine encouraged him that with God all things were possible. This ministry eventually developed into the Salvation Army, to reach the urban masses with the love of Christ.

Catherine and William had eight children, all of whom became leaders in Christian service – a testimony to their Christian home. When Catherine died of breast cancer on 4 October, 1890 thousands came to honor her Christian life. William spoke at the end of her funeral service, saying she was a friend 'who had understood the rise and fall of his feelings, the bent of his thoughts, and the purpose of his existence'.[114] He praised her as a mother who had trained her children for the service for the living God. He praised her as a wife who had stood by his side when the battle was strongest. His heart was full of gratitude that God had lent him such a treasure, one who was a true warrior for Christ.

For this is the message that you have heard from the beginning,
that we should love one another.

~ I JOHN 3:11 ~

112. Quoted in Edith Deen, *Great Women of the Christian Faith* (Uhrichsville, OH: Barbour Books, 1959), p. 220.
113. Ibid, p. 219.
114. Ibid, p. 224.

AUGUST 26

Telling the Story of Jesus

∞ Katherine Hankey, 1834-1911 ∞

At the beginning of the nineteenth century a network of influential Christian reformers in London were important in shaping the spiritual and moral climate of Victorian Britain. Known as the Clapham Sect, since many attended Holy Trinity Church on Clapham Common, the group led the fight against the slave trade and also founded the British and Foreign Bible Society and the Church Missionary Society, as well as tract societies. Led by Member of Parliament William Wilberforce, the group included minister Charles Simeon, economist Henry Thornton, scholar Grenville Sharp, writer and philanthropist Hannah More, director of the British East India Company Charles Grant, and Katherine Hankey.

Katherine was the daughter of a wealthy banker and early had a zeal for bringing others to Christ. She organized a Bible study for girls in her neighborhood, and in her late teens organized Sunday schools for girls working in the London sweat shops. She taught at the schools and wrote poems and gospel tracts for the class. Katherine also visited those in prison and brought them the redeeming truth of the gospel.

In 1866, when she was thirty-two, Catherine had a prolonged illness which kept her confined to her bed from January through November. During that time she wrote a long poem about Jesus called *The Old, Old Story*. The poem was in two parts: *The Story Wanted* and *The Story Told*. The poem was published anonymously in 1867. David Russelll recited the poem at the international convention of the YMCA in Montreal that year. When Bishop William Doane heard the poem, he set the first part to music, which became the favorite hymn, 'Tell me the Old, Old Story':

> Tell me the old, old story of unseen things above,
> Of Jesus and his glory, of Jesus and his love;
> Tell me the story simply, as to a little child,
> For I am weak and weary, and helpless and defiled.

> Tell me the story softly, with earnest tones and grace;
> Remember, I'm the sinner whom Jesus came to save:
> Tell me the story always, if you would really be,
> In any time of trouble, a comforter to me. ...

'I Love to tell the Story' was adapted from the words of the second part of Hankey's poem, with music composed by William Fischer and first published in 1869:

> I love to tell the story of unseen things above,
> Of Jesus and his glory, of Jesus and his love.
> I love to tell the story, because I know 'tis true;
> It satisfies my longing, as nothing else can do. ...

Telling the story of Jesus was a passion for Katherine, and something she needed for her own soul. She once wrote, 'God's remedy for sin is something I want to understand, and I want to hear it often, lest I forget it.'[115] Katherine gave all the royalties of her poem to foreign missions.

> *Come and hear, all you who fear God,*
> *and I will tell what he has done for my soul.*

~ Psalm 66:16 ~

---

115. Leslie Clay, *Sisters in Song: Women Hymn Writers* (Columbus, MO: AKN Publishing, 2013).

Decorating Your Heavenly Home

∞ Sarah Dunn Clarke, 1835-1918 ∞

Born in 1835, Sarah Dunn was raised in a Christian home and enjoyed a very comfortable life. She taught school for a time in New York, then moved with her parents to Waterloo, Iowa in 1861. Sarah enjoyed fine clothes and fabrics and became part of the best society in Waterloo. With a knack for decorating, she was often called on to help others decorate their homes in the finest manner. One day Sarah was designing an elaborate center piece for a party when she heard an almost audible voice ask, 'How are you decorating your eternal home?' Sarah thought of the many homeless, impoverished people and knew she needed to help them and bring them the gospel of Christ.

Sarah moved to Chicago and in 1869, with some other women, organized a Sunday school in a rough part of town. She began working with abused wives and abandoned children, distributing food and sharing the gospel. At first the women supported the work from their own funds. Soon, however, they went to the business community to seek further financing. One person Sarah approached was real estate tycoon George Clarke. The two became friends and were married in 1873.

Though living in an elegant house in the best part of town, Sarah still felt she needed to reach out to the Christless poor with the message of Jesus. She wanted a mission in the middle of the brothels, gambling halls, and saloons. Though George accompanied Sarah on her walks through the town, he was interested in building up his real estate fortune, not in establishing a mission. Then, on a trip to Colorado for another big real estate deal, George telegraphed Sarah that they could establish a mission together.

George and Sarah bought a small store, with room for forty seated in the main room, and opened Clarke's Mission in 1877. George preached the gospel while Sarah tried to keep order among the drunks and wastrels who had wondered into the mission. Sarah could often be found in the back of the room praying fervently for the men's salvation. George was not a great preacher, but God used him to bring four men to Christ in the first four days.

In 1880, the Clarkes bought a much larger building, the Pacific Beer Garden. Dwight L. Moody recommended they take the 'beer' out of the name and add 'mission' at the end, and so the Pacific Garden Mission was born. Many have come to know Christ through the ministry of Pacific Garden Mission, among them Billy Sunday, a Chicago baseball player who became a leading evangelist. Pacific Garden Mission is the oldest continuing operating gospel rescue mission in the United States and continues today to bring the good news to the homeless and downcast. Sarah's decorating for her heavenly home was splendid!

The truth is in Jesus, to put off your old self,
which belongs to your former manner of life and is
corrupt through deceitful desires,
and to be renewed in the spirit of your minds, and to put on the new self,
created after the likeness of God in true righteousness and holiness.

~ EPHESIANS 4:21-24 ~

AUGUST 28

Unselfish Humility

⨳ Amelia Wallinger, 1839-1894 ⨳

From a young age Amelia Wallinger had a love for the Savior and wanted to bring others to Him. Her father, several brothers, and then her mother died when Amelia was still quite young. Though seemingly alone, Amy, as she was called, took comfort in the love of Jesus and the truth found in Psalm 34:22 (KJV), 'None of them that trust in him shall be desolate.'

Having an abundant income from her inheritance, Amy looked for ways to use all she had for the work of the Lord. From 1872 to 1882 she took in fourteen orphan daughters, those of gentle birth who did not have the funds for an education. She hired governesses to teach the girls and taught them the Scriptures herself. Many of the girls came to faith in Christ, and when they became wives and mothers they looked back with thankfulness for the education and Christian nurture Amy had provided for them.

When high schools improved in quality, Amy realized such private tutelage was not as needed. While still keeping a few students, she began a work among the poor. She held mothers' meetings and sewing classes for children, and she called upon friends to bring Sunday evening devotions to the tramps.

When the last aged relative for whom she was caring died, Amy felt free to embark on a missionary career. She had always relished reading 'news from the front' in the missionary magazines. In 1886, when she was forty-seven, Amy went to India under the Church of England Zenana Missionary Society. She paid her own expenses and those of a companion. For the remaining eight years of her life Amy lived in south India, working to bring the truth of Christ to the Todas, a pastoral people who lived on the Nilgiri plateau 7,500 feet above sea level. Amy and her companion, Miss Ling, learned Tamil and trained teachers to begin schools in the region. Amy's thoughts and prayers were always focused on how to better bring Christ to the Nilgiri, and she used her funds to implement many of her plans.

Amy rejoiced to hear the little girls singing the refrain of a hymn in Tamil, 'God is good, God is good'. Amy's always joyous spirit reflected her close communion with her God, and her life reflected humility and Christian service for others. She exemplified what she called for in one of her last letters: 'The loving service of the heart is what is wanted, unselfishness, humility.'[116]

> *The LORD redeems the life of his servants;*
> *none of those who take refuge in him will be condemned.*
>
> ~ PSALM 34:2 ~

---

116. Dona L. Woolnae, 'Amelia Wallinger, From English Lowlands to Indian Highlands' (*The Sunday at Home*, London: Religious Tract Society, Vol. 41, 1893-1894), pp. 711.

Songs for Chautauqua

∞ Mary Artemisia Lathbury, 1841-1913 ∞

When a young girl, Mary Artemisia Lathbury had a talent for composing poems which she illustrated with her own drawings. Mary was born in Manchester, New York in 1841, where her father was pastor in the Methodist Episcopal Church. One day she realized that her illustrated poetry should be consecrated to the Lord's service, and she contributed many works to periodicals for children.

In 1874, Mary became an editorial assistant to Dr John H. Vincent, Secretary of the Methodist Sunday School Union. That same year Vincent organized the New York Chautauqua Assembly as a teaching camp for Sunday school teachers on the shores of Lake Chautauqua in western New York. This quickly grew into the Chautauqua Institution and a pattern for Chautauqua organizations developed around the country. Christian instruction and worship was combined with educational lectures and musical performances on a variety of topics, all in a beautiful outdoor setting. The Chautauqua movement remained important into the twentieth century, and Mary Lathbury was working with Dr Vincent at the Chautauqua's beginning. Not only did Mary continue to write and design children's books and Sunday school material, but increasingly she was asked to compose hymns for various Chautauqua events.

In 1887, Mary wrote what she called a 'Study Song' for students to sing at the camp on the shore of Lake Chautauqua as they began their Bible study:

Break thou the Bread of Life,
Dear Lord, to me,
As thou didst break the loaves
Beside the sea;
Beyond the sacred page
I seek thee, Lord;
My spirit pants for thee,
O living Word!

Bless thou the truth, dear Lord,
To me, to me,
As thou didst bless the bread
By Galilee;
Then shall all bondage cease,
All fetters fall;
And I shall find my peace,
My All-in-All.

The hymn became loved by many. Dr G. Campbell Morgan had his congregation sing the song before his weekly Bible classes in London.

The same year, Mary wrote another hymn for Chautauqua which has now been sung around the world:

Day is dying in the west;
Heaven is touching earth with rest;
Wait and worship while the night
Sets her evening lamps alight.

Through all the sky,
Holy, holy, holy Lord God of Hosts!
Heaven and earth are full of thee!
Heaven and earth are praising thee,
O Lord most high.

Jesus said to them, 'I am the bread of life,
whoever comes to me shall not hunger,
and whoever believes in me shall never thirst.'

~ JOHN 6:35 ~

Jehovah-Jireh

∞ Hannah Norris Armstrong, 1841-1919 ∞

Hannah Norris's journal of 1870 contains the entry:

> Left home June 23rd, returned August 29th. Met 41 appointments with different churches, organized 32 Societies (circles), visited seven Sabbath Schools, attended Central and Eastern Associations and Convention. ... Two circles were also formed in Halifax but I was not present.[117]

So Hannah summarized the remarkable foundation of the United Baptist Woman's Missionary Union. It was a remarkable seven weeks in a day when transportation was not easy.

Hannah had been baptized and joined the Baptist church in Canso, Nova Scotia in 1865 at the age of twenty-three. She was teaching school at a Seminary in Wolfville when, while in prayer, the thought came to her that she was needed in Burma. Staying in Wolfville at the time were Rev. and Mrs Arthur Crawley, Baptist missionaries in Burma. Mrs Crawley encouraged Hannah to go to Burma, even though at that time few single female missionaries were being sent out. When Hannah approached the Board of Foreign Missions of Maritime Baptists, she was told funds were short and nothing was available for her work. Hannah, however, firmly believed that the Lord was able to provide for His own. 'Jehovah-Jireh', 'the Lord will provide', (Gen. 22:14) became her encouragement throughout her life.

Hannah went to a wealthy businessman and asked if he could loan her the funds if she could secure promissory notes from others that he would be repaid. The gentleman agreed, and Hannah quickly secured the sufficient promissory notes from her friends. When she returned to the businessman, however, he had changed his mind. Hannah knew the Lord would provide the funds in another way. She boarded a ship to Boston to apply to the American Baptist Missionary Union there, but several Christian leaders encouraged her to disembark and reapply to the Board of Foreign Missions. Her application was accepted once the funds were secured, and Hannah was encouraged to solicit funds from sisters in the church. With energy and confidence in the Lord's provision, Hannah in seven weeks organized women's missionary societies throughout eastern Canada, forming the United Baptist Woman's Missionary Union.

Hannah herself left for Burma a month later. In 1874, she married fellow missionary William F. Armstrong. The Armstrongs served as missionaries in Burma and India for over forty years. Hannah taught schools, organized orphanages, translated tracts and hymns, while raising three children of her own. She looked forward to celebrating the Jubilee of the UBWMU in 1920, but died the year before the Jubilee. Throughout her life Hannah had trusted Jehovah-Jireh, 'The Lord will provide.'

> *Oh, fear the Lord, you his saints,*
> *for those who*
> *fear him have no lack!*
>
> ~ PSALM 34:9 ~

---

117. As quoted in H. Miriam Ross, 'Women's Strategies for Mission: Hannah Maria Norris Blazes the Trail in 1870', *Historical Papers 1992: Canadian Society of Church History*, p. 5.

Singing the Gospel among the Hindus

∽ Alexina Mackay, 1848-1892 ∾

Alexina MacKay's parents had brought her up to live a life of service to the Lord and to others. Her father, Rev. M. McKay, was Free Church of Scotland minister of Fordyce, on the Banffshire coast of Scotland. Yet when Alexina came to the point of wanting to devote her life to missions, her mother was not enthusiastically behind the move. It would be difficult to part with Alexina, and there would be many hardships in living in the heathen lands.

After completing her schooling Alexina worked some years as a governess. When she was twenty-eight, in 1876, the Committee of the Free Church of Scotland Ladies' Society for Female Education in India and South Africa called for a lady missionary to go to the East. Mrs McKay could not help but recognize this as an answer to Alexina's prayer for mission work and gave her consent. Alexina wrote the Society: 'I feel that it would be a great privilege to be permitted to enter the lists with those favoured few who have been called to bear the "lamp of life" into the dark corners of the earth; and if, in the providence of God, I am called to that honour, I desire to respond, "Here I am!" and to venture forward on the unknown, untrod path.'[118]

Alexina was assigned to the Nagpoor mission in India to work with the women in the zenanas, the women's portion of the house. In Hindu India the women were kept in the inner part of the house and did not freely mingle with outsiders. Alexina went to the zenanas as a woman teaching women. She taught the women how to read as well as the truth of the gospel. Alexina always introduced her lessons by singing a hymn in the native language. She could easily sing the message of the gospel before she was fluent in the native language. With her joyful spirit, obvious love for the people, and eagerness that all know the love of God in Christ, Alexina's evangelistic work among the women bore much fruit.

In 1886, Alexina married Rev. Johan Ruthquist, a Swedish missionary at Amarwara, among the Gonds people. The Ruthquists' home became an example of Christian living among the natives. In their work among the Gonds, Alexina sang hymns and Johan preached. A baby girl was born to the couple in 1889, but she only lived on earth twelve days.

Alexina's strength was failing, and she was compelled to take to her bed while on a journey to Scotland in 1892. She wrote a last message to her husband:

'Jesus Christ, the same, yesterday, to-day, and forever.' They which live should not henceforth live unto themselves, but unto Him who died for them and lived again.

My times are in Thy hand;
My God, I wish them there;
My life, my friends, my all I leave
Entirely to Thy care.[119]

Let the word of Christ dwell in you richly,
teaching and admonishing one another in all wisdom,
singing psalms and hymns and spiritual songs,
with thankfulness in your hearts to God.

~ COLOSSIANS 3:16 ~

118. E. R. Pitman, *Missionary Heroines in Eastern Lands* (London: S. W. Partridge & Co., 1884), p. 11.
119. Ibid, p. 58.

First Women's Hospital and Medical School in Asia

❧ Clara Swain, 1834-1910 ❧

Dr Clara Swain arrived in Bareilly, India in the early morning of 20 January, 1870. Her journey since she left New York on 3 November, 1869, had not been a pleasant one. The sea voyage was very rough, and Clara was sick much of the time. Her luggage didn't arrive in Bombay with her. Because of delays in the horse-drawn carts, she missed the train connection to Cawnpore. Not knowing the language, she had difficulty obtaining food. However, when she arrived at the mission station in Bareilly, a group of native Christian women eagerly awaited 'Doctor Miss Sahiba'.

Women in India led very restricted lives and were not allowed contact with men other than close relatives. When ill or in need of medical attention, a male doctor could not attend to them. When Mr & Mrs Thomas, missionaries who ran a girls' orphanage in Bareilly, had written Clara asking if she would come to India, she quickly agreed to go. Never in all her years of medical training to become a doctor did she imagine she would go to India!

In her first year in Bareilly Clara treated 1,300 patients. She also trained seventeen medical students, lecturing particularly in anatomy, physiology, medicines, and diseases of women and children. The medical work soon grew beyond what the mission station could house; a hospital was needed. Clara and Mr and Mrs Thomas went to Rampore to ask the Nawab of the province to sell them land next to the mission to build the hospital. The Nawab was a Muslim who had bitterly opposed Christianity. When they arrived, they were told the Nawab was in prayer and they could not see him until the next day. For their entertainment he sent over two music boxes and trained athletes to perform!

When the missionaries made their proposal to the Nawab to purchase property for the hospital, he amazingly told them, 'Take it, take it. I give it with pleasure for such a purpose.' Clara later wrote, 'We accepted the gift with gratitude not to this prince alone, but to the King of the Universe, who, we believe, put it into his heart to give it to us.'[120]

The hospital built in Bareilly was the first women's hospital and medical school in Asia, and continues today as the oldest and largest Methodist hospital in India. Apartments were provided at the hospital for families to live together, cook, and care for the patients.

In 1885, when the Rajah of Khetri, Rajputana asked Clara to become physician to his wife and other ladies of the palace, Clara accepted, knowing that the hospital was on a sound footing and could run without her. In Rajputana Clara began caring for the women of the surrounding country. She taught Christianity to the women and distributed copies of the Bible in her work, bringing both physical and spiritual healing to the women of India.

> 'I was sick and you visited me, I was in prison and you came to me. ...
> Truly, I say to you, as you did it to one of the least
> of these my brothers, you did it to me.'
>
> ~ MATTHEW 25:36, 39 ~

---

120. Edith Deen, *Great Women of the Christian Faith* (Uhrichsville, OH: Barbour Books, 1959), p. 381.

Early Women's Medical Mission in India

∞ Sarah Seward, 1833-1891 ∞

When a woman's hospital was built in Allahabad, India in 1893, it was named the Sarah Seward Hospital, after the American medical missionary who first had the vision for such a medical institution to serve the women of the region. Sarah Seward was born in 1833 in Florida, New York. The Sewards had always shown a concern for community affairs. Sarah's grandfather was a physician and active in politics. Her uncle was William Seward, governor and senator from New York and Secretary of State for Abraham Lincoln.

Sarah attended Mrs Willard's famed Troy Female Seminary and then studied medicine at the Women's Medical College in Philadelphia, graduating in 1871. When a call came for female doctors to practice among the women of India, Sarah was the first to answer the call. She left New York in December 1871 and went to Allahabad under the Women's Union Missionary Society. Sarah began the medical work in Allahabad in connection with the zenana work. In 1873, Sarah transferred to the Board of Foreign Missions of the Presbyterian Church, but continued to work in Allahabad. The same year Sarah began a Dispensary as part of the mission, with all products compounded at the site. Funds for the building of the Dispensary were raised from women in the United States. When the Dispensary opened in August, Sarah thought the attendance would be small, but the first morning there were seventy-five patients waiting!

Every morning, when the women first came, Sarah and her helpers talked with the women and read from either the Bible or a Christian book which would explain the truth of Christ in a plain, direct way. Many of the women asked for books which they could take to their homes and read further, sharing with others in their homes. In 1890, the year before Sarah's death from cholera, 3,738 patients were treated at the Dispensary, all of whom heard the words of life while receiving physical help for their ailments.

Sarah spent almost twenty years in India, treating the sick and bringing the gospel to the women of Allahabad. In the 1880s, Sarah began raising funds for a women's hospital to be built in Allahabad; the hospital named in her honor opened two years after her death.

Put on then, as God's chosen ones, holy and beloved,
compassionate hearts, kindness, humility, meekness, and patience …

~ COLOSSIANS 3:12 ~

SEPTEMBER 3

Alone in the Xolobe Valley

∽ Christina Forsyth, 1844-1919 ∾

Born in 1844 in Glasgow, Scotland, Christina Moir had godly parents who taught her the Scriptures from an early age. After the death of her mother when she was ten and her father when she was twenty, Christina continued to look to the Lord for direction and protection in her life. She met a young man, a banker's son, who shared her Christian faith, and the two became close. When he had to go to India on business, they agreed to write each other. However, his sisters began receiving letters, but she did not. She was sad, but took her pain to the Lord.

Christina's brother was a pastor, and before his marriage Christina lived with him and served as hostess in the parsonage. After his marriage Christina applied to the Presbyterian mission and offered to be an unpaid volunteer in South Africa. The Zulu wars were going on and many churches and businesses were being burned, but Christina worked tirelessly assisting teaching in the mission schools there.

In 1884, Christina returned to Scotland to marry Allan Forsyth. The two had become engaged before Christina went to South Africa, but Allan had to travel to South America on business for several years before they could be married. When Christina came home, she discovered the banker's son, whom she had loved, was mystified and heartbroken that she had never written him when he was in India. The two discovered that a jealous admirer had intercepted their letters and kept them from being delivered. The two remained friends, though Christina kept her engagement with Allan.

After their wedding the Forsyths set off for South Africa, where Allan had an interest in the Transvaal gold mines. Less than a year after their marriage, Allan was crossing the Komati River, slipped from the saddle of his horse, and drowned in the raging river. The banker's son offered Christina a home with his sisters, but she decided to stay in Africa as a missionary. She chose to work among the Mfengu people in the Xolobe Valley, a people called 'wolves' because of their viciousness. Christina was forty-one. For the next thirty years her home was with the Mfengu. She taught the children about Jesus, treated ailments among the people, and made herself helpful to the people, all the while showing them the love of Jesus. Her consecrated life drew the Mfengu to the gospel, and in time a Christian mission grew in the Xolobe. Though the people wanted her to stay with them, ill health forced her return to Scotland in 1917, when she was seventy-four. At that time the Xolobe had a school with four teachers and about 140 students. There were Sunday services, a young woman's class, and a weekday prayer meeting, all led by native people Christina had trained. At her death, *The Missionary Review of the World* noted that she had 'civilized the district, gave the people a knowledge of God and brought many scores to the feet of Christ'.[121]

> *The nations that are left all around you shall know that I am the LORD; I have rebuilt the ruined places and replanted that which was desolate. I am the LORD; I have spoken, and I will do it.*
>
> ~ EZEKIEL 36:36 ~

---

121. 'Christina Forsyth of Fingoland', *The Missionary Review of the World*, August 1919, p. 637.

Westminster Sisters

∞ Agnes Smith Lewis, 1843-1926 and Margaret Smith Gibson, 1843-1920 ∞

A few weeks after twins Agnes and Margaret Smith's birth in Irvine, Scotland on 11 January, 1843, their mother died. Their father surrounded his girls with love, teaching them the Scriptures from an early age and giving them the best education. Early he noted the girls were gifted in languages. He promised them he would take them to whatever country they wanted if they learned the language of the country. Agnes and Margaret mastered French, German, Spanish, and Italian; their father took them throughout Europe.

Their father died when they were twenty-three, leaving them vast wealth he had inherited from a distant relative. Agnes and Margaret always sought to use their wealth in a way which would give God glory. They taught Sunday school and reached out to help others in many different ways. They also continued to travel and increase their linguistic skills – learning modern and ancient Greek, Arabic and Syriac. Agnes published accounts of some of their travels in *Eastern Pilgrims*, a description of their early travels in the Holy Land, *Through Cyprus*, and *Glimpses of Greek Life and Scenery*.

In 1892, the sisters traveled to Sinai to visit St Catherine's monastery, where Constantine Tischendorf had discovered the early biblical manuscript, *Codex Sinaiticus*. Several doubted the monks at the monastery would allow the sisters into their library, but their linguistic skills attested to their scholarship, and the monks did grant them entry. The next year the sisters returned to Sinai with a larger group of scholars. The monks became so accepting and appreciative of Agnes and Margaret that they allowed them to catalogue the Syriac and Arabic manuscripts in the library. The sisters made important manuscript discoveries at St Catherine's as well as in Egypt. The travels and studies of the Smith sisters were amazing for their day, when women were not even admitted to many universities. However, several European universities did award them honorary degrees.

Agnes and Margaret settled in Cambridge, England. Each happily married a clergyman, though both of their husbands died after only a few years of marriage. They used their wealth to endow Westminster College in Cambridge and the Presbyterian chaplaincy of the University of Oxford.

If you seek [wisdom] like silver and search for it as for hidden treasures,
then you will understand the fear of the LORD *and find the knowledge of God. For*
the LORD *gives wisdom; from his mouth come knowledge and understanding ...."*

~ PROVERBS 2:4-6 ~

Trusting in Jesus

∽ Louisa M. R. Stead, c. 1850-1917 ∽

Born in Dover, England, Louisa had wanted to be a missionary to China since a teenager. When she was twenty-one she moved to America, and at a camp meeting in Urbana, Ohio, she felt the missionary call even stronger. Frail health, however, prevented her from fulfilling her dream. In 1875, Louisa married a Mr Stead, and the couple had a little girl whom they named Lily. In 1882, the little family was enjoying a picnic on the beach of Long Island Sound when they heard a cry for help. A little boy was struggling in the water, and Mr Stead ran to help him. The flailing boy pulled Mr Stead under the water, and they both drowned, with Louisa and her little four-year-old girl helplessly watching.

In the days following, full of sorrow and grief, Louisa learned to simply trust in Jesus. Out of her tragedy, she wrote the words:

> 'Tis so sweet to trust in Jesus,
> Just to take Him at His word,
> Just to rest upon His promise,
> Just to know, 'Thus saith the Lord.'
>
> Jesus, Jesus, how I trust Him!
> How I've proved Him o'er and o'er!
> Jesus, Jesus, precious Jesus!
> O for grace to trust Him more!
>
> O how sweet to trust in Jesus,
> Just to trust His cleansing blood,
> Just in simple faith to plunge me
> 'neath the healing, cleansing flood!
>
> I'm so glad I learned to trust Thee,
> Precious Jesus, Saviour, Friend;
> And I know that Thou art with me,
> Wilt be with me to the end.

Louisa and her small daughter were in very difficult circumstances after her husband's death. Louisa had no family in America and had little means to support herself and her daughter. There were times when they both were hungry and without food, but then someone would bring them a meat pie or some extra food. However, in time, things improved, and Louisa was even able to fulfill her missionary dream. She and Lily went to South Africa. There Louisa married Methodist minister Robert Wodehouse. After fifteen years Louisa's health required them to return to the United States. When her health improved they returned to Rhodesia and served there from 1901-1911 until poor health forced Louisa to retire from work, though she remained in Rhodesia, where her daughter had married and continued missionary work.

When Louisa died in 1917, her fellow-missionaries wrote that her influence continued, as the five thousand native Christians often sang 'Tis so Sweet to Trust in Jesus' in their native language.

> *Trust in him at all times, O people;*
> *pour out your heart before him;*
> *God is a refuge for us.*
> ~ PSALM 62:8 ~

Grace' Greater Than Our Sins

Julia H. Johnston, 1849-1919

In 1856, when she was six, Julia Johnston moved to Peoria, Illinois with her family. Her father was pastor in the First Presbyterian Church of Peoria. When she came to personal faith in Christ, Julia found numerous ways to serve her Lord. She became a Sunday school teacher and was head of the infant class at the church for over forty years. Her experience in teaching the elementary children led her to write Sunday school lessons for David C. Cook Publishing. Julia also wrote several books, including *Indian and Spanish Neighbors*, *School of the Master*, and *Fifty Missionary Heroes Every Boy and Girl Should Know*. Julia's mother had founded the Presbyterian Missionary Society in Peoria; Julia became an active member of the society and served as President for twenty years.

Julia wrote about five hundred hymns, and here she continues to influence Christians today. Her most well-known hymn, 'Grace Greater Than Our Sin', was written in 1910. In it Julia describes our sinful condition which can be relieved only through the grace of the cross, the blood of Christ:

> Marvellous grace of our loving Lord,
> Grace that exceeds our sin and our guilt!
> Yonder on Calvary's mount outpoured,
> There where the blood of the Lamb was spilled.
>
> *Refrain:* Grace, grace, God's grace,
> Grace that will pardon and cleanse within.
> Grace, grace, God's grace,
> Grace that is greater than all our sin.
>
> Sin and despair, like the sea waves cold,
> Threaten the soul with infinite loss;
> Grace that is greater; yes, grace untold,
> Points to the refuge, the mighty cross.
>
> Dark is the stain that we cannot hide.
> What can avail to wash it away?
> Look! There is flowing a crimson tide,
> Brighter than snow you may be today.
>
> Marvellous, infinite matchless grace,
> Freely bestowed on all who believe!
> You that are longing to see His face,
> Will you this moment His grace receive?

*Therefore, since we have been justified by faith, we have peace with
God through our Lord Jesus Christ. Through him we have also
obtained access by faith into this grace in which we stand, and we
rejoice in hope of the glory of God.*

~ ROMANS 5:1-2 ~

'Cook' and Charles Spurgeon

✑ Mary King, 19th century ✑

Charles Spurgeon was undoubtedly the most famous of nineteenth-century preachers, drawing thousands to his sermons at the London Tabernacle. Spurgeon recounted his conversion as occurring at age fifteen on 6 January, 1850. Hurrying to an appointment, a snow storm forced him to take shelter in a Primitive Methodist Chapel. The preacher's text was Isaiah 45:22 (KJV), 'Look unto me, and be ye saved, all the ends of the earth: for I am God, and there is none else.' The young Spurgeon felt God speaking directly to him in that verse, and he came to faith in Christ.

An important person in Spurgeon's spiritual growth was Mary King, the housekeeper at the school in Newmarket, Cambridgeshire which Spurgeon began attending in August 1849. The students simply called Mary 'Cook'. She loved all the students and had an influence on many of them, including Charles Spurgeon. Mary wasn't theologically trained in a formal sense, but she knew the Scriptures and had a logical mind. She also had an affection for Charles Spurgeon and spent much time instructing him in the Christian faith. Charles later wrote of Mary:

> The first lessons I ever had in theology were from an old cook in the school at Newmarket .... She was a good, old soul, and used to read *The Gospel Standard*. She liked something very sweet indeed, good strong Calvinistic doctrine; but she lived strongly as well as fed strongly. Many a time we have gone over the covenant of grace together, and talked of the personal election of the saints, their union to Christ, their final perseverance, and what vital godliness meant; and I do believe that I learnt more from her than I should have learned from any six doctors of divinity of the sort we have nowadays. There are some Christian people who taste, and see, and enjoy religion in their own souls, and who get at a deeper knowledge of it than books can ever give them, though they should search all their day. The cook at Newmarket was a godly experienced woman, from whom I learned far more than I did from the minister of the chapel we attended.[122]

Spurgeon asked Cook once why she went to the chapel she attended since there was not much there. Cook replied she liked to go to worship even if she got nothing by going: 'You see a hen sometimes scratching all over a heap of rubbish to try to find some corn; she does not get any, but it shows that she is looking for it, and using the means to get it, and then, too, the exercise warms her.' Spurgeon noted that for Cook 'scratching over the poor sermons she heard was a blessing to her because it exercised her spiritual faculties and warmed her spirit'.[123]

Mary King, a member of Bethesda Strict Baptist Church, later lived in a little cottage facing St Margaret's Anglican Church in Ipswich. In those years, when Spurgeon learned she was having a hard time financially, he provided her with regular support to meet her needs.

> *And let us consider how to stir up one another to*
> *love and good works,*
> *not neglecting to meet together, as is the habit of*
> *some, but encouraging one another,*
> *and all the more as you see the Day drawing near.*
>
> ~ HEBREWS 10:24-25 ~

---

122. Lewis A. Drummond, *Spurgeon: Prince of Preachers* (Grand Rapids: Kregel Publications, 1992), p. 101.
123. Ibid, p. 102.

Singing through Suffering

∽ Eliza Hewitt, 1851-1920 ∽

Eliza Hewitt had a love for learning all her life. When she graduated from the Girl's Normal School in Philadelphia at the top of her class, it was natural for her to become a schoolteacher. One day when she was disciplining a wayward student, the boy angrily picked up a slate and hit Eliza on the back with it. The doctor put Eliza in a body cast for six months. When he removed the cast, he told Eliza to take a short walk, and she was filled with gratefulness to God. Returning home, Eliza put her thoughts into a song:

> There's sunshine in my soul today,
> More glorious and bright
> Than glows in any earthly sky,
> For Jesus is my light. ...
>
> *Refrain:* O there's sunshine, blessed sunshine,
> When the peaceful, happy moments roll;
> When Jesus shows His smiling face,
> There is sunshine in the soul.

> There's gladness in my soul today,
> And hope and praise and love,
> For blessings which He gives me now,
> For joys 'laid up' above.

Eliza never fully recovered from her injury, however, and there were times of painful relapse. Eliza's suffering only drew her closer to God. She assiduously read and studied the Bible, and expressed her deep desire in her hymn 'More about Jesus':

> More about Jesus would I know,
> More of His grace to others show;
> More of His saving fullness see,
> More of His love Who died for me. ...

> More about Jesus let me learn,
> More of His holy will discern;
> Spirit of God, my teacher be,
> Showing the things of Christ to me. ...

Eliza expressed her confidence in Jesus in the hymn, 'My faith has found a resting place':

> My faith has found a resting place,
> Not in device nor creed;
> I trust the Ever-living One,
> His wounds for me shall plead.

> I need no other argument,
> I need no other plea;
> It is enough that Jesus died,
> And that He died for me.

Eliza's strength returned for her to teach a weekly Sunday school class, and she wrote children's books and Sunday school literature as well as hymns. Her hymn, 'When we all Get to Heaven', was based on many Scriptures:

> Sing the wondrous love of Jesus,
> Sing His mercy and His grace;
> In the mansions bright and blessed
> He'll prepare for us a place.

> When we all get to heaven,
> What a day of rejoicing that will be!
> When we all see Jesus,
> We'll sing and shout the victory!

*'In my Father's house are many rooms. If it were not so, would I
have told you that I go to prepare a place for you? And if I go and
prepare a place for you, I will come again and will take you to
myself, that where I am you may be also.'*

JOHN 14.2-3

Cheerful in the Lord's Work

∽ Marilla Baker Ingalls, 1827-1901 ∽

When missionary Lovell Ingalls asked Marilla Baker's mother if he could marry Marilla, Mrs Baker replied that Marilla was not fit to be a missionary's wife; she was too light-hearted and full of fun. With long curls and ringlets about her face, Marilla was always laughing and cheerful. In spite of Mrs Baker's reservations, Lovell and Marilla were married on 23 December, 1850.

Marilla was nine years old when she first heard an appeal for missionaries to Burma and saw an idol from that country. She told some friends that if she were grown, she would go and tell those heathen that worshiping an idol was not worshiping God. That youthful passion of wanting the Burmese to know the truth of the gospel continued with Marilla throughout her fifty years as a missionary.

Lovell and Marilla sailed for Burma on 9 July, 1851. They worked for six years together, until God took Lovell home. With his dying breath, he urged Marilla not to neglect the missionary work, but to do all she could for 'the poor Burmans'.

Marilla returned to the United States briefly, but in 1861 settled in Thongze. She was the only western person within a hundred miles, and there were only two or three Christians in the village. By the time of her death there were two churches with 400 members, as well as several outstations. Marilla was a cheerful evangelist and teacher who trained the natives to do the work of the ministry themselves. In one missionary report she wrote:

> I have ten preachers under my care. All send or bring me a monthly report of their work, I have a meeting each Saturday morning for the workers in the vicinity. I have four colporteurs, whom I send on trips or to work among the heathen. They attend funerals, give books, and discuss doctrine, but are not able to perform pulpit duties. The laymen and their families do much colportage work. Each man and woman free from disease and care of infants is expected to make some trips for special teaching among the heathen.[124]

Through her personal conversation and witness, over 160 Buddhist priests came to Christ. When the railroad came through, Marilla set up lending libraries in the train stations for the railroad workers, stocking the library with Christian materials and tracts.

The Dacoit, robbers and marauders, murdered the Karen people and pillaged their homes; twice they burned the mission compound in Thongze. Marilla organized the Karen, gave them weapons, drilled them, and told them to remember the Lord and fight for their families and homes. The Dacoit put a price of 10,000 rupees on Marilla's head. One missionary later said, 'All who know her will agree the price was quite too small.' Marilla determined that if she were captured she would preach the gospel to her captors. When they did come, she pulled out a revolver and showed them she could put successive bullets into a mark. The Dacoits departed and left her alone.

Marilla placed an iron dog in the front of the mission, which she told the people was for protection. The people said the dog would never do anything and was no protection at all. Marilla thus made her point – the iron dog was just like their idols, lifeless and powerless. She fulfilled her desire as a nine-year-old to show the people their idols were not the true God.

We know that 'an idol has no real existence',
and that 'there is no God but one'.

~ 1 Corinthians 8:4 ~

---

124. Mrs J. T. Gracey, *Eminent Missionary Women* (New York: Eaton & Mains, 1898), p. 198.

Remembering Deliverance from Bondage

∞ Octavia Rogers Albert, 1853-1890 ∞

Born a slave in Georgia in 1853, after emancipation Octavia Rogers was able to pursue an education. She studied at Atlanta University to become a teacher and began teaching in Montezuma, Georgia in 1874. Octavia married A. E. P. Albert, also a teacher. Albert later became a minister with the African Methodist Episcopal Church, and the couple moved to Houma, Louisiana.

Octavia considered teaching a form of Christian service to her Lord. In Louisiana she conducted interviews with former slaves, encouraging them to reflect on their deliverance from slavery as Israel had been delivered from bondage in Egypt. Octavia recounted the stories she heard from the freed slaves in *The House of Bondage, or, Charlotte Brooks and Other Slaves, Original and Life-Like, As They Appeared in Their Old Plantation and City Slave Life*. The book was published in 1890 by her husband and daughter shortly after Octavia's death.

As a minister's wife, Octavia opened her home to all. She taught former slaves to read and write, read the Scriptures to them, and listened to their stories. She spent hours listening to their stories and offering spiritual counsel. She became especially close to Charlotte Brooks. Octavia wept with Charlotte as she told that all of her children were gone and she had no one to care for her in her old age. Knowing of Charlotte's faith in Christ, Octavia asked her if she felt lonesome in this world. Charlotte answered, 'No, my dear, how can a child of God feel lonesome? My heavenly Father took care of me in slave times. He led me all the way, and now he has set me free, and I am free in both body and soul.'[125]

One day when Charlotte described the brutal treatment from her slave masters, Octavia read her Fanny Crosby's hymn, 'All the Way the Savior Leads Me'. Charlotte exclaimed that suited her case perfectly and she wanted to sing that hymn in glory!

There is therefore now no condemnation for those who are in Christ Jesus.
For the law of the Spirit of life has set you free in Christ Jesus
from the law of sin and death.

~ ROMANS 8:1-2 ~

---

125. Octavia Albert, ed. *The House of Bondage, or, Charlotte Brooks and Other Slaves, Original and Life-Like, As They Appeared in Their Old Plantation and City Slave Life*, reprint ed. (New York: Oxford University Press, 1988), p. 16.

United Together in Christ

∽ Susannah Spurgeon, 1832-1903 ∾

Susannah Thompson was not at all impressed by the young, nineteen-year-old preacher at New Park Street Church in London that Sunday evening, 18 December, 1853. While others in the small congregation were pleased with Charles Spurgeon's eloquence, Susannah thought:

> So this is his so-called eloquence! It does not impress me. What a painful countrified manner! Will he ever quit making flourishes with that terrible blue silk handkerchief? And his hair – why, he looks like a barber's assistant![126]

Yet, when Spurgeon became pastor of New Park Street Church, a bond developed between Susannah and the preacher. On 20 June, 1854, the two attended the opening of London's Crystal Palace. As they walked through the Crystal Palace, the gardens, and down to the lake, Spurgeon read Susannah selections from Martin Tupper's *Proverbial Philosophy*, 'If thou art to have a wife of thy youth, she is now living on the earth; therefore think of her, and pray for her weal.' Spurgeon asked Susannah softly, 'Do you pray for him who is to be your husband?' Years later Susannah wrote, 'During that walk, in that memorable day in June, I believe God Himself united our hearts in indissoluble bonds of true affection, and though we knew it not, gave us to each other for ever.'[127]

Susannah and Charles pledged their love on 2 August, 1854, in her grandfather's garden. That evening, Susannah knelt and thanked God with tears that He had given her the love of so great a man. Susannah Thompson and Charles Spurgeon were married 9 January, 1856. Their love grew in their thirty-six years of marriage, and they faced many trials and troubles together. Both were often in ill health, Susannah to a degree that she didn't leave the house for fifteen years. In her weakness, however, Susannah continued a strong support to Spurgeon's Christian work and ministry. In describing a model marriage, Spurgeon described his with Susannah, 'founded on pure love, and cemented in mutual esteem. Therein, the husband acts as a tender head; and the wife, as a true spouse, realizes the model marriage-relation, and sets forth what our oneness with the Lord ought to be.'[128]

At Spurgeon's death in 1892, Susannah wrote, 'for though God has seen fit to call my beloved up to higher service, He has left me the consolation of still loving him with all my heart, and believing that our love shall be perfected when we meet in that blessed land where Love reigns supreme and eternal.'[129]

> *For this is how the holy women who hoped in God used to adorn themselves, by submitting to their own husbands, as Sarah obeyed Abraham, calling him lord. And you are her children, if you do good and do not fear anything that is frightening.*
>
> ~ 1 PETER 3:5-6 ~

---

126. Richard Ellsworth Day, *The Shadow of the Broad Brim* (Valley Forge: The Judson Press, 1965), p. 107.

127. *The Autobiography of Charles H. Spurgeon* compiled by his wife and private secretary (Philadelphia: American Baptist Publication Society, n.d., Vol. II), p. 11.

128. Ibid, Vol. II, p. 52.

129. Ibid, Vol. II, p. 8.

First Chinese Woman Doctor

✿ Hu King Eng, 1865-1929 ✿

Hu King Eng's grandfather, Hu King Hi, the military mandarin of Foochow, was the second convert to Christianity in south China. King Eng's father, Hu Yong Mi, at first opposed Christianity, but in time the truth of Christ penetrated his heart; he also converted from Buddhism to Christianity. Yong Mi became a lay preacher with the Methodist church. One of King Eng's earliest memories as a child was lying in bed and hearing her father talking to someone about Jesus.

King Eng's mother had a wealthy, aristocratic background. As was the custom, her feet had been bound as a child and were only three inches, making walking difficult. Mrs Hu also had become a Christian and helped Yong Mi in his missionary work by teaching the women. Yong Mi was convinced that it was wrong to bind the feet of the Chinese girls, and he had the bandages removed from King Eng, at first over her mother's protest. For some time King Eng was very embarrassed she didn't have bound feet. Her aunts and others would ridicule her, pointing to 'those feet', but later she was pleased with her father's protection of her in this way.

King Eng attended the Foochow Boarding School for Girls, then when she was eighteen the Methodist Women's Foreign Missionary Board offered to send her to the United States for medical training. This was a wonderful opportunity, but accepting required courage. King Eng would be one of the first to leave China to seek a foreign education. She looked to the Lord and felt God's 'Fear not, for I will go with you wherever you go'. In 1884, King Eng left for the United States with the Rev. Dr Whitney, a missionary at Foochow.

Her first task was learning English; then she went to Ohio Wesleyan university for four years, then to the Women's Medical College in Philadelphia. All who met King Eng were warmed by her gentleness and Christian character. Her first year at Ohio Wesleyan, she spoke at a prayer service, and many came to Christ through her testimony. One mother later wrote, 'Little did I think when I was giving money for the work in China, that a Chinese girl would come to this country and be the means of leading my daughter to Christ.'[130]

In 1895, King Eng returned to Foochow and began working in the Methodist Foochow Hospital, especially overseeing the women and children. Morning services were regularly held in the hospital, and former patients often returned for these morning services. King Eng recognized that helping the Chinese physically and bringing them healing caused many to trust Christianity rather than idols. One patient told King Eng, 'The Jesus doctrine is truly good. What the leader said is nothing but the truth. Idols are false.'[131]

> 'For I, the Lord your God, hold your right hand; it is I who say
> to you, "Fear not, I am the one who helps you".'
>
> ~ ISAIAH 41:13 ~

---

130. Margaret Ernestine Burton, *Notable Women of Modern China* (New York: Fleming H. Revell Co., 1912), p. 31.
131. Ibid, p. 59.

Go Forward!

∞ Annie Armstrong, 1850-1938 ∞

Words such as 'indomitable' and 'indefatigable' come to mind when considering the life of Annie Armstrong. Born in Baltimore in 1850, Annie lived in the city until her death in 1938. At nineteen she came to faith in Christ, was baptized, and soon afterwards became a founding member of Eutaw Place Church, where she remained a member throughout her life. From the powerful preaching of Pastor Richard Fuller, Annie was encouraged always to give her best in Christian ministry, seeking God's energy through prayer to accomplish the work. Fuller frequently said, 'never insult the Master with indolent preparation or superficial and ineffectual performance'.[132] Annie taught the Primary Department classes at Eutaw Place Church for fifty years, but she also developed a concern for missions, both at home and abroad.

In 1880, Annie served as the first president of the Woman's Baptist Home Mission Society of Maryland. She was particularly moved when she heard a speaker describe how many of the Native Americans had been forced onto reservations. When she learned that 240 Native Americans at the Levering Manual Labor School needed clothes, Annie organized the women in several Baltimore churches to collect clothing and send barrels of clothing to the needy. Annie continued this concern for the Native Americans in Oklahoma throughout her life, even as her missionary interests broadened.

In 1888, Annie led in the formation of the Woman's Missionary Union (WMU) of the Southern Baptist Convention. 'Go forward!' was the motto she chose for the organization. She served as the corresponding secretary until 1906, always refusing a salary, as she worked to spread the gospel. Every year Annie hand-wrote thousands of letters to missionaries and to various church groups encouraging the work of missions. When Lottie Moon asked for an assistant in China, Annie organized a Christmas offering that raised enough funds for three assistants.

With great organizational skills, Annie was tireless in whatever work lay for her to do. She wrote articles and curriculum for young people as well as for missions' publications. When she resigned from the WMU, she continued actively supporting missions and the needy through her church. Annie believed, 'The future lies all before us ... shall it only be a slight advance upon what we usually do? Ought it not to be a bound, a leap forward, to altitudes of endeavor and success undreamed of before?'[133]

> 'The harvest is plentiful, but the laborers are few; therefore pray earnestly to the Lord of the harvest to send out laborers into his harvest.'
>
> ~ MATTHEW 9:37-38 ~

---

132. 'Biography of Annie Armstrong', *Baptist Convention of Maryland/Delaware*, http://bcmd.org/annie-armstrong.

133. 'Annie Amrstrong', *Maryland's Women's Hall of Fame*, http://msa.maryland.gov/msa/educ/exhibits/women-shall/html/armstrong.html.

Evangelizing the South Sea Islanders

∞ Florence Young, 1856-1940 ∞

Born in Motueka, New Zealand on 10 October, 1856, Florence Young grew up on the isolated farm her parents had purchased after they emigrated from England. With no schools nearby, Florence received most of her education at home, before being sent to a boarding school in England for two years when she was fifteen. When she was eighteen Florence was at a prayer meeting when the words of a hymn aroused fears that she was not ready to meet Christ. She found lasting peace from Isaiah 43:25, 'I, I am he who blots out your transgressions for my own sake, and I will not remember your sins.'

In 1880, two of Florence's brothers began establishing a sugar plantation in Queensland, Australia. When Florence came for an extended visit she began holding prayer meetings for the families of the planters, which developed into the Young People's Scriptural Union. Membership eventually rose to 4,000!

Many of the workers on the plantations were migrants from the Sea Islands with little exposure to Christianity. Florence began a small class on Sundays to teach them the Scriptures. In 1885, Florence rejoiced to record Jimmie Aoba as the first convert from these meetings. In 1886, Florence founded the Queensland Kanaka Mission and sent a letter to Christians seeking support. George Müller of Bristol, whose orphanages were the beautiful fruits of trusting God by faith, was visiting Sydney and gave Florence's sister the first contribution to the Kanaka Mission. He said, 'Tell your sister to expect great things from God, and she will get them.'[134]

The Queensland Kanaka Mission continued as a faith mission, bringing many of the sea islanders to faith in Jesus Christ and training the converts in Bible classes to share their faith when they returned to their islands.

In 1901, the Commonwealth Parliament passed a law saying all Pacific Islanders must be sent home from the plantations within five years. This led to the close of the Queensland Mission after twenty-five years and the opening of the South Sea Evangelical Mission in 1907. Florence continued to oversee the mission, but the work of evangelizing and establishing self-supporting churches was mostly done by the island Christians. Yearly she made a trip to the islands, radiating the joy and hope of Christ and encouraging the islanders in their Christian faith.

> 'I, I am he who blots out your transgressions for my own sake,
> and I will not remember your sins.'
>
> ~ ISAIAH 43:25 ~

---

134. Florence Young, *Pearls from the Pacific* (London: Marshall Brothers, 1925), p. 43.

Turn Your Eyes Upon Jesus

∽ Lilias Trotter, 1853-1928 and Helen Lemmel, 1864-1961 ∽

Lilias Trotter's mother was justly proud of Lilias' artistic talents. When she and Lilias were traveling in Venice, John Ruskin, the famous art critic, was staying near them. Mrs Trotter sent Ruskin some of Lilias's drawings and asked for his honest opinion. Ruskin was very impressed, saying, with training, Lilias could become the world's greatest living painter. Lilias became Ruskin's informal student, and the two became lifelong friends. But Lilias felt another calling. She volunteered and served as secretary of the Welbeck Street YWCA, teaching Bible studies and walking the streets at night talking to prostitutes to persuade them to another life in Christ. Ruskin encouraged her to devote more time to her art and not spend so much time in social work, but to no avail.

Lilias felt a call to mission work. Her health was so poor, however, she couldn't pass the physical for the mission agency. Being financially independent, she and friends Lucy Lewis and Blanche Haworth set forth on their own for Algeria on 5 March, 1888. For the next forty years Lilias lived among the Algerians, often living in very primitive conditions to better identify with the natives. The women often traveled into the desert to villages which had never heard the gospel, bringing the people the truth in Christ. Lilias published many tracts and books for the Arab people, illustrating them in a style which would be attractive to them.

One tract Lilias wrote, published in English, was called 'Focused'. She wrote that it was so easy to live in many good worlds of art, music, social science, motoring, or some profession. But often we drift about and let the 'good' hide the 'best':

> It is easy to find out whether our lives are focussed, and if so, where the focus lies. Where do our thoughts settle when consciousness comes back in the morning? Where do they swing back when the pressure is off during the day? Does this test not give the clue? Then dare to have it out with God .... Dare to lay bare your whole life and being before Him, and ask Him to show you whether or not all is focussed on Christ and His glory. Dare to face the fact that unfocussed, good and useful as it may seem, it will prove to have failed of its purpose. ... How do we bring things to a focus in the world of optics? Not by looking at the things to be dropped, but by looking at the one point that is to be brought out. ... Turn full your soul's vision to Jesus, and look at Him, and a strange dimness will come over all that is apart from Him. ...[135]

In 1918, Helen Lemmel read Lilias' tract and was inspired to write and compose the hymn, 'Turn Your Eyes Upon Jesus':

O soul, are you weary and troubled?
No light in the darkness you see?
There's light for a look at the Saviour,
And life more abundant and free!

His word shall not fail you, He promised;
Believe Him, and all will be well;
Then go to a world that is dying,
His perfect salvation to tell!

Refrain: Turn your eyes upon Jesus,
Look full in His wonderful face,
And the things of earth will grow strangely dim,
In the light of His glory and grace.

> ... *looking to Jesus, the founder and perfecter of our faith, who for the joy that was set before him endured the cross, despising the shame, and is seated at the right hand of the throne of God.*

~ HEBREWS 12:2 ~

---

135. Miriam Huffman Rockness, *A Passion for the Impossible: The Life of Lilias Trotter* (Wheaton, IL: Harold Shaw Publishers, 1999), pp. 288-289.

SEPTEMBER 16

Brahmin Lady

∞ Ellen Lakshmi Goreh, 1853-1937 ∞

Ellen Lakshmi Goreh was born into the highest caste, Mahratta Brahmin, in the Hindu holy city of Varanasi on 11 September, 1853. A little over a year before, her parents had become Christians, and they remained joyous in their faith. Ellen's mother became ill soon after Ellen's birth, but her suffering did not diminish her joy in Christ. On 3 December, with death imminent, she looked forward to being with her Savior whom she loved.

After her mother's death Ellen was cared for by Rev. and Mrs W. T. Storrs, who adopted her as their own. When they went to England in 1865, they placed Ellen in school, where she flourished scholastically and spiritually. In October 1880, she returned to India to bring the truth of Christ to her people, especially the women of India.

Ellen had a poetic gift, and before she left England she sent the hymn writer Frances Ridley Havergal one of her poems, signing it anonymously as an 'Indian sister'. Miss Havergal was touched by the poem and recognized it was not just doggerel, but expressed Christian truth in an elegant form. She wrote her 'Indian sister' a letter of encouragement. In later correspondence, Miss Havergal told Ellen that:

> God has given you a real gift, which may be, and ought to be, used for His glory. … I believe that if you will lay your gift at His feet, and let your verses go forth as no Englishman's work, but as that of a Brahmin who is now one with us in Christ, you will be giving help to the case of Zenana Missions and Female Education in the East, which, so far as I know, none but yourself can give! It will be a testimony to many thousands of what His grace can do and has done. … I do not want you to hurry; you must take pains and pray much; you must cultivate and develop by study and patient practice the gift which is yours; but then, always letting Him, as it were, hold your pen, you may do great things for Him. … I want you to feel ever so glad and happy in the thought that Jesus has given you a special gift which you may use for Him; and which He may use for His glory and for the furtherance of the knowledge of His salvation among those who are sitting in darkness in your own land.[136]

A collection of Ellen's beautiful poems were published in 1883, just as Miss Havergal had suggested, with the notice they were by a 'Brahmin Lady'. The poem 'My Refuge' became a gospel hymn often sung in Dwight L. Moody's evangelistic services:

> In the secret of His presence how my soul delights to hide!
> Oh, how precious are the lessons which I learn at Jesus' side!
> Earthly cares can never vex me, neither trials lay me low;
> For when Satan comes to tempt me, to the secret place I go. …
>
> Would you like to know the sweetness of the secret of the Lord?
> Go and hide beneath His shadow; this shall then be your reward.
> And whene'er you leave the silence of that happy meeting-place,
> You must mind and bear the image of your Master in your face.
>
> You will surely lose the blessing, and the fullness of your joy,
> If you let dark clouds distress you, and your inward peace destroy;
> You may always be abiding, if you will, at Jesus' side;
> In the secret of His Presence you may every moment hide.[137]

In the cover of your presence you hide them …

~ PSALM 31:20 ~

---

136. Charles Bullock, *From India's Coral Strand: Hymns of Christian Faith by Ellen Lakshmi* (London: Home Words Publishing Office, 1883), pp. xiii-xiv.

137. Ibid, p. 25.

God Will Take care of You

∞ Civilla Durfee Martin, 1866-1948 ∞

Civilla was a schoolteacher married to minister Walter Stillman Martin. Walter taught for a time at Atlantic Christian College in Wilson, North Carolina, while also leading revival meetings. In 1904, the Martins were at the Practical Bible Training School in Lestershire, New York, where Walter was helping the principal put together a song book. One Sunday Walter was scheduled to preach in a church some distance away, but Civilla was not feeling well and could not go. Walter thought about cancelling his preaching, but their nine-year-old son said, 'Don't you think God will take care of her?' So, Walter went and preached as scheduled. When he came home, he found Civilla had written a poem about what their son had said. Walter then sat down to the organ and composed the music to this comforting hymn:

> Be not dismayed whate'er betide,
> God will take care of you;
> Beneath His wings of love abide,
> God will take care of you.
>
> *Refrain:* God will take care of you,
> Through every day, o'er all the way;
> He will take care of you,
> God will take care of you.
>
> Through days of toil when heart doth fail,
> God will take care of you;
> When dangers fierce your path assail,
> God will take care of you. ...
>
> No matter what may be the test,
> God will take care of you;
> Lean, weary one, upon His breast,
> God will take care of you.

Some months later, in the spring of 1905, Civilla and Walter were in Elmira, New York and developed a deep friendship with a Mr and Mrs Doolittle. Mr Doolittle was a cripple confined to a wheelchair, and Mrs Doolittle had been bedridden for close to twenty years. Faced with such afflictions, they were happy Christians who inspired and comforted all who knew them. One day Walter asked them the secret of their bright outlook, and Mrs Doolittle replied, 'His eye is on the sparrow, and I know He watches me'. Civilla and Walter were both moved by this simple yet profound faith, and Mrs Doolittle's words became the basis of Civilla writing that song with the constant refrain, 'His eye is on the sparrow, and I know He watches me'.

> *Cast your burden on the Lord, and he will sustain you;*
> *he will never permit the righteous to be moved.*
>
> ~ Psalm 55:22 ~

Lead Me to Calvary

⊂◦ Jennie Hussey, 1874-1958 ◦⊃

Jennie Hussey spent almost her entire life on the farm where she was born in Henniker, New Hampshire on 8 February, 1874. She devoted her life to caring for an invalid sister, and battled with crippling arthritis herself. In spite of her personal suffering and the burden of caring for her sister, Jennie was always cheerful. One day, when the pain was especially intense, she prayed that the Lord would make her willing to bear her cross daily, since Christ bore His cross for her. She then wrote her prayer in verse, which became the last verse of her well-known hymn:

> May I be willing, Lord to bear
> Daily my cross for Thee;
> Even Thy cup of grief to share,
> Thou hast borne all for me.

In ensuing days, as Jennie meditated on the cross, she thought of the tomb and Mary seeing the risen Lord, and wrote what became the middle verses of the hymn:

> Show me the tomb where Thou wast laid,
> Tenderly mourned and wept;
> Angels in robes of light arrayed
> Guarded Thee whilst Thou slept.

> Let me like Mary, through the gloom,
> Come with a gift to Thee;
> Show to me now the empty tomb,
> Lead me to Calvary.

The opening verse of adoration and praise, as well as the refrain, were the last to be written:

> King of my life, I crown Thee now,
> Thine shall the glory be;
> Lest I forget Thy thorn crowned brow,
> Lead me to Calvary.

> *Refrain:* Lest I forget Gethsemane,
> Lest I forget Thine agony;
> Lest I forget Thy love for me,
> Lead me to Calvary.

Jennie was a fourth generation Quaker but later in life submitted to believer's baptism and joined the First Baptist Church in Concord, New Hampshire. She told the pastor she had spent so much of her life hidden in the country she wanted in baptism to tell everybody that she loved Jesus.

> *'If anyone would come after me, let him deny himself and take up his cross
> and follow me. For whoever would save his life will lose it, but whoever loses
> his life for my sake and the gospel's will save it.'*

⊶ Mark 8:34-35

Hallelujah Lassies come' to the' United States

∞ Eliza Shirley, 1863-1932 ∞

When she was fifteen Eliza Shirley first saw a group of women evangelists march into Coventry, England and hold open-air meetings in the poorest neighborhoods, proclaiming the saving message of Jesus Christ. Since a child, Eliza had been drawn to Scripture and the truth of Christ. Her father, Amos, was a part-time preacher, and Eliza memorized his sermons as a girl. Hearing the women of the young Salvation Army, Eliza dedicated her life to God's service. When an outdoor meeting was held to celebrate the 35th Corps of the Salvation Army coming to Coventry, fifteen-year-old Eliza was one of the speakers. William Booth was so impressed that he encouraged Eliza to come and work with the Salvation Army, which she did, after her parents' hesitant approval.

The following year, 1879, Eliza's father moved to the United States to find work in Philadelphia. He wrote back to his family that they could not imagine the great number of people in America who never went to church. When Amos Shirley was ready for his wife Anne and his daughter Eliza to join him in America, Eliza asked William Booth if she could start a work for the Salvation Army in the United States. Booth hesitated, but at last gave his approval. He gave Eliza a hundred copies of penny song books to be used in the meetings.

By the time they reached the United States, Eliza's mother agreed to work with Eliza in her ministry. The two women looked for an appropriate building to house the project and organized an event for 5 October, 1879. They placed posters throughout the community advertising 'Two Hallelujah Females' in an open-air meeting. They didn't have all the drums and uniforms which attracted people in England, but many people came out of curiosity. The first evening, twelve people came. On some occasions the rowdy crowd threw mud, stones, sticks, or rotten vegetables at the women. One evening a group of miscreants set fire to the lot where they were to meet. Eliza and her mother took advantage of the crowd watching the fire and the firemen and began preaching the gospel. That evening, a notorious drunk named Reddy came forward and asked if God could forgive a drunk like him. That night he gave his life to the Lord, and he was transformed into a testimony of God's grace. Reddy's conversion was so noticeable that newspapers wrote stories about him, and more people flocked to the Salvation Army meetings.

So began the work of the Salvation Army in the United States. Today there are 7,546 Salvation Army centers in the country, distributing food, providing disaster relief, operating rehabilitation centres and children's programs, and always sharing the transforming good news of Jesus.

Therefore, if anyone is in Christ, he is a new creation.
The old has passed away; behold, the new has come.

~ 2 CORINTHIANS 5:17 ~

Face to Face

∞ Carrie E. Breck, 1855-1934 ∞

In 1898, Rev. Grant Tullar was staying with the Methodist pastor and his wife during a series of evangelistic services in Rutherford, New Jersey. The three had spent the afternoon visiting members of the congregation and barely had time for a quick supper before the evening service. In her haste the hostess hadn't replenished the jelly dish, but knowing Rev. Tullar's fondness for jelly, the pastor and his wife would not take any, leaving all for Tullar. Tullar said, 'So this is all for me, is it?' A composer of gospel music, Tullar quickly thought 'All for me' was a good theme for a gospel song. He sat down to the piano and quickly picked out a tune, which he put to the words, 'All for me the Savior suffered, All for me he bled and died'. The pastor wanted the song sung at the evening service, but Tullar thought the words needed more polishing.

The next morning Tullar received a letter from Mrs Frank A. Breck enclosing several poems for his musical composition. Mrs Breck, born Carrie Ellis in 1855, had been raised in a Christian home, and Bible reading and prayer were always a part of her life. From a youth she had written poetry which was published in religious publications. In 1884, Carrie married Frank Breck, and the couple went on to have five daughters. Throughout her household duties Carrie wrote poetry – over a mending basket, with a baby in her arms, washing dishes, or sweeping. Carrie wrote over two thousand poems, and her first published hymn was, 'You ought to do something for Jesus'. Carrie admitted she could not sing a tune and had no sense of pitch, but she did have a good sense of rhythm, and many of her poems were matched with tunes and placed in hymnals. She frequently sent her poems to Rev. Tullar for his musical composition. When he received Carrie's letter with poems that morning in 1898, he immediately recognized the words to one poem fit the tune he had composed the evening before much better than his own words. Carrie's hymn with Tullar's tune continues a favorite today:

Face to face with Christ, my Saviour,
Face to face – what will it be,
When with rapture I behold Him,
Jesus Christ who died for me?

Refrain: Face to face I shall behold Him,
Far beyond the starry sky;
Face to face in all His glory,
I shall see Him by and by!

Only faintly now I see Him,
With the darkened veil between,
But a blessed day is coming,
When His glory shall be seen.

What rejoicing in His presence,
When are banished grief and pain;
Death is swallowed up in vict'ry,
And the dark things shall be plain.

Face to face – oh, blissful moment!
Face to face – to see and know;
Face to face with my Redeemer,
Jesus Christ who loves me so.

Beloved, we are God's children now, and what we will be
has not yet appeared;
but we know that when he appears we shall be like him,
because we shall see him as he is.

~ 1 JOHN 3:2 ~

SEPTEMBER 21

Devoted to Good Works

∽ Elizabeth Fedde, 1850-1921 ∾

On Christmas Day 1882, her thirty-second birthday, Elizabeth Fedde received a letter from her brother-in-law in Brooklyn, New York inviting her to come and work among the Norwegian immigrants in the city. Elizabeth had worked as a deaconess in Christiana, Norway since she was nineteen, providing nursing and spiritual succour to those in need. For four years she had pioneered work in Tromsø, a difficult region where the summers were three months long and the winters nine. Elizabeth accepted the invitation to serve the Norwegians in America, an invitation which had been sent at the request of Mrs Christian Børs, wife of the Norwegian consul.

Elizabeth arrived in the United States on 9 April, 1883, and within nine days had helped establish the Norwegian Relief Society and began operating a relief program in New York. Within two years, she rented quarters for a nine-bed hospital and set up a program to train deaconesses to provide physical and spiritual help for poor Norwegians. In 1889, a thirty-bed hospital was erected in Brooklyn – the beginning of what is now the Brooklyn Lutheran Medical Center.

Though Elizabeth was an excellent organizer and enlisted the aid of others in her effort, she never lost her personal involvement with the poor and suffering or her sense of the spiritual needs of the people she helped. Her diary is replete with examples of her trust in God to accomplish His purposes. When visiting one poor family, she gave them $5, bringing tears of thankfulness to the eyes of the mother, who then asked her to come the next week with some baby clothes for the baby arriving soon. Elizabeth didn't have any baby clothes, but she knew they were needed and trusted God would provide them. The next day a lady came to the door with a package of children's clothes and asked if she knew of anyone who could use them.

One day, after she had spent some time talking with a very sceptical unemployed young Norwegian, she told him that she regularly prayed that God would bring her to talk to those whom He wanted her to see and share the love of Jesus. Tears streamed down the young man's cheeks as he realized he was the object of God's love and salvation.

Elizabeth went on to establish a Lutheran Deaconess home in Minneapolis and helped plan hospitals in Chicago and North Dakota. After thirteen years in the United States, Elizabeth was exhausted and returned to Norway in 1895. Soon after, she married Ole Slettebo, a suitor who had waited for her thirteen years while she answered God's call in America.

Insist on these things, so that those who have believed in God may be careful to devote themselves to good works.

~ TITUS 3:8 ~

Pioneer in Medical Missions

∞ Anna Sarah Kugler, 1856-1930 ∞

Anna Sarah Kugler, the first medical missionary of the Evangelical Lutheran Church in the United States, arrived in India on 29 November, 1883, after a three month voyage. Rev. Adam Rowe, a Lutheran missionary in India, had written Anna, a graduate of Woman's Medical College of Pennsylvania, suggesting that India needed medical missionaries serving Indian women. However, when Anna applied to the Woman's Home and Foreign Missionary Society of the General Synod of the Lutheran Church in America, the Synod wasn't ready to undertake a medical mission at that time, though it would send Anna as a teacher for the women living in harems. Anna accepted, convinced she could do some medical work on the side and that she would be able to convince the Synod to establish medical work in India.

Anna was assigned to teach in Guntur, Andhra Pradesh, in South India. As Anna began performing medical work for the women of the region, there were many cultural adjustments which had to be made. An example of one simple problem: spoons were not used among the local people, so to instruct a patient to take a spoonful of medicine was meaningless. Instead, markings were placed on the side of the medicine bottle to show how much each dose of medicine should be.

A major problem for Anna was the problem of caste. The upper caste Hindus considered Anna, a white woman, without caste and thus unclean. It was humiliating to be considered polluting the people when trying to help them medically:

> It was not pleasant to be constantly reminded as one entered high-caste Hindu homes, that one was an unclean object, defiling everything one touched. It was not pleasant to have all the bedclothes put to one side while one examined the patient or to have a very ill patient taken out of bed and brought into the courtyard because the doctor was too unclean to go inside. ... Neither did one enjoy stooping down and picking up the medicine bottle because one was too unclean to take it directly from the hand of the Brahman. But it was all in the way of opening the path for those who came later.[138]

Anna was also greatly disturbed by the practice of child brides. One day she treated a twelve-year-old for convulsions who was told she had to leave her parents and go live with her husband. The average age for arranging marriage for girls was six or seven years. Anna ministered to both the body and spiritual needs of her patients, showing and sharing the love of Jesus with them.

In 1897, Anna opened the American Evangelical Lutheran Mission Hospital in Guntur, a fifty-bed hospital which for many years was considered the best in India. She raised funds and was able to add a children's ward, maternity ward, and operating room in the hospital.

Anna came to be highly loved and respected by the colonial officials and the local people. Shortly before her death, in 1930, she told Dr Ida Scuder, a close associate, she would like to get well and work longer so she could serve India for fifty years, for she had only served forty-seven.

As each has received a gift, use it to serve one another,
as good stewards of God's varied grace.

~ I Peter 4:10 ~

---

138. Maina Chawla Singh, 'Women, Mission, and Medicine: Clara Swain, Anna Kugler, and Early Medical Endeavors in Colonial India', *International Bulletin of Missionary Research*, Vol. 29, No. 3, p. 132.

Saved to Serve

༄ Mary Reed, 1854-1943 ༄

Mary Reed came to faith in Jesus early in her life and developed a servant's heart. When she read about the plight of the women in India – uneducated and restricted to the women's quarters of the house, Mary had a great desire to bring them the light of the gospel. The Woman's Foreign Missionary Society of the Methodist Church appointed her to India, and in November 1884, at the age of thirty, she left her dear parents and seven siblings for India. She began visiting women in the zenanas in Cawnpore, but was soon taken ill. Sent to Pithoragarh in the Himalaya Mountains to regain her health, Mary spent her time at rest studying the language and observing the mission school in the mountain region. Nearby was a leper colony where 500 people afflicted with the disease lived and were cared for.

Mary rejoiced when she was able to return to the plains and resume her work in the zenanas. After four years in Cawnpore, Mary was sent to a girls' boarding school in Gonda. Her health broken, in 1890 she returned to Cincinnati to recuperate. She had surgery at the Methodist Episcopal Hospital and while convalescing was bothered by a tingling sensation in her right forefinger and a peculiar spot appeared on her cheek, near the ear. One day, in a moment, as if from her heavenly Father himself, she suspected she had leprosy and the Lord wanted her to minister to the lepers in India. Physicians in America and London confirmed Mary did indeed have leprosy.

Revealing her malady to only one sister, Mary returned to India. After prayerful consideration, she later wrote her family:

> Our loving heavenly Father, Who is too wise to err, has in His infinite love and wisdom chosen, called, and prepared your daughter to teach lessons of patience, endurance, and submission, while I shall have the joy of ministering to a class of people who, but for the preparation that has been mine for this special work, would have no helper at all. And while I am called apart among these needy creatures who hunger and thirst for salvation and for comfort and cheer, He who has called and prepared me promises that He himself will be as a little sanctuary where I am to abide. And abiding in Him I shall have a supply of all my needs. Jesus has enabled me to say not with a sigh but with a song, 'Thy will be done.'[139]

Mary was appointed superintendent of the Chandag Heights Leprosy Home in the Himalaya Mountains. It was a beautiful site, which others referred to as 'one of the fairest spots on God's beautiful earth'. Within eight years Mary had overseen the building of better houses for the lepers, a chapel, and a small hospital. The Indian government gave forty-eight acres of land which were used for grazing and garden plots. With the help of a native Indian minister, Mary brought the hope of Christ to the lepers, and most in the Home became Christians.

Separated from much of the outside world, Mary named her little cottage 'Sunny Crest Cottage'. Trusting in the Lord's care and direction, Mary did not seek medical treatment for her disease, for which there was no known cure at the time, but by 1906 she had no sign of the disease. Mary took advantage of her renewed health to visit her family in Ohio before returning to work among the lepers in India. She died of heart failure at the age of eighty-eight and is buried in front of the Chapel at Chandag.

And my God will supply every need of yours
according to his riches in glory in Christ Jesus.
To our God and Father be glory for ever and ever. Amen.

~ PHILIPPIANS 4:19-20 ~

---

139. Mrs J. T. Gracey, *Eminent Missionary Women* (New York: Eaton & Mains, 1898), pp. 129-130.

Meeting and Marrying a Man Devoted to the Lord

∞ Rosalind Goforth,1864-1941 ∞

When she was twenty Rosalind prayed that if the Lord wanted her to marry, He would lead her to a man wholly devoted to the Lord and His service. Rosalind had yielded herself to the Lord when she was twelve. After hearing Alfred Sandham speak at a revival meeting on John 3:16, she stood up at the meeting, publicly confessing Christ as her Master. On the way home, she was told it was foolish to think that she could be certain Christ had received her. In the morning Rosalind began reading the Bible, praying for some assurance that Christ had indeed received her. Reading John 6:37 (KJV), 'Him that cometh to me I will in no wise cast out,' gave her the assurance she sought. Then, someone told her she was too young for salvation. Again, she went to the Scriptures. After searching for a long time, she came to Proverbs 8:17 (KJV), 'Those that seek me early shall find me.' Rosalind never afterwards doubted that she was the Lord's child.

Rosalind's father was an artist, and she grew up spending much time watching and learning from her father. She graduated from the Toronto School of Art in May 1885, and was preparing to go to London in the autumn to continue her art studies. On a summer boat ride to Niagara Falls, Rosalind was with a group of artists; another group on the boat were going to the Niagara-on-the-Lake Bible Conference. Rosalind's heart was with the group going to the Bible Conference. In the evening, on the return boat trip, the guest speaker who had been at her church the previous Sunday recognized Rosalind as the organist at church, and he invited her to come to the Toronto Mission Union the following Saturday. He introduced Rosalind to Jonathan Goforth, the City Missionary. Rosalind thought him a shabby looking fellow until she looked into his vibrant eyes.

At the City Mission meeting the following Saturday, as people were seated around the room waiting for the meeting to begin, Jonathan Goforth stepped out of the room, leaving his Bible on his chair. Inexplicably, Rosalind got up to look through his Bible. It was worn almost to shreds and marked throughout. She put the Bible back and quickly returned to her seat, saying to herself, 'This is the man I would like to marry!' Rosalind and Jonathan were chosen to be on the same committee to open a new mission in the east end of Toronto. As they worked together, Rosalind had many opportunities to see Jonathan's greatness, underneath his outward shabbiness.

Rosalind never continued her art studies in London. When Jonathan asked her, 'Will you join your life with mine for China?' she answered 'Yes' without hesitation. Rosalind and Jonathan were married forty-nine years and served as Canadian Presbyterian missionaries to China and Manchuria for forty-six of those years, bringing the gospel to many.

*'Have you not read that he who created them from the beginning
made them male and female, and said, "Therefore a man shall leave
his father and his mother and hold fast to his wife; and the two shall
become one flesh?" So they are no longer two but one flesh. What
therefore God has joined together, let no man separate.'*

~ MATTHEW 19:4-6 ~

Preserving and Passing on a Heritage of Faith
Geraldine Guinness Taylor, 1862-1949

When Geraldine Guinness was born on Christmas Day, 1862, her father, famous evangelist H. Grattan Guinness, wrote his little daughter a poem and prayer:

> One cloud remains, that by thy birth
> Thou enterest a ruined earth,
> My little One.
>
> But thou shalt find with sweet surprise,
> Earth but a pathway to the skies,
> My little One.
>
> Such is our trust, for, Lord, we give
> Thy gift to thee! O then receive
> Our little One.
>
> Receive her Lord and let her be
> Thine own to all eternity –
> Thy little One.[140]

The father's prayer was abundantly answered in Geraldine's life.

In 1873, Rev. and Mrs Guinness founded the East London Missionary Training Institute, which in following years went on to train 1,330 missionaries. As a young person, Geraldine was constantly in contact with missionaries from around the globe, including Hudson Taylor, the founder of China Inland Missions and good friend of her father. Having great compassion for the poor girls working in the factories of East London, Geraldine began working among them, establishing Sunday schools and counseling them in their young Christian lives. She took as her motto, 'Live for the glory of God and for the good of many'.

In 1888, Geraldine went to China under the China Inland Mission (CIM). The same year, Howard Taylor, son of Hudson Taylor and a talented medical doctor, joined CIM. Geraldine and Howard, who had known each other in England, became engaged in China and were married in 1894. Together they had a fruitful ministry in China and speaking on the part of missions around the world.

Geraldine had a gift for writing, and her well-researched and beautifully-written books on missions continue to enrich many in their Christian walk. Hudson Taylor first asked her to write a history of the China Inland Mission. Later she spent thirteen years researching and writing a life of Hudson Taylor himself. She traveled to every province in China in compiling her research, and in the process ministered to many Chinese women. Geraldine's *Hudson Taylor's Spiritual Secret* continues to be a Christian classic and encouragement in the Lord's work. She wrote numerous other missionary biographies which tell the story of God's message of salvation in many lands. As she once wrote, 'There is only time, only strength for one thing, to learn of Him and to make Him known.'

> *In this the love of God was made manifest among us, that God sent his only Son into the world, so that we might live through him.*
>
> ~ 1 JOHN 4:9 ~

---

140. 'Mrs Howard Taylor', *Gospel Fellowship Association*, http://gfamissions.org/pages/learn-and-promote/detail/3/68/.

SEPTEMBER 26

He Giveth More Grace

∞ Annie Johnson Flint, 1866-1932 ∞

Born on Christmas Eve, 1866, in Vineland, New Jersey, Annie Johnson as a young girl, along with her baby sister, was orphaned. Mr and Mrs Flint adopted the two children, surrounding them with Christian nurture and love.

When she was eight Annie attended a revival meeting where she was converted to faith in Christ. She read avidly and began to realize she had some poetic talent. She loved the open woods and fields around Vineland, and developed a sensitivity to the natural world around her. She could even tell that rain was on the way from the change in a robin's song.

After she finished high school Annie attended a normal school and began teaching a primary class in the same school she had attended as a girl. In her second year of teaching she began to have pain from arthritis. She barely completed her third year of teaching when she had to quit. Walking had become very difficult, and Annie became increasingly helpless. To add to her difficulties, Annie's adopted parents died within months of each other, leaving her and her sister all alone.

With her joints swollen and fingers twisted, Annie managed to write her uplifting poetry; she also made hand-decorated cards and gift books with her verses in them. Card publishers began publishing her cards, and her poems began appearing in Christian publications. Annie began receiving testimonies from many around the world who were blessed by her poems. In 1919, a collection of her poems was first published. As the years passed, and her affliction worsened, Annie was unable to write and had to dictate her poems and letters.

Even in the midst of her pain Annie kept her cheerful disposition and wit. When someone wrote Annie she was feeling blue and didn't understand why God allowed such difficulties in her life, Annie wrote her the little poem, 'What God Hath Promised':

God hath not promised skies always blue,	But God hath promised strength for the day,
Flower strewn pathways all our lives through;	Rest for the labor, light for the way.
God hath not promised sun without rain,	Grace for the trials, help from above,
Joy without sorrow, peace without pain.	Unfailing sympathy, undying love.

Though crippled, Annie believed God had work for her to do and considered her poetry a ministry for her Savior. For over forty years she was in constant pain, and much of that time she was helpless, yet she was able to comfort others as she had been comforted. The following poem of comfort in God's care is found in many hymnals:

He giveth more grace as our burdens grow greater,
He sendeth more strength as our labours increase;
To added afflictions He addeth His mercy,
To multiplied trials he multiplies peace.

His love has no limits, His grace has no measure
His power no boundary known unto men;
For out of His infinite riches in Jesus
He giveth, and giveth, and giveth again.

He gives power to the faint,
and to him who has no might he increases strength.

ISAIAH 40:29

God's 'Perfect 'Peace'

∞ Frances Ridley Havergal, 1836-1879 ∞

Frances Ridley Havergal devoted her life and talents, which were considerable, to serving Jesus and others in His name. Like her father, she had a poetic gift as well as musical talent. Trained as a concert artist (Charles Spurgeon said she sang like an angel), she rejected a life of worldly fame to serve her Savior. Frances loved the Scriptures and by the age of twenty-two had memorized the Gospels, Epistles, Revelation, Psalms, and Isaiah. Her numerous books of poetry and devotion are permeated with Biblical references.

Frances was often ill. In 1874, she suffered from typhoid fever. In 1876, her lungs were greatly inflamed and death seemed imminent. At the news that she might die, Frances had perfect peace, anticipating a glorious reunion with her Savior. Frances recovered from this illness and wrote a hymn on God's perfect peace still sung and loved by many:

> Like a river glorious is God's perfect peace,
> Over all victorious in its bright increase;
> Perfect, yet it floweth, fuller ev'ry day;
> Perfect, yet it groweth deeper all the way.
>
> Stayed upon Jehovah,
> Hearts are fully blest –
> Finding as He promised,
> Perfect peace and rest.

Numerous Scriptures lay behind Frances's hymn. In Isaiah 48:18, God said, 'Oh that you had paid attention to my commandments! Then your peace would have been like a river, and your righteousness like the waves of the sea. ...' The chorus reflects Isaiah 26:3: 'You keep him in perfect peace whose mind is stayed on you, because he trusts in you.'

Charles Spurgeon admired Frances's hymns and told a friend:

> There is a centre to every storm where perfect calm reigns. There is a point within the circle of the most consuming flame where life is possible without any danger of its being consumed. Miss Havergal seems to me to have got into the very centre of the storms that are disturbing others, and abides in perfect peace. She seems to have penetrated to the very heart of God who is a consuming fire, and rests absolutely in His love.[141]

Frances died suddenly from peritonitis on 3 June, 1879; she was forty-two. Songs written in suffering and trial gave way to a new song sung around the throne of the Lamb forever.

> Sing to the LORD a new song,
> his praise from the end of the earth ... .
> ~ ISAIAH 42:10 ~

---

141. William Williams, *Personal Reminiscenes of Charles Haddon Spurgeon* (London: Spottiswoode and Co), p. 81.

Consecrated for the Savior

∞ Frances Ridley Havergal, 1836-1879 ∞

Frances Ridley Havergal, daughter of an Anglican minister, committed her soul to the Savior during her teenage years. Receiving an excellent education, Frances was fluent in German, French, Greek, Hebrew, and Latin, as well as her native English. With her musical talents as a pianist and with a lyrical voice, she might have had worldly acclaim, but Frances wanted to use her talents for Jesus.

In February 1874, she was on a visit of five days in a house where there were ten people staying. Some were unconverted; others were converted but not rejoicing in their Savior. Frances prayed, 'Lord, give me all in this house.' And He did –

> Before I left the house, everyone had got a blessing. The last night of my visit I was too happy to sleep and passed most of the night in renewal of my consecration, and these little couplets formed themselves and chimed in my heart one after another till they finished with 'ever only, ALL FOR THEE!'[142]

From this experience, Frances wrote 'Take My Life and Let it Be', a hymn of consecration:

Take my life and let it be
Consecrated Lord, to Thee;
Take my hands and let them move
At the impulse of Thy love,
At the impulse of Thy love.

Take my feet and let them be
Swift and beautiful for Thee;
Take my voice and let me sing
Always, only, for my King,
Always, only, for my King.

Take my lips and let them be
Filled with messages for Thee;
Take my silver and my gold –
Not a mite would I withhold,
Not a mite would I withhold.

Take my love – my God, I pour
At Thy feet its treasure store;
Take myself – and I will be
Ever, only, all for Thee,
Ever, only, all for Thee.

A few years later, in 1878, Frances took her silver and gold jewelry and sent it to the Church Missionary House. She wrote a friend, 'Nearly fifty articles are being packed up. I don't think I ever packed a box with such pleasure.'

So, whether therefore you eat or drink, or whatever you do,
do all to the glory of God.

~1 Corinthians 10:31 ~

---

142. Kenneth W. Osbeck, *101 Hymn Stories* (Grand Rapids, MI: Kregel Publications, 1982), p. 240.

Sixty-one Years as a Missionary

∞ Anne Luther Bagby, 1859-1942 ∞

Descended from French Huguenots, Anne Luther and her family were proud of their Christian heritage. Anne's father, Rev. John J. Luther, was a pastor in Missouri at the time of Anne's birth on March 20, 1859. Anne was named after her mother, who was named after Ann Hasseltine Judson, wife of Adoniram Judson and the first American woman who went abroad as a missionary.

When she was eleven Anne confessed her faith in Jesus and was baptized in the Mississippi River. Her father had always had a heart for missions, but because of his poor health, he refrained from applying for missionary service. In a sermon one Sunday he declared that God had so blessed America, Christians must share this blessing with the world. He promised that anyone who went out as a missionary would have the church's prayers and support. When he gave an invitation for those who wanted to serve as a foreign missionary to come forward, twelve-year-old Anne was the only one to answer the call. Her father whispered to her, 'Child, I didn't mean *you*!' But Anne's desire to serve as a missionary had been implanted in her heart.

When she was nineteen Anne moved with her family to Texas, where her father became President of the Baylor Female College. Anne taught at the school, while her desire to serve as a missionary grew. In her diary she described becoming acquainted with William Bagby at a Baptist state convention in 1878:

> I saw in the front of the church a young man whose eyes always met mine and after the close of the session had the pleasure of an introduction to him. The convention closed all too soon, and, as we prepared for our homegoing, I remarked that my only regret was that I had not become acquainted with a certain young minister. What was our surprise when a note was handed to me at the next moment requesting an immediate interview. … I must have done all the talking, for I spoke of my desire, even purpose of becoming a foreign missionary.[143]

Anne and William were married in October 1880 and in January set sail for Brazil, where they became the first Baptist missionaries. Texas Baptist Women organized the Women's Missionary Union in part to raise funds for the Bagbys' work in Brazil. In their years in Brazil, William labored as an evangelist, church planter, and seminary instructor. In the early years Protestant meetings were illegal, and Brazilians attending services could be arrested. One time William himself was arrested and imprisoned for preaching. Anne demanded that she be imprisoned with him, and she shared his time of imprisonment. In 1889, when church and state were separated in the new constitution, there was more religious freedom and the Protestant churches grew in number. In 1901, Anne established a school for girls in Sao Paulo which became a leading Southern Baptist school.

Anne and William had nine children; two died as toddlers and one drowned rescuing a friend from drowning. Five of the children became missionaries in Brazil and Argentina, establishing a family legacy of mission work in South America.

Sing to the LORD, bless his name;
tell of his salvation from day to day.

~ PSALM 96:2 ~

---

143. Quotes from *Anne Luther Diary: The Bagby-Luther Family papers, 1838-1980* (The Texas Collection at Baylor).

First Girls College in South Africa

⨯ Abbie Ferguson, 1837-1919 and Anna Bliss, 1843-1925 ⨯

After Andrew Murray (1828-1917), the Dutch Reformed minister of Wellington, South Africa, read a biography of Mary Lyon and her founding of Mount Holyoke College, he decided a college on the Mount Holyoke plan was exactly what South Africa needed to improve women's education. The expense of the boarding school was reduced by the girls performing all the domestic work, and the Christian life of the students was combined with the best intellectual training. Murray appealed to Mount Holyoke to send a teacher to South Africa who could establish a similar college.

Abbie Ferguson, the daughter of a Massachusetts clergyman and an 1856 graduate of Mount Holyoke, answered Murray's appeal. Abbie had been teaching school and working in city missions. Abbie was joined by Anna Bliss, also a minister's daughter and an 1862 graduate of Mount Holyoke. Anna had been teaching in rural schools in Massachusetts.

In September 1873, the two women sailed for Cape Town, South Africa. In November, they were warmly welcomed by Andrew Murray and the leaders of the Dutch Reformed Church. In January 1874, Abbie and Anna opened the school, named the Huguenot Seminary, honoring French Protestants who had settled in the area 200 years previously. Huguenot was the first women's college in South Africa. Fifty-four girls were enrolled the first year. Abbie had an eye infection for several months which made her almost blind, but she managed to teach along with Anna. By the end of February, Abbie wrote to her sister that every girl in the school had professed faith in Christ. By April the girls, eager for something to do, began a Sunday School for children of color.

The next year the enrollment expanded, and three more teachers arrived from Mount Holyoke. The school was divided into a lower department under Anna Bliss and a higher department under Abbie Ferguson. By 1875, ten of the graduates passed the examinations for a teaching certificate (out of thirty in the colony)!

Abbie and Anna were totally welcomed in their new home. They founded a Women's Missionary Society at Huguenot College which grew into the Vrouwen Zending Bond, a church-wide missionary organization. Abbie had a heart for the people of Africa, 'This great, great Continent, with its two hundred million of heathen.' She thought seriously of moving inland to work among the natives, but she was persuaded to stay at Huguenot. When the population grew from the gold rush of 1885, and the enrollments at Huguenot multiplied, Abbie thought, 'Africa for Christ, our girls in the vanguard of the conquering army.'[144]

But the wisdom from above is first pure, then peaceable, gentle, open to reason, full of mercy and good fruits, impartial and sincere.

~ JAMES 3:17 ~

---

144. 'Abbie Oark Ferguson', in Gerald H. Anderson, ed., *Biographical Dictionary of Christian Missions* (Grand Rapids: Wm. B. Eerdmans, 1999), pp. 209-210.

At the End of Two Millennia

On the Alaskan Frontier

∽ Amanda McFarland, 1833-1913 ∾

After her husband's death in 1876, Amanda McFarland moved to Portland, Oregon. She and her husband David had spent nine years as missionaries in Santa Fe, New Mexico and then among the Nez Percé in Idaho before David died of cancer. Amanda had a heart for missions but was unsure of what step to take next when she met Sheldon Jackson in Portland. Jackson had been superintendent of the western Presbyterian missions when Amanda and her husband were in New Mexico. Sheldon encouraged Amanda to come with him to Alaska where he was opening a Presbyterian mission.

On 10 August, 1877, Sheldon and Amanda arrived in Wrangel, two days before Amanda's forty-fourth birthday. The army had left Fort Wrangel shortly before Amanda's arrival, and there was no law enforcement in the town at all. Sheldon arranged for Amanda to use an empty dance hall for a school, then left for the East Coast to raise funds for the Alaska mission.

Thirty pupils attended Amanda's school in the dance hall when it first opened, but soon the number grew to around ninety-four. Amanda had few supplies – four Bibles, four hymnals, three primers, and thirteen first readers; but the students were eager to learn, and Amanda had a heart for sharing the truth of Christ with the students. There were about forty Christian Indians in the town who were eager to learn from Amanda. They had been converted by a Canadian Indian whose name was Clah. Clah was ill with tuberculosis, but continued to shepherd the Christians as long as his health allowed. On his death, Amanda became the teacher for the Tlingit Christians until a pastor, Rev. Samuel Young, arrived the following year.

In his early reports Rev. Young described the lawlessness of Wrangel, including the slavery of the Indians and the prevalence of witchcraft. Amanda struggled against the white men buying the Indian girls from the parents. One day a store owner bought one of Amanda's students, a girl of thirteen, from her parents for twenty blankets. Amanda was able to rescue the girl and return her to her parents, but she feared what could yet happen to the girl. Another time she rescued an eleven-year-old from a man in the street who was trying to get her to come to his house. When two of Amanda's pupils disappeared from school, she learned that they had been accused of witchcraft and were being tortured. Amanda set out to rescue them, though her students warned her they were having a devil dance and would kill her. Amanda found the two poor girls on the beach, stripped with their hands and feet tied at the center of a fiendish dance; the dancers were cutting them with knives. Amanda went to the center of the dance, and warned and pled with the dancers to cease or she would call out the United States gunboats. She was able to rescue the girls, though one was recaptured and killed later.

Amanda, the first woman missionary in Alaska, became known by the native chiefs as 'the woman who loved their people', and was looked to for advice and counsel by tribal leaders as well as her many students.

> *But let all who take refuge in you rejoice; let them ever sing for joy, and spread your protection over them, that those who love your name may exult in you.*
>
> ~ Psalm 5:11 ~

On a Royal Mission

∽ Mary Slessor, 1848-1915 ∾

Mary Slessor, born in Scotland in 1848, gained her enthusiasm for missions from her mother, who eagerly read each issue of the *Missionary Record* to her children. Mary's father was a shoemaker, but was frequently drunk and unable to support the family. Mary's mother was a skilled weaver and went to work in the mills. At the age of eleven Mary began working in the mills too, working ten to twelve hours a day. Mary was an avid reader, reading Milton, Carlyle, and others. She also became an eager Bible student and gave her life to God's service. When a teenager, she began teaching Sunday school and worked with a youth group.

During one lesson she taught in 1874, Mary unwittingly described her own life:

> Thank God! For such men and women here and everywhere, who in the face of scorn, & persecution ... dare to stand firmly and fearlessly for their Master. Their commission is today what it was yesterday, 'Go ye into all the world, & preach the Gospel to every creature' ... not the nice easy places only, but the dark places, the distant places ... to the low as well as the high, the poor as well as the rich, the ignorant as well as the learned, the degraded as well as the refined, to those who will mock as well as to those who will receive us, to those who will hate as well as to those who will love us.[1]

Following the death of David Livingstone in 1874, a wave of missionary enthusiasm swept over Scotland and Mary was among those who applied to the Foreign Mission Board. The Board agreed to send Mary to Calabar in West Africa, and she set sail 6 August, 1876. She first worked under missionary Euphemia Sutherland, learning to be a 'female agent', visiting the women around Duke Town, the mission headquarters in Calabar, teaching and dispensing medicines. She learned the Efik language and could speak like a native; the Africans said she had an Efik mouth.

Mary longed to take the gospel beyond the coastal settlements and moved into the interior, into regions known for drunkenness, human sacrifice, and cannibalism. She walked miles through the jungle to conduct Sunday services among the people, telling them of the love of Jesus and His saving grace. Here too she began rescuing infants left to die or orphaned. The Africans thought twins were bad luck, and whenever twins were born, they were left to die. Mary saved many, taking them into her home and raising them as her own. Mary lived among the people and showed the love of Christ in all she did. Though often sick and weak, she bravely confronted chiefs and negotiated peace between warring tribes. How could a lone woman survive in such dangerous conditions? Mary's confidence and strength was from Christ. She said, 'Why should I fear? I am on a Royal Mission. I am in the service of the King of kings.'

> *'Truly, truly. I say to you, whoever hears my word and believes him who sent me has eternal life. He does not come into judgment, but has passed from death to life.'*
>
> ~ JOHN 5:24 ~

---

1. 'Mary Slessor', *Dictionary of African Christian Biography*, http://dacb.org/stories/nigeria/slessor_mary.html.

On Earth to Serve

∽ Isabella Thoburn, 1840-1901 ∽

In 1866, Isabella Thoburn received a letter from her brother James, a Methodist missionary in India. He wrote, 'How would you like to come take charge of a school [for girls] if we decide to make the attempt?' Women had a lowly position in India; someone said they were 'unwanted at birth, unhonored in life, unwept in death'. James and his wife had gone to India in 1859, and hoped to improve the lot of the women in India through education and the gospel of Christ. When James's wife died in childbirth, the dream of establishing a school for girls waned – then James thought of his sister Isabella. Perhaps she would come to India and run a girls' school there. James wrote Isabella that through a girls' school, 'light might gradually be diffused among all the homes of the future Christian community'.[2]

Isabella was quite willing to undertake the enterprise. One of her mother's maxims was that we are on earth to serve, not be served. However, getting support might be difficult. Missions organizations at that time did not support unmarried women on the mission field, so in 1869 a group of Methodist women in Boston organized the Woman's Foreign Missionary Society for the support of women missionaries. They sent their first missionaries, Isabella Thoburn and Dr Clara Swain, to India in 1870. Swain was the first female medical missionary doctor.

On 18 April, 1870, Isabella opened a school for girls: Lucknow, the first girls' school in North India. She had only seven students to begin with. The priests told the girls that education was a sin for women. Isabella hired a man to guard the door of the school, protecting the girls from anyone trying to break up the class! The following year, Isabella was able to acquire a beautiful house called Lal Bagh ('Ruby Garden') and converted it into a boarding school. The school later became a high school and, in 1886, Lucknow Women's College, the first women's college in the eastern world. Isabella chose the motto of the college, 'We receive to give', based on her mother's words of wisdom. In 1898, Isabella began a teacher's training program, the first of its kind in India. Following Isabella's death in 1901, the school was renamed the Isabella Thoburn College.

Isabella labored over thirty years in educating Christian women in India. Her brother wrote of Isabella:

> My sister was an exceptional woman, one among ten thousand. Her strong character was notable for its simplicity. Her splendid courage was in striking contrast with her quietness of spirit. ... Her faith was like a clear evidence, her hope like an assurance of things not seen, her absolute devotion to the welfare of those who seemed to be thrown in her way was simply Christ-like.[3]

Do not use your freedom as an opportunity for the flesh, but through love serve one another. For the whole law is fulfilled in one word: 'You shall love your neighbor as yourself.'

~ GALATIANS 5:13-14 ~

---

2. J. M. Thoburn, *Life of Isabella Thoburn* (Cincinnati: Jennings & Pye, 1903), p. 34.

3. William F. Oldham, *Isabella Thoburn* (Chicago: Jennings & Pye, 1902), p. 2.

Woman of Prayer

∞ Ni Kwei-tseng, 1869-1931 ∞

Ni Kwei-tseng was a descendant of Wen Ting-King, prime minister in the Ming Dynasty who was converted to Christianity in 1601 by a Jesuit missionary. Ni Kwei-tseng's mother and father, converted by missionaries with the London Missionary Society in Shanghai, provided Ni a loving Christian home. The Chinese considered small feet beautiful and had developed the custom of tightly binding the feet of young girls to keep the feet extremely small – so small that when they grew up, walking was very difficult. When Ni was four she became very ill and screamed with pain from her bound feet, so her parents loosened her bindings and no longer bound her feet, allowing them to grow normally. By Chinese standards, Ni had 'big feet'.

In 1886, when she was seventeen, Ni married Methodist minister Charles Jones Soong. Soong was born in China. When he was nine he had gone to the United States; there he was converted by Methodist missionaries. He attended Vanderbilt University, was ordained, and returned to China as a Methodist missionary. Soong later became an agent for a Bible society and published and distributed Chinese Bibles.

Ni and Charles had six children and regularly had a family time of Bible reading, prayer, and hymn singing. Ni also spent much time in private prayer, often beginning her prayers at dawn, and the children came to especially respect their mother's prayer time. Many of those prayers were for her children, who came to be important leaders in China. The children were educated in Christian schools and then sent to the United States for their college training. The oldest daughter, Eling, married H. H. King, who became minister of finance for the government. Daughter Chingling married Sun Yat-sen, father of the Republic of China. Son, T. V. Soong, was a leader in international finance. Youngest daughter Mayling married Chiang Kai-shek, leader of the Republic of China. Chiang began regular Bible reading and was converted to Christianity through Ni's example and influence. All of Ni's children knew they were upheld by their mother's prayers, which they missed greatly when she died of cancer in 1931.

Mayling noted that 'whenever mother prayed and trusted God for her decisions, the undertaking invariably turned out well'. She said that, 'Asking God was not a matter of spending five minutes to ask Him to bless … and grant her request. It meant waiting upon God until she felt His leading.' Mayling later wrote a *Confession of Faith* which was distributed throughout China and spoke of the importance of prayer. She wrote. 'Prayer is more than meditation. In meditation the source of strength is one's self. But when one prays he goes to a source of strength greater than his own. … Prayer is our source of guidance and balance. God is able to enlighten the understanding.'

But I, O Lord, cry to you; in the morning my prayer comes before you.

~ Psalm 88:13 ~

World's Largest Women's University

ᖇ Mary Scranton, 1832-1909 ᖇ

In 1882, the *Christian Advocate* published an article on Korea, entitled 'A New Mission Field'. The article told of the secluded life of Korean women, their lack of education, and the fact that Korean girls were not even given names of their own. They were known as the 'daughter of ...' or 'sister of ...' or by some other descriptive related to the men in the family. Mrs L. B. Baldwin of Ravenna, Ohio, read the article and sent $88 to the Women's Foreign Missionary Society (WFMS), 'as a nucleus, around which the contributions of the church shall gather, until that dark land "where woman has no name" is reached, and one more fire lighted never to go out until the knowledge of God covers the whole earth'.[4] Two years later the WFMS sent Mary Scranton to Korea as a missionary among women.

Born in 1832 in Belchertown, Massachusetts, Mary Fletcher's ancestors had been Methodist ministers for three generations. Mary married William T. Scranton, and the couple had one son, also named William. Her husband died when she was about forty, and Mary moved to Ohio to be near her son. There she was active in the Methodist Church and the Women's Foreign Missionary Society. When Mary's son was appointed as a medical missionary to Korea, the WFMS asked Mary to go to Korea as their first female missionary to the country. On 1 February, 1885, William, his wife, and his mother left for Korea.

Mary established a school for Korean girls, though at first she had difficulty getting students. Koreans were superstitiously afraid of foreigners, and people often avoided Mary, running from her. Yet she continued to reach out with the love of Christ to the women in Seoul. One day walking through the city she came across a poor child covered with sores whose mother had just died of typhus. Mary took her up and brought her to her son who gave her medical care. As women began to see the love Mary showed to the girls in her care, they began bringing their daughters to Mary for an education.

On 31 May, 1886, Mary began the first classes for women in her home in Jeong-dong, Seoul. The king named the school 'Ewha Haktang', meaning 'pear blossom'. Many Christian Korean women received their education at Ewha, including Dr Esther Park, the first woman doctor in Korea. In 1909, the year of Mary's death, Ewha opened a woman's college in addition to the high school. Today Ewha University is the world's largest woman's university – and it all began with Mrs Baldwin's $88 contribution.

'Give, and it will be given to you.
Good measure, pressed down, shaken together, running over,
will be put into your lap.
For with the measure you use it will be measured back to you.'

~ LUKE 6:38 ~

---

4. 'Supplement No. 6, Study for July: Korea', *The Heathen Woman's Friend*, June 1890, vols. 21-22.

Crucified with Christ

∽ Jessie Penn-Lewis, 1861-1927 ∽

When Jessie Jones was born in Neath, South Wales, 8 February, 1861, her parents dedicated her to the Lord. Their first child had died, and not wanting to lose another, they gave Jessie to the Lord's protection and care. Jessie was a precocious little girl who was reading the Bible by the age of four. Jessie's grandfather had been a Calvinist Methodist preacher, and Christian teaching and church activities were always part of Jessie's home life growing up.

When she was nineteen Jessie married William Penn-Lewis, an accountant and a descendant of William Penn, the founder of Pennsylvania. Jessie was of frail health, yet the two enjoyed forty-five years of marriage.

About eighteen months after her marriage, Jessie began to feel ill at ease about the Lord's coming again. She did not feel she was prepared to meet Him and began seriously seeking the Lord for peace. She became especially impressed by Isaiah 53:6 and accepted that her sins and iniquities were borne by Jesus on the cross.

When tuberculosis weakened Jessie's lungs, doctors predicted she could not live six months. Yet the Lord healed her, and she was able to serve Him far beyond what her weak condition would expect. At times throughout her sixty-six years Jessie seemed to be on the verge of death, yet she recovered against all the doctors' expectations. Jessie knew her times were in the Lord's hands, and she grew spiritually during those times of illness and suffering.

Though somewhat shy and retiring, Jessie taught at the local YWCA and became a powerful speaker. Invitations began arriving for her to speak at other Christian meetings, and in 1895 she spoke at the China Inland Mission. She spoke in countries around the world – Sweden, Russia, Finland, Denmark, Canada, United States, and India – as well as at Keswick Conventions in England. She was an important part of the Welsh revival of 1904-1905, chronicling its history in *The Awakening in Wales*. Jessie corresponded and was respected by leading Christians of her day, including F. B. Meyer, Andrew Murray, R. A. Torrey, D. L. Moody, and Oswald Sanders. Her tracts and books were widely read. *The Word of the Cross* has been translated into over one hundred languages and continues in print today.

Always Jessie's focus was on the cross of Christ. The cross was not just the place of forgiveness for sins, but the source of power for the Christian life. By identifying with Christ in His death, dying to sin and the world, the Christian lived in newness of life. For the Christian to take up the cross and follow Jesus meant to die to self and live for Him. The cross was the energy of God for the Christian.

We know that our old self was crucified with him in order that the body of sin
might be brought to nothing, so that we would no longer be enslaved to sin.
For one who has died has been set free from sin.

~ ROMANS 6:6-7 ~

OCTOBER 7

Gospel Wagon

◌◦ Malla Moe, 1863-1953 ◦◌

Malla Moe, born in Hafslo, Norway on 12 September, 1863, first became aware of her need for Christ when she was twelve and attended an evangelistic meeting. The deaths of her aunt and then her father deepened Malla's sense of the need for a Savior. When she was twenty-one she and her sister Dorothea moved to Chicago at the invitation of another sister, Karin. There she attended Trinity Lutheran Church and Moody Church. One of R. A. Torrey's sermons at Moody challenged Malla to become a missionary, but she was concerned she lacked the education necessary. She thought about attending Moody Bible Institute for two years, but Fredrik Franson, founder of the Scandinavian Alliance Mission, told Malla that 'if God said go, and the heathen said come', she needed to go now, not in two years. After a two-week training course, Malla sailed for Africa, arriving in June 1892. She began language study with the Africa Free Mission in Natal and gained some acquaintance with the native customs and foods.

An African native, Mapelepele Gamede, was converted and became Malla's assistant, helping her understand the native customs and helping train the native Christians. In 1898, a permanent mission station was built in Bulunga. Named Bethel, this became Malla's base for the next fifty-six years, with only three furloughs. Malla realized she didn't have the special medical or educational skills some of the other missionaries had, but she learned to live among the natives, becoming one with them as she shared the truth of the gospel. Living in a grass-roofed hut with other native women, Malla became part of the day-to-day village life and prayed and shared Bible stories with the villagers. At mealtimes, when Malla bowed her head to thank the Lord for the food, the natives at first laughed at her and wanted to know what she was doing. She tried to explain to them, but it was difficult for them to understand. She realized that they would not understand until God Himself opened their hearts. In 1894, she wrote her supporters:

> Pray to God for Swaziland, that the Love of God may be seen here, that it may start a fire here which will burn continually, and enlighten their darkened minds. And may he also give me zeal and power to do his work which he has given me, so that nothing will be undone when I am called home.[5]

In 1928, when she was sixty-five, Malla found it more difficult to get to the villages. Also she wanted to travel to the unevangelized regions farther away. She devised a house wagon pulled by eight donkeys. With a driver and a girl to help with the cooking, Malla traveled throughout Swaziland and into Tonga. Faithful Gamede also accompanied her on these trips, which she continued for ten years. Once the team set up camp they then evangelized the surrounding countryside. When she was eighty Malla settled in Bethel. She died ten years later, October 16, 1953, surrounded by African Christians.

To the weak I became weak, that I might win the weak.
I have become all things to all people, that by all means I might save some.
I do it all for the sake of the gospel, that I may share with them in its blessings.

~ 1 CORINTHIANS 9:22-23 ~

---

5. 'Missionary Malla Moe's Letter of January 1, 1894', *Billy Graham Center*, www2.wheaton.edu/bgc/archivesdocs/ Moe.htm.

Living for Christ and Serving Others

∞ Katharina Lohrenz Schellenberg, 1870-1945 ∞

Born in 1870 in Tieggerwilde, South Russia, Katharina Schellenberg emigrated to America with her family when she was eight. Her father, Elder Abraham Schellenberg, was a Mennonite Brethren preacher important in building up the church in Kansas. Katharina's mother died when she was fourteen, and Katharina then cared for her three brothers and three sisters. When she was nineteen Katharina committed her life to Christ and joined the Mennonite Brethren Church in Buhler, Kansas. Her father kept in contact with the Brethren in Russia as well as elsewhere in the world, and Katharina imbibed an interest in missions from an early age. As a young adult she worked in an orphanage and two hospitals before volunteering as a missionary. Advised to obtain further medical training beyond her nursing studies, Katharina took a four-year course in homeopathic medicine.

In 1907, Katharina left for India, very sure that this was the field God would have her work in. She was the only American medical doctor in the India Brethren mission until her death in 1945, and she only took two furloughs during those thirty-eight years. Katharina worked in several different locations. In each she had to demonstrate to the Indians that the medicines could be trusted. She especially treated Muslim women who could not be seen by a male doctor. After ten years in the field, Katharina wrote her father, 'the problems are so severe that one can hardly stand it, and one does not know where it will end. But God sees and knows all, and He can change things!'[6]

In 1928, Katharina opened a hospital at Shamshabad which treated an average of 8,000 patients a year. With the many prevalent diseases, Katharina educated the people on the importance of hygiene, clean water, and proper sewage disposal. Concerned for the spiritual needs of her patients and staff, each morning there was a devotional time for everyone in the hospital. Sunday afternoons Katharina would play her autoharp and sing with the patients. Though she never married, Katharina did take in homeless children and cared for them. For relaxation she had a fruit and flower garden, did some farming, and raised chickens, turkeys, and milk cows. She said these were like a holiday and she didn't need a vacation in the hills.

Katharina was greatly mourned at her death on 1 January, 1945. She is buried in the St George Cemetery at Hyderabad, India. The memorial stone reads,

> She lived for Christ.
> She served others.
> She sacrificed herself.

Beloved, I pray that all may go well with you
and that you may be in good health, as it goes well with your soul.

~ 3 JOHN 2 ~

---

6. 'Katharina Schellenberg: Continuously on Call', *Mennonite Brethren Historical Commission*, http://www.mbhistory. org/profiles/schell.en.html.

Lady of the Camps

Minnie had long desired to become a missionary and was delighted to come to Kenya in 1899, to be the wife of missionary Thomas Watson. Watson was among the first six missionaries of the East African Scottish Mission (EASM) to come to Kenya in 1891; Minnie became the first woman missionary for the EASM. Thomas met Minnie's ship in Mombasa, and the two were married a few days later at the Church Missionary Society station at Freretown, on 16 December, 1899.

Conditions were dire as the newlyweds rode to Kikuyu, northwest of Nairobi, by train. Minnie undoubtedly was dismayed at the scenery of the countryside. Invasions of locusts had consumed the vegetation a few years before, and a viral disease had decimated the cattle. Starvation was everywhere, and dead bodies were just lying about. The ship which brought Minnie to Kenya also brought famine relief to the Kikuyu. On 8 January, 1900, the Watsons set up a relief camp. The next day, a smallpox epidemic broke out. Within weeks the Watsons were feeding 200 to 300 people and caring for over eighty people with smallpox in tent camps. Minnie became affectionately known as Bibi na Ngambi, Lady of the Camps, a name she bore in her over forty years among the Kikuyu people.

Two weeks before their first anniversary, Thomas contracted pneumonia and died. Minnie was the only European at the Kikuyu mission then, but she wouldn't abandon the work. Shortly, the Church of Scotland agreed to oversee the mission, and other missionaries were sent to the region. For over thirty years Minnie worked as a teacher and evangelist among the Kikuyu. In 1907 she began a boys' boarding school. The first President of Kenya, Jomo Kenyata, and several other later leaders of Kenya, were educated in Minnie's school. Minnie encouraged girls to attend the school as day students, but many parents opposed girls being educated, thinking it would make them less eligible for marriage. A kind yet strict teacher, Minnie expected the students to be able to recite the previous day's lessons perfectly.

As director of the church choir, Minnie also led an evangelism team of students out into the villages. On Sunday and Thursday evenings, Minnie and the students would go to a village, build a fire, and as the people assembled, sing hymns and tell the gospel story. Through the faithfulness of teachers such as Minnie, the Kikuyu saw the darkness of superstition flee before the light of Christ and His Word.

Now therefore fear the LORD
and serve him in sincerity and in faithfulness.

~ JOSHUA 24:14 ~

Evangelist to Women

⊙ Virginia Healey Asher, 1869-1937 ⊙

Born in Chicago in 1869, Virginia Healey attended Moody Bible Church as a child. When eleven Virginia came to faith in Christ and became active in the Sunday school ministry of the church. Here she also met William Asher, who was converted at the same evangelistic meeting as Virginia. The two were married on 14 December, 1887.

The Ashers were both gifted evangelists, and during the 1890s they held open-air evangelistic meetings near the Ferris wheel built for the World's Columbian Exposition in Chicago. William also served as assistant pastor of Jefferson Park Presbyterian Church. The Ashers then moved to Duluth, Minnesota, where they evangelized in the slums and at Duluth Bethel, a ministry to seamen, miners, and lumberjacks. They became assistants to evangelist J. Wilbur Chapman, focussing on sailors, prisoners, and the working poor.

In 1911, the Ashers were invited to become part of Billy Sunday's evangelistic team. William was an advance man for the team and taught men's Bible studies, while Virginia organized a ministry to businesswomen. At the turn of the twentieth century more women were leaving the farms and finding work in the cities' shops, hospitals, and factories. Before Billy Sunday began evangelistic services in a city, Virginia contacted local church women to help organize luncheons for the young businesswomen, encouraging them to attend the Billy Sunday services. Often the businesswomen were counseled about the temptations they faced in the cities – extramarital sex, drinking, drugs, abortions, and materialism. Bible study meetings were organized and continued after the evangelistic services had ended, encouraging the women to continue in their Christian walk.

These Bible study meetings came to be organized as the Virginia Asher Business Woman's Bible Councils and could be found in major cities throughout the United States. In 1922, a national organization was formed and annual conventions were held in Winona Lake, Indiana. The Councils were to promote Bible study and personal loyalty to Jesus Christ.

Virginia had a lovely contralto voice and often sang duets with Homer Rodeheaver, director of music for the Sunday evangelistic meetings. As sound recording was just beginning, Virginia recorded a number of songs such as 'Old Rugged Cross' and 'Tell me the Story of Jesus', bringing gospel songs into the home.

And do not get drunk with wine, for that is debauchery, but be filled with
the Spirit, addressing one another in psalms and hymns and spiritual songs,
singing and making melody to the Lord with your heart.

~ EPHESIANS 5:18-19 ~

The Lord Had Need of Me in Africa

∽ Louise Cecilia Fleming, 1862-1899 ∽

Louise Fleming was filled with excitement when she sailed for Africa on 17 March, 1887. She was twenty-five and felt particularly that 'The Lord had need of me in Africa'.[7]

Born into slavery in Florida in 1862, Louise never knew her father, who died fighting for the Union in the Civil War. Growing up she attended Bethel Baptist Church with her mother. Interestingly, there were forty whites and 250 slaves in the congregation before the Civil War. After the War, when slaves had received their freedom, the congregation segregated and the whites formed another church.

An unnamed white lady, possibly the plantation owner to whom the Flemings had once belonged, paid for Louise to go to school and train as a teacher. Louise taught school in North Carolina for several years when she was accepted at Shaw University, one of several schools established by the American Baptist Home Mission Society for the recently freed blacks. Louise graduated Valedictorian of her class in 1885.

Since her childhood Louise had heard stories about her grandfather who was born near the mouth of the Congo River, where he had been captured by a slave trader. She appealed to the Women's American Baptist Foreign Mission Society for an appointment to Africa. When she received her appointment in May 1886 she wrote, 'I believe this is the day for which I was born. Can you not see God's hand in allowing [that sinful deed of my grandfather's capture, similar to Genesis 37:28], and raising up from that Joseph a daughter who would return to this people with a message of peace?'[8]

Louise worked in the Congo for five years, teaching in the mission school in the morning and sharing the gospel with women in their homes in the afternoon. At first only men were responding to the gospel, but, in 1888, Louise was delighted to report a woman convert. The people were very superstitious and had all types of fetishes to ward off evil spirits. Once the woman had believed in Jesus, she brought her fetishes to Louise. One fetish was to keep her pulse beating, one to ward off Satan, and the third to cure headaches. She told Louise she wanted to trust Jesus and not in such things. She had heard the story of the cross for years, and Louise rejoiced at the Holy Spirit's work in her heart.

When Louise had to return to the United States because of illness, she brought several Congolese young people with her to place in American schools. While recuperating from her sickness, she also attended Women's Medical College in Philadelphia. In 1895, as soon as she received her M.D., she returned to the Congo. Sadly, she soon became sick with sleeping sickness and had to return to Philadelphia, where she died in 1899 at the age of thirty-seven. She had touched the lives of many Africans with her teaching, the example of her life, and her gospel witness.

> *Here there is not Greek and Jew, circumcised and uncircumcised,*
> *barbarian, Scythian, slave, free;*
> *but Christ is all, and in all.*
>
> ~ COLOSSIANS 3:11 ~

---

7. 'Lulu Fleming', *International Ministries – On Location*, Winter 2010, p. 1.

8. Ibid, p. 1.

'Bible' for the' People'

∞ Suzanne de Dietrich, 1891-1981 ∞

Suzanne de Dietrich was born into a noble family of industrialists in Alsace, France at the end of the nineteenth century. Severely handicapped in her arms and legs and having to use two walking sticks throughout her life, she nevertheless lived a long life and led many to the Bible as the source of truth and life. In 1907-1908, she had a 'resolute turning to Christ', and Bible study and prayer became central to her. Since there was no male heir in her family Suzanne studied engineering in Lausanne, becoming, in 1913, only the second French woman to ever graduate in engineering. The following year she attended the congress of the French Federation of Christian Student associations (the Féde) and became more active in the Christian student movement. She began Bible studies at the Féde, showing the Bible was not just a devotional book but important for strengthening faith and the spiritual life. Bible study, not engineering, became the focus of Suzanne's work.

Suzanne recognized that:

> The written word is only the medium through which God speaks his living word to us here and now, but it is the necessary medium, chosen by God for this purpose. The whole Bible tells about the redeeming activity of God, and its centre is the incarnation, death and resurrection of Jesus Christ. The parts must be interpreted in the light of the whole, starting from the centre, which is God in Christ.[9]

Suzanne was appointed to a number of positions in the student movement after World War I. In 1929, she was appointed vice-president to the Universal Federation of Christian Students and kept this position through 1946. In 1939 she, along with Madeleine Bart, founded CIMADE, a committee dealing with the growing Jewish and other refugees from Nazi Germany. In 1941, she was one of three women, out of sixteen pastors and lay people, who wrote the declaration advocating resistance of the French Reformed Church to Nazism.

In addition to her Bible studies for student groups, Suzanne wrote a number of small books, such as *God's Will*, *Discovering the Bible*, and *God's Unfolding Purpose: A Guide to the Study of the Bible*, all of which encouraged a return to the Reformation principle of *sola scriptura*, the Bible alone as a source of truth. Suzanne resisted the theological liberalism of the nineteenth century. She taught that the Bible was foundational to the church, and it was for the people, not just for professional scholars and theologians.

Suzanne died 24 January, 1891, five days before her ninetieth birthday. On her tombstone is a cross with the words from Psalm 103:1, 'Bless the Lord, O my soul'.

For the word of God is living and active, sharper than any two-edged sword,
piercing to the division of soul and of spirit, of joints and of marrow,
and discerning the thoughts and intentions of the heart.

~ HEBREWS 4:12 ~

---

9. Quoted in Douglas John Hall, *Remembered Voices: reclaiming the legacy of 'neo-orthodoxy'* (Louisville, Kentucky: Westminster John Knox Press, 1998), p. 110.

First European Woman in Tibet

∞ Annie R. Taylor, 1855-1922 ∞

Soon after her conversion to Christ at the age of thirteen, Annie Taylor determined to become a missionary. Her father, director of the Black Ball Line of sailing ships, strongly opposed such a future for his daughter. For several years Annie worked in the slums of Brighton and London as well as studying medicine in London. Persisting in her desire to be a missionary, Annie was accepted by the China Inland Mission and sailed for Shanghai on 12 September, 1884.

Annie was stationed in Lanzhou in northwest China and close to the Tibetan frontier. The controlling Buddhist priesthood had closed Tibet to foreigners, but Annie had always been extremely interested in this forbidden land. No one had told the Tibetans of Jesus, and she felt called to bring the name of Christ to them. She left China and studied the Tibetan language for a year in a Sikkim monastery in India, near the Tibetan border. While there Annie treated a serious injury of Pontso, a teenage native of Lhasa, the sacred city of Tibet, and led him to the Lord. Pontso became Annie's companion and guide into the Tibetan region.

Annie returned to Shanghai to begin her journey to Lhasa. Along with Pontso, Annie hired three other men, ten horses, two months' supply of food, presents for chiefs met along the way, and a few trade items. She sewed four books into her clothing: *New Testament and Psalms, Daily Light*, a hymnbook, and a diary. Early in the trip robbers took their horses and many of their goods. Two of the hired men died, and Noga, the Muslim who survived, turned duplicitous, even attempting to poison Annie. Early in 1893, when they approached Lhasa, Noga left the party and went ahead to report them to the Tibetan authorities. Annie and Pontso were arrested and required to appear before the authorities, who demanded that they leave the territory. Annie in return demanded that they be given renewed horses, provisions and safe conduct for her remaining party. Her demands were met, and Annie began the arduous return to China. Again robbers took most of her goods, and she slept in the open for three weeks. After seven and a half months and traversing 1,300 miles, Annie returned to China on 15 April, 1893. Annie accepted her failure to reach Lhasa as from the Lord, but she continued to have a burden for the Tibetan people.

Annie decided that if Paul could make tents for Christ, she could become a shopkeeper for her Lord. She, along with a Miss Ferguson and Miss Foster, established a small trading business and medical clinic in Yatung, near the Indian border. The small organ in the shop and the singing of hymns delighted the people, and no one ever came without hearing about Jesus or being given a copy of one of the gospels. Making Christ known was Annie's greatest joy.

For the love of Christ controls us, because we have concluded this: ... he died for all, that those who live might no longer live for themselves but for him who for their sake died and was raised.

~ 2 CORINTHIANS 5:14-15 ~

Consecrated to God

⤳ Elsie Marshall, 1869-1895 ⤳

The little girl born 9 November, 1869, in Birchfield, near the English city of Birmingham, was named 'Elsie', meaning 'consecrated to God'. All would agree it was a most fitting name for the little girl and then the young lady. Elsie's father, Rev. J. W. Marshall, was the vicar of St. John's in Blackheath, where Elsie taught the Sunday school class from an early age. Her family recognized that Elsie's brightness and sunshine was a reflection of God's love; she always loved to sing and speak about Christ.

Elsie was inspired by reading missionary biographies, and decided she wanted to be a missionary to India. However, in 1891, Robert and Louisa Stewart spoke in Elsie's father's church and shared the need for women missionaries in China. Elsie applied to serve in China with the Church of England Zenana Missionary Society. She set sail for China with the Stewarts on 14 October, 1892. Those traveling with her during the six weeks voyage noted her earnest devotion to God. She prayed for the sailors and fearlessly shared the gospel with them on the voyage.

Elsie's first year in China was spent learning the language. Whenever she began to feel homesick or troubled she would remind herself she was in the will of Jesus, which renewed her strength. When the missionaries planned a retreat in Huasang during the summer of 1895, Elsie asked Robert Stewart if she could come later in August rather than July, since she had so much work to do. Stewart knew she needed the time away and encouraged her to come to the retreat with them in July. As Elsie looked forward to the retreat, she wrote in a letter:

> I know He has some very precious lessons to teach us. One thing, I think, is to look on and see how God works. Another thing, not to be too much engrossed in the work itself to forget the Master, but to remember if He likes to call us away to other work He is at liberty to do so. We are His bond-slaves, just to go here and there as He pleases, and He has made me so glad to leave it all with Him now, and there's not a shade of worry.[10]

On the morning of 1 August, 1895, a Buddhist movement called Zhaijiao, which was attempting to take over the Qing dynasty government in the Gutian, violently attacked the missionary compound, spearing the victims to death – killing eleven, and burning down two houses. Elsie was among those massacred. She was dragged from the house and hacked to pieces; she was seen clasping her Bible to the end, until her hand itself was severed. When Elsie's father in England learned of his daughter's death, he preached to his congregation from John 11:4. On her coffin was inscribed, 'Miss Elsie Marshall, whose young bright life sparkled with devotion to God and His work. She asked life of Thee, and Thou gavest it, even life for ever and ever.'

'This illness does not lead to death. It is for the glory of God,
so that the Son of God may be glorified through it.'

~ JOHN 11:4 ~

---

10. Elsie Marshall, *For His Sake: A Record of a Life Consecrated to God and Devoted to China* (Religious Tract Society, 1897), p. 43.

God Speaks Navajo

∞ Faye Edgerton, 1889-1968 ∞

Faye Edgerton, born in 1889, was a joyful child with musical talent whose life was carefree until scarlet fever brought her to the door of death. Faye lost her hearing and realized she had been living a purposeless life apart from God. When she recovered and her hearing returned, Faye praised God and determined to live her life for Him. She trained for work as a missionary at Moody Bible Institute and, in 1918, was sent to Korea by the American Presbyterian Mission. She diligently studied Korean on board the ship, so that when she arrived in Korea she could read the language well.

The first winter in Korea, Faye suffered severely from sinusitis. In the following spring the violence and terror of an independence movement in Korea took a toll on Faye's nerves. Though she tried to keep going at her station, in 1922 Faye's health forced her to return to the United States. After her recovery the Presbyterian Board assigned Faye to work at a Navajo school in Arizona, hoping the climate would solve her sinus problem.

As Faye taught the Navajo children she became increasingly convinced that the Navajo needed the Scriptures in their own language. The Navajo was the largest Native American tribe in the United States, and at that time 70 per cent spoke no English. In 1944 Faye left the Presbyterian mission to join Wycliffe Bible Translators and work on translating the New Testament into Navajo. She prayed that she would be able to have the light of the gospel translated into the Navajo tongue.

Earlier missionaries had translated portions of the Scripture into Navajo, but Faye sought to have the entire New Testament translated. She and her Wycliffe associate Faith Hill worked closely with Navajo Geronimo Martin to revise the older translations and complete the New Testament. The complete New Testament was published by the American Bible Society in 1956. Four editions, 9,000 volumes in all, were published in three years, showing the Navajos' hunger for the Scriptures. The Navajos felt this was no longer missionaries talking, but God talking to them.

Faye began learning Apache and, together with Faith Hill, translated the New Testament into the Apache language. She continued working on revisions and new translations into Hopi and Inupiat until her death in 1968.

The grass withers, the flower fades,
but the word of our God will stand forever.

~ Isaiah 40:8 ~

OCTOBER 16

Shining Light in the Darkness

∽ Alice Seeley Harris, 1870-1970 ∽

Alice Seeley entered the Civil Service in London when she was nineteen, but she donated her spare time to mission work at F. B. Meyer's Regent's Park Chapel and later at Christ Church, in Lambeth. Alice left the Civil Service to enter the Congo Balolo Mission's Training College, where she met John Harris; the two were married on 6 May, 1898. A few days later, on 10 May, Alice and John left on the *S.S. Cameroon* for the Congo Free State – their three-month voyage was their honeymoon.

From 1898-1901 Alice and John were at the Mission Station at Ikau, close to the River Lulanga, a tributary of the Congo River; from 1901-1905 they were at the Mission Station at Baringa, on the banks of the Maringa River. Alice taught English to the local children, showing them as well the love of Christ. She taught school in the morning and visited the villages in the afternoon. Often she took some of her students visiting with her, and they would read the Scriptures to the gathered tribesmen.

Alice was appalled at the treatment of the Congolese by the agents of King Leopold II of Belgium, who held the Congo as a private possession. With the development of inflatable tyres by John Dunlop, in 1887, rubber was a prime commodity, and the Congo had a rich supply of wild rubber plants. Overseers for Leopold established quotas for the natives to extract rubber. If the quotas were not met, punishment was severe – whippings, hostage-taking, or even death. The most common punishment, however, was cutting off a hand or foot of a child or relative. In her travels Alice took numerous photos of handless children and natives brutally beaten. One of the most moving photos was of a father sitting on the ground looking at the severed hand and foot of his dead daughter in front of him.

Alice's photos were first used in *Regions Beyond*, the magazine of the Congo Balolo Mission; soon they were used by other publications to raise awareness at the inhumane treatment of the Congo natives. In 1905, Alice and her husband toured the United States presenting lantern-slide lectures about the suffering in the Congo at 200 meetings in forty-nine cities.

Under great pressure, in 1908, Leopold relinquished his ownership of the Congo Free State to the Belgium government, which then created the Belgian Congo. Alice and her husband helped organize the Congo Reform Association to bring reform to the region. Alice was among the first to use photography to bring about humanitarian relief.

For God, who said, 'Let light shine out of darkness', has shone
in our hearts to give the light of the knowledge of the glory of
God in the face of Jesus Christ.

~ 2 Corinthians 4:6 ~

OCTOBER 17

Lo Mo, Beloved Mother

∞ Donaldina Mackenzie Cameron, 1869-1968 ∞

As Donaldina Cameron walked quietly through the night streets of San Francisco's China-town, passing opium dens and gambling halls, she looked for girls being held as slaves or prostitutes she could rescue from such degradation. Men in the Tongs, secret brotherhoods, called her the 'White Devil'; others called her the 'Jesus Woman'. To the women and girls she rescued, she was Lo Mo, beloved mother.

Donaldina Cameron was born in New Zealand in 1869, the youngest of seven children in a devout Presbyterian family. Her parents were Scottish sheep ranchers. In 1871, Allen Cameron moved his family to California, where he worked on ranches in the San Joaquin Valley. When Donaldina was five her mother died, and her older sisters cared for her. When she was fifteen her father began managing a sheep ranch in the San Gabriel Valley and moved the family near Los Angeles. After graduation from high school Donaldina planned to go to a teacher training school, but her father's death, in 1887, ended her plans.

Donaldina was looking for something to do when a mother of a schoolmate invited her to work at the Mission Home in San Francisco. The Home was sponsored by the Woman's Occidental Board of Foreign Missions as a refuge for Chinese women who were abused or had been sold into slavery or prostitution. Donaldina came to the Home in 1895 as a sewing teacher and assisted Margaret Culbertson, the Director. After Culbertson died in 1897 and her replacement served only briefly, Donaldina became superintendent in 1900, and guided the mission for the next thirty-four years, becoming a legend in her own lifetime.

In the early 1900s, Chinese women and girls, some of whom had been sold by their own fathers, were smuggled into California to become slaves and prostitutes. Donaldina worked actively to rescue them and bring them to the Mission Home to be cared for. She went to court to gain legal custody for the girls in her foster care to prevent them from being returned to their masters. At the Mission Home the girls were washed, dressed, and given needed medical care. Educational programs for the women and girls had a strongly Christian component. Donaldina's mothering care for the girls included finding staff positions for them, as well as Christian husbands. When the 1906 San Francisco earthquake with its resulting fires set the Mission Home ablaze, Donaldina rushed back into the burning building to rescue the documents and court papers which guaranteed the girls' continued freedom. The Home was totally burned, but rebuilt within two years.

Donaldina helped more than two thousand Chinese women and girls, many of whom found not only a refuge from a life of slavery, but a new freedom in Jesus Christ.

Now the Lord is the Spirit,
and where the Spirit of the Lord is, there is freedom.

~ 2 CORINTHIANS 3:17 ~

Three Knocks in the Night

∞ Ida Scudder, 1870-1960 ∞

The Scudder family has a rich missionary heritage. In four generations, forty-two of their family became missionaries, with over one thousand years of combined years of missionary service among them! John Scudder with his wife Harriet led the way, sailing from New York for Ceylon in 1819 and becoming the first medical missionary of the American Board of Commissioners for Foreign Missions. The Scudders served thirty-six years in Ceylon and India. Seven of their nine children who survived to adulthood became missionaries. John and Harriet's youngest son, also named John, was also a medical missionary in India. He was the father of Ida Scudder, born in India in 1870.

Ida enjoyed the furloughs to America but did not like the heat, dust, and smells of India. She definitely had no interest in becoming a missionary like her parents or grandparents. Ida was attending Dwight L. Moody's Northfield Seminary for Girls when she received news her mother was seriously ill. Ida returned to India to care for her mother, intending to return to America as soon as she was well. Three knocks at the door one night changed Ida's direction.

A Brahmin man came requesting Ida to assist his wife in a difficult childbirth. Ida could not come, but offered to send her father, a physician. The man would not allow Ida's father to come; custom prohibited his wife be seen by another man. Later in the night, another Hindu and then a Muslim came to the door with the same request; each refused the help of a male doctor. Ida was in great anguish and prayer throughout the night, not wanting to stay in India, but sensing God placing the need of India's women before her. In the early morning Ida heard the 'tom-tom' announcing death in the village. All three of the women had died in the night. Ida was convinced she must study medicine and return to India as a doctor.

After receiving her M.D. from Cornell Medical College and a cheque for ten thousand dollars for a hospital from a wealthy donor, Ida Scudder returned to India. Except for fundraising trips to America and Britain, India would be her home for the next sixty years. During that time she established a hospital at Vellore, a training school for nurses and a Christian Medical College at Vellore, in addition to numerous clinics and dispensaries throughout the countryside. Ida always prayed and brought a Christian message of hope to her patients, and she held regular Bible study at the medical school.

The Vellore Christian Medical College and Hospital today is one of the largest Christian hospitals in the world, bringing healthcare and Bible instruction to many. Ida had not wanted to live her life in India, but three knocks in the night redirected her life.

To this end we always pray for you,
that our God may make you worthy of his calling
and may fulfill every resolve for good and every work of faith by his power.

~ 2 THESSALONIANS 1:11 ~

Streams in the Desert

∞ Lettie Cowman, 1870-1960 ∞

Lettie and Charles Cowman met in Lettie's hometown of Thayer, Iowa when she was fifteen; he was twenty-one. Four years later, in 1889, they were married and moved to Chicago, where Charles was a telegraph operator. They both were converted at Grace Methodist Episcopal Church. When they heard a missionary challenge from A. B. Simpson, founder of the Christian and Missionary Alliance, they dedicated themselves to missionary work. After training at a Bible school they went to Japan, arriving on 22 February, 1901.

The Cowmans had met Juji Nakada when he was a student at Moody Bible Institute and teamed up with him in Japan to found the Oriental Missionary Society (today OMS International). They conducted nightly evangelistic services and established a Bible training school during the day. Soon they launched the 'Every Creature Crusade', to bring the gospel to every house in Japan. They printed Scriptures and gospel tracts and organized workers to distribute them throughout Japan. Charles was a great administrator, but his health broke down over the load of work. He and Lettie had to return to the United States in 1917. They settled in Los Angeles, where Lettie cared for her husband, whose health continued to worsen.

During this time of difficulty and suffering Lettie and Charles read through the Bible together and read many of the writings of leaders of the nineteenth century evangelical movement – A. C. Dixon, A. T. Pierson, F. B. Meyer, Andrew Murray, A. B. Simpson, and others. Lettie extracted the richest passages from their writings which she found most helpful and comforting during her trials. After her husband died in 1924, she published the extracts, interwoven with her own comments, as *Streams in the Desert*. For all those troubled in spirit, she wanted to 'comfort them with the same comfort wherewith we have been comforted of God'. The little devotional has gone through numerous printings and continues to comfort many today.

After Charles' death Lettie continued her concern with missions, serving as President of OMS from 1928-1949 and speaking throughout the world on behalf of Christian missions.

*Blessed be the God and Father of our Lord Jesus Christ, the Father of mercies
and God of all comfort, who comforts us in all our affliction, so that we may
be able to comfort those who are in any affliction, with the comfort with which
we ourselves are comforted by God.*

~ 2 Corinthians 1:3-4 ~

In the Potter's Hands

∞ Sarah Adelaide Pollard, 1862-1934 ∞

Sarah Pollard lived an active life as a teacher and evangelist. She didn't like her given name, so she adopted the name 'Adelaide', by which she was always known. Adelaide taught in several girls' schools and at the Christian and Missionary Alliance School in Nyack, New York.

Adelaide wanted to go to Africa as a missionary, but was frustrated that she could not raise the required funds. In 1902, at a prayer meeting, an elderly woman prayed, 'Lord, it doesn't matter what you bring into our lives – just have your way with us.' The phrase struck in Adelaide's mind as she made her way home that evening. She thought of Scripture passages which described God as a potter, and wrote a hymn which continues to encourage many:

> Have Thine own way, Lord! Have Thine own way!
> Thou art the potter; I am the clay.
> Mold me and make me after Thy will,
> While I am waiting, yielded and still.
>
> Have Thine own way, Lord! Have Thine own way!
> Search me and try me, Master, today!
> Whiter than snow, Lord, wash me just now,
> As in Thy presence humbly I bow.
>
> Have Thine own way, Lord! Have Thine own way!
> Wounded and weary, help me, I pray!
> Power, all power, surely is Thine!
> Touch me and heal me, Saviour divine.
>
> Have Thine own way, Lord! Have Thine own way!
> Hold o'er my being absolute sway!
> Fill with Thy Spirit 'till all shall see
> Christ only, always, living in me.

Adelaide did finally make it to Africa. However, World War I soon broke out, and she had to leave and spend the war years in Scotland. When she did return to the United States, she continued her ministry as a Bible teacher and evangelist.

> *So I went down to the potter's house, and there he was working at his wheel.*
> *And the vessel he was making of clay was spoiled in the potter's hand, and*
> *he reworked it into another vessel, as it seemed good to the potter to do.*
> *Then the word of the LORD came to me: 'O house of Israel, can I not do*
> *with you as this potter has done?' declares the LORD. 'Behold, like the clay*
> *in the potter's hand, so are you in my hand ... .'*
>
> ~ JEREMIAH 18:3-6 ~

Trio of Women in the Desert

∞ Mildred Cable, 1878-1952 ∞

Believing the church in China needed educated women to be Christian wives and mothers, as well as Bible women and evangelists, Mildred Cable and Eva French opened a girls' school in Huozhou, China in 1904. They began with twenty-four students, but before the year was out they had seventy women and girls in attendance. In 1908 Eva's sister Francesca joined the work, and the three women worked together for the rest of their lives, becoming known as 'The Trio'.

The school continued to grow and graduated its first class of teachers in 1913. Over a period of twenty years, approximately 1,000 girls were educated at the school. Many of the girls went on to become teachers themselves, impacting Chinese education throughout the region. In 1923, when the Governor of Shanxi decided to open seventy new provincial schools for girls, he called on the Trio's students and teachers to staff the schools.

At that time Dr Kao, a Christian Chinese doctor, invited The Trio to come and help in reaching out to Muslim, Tibetan and Mongolian people in the interior. When the women heard of the Silk Road, stretching a thousand miles from Gansu province to Xinjiang province, and the need for evangelism among the people in remote areas, they answered the call. The three traveled by mule cart. Eight hundred miles and nine months from Huozhou, they arrived at their first stop, Zhangye. The pastor at the small church there said they were an answer to prayer. In the coming months The Trio conducted a Bible school for men and women, taught reading classes, and traveled into the surrounding villages to preach the gospel. They set up a tent at the village fairs, and people gathered to listen to the Christian message. The size of the church congregation doubled, and many natives were trained in the work of evangelism.

The Trio then moved on to Jiuquan and Dunhuang, which was a crossroads for people from India, China, and Tibet and had a heavy Muslim population. They later followed the Silk Road to the Russian border, crossing portions of the Gobi Desert. After a furlough in England, The Trio returned to China in 1928, in the midst of a civil war. They retraced their steps along the Silk Road, encouraging the Christians in their faith, visiting 2,700 homes, conducting 665 meetings, and selling 40,000 copies of Scripture.

During the war Muslim forces gained control of 600 miles of the Silk Road and the city of Dunhuang. The Muslim general, noted for his cruelty, summoned The Trio to his army headquarters eighty miles away and asked them to bring their medical supplies. They treated the general's wounds. Once they had healed, Mildred asked permission for them to leave. She also asked him to consider the life he led, and he accepted from her a New Testament.

In 1936, the communists required The Trio, along with other foreigners, to leave China. Mildred and Francesca later wrote of their travels in *The Gobi Desert*, which continues to be an excellent guide into that remote region today.

Declare his glory among the nations, his marvelous works among all the
peoples! For great is the LORD, and greatly to be praised … .

~ PSALM 96:3-4 ~

Representative of the Heavenly City

⌒ Dora Yu, 1873-1931 ⌒

Dora Yu was born in 1873 on the American Presbyterian Mission compound near Hangzhou, China. Her father, a physician, was studying to be a preacher. From her earliest years Dora had a love and affection for Christ and a desire to serve him. When she was fifteen, in 1888, Dora went to a medical school established by American missionaries and attached to the Soochow Hospital. During that time Dora was engaged to be married, but she chose to relinquish the engagement, wanting to give her undivided love and will to God.

Graduating from medical school in 1896, Dora accompanied the Texas missionary Josephine Campbell to Korea and the two began the first Methodist mission to women in that country. Dora's medical skills were often an opening to the Korean women, whom Dora then personally evangelized. She trained native women to be 'Bible women', who visited women in the villages with copies of the Scriptures, teaching them to read as well as the basic truths of the Christian faith. Dora daily led the staff prayer meetings at the Paiwha School and spoke at the thrice-weekly chapel services, while also visiting the women and children to encourage them in the Scriptures. In 1903 alone, she visited 925 women and 211 children and gave them the good news of Jesus. In that year, Dora also returned to China and continued her evangelistic work among the Chinese, trusting God in faith to provide her needs, and cooperating with the YMCA and other missionary organizations in their work.

In 1915, Dora opened a Bible school and prayer house to train Christian women in Jiangwan, a southern suburb of Shanghai. Dora also spoke in evangelistic meetings throughout eastern China. Many of the next generation of Chinese Christians came to faith in Christ under her ministry, including a seventeen-year-old Ni Tuoseng. In 1920, Ni's mother attended one of Dora's meetings, repented of her sins, and came to faith in Christ. When she apologized to Ni for a harsh punishment she had inflicted on him, Ni was so impressed that he went to the evangelistic meetings, returned to his room in deep thought and prayer, and believed in Jesus. Ni, who became known as Watchman Nee, was an influential church leader in China during the twentieth century and planted over four hundred churches during a thirty-year period. His last twenty years were spent in a communist prison for his Christian faith.

In 1927 the director of China Inland Mission invited Dora to be the main speaker at the Keswick Convention in England. In her address Dora pled with the people to stop sending modernist missionaries to China who would destroy the faith of the Chinese believers. Those who opposed Christ's incarnation and divinity, His atoning death on the cross, His resurrection, and His coming again were not true Christians. When she was introduced as the 'voice of China', Dora replied, 'I am not the representative of China but of the Lord Jesus Christ. I belong to a Heavenly City.'[11] Four years later, in 1931, Dora died of cancer and entered the Heavenly City.

For here we have no lasting city,
but we seek the city that is to come.

~ HEBREWS 13:14 ~

---

11. Mark A. Noll and Carolyn Nystrom, *Clouds of Witnesses: Christian Voices from Africa and Asia* (Downers Grove: Intervarsity Press, 2011), p. 197.

Looking for Christ's Soon Return

∞ Christabel Pankhurst, 1880-1958 ∞

Christabel Pankhurst, along with her mother Emmeline and her sisters Sylvia and Adela, was a leader of the militant suffrage movement in Britain. Raised in a family with socialist leanings, Christabel and her mother founded the Women's Social and Political Union (WSPU) in 1903. The WSPU became known for its militant tactics including hunger strikes, mass protests, and vandalism, in promoting women's suffrage and equality. Christabel became known as the 'Queen of the Mob' and was arrested frequently for her militant protests.

Though women gained the right to vote in England after World War I, Christabel was disillusioned by the inability of politics to bring about true reform. Picking up a book on prophecy by F. B. Meyer in a bookshop, she was awakened to her need of a Savior and the reality of Christ's return. She read the Bible's diagnosis of the world's ills and the promise they would be cured with the return of Jesus Christ:

> 'Ah! That is the solution!' My heart stirred to it. My practical eye saw that this Divine Programme is absolutely the only one that can solve the international, social, political, or moral problems of the world. The only trouble was, that it seemed too good to be true. ... For a long time, too, mine seemed too fragile a flower of belief to speak of, and expose to the cold wind of other people's possible scepticism.[12]

She realized that in campaigning for suffrage, she was trying to build a human-made Utopia – an impossible achievement.

Christabel became an evangelist, lecturing in both England and the United States. Writing Christian books, especially on the Second Coming of Christ, she bemoaned the liberalism in the churches which saw Jesus as merely a moral example without 'the power of the Lord Jesus Christ in His deity, His Incarnation, His Death, and real Resurrection'. Christabel's favorite passage of Scripture was Philippians 2, 'for it tells me of the One who came down from heaven the first time, and died for my sins, and who is coming again that He may be glorified and obeyed throughout the world'. In her lectures Christabel spoke of 'the Cross of Christ for redemption of sin and His second coming to deliver the world from war and unrighteousness'.[13]

Her lectures were widely attended, as she spoke of her disillusionment with politics and her expectation of the return of Jesus Christ.

Though Christabel is still remembered today as a leader of the suffragette movement (in 1936 she was appointed Dame Commander of the Order of the British Empire for her work for women's rights), the greater part of her life was spent as a Bible student, Christian writer and lecturer. Upon her death in California in 1958, *The Santa Monica Evening Outlook* described her as 'Dame Christabel Pankhurst, militant campaigner for Christ and women's suffrage'.[14]

> *... so that at the name of Jesus every knee should bow, in heaven and on earth and under the earth, and every tongue confess that Jesus Christ is Lord, to the glory of God the Father.*
>
> ~ PHILIPPIANS 2:10-11 ~

---

12. Timothy Larsen, *Christabel Pankhurst: Fundamentalism and Feminism in Coalition* (Woodbridge: The Boydell Press) p. 21.

13. Ibid, p. 45.

14. Ibid, p. vii.

'I Must Go'

∞ Mary Slessor, 1845-1915 ∞

The village chief lay dying, and a hush hung over the village in Calabar. The chief's wives knew that with his death they too would die, sacrificed to become the chief's attendants in the spirit world. A woman from a neighboring village urged them to send to the white woman who lived at Ekenge. She had potions which healed her child and perhaps could heal the chief.

Messengers were sent to Mary Slessor in Ekenge, known as 'the white Ma' among the people. Mary's friend, Chief Edem, urged her not to go. The way was dangerous; warriors were in the woods along with wild beasts; and the rains had made the streams deep. Mary thought of the lives which would be spared if the chief were healed and replied, 'I must go.' She prayed through the night that she would know the Lord's will. In the morning she knew the Lord would be with her and set out on her journey. The rain and mud was so deep, her boots were an impediment, and she threw them into the bushes, walking barefoot. Her head throbbed with a fever, but her spirit was tireless. She walked eight hours to find the chief still clinging to life, though unconscious. Mary examined him, then gave him some medicine from her medicine chest. She remained with him throughout the next day, when he gained consciousness and began to eat. In a few days, he was quite well. The entire village rejoiced and wanted to know Mary's powers. Mary said,

> I have come to you because I love and worship Jesus Christ, the Great Physician and Saviour, the Son of the father God who made all things. I want you to know this Father and to receive the eternal life which Jesus offers to all those with contrite and believing hearts. To know Jesus means to love Him, and with His love in our hearts we love everybody. Eternal life means peace and joy in this world and a wonderful home in the next world. My heart longs for you to believe in Jesus, to walk in His paths and to know the blessings of eternal life through him.[15]

For forty years, Mary Slessor tirelessly loved the people of the Calabar region – rescuing twins abandoned to death, caring for orphans, establishing schools, providing medical care, and mediating peace between warring tribes. When she received a message that two villages were holding councils of war over a man of one village wounding the chief of another, she said, 'I must go.' She herself was ill and could hardly walk, but she took two men with lanterns and walked through the night. When she reached the village, warriors were preparing to attack. Mary ran to the warriors and demanded they stop. In their amazement, they did stop. Mary then walked to the village warriors and said she was to help them settle the matter peaceably. An old chief stepped forward and said, 'Ma, we are glad you came. We admit that one of our drunken young men wounded the chief over there. It was an act in which the rest of us had no part. We are glad for you to speak with our enemy and help make peace.' Looking in the old man's face, Mary recognized the dying chief she had cured several years before. Mary was able to restore peace, again saving many lives.

> 'Go therefore and make disciples of all nations, baptizing them in the name of the Father and of the Son and of the Holy Spirit, teaching them to observe all that I have commanded you. And behold, I am with you always, to the end of the age.'
>
> ~ MATTHEW 28:19-20 ~

---

15. Eugene Myers Harrison, 'Mary Slessor: The White Queen of Calabar', in *Blazing the Missionary Trail.* (Chicago: Scripture Press Book Division, 1949), as found at *Wholesome Words*, www.wholesomewords.org/missions/bioslessor2.html.

Treasures in Heaven

∽ Maria Fearing, 1838-1937 ∽

Maria was born into slavery in 1838. Her mother was a house servant on William Winston's Oak Hill Plantation near Gainesville, Alabama. Maria grew up playing with the Winston children and learning to help her mother in the big house. Maria especially enjoyed bedtime, when Mrs Winston would read Bible stories to her children. Maria would later vividly retell the stories to her family in the slave quarters. She longed to be able to read the Bible, but it was against the law to teach slaves to read.

Maria was twenty-seven when slavery was abolished. Learning of a Freedmen's Bureau school in Talladega, Alabama, Maria enrolled, earning her expenses by working at the school. Maria was placed in a beginner's class full of children. Some made fun of her, a grown woman, just learning to read, but Maria learned quickly and soon was helping the children in their lessons. She completed ninth grade and began teaching in a rural school, saving enough money to buy a small house. She even helped support a student at Talladega College. Talladega then asked her to be a matron in the boarding school. In 1894, Maria heard William Henry Sheppard speak at Talladega, calling for others to join him in missionary work in the Congo. Maria was moved to go. She remembered from her childhood the stories Mrs Winston had told about missionaries in Africa and how she then had wanted to work on the mission field. Maria applied for mission work in the Congo, but was not accepted because of her age – she was fifty-six. Maria was healthy and active, and had never considered age a hindrance. Firmly convinced God had called her to the mission field, Maria asked if she could accompany the missionaries if she paid her own way. Accepted on that basis, Maria sold her house and accepted donations from the Women of the Congregational Church of Talladega.

On 26 May, 1884, William Sheppard, five African American missionaries, and Maria left for Africa. The mission station was located twenty miles inland at Luebo, which would be Maria's home for the next twenty years. Maria learned the Baluba-Lulua language and within a year was able to converse freely and tell Bible stories to the children. She also began helping with Bible translation. Maria established the Pantops Home for Girls, rescuing many girls who had been kidnapped, caring for orphans, and buying and freeing some girls sold into slavery. She taught the girls reading, writing, homemaking skills, and the Bible. She hoped the girls would then be better able to establish Christian homes in Africa. Many of the girls did become wives of pastors. The people loved Maria calling her 'mama wa Mputu', mother from far away.

Encouraged by the mission agency to retire, Marie returned to Alabama when she was seventy-eight. She continued active in teaching Sunday School until her death at age ninety-nine.

> *'If you would be perfect, go, sell what you possess and give to the poor,*
> *and you will have treasure in heaven; and come, follow me.'*
>
> ~ MATTHEW 19:21 ~

Grace of the Savior for life

∞ Anna Bowden, d. 1890s ∞

Sensing a call to missionary work in a foreign land, Anna Bowden enrolled in Henrietta Soltau's mission training school in London. The school had been established to help screen and train women for overseas mission work. In 1891, Robert Campbell-Green, an evangelist working in southern India, gave a series of devotional messages at the school. He told of the brutality of the Hindu culture to the poor and weak as well as the spiritual darkness that held many captive. Anna was so moved by the need in India that she arranged to leave for India immediately, though only half way through her training. Within a month she set sail for Conjeeveram, India. She wrote in her journal, 'I know not the challenges that face me among peoples who live but for death. I do know the grace of the Savior that has called me to die but for life.'[16]

When Anna arrived in Conjeeveram, she discovered that the mission compound there had been abandoned. No one seemed to know what had happened. A community of English merchants nearby said the mission residents had suddenly disappeared and the compound had been vacant for some time. Anna managed to get the English merchants to help her refurbish the mission, and she reopened a tiny clinic and school there. Many children and 'untouchables' began to come to the mission for assistance, drawn in part by Anna's love and warmth.

The *Arya Samaj* movement had begun to spread in Southern India and soon opposed Anna's mission. Seeking to purify Hinduism and return to its ancient practices, the *Arya Samaj* opposed westerners in India, and especially opposed Christianity. The group followed the ancient practice of *sati*, burning the widow on the funeral pyres of their husbands, and female infanticide. Anna set up a network to rescue women and babies from such practices, believing 'The mandate of Holy Writ is plain. We must clothe the naked, feed the hungry, shelter the shelterless, succour the infirmed, and rescue the perishing. I can do no less and still be faithful to the high call of our Sovereign Lord.'[17]

Dayanand Sarasvati, leader of *Arya Samaj*, appealed to the English viceroy to stop Anna from activities not directly related to the missionary compound. Anna replied that rescuing innocent life was directly related to her mission work and was 'directly related to any form of Christian endeavor, humanitarian or evangelistic'. Sarasvati stirred up a mob to attack the mission compound. Several of the buildings were burned to the ground, some of the young girls living there were raped, and Anna was tortured and killed. The mob activity was itself evidence of the gulf between the Christian and heathen ethics. Anna's example and her journals, published shortly after her death, led to a revival within the missionary community in India and strengthened the British colonial rulers in their value of all human life.

Do not be overcome by evil, but overcome evil with good.

~ ROMANS 12:21 ~

---

16. Quoted in George Grant, *Third Time Around, A History of the Pro-Life Movement from the First Century to the Present* (Brentwood, TN: Wolgemuth & Hyatt, Publishers, Inc., 1991), p. 70.

17. Ibid, p. 72.

Through Gates of Pearly Splendor

∞ Edith Gilling Cherry, 1872-1897 ∞

In 1956, the five missionaries and their wives had a final prayer meeting before the five attempted a meeting with the Auca Indians in Ecuador. They sang the hymn 'We Rest on Thee' as they closed their meeting:

> We rest on Thee, our Shield and our
> Defender!
> We go not forth alone against the foe;
> Strong in Thy strength, safe in Thy keeping
> tender,
> We rest on Thee, and in Thy Name we go.
>
> Yes, in Thy Name, O Captain of salvation!
> In Thy dear Name, all other names above;
> Jesus our Righteousness, our sure
> Foundation,
> Our Prince of glory and our King of love.

> We go in faith, our own great weakness feeling,
> And needing more each day Thy grace to
> know:
> Yet from our hearts a song of triumph
> pealing,
> 'We rest on Thee, and in Thy Name we go.'
>
> We rest on Thee, our Shield and our Defender!
> Thine is the battle, Thine shall be the praise;
> When passing through the gates of pearly
> splendour,
> Victors, we rest with Thee, through endless days.

When the five missionaries met with the Auca on 8 January, they were attacked and killed. Their wives and children would indeed look to Jesus as their Shield and Defender in the days ahead.

'We Rest on Thee', sung to the tune of *Finlandia*, was one of many beautiful hymns written by Edith Gilling Cherry. Edith was born in England on 9 February, 1872. When she was sixteen-months old she suffered from infantile paralysis, leaving her crippled throughout her life. When she was twelve she suffered another stroke, leaving her weakened, yet allowing her heart to sing. Poetry often flowed from her effortlessly, and Edith recognized this as a gift from God she should use for His glory. All were amazed at the depth of thought in her poems as well as their beauty. Though she could walk only with the aid of crutches, which she called her 'ponies', Edith was happy and cheerful.

One of her favorite Scripture passages was in 1 Corinthians, that God had chosen the foolish things, the base and despised things for His honor and glory. On 29 August, 1897, when she was twenty-five, Edith suffered another stroke which brought on her death within hours. In her last hours she told her mother, 'it all seems so *small*, all I have tried to do – so small to Him'. Her mother replied, 'But there are your songs, dear, they will carry on your work.' Edith quickly replied, 'Ah, but *they* were not *mine* at all, they were just given to me all ready, and all I had to do was to write them down.' Just before she stepped into eternity Edith told her mother, just as she used to do when leaving home through the garden gate. 'I'm all right mama; I'm trusting in God, and He will undertake for me.'[18]

> *God chose what is foolish in the world to shame the wise; God chose what is weak in the world to shame the strong; God chose what is low and despised in the world … so that no human being might boast in the presence of God.*

~ 1 CORINTHIANS 1:27-29 ~

---

18. 'Edith Gilling Cherry', http://stempublishing.com/hymns/biographies/cherry.html, accessed 11/10/2014.

OCTOBER 28

Rescue the Perishing

⤝ Amy Carmichael, 1867-1951 ⤞

Amy Carmichael's mother heard a wail coming from her daughter's room and went to see what had happened to the child. When Amy's mother had told Amy that the Lord would answer her when she prayed to him, Amy prayed for blue eyes and went to bed thinking her eyes would be blue in the morning. She was greatly disappointed to find her eyes still brown when she woke up! Amy's mother told her that 'No' was just as much an answer from God, even if she didn't understand why. Later, when Amy became a missionary in India and sought to dress and look Indian in her work, she realized that brown eyes were a blessing.

Amy was born in 1867 into a Christian family in Northern Ireland. As a young woman, Amy began visiting the slums of Belfast and began a ministry among the women and girls there. Amy also worked as a secretary for Mr Wilson, one of the leaders of the Keswick Movement, which impacted her spiritual growth greatly. One conversation she overheard between Dwight L. Moody and Mr Wilson deepened Amy's faith. Moody had just preached on the prodigal son and commented on the father telling the older son, 'Son, thou art with me and all that I have is thine.' Tears streamed down Moody's face as he realized the depth of God's love. The thought that 'all I have is thine' remained with Amy in later years. God knew and would supply her needs.

In 1895, when she was twenty-eight, Amy left England to serve as a missionary in India; She would spend her remaining fifty-five years in India, never returning to England on a furlough. For a time Amy worked in the traditional missionary manner – visiting villages, speaking to clusters of women about the gospel, supplying physical needs where possible. On 7 March, 1901, the direction of Amy's work changed. An Indian woman brought Amy a little seven-year-old girl named Preena. The little girl's mother had sold Preena when she was five to the Hindu Temple, where she was to become a temple prostitute. Preena had run away twice, but was recaptured and brought back to cruel perversions. The Indian woman had found Preena running away again at night, and brought her to Amy for protection. Preena used a rag doll to show Amy what the Temple priests had done to her. This led Amy to establish the Dohnavur Fellowship to rescue temple children from such corruption and slavery. Thousands of children, girls and boys, have been rescued over the years, bringing them to the love of Christ.

Seriously injured in a fall in 1931, Amy was an invalid the last twenty years of her life and rarely left her bed. Many of the thirty-five books Amy wrote were written during this time, works filled with the Father's love.

> But Jesus called them to him, saying, 'Let the children come to
> me, and do not hinder them, for to such belongs the kingdom of
> God. Truly, I say to you, whoever does not receive the kingdom
> of God like a child shall not enter it.'
>
> ~ LUKE 18:16-17 ~

Radiating the Joy of Christ

∽ Salamo, c. 1881-1903 ∽

When Salamo was about six, Arab traders came into her village near the River Congo, set fire to the houses, and captured the villagers to sell as slaves. Saloma's father and uncle were away hunting, but Salamo and her mother were among the captives. Salamo was bought by some Dutch traders, who later gave her into the care of Mr and Mrs Darby of the Baptist Missionary Society.

Missionary William Balfern visited the Darbys in 1891 when he first came to the Congo, and admired Salamo's beautiful smile. Back in England Balfern had been given ten shillings to spend as he saw fit when he arrived in the Congo, and he gave the shillings to Mrs Darby for Salamo. Balfern wrote his fiancé, Mary Grigg, about the charming girl and asked her to pray for her. Balfern died in Africa before ever returning to England.

When Mrs Darby returned to England she placed Salamo in the care of Edith Stapleton, a young missionary wife who had just arrived in Africa. Edith suffered from illness and disease for several years after she came to Africa, and Salamo lovingly cared for her. Salamo joyfully embraced Jesus as her Savior. When she was fourteen she was among the first four Christians baptized at Monsembe. She was full of joy and regularly evangelized the young people in the village.

When Edith returned to England on furlough Salamo, then about sixteen, went with her. Through amazing circumstances, in England they met Mary Grigg, whose fiancé had written her about Salamo. She and her Sunday school class had been praying for Salamo for five years, though they had not heard anything more about the girl. Salamo was quite moved that these people had been praying for her.

Salamo had been praying too – that she could find her father to tell him about Jesus! In 1897, when the Stapletons were developing the missionary station at Yakusu, Salamo recognized the language of her young childhood there. Realizing this must be her tribe's home, she searched for her father, and did indeed find him and told him about Jesus.

Salamo became an important part of the early church at Yakusu. She married and had a little daughter, but her husband died shortly after the daughter was born. Salamo was a translator for the missionaries and helped in the early translation of the Gospel of Mark and an early hymnal. With her joyous spirit, Salamo also wrote hymns herself, which are still sung among the Christians at Yakusu. Salamo contracted sleeping sickness and died August, 1903; she was only twenty-two. Her life had seen much tragedy and difficulty, but to the very end, she radiated a Christian joy to all she met.

Continue steadfastly in prayer,
being watchful in it with thanksgiving.

~ COLOSSIANS 4:2 ~

Life of Compassion

∞ Eleanor Chestnut, 1868-1905 ∞

Eleanor Chestnut's difficult childhood seemed to prepare her for a life of compassion and service to others. Her father had left the family before Eleanor's birth in 1868, and her mother died when she was three. She was cared for by relatives, but felt some resentment at being a charity case. Eleanor applied to Park College and Academy in Missouri, a Christian school with a work-study program that would allow her to provide for her own high school and college education. When Eleanor entered the school at fifteen, she was so poor she had to wear clothing taken from the box of clothes donated for the poor.

Besides their normal classes, students at Park College went to chapel three times a day and were required to attend church. During her eight years at Park College, Eleanor's faith in Christ took root and began to grow. The bitterness from her childhood experiences was replaced with a sympathy and compassion for others who were suffering. Several speakers at the College chapel sparked Eleanor's interest in missions. To prepare for missionary work, after graduation from Park College she attended the Women's Medical College in Chicago, followed by a year of training at Moody Bible Institute. In 1894, she sailed for south China to take up work in the city of Lienchow.

Eleanor eagerly entered into the life of the community, learning Mandarin, Cantonese and the local dialect of Lienchow. Besides building and overseeing a hospital and dispensary at Lienchow, Eleanor trained students in medicine and traveled into surrounding villages to hold medical clinics, especially talking to women about the evils of footbinding. Her medical care was a means of showing the Chinese the love of Christ. One time, she had to amputate a man's leg to save his life. When he needed a skin graft to heal properly, she took skin from her own leg to graft on his. Not only did the man heal well, but he became a Christian through Eleanor's witness.

It was an unsettling time in China. Some blamed the problems China faced on the neglect of the native gods and the influence of foreigners. Missionaries and native Christians especially became the target of attacks. In 1900, during the Boxer Rebellion in Northern China, 189 Christian missionaries and 2,000 Chinese Christians were martyred. In spite of danger, Eleanor remained in Lienchow, thinking she might as well die suddenly in God's work as by some long illness at home.

On 29 October, 1905, a riot started in Lienchow against the missionaries. During the rioting, a Chinese boy suffered a head wound, and Eleanor tore her dress to make a bandage for the boy – her last act of kindness to the Chinese people. The rioters beat Eleanor, threw her into the river and stabbed her to death with a pitchfork. They also killed three other missionaries and a ten-year-old girl. The story of Eleanor Chestnut's courageous death at the age of thirty-seven inspired others at home to come and take up the work of Lienchow's women's hospital as well as the gospel work among the people.

They loved not their lives even unto death.

~ REVELATION 12:11 ~

Dying and Raised with Christ

∾ Bertha Smith, 1888-1988 ∾

Bertha Smith first went to China in 1917, five years after Lottie Moon died in China after almost forty years of service as a missionary. Bertha served in China and Taiwan for forty-two years, leaving at seventy only because the Baptist Foreign Mission Board had set that for the retirement age.

On 5 September, 1905, Bertha came to faith in Christ at a revival meeting in Cowpens, South Carolina. There for the first time she realized that Christ took her sins on his own body on the tree. Trusting in Christ, the burden of sin rolled away. The revival preachers, Revs. Troy and Luther Manness,

> preached that people who are saved belong to the Lord – mind, body and soul – that we should acknowledge that fact, confess all of our sins of failing the Lord, so as to be cleansed, and then hand over ourselves and let the Holy Spirit fill us. We would then be empowered to live to please the Lord all the time.[19]

When she felt called to mission work, Bertha also felt she was to serve the Lord as a single woman. In China, however, there were times of great loneliness, and she struggled as she saw other missionaries with children and families. One day she made a covenant with God. Looking to Him for grace, she prayed for Him to take away her longing for a family and fulfill that by spiritual children as she won others to Christ. It became a privilege for her to have the salvation of others take first place in her heart.

Important to Bertha was the understanding that she had been crucified with Christ, and as she died to self, so she also lived in newness of Christ's resurrected life. Christ living in and through her was her greatest desire. These truths were important for the Shantung Revival of 1927-1937, of which Bertha was a part. The revival strengthened the missionary community and brought many Chinese to faith. Through prayer, repentance and humbling themselves before God, the missionaries renewed their Christian testimony among the Chinese themselves, who they now treated with equality as brothers in Christ.

When wars came to North China, Bertha learned to pray, "'Now, Lord, you are equal to this!' And He always was! ... You may say this is not natural. Whoever thought the Christian life is natural. The Christian life is supernatural.'[20]

After her forced retirement Bertha traveled throughout the world – Australia, Burma, Ghana, India, Indonesia, Israel, Japan, Korea, Lebanon, Nigeria, the Philippines, South America and Zimbabwe – speaking on evangelism and Christian revival. She went to be with her Savior in 1988, five months before her hundredth birthday.

I have been crucified with Christ.
It is no longer I who live, but Christ who lives in me.
And the life I now live in the flesh I live by faith in the Son of God,
who loved me and gave himself for me.

~ GALATIANS 2:20 ~

---

19. Bertha Smith, *How the Holy Spirit Filled My Life* (Nashville: Broadman, 1973), p. 3.
20. Ibid, p. 216.

I'd Rather Have Jesus

❧ Rhea F. Miller, 1894-1966 ❧

Rhea Ross's mother was a pious woman, but her father was an alcoholic with no interest in the things of Christ. Bertha Ross continued faithful to her God and prayed for her husband's salvation. Bertha's prayers, as well as those of other family members and friends, were answered. Martin Ross came to faith in Christ, quit drinking, and eventually became pastor of the Baptist Church of Brooktondale, New York, about eight miles from Ithaca.

It was at church that Rhea Ross met Howard Vassar Miller. After Howard graduated from Colgate University, he and Rhea were married and made their home in Brooktondale. One day, in 1922, Rhea was walking in the meadows around her home and thinking about her father's testimony. He often said he would rather have Jesus than all the gold and silver in the world or all the lands and houses that money could buy. Rhea put these thoughts into a hymn:

I'd rather have Jesus than silver or gold;	I'd rather have Jesus than men's applause;
I'd rather be His than have riches untold;	I'd rather be faithful to His dear cause;
I'd rather have Jesus than houses or land;	I'd rather have Jesus than world-wide fame;
I'd rather be led by His nail-pierced hand:	I'd rather be true to His holy name:
Refrain: Than to be the king of a vast domain	He's fairer than lilies of rarest bloom;
Or be held in sin's dread sway!	He's sweeter than honey from out the comb;
I'd rather have Jesus than anything	He's all my hungering spirit needs –
This world affords today.	I'd rather have Jesus and let Him lead.

Rhea, an accomplished pianist, also wrote music for the hymn, though it's the music by another composer that the hymn is most known by today.

Rhea's husband Howard became a pastor and the Millers lived in Rhode Island, and Connecticut over the next several years. In 1939, Howard became the Dean of Religion at Northwest Nazarene College in Idaho. The same year George Beverly Shea was a twenty-three-year-old young man working in insurance in Ottawa, Canada. George's dad was a Methodist minister and George, who had a great voice, had sung in church services since a youngster. When he was offered an audition for a secular singing position in New York, he recognized this would bring him wider recognition and a bigger income. His mother placed a copy of Rhea Miller's hymn on the piano, hoping to guide her son's decision. When George read the poem, he was moved by its message and set it to music. The words did guide George away from secular fame and into a life of service for Christ as a gospel singer. He began singing in evangelistic meetings, and sang with the Billy Graham Crusade for sixty-six years. 'I'd Rather Have Jesus' became his signature song. He once commented, 'Over the years, I've not sung any song more than "I'd Rather Have Jesus," but I never tire of Mrs Miller's heartfelt words.'[21]

Indeed, I count everything as loss because of the surpassing worth of knowing Christ Jesus my Lord. For his sake I have suffered the loss of all things and count them as rubbish, in order that I may gain Christ and be found in him … .

~ PHILIPPIANS 3:8-9 ~

---

21. Kenneth W. Osbeck, *Amazing Grace: 366 Inspiring Hymn Stories for Daily Devotions* (Grand Rapids, MI: Kregel Publications, 1990).

Shelter for Women

∞ Pandita Ramabai, 1858-1922 ∞

Named after the Indian goddess Rama, Ramabai was born in India in 1858. Her father was a Brahmin priest who instilled a love for learning in his daughter. Ramabai early memorized the Sanskrit puranas and learned the languages of Marathi, Kanarese, Hindustani, and Bengalese. Her family went on pilgrimage across India to the shrines and temples for the numerous Indian gods. When her family fell into poverty and Ramabai's parents died, her faith in the idols of the shrines was shaken. In a youth meeting in Calcutta she heard for the first time about Jesus. That he loved all, regardless of their caste, brought hope to Ramabai. Women had a lowly status in India, but to Christ they had worth and value.

Ramabai married a lawyer, but he died within a year and a half of cholera, leaving Ramabai with an infant daughter. She was reading the Bible in Sanskrit now and began speaking out about the poor plight of Indian women – many of whom were child brides who then were early widowed and left in poverty. Ramabai traveled to both England and America to raise awareness of the condition of women in India. In England she continued her education and was baptized as a member of the Church of England. A group of Christians in Boston raised support for her to found a school to educate child widows in India. During her work in building the school, she came to realize that Christianity was not just a religion and she needed Christ himself. She wrote, 'I had at last come to an end of myself and unconditionally surrendered myself to the Savior; and asked Him to be merciful to me, and to become my righteousness and redemption, and to take away all my sin.'[22] Ramabai expanded her school to provide a home for destitute women and children and called it the Mukti (meaning Salvation) Mission, which still exists today. In the last years of her life she taught herself Greek and Hebrew and translated the Bible into Marathi, completing the work ten days before her death on 5 April, 1922.

> *... that I may gain Christ and be found in him, not having a righteousness of my own that comes from the law, but that which comes through faith in Christ, the righteousness from God that depends on faith ... .*
>
> ~ PHILIPPIANS 3:8-9 ~

---

22. Mark Noll and Carolyn Nystrom, *Clouds of Witnesses: Christian Voices from Africa and Asia* (Downers Grove, IL: Intervarsity Press, 2011), p. 138.

Living in the Love of God

∞ Lydia Vins, 1907-1985 ∞

Peter Vins' marriage proposal to Lydia Zharikova was an unusual one. He told her, 'My life is dedicated to the Lord. If you are willing to die in the mud, the swamps, and the forests of Siberia, then marry me.'[23] Lydia accepted, and the two were married in 1927. Lydia was twenty and Peter twenty-nine.

Lydia was born in Blagoveshchensk, which means 'City of Good News'. Christian revival swept through this area on the Russian-Chinese border during Lydia's youth, and she gave her life to the Lord when twelve years old. When she was fifteen she began teaching Sunday school.

Peter was the son of American missionaries and was born and grew up in Russia. He finished high school in the United States, went to college, and then studied theology. He pastored Russian Baptist churches in Detroit and Pittsburgh, but always longed to return to Russia, for he loved the Russian people. In 1926, he returned to the land of his birth and became pastor of the Baptist Church in Blagoveshchensk.

A year after they were married, Lydia and Peter had a son named Georgi. The communist government was increasingly restricting religion. Sunday schools had been banned, and a struggle against religion was growing. Lydia and Peter considered leaving and going to America, but Peter felt he had been called to minister to and suffer with the Russian people. In 1929, the authorities gave Peter a choice – either leave the country, or surrender his American passport and become a Russian citizen. After much prayer Peter surrendered his passport. Less than a year later he was arrested and then sentenced to three years in labor camps for 'counter-revolutionary activities'.

Lydia and two-year-old Georgi were thrown out of their home. Lydia was not allowed to visit Peter or even correspond with him. Lydia raised her son to follow in his father's footsteps, to know that whatever suffering or pain came his way, Jesus was greater. In 1934, Peter was exiled to Siberia, and the family was reunited for a time. But in 1937, Peter was arrested the third and final time.

Lydia always sought to share the love and care of Christ with others and formed the Council for Prisoners Relatives to help other women in the persecuted church. She traveled around to churches and started Bible studies for women. In 1967, Lydia learned Peter had died years before in Siberia. Actually, he had been executed in 1937, but that fact was not disclosed until records were released in 1995.

In 1970, when she was sixty-three, the police arrested Lydia and imprisoned her for three years. Even in prison she continued to speak of the love of Jesus to all around her. Her son Georgi was arrested for printing Bibles the next year. In 1979, Georgi and his family, including Lydia, were expelled from the Soviet Union. Lydia continued to speak to Christians in Europe and America about the persecuted Christians, challenging them to pray for their persecuted brethren and have an uncompromising faith in their Savior.

Who shall separate us from the love of Christ? Shall tribulation, or distress, or persecution, or famine, or nakedness, or danger, or sword?... For I am sure that neither death nor life, nor angels nor rulers, nor things present nor things to come, nor powers, nor height nor depth, nor anything else in all creation, will be able to separate us from the love of God in Christ Jesus our Lord.

~ ROMANS 8:35, 38-39 ~

---

23. Barbara Hitching, 'Valiant in Life and Death', *Moody Monthly*, November 1985, p. 62.

Joy to the World

When Robert C. McQuilkin spoke to Joy Ridderhof's church in Los Angeles, he called worry a sin and encouraged the people to rejoice as they trusted God. McQuilkin told Joy he was opening a Bible College in Columbia, South Carolina. Joy wanted to enroll, but it seemed impossible. McQuilkin encouraged her and told her the Lord would guide her. Joy prayed and asked the Lord that if He wanted her in Columbia, He would pay her fare. Shortly afterward, Joy's married sister in Minneapolis asked Joy to come and help her a few weeks; she would pay her way. Joy realized that the cost to her sister would be the same if she returned to Los Angeles or Columbia – God had indeed provided her way to Columbia Bible School (today's Columbia International University)!

Joy was in the first class of three students at the school and graduated in 1925. Throughout her time in school she learned to trust God for all her needs, praying for Him to provide, as He always did. After graduation, Joy went to Honduras, where she worked in the village of Marcala. Her habit of trusting God at all times was strengthened, as at times she was threatened by unbelievers, and often food supplies were short. After five years in Honduras, Joy was very ill after bouts with the flu, malaria, and smallpox and had to return to the United States.

It seemed as if Joy's missionary career was over, but she again trusted God, remembering Paul's repeated Scriptural commands to 'rejoice'. Wanting to encourage the believers she had left behind in Honduras, Joy recorded some gospel messages, Scriptures, and songs to send to them. The recordings were so well received that Joy began making more Spanish recordings, using native speakers, which could be used throughout Latin America. She was then enlisted to make some Navajo recordings. This spurred the formation of Gospel Recordings in 1939.

Today the organization is called Global Recordings Network. With hand-operated record players, recordings make the Word of God available to illiterate people in Africa, South America, Asia, Australia, and Central America. With centers and bases in over thirty countries, Global Recordings Network now provides recordings of Scripture readings in over 4,000 languages. The recordings can be listened to under a tree, in a medical clinic, a school, or in the market place. Though Joy had to leave Honduras from illness, she found the Lord had opened up for her a ministry to the peoples of the world.

How then will they call on him in whom they have not believed? ... And how are they to hear without someone preaching?... So faith comes from hearing, and hearing through the word of Christ.

~ ROMANS 10:14, 17 ~

NOVEMBER 5

Model of Good Works

⚭ Althea Brown Edmiston, 1874-1937 ⚭

Althea's parents, Robert and Mary Brown, were born in slavery, though she was born in freedom in 1874 in Alabama. The Browns were industrious and enterprising, raising ten children on a family farm they purchased in Mississippi. Though not having any formal schooling himself, Robert taught his children to read and encouraged their education. Seven of the children, including Althea, went to college. Althea learned many agricultural techniques working on the family farm. When she was ten she began caring for the sick in neighboring families.

When Althea began attending Fisk University in 1892, she feared her rural, unsophisticated ways would not be at home in the university. Yet she graduated with highest honors in 1901, and delivered the valedictory address. During her time at the university Althea earned money by selling home-made fudge, running a beauty shop in her dorm room, and working as a domestic for various faculty members. A few months after entering Fisk, Althea was brought to faith in Christ, and she determined to use her education to help others. Shortly after graduation she was commissioned by the Foreign Missions of the Presbyterian Church to be a missionary in Africa's Congo Free State. Althea left for the Congo on 20 August, 1902, expecting never to see her family again.

Althea began work in Ibanche, deep in the African continent, where Dr William Sheppard, another African-American, had co-founded a mission. Althea worked as a mistress in the day school, a Sunday school teacher, and a matron of the Maria Carey Home for Girls. She also organized the women's work. During an uprising against the Congo government in November 1904, the rebels ordered all white inhabitants to be burned, and their leader demanded the heads of missionaries be delivered to him. A runner brought a blood-covered branch to Ibanche saying that it was the blood of a murdered Christian. Fighting could be heard around the village. Althea thought she would be killed that night. After another fearful night, Congolese soldiers came to march the women and children to Luebo to safety. Althea survived the gruesome march.

On 8 July, 1905 Althea married Alonzo Edmiston, a fellow American who had come to support the missionaries in scientific farming. The couple had two sons and continued to work in the Congo missions. The Bakuba people had no written language, so Althea developed a written language for the Bakuba and wrote a grammar and dictionary. In addition, she translated school books and hymns for the Bakuba. When Althea died in 1937 there was an outpouring of respect and love for her, and over two thousand attended her funeral in Mutoto.

Show yourself in all respects to be a model of good works,
and in your teaching show integrity, dignity, and sound speech
that cannot be condemned … .

~ Titus 2:7-8 ~

NOVEMBER 6

Beloved Disciple

∞ Gertrude Hobbs Chambers, 1884-1966 ∞

Gertrude Hobbs met Oswald Chambers briefly during Christmas of 1905, when Chambers led a mission at Eltham Park Baptist Church in East London. But the two became better acquainted the summer of 1908 on the SS *Baltic's* voyage from Liverpool to New York. Gertrude had a job in New York as a stenographer, and Oswald was leading a series of summer camps in Ohio.

The two enjoyed eating and walking around the ship together. Gertrude admired Oswald's sharp mind, sense of humor, and deep love for Jesus Christ. Oswald admired Gertrude's determination and caring interest in people. Oswald's sister was also named Gertrude, so he developed a nickname for Miss Hobbs to keep the Gertrudes separate in his mind. Miss Hobbs would be the Beloved Disciple, which Oswald shortened to B. D., which became Biddy, the name by which everyone later knew her.

After landing in New York the pair went their separate ways but kept in touch by correspondence. Oswald returned to England at the end of the summer; Biddy didn't return until November. Oswald was busy leading meetings, preaching, and teaching with the League of Prayer, and Biddy shared his passion for serving Christ. Oswald wrote to Biddy, 'I have nothing to offer you but my love and steady lavish service for Him.'[24] They pledged their love to each other and became engaged in front of Holman Hunt's painting of Jesus, *The Light of the World*, in St. Paul's Cathedral. It was a way of also pledging their love to Jesus and the dedication of their lives to bringing the light of the gospel to a dark world. Oswald and Biddy were married 25 May, 1910.

Together they established the Bible Training College in Clapham Common. While Oswald taught, Biddy exercised her gift of hospitality to the students and the numerous missionaries and preachers passing through. Daughter Kathleen brought joy to all when she arrived in 1913. When World War I began Oswald was accepted as a YMCA chaplain and assigned to Cairo, Egypt. He left in August 1914, with Biddy and Kathleen arriving two months later. The Chambers were a great encouragement to the soldiers. Biddy had tea for the soldiers every Sunday, and often 700 soldiers were in attendance. Oswald's preaching brought them spiritual nourishment, and Biddy used her shorthand skills to take notes on all his sermons.

In the fall of 1917, Oswald became ill and died on 15 November during surgery for a ruptured appendix. Biddy sent home the telegram 'Oswald, In His Presence'. He was buried with full military honors in the British cemetery in Cairo.

In the following months Biddy continued her hospitality to the soldiers and began transcribing her shorthand notes of Oswald's sermons. Soon the YMCA was sending out 10,000 copies of Oswald's messages each month. When the last soldier left Egypt, in June 1919, Biddy and Kathleen returned home. Biddy continued to provide Oswald's sermons to the public. In 1927, she compiled key portions into the devotional *My Utmost for His Highest*, which continues to be widely read to this day.

> *Let brotherly love continue.*
> *Do not neglect to show hospitality to strangers,*
> *for thereby some have entertained angels unawares.*
>
> ~ HEBREWS 13:1-2 ~

---

24. David McCasland, *Oswald Chambers: abandoned to God* (Nashville, TN: Thomas Nelson Publishers, 1993).

Teacher

∽ Henrietta Mears, 1890-1963 ∾

When Henrietta Mears was a child she had extreme myopia, and a doctor told her mother Henrietta would be blind by the time she was thirty. Decades later, when wearing thick glasses but not blind, Henrietta remarked that her failing eyesight had been a great spiritual asset, for it kept her absolutely dependent on God.

Both of Henrietta's grandfathers had been ministers, and her parents provided a solid Christian home for her and her six older siblings. Henrietta attended the University of Minnesota, graduating with high honors and a degree in chemistry. While at the University, she began a Bible study and prayer time in her room which soon had sixty women attending. In the ensuing fifteen years Henrietta taught in various schools in Minnesota; wherever she went, she also taught a vibrant Sunday school class in her church. Her life took a totally new direction when, in 1928, Dr Stewart McLennan invited Henrietta to be the Director of Christian Education at Hollywood Presbyterian Church. Henrietta and her older sister Margaret made the move to Los Angeles. Margaret was always Henrietta's best friend and managed the house while Henrietta worked in Christian education.

When Henrietta arrived at Hollywood Presbyterian the Sunday school attendance was 400; within three years it had grown to 4,000. Henrietta reviewed all the Sunday school material then used and was appalled at the lack of Biblical truth in the lessons. When she read in one lesson that Paul survived shipwreck because he had eaten carrots and was strong, she sent all the material back and began writing the lessons herself. She designed a curriculum so that students from age two through high school would go through the Bible four times. From her experience teaching school, Henrietta realized the need for graded lessons to fit the abilities of each age group. When others began requesting copies of the lessons, Henrietta began Gospel Light Press in 1933, which became the first publisher of closely-graded Bible lessons. Within the year, 13,366 copies were sold to 131 Sunday Schools in thirty-five states; by 1937 more than a quarter-million books had been sold.

Henrietta soon began lecturing on Christian Education across America to tens of thousands of people and became co-founder of the National Sunday School Association. She emphasized that the goal of Sunday school was not just to lead the young to faith, but to train them to serve the Master. Henrietta herself taught the College Department, showing a personal interest in the students and training many young people for Christian ministry, including Bill Bright, founder of Campus Crusade, and Richard Halverson, later chaplain of the U.S. Senate. She taught the Scriptures and trained the collegians to witness in jails, in hospitals, and in their colleges. In 1938, Henrietta founded Forest Home Christian Conference Grounds, where many would come for spiritual nourishment and refreshment in a beautiful setting of God's creation. Her Bible handbook, *What the Bible is All About*, has sold over four million copies.

While an indefatigable worker, Henrietta daily spent time alone with the Lord in prayer and Bible study. She died quietly in her sleep in 1963, slipping through the veil between the present and hereafter she had described over the years as being very thin. Someone remarked, 'It was nothing new for her to meet her Lord alone, for she had often done so. This time she just went with Him.'[25]

I can do all things through him who strengthens me.

~ PHILIPPIANS 4:13 ~

---

25. Earl O. Roe, ed., *Dream Big: The Henrietta Mears Story* (Ventura, California: Regal Books, 1990), p. 334.

Door of Hope

∞ Emma Whittemore, d. 1931 ∞

Emma and Sidney Whittemore were part of the wealthy social elite in New York during the Gilded Age. Regular church-goers, their lives were prosperous, peaceful, and happy. One day, a friend of Emma's invited her to come to hear an evangelist speak at the YMCA. Unknown to Emma, Sidney also attended the meeting. Both were deeply moved by the gospel presentation and resolved to live lives more committed to Christ.

Emma's friend later invited her to hear Jerry McAuley, a former drunkard and ex-convict who had opened a rescue mission in a former dance hall on Water Street, the first rescue mission in the United States. Sidney did not think Emma should attend the meeting, but he finally agreed to go with her one night. Emma had never seen such scenes as she witnessed that night – curses, street fights, women being dragged off to the police station. There was a stench in the hall from the impoverished people there. Jerry McAuley was at the front, hollering in a rough voice. Gradually, however, both Emma and Sidney were convicted by the words of the rough preacher, and they sensed the uselessness of their own lives. When several of the poor people in the crowd stood up and gave their testimonies of being transformed by Christ, Sidney stood up with tears streaming down his face and asked for prayer. Sidney and Emma both came forward at the end of the service to kneel in prayer with tramps, thieves, and drunkards. They desired to live their lives for God's glory and praise.

When Emma prayed for God to show her what she should do with her life, she felt that she should help the girls who had fallen into prostitution. Though she cringed at the thought of working with the unclean tramps she had seen on the streets, the love of God compelled her to seek to rescue them from their lives of sin. Emma's heart was often broken at the terrible sights she saw on her evening walks, and she prayed for God to give her strength for His service.

Minister A. B. Simpson owned a house he gave to Emma for use in providing a home to the rescued girls. On 25 October, 1890, Emma opened the Door of Hope. She never asked for funds but relied upon the Lord's leading others to give in the work. In the first four years, Door of Hope provided help and sustenance for 325 girls. Emma realized that showing the girls the power of Christ was most important. You could remove the girls from their sinful environment, but only Jesus could get the sin out of the girls. Once converted to Christ, Emma worked to train the girls to evangelize and rescue others who had fallen into prostitution.

At the time of Emma's death, in 1931, there were ninety-seven Door of Hope homes in the United States, Canada, Great Britain, Africa, Japan, and China. The love of Christ had not only transformed Emma, but many around the globe came to know the Door of Hope that is in Jesus.

Jesus again said to them, 'Truly, truly, I say to you,
I am the door of the sheep. … If anyone enters by me, he will be saved
and will go in and out and find pasture.
The thief comes only to steal and kill and destroy.
I came that they may have life and have it abundantly.'

~ JOHN 10:7, 9-10 ~

Calvary Covers it All

⚭ Ethel Taylor, 1934 ⚭

Walter and Ethelwyn Taylor were known as 'Pa' and 'Ma' to the men of Chicago's Pacific Garden Mission, which they had directed since 1918. The couple had served as missionaries to railroad men and miners in Colorado and had spent sixteen years in the Old Brewery Mission in Montreal before returning to Pacific Garden Mission, where Walter had volunteered while attending Moody Bible Institute.

The Taylors were at the Mission in 1923, when it moved to South State Street, to an area known as 'Murderer's Row' because of the many murders committed in the region. In the midst of immorality and crime, the Mission offered food, overnight accommodations, and the gospel to all who came. 'Pa' Taylor preached the gospel and forgiveness through Jesus Christ; 'Ma' prayed for the men and played the piano during the invitation.

In 1934, Walter MacDonald, a vaudeville dancer known as 'Happy Mac', came several nights in a row to the mission. He never responded to the gospel, but he kept coming back. Ethel prayed that his heart would be opened to the Truth and they would be able to say the right things to him. One evening, Happy Mac opened up, and when he prayed told the Lord he was the worst man in the world and just too bad for the Lord to save him. Ethel remembered a message she had heard a few weeks before; the evangelist Percy Crawford's theme was 'Calvary covers it all'. When Ethel asked Happy Mac to repeat those words, the light dawned in his face. He was so thankful that Calvary did cover it all – his whole past of sin and shame.

A few days later, with Happy Mac's words echoing in her mind, Ethel wrote the words and music for the beloved gospel song on the atonement of Christ:

> Far dearer than all that the world can impart
> Was the message that came to my heart;
> How that Jesus alone for my sin did atone,
> And Calvary covers it all.
>
> *Chorus:* Calvary covers it all,
> My past with its sin and stain;
> My guilt and despair
> Jesus took on Him there,
> And Calvary covers it all.
>
> The stripes that He bore and the thorns that He wore
> Told His mercy and love evermore;
> And my heart bowed in shame as I called on His name,
> And Calvary covers it all.
>
> How matchless the grace, when I looked in the face
> Of this Jesus, my crucified Lord;
> My redemption complete I then found at His feet,
> And Calvary covers it all.
>
> How blessed the thought, that my soul by Him bought,
> Shall be His in glory on high;
> Where with gladness and song,
> I'll be one of the throng
> And Calvary covers it all.

Blessed is the one whose transgression is forgiven, whose sin is covered.

~ PSALM 32:1 ~

May God be Glorified, by Life or Death

∽ Betty Stam, 1906-1934 ∽

A descendant of Pilgrims who came to America on the *Mayflower*, Betty Stam was born in Albion, Michigan on 22 February, 1906, and grew up in China, the daughter of missionaries. While attending Wilson College in Pennsylvania Betty prayed to God, 'If it is Your will, please allow me to return to China without any obstacle.' While attending the Keswick Convention in England in 1925, Betty was particularly affected by Philippians 1:21, 'For me to live is Christ and to die is gain.' In preparation for the mission field Betty attended Moody Bible Institute, where she met John Stams at a Monday evening missions prayer service. Both hoped to go to China with China Inland Missions (CIM).

John and Betty were married on 25 October, 1933, at Betty's parents' mission station at Jinan, Shandong, with over two hundred missionaries in attendance along with over one hundred and forty Chinese Christians. After a honeymoon in Qingdao, where Betty had lived as a child, the couple was assigned to the mission station at Jingde.

China was in the throes of a civil war, but both Betty and John had peace they were in the Lord's will. Betty wrote,

> When we consecrate ourselves to God, we think we are making a great sacrifice, and doing lots for Him, when really we are only letting go some little bitsie trinkets we have been grabbing, and when our hands are empty, He fills them full of His treasures.[26]

Among the treasures placed in the Stams hands was little Helen Priscilla, born in the fall of 1934.

On 7 December, a city official came to the Stams' home and warned them the Communists were taking over the city. As the Stams gathered some of their effects together and prepared to flee they had a moment of prayer, when the Communists burst into the room. They took all the Stams' money and took them away, eventually to Miaosheo. Terror reigned throughout the region. On the morning of 8 December the Stams were marched out to a hillside and beheaded. Betty had left baby Helen behind in a sleeping bag at their overnight stop, undoubtedly praying for her protection. Mr Lo, an evangelist who had worked with the Stams, found the baby two days later and was able to bring her to Betty's parents. In a burial service for the Stams, Mr Lo said,

> You have witnessed what took place here today, and feel pity for what has happened to our friends. You should know, however, that they are children of God, and their souls are already at rest in the bosom of their heavenly Father. It was for you that they came to China ... in order to tell you about God's great love and the grace of the Lord Jesus Christ, so that you might believe in Jesus and gain eternal life. You have already heard the message they preached, and have seen their sacrifice, which is certain evidence [of their love]. Do not forget what they said: that you must repent and believe the Gospel![27]

The deaths of John and Betty Stam shocked the Christian world in Europe and America. Their example encouraged many others to consecrate themselves to missionary work in China.

> 'Unless a grain of wheat falls into the earth and dies, it remains alone;
> but if it dies, it bears much fruit. Whoever loves his life loses it,
> and whoever hates his life in this world will keep it for eternal life.'
>
> ~ JOHN 12:24-25 ~

26. 'Betty and John Stam Martyred', Church History Timeline, http://www.christianity.com/church/church-history/timeline/1901-2000/betty-and-john-stam-martyred-11630759.html.

27. 'Betty Stam', *Biographical Dictionary of Chinese Christianity*, www.bdcconline.net/en.

Giving the Words of Life

∽ Helen Watkins, b. 1904 – d. 1990s ∽

Helen Watkins grew up in the El Cajon and Ramona areas of California and was graduated from San Diego State University in 1926. She enlisted with Sudan Interior Mission and served in western Africa over forty years, retiring from the field in 1979. Helen's life was filled with danger, strain, and intrigue. The people in northern Nigeria where Helen worked were largely illiterate. Most were Muslim and in need of the gospel; many were held in fear of demons and evil spirits. One night Helen was chased through a village by a pagan spirit man, before being rescued by a sympathetic chieftain. She and her helper, Ruth Warfield, who worked with Helen, beginning in 1939, persuaded the men of the Kagoro tribe to stop beating their wives. One man, however, wasn't sure if he liked Christianity, since he no longer had a way to free himself of his frustrations!

In 1948, Helen returned to the United States with some unusual symptoms in her hands and feet. The doctor diagnosed leprosy, but Helen refused to accept the diagnosis and returned to Africa to work. As her symptoms worsened, she had to concede that she indeed had leprosy and began receiving treatment, including surgery to her hands and feet to maintain their function.

Helen was an excellent linguist and became a specialist in the Hausa language, the language prominent in northern Nigeria. Hausa is a tonal language, which means words can have different meanings depending on the tone with which they are pronounced. Helen was a linguistic trainer for the missionaries, teaching them the language and regularly testing their proficiency. She worked closely with native speakers in helping with the translation of the Hausa Bible, being one of the final reviewers before the Bible was approved. Even when she returned to the United States she continued perfecting the translation work.

When she was eighty-three Helen, together with Ruth Warfield (then seventy-seven), returned to Africa for a three-month visit. Their heart was very much with the people of Africa. In America they found materialism suffocated the spiritual life. In Africa they distributed a new edition of the four Gospels for the Hausa people, giving them the gift of the words of Life.

'Heaven and earth will pass away,
but my words will not pass away.'
~ MATTHEW 24:35 ~

His Eye is on the Sparrow

∽ Ethel Waters, 1896-1977 ∽

Ethel Waters, born 31 October, 1896, in Chester, Pennsylvania, did not have a promising beginning. She was conceived when her mother was raped at the age of twelve. Her mother, a child herself, sent Ethel to first one relative and then another, and Ethel never lived in one place for long. For a time she attended the Baptist church in the neighborhood, and at twelve believed in Jesus as her Savior. However, when a teenager in the church treated her wrongfully because she was black, Ethel left the church and never went back.

When she was thirteen, Ethel married, but her husband was abusive, and she soon left him. She became a maid in a Philadelphia hotel, singing songs and performing before the mirrors as she cleaned them. At a party when she was seventeen she was persuaded to sing two songs, and was offered work in a theater in Baltimore. Ethel sang on the black vaudeville circuit then joined a carnival, where she enjoyed the loyalty and friendship of the performers. In the 1920s, Ethel moved to Harlem and became a leading performer in the renaissance of black musicians there. Ethel's career as a performer truly took off, as she went on to perform on Broadway and in movies. She married again, but this marriage too was a failure. Though she now had material success and fame, Ethel's life was empty. She gained a tremendous amount of weight (she weighed 380 pounds) as she ate herself out of her sorrows.

In 1957, Billy Graham held a series of evangelistic meetings in Madison Square Garden. Ethel attended one night and felt like she had found something; she attended every meeting for the next sixteen weeks and recommitted her life to her Savior. Jesus became the center of her life, and she began to see everything in relation to Him. The newspapers said Ethel had become religious, but she disagreed, saying, 'I'm not religious. I'm a born-again Christian! That's the most important thing in my life, because I've found my living Savior!'[28] Knowing her Savior brought Ethel the peace and freedom her fame and wealth could never bring her. She felt like the prodigal son, and she now wanted to live her life completely for Jesus. She could no longer sing blues, for the Savior had put sunshine in her life. Ethel left the theater and began traveling, putting on Christian concerts. She sang for Presidents and dignitaries, but the highest dignitary was her Lord and Savior.

The song which became her signature song was, 'His eye is on the Sparrow', which expressed so well Ethel's own assurance of Jesus' love and care:

> Why should I feel discouraged, why should the shadows come,
> Why should my heart be lonely, and long for heav'n and home,
> When Jesus is my portion? My constant Friend is He:
> His eye is on the sparrow, and I know He watches me
>
> I sing because I'm happy, I sing because I'm free.
> For His eye is on the sparrow, and I know He watches me.

'Are not two sparrows sold for a penny? And not one of them will fall to the ground apart from your Father. ... Fear not, therefore, you are of more value than many sparrows.'

~ MATTHEW 10:29, 31 ~

---

28. Juliann DeKorte, *Ethel Waters – Finally Home* (Old Tappan, New Jersey: Fleming H. Revell Co., 1978), p. 74.

Queen of Tonga

∞ Salote Tupou III, 1900-1965 ∞

Salote became queen of Tonga in 1918, when she was only eighteen. Her forty-seven year reign was a period of peace and development for the small Polynesian nation, an archipelago of 177 islands in the Pacific. The Dutch had first visited the islands in the seventeenth century. James Cook stopped on several of his voyages with the British Royal Navy in the eighteenth century. The London Missionary Society sent missionaries in 1797, and the Wesleyan Methodists came to the islands in the early nineteenth century. Salote's great-grandfather was baptized by the Methodists in 1831 and worked to unite the islands into one government. He established a constitutional monarchy with laws shaped by Christian morals.

By the time of Salote's reign, the Tongans were sending missionaries to the Solomon and Papuan Islands. One of the events Salote loved to preside over was the *Misinala*, an annual occasion when people in the villages brought together their savings for missions and had a service of dedication and worship, accompanied by feasting and drama. The year Salote became queen was also the year of the world-wide flu pandemic, which killed 1,800 Tongans. Salote established the Department of Health to encourage better health practices in Tonga. She also encouraged free and compulsory education. By the end of her reign literacy flourished everywhere on the islands.

Salote had a gift for administration and she was noted for her intelligence and wisdom. In September 1917, she married a high-ranking chief, Utliami Tupoulahi Tungi Mailefihi, whom she appointed as her premier. The couple had three sons, one of whom succeeded Salote as ruler upon her death in 1965.

Salote's faith was woven throughout her life. She encouraged Bible study networks and prayers in the churches, especially encouraging chieftains to become lay preachers and trustees of the village churches. She recognized Christianity's importance in elevating the status of the wife in Tongan society. Always working for the peace and unity of the Tongan people, Salote prayed:

> God, our Heavenly Father, we draw near to thee with thankful hearts because of all thy great love for us. We thank thee most of all for the gift of thy dear Son, in whom alone, we may be one. We are different from one another in race and language, in material things, in gifts, in opportunities, but each of us has a human heart, knowing joy and sorrow, pleasure and pain. We are one in our need of thy forgiveness, thy strength, thy love; make us one in our common response to thee, that bound by a common love and freed from selfish aims, we may work for the good of all and the advancement of thy Kingdom.[29]

> *Blessed be the name of God for ever and ever, to whom belong*
> *wisdom and might. He changes times and seasons; he removes*
> *kings and sets up kings; he gives wisdom to the wise and*
> *knowledge to those who have understanding.*
>
> ~ DANIEL 2:20-21 ~

---

29. Dorothy M. Stewart, ed., *The Westminster Collection of Christian Prayers* (Louisville, Kentucky: John Knox Press), p. 36.

Jubilee for Women's Missionary Movement

⌐ 1910-1911 ⌐

As Lucy Peabody read a draft of Helen Montgomery's *Western Women in Eastern Lands*, she had an idea. Helen Montgomery's book summarized the fifty years of the women's missionary movement in the United States, and Lucy thought they should have a Jubilee celebration.

The women's missionary movement was the largest women's movement in America, boasting a membership of at least two million women – more than the General Federation of Women's Clubs, the National Woman's Suffrage Association, or the Woman's Christian Temperance Union. With Lucy's suggestion, Helen added an invitation for a Jubilee celebration to conclude *Western Women in Eastern Lands*. The book sold 50,000 copies within six weeks, and sales eventually reached 132,000 copies; the readers quickly embraced the idea of a Jubilee. Teas, luncheons, and missionary festivals were organized throughout the country. A group of speakers were chosen, headed by Helen Montgomery and including Dr Mary Riggs Noble, a Presbyterian doctor who served as a missionary in India; Kate Boggs Schaffer, a Lutheran missionary in India; and Jennie Hughes, a Methodist missionary in China.

The tour began on 12 October, 1910, in Oakland, California and included thirty-three cities, with smaller celebrations across the land. Meetings included general sessions for all as well as smaller denominational meetings. By the time the celebration reached the East coast, attendance was quite large. The Jubilee luncheon in Pittsburgh had 4,800 in attendance. President Taft had a reception for the Jubilee speakers at the White House, where Helen presented him with a leather-bound, autographed copy of *Western Women in Eastern Lands*.

The grand finale, in 1911, was in New York City, where 6,000 women, including some of the most notable in the city, attended the luncheon. Events were held at the Metropolitan Opera House, the Astor, Waldorf-Astoria and Plaza Hotels, and Carnegie Hall, as well as several churches. At the Met a 'Pageant of Missions' was performed with more than a thousand actors and a sixty-six piece orchestra. Helen gave the closing address in Carnegie Hall to an overflow crowd. She saw the missionary movement as important to the freedom and dignity of women, removing the oppression under which they lived in many cultures. Christ was drawing a redeemed humanity to Himself and providing opportunities for women to minister to other women across the globe.

By the end of the Jubilee year the women had collected over $3 million for world missions, which went to the support of 2,000 missionaries and 3,000 schools.

Their voice goes out through all the earth,
and their words to the end of the world.

~ PSALM 19:4 ~

NOVEMBER 15

World Tour for Missions

∞ Helen Montgomery and Lucy Peabody, 1914 ∞

Helen Montgomery and Lucy Peabody were good friends and leaders of the women's missionary movement in the United States. They had worked together in organizing the International Jubilee of Missions in 1910, with its coast-to coast speaking tour, in which Helen challenged the 'privileged educated woman of leisure to form a great sisterhood of service and league of love'. Lucy noted that missionaries brought an alternative to the militarism, oppression, and violence in the world by providing 'arrangements for the care of mothers, for the upbringing of children, for the kindly progress of the community under the influence of Christ'.[30]

After the 1910 World Missionary Conference in Edinburgh, John Mott formed a Continuation Committee to encourage native evangelism among non-Christian lands. In November, 1913, the Edinburgh Continuation Committee was to meet in the Hague. Lucy Peabody, a member of the Committee, and Helen Montgomery, decided to make the meeting the beginning of a world tour examining the condition of missions. Their college age daughters accompanied them.

At The Hague meeting, the ladies were graciously received by Queen Wilhelmena, who had a luncheon for all the delegates. In a thoughtful address the Queen told the delegates,

> It is my desire that the unity of all Christ's followers, members of his invisible fellowship, may be deeply felt, and that our Savior may stir our hearts to more and more fervent prayer.
>
> May our zeal be roused and hollowed, and may all the labourers in God's vineyard be fitted for the tasks to which we are personally called. May the truth which is in Christ enlighten the darkness of human misery, and may the unsearchable riches of His Divine Love awaken joy and gladness in the hearts of all God's creatures.[31]

After the meeting in The Hague, Helen, Lucy, and their daughters traveled for six months from London to Tokyo, visiting key missionaries along the way. They visited Egypt, went through the Suez Canal on their way to India, then visited Burma, China, Korea, Japan, and Hawaii before reaching San Francisco. They noted the degradation of women in many of the countries, especially Egypt and India, and the lack of education afforded to women in all the lands. In India they saw girls who were grandmothers at twenty-five, numerous child-mothers, and many girls in temple prostitution. They also noted the happy childhood many found in the Christian mission schools and the lovely ladies whose lives were uplifted by the gospel of Christ.

After their worldwide tour, Helen and Lucy raised funds for seven girls' schools in India, China, and Japan. Helen's book, *The King's Highway*, with a title taken from Isaiah 35, eloquently described their journey and the lessons from their travels.

> *And a highway shall be there, and it shall be called the Way of Holiness ...*
> *the redeemed shall walk there. And the ransomed of the LORD shall return*
> *and come to Zion with singing; everlasting joy shall be upon their heads;*
> *they shall obtain gladness and joy, and sorrow and sighing shall flee away.*

~ ISAIAH 35:8-10 ~

---

30. William H. Brackney, 'The Legacy of Helen B. Montgomery and Lucy W. Peabody'. *International Bulletin of Missionary Research*, October 1991, p. 175.

31. Helen Montgomery, *The King's Highway* (West Medford. MA: Central Committee of the United Study of Foreign Missions, 1915), pp. 11-12.

Keeping the Faith

Ꮳ Eliza Davis George, 1879-1980 Ꮳ

Eliza Davis' parents had been born slaves, but by the time of Eliza's birth they were enjoying the freedom of emancipation and were sharecroppers in east Texas. Raised in a Baptist Church, Eliza came to faith in Christ at a revival meeting when she was sixteen. As she heard the preacher's sermon on John 3:16 her heart was opened and she believed in Jesus. Great joy flooded her soul, and immediately she wanted to do something for Jesus – but she didn't know what the 'something' might be.

Eliza earned a teaching certificate from Central Texas College and then joined the faculty. At a college prayer meeting in 1911, Eliza was filled with a distinct desire to go to Africa. The president of the College and the board president of Texas Baptist Missions Convention both tried to discourage Eliza from going to Africa. Eliza waited two more years, developing a life of prayer for the lost souls in Africa. Though the local Baptists were not interested in sending a black single woman as a missionary to Africa, Eliza was successful in achieving support from the National Baptist Convention. With six other missionaries she arrived in Monrovia, Liberia on 20 January, 1914.

Eliza and another missionary opened a Bible Industrial Academy in Liberia's interior where they taught children to read the Bible as well as life skills. By the end of two years there were fifty children attending the Academy. Eliza also went to the surrounding villages evangelizing, teaching, and planting churches. She trained native Liberians to take the Word of God to their own people and educate their children. When support from the mission board waned, Dr Charles George, a native of British Guyana, proposed marriage, hinting that his support would allow her to stay in Africa. After prayer, Eliza accepted Dr George's proposal, and the two were married in 1919. They adopted three children together.

When Dr George died, in 1939, supporters of Eliza organized Eliza George Clubs in the United States to continue supporting her work in Africa. By the 1960s, there were twenty-seven churches as part of the Eliza George Baptist Association. Eliza continued her work for the Lord in Africa until she was in her nineties. Twice the Liberian President honored Eliza for her service to the Liberian people. Though almost blind and suffering from a large tropical cancer on her leg, she continued to tell others of Jesus and his love for them. Finally, when she was 92, ill health forced Eliza to return to Texas, where she died at the age of 100.

I have fought the good fight, I have finished the race, I have kept the faith.
Henceforth there is laid up for me the crown of righteousness,
which the Lord, the righteous judge, will award to me on that Day,
and not only to me but also to all who have loved his appearing.

~ 2 TIMOTHY 4:7-8 ~

Nile Mother

∽ Lillian Trasher, 1887-1961 ∽

One day, walking in the woods near her Georgia home, little Lillian Trasher knelt by a log, as if it was an altar, and prayed to the Lord, 'I want to be your little girl.' As she continued in prayer, she said, 'Lord, if ever I can do anything for You, just let me know and – and I'll do it!'[32] At sixteen, Lillian's family moved to Ashville, North Carolina. Lillian met Mattie Perry and worked for a time in the orphanage she had founded in Marion, North Carolina. Lillian learned to feed and clothe the children and gained an appreciation of how to operate a faith-based mission.

Pastor G. S. Brelsford invited Lillian to join him and his wife in their work in Assiout, Egypt, 230 miles south of Cairo. Lillian sailed for Egypt in 1910. Some months after her arrival, on 10 February, 1911, a man came to the mission seeking someone to visit a dying woman nearby. Lillian and an older woman went to see the woman, who died soon after they arrived, leaving behind a malnourished baby girl. When the Arabic translator said the grandmother planned to throw the baby into the Nile, Lillian offered to take the child and care for her as her own. So began the Assiout Orphanage. By 1918, the orphanage cared for fifty children and eight widows. By the time of Lillian's death fifty years later, 1,200 children were being cared for and thousands who had been cared for by the orphanage over the years were living lives for Christ.

For many years Lillian traveled throughout the surrounding villages on a donkey, asking for money to support the orphanage. She became well acquainted with many in the villages, who appreciated the care and love she bestowed on the poorest of the Egyptian children. Lillian could give many accounts of times she turned to the Lord to provide provisions for the orphans, and supplies came through in unexpected ways. During World War II, the fighting cut off shipping, and the mail which brought funds from abroad could not get through. The children's clothing was in tatters, bath towels and bed sheets were full of holes, and Lillian had to ration food for the children. She told the children to 'pray as long and as hard as the Lord puts it on them. We have nothing. The need is very great indeed, but our God is greater. "Ask and it shall be given."'[33] Lillian soon received an urgent message to come to Cairo and meet the American ambassador. When she arrived in Cairo, she was told a Red Cross ship loaded with relief supplies for Greece had been turned back and came to Alexandria. The cargo included clothing for men, women, children, and babies, towels, bedding and kegs of powdered milk, sacks of rice, flour, and beans. The ambassador asked if she could use these supplies. With these, all the children would have new clothes, sleep in fresh beds, have ample food, and witness the answer to their prayers.

The Lord is my shepherd; I shall not want.
He makes me lie down in green pastures.

~ PSALM 23:1-2 ~

---

32. Beth Prim Howell, *Lady on a Donkey* (New York: E. P. Dutton and Company, 1960), p. 22.

33. 'Orphanage celebrates 100 Years', *Assemblies of God World Missions*, http://worldmissions.ag.org/regions/eurasia/__.cfm?targetbay=4bab7a5e-cb12-48a0-8788-486b7cfbbfb7&modid=2&process=displayarticle&rss_rsscontentid=18467&rss_originatingchannelid=1164&rss_originatingrssfeedid=3689&rss_source=.

Comforting the Persecuted

∞ Mary Graffam, 1872-1921 ∞

Missionaries in Turkey were the first to open schools for girls, and by the early twentieth century thousands of young girls were receiving an education in the missionary schools. Mary Graffam, principal of the Girls' School at Sivas, was also head of the Industrial Work for Women and Girls. There girls and young women were taught sewing and other skills which could be marketed and which could aid in their support.

When war between Russia and Turkey raged on the eastern border in 1914, Mary volunteered to help open a hospital for the Red Crescent (the Muslim counterpart to the Red Cross) in Erzurum. She thought this volunteer work helping the Turkish troops might gain her respect and a hearing among the government officials in Sivas. She left in the fall, but returned to Sivas in time for the spring commencement. On the way back to Sivas she heard stories of Christian Armenians being imprisoned, people shot in the fields, and massacres in some village streets. Back in Sivas, she found that many of the Armenian men had been imprisoned. Mary went to the provincial governor to protest the imprisonment. She was told they would be released in a few days, but on 5 July, 1915, the Turkish authorities rounded up the Armenians in the town, about 3,000, and began their deportation march South. When Mary was told these Armenians were being taken to safety, she told the governor she was going with them, and he did nothing to stop her.

Mary went with her students and the Armenian teachers from the school, who tried to stay together on the march South. She said they were all heroes in the Christian encouragement they gave to each other. About the third day out, about 200 men were separated out and killed. Any laggers who fell behind on the march were bayoneted. Mary asked one of the teachers from the college how it felt with death approaching him. He told her, 'It is nothing, but when I think of this whole nation, I cannot stand it or see the right and justice in it all'.[34] The man was thirty-three. Mary reminded him that 1,900 years ago Jesus was sacrificed at that age, but his death and resurrection became the cornerstone of the Christian faith and gave Christians the hope of a resurrection.

The roadside was strewn with dead bodies, and Mary saw hundreds die in a day. Finally the Turks would not allow Mary to continue on the deportation march, and she returned to Sivas. Through all she endured she could testify that God came near to many during those days of death and suffering. In a report prepared for President Wilson on the Armenian massacre, Mary Graffam was particularly praised, noting her 'knowledge of Turkish, Armenian, and German enabled her to play a part in the stirring events of the past six years which has probably never been equaled by any other woman in the chronicles of missionary effort'.[35]

Now may our Lord Jesus Christ himself, and God our Father, who loved
us and gave us eternal comfort and good hope through grace, comfort your
hearts and establish them in very good work and word.

~ 2 THESSALONIANS 2:16-17 ~

---

34. Gordon and Diana Severance, *Against the Gates of Hell* (Wipf and Stock, 2012), p. 343.
35. Ibid, p. 355.

World Day of Prayer

∽ 1920 ∽

The nineteenth century saw, not only a growth in foreign missions, but also a growth in women's organizations supporting missions. From cent societies to denominational auxiliaries, women collected funds and supported missions both at home and in foreign lands. The women's boards were especially concerned with evangelization and Christian nurture of women and children. The women encouraged one another in prayer for the various areas of missions. Individual boards often held special days and weeks of prayer. In 1887, Presbyterians called for prayer for Home Missions, while Methodist women called for a week of prayer and self-denial for foreign missions. Baptist women began a day of prayer for foreign missions in 1891. Anglican women in Canada also began organized prayers for missions. By 1897 women's organizations from six denominations had some form of prayer emphasis for missions.

When Helen Montgomery and Lucy Peabody made their tour of the world studying missions in 1914, repeatedly the women in the various countries of the Middle East or the Orient asked for prayer for their work and for the women and children. When Helen and Lucy returned to the United States, the Federation of the Woman's Boards of Foreign Missions adopted a resolution for a 'Day of Prayer for the Women of the World'.

World War I broke out soon thereafter. Faced with the horrors of war, many believed Christian missions and prayer were vital to the establishment of peace. For the first time, on 20 February, 1920, the first Friday in Lent, a joint, interdenominational women's day of prayer for missions was established in the United States. In 1922, women's groups in Canada and the United States cooperated in a common day of prayer. In 1926, the North American women distributed a prayer worship service to women and missions groups in many countries.

The World Day of Prayer has grown to a worldwide, interdenominational movement of Christian women in 170 countries, with the first Friday in March being the annual day of celebration. National committees are established in these countries, and each year Christian women of a particular nation prepare the prayer service to be used for the Day of Prayer.

In prayer, women affirm their faith in Jesus Christ, are enriched by the faith of Christians in other countries, and share the burdens of fellow Christians around the globe. Informed prayer also leads the women to prayerful action, reaching out to the needs of women and children around the globe.

The prayer of a righteous person
has great power as it is working.

~ JAMES 5:16 ~

Pastor's Wife Converted

⌘ Bethan Lloyd-Jones, 1898-1991 ⌘

Bethan Phillips was born into a family with strong Christian roots. Descended from the great Welsh preacher Christmas Evans, Bethan's grandfather had been a leading Welsh preacher at Newcastle Emlyn during the 1859 and 1904 revivals. Bethan's dad, an eye surgeon in London, taught a Bible study at the Welsh Calvinistic Methodist Church in London, which Bethan continued to attend as a young medical student. A young Dr Martyn Lloyd Jones, who was assistant to Sir Thomas Heder, the Royal Physician, attended Dr Phillips' Bible class for seven years. Bethan, who received her Bachelor of Surgery from the University College Hospital in London and was certified to practice medicine, seemed to have much in common with Dr Lloyd-Jones. The two had first met when Martyn was fourteen and Bethan eighteen months older. The couple were engaged in 1926 and married at Charing Cross Chapel, London, on 8 January, 1927.

For two years Martyn had struggled with the sense that God was calling him to preach. When they married, both Bethan and Martyn gave up their medical ambitions for Christian service. After a honeymoon at Torquay, on 4 February, they moved to Aberavon, Wales where he became minister of a debt-ridden, struggling church at Sandfields. The first sermon Bethan heard Martyn preach was on Zacchaeus in Luke 19. The sermon made Bethan very uncomfortable. She was disturbed when she heard that all people are in need of salvation from their sins. She had always been a religious person and resisted the idea that she too was in need of salvation. She rejoiced when at the end of the service drunkards or prostitutes were converted, but she grappled with the thought that she too must be converted. As Martyn preached each Sunday, Bethan felt a growing conviction of her own sin and wondered if her sin might be greater than the blood of Christ. Martyn suggested she read John Angell James' *The Anxious Inquirer Directed*. Bethan at last came to understand the true meaning of the gospel and the sufficiency of Christ to clear away her sins. Though she thought she was a Christian previously, she realized she needed to trust Christ alone for her salvation.

Bethan and Martyn enjoyed eleven and a half beautiful years at Sandfields, during which their two daughters were born. Their love deepened as they each used their gifts in the Lord's service. In 1939, Martyn took the position of assistant pastor at Westminster Chapel in London, where he became pastor in 1943 and remained until his retirement in 1968. Dr Martyn Lloyd-Jones became one of the leading evangelical ministers of the twentieth century. Together Bethan and Martyn rejoiced to see God's providence work in their lives, for His glory and honor.

'The Son of Man came to seek and to save the lost.'

~ LUKE 19:10 ~

Beautiful Happiness

∽ Edith Schaeffer, 1914-2013 ∾

On 26 June, 1932, Edith Seville went to the young people's meeting at the Presbyterian Church ready to forcefully dispute the topic for the evening: 'How I know that Jesus is Not the Son of God, and How I know that the Bible is not the Word of God.' In this church, which had abandoned some of the key beliefs of the Christian faith and embraced liberalism, Edith suspected she was the only member of the youth group who still accepted the Bible as the Word of God. She listened carefully to the speaker, mentally preparing what she would say in refutation. After the speaker finished, before Edith had an opportunity to respond, a young man named Francis Schaeffer stood up saying he knew Jesus Christ was the Son of God and described his personal experience of knowing Jesus as Savior. Edith then stood up and gave a brief defense of the Bible as God's Word. Edith and Francis met that night and began dating. They were married in 1935, just after Francis' graduation with highest honors from Hampden-Sydney College.

Edith was born in Wenzhou, China, where her parents ran a school for girls and taught the Bible in Mandarin. Her parents gave her the Chinese name Mei Fuh, meaning 'beautiful happiness', and she brought beauty to many as the wife of Francis Schaeffer. Edith helped pay for Francis's training at Westminster Seminary by tailoring men's suits and making ball gowns and wedding dresses. After graduation Francis became a pastor, and Edith taught children's Bible classes at home.

In 1948, the Schaeffers were sent to Switzerland by the Independent Board for Presbyterian Foreign Missions. There they sought to strengthen churches in their gospel faith, at a time when many churches had fallen into modernism. In 1955, the Schaeffers founded L'Abri, which means 'The Shelter', as a community for those with intellectual questions about the gospel. Young people from throughout Europe, the United States, and the farther reaches of the globe found their way to L'Abri, where Edith offered beautiful hospitality and Francis lectured, answering intellectual questions from a biblical worldview. While many of Francis' books became important apologetic works in the twentieth century, Edith wrote about the Christian artist creating beauty, reflecting the Creator, and about Christian homemaking and family. Together Francis and Edith Schaeffer mirrored an intellectually vibrant faith in Christian truth. Author Os Guinness, who lived at L'Abri for a time and knew the Schaeffers intimately, said of Edith:

> Edith Schaeffer was one of the most remarkable women of her generation, the like of whom we will not see again in our time. I have never met such a great heart of love and such indomitable faith, tireless prayer, boundless energy, passionate love for life and beauty, lavish hospitality, irrepressible laughter, and seemingly limitless time for people – all in a single person … . To many of us she was a second mother, and in many ways she was the secret of L'Abri.[36]

In your hearts honor Christ the Lord as holy, always being prepared
to make a defence to anyone who asks you for a reason for the hope that is in you;
yet do it with gentleness and respect … .

~ 1 PETER 3:15 ~

---

36. Os Guinness, 'Fathers and Sons', *Books and Culture*, March/April 2008, http://www.booksandculture.com/articles/2008/marapr/1.32.html?start=2.

Using Her Talents for the Lord's Glory

∽ Mary Nanwar Lar, c. 1935 – ∽

When the gospel was brought to the Taraok people of the Plateau State of Nigeria in the early 1900s, Lar Mbamzhi was among the first converts. Some in his tribe attacked him for going over to the white man's religion, even burning down Lar's house. Missionaries H. I. and Mary Cooper had no children of their own, so they took Lar's two sons, Nansheo and Zingoyen, into their home and educated them. Nansheo married a Christian woman named Mbai Dadi, and their first child was born in 1935; she was named Mary after Mary Cooper, who had done so much to help their family.

When she was about twelve, Mary Lar was converted to Christ through a sermon she heard from John 1:12, 29. Mary later wrote, 'Like Christian in *Pilgrim's Progress*, I saw myself as a sinner who was carrying a load of sin.' Mary stepped forward at the invitation, trusted Christ, and began a walk with God. It was 'a most joyful experience as I went home happy that my sins had been washed away'.

Mary continued her education in missionary schools, receiving a Teaching Certificate. As a college student she participated in the Man O'War Bay Course in Cameroon and became one of the first African women to climb Mount Cameroon, an example of her determination to excel. On 30 January, 1960, Mary married Solomon Lar, a young man from her tribe who was deeply committed to serve the Lord. Solomon encouraged Mary to continue her education, knowing that it would equip her to better serve her family and community. Mary continued her educational studies in England, at the Ahmadu Bello University in Nigeria, and at the University of Jos, where she became a university professor – the first woman in northern Nigeria to do so. The Ministry of Education enlisted Mary to establish several public schools, and she followed the pattern of education she had learned from the missionaries.

In 1974, Mary was one of the Nigerian delegates to the World Congress on Evangelism in Lausanne, Switzerland. Returning to Jos, she began a home Bible discussion group to reach the elites with the message of the gospel. For several years she had a weekly educational television program. With Wycliffe Bible translators, she worked in translating the Tarok language into written form and helped with the translation of the Bible, translating the books of John and James. When her husband Solomon became Governor of the Plateau State, Mary worked with others to organize a school in Langtang, which opened in 1981 as the Mary Cooper Girls School. When the military again took over the government in 1984 Solomon was imprisoned for several years. Mary organized a weekly prayer vigil for him and others imprisoned.

Mary Lar worked tirelessly for her people and the Lord, as a Sunday school teacher, organizer of literacy programs, a patron of Children's Evangelism Ministry International, member of the Nigerian Bible Translation Trust, prayer secretary of the National Congress on Evangelization, the Nigeria President of the Pan African Women's Assembly, and even serving as Nigeria's ambassador to the Netherlands in 2004. She used her many talents to serve her people and her Lord.

> But to all who did receive him, who believed in his name, he gave
> the right to become children of God. ... 'Behold, the Lamb of
> God, who takes away the sin of the world!'
>
> ~ JOHN 1:12, 29 ~

Crying out against 'Injustice'

∞ Elisabeth Schmitz, 1893-1977 ∞

The Nazi rule in Germany, in attempting to establish a pure 'Aryan' government, began restricting the Jews and trying to control the teachings of the Christian church. In 1933, civil service laws included the 'Aryan Paragraph', which said only those of Aryan descent, without Jewish parents or grandparents, could serve in the government. The law soon extended to all areas of employment and even to the church. In November 1933, a rally of German Christians in Berlin embraced the Nazi program, accepted the Aryan Paragraph in the church, and even removed the Jewish Old Testament from the Bible. In May 1934, an opposition group, calling itself the Confessing Church, met in Barmen and adopted what became known as the Barmen Declaration. The Barmen Declaration declared the Nazi Church heretical and stated the State had no authority over the church.

In September 1935, the Reichstag's Nuremburg laws officially excluded Jews from citizenship in the German nation and prohibited mixed marriages with Jews. Soon after passage of the Nuremburg Laws, on September 23-26, 1935, a synod of the Confessing Church met in Berlin. Elisabeth Schmitz wrote an anonymous memorandum for the synod's consideration, to rally opposition against the anti-Jewish measures. Elisabeth, born in 1893, grew up in a Christian family of teachers. Her father encouraged her in her academic career, and Elisabeth received her doctorate in history in 1920 then studied theology. In 1929, she began teaching at the Luis School for Girls in Berlin. Elisabeth was a member of the Jesus Christus Kirche pastored by Martin Niemöller in Dahlem, a suburb of Berlin. She fully supported Niemöller's work against the Nazification of the German Church, but she thought there should be a protest against the discrimination against the Jews. In her memorandum, 'Situation of the German non-Aryans', Elisabeth asked why the Confessing Church had not reacted to what was happening to the Jews in Germany. The church had an obligation to both Jewish Christians and Jews suffering at the hands of society. Why was the church not protesting the Nazis' Jewish policies? The Barnum Declaration was a good confession, but it was silent on the Jewish issue. Why doesn't the church at least pray for the Jews? What is the church to say when asked, '"Where is your brother, Abel?"' She wrote, 'this sin against the Jews becomes our sin if German Christians do not speak out'. Though the synod never considered Elisabeth's memorandum, it was widely circulated among the leaders of the Confessing Church.

In 1938, Elisabeth resigned her teaching position; she did not want to work for a state persecuting the Jewish people. Throughout the war, she hid Jews and protected them in any way she could. After the war, she returned to teaching in her hometown of Hanau.

Learn to do good; seek justice, correct oppression;
bring justice to the fatherless, plead the widow's cause.

~ ISAIAH 1:17 ~

By Grace Made Strong

∞ Margaret Clarkson, 1915-2008 ∞

Margaret Clarkson knew a life full of every form of suffering. Her mother told her the first words she ever spoke were, 'My head hurts', and she suffered from migraine headaches and arthritis throughout her life. Her family was full of strife and discord, leading to her parents' divorce when she was thirteen. She suffered financial difficulties during The Great Depression and lived a life of loneliness teaching in an isolated mining camp. Through her many difficulties, Margaret learned to trust in God's sovereign love and care.

Growing up, Margaret attended St. John's Presbyterian Church in Toronto. After she won a hymnbook in Sunday school for her memorization, she used to climb a tree to the highest point and sing in the treetop. The hymns of the church always strengthened her, and she frequently leafed through the pages of the hymnal in church. Noting the names of people such as John and Charles Wesley, Martin Luther, William Cowper, John Newton, Paul Gerhardt, Isaac Watts, Fanny Crosby, Francis Havergal, and others, Margaret became familiar with the 'community of saints' and realized she was a part of a large body of people touched by God's grace.

After a series of children's lessons on Bunyan's *Pilgrim's Progress*, Margaret came to faith in Christ and officially joined the Church. She had memorized all 107 questions and answers to the Westminster Shorter Catechism, so she had a strong foundation in the truths of Scripture. She regularly began writing poems, many of which were published in church magazines or Sunday school papers.

Margaret taught school for over thirty-five years and wrote numerous books, from a children's book on reproduction to books on suffering. But always Margaret was writing hymns. In her first teaching job isolated in a mining camp, she first wrote 'So send I You', which became a favorite missionary hymn. Revised in later years, as her trust in God's sovereignty strengthened and increased, Margaret's hymn has a victorious tone:

> So send I you by grace made strong to triumph
> O'er hosts of hell, o'er darkness, death, and sin,
> My name to bear, and in that name to conquer –
> So send I you, my victory to win.
>
> So send I you to take to souls in bondage
> The word of truth that sets the captive free,
> To break the bonds of sin, to loose death's fetters –
> So send I you, to bring the lost to me.
>
> So send I you – to bear My cross with patience,
> And then one day with joy to lay it down,
> To hear My Voice, 'well done, My faithful servant –
> Come share My throne, My kingdom, and My crown!'
> 'As the father hath sent Me, so send I you.'

Jesus said to them again, 'Peace be with you.
As the Father has sent me, even so I am sending you.'

~JOHN 20:21~

Prisoner of War

∽ Carol Terry Talbot, 20th century ∽

After Carol Terry completed her studies at Biola in Los Angeles, she eagerly boarded the *S.S. Grant* to sail for missionary work in India. The Japanese bombed Pearl Harbor in December 1941, and the war stranded the *S.S. Grant* in Manila Bay in January 1942. The Japanese captured the Philippines and made all on board the ship prisoners of war. Carol and her shipmates were taken to a prisoner camp in Los Banos, forty miles from Manilla. This would be Carol's home for the next three and a half years.

Conditions in the camp were grim. Many died of starvation, and the prisoners took to eating worms and grubs for some kind of nourishment. Some were tortured in the cruelest ways; others were executed. At one point, Carol told a fellow prisoner that she supposed someday she would see God's purpose in their imprisonment and thank Him for it. The friend replied it would be better to thank God now for their condition and trust Him in faith for the purpose to glorify Him.

One day, sores began breaking out all over Carol. She had contracted impetigo, a highly infectious skin disease. She became like a leper to others in the camp, was isolated and not allowed to touch anything. She was not allowed to bathe or wash her clothes for fear of infecting others with the water or tub. Carol thanked God for her condition, miserable as it was. Soon a nurse came to offer a more successful treatment to the malady. One couple risked the disease themselves and washed Carol's clothes and sheets.

On 23 February, 1945, at seven in the morning, the Japanese lined up the prisoners four deep for roll call. Rumor was that they were to be executed soon. As planes flew overhead, Carol and the other prisoners wondered if they would be shot by the planes as they flew by. Then they realized they were American planes. Paratroopers from the 11th Airborne Division dropped into the camp, like angels from the sky, and freed the 2,121 remaining prisoners from their captors.

After some recuperation in the United States Carol did make it to India and was with the Ramabai Mukti Mission for over twenty years. The mission took care of unwanted baby girls, child wives, needy widows, and a number of blind women and children. Carol saw that her three and a half years as a P.O.W. prepared her to minister to those who were imprisoned by other circumstances. From her own experience she had come to see the sufficiency of God's Word in the most desperate of situations.

Carol returned to the United States in 1963 because of a chronic eye infection. She then married Dr Louis Talbot, former pastor of the Church of the Open Door and President of Biola University.

Though I walk in the midst of trouble, you preserve my life;
you stretch out your hand against the wrath of my enemies,
and your right hand delivers me.

~ PSALM 138:7 ~

NOVEMBER 26

Never Forsaken

Darlene Deibler Rose, 1917-2004

At the beginning of World War II, the Christian and Missionary Alliance had 476 missionaries in the field; 252 of those remained overseas during the war. When China, Indonesia, the Philippines, and Vietnam became closed to missions, 121 Christian and Missionary Alliance men, women, and children were placed in internment camps. Among those was Darlene Deibler, a missionary in the Netherland East Indies.

In March 1942, the Japanese Imperial Army invaded the island of Celebes and placed the Christian and Missionary Alliance team under house arrest. On 13 March, they came and took all the men to Pare Pare prison camp. Darlene grabbed a pillow case and filled it with clothes, a Bible, pen, and notebook for her husband Russell, who was already on the back of the truck. As Russell took them, he looked at her and quietly said, 'Remember one thing, dear: God said that He would never leave us nor forsake us.' This was the last Darlene saw of her husband.

In May, she and the remaining missionaries were taken to a prison camp in Kampili. Darlene, who was fluent in English, Dutch, and Indonesian, was chosen as the barrack's leader. She helped organize the work details of the women and also began reading Scripture and having prayer each night with the women. In command of the camp was Commander Yamaji, who had a terrible temper and made unreasonable demands on the women. About a year after Russell had been taken to prison camp, Darlene heard he had died of dysentery. She briefly felt forsaken, but remembered that God had promised He would be with her.

Commander Yamaji then called her to his office and told her that many women in Japan had heard what she had heard. After the war was over, she would be able to have a life again and the pain would leave. Darlene took the opportunity to tell the Commander about Jesus, the Son of Almighty God, the Creator of heaven and earth. When she told him that Jesus had died for him and that Jesus said we were to love even our enemies, tears streamed down the Commander's face, and he left the room. Darlene was later accused of being a spy and placed in solitary confinement with only a small amount of rice each day. She remembered that Paul had testified that God's grace *is* sufficient, not *was* or *shall be*.

After the war was over, Darlene returned to the United States and married Rev. Gerald Rose; they returned as missionaries to New Guinea in 1949, where they worked among the Kapauku for thirty years. Whenever she told others about her prison experience, Darlene always said she would do it all again for her Savior.

> *He has said, 'I will never leave you nor forsake you.'*
> *So we can confidently say 'The Lord is my helper;*
> *I will not fear; what can man do to me?'*
>
> ~ HEBREWS 13:5-6 ~

Confident in God's Word

∞ Audrey Wetherell Johnson, 1907-1984 ∞

Although born into a devout Christian family in Leicester, England, as a young woman Audrey came under the influence of secular philosophers and intellectuals during her studies in France. Her agnosticism only led her to despair. In the midst of her hopeless dejection, Audrey recalled Jesus' words, 'And whosoever liveth and believeth in me shall never die. Believest thou this?' (John 11:26, KJV). She cried out to God in prayer and, as she wrote later:

> Suddenly God's mysterious revelation was given to me. I can only say with Paul, 'It pleased God to reveal His Son in me.' I could not reason out the mystery of the Incarnation, but God caused me to know that this was a fact. I knelt down in tears of joy and worshipped him as Saviour and Lord, with a divine conviction of this truth which could never be broken.[37]

The importance of Scripture in her conversion taught Audrey the importance of the authority of Scripture, a truth which became a foundation of her Christian life.

In 1936, Audrey went to China as a missionary with China Inland Mission. During World War II, she became a prisoner of war of the Japanese when they invaded China. By the time the war ended, Audrey had spent thirty months as a prisoner, sharing a horse stable with almost ninety other prisoners. After a time of recuperation in England, Audrey returned to China, in 1947, to teach at the China Bible Seminary in Shanghai. The following year, the Communists placed her under house arrest, and she was forced to flee the country in 1950.

In the United States and under a doctor's care, Audrey was uncertain where the Lord would lead her. Her heart was in China, but a group of five women asked her to lead them in a Bible class. Audrey was not enthusiastic, but she agreed to do so if the women would agree to study the Bible beforehand and share their studies with each other. As they read the Bible passage, the women were to answer three simple questions: What does the passage say? What did it mean when it was written? What does it mean to me? Audrey closed the women's discussion with a summary lesson on the passage. The study grew. In 1958, Audrey was asked to organize a follow-up Bible study for those who were expected to come to Christ during a Billy Graham Crusade in California's Bay area. The results were so encouraging that Audrey incorporated Bible Study Fellowship in 1959. The goal always was for people to study the Bible for themselves. Audrey developed a series of five studies which covered nearly the entire Bible. Each series was thirty weeks or lessons, corresponding to the school year. Audrey's notes focussed on Jesus and the practical application of Bible truths. Today, Bible Study Fellowship has classes in thirty-nine countries.

After several struggles with cancer, Audrey went to be with her Lord on 22 December, 1984. The nurse heard her say, 'The Lord is coming for me today. He's at the foot of my bed now.' At the end of her earthly life, she did not see death but the face of her Lord Jesus Christ.[38]

My soul longs for your salvation;
I hope in your word.

~ PSALM 119:81 ~

---

37. Quoted in 'Miss J: A. Wetherell Johnson and the Bible Study Fellowship', John Woodbridge, ed., *More Than Conquerors* (Chicago: Moody Press, 1992), p. 80.

38. 'Miss J: Audrey Wetherell Johnson', p. 83.

Mother of the Year

∞ Evelyn LeTourneau, 1900-1987 ∞

Twelve-year old Evelyn Peterson was attending a tent revival with her parents near her house in Stockton, California when she came to know the Lord Jesus Christ as her Savior. She also met Bob LeTourneau at the revival meetings. He was a mechanic and race-car driver. During one race he lost control of the car, crashed into a fence and broke his neck. Unconscious for several days, the doctors were amazed he was even alive after the accident. When he did recover, Evelyn's mother invited the young man to board with the family. Evelyn quickly came to love him and prayed to the Lord that he would wait for her, since she was twelve and he twenty-four. In 1917, when she was sixteen, Bob asked Evelyn to marry him and she gladly accepted, thankful he had waited for her!

The death of their first child focussed Evelyn and Bob more on spiritual values and they dedicated their lives to the Lord, asking Him to take over their lives in every way.

Evelyn noticed that many of the children in the neighborhood were not churchgoers. She began inviting them to Sunday school and church, eventually taking about thirty every Sunday! In the summers Evelyn began to take neighborhood children, as well as her growing family of six children, to Mount Herman camp. Evelyn was always counseling young people and seeking to lead them to Christ or deepen their Christian walk.

In 1929, Bob established R. G. LeTourneau, Inc. to manufacture earth-moving machinery. As the company prospered, in 1935 Evelyn gently suggested that they increase their giving to the Lord's work to 90 per cent, keeping 10 per cent for their living expenses. This became their pattern the rest of their lives.

When they established a factory in Illinois, Evelyn bought Bethany Camp at Winona Lake, Indiana, and for ten years she ran a camp for young people during the summer. Many young people came to know the Lord during those summers, realizing for the first time that simply going to church didn't make one a Christian.

When Evelyn and Bob moved to Georgia to open another factory, they also established a mechanical training program for the workers, and Evelyn frequently mothered and counseled the young men in spiritual matters. Needing to expand again, in 1946 the LeTourneaus were looking to build a plant in Longview, Texas. Flying over the area, Evelyn spotted the buildings of a military hospital which she thought would be a perfect site for a training school. They bought the land and established LeTourneau Technical Institute. The school has since become LeTourneau University, offering a Christian education in numerous degree fields.

Evelyn had shown the love of Christ to many young people over the decades. In 1969, she was chosen national 'Mother of the Year', opening up numerous opportunities to share her biblical wisdom in being a mother to younger women across the United States.

She opens her mouth with wisdom,
and the teaching of kindness is on her tongue.

~ PROVERBS 31:26 ~

Prayers for a Loved One Answered

∞ Amy George, 1934 – ∞

Amy could not remember her father. In the spring of 1936, when Amy was a year and a half, the Russian secret police pushed in the door of their home in Drushkovka, a little village in Ukraine, and ransacked the house. The police took Amy's father away as her mother, older sister and brother stood by helpless. Fyodor was in jail for a year, frequently beaten, then was deported to Siberia. The family never knew why he was taken.

Life became more difficult as Maria, Amy's mother, had to find work and care for her small children. Maria finally got a job shoveling coal in a tunnel. The only food available was what they raised, and hunger was constant. When the war came fear gripped the village as bombers flew overhead and fighting could be heard in the distance. During the fighting between the Germans and Russians, the Germans took over their house. In the spring of 1943, the people of the village were deported to Germany on cattle trains, having only the clothes on their backs.

Amy and her family were taken to a concentration camp in Germany, where Maria worked in a munitions factory. When the war ended her family escaped to the American sector of Germany. It was then, in 1945, that Amy first went to church and heard about God. She learned that God can look into people's hearts and loves them. Amy wanted to know more about this God and rose early each Sunday for church. She learned about Jesus and memorized the verse on the wall of the church, 'I am the way, the truth, and the life: no man cometh unto the Father, but by me' (John 14:6, KJV). Amy began praying to God and Jesus, alternating her prayers to one each day, not realizing at first that Jesus was God.

Amy met a tall, handsome American soldier, Bob George, and the two were married in 1958. Amy's brother and sister had already immigrated to America, and Amy followed them with her new husband. The Georges had two children, but there was unhappiness in their lives. After ten years they considered divorce, but they reconciled, surrendered their lives to Jesus, and began living for Him. They prayed together as a family, and they prayed for Amy's father, who they heard had survived the war. They prayed that someone in Russia would be able to share the gospel of Jesus with him so that he would have life eternal. Amy exchanged letters with her father, but knew all letters were censored. Her father tried to receive permission from Moscow to visit his family in America, but his request was always denied.

One day, in 1977, Amy received a phone call from her mother saying her father would soon be in the United States. It was a joyous visit to be reunited, even briefly, with her father after forty years. It was a special joy to share the Bible with him in Russian. Bob and Amy had him read John 3:16 inserting his own name in the verse. His heart was opened to the truth, and he received eternal life in Jesus. When Fyodor returned to Russia, he returned as a new man in Christ. Amy knew when she told him goodbye, this goodbye was not forever.[39]

> As high as the heavens are above the earth,
> so great is his steadfast love toward those who fear him;
> as far as the east is from the west,
> so far does he remove our transgressions from us.
>
> ~ PSALM 103:11-12 ~

---

39. *Goodbye is not Forever* (Eugene, Oregon: Harvest House Publishers, 1994) is Amy George's account of her story.

Ai Wei De, 'Virtuous One'

∞ Gladys Aylward, 1902-1970 ∞

At the age of fourteen, Gladys Aylward went to work as a parlor maid for a wealthy family. When she was eighteen she attended a service where the preacher taught about giving your life to the Lord. The message began to awaken in Gladys a desire to be a missionary, and she began reading books on China. In her mid-twenties Gladys applied for a position with China Inland Mission (CIM), but she was rejected. CIM did not find she had the educational background expected, and thought she was probably too old to begin learning the difficult Chinese language. Nevertheless Gladys, feeling called to serve God in China, began saving money to go there. Though she could not afford passage by ship, she was eventually able to buy overland train transport across Europe and Russia to China. On 15 October, 1932, Gladys left the Liverpool train station for the Orient.

Gladys went to Yangcheng, where an elderly missionary, Jeanie Lawson, needed assistance. Yangcheng was a stopping-off point for the mule caravans, and Gladys and Mrs Lawson decided to open an inn for the mule teams. While providing food and shelter for the mule drivers and the mules, they also told Bible stories to the men after dinner.

Gladys easily adapted to Chinese dress and culture, and, in 1936, became a naturalized Chinese citizen. She was well respected by all, including the governor, who made her a foot inspector. The Chinese thought very small feet in women were beautiful and bound the feet of girls to keep them small. Laws had recently been passed, however, forbidding this practice. Gladys' job as foot inspector was to travel to the villages, educate the people on not binding the feet, and see the new law was complied with. Gladys was amazed she was being paid to travel to the villages, where she could also tell the people about the gospel of Christ. Gladys also served as a spy for the Chinese as the Sino-Japanese War intensified. In her travels she encountered many unwanted children and orphans, whom she took to herself and cared for. In time she had one hundred children in her care. The Chinese gave her the name 'AiWeiDe', which sounded somewhat like her name 'Aylward' and meant 'Virtuous One'.

As Japanese bombings intensified in 1940, Gladys was forced to leave Yangcheng for a safer haven in Sian province. Gladys led the one hundred children across mountains and the Yellow River, a journey of over one hundred miles. Singing hymns to keep up their spirits during the twenty-seven days, Gladys collapsed when they reached Sian safely. She was ill with pneumonia, typhus, and exhaustion, but all the children had been brought to safety. In her incredible journey leading the children across the mountains, Gladys had trusted God's guidance and protection as she had on her journey from England to China.

Lead me, O LORD, in your righteousness because of my enemies;
make your way straight before me.

~ PSALM 5:8 ~

DECEMBER 1

Legacy of Faith

∞ Ruth Bell Graham, 1920-2007 ∞

Ruth Bell was born 10 June, 1920, in Qingjiang, Kiangsu, China, where her parents were medical missionaries. Her father, Dr Nelson Bell, who was surgical chief and administrative superintendent at the hospital, also showed a pastor's heart for his patients and their spiritual needs. Daily prayer and Bible study were part of the Bells' family life, and Ruth found in her parents an example of Christian service on which to model her own life. Ruth later noted her mother, 'built a house, had three children, buried one, had two more, taught her children at home through fifth grade, ran the women's clinic, always had a missionary or two in the home … entertained well and often, and wrote home faithfully'.[40]

When she was thirteen, Ruth went to a boarding school in Pyongyang, in what is now North Korea. She had to overcome terrible homesickness and tremendous loneliness being away from her family. At seventeen she returned to the United States with her parents on furlough, finished high school, and entered Wheaton College, where she majored in Bible – planning on becoming a missionary in Tibet. During her second year at Wheaton, Ruth heard a student pray one Sunday morning during prayer meeting and thought, 'There is a man who knows to Whom he is speaking.' Friends had told Billy Graham that Ruth was one of the prettiest and most spiritual girls on campus, so he gathered up courage and asked Ruth to a performance of Handel's *Messiah*. When Ruth returned to her room after the date, she prayed, 'Lord, if You'd let me serve You with that man, I'd consider it the greatest privilege of my life.'

Ruth and Billy Graham were married 13 August, 1943. As Billy went on to become a world-renowned evangelist and a confidant of presidents, Ruth was always encouraging him to remain true to his calling and ministry and not become side-tracked by offers of worldly gains. When asked where he went for spiritual guidance, Billy once answered, 'my wife, Ruth. She is a great student of the Bible. Her life is ruled by the Bible more than any person I've ever known.'[41] While Billy had often to be away preaching, Ruth stayed at their home in Montreat, North Carolina with their five children, providing nurture and guidance to them as well as hospitality to others. Ruth also found time to write poetry and numerous books as outpourings of her walk with the Lord.

Ruth's life serving her family and husband became a model and example for many. Ruth's daughter, Anne Graham Lotz, believed, 'our heavenly Father, our Savior, saved my mother from loneliness because of her daily walk with the Lord Jesus – He was the love of her life. I saw that in her life. It was her love for the Lord Jesus, with whom she walks every day, that made me want to love Him and walk with him like that.'[42]

> *The heart of her husband trusts in her,*
> *and he will have no lack of gain.*
> *She does him good, and not harm,*
> *all the days of her life.*
>
> ~ PROVERBS 31:11-12 ~

---

40. Kristen Driscoll, 'Ruth Bell Graham: A Life Well Lived', *Decision Magazine*, June 2013 as posted on *Billy Graham Evangelistic Association*, http://billygraham.org/decision-magazine/june-2013/ruth-bell-graham-a-life-well-lived/.

41. Meghan Kleppinger, 'Ruth Bell Graham: A Legacy of faith', *Christianity.com*, 18 June 2007, http://www.christianheadlines.com/news/ruth-bell-graham-a-legacy-of-faith-11544172.html.

42. Kleppinger, ibid, 'Ruth Bell Graham.'

Hiding Place

⊙ Corrie ten Boom, 1892-1983 ⊙

The old house on Barteljorisstraat in Haarlem, Holland had been the home of the ten Booms since 1837, when Willem opened a watch shop in the house. The family lived in the rooms above the shop. Willem's son, Casper continued to operate the watch shop and raised four children there. The youngest, Corrie, trained as a watchmaker and became the first licensed female watchmaker in the Netherlands. Though enjoying her work, Corrie's passion was helping others in the name of Christ. She organized clubs for teenage girls in the neighborhood, training them in sewing, handcrafts, and performing arts and providing them Christian instruction. She also began a church for the mentally disabled and raised foster children in the ten Boom home.

When the Nazis invaded the Netherlands in the spring of 1940, the club for girls was banned. Corrie, with her father and sister Betsie, began helping Jews who were being rounded up and arrested by the Nazis. They built a secret room behind Corrie's bedroom where Jews could hide if the house was raided. Corrie became part of the Haarlem underground, working with others to protect Jews and resistance workers from the Nazis. It is estimated she and her friends saved the lives of 800 Jews during the Nazi occupation.

A Dutch informant betrayed the ten Booms, and the Gestapo raided their house on 28 February, 1844. Six Jews managed to take refuge in the back hiding place, but the ten Booms were arrested and taken to Scheveningen prison. Casper, eighty-four years old and in failing health, died within ten days. Corrie and Betsie were taken to three different prisons, the last being Ravensbruck Concentration Camp. At Ravensbruck, Betsie and Corrie had a Bible study and prayer time for the women, and many found Christ as Savior in the camp. They were surprised that the guards never bothered them in the large room where they held the Bible study. Then, they learned the guards stayed away from the room because of the fleas there. The fleas gave them more freedom for their Bible study!

Betsie died at Ravensbruck. As she lay dying, she told Corrie that she 'must tell people what we have learned here. We must tell them that there is no pit so deep that He is not deeper still. They will listen to us, Corrie, because we have been here.'[43] Corrie was released on Christmas Day, 1944, probably due to a clerical error. All the women in the camp her age were killed the following week.

After the war Corrie returned to the Netherlands and established rehabilitation centers for war prisoners. She also traveled the world telling the story of God's love, the forgiveness for sins in Christ, and victory in Jesus.

You are a hiding place for me;
you preserve me from trouble;
you surround me with shouts of deliverance.

~ Psalm 32:7 ~

---

43. Corrie ten Boom, *The Hiding Place* (Peabody, MA: Hendrikson Publishers, Inc., 2006), p. 240.

Giving *Voice* to the *Martyrs*

∞ Sabina Wurmbrand, 1913-2000 ∞

It was easy for Sabina Oster to agree to marry Richard Wurmbrand. Tall, handsome, and with clear blue eyes, he was a successful stockbroker who could provide her a life of fun and luxury. Both were Jewish; the two were married on 26 October, 1936. Shortly after their marriage, Richard became ill with tuberculosis and went to a mountain sanatorium to recover his health. After a German carpenter gave him a Bible to read and told him about the salvation that was to be found in Jesus Christ, Richard became a Christian. Sabina soon followed him into the Christian faith. They joined an evangelical mission to the Jewish people in Romania and soon were engaged in evangelistic work. Richard became an ordained Anglican minister for their Christian community.

While World War II brought much suffering to the Wurmbrands, they did all they could to bring comfort and help to others, including rescuing Jewish children from the ghettos and caring for them as their own. They were repeatedly arrested and beaten, but continued their Christian work of evangelism, encouragement, and aid. Even when beaten Sabina learned to give thanks – that they were the beaten and not the ones beating others. Sabina's parents and three siblings were killed in the Holocaust, bringing more sorrow. When the Russian troops occupied Romania in 1944, Sabina and Richard had Russian Bibles printed and distributed them to the Russian soldiers, who had little knowledge of Christianity living under their communist government. As famine settled on the country, the Wurmbrands opened a canteen to help feed the hungry. These years of difficulty and suffering were preparing them for what was to come.

In October 1945, the Romanian Communist government organized the Congress of the Cults for all religious leaders, encouraging them to follow the communist system as their salvation. Richard and Sabina were in attendance as many religious leaders pledged loyalty to communism. Sabina told Richard he should speak up and 'wash away this shame from the face of Christ'. Richard told her, 'If I do so, you lose your husband.' She replied, 'I don't wish to have a coward as a husband.' Richard stood up and spoke to the four thousand in the Congress, and to a broadcast across the nation, challenging the leaders to glorify God and Christ alone, not any man or human system.

Months later, Richard was arrested on his way to church. Sabina didn't know where he was for years and was even told he was dead. Sabina herself was arrested two years later and spent two years in a penal prison for working against the communist regime and for her 'fanatical faith'. Throughout their imprisonments both Richard and Sabina shared the love of Christ with others and encouraged them with Scriptures. Richard was released after eight and a half years, but was soon re-arrested for preaching contrary to Communist doctrine. When he was granted amnesty and released in 1964, the Wurmbrands immigrated to Norway, then England, and the United States. They worked tirelessly to awaken awareness to the persecution of Christians around the world, establishing Voice of the Martyrs in 1967.

> 'For whoever would save his life will lose it,
> but whoever loses his life for my sake will find it.'
> ~ MATTHEW 16:25 ~

DECEMBER 4

Littlest Lady with the Biggest Heart

∾ Lillian Dickson, 1901-1983 ∾

When James and Lillian Dickson first came to Taiwan in 1927, the island was under Japanese control. James taught at the Taiwan Theological College, founded by the Canadian Presbyterian Church in 1872, to train pastors for the island. On the weekends he visited the mountain tribes, becoming the first to bring the gospel to many. During those early years Lillian was devoted to caring for their two children, Marilyn and Ronald.

During World War II, the Dicksons were re-assigned to British Guyana, but as soon as the war was over they eagerly returned to Taiwan. James was now Principal of the Taiwan Theological College. With their children grown, Lillian had more time to devote to mission work. She bought an accordion and taught herself to play. She would then go into a village and begin playing and singing to gather a crowd, then she would present the gospel to the people. When James was not able to go into the mountains because of his other work, Lillian often went with the pastoral team. Her heart was moved by the suffering of many due to poverty and the prevalence of leprosy and tuberculosis.

Taiwan was a scene of turmoil after the war, with refugees fleeing Communist China by the thousands. Lillian helped care for many refugees, but the numbers were overwhelming. At one time the Dicksons were asked to provide shelter for an orphanage and students from an entire theological college! Lillian was tireless in seeking help for the needy. When she went to the American Aid office seeking help for the mountain people with tuberculosis, she was told that the problem was as big as the ocean. Anything she did would be like dipping a bucket to remove the ocean water. Lillian replied, 'Because I am a Christian, I must take out my bucketful.'[44] Whenever she was told that she wouldn't be able to manage a large aid project, she replied, 'I can't, but God can.'

In her circular letters, as well as in speaking opportunities back home, Lillian reported on the many physical needs of the Taiwanese as well as the opportunities for evangelism and building up the churches. In 1954, she formed The Mustard Seed to oversee the funds for the many projects needed. A simple listing of the many projects Lillian began or oversaw is staggering: she took over the government Leprosarium; established the An-Loh children's home for the children of lepers; established schools for mountain people as well as teacher training schools; established a boy's home for street boys, so they would not be placed in prison with hardened criminals; established the Ira-Iro orphanage; set up a chain of Reading Rooms in villages; sponsored mobile medical teams for the villages; Rooms for Mary, clinics for expectant and new mothers; and rest hospitals for those with tuberculosis. In all of these settings the gospel was always proclaimed. Lillian's love for the people was boundless, so that the Taiwanese called her the 'littlest lady with the biggest heart'. Hollington Tong, one time Nationalist Chinese ambassador to the United States, said that 'Christianity's leaping growth in Taiwan, tenfold since 1945, is largely due to the tireless woman who can't say no to human need'.[45]

> 'Blessed are the merciful,
> for they shall receive mercy.'
> ~ MATTHEW 5:7 ~

---

44. Jean H. Young, *Would You Dare!* (Scottsville, MI: Shark Enterprise, 2004).

45. Ralph R. Covell, *Pentecost of the hills in Taiwan: The Christian Faith Among the Original Inhabitants* (Pasadena, CA: Hope Publishing House, 1998), p. 204.

If I Perish, I Perish

∞ Esther Ahn Kim, born c. 1918, d. 1990s ∞

Ei Sook Ahn was born around 1918 into a prosperous family in the town of Bhak Chon, Korea. Her mother had become a Christian as a child, but had no church or Bible. She did, however, cling to four principles she had learned from a missionary:

1. Jesus is the Savior and only Son of God.
2. Jesus will never forsake those who believe in him.
3. Jesus is able to turn believers' misfortunes into good.
4. Jesus hears his children's prayers.

While Ei Sook's mother taught her these principles and strengthened her to follow Jesus, Ei Sook's grandmother continued to worship and offer food to the pagan gods. These gods didn't seem to do much for grandmother, for she was always disgruntled. Ei Sook's mother, however, always lived for others and was helping those in need. When a Bible became available, Ei Sook's mother encouraged her in the memorization of Scripture.

The Japanese occupation of Korea brought much hardship among the people. Korean became a forbidden language, and Japanese culture was imposed upon the Koreans. Ei Sook's mother wanted to send her to a Christian college in America, but her father insisted she attend a Japanese University. Becoming fluent in Japanese and the Japanese culture would help her live more successfully under the occupation.

After completing her university schooling Ei Sook became a music teacher in a Christian school in Pyongyang. The Japanese were requiring everyone to participate in ceremonies at the Shinto shrines, bowing before the Japanese sun goddess and a picture of the Emperor of Japan, who himself was considered a god. Shinto shrines were placed throughout Korea, even in the churches. Ei Sook wrestled with what she should do. How could she bow to a worthless idol when Jesus said he was the way, the truth and the life? She recalled a similar trial put before the Jewish young men Shadrach, Meshach, and Abednego in ancient Babylon, who were required to bow before the statue of Nebucahdnezzar and were thrown into a fiery furnace for refusing. Their words gave courage to Ei Sook:

> Our God whom we serve is able to deliver us from the burning fiery furnace, and he will deliver us out of your hand, O king. But if not, be it known to you, O king, that we will not serve your gods or worship the golden image that you have set up. (Dan. 3:17-18)

She knew God could deliver her, but even if not, she would not worship idols.

When the day came for all students and teachers to attend the school rally at the shrine at Namsan Mountain in the center of Seoul, Ei Sook resolved to stand alone if necessary, knowing that imprisonment and death could be her punishment. When the command came to bow, she was the only one who remained erect, looking up at the sky.

Ei Sook was later arrested and imprisoned for six years, enduring hunger, cold, filthy prisons, and torture. Throughout she was encouraged and strengthened by the Scripture she had memorized and the hymns she had learned. After her release Ei Sook met and married Kim Dong Myung, who 'burned with God's love'. They immigrated to the United States, where Dong became a pastor in California.

> *I will go to the king, though it is against the law,*
> *and if I perish, I perish.*
>
> ~ ESTHER 4:16 ~

Dealing with Pain

∞ Cicely Saunders, 1918-2005 ∞

Cicely Saunders had wanted to be a nurse, but when her father objected, she went to St. Anne's College, Oxford to study politics, philosophy, and economics. With the outbreak of World War II, Cicely turned again to her nursing dream and became a student nurse at the Nightingale Training School in London's St Thomas Hospital. A back injury, in 1944, led her to return to St Anne's, where she took her degree and qualified as a medical social worker. In 1945, on a holiday with some Christians, Cicely moved from agnosticism to faith in Christ. Ever after, her Christian faith guided her and set the path she followed.

In 1948, while working in the hospital, Cicely fell in love with a patient, David Tasma, a Polish-Jewish refugee who had escaped from the Warsaw ghetto and was dying of cancer. The two often discussed Cicely's dream of establishing a home where those near death could find peace and care. Tasma left his entire funds, £500 (a sizeable amount in 1948!), to Cicely to be a 'window in your home'. Realizing she could best help dying patients by being a good doctor, Cicely enrolled in medical school at the age of thirty-three.

After qualifying as a doctor, Cicely studied pain management for the incurably ill and worked at St Joseph's, a hospice for the dying poor run by nuns. She introduced a system of pain control where patients were given regular pain relief and not forced to wait until their pain returned, believing that 'constant pain needs constant control'. Cicely recognized that there was mental pain as well as physical pain and that the mental pain and anxiety could be reduced if the physical pain was cared for. Recognizing that the medical and spiritual were inextricably mingled, Cicely wrote that she longed:

> to bring patients to know the Lord and to do something towards helping many of them to hear of him before they die, but I also long to raise the standards of terminal care throughout the country from a medical point of view at least, even where I can do nothing about the spiritual part of the work.[46]

After eleven years of planning, Cicely had drawn up a plan for the first purpose-built hospice. Encouraged by Psalm 37:5, she began raising funds and, in 1967, St Christopher's Hospice was established in London. Its principles of pain relief and care for the physical, social, psychological, and spiritual needs of its terminal patients, their families, and friends, became a pattern duplicated throughout England, the United States, and indeed the world.

Cicely spent a lifetime dealing with pain and suffering and worked to bring peace and comfort to many during their dying days. She recognized that:

> The fullest consideration of the problem of innocent suffering is given in the book of Job. Job was not given any answer to his questions, but instead was given a vision of God which silenced his asking. We are given the vision of Jesus crucified, 'bearing our griefs and carrying our sorrows'. That vision brings us to the point where we change our questions. 'Why should this happen …?' changes to 'How can I help – with God's grace?' or 'What can I do in this situation – which He shares with me?'[47]

Commit your way to the LORD;
trust in him, and he will act.

~ PSALM 37:5 ~

---

46. Cicely Saunders letter to Bruce Reed, 14 March 1960.
47. *Cicely Saunders: Selected writings 1958-2004* (Oxford University Press, 2006), p. 135.

Wife of a P.O.W.

When Florence Matheny chose to attend Seattle Pacific College, she did so because she thought the college would prepare her for the missionary work to which she felt called. As she was getting ready for her freshman year, she read that Jake DeShazer planned to get a theological education to bring the message of Christ to Japan. Newspaper reports had told about Jake's wartime experience. He had been a member of Doolittle's Raiders in World War II, who bombed Japan shortly after the attack on Pearl Harbor. When Jake's plane had trouble, he parachuted out over China and was captured by the Japanese. Filled with hatred and bitterness for the Japanese, Jake was in a prisoner-of-war camp where he was often tortured. At one point during his imprisonment, Jake was given a Bible. In three weeks he read the Bible three times, and he began memorizing entire chapters. The bitterness he had against the Japanese disappeared as he realized Jesus had died for them as well as for him. He determined that if he survived the war and was released, he would get a theological education and return to Japan to tell the Japanese about Christ.

Florence read Jake's story and thought it would be a great coincidence if he attended Seattle Pacific College. Maybe she could even shake his hand! Seattle Pacific indeed was the school Jake attended, and Florence and Jake met at a Youth for Christ service early in 1946. Jake thought Florence 'was a very attractive young lady, the most attractive … I had ever met.'[48] As she wanted to go into full-time work for the Lord, they felt a 'oneness of purpose'. Florence and Jake were married and sailed for Japan in 1948, beginning thirty years of missionary work in that country.

The Japanese were curious about this 'Doolittle Raider', and large crowds came to hear Jake speak in factories, schools, mines, and churches. Thousands came to faith in Christ as they saw how the love of Jesus transformed Jake so that he could even love those who had tortured him. The DeShazers established numerous churches during their years in Japan. Florence held children's Bible lessons in their home as a way of building bridges with their neighbors as well as sharing the love of Christ. Once a group of believers became a growing congregation, a Japanese pastor was brought in and Jake, Florence, and their five children would move to begin a church elsewhere. Florence's dream of shaking the hero Jake DeSahzer's hand was transformed into being his wife and partner in the Lord's work.

> 'Love your enemies and pray for those who persecute you,
> so that you may be sons of your Father who is in heaven.'
>
> ~ MATTHEW 5:44-45 ~

---

48. Charles Hoyt Watson, *DeShazer* (Salt Box Press, 1992), p. 145.

First Missionary Aviation Fellowship Pilot

∞ Betty Greene, 1920-1997 ∞

Betty Greene always had a passion for flying. When her uncle gave her $100 for her sixteenth birthday, she spent it on a few flying lessons. In 1937, Betty went to the University of Washington to study nursing, but she really didn't like nursing and wondered what God wanted her to do with her life. One day, pondering the possibilities, an older Christian friend suggested Betty combine flying with her love for God. Betty began to have the idea that pilots could bring important support to Christian missions. Thrilled with the thought, Betty enroled in a pilot training course and went to college to major in sociology. Shortly before graduation she read about the Women's Flying Training Detachment (later called Women Airforce Service Pilots, or WASP), applied for the training, and was accepted. During her six months of training, Betty wrote a couple of articles for Christian magazines exploring her ideas about how pilots could assist missionaries.

In January 1944, Betty was assigned to Wright Field, where she tested high altitude equipment, flying at 40,000 feet. In July of that year, Betty received a letter from Jim Truxton about a new organization, Christian Airmen's Missionary Fellowship (CAMF), which planned to use war-trained pilots to help missionaries. Truxton wanted to meet Betty in Washington, D.C. About two weeks later, Betty providentially received an assignment which sent her to the Pentagon; she would be in D.C. to meet with Truxton. Truxton asked Betty to open the first CAMF office and headquarters in Los Angeles. This would be fulfilling Betty's dream, but she couldn't just quit WASP. However, by mid-August, the announcement came that WASP was being disbanded. The way was open for Betty to work with CAMF.

Betty spread the word about CAMF and enlisted support from churches and individuals. CAMF was able to join with Wycliffe Bible translators, and Betty flew to Mexico to meet Wycliffe's staff there. She clearly saw how important an airplane could be in reaching isolated tribes and peoples. CAMF bought a first plane, a 1933 Waco Biplane, and Betty became CAMF's first pilot. Her CAMF first flight, 14 February, 1946, took her into a jungle camp in Southern Mexico.

In 1946, CAMF changed its name to Mission Aviation Fellowship (MAF). Betty served as a MAF pilot for sixteen years, flying in twelve countries and touching down in twenty others on three continents. Betty found the passion she had for flying could be used for God's glory in helping bring the love of Christ to the isolated peoples of the world.

Therefore, my beloved, as you have always obeyed, so now ...
work out your own salvation with fear and trembling,
for it is God who works in you,
both to will and to work for his good pleasure.

~ PHILIPPIANS 2:12-13 ~

Discovering the Kingdom of Heaven

∽ Miss Wang and Bertha Smith, 1950s ∽

After the Communist takeover of China, missionary Bertha Smith moved to Taiwan and began Bible studies among the people on the island. One morning a young lady knocked on Miss Bertha's door and asked when she held church services. Bertha invited the young lady in and said they could have a service right then.

Miss Wang was a teacher from Peking who had never heard of Jesus until during her journey from Peking to Taiwan, fleeing the communists. In Nanking she had spent one night near a Baptist chapel. In her deep loneliness, Miss Wang was attracted by the singing at the chapel and went in. When she later saw the word 'Baptist' on Bertha Smith's sign, she thought this was the same word she had seen on the Nanking chapel. She would see what else she could hear there. Miss Bertha gave Miss Wang a Chinese Bible and began to show her her own sinfulness and need to die to self and receive Christ. After some conversation, Miss Bertha realized the lady was not ready for that and told her she didn't want the Lord, she just wanted his blessings – like a job, money and a place to live. There was a long, thoughtful pause, and then Miss Wang said, 'I must have the Lord at any cost.' She and Miss Bertha knelt by the sofa in prayer; Miss Wang repented and gave herself completely to Christ, rising from her knees with a new life in Christ.

Miss Bertha always recorded the date and name of those she was privileged to lead to Christ. Recording Miss Wang's conversion, she noticed it was 12 October – the day Christopher Columbus discovered America. Miss Wang exclaimed her discovery was greater. Columbus had only discovered a continent; she had discovered the kingdom of heaven!

Miss Wang became regular in attending Miss Bertha's mission for Bible study and prayer. Miss Bertha found her prayers so refreshing as she talked to the Lord about everything that concerned her. She always closed her prayers by saying, 'Lord, I am just delighted to talk to you!'[49]

Miss Wang was one of many who prayed kneeling beside Miss Bertha's sofa. Miss Bertha worked at the mission in Taiwan for ten years, after serving thirty years in China. When she was seventy, the mission board required her to retire. Miss Bertha lived another thirty years in America, continuing to share the gospel of her Savior.

> Then Jesus told his disciples, 'If anyone would come after me, let him deny himself and take up his cross and follow me. For whoever would save his life will lose it, but whoever loses his life for my sake will find it.'
>
> ~ MATTHEW 16:24-25 ~

---

49. Lewis and Betty Drummond, *Women of Awakenings: The Historic Contribution of Women to Revival Movements* (Grand Rapids, MI: Kregel Publications, 1997), p. 293.

Tentmaker Training Tentmakers

∽ Ruth Siemens, 1925-2005 ∾

Lying on the hospital bed after three surgeries and with only one functioning lung, Ruth knew no missionary agency would accept her. It seemed the end of what she thought God had planned for her. Ruth came to a personal faith in Christ and was baptized when she was thirteen. She early became strongly interested in missions by listening to the many missionary speakers at the Mennonite Brethren Church where she grew up as well as reading numerous missionary biographies.

In college, Ruth learned that to live in obedience to Christ she needed to daily renew her commitment to Him. Active in the Student Missionary Union, she signed a promise card that she would serve God abroad if He would open the door. Then, as World War II was coming to an end, Ruth contracted tuberculosis and became seriously ill. Her road to recovery was slow.

Thinking being a missionary was no longer an option, Ruth enrolled at Chico State to get a degree in education and English. On the secular campus she found herself on the mission field! She became active in InterVarsity Christian Fellowship (IVCF) and learned to study the Bible inductively. Upon graduation she began teaching elementary school. She and two other Christian teachers started a teachers' Christian fellowship with Bible study groups. Ruth was learning to reach others with the gospel and the truth of Christ wherever she was.

In 1954, Ruth had the opportunity to teach third grade at a bi-national school in Peru. Ruth began a Bible study for Peruvian teachers in her home, taught a sixth-grade Sunday school class at a nearby church, and began a Bible club for high school girls. To improve her Spanish she audited classes at San Marcos University. Language lessons with fellow-students turned into Bible studies. Without the sponsorship of a missionary agency and while being paid working at her secular teaching job, Ruth discovered she was doing the work of a missionary!

Ruth went on to develop student work in Spain and Portugal and to conduct training in evangelism in France, Switzerland, Austria, and even communist Poland. In 1976, she began Global Opportunities, an organization to recruit and train missionary 'tentmakers' – people who, like the apostle Paul, might support themselves in secular work while carrying on the work of evangelism and discipleship.

One of the college students Ruth met in Spain was Rebecca Manley, who learned much about evangelism and the Christian life from Ruth. For Ruth's eightieth birthday, Rebecca wrote Ruth:

> In observing you I saw what a walk of faith looked like up close. Everything you thought, felt, delighted in, or regretted was viewed in relationship in the Living God. Your relationship to Christ was one of such delight and awe that it was impossible to understand you unless one knew the God that you worshipped. And that, I believe, is your epitaph. Your life has been a clarion call to everybody you ever encountered that we must give our lives unreservedly to Christ – for it is only in radical surrender to Him that we find our true joy and freedom.[50]

Walk in wisdom towards outsiders, making the best use of the time.
Let your speech always be gracious, seasoned with salt,
so that you may know how you ought to answer each person.

~ COLOSSIANS 4:5-6 ~

---

50. 'Ruth Siemens – In His Presence', January 9, 2006, *Intervarsity Christian Fellowship*, http://www.intervarsity. org/news/ruth-siemens-in-his-presence.

Among the Lisu

Isobel Kuhn, 1901-1957

The Lisu people live in the mountainous area of south-west China, Burma, Thailand, and North-east India. With richly colored dress and a rich oral culture, the Lisu were originally animists, believing everything, including plants, animals, and inanimate things, had a spirit. Today, however, Christianity is so prevalent among the Lisu in the Yunnan province of China that the Chinese government's Religious Affairs Bureau proposed considering Christianity the official religion of the Lisu.

Missionary work among the Lisu in Yunnan province was begun in the early twentieth century by James O. Fraser of the China Inland Mission. Fraser developed an alphabet and written language for the Lisu as well as working on Bible translation. In 1924, Fraser spoke at a summer missions conference in Bellingham, Washington and deeply affected twenty-five-year-old Isobel Miller. From Vancouver, Canada, Isobel was an honors graduate from the University of British Columbia. Fraser's descriptions of his work among the Lisu encouraged Isobel in her calling to become a missionary. After further training at Moody Bible Institute, Isobel was accepted as a missionary with the China Inland Mission. On 11 October, 1928, she sailed out of Vancouver to China. On 4 November, 1829, Isobel married fellow missionary John Kuhn, whom she had met at Moody Bible Institute. The couple worked in Yunnan province beside James Fraser until his death in 1938.

Isobel wrote eight inspirational books about her missionary experiences which not only awakened many to an interest in missions but also encouraged them to consecrate their entire life to the Lord. *By Searching: My Journey Through Doubt into Faith* recounted Isobel's own doubts and her coming to faith in Christ. *Nests Above the Abyss* described the fear and darkness of the Lisu people in their animistic beliefs and the beauty, joy, and hope found in Christ. Isobel recounted how important prayer was in the advance of the gospel. When one tribal leader renounced a long-standing feud, Isobel noted the exact time this occurred, knowing this must be an answer to prayer. Some months later, an elderly lady wrote and asked what had happened on that date and time. She had a burden then to pray for the Three Clans village and had phoned two friends to pray as well. They all put off their morning chores to pray for the feuding clans. These frail saints by their prayers had affected peace half a world away!

Isobel established the 'Rainy Season Bible School', which greatly strengthened the faith of the Lisu. Conducted during the Rainy Season when little agricultural work could be done, the School trained Lisu in the gospel and the historic truths of Christianity. Numerous Lisu pastors and evangelists then took the gospel to others throughout China.

The Kuhns had to leave China in 1950, when the Communists took over, and spent a few years among the Lisu in Thailand. The reason the Lisu Church in China remains vibrant today is due to the firm foundation in the gospel laid by the missionaries in the first half of the twentieth century.

> 'But seek first the kingdom of God and his righteousness, and all
> these things thiswill be added to you.'
>
> ~ MATTHEW 6:33 ~

People's General

∞ Eva Burrows, 1929-2015 ∞

In 1991, as the communist party went to its demise in the old Soviet Union, General Eva Burrows marched with the Salvation Army's Oslo Temple Band through the streets of Leningrad. Since 1923, the Salvation Army's work in Russia had been prohibited. Eva Burrows, General of the Salvation Army since 1986, eagerly brought the message of salvation again to the Russian people. The Army distributed Bibles and tracts in Moscow to counter the spiritual deadness of atheistic communism which had ruled the land for most of the century. Within two years the Salvation Army had ten post-communist recruits, including a former Soviet army colonel, a doctor, lawyer, and a university professor. Eva considered being able to return the gospel to eastern Europe one of the high points of her life.

Born into a Salvation Army family on 15 September, 1929, in Newcastle, Australia, Eva was the eighth of nine children. The day of her birth, her father rushed home from a Sunday service, picked up his new little daughter and declared, 'I dedicate this child to the glory of God and the salvation of the world.'[51] She was named after Evangeline Booth, the daughter of William and Catherine Booth. As a teenager, however, Eva rebelled against the strict Salvation Army life and refused to go to church with her parents. She needed to 'fly her own wings' was the expression she used. While attending Queensland University, reading English and History, she attended an evangelistic service and returned to her Christian roots, asking God to forgive her rebelliousness and submitting her life to His will.

After training at the William Booth Memorial Training College in London, Eva held many positions within the Salvation Army, beginning with teaching and training teachers in what is now Zimbabwe. She then ran social service programs for women in Britain and served as territorial commander in Sri Lanka, Scotland, and Southern Australia, before being named the 13th General of the Salvation Army. With superb administrative skills, Eva was always most interested in individuals, gaining her the nickname of the 'People's General'.

As an evangelist Eva said she never preached Christianity, but preached Christ as a living Savior: 'The focus and dynamic of my life is Jesus Christ. I will lift up Christ and would challenge all Salvationists to a commitment to Christ which makes them a powerful witness for him in the world today.'[52]

> *'And I, when I am lifted up from the earth,*
> *will draw all people to myself.'*
>
> ~ JOHN 12:32 ~

---

51. Sam Roberts, 'Eva Burrows, Salvation Army's "People's General" dies at 85', *The New York Times*, 24 March 2015.

52. 'Celebrating the life of General Eva Burrows,' *AUE mySalvos*, http://salvos.org.au/mysalvos/news/2015/03/23/celebrating-the-life-of-general-eva-burrows/ accessed 4/13/2015.

God's 'Beauty Parlor'

∽ Sabina Wurmbrand, 20th century ∾

After Sabina Wurmbrand and her husband Richard were released from prison and received amnesty, they left communist Romania, eventually settling in the United States. They traveled the world awakening people to the persecution of Christians happening in many places.

Sabina movingly told of the horrible conditions thousands of women faced in the communist prisons and slave labor camps because of their faith in Christ. At one camp, Sabina and other women worked building a canal. Their hands were cut and bleeding from moving and throwing the heavy stones into the rivers. Sometimes in a cell next to theirs they could hear children being beaten, and their mothers' hearts wept for their children. In prison they never knew what day it was, though occasionally someone would whisper, 'It is Sunday,' and they would remember the beautiful times of worship in church they had once known. One such Sunday the women were brought back to their cells and wanted to read the Bible. Yet, having no Bible, each would recite Scriptures they could remember, and they prayed together. In communist prison Sabina came to realize what a treasure there was in having a Bible. The communists took away their loved ones and their children, but they could not take away their faith and hope or Scriptures they had in their hearts. The Bible's words gave richness to those despairing in prison.

One lady in prison knew many chapters of the Bible by heart, and one day she recited Acts 6, about the stoning of Stephen. The chapter ends with Stephen's face shining like an angel as he was facing death. Another lady in the group had been quite wealthy and was a political prisoner because her husband had been a Romanian ruler. She was not a Christian and couldn't imagine that Stephen could so glowingly face death. A Christian lady replied,

> I am sorry for you. You do not know Jesus, the Son of God. But whenever Jesus comes in a heart, he never comes alone, He always comes with all His richness. … He comes with the glory of heaven and so when you open your heart and Jesus comes in your heart to be your Lord and Saviour, He brings His beauty. And so Stephen could be so beautiful like an angel.

A communist guard came in at that moment, took out the women, gave them a beating and threw them back into the prison cell. The rich lady was beaten and bleeding all over her face. She said that the communists were beating the Christians was proof enough that God is God, and she took Jesus as her Savior. Sabina said the woman's face, smeared with blood and tears, was beautiful like the face of an angel:

> It is wonderful to pass in the beauty parlor of Jesus, the Son of God, who has given His life for you and wishes to be Lord and master in your heart. He forgives your sins, He takes over your problem. He brings His grace and peace and His richness in your life. And you become beautiful like the angels in heaven. It is quite a beauty parlor … the best which can exist.[53]

And Stephen, full of grace and power, was doing great wonders and signs
among the people. … But they could not withstand the wisdom and the Spirit
with which he was speaking. … And gazing at him, all who sat in the council
saw that his face was like the face of an angel.

~ ACTS 6:8, 10, 15 ~

---

53. 'In God's Beauty Parlor', a talk given by Sabina Wurmbrand, transcribed by Andrea King Hendrix, http://www. reavivamentos.com/en/books/RICHARD_WURMBRAND/beauty_parlor.html, accessed January 13, 2015.

Sister in Christ from a Murderous Tribe

∞ Dayuma, c. 1930-2014 ∞

In 1956, the whole world was shocked with news of five missionaries murdered in the jungles of Ecuador – their bodies found face down in a stream, pierced with spears and wounded by machetes. The five were preparing to build a base camp near the Waodani village to bring the gospel to the natives. To learn some of the Waodani language, they had earlier met with Dayuma, who was living in a nearby Quechua village.

Dayuma was a member of the Waodani tribe, but she had fled to live among the Quechua. Waodani were very fierce and had killed many in her own family, including her father. Living among the Quechua, Dayuma met Rachel Saint, a missionary with Wycliffe Bible Translators and sister of one of the slain missionaries. Hearing the good news of Jesus Christ, Dayuma became a Christian and was baptized on 15 April, 1958. Members of Dayuma's family found her and urged her to return home, saying her mother was still alive and those who sought to kill her were dead. Dayuma went back to the Waodani but soon returned to the Quechua village with an invitation for Rachel Saint and Elizabeth Elliot to come live with the Waodani – the very people who had killed their brother and husband! The women accepted the invitation and opportunity to spread the love of God among the people. They taught the Bible to Dayuma, and she in turn taught her people. She told them, '... just like you speared the good foreigners, that's how they killed Jesus, God's good son.' Gikita, the leader of the attack on the missionaries, responded, 'Not understanding I killed, but Jesus' blood has washed my heart clean – I used to hate, but now my heart is healed.' Another of the murderers prayed, '... we shall see them again in the hut you are thatching for us in the sky, and seeing them, we will be happy.'

When Dayuma died on 1 March, 2014, Steve Saint, son of slain missionary Nate Saint, wrote, 'A beautiful daughter of Christ has joined Him in heaven today. Dayuma was the first Waodani that reached out to her own people along with Aunt Rachel. She made God's story known to these people in a way only a Waodani could. Praise God for her life!'[54]

> *In this is love, not that we have loved God but that he loved us*
> *and sent his Son to be the propitiation for our sins.*
> *Beloved, if God so loved us,*
> *we also ought to love one another.*
>
> ~ I JOHN 4:10-11 ~

---

54. 'Died; Dayuma, First Convert from Tribe that Martyred "Gates of Splendor" Missionaries', *Christianity Today Gleanings*, 3 March 3 2014, http://www.christianitytoday.com/gleanings/2014/march/died-dayuma-convert-gates-of-splendor-elliot-saint-auca.html.

Prayer of a Child

ன Helen Roseveare, 1925- ன

Helen Roseveare spent twenty years in the Congo as a medical missionary. From her earliest days as a Christian she was convinced that she should be a missionary abroad. Her studying medicine at Newnham College, Cambridge and her further study of French and tropical medicine in Belgium all were preparatory to her leaving for Africa as a medical missionary in 1953. Helen began work at Iambi, where she started a nurses' training school while also overseeing the medical work at the station. After eleven years she moved to Nebobongo, where she took over the maternity and leprosy center. Throughout Helen struggled with overwork and a tendency to be short-tempered. One day, the prayer of a little child taught her a lesson in trusting God.

One night, in the maternity ward, Helen had worked hard helping a mother in labor, but the mother died, leaving a premature baby and a forlorn two-year-old daughter. Keeping the baby alive would be difficult, since the ward had no incubator. One assistant wrapped the little one in cotton wool while another went to fill the hot water bottle. She came back quite upset, for the water bottle had burst (rubber decays quickly in the tropics), and that was their last one.

At noon, Helen had her normal time of prayer with some of the orphanage children. As they talked about what they needed to pray about, Helen told them about the little newborn and her two-year-old sister now without a mother. During the time of prayer, ten-year-old Ruth prayed that God would send a water bottle that afternoon (tomorrow would be too late) and a dolly for the little girl so she would know God loved her. Helen hesitated to say 'Amen', for such a particular prayer seemed virtually impossible to be answered. She had been in Africa four years and had never received a package from home, and who would send a hot water bottle?

Later in the afternoon, as Helen was teaching in the nurses' training school, a message came that there was a car at the front door. When she reached the veranda, a large package had been left. Helen sent for the orphanage children, and together they began opening the package. There were beautifully colored little clothes, bandages for leprosy patients, raisins – and then Helen amazingly pulled out a brand new rubber hot water bottle! Tears came to her eyes. Little Ruth said, 'if God had sent the hot water bottle, there must be a dolly in there too'. Digging into the box, she pulled out a beautifully-dressed doll. With shining eyes she begged to go and give the doll to the little girl so she would know Jesus loved her.

The package had been sent by Helen's former Sunday school class. It had been sent five months before, but arrived in God's perfect timing.

Before they call I will answer;
while they are yet speaking I will hear.

~ Isaiah 65:24 ~

Loved with an Everlasting Love

∞ Elisabeth Elliot, 1926-2015 ∞

For over a decade, the radio program 'Gateway to Joy' opened with the words, 'You are loved with an everlasting love. That's what the Bible says. And underneath are the everlasting arms. This is your friend, Elisabeth Elliot.' Elisabeth Elliot became an exemplar and counselor to thousands of Christian women as she showed the way to trusting God and His Word in every circumstance of life.

When Elisabeth Howard met Jim Elliot at Wheaton College, both planned to be missionaries. The two were married in Quito, Ecuador in 1953. While working among the Quichua Indians, Jim and his fellow missionaries planned to reach out to the Aucas, who had no contact with the outside world. When they made an attempted contact, the Aucas thought the five misionaries were cannibals and killed them in January of 1956. Elisabeth was now a widow with a little girl, Valerie.

Confident that it was God's will for them to reach the Aucas, Elisabeth and Rachel Saint, sister of slain missionary Nate Saint, remained to work among the people, translate the Bible into their language, and bring them the good news of Jesus. One day little Valerie asked if one of the men was her daddy. Elisabeth replied, 'No, he's one who killed your Daddy.' Valerie simply said, 'Oh.' Through Elisabeth and Rachel's sacrificial love, the gospel did come to the tribe, and some of those who had first murdered the missionaries now became followers of Jesus.

Elisabeth and Valerie returned to the United States in 1963, and Elisabeth began her career as a writer: *Through Gates of Splendor* told the story of the slain missionaries; *Shadow of the Almighty* was the life of Jim Elliot; *The Savage My Kinsman* told of Elisabeth's life among the Aucas and their becoming her brothers and sisters in Christ.

Elisabeth was called upon frequently as a speaker. She spoke out against the rising feminism of the day and encouraged a woman's proper submission to her husband in marriage. Always she sought to ground her counsel and advice in the Word of God. In *No Graven Image* she noted that God works through our experiences to bring us closer to Himself, breaking down and destroying the false gods we have created to replace them with the truth of Himself. In the midst of a sexual revolution, Elisabeth wrote *Passion and Purity*, encouraging sexual purity within biblical marriage.

A skillful writer, Elisabeth's words often reached the heart:

Leave it all in the hands that were wounded for you.

If you believe in a God who controls the big things, you have to believe in a God who controls the little things.

We have proved beyond any doubt that He means what He says – His grace is sufficient, nothing can separate us from the love of Christ.[55]

'I have loved you with an everlasting love;
therefore I have continued my faithfulness to you.'

~ Jeremiah 31:3 ~

---

55. Kate Shellnutt, 'Missionary Pioneer Elisabeth Elliot Passes Through Gates of Splendor', *Christianity Today* Gleanings, http://www.christianitytoday.com/gleanings/2015/june/died-elisabeth-elliot-missionary-author-gates-of-splendor.html.

‘Very Present Help in Trouble’

∞ Ruth Hege, c. 1905 – ? ∞

In 1960, the Belgian Congo gained independence as the Republic of Congo. Soon after, various provinces attempted to secede, and there was a political struggle for control of the country. In 1964, the Simba Rebellion, led in part by Pierre Mulele, a communist who received guerrilla training in China, brought further unrest, especially in the Kwilu District. Pierre had trained many of the youth, the Jeunesse, in guerilla warfare and terrorism

Ruth Hege and Irene Ferrel were two single missionaries in Mangungu. Ruth first came to the Congo in 1933, with Baptist Mid-Missions. After three years in the Congo she spent eighteen years in Venezuela, then in 1957 returned to the Congo. With the upheavals at independence in 1960 she left the country, but returned the following year with Irene Ferrel. The two single missionaries went to Mangungu, where they operated a Bible school, a primary school, and a dispensary, which became the center for a small hospital.

With the Simba rebellion many foreigners left the country. Ruth and Irene made preparations to evacuate, but before the helicopter came the Jeunesse attacked, on 25 January, 1964. The Jeunesse, armed with clubs, hatchets, arrows, and knives, broke into their house, looting and taking whatever they chose. The drug-crazed youth then dragged the women outside. Irene was shot in the neck with an arrow, which she pulled out, saying 'I am finished' as she fell to the ground dead. Ruth also had an arrow wound and was bleeding, but not as severely. She lay on the ground as if dead; thankfully the Jeunesse decided she was dead and left her alone. The school house was set ablaze before the Jeunesse left in the morning light.

The next three days were filled with terror, as Ruth went into hiding, then was twice discovered by Jeunesse who said they were going to kill her. Each time she was able to remain calm and share the love of Christ with the young man. Each time she could see his face change, and he left her alive. Finally, four days after the initial attack, the helicopter came to evacuate Ruth. She recognized her deliverance was all from the Lord:

> It is all the work of the Lord. When I was afraid, He gave me peace. When I was weak, He gave me strength. When, many times, men threatened to kill me, I spoke to them the message of Our Savior and the Lord changed their hearts. … I could see the change come over their faces.[56]

Ruth's trust was in God, and she found strength from Psalm 46, 'God is our refuge and strength, a very present help in trouble. Therefore we will not fear.'

> *God is our refuge and strength,*
> *a very present help in trouble.*
>
> ~ Psalm 46:1 ~

---

56. Arthur Vesseu, 'Lord Saved Me, Missionary Says of Congo Rescue', *Chicago Tribune*, 30 January 1964.

Fellowship of His Suffering

∞ Helen Roseveare, b. 1925 ∞

During Christmas break 1945, Helen Roseveare came to the place of repentance and resting in God's forgiving grace. Peace and joy flooded her soul as she revelled in a friendship with Christ. When Helen told what had happened to her Christian friends, a Bible teacher in the group took her Bible and wrote Philippians 3:10 (KJV) inside: 'That I may know him, and the power of his resurrection, and the fellowship of his sufferings, being made conformable unto his death.' He told Helen that she had entered into the first part of the verse, 'That I may know him,' but that was only the beginning. He prayed that in her Christian journey she would come to know 'the power of his resurrection' and, perhaps, 'the fellowship of his sufferings, being made conformable unto his death'. Decades later she would indeed come to know the fellowship of his suffering.

Helen came to the Belgian Congo in 1953 as a medical missionary. She worked tirelessly, often as the only missionary doctor in a vast area. In 1960, the Congo gained its independence from Belgium. Fearing unrest to follow, many European governments removed their people from the Congo; Helen remained and was the only European in Nebobongo. One evening national Army troops drove through the town laughing and threatening to return in the night to 'enjoy the white lady's company'. Fear took possession of Helen and she prayed for God to keep her close, praying He would send someone to stay with her. When there was banging at the door she knew the Army had returned, but then she heard female voices. An evangelist's wife and a midwife had come to stay with her, saying they had awakened from sleep and sensed the Lord wanted them with her.

Four years later guerrilla forces seeking to overthrow the Congolese government came to the village. Practising witchcraft, drunk and using drugs, they thought themselves invincible. One night the guerrillas attacked and ransacked her house. They seized her, beat her, knocked out her teeth, raped her and imprisoned her for five months. At first Helen felt abandoned by God, but then she lost all fear and had a strong sense that God had her in His arms. She remembered Philippians 3, and that she had been called to the fellowship of his suffering. As she had anticipated the terrors which befell her she was filled with fear, but in time of trial His grace was sufficient, and she enjoyed an indescribable peace.

Later, back in England, a woman whom Helen had not known asked her if a particular night in October during the trouble had any significance. It was the night Helen had been attacked. The woman had awakened with a strong sense to pray for Helen and continued praying until a certain time she told Helen – which was the time Helen had been washed free of fear and surrounded with God's peace.

> *That I may know him and the power of his resurrection,*
> *and may share his sufferings,*
> *becoming like him in his death.*
>
> ~ PHILIPPIANS 3:10 ~

Learning to Pray

∞ Joanne Shetler, b. 1936 ∞

Wanting a Bible in their own language, the Balangao tribe in the Natonin Mountain Province of the Philippines asked missionaries in neighboring tribes to send them someone who could translate the Bible for them. Wycliffe Bible Translators sent two women, Joanne Shetler and Anne Fetzer, to work on the translation. The Balangaos, expecting men to come and do the translation, were not pleased when two tall women were sent to them. The Balangaos couldn't understand that they had come to translate God's Word so they could know God. Somehow they thought the women were coming to take back their language to America and sell it to help them get husbands. One of the elders of the tribe 'adopted' the women into his family and served as their protector; he later became a Christian and a teacher of the tribe.

There were no midwives among the Balangao, and the death rate of children and mothers at childbirth was high. The missionaries gained the trust of the people in part by helping them as midwives and preserving their lives. The people were often in fear of the evil spirits and made regular sacrifices to appease the evil spirits. Tekla was one of the few people who would not sacrifice to the evil spirits. She knew it was evil and wanted to know the true God. Tekla became one of the early converts and helped with Bible translation.

Soon Anne received a marriage proposal from a friend at home and returned to America. Wycliffe didn't want Joanne to stay in the remote area alone, but she insisted that she had to finish the translation work for Balangao. As more and more of the Balangao became Christians, Joanne tried to teach them to pray, but they didn't understand what to pray, when or why. On a furlough, Joanne asked her home church to pray for a breakthrough in prayer for the people, no matter what the cost. When Joanne returned to the Balangao, she brought a medical doctor and an airplane full of supplies to build a hospital. However, the airplane crashed just before landing, and the doctor was killed. Joanne was severely injured with broken ribs, a collapsed lung, and damage to her eyes. She was in intense pain, but she also had great joy. For, all night long the Balangao people came, stood by her and prayed repeatedly, 'God, don't let her die, the Book's not done yet.' The Lord was using her injuries and pain to teach the people to pray.

In 1982, a ceremony of celebration was held for the completion of the Balangao Bible. Now having their own Bible, the Balangaos began translating God's Word into the languages of neighboring tribes.

'You will call upon me and come and pray to me, and I will hear you. You will seek me and find me, when you seek me with all your heart.'

~ JEREMIAH 29:12-13 ~

Good Seed

ꙮ Marianna Slocum, 1917-2008 ꙮ

In 1941, Marianna Slocum and her fiancé Bill Bentley were enjoying special days together just weeks before their 30 August wedding. Both were missionaries in Mexico with Wycliffe Bible Translators. Bill worked among the Tzeltals and Marianna among the Chol tribe, both tribes being descendants of the ancient Maya. The couple had returned to the United States for their wedding in Marianna's home in Philadelphia. They traveled to New Jersey where Bill spoke at a 'Keswick' meeting, then spent a day of sight-seeing in New York, returning to Philadelphia six days before the wedding.

When Bill did not come down for breakfast, Marianna's father went up to call him and found him dead. He had died in his sleep from unknown heart problems; he was only twenty-six. Marianna was heartbroken, but when she called Cameron Townsend, founder of Wycliffe Translators to tell him the news, she asked if she could go to the Tzeltal tribe and finish the work Bill began. Townsend could not help but reply in the affirmative. Later in the day Marianne received a telegram quoting John 13:7: 'Jesus answered him, "What I am doing you do not understand now, but afterwards you will understand."'

Marianna went to live among the Tzeltals and began the arduous process of first developing a written language for the tribe, then developing the vocabulary, grammar and translating the Scriptures. Marianna was joined by several helpers, but nurse Florence Gerdel worked with Marianna for decades.

Martin was the first to show much interest in Marianna's work. She began teaching him to read, but he found the process very difficult. He would often forget his earlier lessons, saying, 'I've lost it out of my heart.' Marianna began to realize this phrase could help explain to the Tzeltals about God's forgiveness of sins. When she told Martin that when we believe in Jesus, 'God loses all of our sins out of His heart,' Martin's face lit up with understanding.

After fifteen years Marianna had completed the New Testament in the Tzeltal language. She and Florence then moved to another tribe in Mexico and began the translation of the New Testament in the Bachajon language, which took eight years. Marianna then went to work with the Paez Indians in Columbia, South America. The Tzeltals called the Bible the 'Good Seed', and Marianna faithfully sowed the Good Seed among the native tribes of the Americas.

Jesus answered him,
'What I am doing you do not understand now,
but afterwards you will understand.'

~ JOHN 13:7 ~

Bringing Life to the Mountains of Death

∞ Evelyn Harris Brand, 1879-1974 ∞

Sailing home to England after visiting her sister in Australia, Evelyn Harris began to sense a call to be a missionary. She knew this would not be welcomed news to her protective father. When she heard a missionary from India, Jesse Brand, speak at a missionary meeting, her resolve to become one intensified. Brand was very intense and seemed to look directly at her when he described the dirt and poverty of the mission field. Could she, who had always lived in fashionable comfort, endure such things? She resolved with God's help she would! Her father was resistant at first. Why did she need to go to a foreign land for missionary work when London was filled with lost souls? Finally, he consented to God's call on his daughter's life.

Evelyn's first missionary assignment was to Madras, India, where Jesse Brand had recently been transferred. Brand had a passion to take the gospel to the Kolli range and then beyond to the Pachais, Kalrayn, Peria Malai, and Chitteris ranges. These were sometimes called the Mountains of Death because of the malaria and numerous diseases rampant there. Jesse asked Evie, as Evelyn was called, to join him in the adventure, and the two were married. Their honeymoon journey to the mountains was memorable – thunderstorms, heat, and steep mountain precipices marked the way.

Early in their mission on the Kolli range, a dying man believed in Christ. Then there were no converts for seven years. The Hindu priests, fearing they were losing influence, put up strong opposition. The Brands traveled to the villages together, preaching the gospel, tending the sick, teaching better agricultural methods. When a priest was ill and dying, the Brands tended his needs, leading him to come to faith in Christ. The priest thought Jesus must be the true God, for only the Brands came to help him in his hour of death. As he died he entrusted his children with the Brands, who were caring for many orphans as well as their own two children.

When Jesse died of Blackwater Fever, Evie continued to live and work the mountain region. She and Jesse had vowed to reach the five mountain ranges with the gospel, and four more needed work. When she was nearing seventy and the missionary agency did not renew her appointment, Evie took up an independent work in the mountains to fulfill her vow. She felt young, but everyone called her 'Granny'. For the next twenty-four years Granny Brand visited the mountain villages on a pony, teaching the Scriptures, dispensing medicine, and rescuing abandoned children. Before her death on 18 December, 1974, at the age of ninety-five, the five mountain ranges had been evangelized.

> *How beautiful upon the mountains are the feet*
> *of him who brings good news,*
> *who publishes peace, who brings good news of happiness,*
> *who publishes salvation, who says to Zion,*
> *'Your God reigns.'*
>
> ~ Isaiah 52:7 ~

In Times Like These

∞ Ruth Caye Jones, 1902-1972 ∞

The year was 1943, and World War II was raging in Europe. Ruth Caye Jones, wife of evangelist Bert Jones and mother of five children, was meditating on the Scripture in 2 Timothy 3:1 (KJV), 'This know also, that in the last days perilous times shall come.' 'Perilous times' certainly seemed to describe all the news from those days. What could be done in such times? Ruth took out a notepad from her apron and began writing the words of a song:

> In times like these you need a Saviour,
> In times like these you need an anchor;
> Be very sure, be very sure
> Your anchor holds and grips the solid Rock!
>
> In times like these you need the Bible;
> In times like these O be not idle;
> Be very sure, be very sure
> Your anchor holds and grips the Solid Rock!
>
> *Chorus:* This Rock is Jesus, yes, He's the One;
> This Rock is Jesus, the only One!
> Be very sure, be very sure
> Your anchor holds and grips the solid Rock!

Ruth also wrote the music for her song. Though she had no formal musical training, she had taught herself organ and piano. Some months later she realized that the first notes to her hymn were the first notes of the Westminster Chimes, which the mantle clock regularly rang.

In 1948, Bert and Ruth began a radio broadcast, *A Visit with the Jones*, which was aired for fifty years. The program was recorded in their home in Erie, Pennsylvania and allowed people across the nation to share in their family devotions. Ruth became known to many as 'Mother Jones' through this program.

In 1972, during a rather routine gall stone surgery, Ruth discovered she had cancer. She suffered briefly for five weeks before the Lord took her home. One Bible (and there were several) by her bedside was the Living Bible. In it she had underlined 2 Timothy 4:5-8:

> But you should keep a clear mind in every situation. Don't be afraid of suffering for the Lord. Work at telling others the Good News, and fully carry out the ministry God has given you. As for me, my life has already been poured out as an offering to God. The time of my death is near. I have fought the good fight, I have finished the race, and I have remained faithful. And now the prize awaits me—the crown of righteousness, which the Lord, the righteous Judge, will give me on the day of his return. And the prize is not just for me but for all who eagerly look forward to his appearing.[57]

Out to the side she had written 'August 1, 1972. I am longing to see him. With love my heart o'er flows.' Ruth's longing was granted on 18 August. She had told her family the anchor of faith never failed and the solid Rock never budged.

The LORD is my rock and my fortress and my deliverer, my God, my rock, in whom I take refuge, my shield, and the horn of my salvation, my stronghold.

~ PSALM 18:2 ~

---

57. New Living Translation (NLT).

Because He Lives

∞ Gloria Sickal Gaither, b. 1942 ∞

Gloria Sickal's parents always told her that whatever gifts and talents God had given her should be used for His honor and glory. Gloria went on to Anderson College in Indiana, majoring in English and French and planning to become a missionary in South Africa. When she was nineteen one of her professors asked her to teach three high school classes nearby while the teacher underwent cancer treatment. The same week she began teaching, Bill Gaither became head of the high school English Department, having taught intermediate school for several years. As they became acquainted, Bill and Gloria realized they both had a desire to live their lives for God's glory. They were married on 22 December, 1962.

Bill, also a musician, had written a number of gospel songs and sang in a gospel trio with his brother and sister. Gloria had written some poetry and was able to help Bill improve his lyrics. Soon, Gloria was writing the lyrics; Bill composed the music, and Gloria took Bill's sister's place in the trio. Together the Gaithers have written over six hundred songs, have produced sixty recordings, and have traveled the world giving gospel music concerts. In their ministry they have also encouraged many younger Christian musicians. With three children, family has always been important to Gloria and Bill, and Gloria wrote several books on parenting and the Christian family.

Towards the end of the 1960s, Gloria found herself discouraged. The country was going through a difficult time with the drug culture, racial tensions, and the turmoil from the Vietnam War. Bill was suffering from mononucleosis, and there were some people in the church who had been denigrating them and making false accusations. Gloria was pregnant, and it just seemed such a grim time to bring a child into the world. At this time of discouragement, God brought a peace to their souls and an assurance that the future of their child would be fine in God's hands. From this experience, Gloria wrote, 'Because He Lives':

> God sent His son – they called Him Jesus;
> He came to love, heal and forgive;
> He lived and died to buy my pardon;
> An empty grave is there to prove my Saviour lives.

> *Chorus:* Because He lives, I can face tomorrow,
> Because He lives, all fear is gone;
> Because I know He holds the future
> And life is worth the living – just because He lives.

> How sweet to hold a new-born baby
> And feel the pride and joy he gives;
> But greater still the calm assurance:
> This child can face uncertain days because Christ lives.

> And then one day I'll cross the river;
> I'll fight life's final war with pain;
> And then, as death gives way to victory,
> I'll see the lights of glory – and I'll know He lives.

Gloria only recently visited South Africa, where she had once thought she would be a missionary. While there, a lady came up to her and said, 'I want to tell you that I grew up with your songs. Your songs have been in Africa for forty years.'

'Because I live, you also will live.'

~ JOHN 14:19 ~

DECEMBER 24

Strengthened through Suffering

∽ Joni Eareckson Tada, b. 1949 ∽

Joni Eareckson was a vivacious teenager who had just graduated from high school. A champion horse rider, she was athletic and energetic. She had given her life to Christ at a Young Life camp, but she knew she wasn't living as she should for Him. She prayed that God would do something in her life to change her around. Shortly after, in 1967, she was injured in a diving accident on Chesapeake Bay. Joni became a quadriplegic, unable to move her hands or legs. In the following months, she often was in the depths of despair and asked her friends to help her commit suicide.

A friend introduced Joni to Steve Estes, a high school student three years younger, who was consumed with a love of Christ. He studied the Bible with Joni, exploring the meaning and uses God has for suffering. When considering how her accident, with its painful consequences, could be part of God's will, Steve asked if she believed that Jesus dying on the cross was God's will. They knew that the suffering, injustice, and torture endured by Jesus on the cross was indeed part of God's plan and necessary for our salvation; suffering is connected with our sinful world. Joni came to cling to God's sovereign love, knowing the healing of her soul was more important than her body, and that there were more important things than not being able to walk.

Joni went through two years of rehabilitation learning how to cope with her overwhelming disability. A team was necessary to care for Joni, dressing her, bathing her, combing her hair, even turning her in bed. Artistic before her accident, Joni learned to paint by holding the brush in her mouth. Her paintings gained her national attention, and Joni became a spokesperson for persons with disability. In 1979, she founded 'Joni and Friends' to minister to the disabled around the globe. Joni and Friends provides family retreats for those with disability, collects used wheelchairs which are distributed around the world (after being refurbished by prison inmates!), and sends physical therapists to fit the disabled person with the wheelchair. Joni also began writing and narrating a five-minute radio program, which has received awards from the National Religious Broadcasters. She has traveled around the globe encouraging people with disabilities and has served on the Disability Advisory Committee of the U.S. State Department. She has also written numerous books telling her story and exploring the love and grace of God in suffering.

In 1982, Joni married Ken Tada, a school teacher from Hawaii who actively supports Joni and Friends. Joni's joy in the Lord is irrepressible in spite of her disability, chronic pain, and even battle with breast cancer. Her love for God's Word and Christian hymns permeates her soul. She begins singing even in crowded airports as she rejoices in the Lord and shares His love with all around her. She knows that in this fallen world we will have suffering, but our God provides sustenance and strength even in our darkest hours.

For to this you have been called,
because Christ suffered for you, leaving you an example,
so that you might follow in his steps.

~ 1 Peter 2:21 ~

Magnifying the Lord Together

∞ Anne Sweet Ortlund, 1923-2013 ∞

Anne Sweet met Ray Ortlund in a prayer meeting at the University of Redlands. He was among twenty-two other sailors waiting for deployment in World War II. Anne and Ray got to know each other by listening to each other talk to the Lord before they ever talked together. After a couple of weeks Ray asked Anne on their first date. They went horseback riding in San Bernardino, California. As the moonbeams lit up the rocks and filtered through the trees, Ray began to sing an old hymn:

Far away in the depths of my spirit tonight,	Peace, peace, wonderful peace,
Rolls a melody sweeter than psalm,	Coming down from the Father above!
In celestial strains it unceasingly falls	Sweep over my spirit forever, I pray
O'er my soul like an infinite calm.	In fathomless billows of love!

As Ray sang, Anne joined him, and they both were surprised at the beautiful harmony they made together. Ray wrote his parents that night that he had met the woman he would marry.

Shortly before Christmas 1944, Ray proposed to Anne. He knelt, pulled a pocket New Testament and Psalms from the pocket of his uniform, and read Psalm 34:3: 'O magnify the LORD with me, and let us exalt his name together.' Anne immediately accepted. Ray then was sent overseas for eighteen months; they were married on his return. Ray went on to Seminary and pastored three churches, including Lake Avenue Congregational Church in Pasadena, California for twenty years. Anne was always an encourager and helper in Ray's care and love for the church. At a time of growing liberalism in the churches, Ray stood strongly for the authority and reliability of Scripture. An accomplished musician, Anne for many years was the organist for the 'Old Fashioned Revival Hour' radio program.

In 1979, Ray and Anne formed Renewal Ministries to encourage and train younger Christian leaders. Together they read the Bible each day, reading through it at least once a year. Each evening they prayed together. Bible reading and prayer together intensified their unity in Christ. During these years Anne wrote numerous best-selling books, including *Disciplines of the Beautiful Woman; Disciplines of the Heart; Turning Your Inner Life to God; Fix Your Eyes on Jesus*, and *Disciplines of the Home*. She also wrote a poem for Ray, recalling how their love began:

'I want to train for mission work,' you say.	The hum of leaves and crickets far away.
'That's what I'm praying for,' I answer you.	But a shining thought, a trembling, blazing thing
The rows of lights down Colton Avenue	Hangs over us unspoken, shimmering.
Make buttons for its coat of evening grey.	Because of it your hand is warm on mine,
'I hope for untried fields to conquer, Ray.'	And all the world seems challenging and fine:
And you reply, 'That's just what I want, too.'	'Before us lands of sin-sick millions lie;
Our talk is cool and unexcited through	Oh, why not go together, you and I?'

Ray died in 2007; Anne followed in 2013. After his mother's death their son wrote, 'Their romance was for Christ. Their everything was for Christ. And that way of living always has world-changing impact, because Christ himself is powerfully present in it.'[58]

And it is my prayer that your love may abound more and more, with knowledge and all discernment, so that you may approve what is excellent, and so be pure and blameless for the day of Christ. ...

~ PHILIPPIANS 1:9-10 ~

---

58. Ray Ortlund, Jr., 'Anne Sweet Ortlund, 1923-2013', *The Gospel Coalition*. http://blogs.thegospelcoalition.org/rayortlund/2013/11/05/anne-sweet-ortlund-1923-2013/. The poem is also in Ray's blog.

Peace of *Christ Surrounded by* Army *Tanks*

☞ Shirinai Dossova, 1991 ☜

Born into a Muslim family in Uzbekistan, Shirinai Dossova came to faith in Christ through the witness of Vicktor Pavlovich. Pavlovich had already served twelve years in prison for his Christian beliefs, and he warned Shirinai that because she was a Christian in the Soviet Union, she could be arrested, imprisoned, and drugged in order to elicit a 'confession' from her. Yet God would be with her even in prison, and with Him she would have true freedom. When Shirinai's family learned she had become a Christian, her oldest brother kicked her out of the house.

Shirinai became a street evangelist, preaching on the Arbat in Moscow, the street filled with tourists, trade, and artists. She received threatening letters, and the KGB warned her that if she did not stop, they would kill her. Shirinai entrusted her life to Christ and prayed that she could do more for Him.

The summer of 1991 was a transitional one. Mikhail Gorbachev had proposed a treaty allowing sovereignty for Russia and the other Soviet republics while maintaining a loose central government. The Communist Party opposed this dissolution of the old Soviet Union and organized a coup to take down Gorbachev and preserve the communist system. Tanks were ordered out and surrounded the Parliament building. The Russian Bible Society, hoping to ensure peace, ordered boxes of Bibles and began passing out Testaments to the soldiers in the tanks, urging them not to open fire. The soldiers and others were eager to receive the Testaments. Boris Yeltsin, newly elected Russian President, stood on top of one of the tanks and urged the soldiers not to kill their fellow Russians, ending his speech with 'Thou shalt not kill'.

Masses of people had come to assemble in Red Square and nearby Manege Square, and Shirinai was among them. She climbed on a nearby hill, and with her Bible raised she said,

> Christ called for love and peace, and only he can stop hate and fighting. There is no peace in the lives of people who are not at peace with God, and without him we cannot live in peace with one another. Jesus rose from the dead, he is alive here and now, and knocks at the door of our hearts. This kingdom will end in ruins, but God's kingdom is coming.

The crowd was stunned, and some wondered why Shirinai placed herself in such a dangerous situation. Shirinai said,

> I want to give my life for Christ. I didn't come only for a political statement. If I am going to be killed, then I want to be killed for Christ. The only real freedom is in Christ, not in *perestroika* [openness, or reform].[59]

The coup failed, as the soldiers in their tanks welcomed the Testaments and withdrew from surrounding the government buildings.

Shirinai continued speaking and living for Christ. Eight of her nine siblings became Christians and many planted churches, including the brother who once kicked her out of the house.

> *'Peace I leave with you; my peace I give to you. Not as the world gives do I give to you. Let not your hearts be troubled, neither let them be afraid.'*
>
> ~ JOHN 14:27 ~

---

59. Barbara von der Heydt, *Candles Behind the Wall: Heroes of the Peaceful Revolution that Shattered Communism* (Grand Rapids, MI: William B. Eerdmans Publishing Co., 1993), p. 214.

DECEMBER 27

In the Presence of My Enemies[60]

∽ Gracia Burnham, born c. 1959 ∽

Gracia and Martin Burnham had been in the Philippines seventeen years, serving with New Tribe Missions. Martin was a jungle pilot delivering supplies, mail, and aide to missionaries in remote areas. Gracia helped the aviation program in various ways and home-schooled their three children, ages 15, 12, and 11, all born in the Philippines. For their eighteenth wedding anniversary Gracia and Martin went to the Dos Palmas resort off Palwan Island. There, on 27 May, 2001, they, along with eighteen others at the resort, were kidnapped by the Abu Sayyaf Group, a militant group of Muslims with links to al-Qaeda. The rebels moved the hostages to the island of Basilan and worked to secure large ransoms for the captives.

The Burnhams were sorely tried during their 376 days of captivity, suffering starvation, malaria, exposure, and lack of water. By the spring of 2002 seventeen of the hostages had either been released for ransom or killed; one American had been beheaded. Only Gracia, Martin, and Ediborah Yap, a Filipina nurse, remained. Gracia often wondered why their captivity was going on so long; Martin said, 'I think God's just giving these guys one more day of grace, one more day to turn around, one more day to do the right thing'.[61] Martin used every opportunity to explain the gospel to the Muslim rebels and had lengthy conversations with the ringleader, Abu Sulaiman.

Martin had a premonition that death was near and wrote letters to his three children. On 7 June, he told Gracia their time together was nearing an end: 'The Bible says to serve the Lord with gladness. Let's go out all the way. Let's serve him all the way with gladness.'[62] Lying in a hammock together, they prayed, recited Scripture and sang. Suddenly they heard gunfire. Immediately they rolled out of the hammock to the ground, as they had been taught in missionary training. They slid down a steep hill and waited out the fighting. Gracia had been hit in the leg; Martin was hit in the chest and lay dead. Ediborah was also killed in the fighting; but the rebels fled, and Gracia was free.

Gracia's reunion with her children in Rose Hill, Kansas was bittersweet, but she told the large homecoming crowd, 'We want everyone to know that God was good to us every single day of our captivity.' She has seen her children grow to adulthood and continue strong in their Christian faith. The Martin and Gracia Burnham Foundation was established to support missionary aviation and has a special outreach to Muslims. Several of Gracia's Muslim captors have now come to faith in Jesus Christ, influenced no doubt by the example of Christ-likeness they first saw in Gracia and Martin.

You prepare a table before me in the presence of my enemies ... Surely goodness and mercy shall follow me all the days of my life, and I shall dwell in the house of the LORD for ever.

~ PSALM 23:5-6 ~

---

60. *In the Presence of Mine Enemies* is the name of the bestselling book Gracia Burnham wrote about her hostage experience.
61. Stan Finger, 'Ringleader in Burnham ordeal killed in firefight', *The Wichita Eagle*, January 18, 2007.
62. Ted Olson, 'Two Hostages Die in Attempted Missionary rescue in Mindanao', *Christianity Today*, June 2002.

Mama Maggie

☞ Maggie Gobran, 20th – 21st centuries ☜

As a special outreach at Easter time, Maggie Gobran and friends from her church visited the slums of Cairo, bringing provisions to the garbage pickers, families who lived in the slums and eked out a meager existence collecting, recycling and picking through Cairo's garbage. Maggie was drawn to the impoverished children and enjoyed talking with them and seeing the sparkle come in their eyes with some love and attention.

Maggie began regularly visiting the garbage slums, not just at Easter. She always talked with the people, showing a personal interest in their lives and needs. One day she encountered a little girl selling corn, with worn-out sandals. Maggie took her to buy some shoes. The little girl chose a lovely pair of shoes, then asked if she could have a pair for her mother instead, since she had no shoes. Maggie thought of her own daughter and realized she could have been living in the garbage slums. She knew,

> We don't choose where or when to be born. We don't choose where or when to die. But we can choose either to help others or turn away. We can choose to do nothing or be a hero. If you want to be a hero, do what God wants you to do. He will let you know what that is, as long as you are open to finding out.[63]

Maggie came from a wealthy Coptic Christian family in Cairo. Her father was a doctor and Maggie enjoyed a life of privilege, vacationing in Europe and buying the finest Paris fashions. She married well, had two children, and enjoyed a professional life in marketing and then as a professor of computer science at the American University in Cairo. Yet the children in Cairo's slums tugged at Maggie's heart. In 1989, she resigned her position at the University and established Stephen's Children to help the poor of Egypt, a charity named after Christianity's first martyr.

Stephen's Children aims to bring the love of Christ to Egypt's poor. Trained workers weekly visit homes and bring encouragement and counseling from the Scriptures as well as assistance in health and hygiene. Schools incorporate Christian truths into their curriculum; community centers provide safe places for children to play; literacy classes train adults in reading;, special programs help mothers in child care; and vocational training is provided so youngsters can move beyond the slums. Clothed with humility and the love of Christ, Mama Maggie, as she is affectionately called, can say,

> Indeed, God has truly blessed and given us more than we have hoped for or imagined; the wonderful opportunity to reach so many destitute children in such a closed part of the world. My prayer is that God will continue to draw us closed to Him though thousands of more children who still need the love of Jesus Christ.[64]

'You shall love your neighbor as yourself.'

~ MATTHEW 22:39 ~

---

63. Marty Makary and Ellen Vaughn, *Mama Maggie: The Untold Story of One Woman's Mission to love the Forgotten Children of Egypt's Garbage Slums* (Thomas Nelson books, 2015), p. 11.

64. 'Who is Mama Maggie?' at Stephen's Children website: http://www.stephenschildren.org/about/founder/, accessed 6 May, 2015.

Comfort in Sorrow

∽ Evelyn Husband, 2003 ∾

On 1 February, 2003, Evelyn Husband, with her children Laura and Matthew, eagerly waited at Kennedy Space Center for the return of her husband to Earth after his sixteen days aboard the Space Shuttle *Columbia*. Rick, who had wanted to be an astronaut since the early days of the U.S. space program, was a United States Air Force Colonel and the commander on the *Columbia* flight. The joy and excitement of an anticipated family reunion turned into an inconceivable tragedy when the *Columbia* disintegrated upon reentry into the earth's atmosphere, resulting in the deaths of all seven crew members.

In the days, months, and years to follow, Evelyn was strengthened by Scripture. The evening before the *Columbia's* launch Commander Husband had spoken a few words to the assembled crew and their spouses. With a voice full of emotions he quoted Joshua 1:7, 'Only be strong and very courageous, being careful to do according to all the law that Moses my servant commanded you. Do not turn from it to the right hand or to the left, that you should have good success wherever you go.' This passage repeatedly came to Evelyn's mind after the *Columbia* tragedy. One of the crew members, Ilan Ramon, was from the state of Israel, and when Israel issued a stamp in his honor, the Scripture from Joshua 1:7 was printed on the stamp.

Whenever Rick autographed pictures for people, he always put 'Proverbs 3:5-6' by his name. In the days following the *Columbia's* disintegration, these verses particularly blessed Evelyn: 'Trust in the Lord with all your heart, and do not lean on your own understanding. In all your ways acknowledge him, and he will make straight your paths.' Evelyn didn't understand the tragedy, but she did trust the Lord and was comforted in Him.

In her sorrow, Evelyn repeatedly turned to Jesus for comfort, knowing as 'a man of sorrows, and acquainted with grief' (Isa. 53:3), He knew how she felt. Psalm 147:3 re-assured her that God heals the brokenhearted and binds the wounds. From Revelation 21:4 she knew that her husband now was with Jesus, where there were no tears, no death, no mourning. Psalm 56:8 told her that God keeps track of each one of our sorrows. In the midst of the sorrow of losing her loving husband, the wonderful father of her children, and her best friend, Evelyn Husband became an example of the truth Jesus spoke in Matthew 11:28, 'Come to me, all who labor and are heavy laden, and I will give you rest.'

> 'Come to me, all who labor and are heavy laden,
> and I will give you rest.'
>
> ~ MATTHEW 11:28 ~

Saved to Serve'

∞ Jarmilla, 21st century ∞

Christian apologist Ravi Zacharias tells the moving story of a young lady named Jarmilla. Zacharias was preaching in Tschechian, Poland, near the border of Czechoslavakia, when he heard Jarmilla give her testimony.

As a seventeen-year-old girl, Jarmilla had dreams of being in opera, but it seemed to her nothing was going right in her life. She was angry with God, her family, and all around her. She had lost the capacity to believe. One night she lay in bed and expressed her hatred to God, telling him she would never again fold her hands in prayer to him. Sinking further into despair, she decided to commit suicide. She got on her bicycle and rode towards a train track. When she saw a train coming, she pedaled her bicycle so she would be on the tracks when the train passed. But, when she first hit the tracks, her bicycle flipped and she landed on the other side of the tracks, with only her hands across the track. Though the train came to a screeching halt, it wasn't in time to spare the girl. She was rushed to the hospital with her hands severed.

In the hospital, Jarmilla's grandmother repeatedly came and read Jarmilla the book of Psalms. Jarmilla's heart was softened, and she came to Christ on that hospital bed. Rubber hands were attached to Jarmilla's arms, and she left the hospital desiring to serve God in some Christian ministry.

The first time Jarmilla ever shared her testimony in a public meeting, a woman in the audience began crying just at the time Jarmilla told of the train severing her hands. After her talk, the woman rushed up to Jarmilla and told her she was on that train. When the conductor told them that a young lady had tried to commit suicide and was being taken to a hospital, the woman said she began praying that the young lady's life would be spared and someone would share with her the love of Jesus. Hearing Jarmilla speak, she knew her prayer had been answered.[65]

> But I trust in you, O LORD; I say, 'You are my God.'
> My times are in your hand ... .
>
> ~ PSALM 31:14-15 ~

---

65. Ravi Zacharias, 'Die Geschichte von Jarmila', https://www.youtube.com/watch?v=2ezv0LWWdjI.

'The Glory of Woman is the Fear of the Lord'
∞ 1847 ∞

In 1847, Rev. Charles Colcock Jones, former pastor of the First Presbyterian Church of Savannah, Georgia and then Professor of church history and polity at Columbia Theological Seminary, preached a sermon which gained wide-spread fame and was printed as *The Glory of Woman is the Fear of the Lord*. Rev. Jones began:

> No one thing in social life, more distinguishes a Christian from a heathen country, than the consideration in which *females* are held, and the important and influential station which is assigned them in society. As the farther you depart from Christianity, the deeper is the degradation of females, and the more miserable and polluted the state of society, so the nearer you approach to Christianity, and the purer its nature and the more efficient its influence, the higher is the perfection of female character, and the more virtuous and happy the community at large.
>
> How great is the responsibility of females in Christian lands, to improve the blessings which God confers upon them through his Holy Word!..the true glory of women, and that which they are to prefer before all things else, and which forms the just foundation of their praise, is – *the fear of the Lord* ....
>
> The woman that feareth the Lord, has through grace, been brought to a true sight and sense of her sins: she has repented and sought forgiveness and salvation in the name of the Lord Jesus Christ alone. God hath shed abroad his love in her heart, and she has experienced joy and peace in believing. She has approached the Saviour in humility, and bowed down and washed his feet with the tears of her sincere contrition, and wiped them with the hairs of her head. To her Jesus has said, 'Thy sins be forgiven thee – go in peace.' She hath seated herself with Mary at his feet, to be taught and led, and to be sanctified and saved by him. ... She 'hath chosen that good part which shall not be taken away from her.' Luke 10:38-42 ....
>
> The work of the woman that feareth the Lord is not *inward* only, but it exhibits itself *in her life*. Her fruit is unto holiness. Your observation will convince you that she 'walks with God' daily; that religion is her comfort, her refuge, her strength, and her delight and happiness.

Jones then enumerated and elaborated upon particular characteristics of the woman who has the inward fear of the Lord:

> She giveth herself conscientiously to the *duty and the privilege of secret prayer* ... She giveth herself conscientiously to the *reading and study of God's holy word* .... She giveth herself to *sobriety and watchfulness*. She adorns herself in modest apparel ... even the ornament of a meek and quiet spirit, which is in the sight of God great price. 1 Tim. 2:9; 2 Peter 3:3,4 .... She giveth herself to the *faithful observance of the holy Sabbath* ... She giveth herself to the *services of the house of God* ... She giveth herself to *love the brethren and the ministers of God* ... She giveth herself to *good works* ... She giveth herself faithfully to the duties of her family and household. Here is her peculiar, her delightful, yet responsible field of labour, assigned her by the Lord.

Rev. Jones concluded with this exhortation:

> Set your light upon a candlestick, that it may give light to all that are in the house. Continue, by your pious examples, to cheer and animate your brethren in the Lord, and by your efforts to uphold every good work. Continue, by your prayers, your works of faith and labours of love, to draw down blessings upon your families, your churches, and the world. And when it shall please God to call you from his service here on earth, it will be to enjoy him in heaven for ever. Generations that come after you, shall rise up and call you blessed. 'Favour is deceitful, and beauty is vain; but a woman that feareth the Lord, she shall be praised.'[66]

> *Charm is deceitful, and beauty is vain,*
> *but a woman who fears the LORD is to be praised.*
> ~ PROVERBS 31:30 ~

---

66. Rev. Charles Colcock Jones, *The Glory of Woman is the Fear of the Lord* (Philadelphia: William S. Martien, 1847), pp. 2, 8-20, 60.

Diana Lynn Severance

Feminine
Threads

Women in the Tapestry of Christian History

Feminine Threads
Women in the Tapestry of Christian History
by Diana Lynn Severance

From commoner to queen, the women in this book embraced the freedom and the power of the Gospel in making their unique contributions to the unfolding of history. Wherever possible, the women here speak for themselves, from their letters, diaries or published works. The true story of women in Christian history inspires, challenges and demonstrates the grace of God producing much fruit throughout time.

Diana Lynn Severance has broad experience teaching history in universities and seminaries, She is a Director of the Dunham Bible Museum at Houston Baptist University, (www.hbu.edu/biblemuseum) and is the author of *Feminine Threads: Women in the Tapestry of Christian History*.

"*Feminine Threads* is a must-read for men and women alike, but especially so for young women who need to have a clear view of the contributions that women before them have made to the Christian faith."

Carolyn McCulley, Conference Speaker and Author of Radical Womanhood:
Feminine Faith in a Feminist World, Washington, D.C.

ISBN: 978-1-84550-640-7

SUSANNA WESLEY   ·   FANNY CROSBY

VANCE CHRISTIE

WOMEN *of*

FAITH

& COURAGE

CATHERINE BOOTH   ·   MARY SLESSOR   ·   CORRIE TEN BOOM

Women of Faith & Courage
by Vance Christie

Through some of the best-loved heroines of the Christian faith, God's glory is manifest as He accomplishes significant things through imperfect people. In *Women of Faith* readers discover the remarkable stories of Susanna Wesley, Fanny Crosby, Catherine Booth, Mary Slessor and Corrie ten Boom. Their lives spanned three centuries and their circumstances were each very different, but steadfast faith and courage is the constant resounding theme for each.

In *Women of Faith* engaging narratives with rich historical detail reveal the uncommon faithfulness of these five women in evangelism, missions pioneering, ministries of compassion and the nurturing of their own families. Their giftedness, resilience and compassion shine through, modeling devotion to Christ and sacrificial service in His kingdom.

Across the pages of this book, the legacy of these women lives on to inspire and instruct contemporary believers-in living all of life for the glory of God.

ISBN: 978-1-84550-686-5

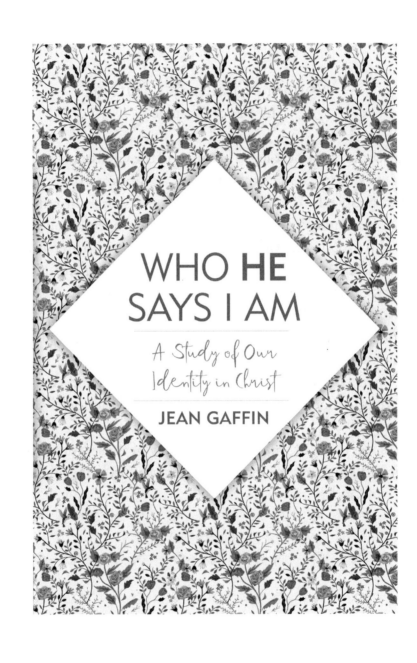

WHO **HE** SAYS I AM

A Study of Our Identity in Christ

JEAN GAFFIN

Who *He* Says I Am
by Jean Gaffin

It is crucial to know who we are. The world loves to label us – by our gender, by our ethnicity, by our job – but as Christians our identity is not in those labels. We are 'in Christ'. We are united to Him by faith. This devotional digs into what that means, how it impacts our lives, and why it matters most who God says we are.

Each chapter looks at one facet of our identity in Christ and includes:

Bible reading

Memory verse

Digging Deeper section

Questions for self–reflection or group discussion

Space for personal journaling and self–reflection

"With biblical wisdom coupled with an endearing modesty and practicality it takes us to the heart of living the Christian life. And, truth to tell, *Who He Says I Am* is simply a transcript of the Christ–reflecting life Jean Gaffin herself lived, as a woman who knew where her true identity was found."

Sinclair B. Ferguson, Chancellor's Professor of Systematic Theology, Reformed Theological Seminary, Jackson, Mississippi

ISBN: 978-1-5271-0480-8

Christian Focus Publications

Our mission statement –

STAYING FAITHFUL
In dependence upon God we seek to impact the world through literature faithful to His infallible Word, the Bible. Our aim is to ensure that the Lord Jesus Christ is presented as the only hope to obtain forgiveness of sin, live a useful life and look forward to heaven with Him.

Our books are published in four imprints:

CHRISTIAN FOCUS

Popular works including biographies, commentaries, basic doctrine and Christian living.

CHRISTIAN HERITAGE

Books representing some of the best material from the rich heritage of the church.

MENTOR

Books written at a level suitable for Bible College and seminary students, pastors, and other serious readers. The imprint includes commentaries, doctrinal studies, examination of current issues and church history.

CF4•K

Children's books for quality Bible teaching and for all age groups: Sunday school curriculum, puzzle and activity books; personal and family devotional titles, biographies and inspirational stories – Because you are never too young to know Jesus!

Christian Focus Publications Ltd,
Geanies House, Fearn, Ross-shire,
IV20 1TW, Scotland, United Kingdom.
www.christianfocus.com